Eugene O'Neill

Eugene O'Neill

A Life in Four Acts

ROBERT M. DOWLING

Yale UNIVERSITY PRESS

New Haven and London

Published with assistance from the foundation established in memory of
Philip Hamilton McMillan of the Class of 1894, Yale College

Yale University Press books may be purchased in quantity for educational, business, or
promotional use. For information, please e-mail sales.press@yale.edu (U.S. office) or
sales@yaleup.co.uk (U.K. office).

Designed by James J. Johnson.
Set in Janson type by IDS Infotech, Ltd.
Printed in the United States of America.

Library of Congress Cataloging-in-Publication Data

Dowling, Robert M., 1970– author.
Eugene O'Neill : a life in four acts / Robert M. Dowling.
pages cm
Summary: "A major new biography of the Nobel Prize–winning playwright
whose brilliantly original plays revolutionized American theater."
— Provided by publisher.
Summary: "This extraordinary new biography fully captures the intimacies of Eugene
O'Neill's tumultuous life and the profound impact of his work on American drama. Robert
M. Dowling innovatively recounts O'Neill's life in four acts, thus highlighting how the stories
he told for the stage interweave with his actual life stories. Each episode also uncovers how
O'Neill's work was utterly intertwined with, and galvanized by, the culture and history of
his time. Much is new in this extensively researched book: connections between O'Neill's
plays and his political and philosophical worldview; insights into his Irish upbringing and
lifelong torment over losing faith in God; his vital role in African American cultural history;
unpublished photographs, including a unique offstage picture of him with his lover Louise
Bryant; new evidence of O'Neill's desire to become a novelist and what this reveals about
his unique dramatic voice; and a startling revelation about the release of *Long Day's Journey
Into Night* in defiance of his explicit instructions. This biography is also the first to discuss
O'Neill's lost play *Exorcism* (a single copy of which was only recently recovered),
a dramatization of his own suicide attempt. Written with lively informality yet a scholar's
strict accuracy, *Eugene O'Neill: A Life in Four Acts* is a biography that America's
foremost playwright richly deserves."
— Provided by publisher.
Includes bibliographical references and index.
ISBN 978-0-300-17033-7 (hardback)
1. O'Neill, Eugene, 1888–1953. 2. Dramatists, American—20th century—Biography. I. Title.
PS3529.N5Z6284 2014
812'.52—dc23
[B]   2014014634

A catalogue record for this book is available from the British Library.

This paper meets the requirements of
ANSI/NISO Z39.48-1992 (Permanence of Paper).

10 9 8 7 6 5 4 3 2 1

To Mairéad Dowling and Chris Francescani

There can be no such thing as an Ivory Tower for a playwright. He either lives in the theater of his time or he never lives at all.

—Eugene O'Neill, 1926

Contents

━━━━

ACT III: "The Broadway Show Shop" 241

ACT IV: Full Fathom Five 351

Acknowledgments

=====

A BLIZZARD-LIKE STORM has engulfed my hometown of New London, Connecticut, as I type these acknowledgments. New London is the town in which this book's subject spent the earliest years of his life, and in 1951, a blizzard in effect ended it, on a spiritual level, at Marblehead Neck, Massachusetts. As the majority of those listed below can testify, for the past decade all such roads—literal and associative, biographical and literary—have in some way, like this storm outside my office window, swung my mental focus back around to Eugene Gladstone O'Neill.

The only person who has had a higher claim on my daily thoughts over these last years is my daughter, Mairéad Dowling, to whom I warmly dedicate this book. I would bet that throughout this period Mairéad, now a teenager, has unwittingly absorbed more facts, figures, anecdotes, and judgments about Eugene O'Neill than many avid theatergoers and drama critics have in their lifetimes. Thank you for your patience and understanding, my darling girl.

I would next like to thank my great friend and fellow "hapless architect of the written word," Chris Francescani, to whom this book is also dedicated. Chris adroitly guided me through the process of how to tell a story, to the best of my ability, as exceptional as O'Neill's.

My mother, Janet B. Kellock, and my friend, colleague, and coeditor Jackson R. Bryer also read complete drafts of this biography, and each of them offered critical insights and editorial acumen. I owe an enormous debt of gratitude to my splendid agent Geri Thoma as well as to my former and current editors Ileene Smith, Eric Brandt, and Steve Wasserman, respectively, and editorial assistants Erica Hanson and Eva Skewes for their steadfast enthusiasm and support. My copy editor Robin DuBlanc, project manager Laura Jones Dooley, and proofreader Jack Borrebach took on the heavy lifting of this book's final hours, and their remarkable fortitude and skill have proved invaluable. I would also like to express my gratitude to the leadership of Central Connecticut State University (CCSU), which has shown abiding interest in my work on O'Neill and provided much-needed resources for this book's completion.

Throughout various stages of this project I've counted on the input and assistance of many other family members, friends, and colleagues, notably my sisters, Susanne Magee and Elisa Olds, my friends Michael J. Peery, Tom Cerasulo, and Yibing Huang, my niece Jenna May Magee and her significant other, Huntley Brownell, my nephews Naoise and Daithi Magee, Burl Barr, Barry H. Leeds, Eileen Herrmann, William Davies King, Kurt Eisen, the late and beloved Deborah Martinson ("Put the man in there!"), Gwenola Le Bastard, Adam Kroshus, Kamal John Iskander, Megan Byrne, Derron Wood, Marc Zimmer, Art Wilinski, Jon and Laura Hexer, and James Scarles, all of whom have read through sections of this book and/or offered essential feedback.

Far too many others to list have lent a hand, but a few more require mentioning: Mary Hartig, for taking on the painstaking work of formatting the text and footnotes of the manuscript; my indexer John Bealle (another magnificent job); George Monteiro and Brenda Murphy, whose original research provided lively anecdotes for this book (I look forward to the publication of theirs); O'Neill's former nurse Kathryne Albertoni, may she rest in peace, for granting me an interview in 2010; my graduate student Erin Sullivan (who, among other things, transcribed the hours-long taped interview of Albertoni); Myles Whalen, whose legal expertise helped me to interpret the mysteries of O'Neill's first divorce papers; Peter Quinn,

Jay Parini, and Gary Greenberg, whose respective enthusiasms for this project were the first three steps toward getting it into print; my fellow members of the Eugene O'Neill Society, for whom I've served with pride on the board of directors, and the editorial board of the *Eugene O'Neill Review*, on which I also serve; those who with such passion run the Tony Award–winning Eugene O'Neill Theater Center of Waterford, Connecticut, and the Flock Theatre of New London; and the other fellows who studied with me under Deborah Martinson at the Norman Mailer Fellowship program.

Countless librarians, curators, and archivists also gave up precious time and resources for this endeavor (some of whom are recognized in the endnotes for specialized advice), but many thanks to Ben Panciera and Nova Seals of the Linda Lear Center for Special Collections and Archives at Connecticut College, Raymond Pun and Jeremy Megraw of the New York Public Library, Edward Gaynor of the University of Virginia's Special Collections Library, Edward Gaynor of the University of Virginia's Special Collections Library, Louise Bernard, Melissa Barton, Anne Marie Menta, and Ingrid Lennon-Pressey of the Yale University Beinecke Rare Book and Manuscript Library, Mary Camezon of the Eugene O'Neill Foundation, and Deborah Herman and Sarah Marek of CCSU's Elihu Burritt Library. My deep gratitude to all of you.

Eugene O'Neill

Prologue
The Irish Luck Kid, 1916

In the rash lustihead of my young powers
  I shook the pillaring hours
And pulled my life upon me; grimed with smears,
I stand amid the dust o' the mounded years—
My mangled youth lies dead beneath the heap.
My days have crackled and gone up in smoke,
Have puffed and burst as sun-starts on a stream.

—FRANCIS THOMPSON, *The Hound of Heaven*, 1893

If tragedies might any Prologue have,
  All those he made, would scarce make one to this.

—HUGH HOLLAND, ELEGIAC SONNET TO
WILLIAM SHAKESPEARE, 1623

Spring 1916, New York City

EUGENE O'NEILL, a despondent twenty-seven-year-old college dropout and ex-sailor, had spent the last six months lost in a whiskey fog of oblivion at a Greenwich Village saloon known as the Golden Swan Café. To the regulars, it was "the Hell Hole," so named after a passerby glanced inside one day and cringed, "This is one helluva hole." O'Neill felt right at home.[1]

The Hell Hole sat on the southeastern corner of Sixth Avenue and Fourth Street, the heart of Greenwich Village, and it served hustlers, pickpockets, prostitutes, bohemians, and the Hudson Dusters, a cocaine-fueled Irish gang that had lorded over the neighborhood for years. If you had a hangover, and nearly everyone did, the Sixth Avenue El that passed just outside the front door rattled the three-story brick building with a head-splitting drum roll. The bar's

1

proprietor, Tom Wallace, hung two massive shillelaghs crossed in the pagan way behind the bar below a photograph of Tammany Hall's Irish-born strongman, Richard "Boss" Croker.[2] Beer was 5¢ a glass in the back room, where O'Neill would retreat to get drunk in relative solitude in the bar's dark corners, undisturbed by the quivering glow of two gas jets mounted on the wall. Patrons rapped on the door three times, and a bouncer named Leftie Louie glared through a slat before deciding whether to let them in. Women weren't permitted to smoke in most places in Manhattan, but at the Hell Hole, they were encouraged to light up.[3]

Just the year before, O'Neill had given himself the nickname "The Irish Luck Kid," but by now the irony of that roguish moniker had become all too clear. His life to date had been a relentless cascade of hopeless hopes: he was thrown out of Princeton freshman year for poor academic standing and drunkenness; he got married, divorced, and in the process fathered a son whom he still hadn't seen since infancy; he fled the conjugal life for the teeming jungles of Honduras to prospect for gold and instead contracted a crippling bout of malaria; he survived nine months as a beachcomber in Buenos Aires, working odd jobs, eating scraps, and swilling gin and cheap beer; he contracted tuberculosis, a minor case, yet one that landed him five months at a sanatorium; he studied playwriting at Harvard University, but the "Old Man," as O'Neill called his father, stopped paying the tuition after two semesters. True, he'd published a book, *Thirst and Other One-Act Plays*, but his father fronted the production costs, and it hadn't made a dime in royalties. Most painfully, for the moment, he'd just published a poem dedicated to his girlfriend Beatrice Ashe in which he compared her to Dante's Beatrice. She was in New London, Connecticut, where they had both grown up, and O'Neill was convinced that she was ready to dump him. (He was right.)

O'Neill was antisocial, alcoholic, a heavy smoker. His father was a domineering overachiever and his brother an underachiever and a world-class drunk. His mother, Ella, had been a morphine addict since the day he was born, all eleven pounds of him.

He'd tried to commit suicide; he'd tried to keep writing. He'd failed at both.

O'Neill shared a room with a sixty-one-year-old anarchist named Terry Carlin in an unfurnished apartment down Fourth Street from the Hell Hole so filthy they called it "the Garbage Flat." Everyone in the Village knew Carlin, an unapologetic drinker who held court in the Hell Hole's backroom and shamelessly sponged off O'Neill, who at the time was living on a small allowance from his father, for as long as he was able. (Carlin was able, it turned out, for nearly two decades.) Born Terence O'Carolan in 1855, Terry Carlin was raised in Chicago but had emigrated as a young boy from Ireland; and he looked the part of the rogue Irishman, with his unkempt shock of silvery hair tucked behind the ears, baggy gray suits, and fedora-style hat tilted back on his head as if he were a leprechaun. He spoke rapidly, at an unnervingly high pitch, and was endowed with preternatural wit; he had the hands of a laborer but long ago had vowed never to work for money. There's a word for what Carlin thought of puritanical drudges who boasted, as O'Neill's father did, that they never missed a day of work in their lives: suckers.

Few at the Hell Hole took Terry Carlin seriously. But to O'Neill, he was nothing less than brilliant and among the best-read men he'd ever met. Like O'Neill, he was a self-styled "philosophical anarchist," someone who believed in nonviolently protesting against all forms of institutional power, mostly by ignoring them. ("I am a philosophical anarchist," O'Neill maintained as late as 1946, "which means, 'Go to it, but leave me out of it.' ")[4] O'Neill resented his father's unsolicited counsel, but Carlin he listened to. Carlin reciprocated his young friend's respect, though he had his number better than anyone: "Every soul is alone," O'Neill would somberly declare. "No one in the world understands my slightest impulse." "Then you don't understand the slightest impulse of anyone else," Carlin would respond.[5]

Hutchins Hapgood, an anarchist friend of Carlin's, rented a summerhouse in Provincetown, Massachusetts, at the outermost point of Cape Cod, where he and a group of his friends holed up to keep cool and let loose their creative energies. Hapgood and his wife, the writer Neith Boyce, had formed an amateur drama group in Provincetown the previous summer and were actively seeking new talent. O'Neill's yearning for a theatrical breakthrough, some political troubles Carlin was up against with New York's anarchist contingent, and the threat of the city's summer swelter combined to make it a good time to leave town.

Summer 1916, Provincetown, Massachusetts

Provincetown is situated fifty miles out from the mainland on a continuously fluctuating spit of sand dunes, pine forests, and weathered houses. "Land's End," as the peninsula's called, twists up and around on itself like a scorpion's tail—east, north, west, south, and east again. Its harbor has a long tradition of attracting pathfinders; and by that time, the seaside village it protects from the brutal storms of the North Atlantic had become a hothouse of creative energy. Over six hundred artists migrated there that summer; by August, the *Boston Globe* would run an article under the headline "Biggest Art Colony in the World at Provincetown."[6] O'Neill and Carlin, the two "wash ashores," as they'd be designated by locals, arrived in late June.

Casting their eyes along the curve of the shoreline, the ragtail Irishmen no longer knew which direction they were facing—and no longer cared. "Sand and sun and sea and wind," O'Neill wrote later of the rolling dunes and seascapes encircling the town, "you merge into them, and become as meaningless and as full of meaning as they are. There is always the monotone of surf on the bar—a background for silence—and you *know* that you are alone—so alone you wouldn't be ashamed to do any good action. You can walk or swim along the beach for miles, and meet only the dunes—Sphinxes muffled in their yellow robes with paws deep in the sea."[7]

But O'Neill and Carlin had a more immediate concern on their minds than the picturesque landscape—their lack of money—and Carlin suggested they "put the bite" on Hutchins Hapgood for $10. Nestled among an endless procession of gray-shingled houses on

Commercial Street, Provincetown's sand-strewn access road, Hapgood's house was located in the arty East End district. Hapgood lent them the money, even though, as he suspected at the time and later confirmed, it would never be repaid.[8] O'Neill and Carlin then temporarily moved into the studio of Bayard Boyesen, an outspoken anarchist they knew from Greenwich Village.

O'Neill, with a good word from Carlin, scheduled an audition with the experimental theater group that would soon become known as the Provincetown Players. The reading was to take place at the radical journalist John Reed's house. Most of the Players knew Carlin from Greenwich Village, but O'Neill was a curiosity, "more unknown then than he's famed now," one of them remembered.[9] They referred to him as the "son of James O'Neill," the brilliant actor who'd sold his talent for the easy money of costumed romances and melodrama.[10]

"Jack" Reed loomed large in O'Neill's imagination, even while O'Neill felt an unconquerable desire for Louise Bryant, Reed's future wife. The journalist had gained notoriety three years earlier when he covered the Mexican Revolution and embedded for four months with the populist Mexican general Pancho Villa and his rebel army. O'Neill, hoping to impress Reed, got to work revising his one-act play *The Movie Man*, a vaudeville-style satire based on an actual 1914 Hollywood venture in the Mexican war, during which filmmakers had paid General Villa to let them film his battles.

On the night of O'Neill's tryout, the brief walk from his new shack on the beach to Reed's cottage must have seemed like a mile. The daunting assembly gathered there included Reed and Bryant, Hapgood and Boyce, labor journalist Mary Heaton Vorse, playwright Susan Glaspell, director George "Jig" Cram Cook (Glaspell's husband), set designer Robert Edmond Jones, Provincetown's "poet of the dunes," Harry Kemp, and the enthralling red-haired actress Mary Pyne (Kemp's wife). The Players had been growing restless; they aimed at nothing less than to upend the stale conventions of American theater. Expectations were high over this newcomer, scion of one of the most legendary matinee idols in America.

The night was a disaster. For nearly an hour, the Players' eyes rolled as O'Neill muddled through *The Movie Man*. After he'd finished, the group eviscerated the work as "frightfully bad, trite and full of the most preposterous hokum." Later, Harry Kemp scoffed at its abysmal plot: "Something about an American movie man who financed a Mexican revolution for the sake of filming its battles. One of the scenes depicted the hero's compelling the commanding generals on both sides—both being in his hire—to wage a battle all over again because it had not been fought the way he liked it!"[11] Not only was the story absurd, the script was borderline racist.[12] Reed must have deplored it more than anyone. He knew Mexico and its struggling people well from firsthand reporting. O'Neill knew next to nothing about the country beyond what he'd learned from barrooms, newspapers, and movie house newsreels, and it showed.

O'Neill was highly sensitive to criticism at the time. The editor of the New London newspaper where he'd worked as a cub reporter four years earlier remembered young "Gene" as the temperamental sort who would "grieve like a stricken collie if you so much as looked an unkind thought at him."[13] Although surely devastated by his defeat, O'Neill wasn't yet beaten.

By mid-July he was ready for a second audition, this time at Susan Glaspell and Jig Cook's house, where he arrived clutching the script of *Bound East for Cardiff*, a one-act sea play based on his real-life experiences working on tramp steamers. The same players had assembled, and O'Neill must have sensed a heavy air of doubt. Near prostrate with dread, he sat stock-still in a wicker chair and slowly began to read, one of the Players recalled, "in his low, deep, slightly monotonous but compelling voice."[14] The Players listened silently—this time utterly enthralled.

"There was no one there during that reading who did not recognize the quality of this play," wrote Mary Heaton Vorse years later. "Here was something new, the true feeling of the sea."[15] O'Neill's dialogue was written exclusively in seamen's banter and foreign dialects, and his stage directions offered, in intimate detail, a porthole into the stifling atmosphere of the seamen's living quarters. *Bound East for Cardiff* signaled to the Players a radical departure: in it, O'Neill conveyed the sublime power of the sea through a profound sympathy for a working-class type that up to then had been voiceless on the American stage—and, fundamentally, in society at large. "We heard the actual speech of men who go to sea," Harry Kemp recalled breathlessly. "We shared the reality of their lives; we felt the motion and windy, wave-beaten urge of a ship. This time, no one doubted that here was a genuine playwright."[16]

Over the next forty years, O'Neill would go on to attain four Pulitzer Prizes and a Nobel Prize—the only American dramatist to be awarded that honor. Those triumphs and a great deal more can be traced back to that single midsummer evening in a crowded New England cottage where what has to be the most legendary story of discovery in American theater history had just come to pass.

Introduction

"Life Is a Tragedy—Hurrah!"

I'm an O'Neill fanatic. . . . If you're a playwright, you go to O'Neill as the source. There's really not much in the way of serious American theatre before he came along. He proved it could exist. He's the father of us all, the first to stake a claim nationally and internationally for American dramatic literature.

— Tony Kushner, 2011

Call me a tragic optimist. I believe everything I doubt and I doubt everything I believe. And no motto strikes me as a better one than the ancient "Hew to the line and let the chips fall where they may!"

— Eugene O'Neill, 1925

Tragic. Bitter. Pessimistic. Fatalistic. Gloomy. Take your pick from the run of adjectives trotted out to describe Eugene Gladstone O'Neill, the Irish American "master of the misbegotten," "dean of dysfunction," "black magician," "apostle of woe," "poet laureate of gloom."[1] O'Neill's plays express profound suffering; no one can dispute that. If it's uplift you're after, he's not your man. But O'Neill himself took umbrage when drama critics and celebrity profilers portrayed him in such morbid terms. In one telling letter written in 1923 to Mary Clark, a nurse at the sanatorium where he'd been treated for tuberculosis a decade earlier, we find a genuine instance of O'Neill's warm-hearted and self-effacing personality, traits that offer a startling contrast to the lugubrious existential being of popular lore: "I know you're impervious to what they are pleased to call my 'pessimism'—I mean, that you can see behind that superficial aspect of my work to the truth.

9

I'm far from being a pessimist. I see life as a gorgeously-ironical, beautifully-indifferent, splendidly-suffering bit of chaos the tragedy of which gives Man a tremendous significance, while without his losing fight with fate he would be a tepid, silly animal. I say 'losing fight' only symbolically for the brave individual always wins. Fate can never conquer his—or her—spirit. So you see I'm no pessimist. On the contrary, in spite of my scars, I'm tickled to death with life! I wouldn't 'go out' and miss the rest of the play for anything!"[2]

This candid self-assessment to his friend and former nurse offers us a far more authentic representation of O'Neill's worldview than his prevailing image. In art as in life, O'Neill embraced suffering as an avenue toward exaltation, and he rejected the label "tragic pessimist," coining for himself the keen phrase "tragic optimist" instead. Just before O'Neill won his first Pulitzer Prize for *Beyond the Horizon* in 1920, an unusually insightful feature story on the rising theatrical star appeared, and the physical description it provides, as with so many reminiscences about him, emphasized his lustrous dark eyes: "These eyes have seen both the sunshine and suffering of the world—they say 'Life is a tragedy—hurrah!' "[3]

On the stage and off, O'Neill confronted tragedy head-on throughout his life. All too often this playwright stood terrified, angry, and alone. But he rarely lost sight of the possibility of escape, that sense of belonging to something larger and more meaningful than himself. "The philosophy," O'Neill said, "is that there is always one dream left, one final dream, no matter how low you have fallen, down there at the bottom of the bottle. I know because I saw it."[4] O'Neill had faith that in time he might arrive at that small blue circle of sky, a dream of salvation he held onto tenaciously. Suffering, for the Irish, is almost an art form, in which psychic and physical pain conjure their greatest adversaries—hope and spirit. Such "pipe dreams," as O'Neill called them—or "abject illusions" or "hopeless hopes"—are prerequisites for enduring the trials of life.

Per aspera ad astra—through difficulties to the stars. James Joyce's memorable evocation of the Latin expression in his autobiographical novel *A Portrait of the Artist as a Young Man* (1916) may best encapsulate O'Neill's life and plays. It's a cliché, undoubtedly, but each theme that cycles over and over in O'Neill's writing—his rejection of accepted morality and social institutions, his disdain for what he regarded as the "eternal show-shop" of Broadway, his intense empathy for outcasts, his Irish pride, his sense of the past informing the present and future—all fall under this central concept. *Through difficulties to the stars*. "The point is that life itself is nothing," he once said. "It is the *dream* that keeps us fighting, willing—living! Achievement, in the narrow sense of possession, is a stale finale. The dreams that can be completely realized are not worth dreaming. . . . A man wills his own defeat when he pursues the unattainable. But his *struggle* is his success! . . . Such a figure is necessarily tragic. But to me he is not depressing, he is exhilarating!" O'Neill's autobiographical character Robert Mayo's dying declaration in *Beyond the Horizon* presents the case with stark clarity: "Only with contact with suffering . . . will you—awaken."[5] In the telling of O'Neill's life, this blend of suffering and awakening, forged in the heat of struggle and the light of the stage, will be shown as the starting place from which to arrive at a sincere understanding of this perennially fascinating man.

There's a sizable constituency of literary critics who have made great sport by sullying, with a dogged persistence, Eugene O'Neill's literary reputation as somehow handicapped in the writing department. This is particularly true as compared to other modern authors like Fitzgerald, Hemingway, or Faulkner. He never quite reached his potential, they say, because he was too self-absorbed, too tortured by familial and conjugal relations, or simply too drunk to do so. It is my hope that *Eugene O'Neill: A Life in Four Acts* will dispel this presumption. Indeed, having scrutinized virtually every review of his premieres, I can say that O'Neill likely received more bad reviews than any other major American author. But even so-called real clunkers—*The First Man, Welded, Dynamo, Days Without End*—were still credited by many as breakthroughs in subject matter and form that had never before been attempted on the American stage.

A cursory glance over some of O'Neill's titles (he was one of the great title makers of his generation or any other) evokes with startling clarity this playwright's expansive vision: *"Anna Christie," The Emperor Jones, The Hairy Ape, Desire Under the Elms, Strange Interlude, Mourning Becomes Electra, Ah, Wilderness! A Touch of the Poet, The Iceman Cometh, Long Day's Journey Into Night*, and *A Moon for the Misbegotten*. These plays are readable, teachable, and spellbinding when done right. But as any actor will tell you, to perform them "right" is not easy. Brian Dennehy, who's acted in countless productions of O'Neill's plays and has become one of his greatest interpreters, understands this well: O'Neill "gets a rap for being not a good writer in the sense of not writing poetry, which is crap," Dennehy remarked in 2009. "He's a beautiful writer, a beautiful writer. . . . It's like Shakespeare. . . . None of us are really familiar with that kind of writing. But we all know it's beautiful, and your job as an actor is to make it work. . . . You have the emotional response, the proper one, and the proper intellectual response, and it's usually the result of an enormous amount of work. Same with O'Neill."[6]

Actor Nathan Lane made a similar observation during the Goodman Theatre of Chicago's 2012 production of *The Iceman Cometh*. At the time, Lane was playing the *Iceman*'s leading role of Theodore "Hickey" Hickman, and he wrote to actress Laurie Metcalf, who was then in London playing Mary Tyrone in O'Neill's autobiographical masterwork *Long Day's Journey Into Night*. "The amazing thing about O'Neill," Lane said, "is that he's daring you to go as far as he does, to jump off the cliff with him into the deepest and darkest of places. And if you're brave enough, you will soar. If you don't give yourself over to him, if you try backpedalling him at times, that's when it feels melodramatic or old-fashioned."[7] Nearly a decade earlier, the British actress Helen Mirren identified her role as Christine Mannon in O'Neill's Civil War–era trilogy *Mourning Becomes Electra*, which she'd played for the British National Theatre in 2003, as "one of the really, truly great roles for a woman in literature in the English language."[8]

Theater people aren't the only ones drawn in by O'Neill's inexorable pull. On the fiftieth anniversary of O'Neill's death in

2003, Cornel West, a prominent African American literary theorist and philosopher, called him "the great American blues man of the theater." West went on to compare O'Neill to three other trailblazers: first, Martin Luther King Jr., because O'Neill's plays were meant, like King's speeches, "to redeem the soul of America"; then jazz great Charlie Parker, because he too created his art in "blood, sweat, and tears"; and third, the producers of the *Matrix* films, the Wachowski brothers, because, like them, O'Neill was a white artist "preoccupied with the humanity of black people." *The Emperor Jones*, with its bold elevation of a black protagonist, had forcefully dramatized what West aptly called the "unmasking of civilization." O'Neill recognized the fact, he went on, that "race is constitutive of American civilization. It's not additive; it's not an appendage. It's integral to American life. Eugene O'Neill affirms that in the way in which Faulkner does, Toni Morrison does, Thomas Pynchon does." T. Coraghessan Boyle, a fiction writer who was first dazzled by O'Neill's plays in college, also demonstrates how the playwright's work transcends artistic genres: "I read them apart from classes, for the sweep and power and enjoyment of them. . . . And I will forever be indebted to his influence, as so many of us are, whether we work as poets, novelists or dramatists."[9]

Much earlier, in 1930, when novelist Sinclair Lewis became the first American to win the Nobel Prize for Literature (O'Neill would become the second in 1936, but the only one for drama to date), Lewis told the Swedish committee in his acceptance speech, "Had you chosen Mr. Eugene O'Neill, who has done nothing much in American drama save to transform it utterly . . . from a false world of neat and competent trickery to a world of splendor and fear and greatness, you would have been reminded that he has done something far worse than scoffing—he has seen life as not to be neatly arranged in the study of a scholar but as a terrifying, magnificent, and often quite horrible thing akin to the tornado, the earthquake, the devastating fire."[10]

To this day, O'Neill's plays demand a great deal of self-examination from audiences. They are not passive entertainment. As was the case for his contemporary audiences, his work forces us to confront tough issues that remain divisive flashpoints of our own time: abortion, war, immigration, prostitution, addiction, the theory of evolution, Western materialism and imperialism, wage slavery, interracial marriage and racism. And yet with all of this, the enduring, misleading image remains: O'Neill was a lost poet howling in the wilderness, an isolated misanthrope who obsessed over "universal" themes and left the contemporary political world to its own devices. (O'Neill himself, as we will see, took the term "universal" to task, particularly with regard to the ancient Greeks.) But this perception of his remove from politics has been challenged by, among other law enforcement and government agencies, the Federal Bureau of Investigation.

In the aftermath of the Red Scare of the late 1910s and early 1920s, after which time O'Neill publicly declared the United States to be "the most reactionary country in the world," an agent from what was then called the Bureau of Investigation sent out a memorandum on O'Neill dated April 22, 1924. Submitted one month before J. Edgar Hoover took over as acting director, the memo was filed under Classification 61: Treason. The Bureau had grasped O'Neill's agenda all too well and took particular note of his preoccupation with racial inequality, "a favorite theme of O'Neil's [sic]."[11]

O'Neill resolved early on to avoid open propagandizing; but along with race plays like *The Emperor Jones* and *All God's Chillun Got Wings*, O'Neill's *The Hairy Ape* aroused the Bureau's interest because it "possesses inferential grounds for radical theories" that even surpassed revolutionary Europeans like the Czech writer Karel Čapek, whose play *R.U.R.* (1920), the Bureau said, "has lately been adopted by the radical fraternity."[12] (Čapek would join O'Neill as a Nobel Prize winner in the 1930s.) O'Neill's resistance to propaganda, however, infuriated outspoken Communist playwrights of the 1930s and 1940s like Mike Gold, Clifford Odets, Lillian Hellman, and Arthur Miller. But to dismiss politics as a by-product of O'Neill's dramas leads to false conclusions, as Arthur Miller came to acknowledge. In his autobiography *Timebends* (1987), Miller expressed frustration over seemingly apolitical writers like O'Neill who appeared to write for "the mystical rich, of high society and the . . . escapist 'culture.' " Then he attended the 1946 premiere of *The Iceman Cometh*: "I was . . . struck by O'Neill's radical hostility to bourgeois civilization, far greater than anything Odets had expressed. . . . It was O'Neill who wrote about the working-class men, about whores and the social discards and even the black man in a white world, but since there was no longer a connection with Marxism in the man himself, his plays were never seen as the critiques of capitalism that objectively they were."[13]

O'Neill was politically outspoken throughout his life, always siding with the disempowered. "I care only for humanity," he said. "I wish to arouse compassion. For the unfortunate. The suffering. The oppressed. . . . If people leave the theatre after one of my plays with a feeling of compassion for those less fortunate than they I am satisfied. I have not written in vain."[14] He believed that agitprop from activist-playwrights would change little and weaken the impact of their drama. "My quarrel with propaganda in the theatre," he wrote Mike Gold in 1926, "is that it's such damned unconvincing propaganda—whereas, if you will restrain the propaganda purpose to the selection of the life to be portrayed and then let that life live itself without comment, it does your trick. I advise this in the name of flesh & blood propaganda!"[15]

O'Neill publicly defended anarchists and socialists and railed against racial injustice. He signed a petition for members of the Industrial Workers of the World to be released from Leavenworth prison for their vocal stance against World War I. He supported Jewish refugees fleeing Europe when the Nazis came to power. He wrote a telegram to the Catholic Interracial Council when the National Theater in Washington, D.C., tried to ban African Americans from attending *The Iceman Cometh*: "I am and always have been opposed to racial discrimination of any kind and I assure you I will insist on a non-discrimination clause in all future contracts. Surely my past record as a dramatist and a producer has shown where I stand on this issue."[16] O'Neill refused, however, to sign an appeal for Ireland to break neutrality during World War II. "It is they who will be massacred by German bombers if they commit this act of war," he said. "If we could promise our country would fight as an ally of

Ireland and defend her independence we might have a right to make this appeal, but as things are I feel we have no right."[17]

O'Neill's tragedies, in their denial of Americans' most cherished desire as a people, hinge on the distressing fact that the American Dream seldom realizes itself. O'Neill never lived the dream the way most believe American "success stories" are supposed to play out. He believed it was a fatuous delusion from the start.

Indeed, one of the more stunning moments in O'Neill's career was a near-treasonous declaration he gave in 1946 during a press conference to promote *The Iceman Cometh*—his first such public appearance in more than a decade. At the height of the patriotic triumphalism that gripped the nation in postwar America, O'Neill lambasted the concept of the American Dream, and it's remarkably easy to imagine the impact of such a statement even today: "Some day this country is going to get it—really get it. We had everything to start with—everything—but there's bound to be a retribution. We've followed the same selfish, greedy path as every other country in the world. We talk about the American Dream and want to tell the world about the American Dream, but what is that dream, in most cases, but the dream of material things? I sometimes think that the United States, for this reason, is the greatest failure the world has ever seen. We've been able to get a very good price for our souls in this country—the greatest price perhaps that has ever been paid."[18]

Many other aspects of O'Neill's career have been sidelined in the past, often with the best of intentions. While praise over his legacy is inevitable, to omit his difficulties would be deceptive. Perhaps most important among them is that O'Neill was in no sense a natural-born genius. Terms like *genius* and *gifted*, so blithely conferred upon our accomplished scientists, artists, musicians, and writers—those with a creative *gene*—presume a gift of nature handed down rather than a skill to be earned through time and hard work. "A horrible word," novelist William Faulkner said of "genius" in an essay on O'Neill's singular contribution to American letters, written well before Faulkner

had published his first book.[19] The indomitable acting impresario
Stella Adler once asked a group of her students, "Do you understand
the difference between craft and the result of craft, which is talent?
Nobody says 'I want to play the piano at Carnegie Hall' before they
take some lessons. You can imagine what it would sound like."[20]

O'Neill's development as a writer was anything but smooth sailing. I have discovered, for instance, new evidence that at the height
of his celebrity in the mid-1920s, he planned to give up playwriting
and become a novelist. "Crowding a drama into a play," he grumbled
to a friend, "is like getting an elephant to dance in a tub."[21] Though
O'Neill became exasperated with the limits of the stage, in the end
he refused to abandon it. Instead, he pushed beyond its conventions
and forever changed its rules. If Tennessee Williams is the poet of
American drama, O'Neill is its novelist, with strong elements of the
composer. For this reason, and unlike most dramatic works, O'Neill's
plays are meant to be read in solitude as much as seen in a crowded
theater.

Contrary to the implied ease of a genius at work, O'Neill's
writing life consisted of uneven stretches of creative doldrums punctuated by flashes of staggering brilliance, a heartrending process in
which he achieved the highest possible stature as a playwright through
sheer force of will. Decades of grueling labor and self-doubt fueled
the creation of his late masterworks: *The Iceman Cometh, Long Day's
Journey, A Touch of the Poet,* and *A Moon for the Misbegotten.* And yet his
earlier plays are still too often dismissed. O'Neill scholar Jackson R.
Bryer told me that while working as a consultant on Ric Burns's 2003
documentary on O'Neill, he was frustrated to discover that once
again the "late great" plays dominated the narrative while O'Neill's
earlier work went largely ignored. "O'Neill won three Pulitzers and
a Nobel Prize before he wrote those late plays," he pointed out to
Burns. "He must have been doing something right!"

In 2004, Tony Kushner professed that "much that an Ameri-
can playwright needs to know can be learned by studying Eugene
Gladstone O'Neill's life and work."[22] Indeed, it is the full sweep of
O'Neill's career, from tyro to titan, that concerns us here. A model for

any unformed artist, O'Neill swore as early as 1914 "to be an artist or nothing."[23] And so he wrote.

"So, why Eugene O'Neill?" My standard line when asked this maddening question—maddening both in its complexity and its rate of recurrence—goes something like this: "Because I'm an Irish-American male who grew up in Connecticut and New York and feels at home in dive bars. I also love plays. And if they're set in dive bars, all the better." There's autobiography in all biography, of course, no matter what purists say. But the deeper question for me is why I feel so reassured in the company of this playwright. It's a great irony that a man so desperately alienated could conjure the feelings of warmth and compassion that make countless others feel they belong. But maybe that's why O'Neill's fans settle into an irresistible comfort zone when we enter his imagination, and also why we don't find his plays as gloomy as others often complain.

My mother first discovered her love of O'Neill's writing in a seminar taught by Professor James Baird, at what was, in the early 1950s, the Connecticut College for Women. (The playwright was alive at the time, wasting away from a neurological illness just a couple of hours north in Massachusetts.) Her bookshelves while I was growing up were stocked with volumes of O'Neill's plays, many of them first editions, and by the time I was in my early twenties, she took me to my first O'Neill production: the Wooster Group's masterful revival of *The Hairy Ape* starring Willem Dafoe as Robert "Yank" Smith. I was sold then and there, forever and for good.

Like O'Neill, I was raised Irish Catholic. I attended Mass on Sundays and holidays, got baptized, took first Communion, and so on. Monks, nuns, and priests were relatives and friends, welcome guests at the dinner table. But I don't ever remember, not for one moment, believing in God. (Jesus I believed in, as O'Neill did, not as a divine being but as an advocate for the misbegotten among us.) In order to avoid going to Mass, I even tried to convince my now-deceased father, whom I loved very much but didn't see eye to eye with on religion, that I was allergic to incense. "That's ridiculous," I can still hear him saying. "Get your coat on, we're going." I realize now that the empti-ness O'Neill felt within him, the desperate lack of a higher power—"without past or future, within peace and unity and a wild joy," as his character Edmund Tyrone calls it in *Long Day's Journey*, "something greater than my own life. . . . God, if you want to put it that way" (*CP*3, 812)—often plagues latecomers to the mindset of the nonbeliever. This spiritual void eternally harassed O'Neill, and it no doubt led to his life-long battle with alcoholism. But it also explains a great deal about his eventual stature as a writer. O'Neill desperately needed to fill that void with something, anything. Writing plays gave him the opportunity to explore what, in the end, might restore some meaning to his existence.

My father's side of the family waxed as romantic about Ireland in my grandparents' living room as the O'Neills had when Eugene was young. My ancestor Michael O'Rahilly (first cousin thrice removed), known to the Irish as "The O'Rahilly," was the only officer who died at Dublin's General Post Office during the Easter Rising of 1916. My family is as proud of our ties to The O'Rahilly as the O'Neills had been about their line to the chieftains of County Tyrone. As late as 1943, when a mysterious neurodegenerative disease arrested O'Neill's ability to write, one of his favorite new books was Seán O'Faolain's *The Great O'Neill* (1942), a biography of "The O'Neill," the sixteenth-century Gaelic chieftain Hugh O'Neill, Earl of Tyrone; the dramatist portrayed his ancestor to the Irish American novelist James T. Farrell as "strong proud and noble, ignoble shameless and base, loyal and treacherous, a cunning politician, a courageous soldier, an inspiring leader—but at times so weakly neurotic he could burst openly into tears (even when sober!) and whine pitiably that no one understood him."[24] One of my own favorite biographies is Aodogán O'Rahilly's *Winding the Clock: O'Rahilly and the 1916 Rising* (1991). The O'Rahilly's rebellion proved futile, as he suspected it would; but the Easter Rising shocked the world just two months before the twenty-seven-year-old playwright's arrival at Provincetown, Massachusetts, where O'Neill was one of the chosen leaders of another kind of revolution. Both men's sides would ultimately triumph, if O'Neill, unlike The O'Rahilly, survived to tell the tale.

O'Neill's proud testimonials about his Irish heritage—in his diaries and letters, public proclamations and idle chatter—together lay bare the weight his Irishness had on his dramas, and thus on American theater. They also reveal how such immigrants as his parents, and my own ancestors who arrived much later, improve upon and integrate our nation's cultural fabric rather than pulling it asunder. I've since spent a good deal of my life in Ireland, visiting family (my sister and her husband run a dolphin-watching boat at the mouth of the River Shannon) and teaching Irish literature in Sligo. It was during my visits there that I adopted the egalitarian impulse, the mistrust of authority, the laughter at pretension, the devotion to storytelling—traits that made their way across the Atlantic to the United States in no small part in the figure of Eugene O'Neill.

O'Neill never visited his parents' homeland, much as he longed to. But paying tribute to the dispossessed on the American stage became a lifelong project for the playwright, one he would explore with his treatment of an unrepentant prostitute in *"Anna Christie,"* a black Pullman porter in *The Emperor Jones*, a coal-stoker on a steamship in *The Hairy Ape*, culminating with his barroom tour de force *The Iceman Cometh*. With these plays and dozens of others, O'Neill reached broadly across the American social matrix—sailors, prostitutes, pimps, gamblers, hustlers, anarchists, socialists, hotel clerks, down-and-outers, black gangsters, tenant farmers, bohemian artists, safecrackers, bartenders, and Broadway "rounders"—unleashing virtually every outcast from America's misbegotten landscape onto the world stage.

The Irish playwright John Millington Synge, commenting on his plays, said he found Mother Ireland as she was, not as she wished to be found; O'Neill, like Synge before him, wrote about his own motherland, the United States, as he found her rather than as she wished to be found. And he inspired countless members of subsequent generations, myself included, to do the same.

Eugene O'Neill: A Life in Four Acts is not an all-inclusive study of O'Neill's life and work, nor does it need to be. But for the general audience—loads of converts, with any luck—I will highlight what are in my opinion the most revealing episodes in an attempt to capture an artist's life with his own medium, drama, in steady view. Each episode shows the ripple effect of this playwright on American theater and culture and how the stories he told interweave with his actual life stories, many of which have lain fallow beneath thousands of pages of scholarship or buried in archives since his death in 1953.

Every word O'Neill wrote—from amateur poet to master playwright—is part of one tale, and decades of grueling labor produced some of the finest plays ever written. So as not to interrupt the narrative with too many historical digressions (which, as a literary historian by trade and temperament, I'm ordinarily inclined to do), I've begun each "act" with italicized vignettes that function something like the program notes of a playbill; each sums up, in broad-brush strokes, the context of American theater writ large overarching the events of O'Neill's life and career. In this way, I hope to show how O'Neill's personal experience was intertwined with the revolutionary theater of his time, a theater that he molded and uncompromisingly urged forward.

I have made use of recent scholarship for this biography, but the book also contributes much that is new to O'Neill studies. Along with bringing to light a wealth of previously overlooked material—including letters, reminiscences, and literary works like his story "The Screenews of War," which contains the first plot he pitched to the Provincetown Players—this book supplies connections between O'Neill's plays and his worldview, "philosophical anarchism"; his role in African American cultural history; photographs that have eluded scholars for generations, including a never-before published image of O'Neill and his lover Louise Bryant and pictures of all three dive bars that inspired *The Iceman Cometh* (Jimmy the Priest's, the Garden Hotel, and the Hell Hole); commentary and anecdotes from the largest stockpile of opening night reviews of O'Neill's plays ever assembled; evidence for the fact that O'Neill was determined to give up playwriting and become a novelist, why he made that decision, and what his envy of novelists tells us about his work as a whole; and, in the postscript, revealing evidence about the mystery of why O'Neill's widow, Carlotta Monterey, might have defied her husband's wishes and authorized the release of *Long Day's Journey* in 1956—this last, despite his proviso, known to the public at the time, that the play not be published until twenty-five years after his death and, what is less known, never produced on stage, screen, radio, or television.

Eugene O'Neill: A Life in Four Acts is notably the first biography to discuss O'Neill's lost play *Exorcism*, an illuminating prequel of sorts to *Long Day's Journey Into Night*, after its recovery in 2011. I was in the research stage of this book when Yale University's Beinecke Library, which holds the Eugene O'Neill Papers, had the great fortune of acquiring the only known script of *Exorcism*, O'Neill's one-act account of his actual suicide attempt in late 1911. O'Neill thought he'd destroyed all copies of the script after its run in 1920, but over ninety years later, *Exorcism* was brought to light at last; and as biographers and scholars have suspected all along, the autobiographical play holds some remarkable new insights into O'Neill's most tragic experience as a young man while at the same time deepening our understanding of *The Iceman Cometh* and *Long Day's Journey*. O'Neill characterizes his avatar in *Exorcism*, Ned Malloy, who later appears in a more sanitized form as Edmund Tyrone in *Long Day's Journey*, as bitter and self-absorbed. He's an emotional bully to friends and family, insensitive to their deep concern for his well-being. In private, O'Neill was so often disgusted with himself and life in general, in fact, that he took his anger out, sometimes cruelly, on those who cared for him most. No document speaks more tellingly to this than *Exorcism*. But the more we grasp Ned Malloy's all-too-common personality defects, the more human his creator's journey becomes.

The college seminar I teach on Eugene O'Neill ends with two simple questions: Which plays did you enjoy the most? Which the least? Without missing a beat, one student a few years back raised his hand and submitted that O'Neill's actual life was his finest drama. His classmates all nodded in agreement. Thinking the matter through, I realized that the dramatic structure of O'Neill's life came into clearer focus when matched to the narrative arc of so many of his plays. Most of us attempt to formulate a meaningful narrative of our lives as they move forward; the difficulty for a biographer lies in comprehending the arc of other people's lives.

O'Neill himself pointed out this difficulty of forming a coherent chronicle of his life to his first biographer, Barrett Clark: "The trouble with anyone else writing even a sketch [about me]," he said after reading Clark's manuscript in 1926, "is that I don't believe there is anyone alive today who knew me as intimately in more than one phase of a life that has passed through many entirely distinct periods, with complete changes of environment, associates, etc. And I myself might not be so good at writing it; for when my memory brings back this picture or episode or that one, I simply cannot recognize that person in myself nor understand him nor his acts as mine (although objectively I can) although my reason tells me he was undeniably I."[25]

By my count, O'Neill lived through four acts, each with its own, as he himself suggests above, idiosyncratic episodes, characters, and mise-en-scène. (Four was O'Neill's chosen number of acts in, among other plays, *"Anna Christie," Long Day's Journey Into Night, The Iceman Cometh, A Touch of the Poet,* and *A Moon for the Misbegotten.*) Within these four acts, O'Neill's life uncannily follows classical dramatic structure as well: the *exposition* during his childhood and theatrical upbringing; the *rising action* as he proves himself as a writer; the *climax* when he reaches his greatest heights as a theatrical giant, but then flees the country to avoid a scandal over his second divorce; the evident *crisis* that took place after the catastrophic failure of his 1933 "God play" *Days Without End*; the *falling action* after he removes himself from the public eye for twelve long years; and the *denouement* with the neurological illness that forced him to quit writing at the height of his mental power and led to his untimely death. The postscript covers the posthumous release of O'Neill's greatest play, *Long Day's Journey Into Night,* in 1956—the catalyst for a "Eugene O'Neill Renaissance," one of the single most astonishing resurrections in American literary history.

* * *

In December 1905 Clyde William Fitch, then America's most famous living dramatist, knocked on the door of 884 Park Avenue, the novelist Edith Wharton's New York residence. Wharton's first best seller The House of Mirth *had just appeared, and Fitch, a flamboyant and prolific playwright rumored to have enjoyed "relations" with Oscar Wilde, asked if he might persuade her to collaborate on a stage adaptation of her new novel. She accepted the offer, though with reservations.*

Wharton had tried to win over theatergoers with original plays before. But she could never descend low enough for the average audience and had rebuffed a friend's advice that if she wanted a hit play, she should consider the century-old costumes and "society gags" that sold at the box office. Many illustrious fiction writers such as herself had taken their turn "on the boards" from the 1880s to the early 1900s— Henry James, William Dean Howells, Mark Twain, Bret Harte, Hamlin Garland, Mary Austin, and Jack London, among others—none of them successfully. "Forget not," Henry James cautioned would-be playwrights, "that you write for the stupid."

Leaving the Savoy Theatre in Herald Square after the New York premiere of The House of Mirth *on October 22, 1906, Wharton remarked to her escort, William Dean Howells, "What the American public always wants is a tragedy with a happy ending." And after the play received several poor reviews, she admitted, "I now doubt if that kind of play, with a 'sad ending,' and a negative hero, could ever get a hearing from an American audience." Nearly three decades later, Wharton agreed to another collaboration, this time with playwright Zoë Akins, based on Wharton's dolorous novella* The Old Maid *(1924). The play was a resounding success, and it beat out Lillian Hellman's thematically parallel* The Children's Hour *and Clifford Odets's* Awake and Sing! *for the 1935 Pulitzer Prize for Drama. By then, even Wharton's play was hotly contested as not original or experimental enough for the award, however, and opponents to the decision consequently founded the New York Drama Critics' Circle Award.*

The following year, 1936, Eugene O'Neill, having already won three Pulitzers in the 1920s, emerged as the only American dramatist to date to win the Nobel Prize in Literature. It was an honor, he told the Swedish Academy, that spoke to the evolution of American drama as a whole: "This highest of distinctions is all the more grateful to me because I feel so deeply that it is not only my work that is being honored, but the work of all of my colleagues in America—that this Nobel Prize is a symbol of the recognition by Europe of the coming-of-age of the American theatre . . . worthy at last to claim kinship with the modern drama of Europe, from which our original inspiration so surely derives."

Whatever one's prejudice about the Nobel or the Pulitzer, and whatever one's opinion of O'Neill's tragic vision, by the 1930s, everyone agreed: American plays like O'Neill's, with "sad endings and negative heroes," even while faced with daunting competition from the lighter forms of entertainment amply provided by the Hollywood studio system and the commercial theater, had at last found their hearing.

* * *

ACT I: The Ghosts at the Stage Door

It is impossible to act in the American play unless we go back and see that
the American play really starts with O'Neill. But in order to get to O'Neill,
you have to know what was before him. . . . Before O'Neill in this country,
the play was for business, for success, for the star who brought in money,
for its fashionableness to an audience. The theater was nothing more, and
not thought of as anything more, than a place of amusement.

—STELLA ADLER, 2010

Before Eugene O'Neill . . . there was a wasteland. . . . Two centuries of junk.

—GORE VIDAL, 1959

The Treasures of Monte Cristo

MARY ELLEN "ELLA" QUINLAN O'NEILL gave birth to
her third and last child, Eugene, at the Barrett House
hotel in Manhattan on October 16, 1888. Situated on
the northeast corner of Broadway and Forty-Third
Street, the Barrett House loomed at the intersection of what would
become Times Square, the theatrical center of the world. Ella's hotel
room had a corner view of the neighborhood where her newborn's
name would burn brightly on electric marquees as a heady draw for
the theatergoing public. Two days after his birth, Eugene was swept
away with his family on the first of many national tours with his father, the matinee idol James O'Neill.

One of the most celebrated actors of his day and a natural successor to the great Shakespearean actor Edwin Booth, James was born in
1845, the son of Edward and Mary O'Neill, Irish immigrants of the
peasant class from County Kilkenny. In 1850, Edward had emigrated
to Buffalo, New York, with his wife and their eight children to escape
the devastation of the potato famine. (James was the seventh child,

The Barrett House, O'Neill's birthplace, at Broadway and Forty-Third
Street, later Times Square. O'Neill responded to the friend who sent
this image to him as a present that the man leaning against the lamppost
obviously "had a bun on" (that is, he was drunk).
(COURTESY OF SHEAFFER-O'NEILL COLLECTION, LINDA LEAR CENTER FOR SPECIAL
COLLECTIONS AND ARCHIVES, CONNECTICUT COLLEGE, NEW LONDON)

✳   ✳   ✳

and his sister Margaret, born in Buffalo in 1851, made nine.) The
transatlantic journey was so harrowing that James rarely spoke of it as
an adult. A few years later, in the mid-1850s, Edward O'Neill returned
to Ireland after his eldest son, Richard, died, leaving the rest of the
family to fend for themselves. Edward himself died of arsenic poisoning in Ireland six years after his departure, most likely a suicide.[1]

James O'Neill, at a mere ten years old, was thus compelled to help
support his family by working grueling twelve-hour shifts making files
at a machine shop. "A dirty barn of a place," James Tyrone (O'Neill)
remembers the shop in his son's autobiographical play *Long Day's Journey Into Night*, "where rain dripped through the roof, where you roasted

in summer, and there was no stove in winter, and your hands got numb with cold, where the only light came through two small filthy windows, so on grey days I'd have to sit bent over with my eyes almost touching the files in order to see! ... And what do you think I got for it? Fifty cents a week! It's the truth! Fifty cents a week!" (*CP*3, 807). By 1858, the O'Neills had relocated to Cincinnati, Ohio, where they were largely supported by James's older sister Josephine, who'd fortuitously married a prosperous Ohio saloonkeeper. It was in Cincinnati that James discovered his talent for acting at age twenty, when he made his debut in 1865 during the final days of the Civil War at Cincinnati's National Theatre and rapidly gained a reputation as a dashing leading man.

The reigning "queen of actresses," Adelaide Neilson, a British performer whose Juliet was thought to be the finest of all time, was

James O'Neill, 1869.

* * *

once asked which Romeo among the many she'd played opposite was best. Neilson replied brusquely, "A little Irishman named O'Neill."[2] In 1872, James found himself onstage with Edwin Booth, "the greatest actor of his day or any other," James Tyrone boasts in *Long Day's Journey* (*CP3*, 809). Booth, the brother of Lincoln's assassin, John Wilkes Booth, and James played *Othello* at McVicker's Theatre in Chicago, each night alternating the roles of Iago and Othello. During one performance, while waiting for his cue in the wings, Booth remarked, "That young man is playing [Othello] better than I ever did."[3] This single evening, after James had been informed of Booth's tribute to him, marked the high point of his acting career, perhaps of his entire life. James would never again experience such a genuine surge of professional gratification.

On February 12, 1883, James accepted a role at New York's Booth Theatre that would thrust him into the national limelight, though he would notoriously become trapped by its very popularity: Edmund Dantès in Charles Fechter's 1870 stage adaptation of Alexandre Dumas's novel *The Count of Monte Cristo*, the title of which, though it's often forgotten, Fechter had reduced to the more straightforward *Monte Cristo*.

James had played Edmund Dantès back in Chicago on April 21, 1875, while a stock actor at Hooley's Theatre, and the reviews for that performance had been excellent. *The Spirit of the Times* newspaper, however, predicted of the new Booth Theatre production that "*Monte Cristo* will not run very long." James had been prevented by heavy snowfall from attending most of the rehearsals, and consequently he'd only had a few days to learn his part. John Stetson, the owner of the Globe Theatre in Boston, ignored the bad notices and kept the production going. Fechter's widow was brought in as a consultant, and she worked enough magic to make it a hit.[4]

The legendary character Edmund Dantès is an upright sailor wrongly accused of treason against the king of France and cast into a dungeon at the Château d'If off the coast of Marseilles. His imprisonment clears the way for the villain Fernand to gain Edmund's betrothed, the Catalan Mercédès (a name that James, who spoke some French, liked to enunciate affectedly with a rolling "r").[5]

After languishing in prison for eighteen years, Edmund makes his getaway with the help of his dying cellmate, friend, and benefactor Abbé Faria. Eventually, he reclaims Mercédès and a son, Albert, who had been conceived before Dantès's imprisonment (without, as the saying goes, the benefit of clergy). Dantès doesn't have many lines; most of the dialogue is reserved for the play's villains pacing about conspiring against one another. But the spectacular prison escape is far and away the most defining scene of James's career: "The moon breaks out, lighting up a projecting rock," the stage directions specify, then "Edmund rises from the sea, he is dripping, a knife in his hand, some shreds of sack adhering to it." He stands up on the stone pedestal and shouts exultantly to the heavens, "The world is MINE!" James would enact this climactic scene to as many as six thousand audiences, thus branding his acting reputation forever.[6]

Far more relevant to James's actual life, however, are the lines that precede the heroic declaration: "Saved! Mine, the treasures of Monte Cristo! The world is MINE!"[7] "The treasures of Monte Cristo" refer to a hidden fortune on a deserted island that Faria bequeaths to Dantès before dying in prison. After his daring escape, Dantès spends years traveling the world spending Faria's money lavishly before, apparently as an afterthought, returning to Mercédès. More than about love, then, *Monte Cristo* is about money, and James soon decided to acquire his own "treasure of Monte Cristo": the rights to

Monte Cristo playbill.
(COURTESY OF SHEAFFER-O'NEILL COLLECTION, LINDA LEAR CENTER FOR SPECIAL COLLECTIONS AND ARCHIVES, CONNECTICUT COLLEGE, NEW LONDON)

✳   ✳   ✳

the Fechter script for $2,000. With sole proprietorship of the play as of the 1885–86 season, James O'Neill would perform the role to packed houses for almost thirty years, earning him a profit of near-ly forty thousand a year. Like Edmund Dantès, James had escaped from a prison of his own—the prison of poverty. And both men were spared horrible fates by dint of their talent, honesty, and charisma.[8]

Charles Fechter's *Monte Cristo* is saturated with doses of mous-tache twirling by evildoers and moral posturing by good-guy swash-bucklers. One line from Edmund Dantès neatly sums up the play's complexity: "Sooner or later believe me, the honest man will meet his reward and the wicked be punished."[9] Those who surrender an after-noon to Fechter's abysmal dialogue will discover their minds drifting off and returning back to a single question: Why would theatergoers choose to see this grossly melodramatic play night after night, year after year? The script was considered just as hackneyed in those days, and the question was the same then as it is today. "The answer, of course, was my father," Eugene O'Neill explained toward the end of his own career. "He had a genuine romantic Irish personality—looks, voice, and stage presence—and he loved the part. . . . Audiences came to see James O'Neill in *Monte Cristo*, not *Monte Cristo*."[10]

O'Neill's vocal contempt for his father's play once he'd grown old enough to have such opinions would be echoed by him years later in a speech by the guileless Marco Polo in the historical satire *Marco Millions* (1928). At one point, Marco repeats the lackluster word "good" six times to emphasize his bourgeois tastes: "There's nothing better than to sit down in a good seat at a good play after a good day's work in which you know you've accomplished something, and after you've had a good dinner, and just take it easy and enjoy a good wholesome thrill or a good laugh and get your mind off serious things until it's time to go to bed" (*CP2*, 431). Shakespeare similarly derided plays designed "to ease the anguish of a torturing hour" in *A Midsummer Night's Dream*, while in O'Neill's earliest satire, *Now I Ask You* (1916), Lucy Ashleigh, a pretentious adorer of Ibsen's *Hedda Gabler* (1890), argues against at-tending vaudeville shows because "those productions were concocted with an eye for the comfort of the Tired Business Man" (*CP1*, 451).

Some of the earliest words O'Neill remembered his father uttering were "The theater is dying." James in fact came to regard his good fortune as a "curse" that had barred him from true theatrical greatness. Although O'Neill later believed that he alone had been told of this family curse, James had been quite open to the press about it. In 1901, for instance, a reporter ran into him in Broadway Alley and asked about his future plans. "My private secretary informs me that I have played Dantes four thousand times," James said. "I have struggled to elaborate my repertoire, but what can a man do when his greatest measure of success seems to lie in a familiar rut? When a treadmill is grinding out big profits, you know, it is rather difficult to step from it."[11]

In fact, the curse of *Monte Cristo* had bedeviled the actor as far back as 1885, before he'd even bought the rights to the Fechter script. Just after his second son Edmund's death, when James was at his most emotionally fragile, he was approached by a meddlesome reporter in a Chicago wine bar and, with his guard carelessly down, confided everything. The article offers a detailed exposition on the "improvidence" of actors like James, whose "great promise has never been realized" and recounts James's wistful, wine-soaked grief for his "early days," when "Jimmy O'Neill" "performed Iago to Booth's Othello with an aptness and clearness of conception that all but eclipsed the star himself." "And yet, in spite of all his successes in the 'legitimate,' " the reporter went on, "he forsook the higher walks of the drama, adopting melodramatic roles which are ephemeral as the day when compared with the true art in which he had given such promise."[12] For the remainder of his life, James lamented his choice of profits over the nobler pursuits of the stage. "That's what caused me to make up my mind that they would never get me," O'Neill said after learning of this. "I determined then that I would never sell out."[13]

Ella O'Neill, like her husband, James, was born into a first-generation Irish home. Her parents, Thomas and Bridget Quinlan, were also famine refugees, but Thomas thrived in the United States as a tobacco and liquor merchant in Cleveland, Ohio. Ella met the impossibly handsome James, who was twelve years her senior and by then a sought-after bachelor, in 1872 through her father, Thomas, whom James had befriended at the Quinlans' liquor shop, a popular hangout for performers within a short walk of the city's Academy of Music. Ella and James were married five years later and had three sons together—James Jr. in 1878, Edmund Burke in 1883, and Eugene Gladstone in 1888. (Charles Fechter, not incidentally, had anglicized Dumas's hero's name from "Edmond" to "Edmund." James's older brother, named Edward after their father, had died in battle during the Civil War. But James didn't choose to name his first two sons after his father or his brother, whose veteran's pension had sustained their mother Mary. Rather, he named them in effect after his dual personae, offstage and on: James and Edmund.)[14]

On March 4, 1885, at four o'clock in the morning, Edmund, only eighteen months, died.[15] The death of a child is an unimaginable horror for any parent, of course, but the cause of his death was especially shocking. The O'Neills had left Edmund and Jamie, as they called their firstborn, in New York under the care of Ella's mother, Bridget, while James was performing in Colorado. Jamie contracted measles in their absence, and the obstreperous six-year-old was under his grandmother's strict orders not to come in contact with his little brother. He went into the child's bedroom anyway, and only a few days later Edmund succumbed to the disease. Ella returned to New York by train straight away while James stayed on to finish the tour. "The vast audience," reported the *Denver Tribune-Republican* the night Ella departed, "did not know that James O'Neill ... was heartbroken. It did not know that at that moment his little child lay dead in far distant New York, and that the agonized mother had just taken a tearful farewell of him to attend the burial of the little one. It laughed and clapped its hands and paid no thought but to the actor's genius, and dreamed not of the inward weeping that was drowning his heart."[16]

O'Neill became convinced in the years to follow that his mother never forgave his older brother Jim, as he called him, for infecting Edmund; and he himself suffered from a tormenting mixture of survivor's guilt and death envy, later naming his autobiographical character in *Long Day's Journey* "Edmund" and the dead child "Eugene." The reversal of names in the play appears to have an even deeper symbolic meaning for the mother, Mary Cavan Tyrone, who makes clear that she gave birth to her third son to replace the deceased Eugene, and only at the insistence of her husband James (*CP*3, 766). Hence O'Neill proposes that his birth was no more than a mistake made out of desperation and that his existence in her eyes was a bedeviling reminder of her guilt over Edmund. It's no wonder, then, that O'Neill later wrote down, without explanation and despite the fact that his mother was a practicing Catholic, that he'd been born in the wake of "a series of brought-on abortions."[17] "I knew I'd proved by the way I'd left Eugene [Edmund] that I wasn't worthy to have another baby," Mary Tyrone says to James while high on morphine, "and that God would punish me if I did. I never should have borne Edmund [Eugene]" (*CP*3, 766).

Worse still, perhaps, a hotel doctor prescribed Ella O'Neill morphine for the intolerable pain of giving birth to Eugene, an

Mary Ellen "Ella" Quinlan O'Neill.
(COURTESY OF SHEAFFER-O'NEILL COLLECTION, LINDA LEAR CENTER FOR SPECIAL COLLECTIONS AND ARCHIVES, CONNECTICUT COLLEGE, NEW LONDON)

✳   ✳   ✳

eleven-pound baby, thus precipitating a drug addiction that would last for well over two decades and haunt Ella and the O'Neill men to all of their deaths. This was the guilt-ridden, blame-laden family substructure that O'Neill would lay bare in *Long Day's Journey Into Night*, a play, he wrote, "of old sorrow, written in tears and blood . . . with deep pity and understanding and forgiveness for *all* the four haunted Tyrones" (*CP*3, 714).

O'Neill toured with his parents around the American theater circuit for the first seven years of his life. "Usually a child has a regular, fixed home," he said decades later, "but you might say I started in as a trouper. I knew only actors and the stage. My mother nursed me in the wings and in dressing rooms."[18] But like any average American lad, one of his earliest memories involved . . . what else? Cowboys and Indians. Most small boys from the Northeast became enraptured by the romantic lure of the Wild West by reading dime novels and magazines. O'Neill's father brought him right to the source.

James O'Neill's advance man, George C. Tyler, marveled at the storybook figures his boss fraternized with across the West. On any given night, Tyler said, he would find James in a saloon chatting with "the biggest poker player in the United States, or Buffalo Bill Cody or somebody like that—the biggest guns in any walk of life were a natural part of his background."[19] Indian-related violence in the Montana Territory had abated after the Great Sioux War (1876–77), and James, the prosperous showman and Civil War veteran Nate Salsbury, and Colonel William F. "Buffalo Bill" Cody together held lucrative shares in a Montana ranch called the Milner Cattle Company. So the three men communed together at barrooms whenever they chanced to find themselves performing in the same Western town.

In his adult years, O'Neill calculated that he'd been around two years old and near death from typhoid in a Chicago hotel room when Sitting Bull, Crazy Horse, and other Sioux "hostiles" from the Dakota Territory gathered around his sickbed. He remembered feather headdresses and blankets draped across imposing, longhaired heads and "big brown" bodies. One of James O'Neill's associates had indeed assembled a troupe of Sioux performers from William Cody's Buffalo Bill's Wild West show to offer the child some respite from the stomach cramps, headaches, and soaring temperatures with which typhoid assails its victims. O'Neill couldn't recollect the words spoken, though he remembered the visits took place over the course of a month. Whatever was said, this memory—maybe his earliest—"left him with the low-down on Custer," he told a friend in 1946, "and an acute sympathy for the redman."[20]

This makes for a great story. But Sitting Bull and Crazy Horse weren't there at O'Neill's sickbed in Chicago. Sitting Bull had performed only one season for William Cody, and that was four years before O'Neill was born. It's unlikely that Crazy Horse would have submitted to the demeaning behavior expected of Cody's performers; but in any case, he couldn't have. Crazy Horse was killed by a prison guard in 1877 after his pyrrhic victory at Little Big Horn. And by the time the O'Neills arrived in Chicago in the late spring of 1891, when Eugene was two and a half, Buffalo Bill's Wild West was on tour in Europe. Cody wouldn't play Chicago again until 1893 at the famed World's Columbian Exposition, better known as the great Chicago World's Fair, commemorating the four hundredth anniversary of Christopher Columbus's discovery of the New World.[21] With these facts in mind, the only plausible story is nearly as good as the one O'Neill recalled.

The Chicago run of James's romantic drama *Fontanelle*, a welcome thirty-week break from *Monte Cristo*, opened on March 12, 1893, after which the O'Neill family spent the last week of March "resting" in the Second City before traveling eastward on Easter Sunday, April 2, 1893.[22] Buffalo Bill's Wild West, whose performers had been in town throughout March preparing for their six-month engagement, opened the following day, April 3. (Cody's act was deemed too mawkish a billing for the official grounds, so the show was performed just outside the gates on the Midway Plaisance leading up to the fair. In the end Cody exacted the perfect revenge for this slight: the Columbian Exposition went bankrupt, while his show took in more than $1 million.) Eugene was four and a half then, which explains his vivid memory of the Indians far better than if he were two or three. Thus O'Neill preceded Mark Twain, Helen Keller, Frederick Douglass, Jack London, Thomas Edison, and countless other illustrious visitors to the Chicago World's Fair. Of course, they all witnessed the spectacle; O'Neill missed it by a day.

The Indians at O'Neill's bedside, then, must have been Sioux warriors known as Ghost Dancers, a cohort of holdouts who called for war after the Wounded Knee Massacre left over 150 tribal members—men, women, and children—dead on December 29, 1890. Just three months after Wounded Knee, William Cody made a deal with Secretary of the Interior John W. Noble for the release of a hundred of these Ghost Dancers imprisoned at nearby Fort Sheridan in order to enlist authentic Indians for another European tour. "The Indians at Fort Sheridan are a nuisance," the press reported, "and it is understood that Secretary Noble was only too glad of an opportunity to get rid of them. . . . The Indians were, of course, glad to do anything to get out of prison."[23] Among those captured were the Lakota Sioux medicine man Kicking Bear, a veteran of the battle of Little Big Horn, and another Lakota named Short Bull—both leaders of the Ghost Dance resistance. Each of them took Cody up on his offer, and each, it's safe to say, would have left young Eugene with "the low-down on Custer."

Nearly two dozen Sioux braves were coerced into playing "savages" for William Cody's show, and the grotesquery involved was never lost on O'Neill. In a scene in his 1920 play *Diff'rent*, a spiteful ne'er-do-well mocks a woman for having "dolled" up with "enough paint on her mush for a Buffalo Bill Indian" (*CP2*, 36). Other than that, O'Neill only once addressed the plight of the American Indian in his plays. *The Fountain* (1922), his first historical drama and a failure at the box office, follows the adventures of the sixteenth-century explorer Juan Ponce de León, who joined Columbus on his second voyage to the New World. Juan is nearly killed in Florida by Seminoles. O'Neill depicts the Native tribesmen, like the novelist James Fenimore Cooper a century before him, as a proud and defiant but ultimately doomed people.

O'Neill related his memory of the Sioux visits over fifty years later in a New York penthouse amid frenzied preparations for the premiere of *The Iceman Cometh*, testifying to the impact of the experience on both his creative imagination and his politics. He passionately spoke out against the injustices visited upon Native tribes by the government, and he would shock an unsuspecting reporter at the time by delighting over the conclusion of Custer's Last Stand: "The great battle in American history was the Battle of Little Big Horn. The Indians wiped out the whitemen, scalped them. That was a victory in American history. It should be featured in all our school books as the greatest victory in American history."[24]

O'Neill's friend the journalist Elizabeth Shepley Sergeant wrote about the tale's evocation of the playwright's cynicism that the American Dream was an insidious myth. "In so far as O'Neill has written of American life," Sergeant's unpublished notes on the subject read, "he has written its *un-success* story, discussed the places where the American dream has broken down into something rather raw and unacceptable."[25] Another interviewer took note of two paintings on the walls of his penthouse, one of a clipper ship and one of Broadway at theater hour. "There's the whole story of the decline of America," O'Neill told him. "From the most beautiful thing America has ever made, the clipper ship, to the most tawdry street in the world."[26]

No single American more than William F. Cody trumpeted the virtues of Euro-American expansion across North America, and his legend only grew, long after his death in 1917, with the heightened mood of triumphalism that followed World War II. And no single writer could have done more to dispel the myth of those very same virtues than Eugene O'Neill, the wide-eyed child gazing up at those "big brown" figures looming over his sickbed in a Chicago hotel room.

School Days of an Apostate

Ella and James O'Neill settled on New London, Connecticut, as their permanent town of residence in 1885. Conveniently located halfway between the theatrical centers of New York and Boston, the whaling city turned summer resort was a sensible choice. Ella's cousins on her mother's side, the Sheridans and the Brennans, had lived in New London for some time, and James had theater friends who owned summer homes there as well. Second in importance only to New Bedford, Massachusetts, in the heyday of the whale oil trade, New London is situated at the mouth of the Thames River, a tidal estuary that connects points inland to Long Island Sound and the Atlantic Ocean. During the Revolutionary War, Benedict Arnold, then a British officer, personally orchestrated the town's desolation by fire in one of the infamous traitor's most vicious acts of betrayal against the revolutionary forces. But the townspeople rebuilt and soon after transformed the waterfront into a patchwork of multitiered clapboard, red brick, and granite shops and dwellings, bestowing on the port city one of the more picturesque skylines in New England.

New London's economy foundered after the Civil War, by which time whale oil had been replaced by petroleum and natural gas; ever since, the citizenry of the "large small-town," as O'Neill refers to it in *Ah, Wilderness!* (*CP*3, 5), has taken the fantasy of an imminent "renaissance" for granted. Real estate in New London was thus considered a strong bet in the late nineteenth century, and James O'Neill, with his Irishman's faith in the surety of land to ward off poverty, was game to try his luck. After buying and inhabiting several rental properties, by the summer of 1900, when Eugene was eleven, the family occupied a Victorian-style residence at 325 Pequot Avenue. Horse-drawn carriages clopped back and forth along the west bank of the Thames from the majestic Pequot House resort hotel and the Pequot Summer Colony, the bailiwick of the town's most elite families, to the downtown "Parade" a couple of miles north. For a few thousand dollars, James had Monte Cristo Cottage, as the house was soon called, renovated and enlarged using the abandoned structures of a schoolhouse and a general store. The O'Neills would spend their summers there, from June to September, for the next two decades. Monte Cristo Cottage was as close as the family would ever come to a true home.

When O'Neill was in his late thirties, he sketched out a diagrammatic account of his childhood development using what the founder

Eugene O'Neill in New London. Photo signed to "Carlotta Monterey O'Neill."

* * *

of American psychiatry Adolf Meyer called a "life chart."[27] (Today a similar tool is referred to as a genogram.) O'Neill's psychiatrist Dr. Gilbert V. Hamilton believed the exercise might help his patient at long last understand the painful and abiding resentments he'd clung to since childhood; in that way, perhaps, he might be released from over two decades of bondage to alcohol, which had by that time become untenable. O'Neill revealed in his chart that as a toddler, it was his English nurse Sarah Sandy, not his aloof mother Ella, who'd provided him with "mother love." Sandy also brought him to novelty museums that displayed "mal-formed wax dummies" and enjoyed watching as the boy recoiled in horror. The nurse also, perversely, instilled in him an acute fear of darkness as a result of the ghoulish "murder stories" she delighted in telling before turning out his lights at bedtime, after which she coddled him with motherly love as he howled in fear. "Father would give child whiskey + water to soothe child's nightmares caused by terror of dark," O'Neill recalled in his chart. "This whiskey is connected with protection of mother—drink of hero father."[28]

Sarah Sandy was relieved of duty in the fall of 1895, not because of her unorthodox ideas of child rearing but rather because Eugene, not yet seven years old, was sent to St. Aloysius Academy in the Bronx, where he was instructed for four years by the Sisters of Charity. This point on O'Neill's life chart reads, "Resentment + hatred of father as cause of school (break with mother). . . . Reality found + fled from in fear—life of fantasy + religion in school—inability to belong to reality."[29] O'Neill looked back on his exile as a cruel act of abandonment on the part of his parents, though his brother Jim had fared much better: he too was sent away before he turned seven, to Notre Dame's preparatory school in South Bend, Indiana, but while there he blossomed socially and academically. It was a period of success for Jim that would constitute a painful reminder of his wasted intellectual potential once he reached adulthood.

Eugene O'Neill with James O'Neill Jr. and James O'Neill, left to right, in 1900 on the porch of Monte Cristo Cottage.
(COURTESY OF THE YALE COLLECTION OF AMERICAN LITERATURE, BEINECKE RARE BOOK AND MANUSCRIPT LIBRARY, NEW HAVEN)

✳   ✳   ✳

In 1900, O'Neill entered Manhattan's De La Salle Institute on Central Park South and boarded with his family close by at a rented apartment on West Sixty-Eighth Street. One afternoon, arriving back from school early, he walked in on his mother holding a hypodermic needle. Indignant over the disruption, Ella accused him of spying; with little explanation, he was sent back to De La Salle the following fall as a boarder rather than a day student.[30] A year later, O'Neill transferred to Betts Academy, a prep school in Stamford, Connecticut.

One summer night in 1903 after his freshman year of high school, the fourteen-year-old Eugene, his brother Jim, and his father all looked on, horror-stricken, as Ella made a desperate attempt on her life. Having run out of morphine, she ran headlong, wearing only a nightgown and shrieking like a madwoman, toward the Thames River across Pequot Avenue. The men rushed after her and stopped her before she could leap from the dock. James and Jim had been aware of Ella's "problem" for years; but they had, right up to that moment, kept the truth from Eugene. "Jamie told me," Edmund recounts bitterly of the incident in *Long Day's Journey Into Night*. "I called him a liar! I tried to punch him in the nose. But I knew he wasn't lying. (*His voice trembling, his eyes begin to fill with tears*.) God, it made everything in life seem rotten!" (*CP3*, 787).

O'Neill's life chart makes it clear that this traumatic revelation triggered an instantaneous "discovery of mother's inadequacy," and here the "mother love" line on the chart drops off. The shock of Ella's drug addiction, which in O'Neill's mind was reserved for prostitutes and derelicts (though morphine use was endemic among well-heeled women at the time), along with the possibility that she might be insane, activated an addiction of the young man's own: alcoholism, which began when he was fifteen and was eagerly reinforced by his ne'er-do-well brother Jim.[31] (Only his parents and close family relations referred to him as "Jamie"; after O'Neill's adolescence, he unvaryingly calls him "Jim.") Jim also arranged for his younger brother's loss of virginity to a prostitute in a two-bit Manhattan brothel. "Gene learned sin more easily than other people," he boasted years after this event, which was severely traumatizing for his teenage brother. "I made it easy for him."[32] "The girls were such terrible creatures they forced whiskey down his throat," O'Neill's third wife, Carlotta Monterey, related of the incident decades later: "with Jamie helping them," according to Monterey, "they tore off his clothes—he was fighting them. He wasn't ready for that. He was reading a lot of poetry in those days. But later on he made himself at home in them, in the whorehouses."[33]

Alcohol, often combined with sex, became a psychic painkiller for O'Neill, and over the years, drunkenness and even hangovers occupied his imagination as more reliable companions than the people who ostensibly loved him. For over two decades, O'Neill would drink himself into a stupor from morning to night, then dry out for weeks at a time in a state of utter loneliness and despair.

O'Neill also openly renounced his parents' Catholicism after his mother's breakdown—all religions, in fact—and became a confirmed atheist. "He rejected God," O'Neill's onetime girlfriend the Catholic Worker activist Dorothy Day wrote soon after his death. "He turned from Him." That first Sunday morning after his mother's attempt on her life, O'Neill refused to join his parents for Mass. A fight erupted between Eugene and James on the staircase in the front hall until the full-bodied James, who could have handily drubbed his son, abruptly stopped, straightened his cuffs, and said, "Very well. The subject is closed."[34] Though Ella would eventually conquer her morphine habit for good in 1917, thanks in part to the Sisters of Charity, her son never looked back.

O'Neill's loss of faith was truly a loss—a profound emptiness, a breach in spirit. In *Long Day's Journey Into Night*, O'Neill dramatizes a period when his mother had given up Mass as well. Her character, Mary Tyrone, longs to return to her convent schooldays when she embraced Catholicism. "If I could only find the faith I lost," she laments, "so I could pray again!" (*CP*3, 779). In the final scene, locked in a morphine-induced dream state, Mary searches helplessly through the living room for something she's misplaced, "something I need terribly. I remember when I had it I was never lonely nor afraid. I can't have lost it forever, I would die if I thought that. Because then there would be no hope" (*CP*3, 826). O'Neill himself experienced this desperate search for hope and spirit. Had he been able to regain his Catholic faith, and his mother's affection, or find a meaningful substitute, he would have felt safer and less alienated through life—but it's more than likely he would never have achieved his stature as an artist.

The Greek philosopher Diogenes the Cynic made up his mind in the third century B.C. to cast off his worldly possessions and live the rest of his days in a bathtub. O'Neill viewed the tedium of life as a teenager at Monte Cristo Cottage in New London as even less exciting than this "Cynic Tub." O'Neill would read in the morning, swim in the Thames in the afternoon, and read again at night, with little variation for weeks. Although his peripatetic childhood on the road instilled a powerful urge to find a "home" in the truest sense, it also intensified his view of Connecticut's cultural life as impossibly parochial. At sixteen, he sneeringly claimed that each passing hour in New London was "equivalent to ten in any other place." "Bored to death" with the dance "hops" at the Pequot House down the road, O'Neill would grumble that at least "in a graveyard there is some excitement in reading the inscriptions on the tombstones."[35]

A welcome respite from this drowning ennui arrived in the summer of 1905 in the form of Marion Welch, a well-read teenager from the state capital of Hartford. Visiting a friend in New London that July, Welch was a couple of years older than Eugene, athletically built and, most important, intellectually curious. O'Neill would always think of their days together in his rowboat on the Thames as some of the happiest of his life. The surviving love letters to Marion read like those of a typical lovesick sixteen-year-old boy—thick with sarcasm and braggadocio, more Tom Sawyer than Baudelaire (that would come later). Written to impress more than woo, the letters boasted of joining his wayward brother Jim to bet on the "ponies," play the slot machines, and carouse generally in upstate New York at Canfield's Saratoga Club, "a refined name for one of the most fashionable (and notorious) gambling joints in the world." He regarded Welch as his intellectual peer, and their letters over the course of their short-lived relationship reveal what books they were reading, which they planned to read next, and which weren't worth reading at all. They shared what plays to see too: "So you went to see the old worm eaten *Monte Cristo*," he responded to a letter from Marion. "It may be all right for those who have never seen it before."[36]

Graduating from Betts Academy in the following spring of 1906, O'Neill next entered Princeton University, where he was determined to make up for lost time in New London and Stamford. His fellow students remembered him as a "loner," though sarcastic and "foul-mouthed." Most college boys in those days drank beer or wine; O'Neill, who was also a heavy smoker by this time, drank hard liquor, a choice his to-the-manner-born classmates associated with "bums." O'Neill made them cringe with his blasphemy, and he regarded the school's mandatory Sunday sermons as "so irritatingly stupid that they prevented me from sleeping." On at least one occasion O'Neill, who by eighteen was nearly six feet tall, stood up on a chair and crowed at the ceiling with arms outstretched, "If there be a God, let Him strike me dead!" (Witnesses to this recalled that his ethnic pride surpassed his atheism, however, and "if anyone spoke disparagingly of Catholicism he would spring furiously to its defense.")[37]

For the most part O'Neill kept a low profile during his first semester, when he was a resident of University Hall, now Holder Hall, and few Princetonians could claim they knew him well (though he was nicknamed "Ego" for his lack of humor concerning all things Eugene Gladstone O'Neill). His study was decorated with a fisherman's net festooned with cork floats and sundry souvenirs, including, according to a fellow dormer, "actresses' slippers, stockings, brassieres, playbills, posters, pictures of chorus girls in tights . . . and a hand of cards, a royal flush. But what got me was that among all this stuff he had hung up several condoms—they looked like they'd been used. Very gruesome." The remainder of his suite contained a simple round table and chairs and a cramped bedroom with an iron cot, a washbowl, a water pitcher, and a commode. He retained his voracious reading habits, and he wrote some poetry, though not of the "highbrow" sort. One typical bit of doggerel composed during his short-lived period at the Ivy League school went something like this:

Cheeks that have known no rouge,
Lips that have known no booze,
What care I for thee?
Come with me on a souse,
A long and lasting carouse,
And I'll adore thee.[38]

Pressed by classmates as to why he preferred the "stinking garbage pail" over a vase of fragrant roses, O'Neill replied enigmati-
cally, "Both are nature," a phrase that brings to mind one of O'Neill's
literary heroes, the French journalist and naturalist author Émile
Zola. "When I go into the sewer, I go to clean it out," the Norwegian
"father of modern realism" Henrik Ibsen complained. "When Zola
goes into the sewer, he takes a bath." Zola countered such attacks
by citing the physiologist Claude Bernard who, when asked about
his "sentiments on the science of life," responded that "it is a superb
salon, flooded with light, which you can only reach by passing through
a long and nauseating kitchen."[39]

Broadly speaking, "realism" refers to the nineteenth-century
revolt against melodrama and romanticism toward dramas that end
with calculated ambiguity and reflect the contemporary lives of run-
of-the-mill characters who, unlike in naturalism, exhibit free will.
(It was this movement, led by Ibsen, that precipitated the end of the
soliloquy.) "Naturalism" vaguely connotes a grittier, more perverse
form of realism in common theater parlance. But once we remove
realistic "slice-of-life" plays that share the "fourth-wall" illusion of
most naturalistic dramas, naturalism distinguishes itself as a tradition
of tragic endings, the exposure of sublime truths existing beneath
surface realities, and the philosophical idea that individuals' fates are
determined by biological, historical, circumstantial, and psychological forces beyond their control. O'Neill's future dramas would con-
flate naturalism with other techniques, but the naturalist tradition
nearly always predominates.[40]

On the weekends, O'Neill divided his time between boozing at
"Doc" Boyce's nearby tavern and another local dive on Alexander

Street with a noxious atmosphere that only he among his classmates could apparently stomach. But, as he had while at Betts, he also commuted to New York City every chance he got. He attended Ibsen's *Hedda Gabler* that spring at the city's Bijou Theatre on ten successive nights. Though as a playwright O'Neill would follow Zola's naturalist path, Ibsen's revolt against Victorian convention spoke to O'Neill more than any play he had yet seen: "That experience discovered an entire new world of the drama for me. It gave me my first conception of a modern theatre where truth might live."[41]

Louis "Lou" Holladay, a New Yorker O'Neill had met during a sojourn to the city, arrived at Princeton's campus one weekend armed with a handgun and a quart of absinthe, a potent liquor distilled from the toxins of the wormwood plant. O'Neill was enthralled by the hallucinogenic properties of the soon-to-be outlawed drink; he'd read about it in *Wormwood: A Drama of Paris* (1890) by the British novelist Marie Corelli and asked Holladay to bring a bottle down from the city. After consuming too much of the green-hued tincture in his room, O'Neill turned "berserk"—smashing furniture, hurling a chair through his window, and aiming Holladay's revolver at its owner, then pulling the trigger. Luckily, the gun wasn't loaded. It took three classmates to pin him down, tie him up, and heave him into bed.[42] No lessons were learned, however, and his heavy drinking and unruly behavior only worsened that winter and spring.

O'Neill left the distinct impression among his classmates that he'd derived his cynicism from his "wild" and "worldly" older brother Jim. "There is not such a thing as a virgin after the age of fourteen," O'Neill told them, sounding much like his brother; although when he dated a local girl from Trenton, the closest urban center to Princeton's campus, he would "expiate in high dudgeon" if anyone uttered a disrespectful word about her. Once he took a couple of Princeton students to New York's Tenderloin district, where the notorious Haymarket bar was located on the same block as an assortment of brothels in which he'd been initiated by Jim. ("Those babes gave me some of the best laughs I've ever had, and to the future profit of many a dramatic scene," O'Neill said later.) His companions got cold feet and hastily retreated back to school.[43]

Late that spring semester, 1907, O'Neill went on a drunken spree through Trenton with a pack of like-minded students, and they missed the last trolley to Princeton. Instead, they caught the train to New York, which dropped them off at Princeton Junction; but the drawbridge was up, and they had to swim across Carnegie Lake. When a dog started barking on a railroad embankment leading down to a group of houses, O'Neill, drunk as a lord, began hurling stones at the animal. As the dog's fury grew, so did O'Neill's, and one of his stones went wide of its mark and crashed through a window of the house. Undeterred, he threw outdoor furniture next, thus rousing from bed the homeowner, a division superintendent of the Pennsylvania Railroad. The boys were suspended for three weeks.[44]

O'Neill's academic standing had already been declining precipitously, and the incident proved a convenient excuse to end relations between O'Neill and the hallowed Ivy League school. (This would not be a permanent break, as decades later O'Neill would donate to its library a substantial cache of his manuscripts and letters.) "Princeton was all play and no work," O'Neill said, "so much so that the Dean decided I had, by enormous application, crowded four years' play into one, and he graduated me as a Master Player at the end of that year." No love was lost between the two parties, nor was expulsion from college new to the O'Neill family: a decade earlier, Jim had been attending Fordham University, a Jesuit school, when he was expelled for hiring a prostitute, then introducing her to classmates and at least one priest on campus as his sister. At Princeton, O'Neill had been charged with "conduct unbecoming a student." When asked later by a reporter why he was thrown out, he just chuckled and said, "General hell-raising."[45]

Anarchist in the Tropics

James O'Neill landed his unrepentant son a position that summer making $25 a week in Manhattan as a secretary at the mail order house of the New York–Chicago Supply Company. O'Neill held the position for nearly a year but, he said, "never took it seriously."[46] His friend Lou Holladay's sister Paula, known as Polly, ran a café on Macdougal Street in Greenwich Village that catered to the Village's burgeoning avant-garde artistic and bohemian set. Without responsibility or purpose, O'Neill referred to this time as his "wise guy" period.[47]

Along with frequenting Polly's, O'Neill and Holladay combed the bars and brothels of the Tenderloin district and soaked up the music of the era, O'Neill thus initiating his lifelong obsession with ragtime piano and early jazz. They also formed a close relationship with Benjamin R. Tucker, an iconoclastic publisher and editor of the anarchist journal *Liberty*. Tucker's Unique Book Shop at 502 Sixth Avenue near Thirtieth Street was a preferred haunt for the growing cohort of what one reporter characterized as "well dressed, seemingly well-educated young men, whose mental processes have led them into out of the way or unconventional channels."[48] Tucker dedicated his life to promoting intellectual freedom and preached, in opposition to the "Communist anarchism" of Emma Goldman and Alexander Berkman, nonviolent social and political protest. O'Neill thus adopted what became his only self-professed, lifelong worldview: "philosophical anarchism," also known as "individualist anarchism" or "egoism."

Philosophical anarchists maintained three chief principles: unconditional nonviolence, one-on-one instruction rather than mass propaganda, and the complete disregard of all social and political institutions (the press, organized religion, government, law enforcement, the military) as "phantasms," "ghosts," or "spooks" to exorcise from one's mind. This last became a unifying theme in nearly all of O'Neill's work. The anarchist Hartmann in O'Neill's early play *The Personal Equation* (1915), for instance, refers to American notions of "fatherland or motherland" as a "sentimental phantom," and he goes on to say that "the soul of man is an uninhabited house haunted by the ghosts of old ideals. And man in those ghosts still believes!" (*CP1*, 321). Over a decade later, O'Neill's character Nina Leeds in *Strange Interlude* (1927) snarls at her upright friend Charlie Marsden about her desperate attempt to "believe in any God at any price—a heap of stones, a mud image, a drawing on a wall, a bird, a fish, a snake, a baboon—or even a good man preaching the simple platitudes of truth, those Gospel words we love the sound of but whose meaning we pass on to spooks to live by!" (*CP2*, 669). And by the 1930s, in his Faustian mask play *Days Without End* (1933), the protagonist's masked doppel-gänger scorns his alter ego's longing for the "old ghostly comforts" of religion (*CP3*, 161).[49]

Tucker's Unique Book Shop offered over five thousand volumes of what its proprietor advertised as "the most complete line of ad-vanced literature to be found anywhere in the world," and O'Neill later professed that his access to this eclectic library through this period had unalterably molded his "inner self." Tucker translated a good deal of this outlaw literature for the first time into English and debuted American editions through his independent press; but he made a point to champion American philosophies as well: Thomas Jefferson's suspicion of government power, Henry David Thoreau's civil disobedience, and the intrepid poet Walt Whitman's heightened individualism and lyrical call for radical democracy. The good gray poet responded in kind. "Tucker did brave things for *Leaves of Grass* when brave things were rare," Whitman said. "I could not forget that. . . . I love him: he is plucky to the bone."[50]

But the most vital source of Tucker's philosophy could be found in the German philosopher Max Stirner's radical manifesto *The Ego and His Own: The Case of the Individual against Authority* (1844), a volume listed on Edmund Tyrone's bookshelf in *Long Day's Journey Into Night*. Tucker had been obsessing over *The Ego and His Own* at the time O'Neill regularly frequented his shop in 1907, and his imprint published its first English translation that same year. Saxe Commins, the notorious anarchist Emma Goldman's nephew and later a man O'Neill would identify as one of his "oldest and best of friends," described Stirner's book as "an anarchical explosion of aphoristic generalities, defiant and iconoclastic."[51] Stirner railed against "fixed ideas" the same way Ralph Waldo Emerson denounced "foolish con-sistency [as] the hobgoblin of little minds." The Unique Book Shop stocked volumes by Proudhon, Mill, Thoreau, Tolstoy, Zola, Gorky,

Kropotkin, Schopenhauer, Nietzsche, and Shaw, but when O'Neill took his New London pal Ed Keefe to Tucker's store, according to Keefe, O'Neill breezed past several packed shelves and "made" him buy *The Ego and His Own*.[52]

This steady drumbeat of the "self" that resounded through the cafés, barrooms, and alleyways of Manhattan emboldened O'Neill to quit his humdrum desk job at the shipping company. In the summer of 1908, scraping by on $7 a week from his father, he rented a studio in the Lincoln Arcade Building at Sixty-Fifth Street and Broadway with Ed Keefe, the painter George Bellows, and the illustrator Ed Ireland. Early in 1909, the bohemian cabal also lived for a month on a farm O'Neill's father owned in Zion, New Jersey. As they cooked for themselves and tried to keep warm, Bellows and Keefe painted while O'Neill, according to him, "wrote a series of sonnets" that were little more than "bad imitations of Dante Gabriel Rossetti."[53]

Bellows was a contributor to the radical organ the *Masses* and a student of the "Ash Can" painter Robert Henri (pronounced "Hen-Rye").[54] According to another of his students, Henri was considered a sort of mystic who lectured "with hypnotic effect." He and other philosophical anarchists taught O'Neill and his cohort that by their example of "owning" their lives, Victorian moralists might follow suit and cease their meddling in the lives of others. The famed Ash Can School of painting was Henri's invention, and he mentored a number of first-rate artists, including Bellows and a young Edward Hopper. O'Neill thus found himself among true believers in his naturalistic "stinking garbage pail" aesthetic—Henri taught his art students that painting must be "as real as mud, as the clods of horse-shit and snow, that froze on Broadway in the winter." That year Bellows completed what would be his most famous painting, *Stag at Sharkey's*, which featured an illegal boxing match at Tom Sharkey's Athletic Club, a work of brutal realism meant to capture, Bellows explained simply, "two men trying to kill each other."[55]

O'Neill reproduced this art-studio milieu in his first full-length play, *Bread and Butter* (1914), a tragedy about an artist in desperate revolt against bourgeois tastes. (In this way, *Bread and Butter* joins the tradition of George du Maurier's *Trilby* [1894] and its American counterpart, Stephen Crane's *The Third Violet* [1897].) The play's master painter Eugene Grammont (based on Henri) declaims the philosophical anarchist's credo to O'Neill's loosely based alter ego, John Brown: "Be true to yourself . . . remember! For that no sacrifice is too great" (*CP1*, 148).

During that summer of 1909, O'Neill made the acquaintance of Kathleen Jenkins, the upright daughter of a respectable Protestant mother. (Her father, an alcoholic, had long ago abandoned them.) George Bellows encouraged the match, certain that O'Neill needed a "nice girl" like her for stability. At first Jenkins was attracted by the idea of a romance with a raffish intellectual like O'Neill, even if he had no job and few prospects for one. "The usual young man sent you flowers, a box of candy, took you to the theater, but mostly," she said, since O'Neill never had any money, "we talked and walked. . . . He was always immaculately groomed, in spite of being unconventional; he led a bohemian sort of life. . . . The books he read were 'way over my head.' "⁵⁶ Jenkins was stable but not too "nice," at least according to the standards of the day. She soon became pregnant, and as a result, they got married in a clandestine ceremony at Trinity Protestant Episcopal Church in Hoboken, New Jersey, on October 2, 1909.⁵⁷

James and Ella were soon confronted at their suite at the Prince George Hotel on East Twenty-Eighth Street by Kathleen's mother, Kate Jenkins, who told them about their children's secret marriage and demanded to know what they planned to do about it. James was at first startled at Jenkins's impudence, then infuriated. His solution for ending the relationship was to pack his son off on a mining expedition to Spanish Honduras with a gold-prospecting associate of his, Earl C. Stevens. James and Kathleen accompanied O'Neill to Grand Central Station to see him off on a train to San Francisco, and by his twenty-first birthday, October 16, O'Neill found himself contentedly drifting southward on a banana boat off the coast of Mexico.⁵⁸

After traveling by mule from Amalpa for nearly a hundred unmapped miles through jungles and mountain passes, O'Neill and

Eugene O'Neill with Earl C. Stevens on a banana boat en route to
Honduras, October 16, 1909, O'Neill's twenty-first birthday.
(COURTESY OF THE YALE COLLECTION OF AMERICAN LITERATURE, BEINECKE RARE BOOK
AND MANUSCRIPT LIBRARY, NEW HAVEN)

*   *   *

Stevens's party finally arrived at the Honduran capital, Tegucigalpa.
He had passed through stunning territory but was harassed, he reported back to his parents, by an endless horde of fleas and ticks "that
burrow under your skin and form sores." And in spite of his predilection for "the stinking garbage pail," he found the squalor appalling: "Pigs, buzzard[s], dogs, chickens and children all live in the same
room and the sanitary conditions of the huts are beyond belief."[59] The
tropical climate, on the other hand, suited him just fine. It never went
above eighty-five degrees during the day or below seventy at night.
He enjoyed listening to the local bands in town squares while observing the "funny way everyone . . . struts around with a six-shooter and
a belt full of cartridges on their hip—just like a 30 cent Western melo-

drama." (O'Neill later penned his own cheap western melodramas, the one-act plays *A Wife for a Life* in 1913, the first play he ever wrote, and *The Movie Man* in 1914, and the latter's 1916 short story version, "The Screenews of War.") He also embraced the languorous pace of life in Central America: "If we don't do it today why we can tomorrow—that is the way they seem to feel about it." To fit in, O'Neill loaded himself down "like an arsenal with ammunition, knives, and firearms" and first cultivated what would become his iconic moustache, a disguise meant for circulating in the plazas, with the goal "to look absolutely as shiftless and dirty as the best of them."[60]

O'Neill's pumped-up spirit of adventure rapidly deflated, however, and after a couple of months he wrote his parents, "I give it as my candid opinion and fixed belief that God got his inspiration for Hell after creating Honduras." At the same time, the ambiguous nature of his marital responsibilities still nagged at him. "It sure would be some shock to find out I was enduring all this for love," he wrote them. "Better find out for me." By Christmas in Guajiniquil, O'Neill was mired in self-pity. He hated the food—the meat rotten, everything fried and wrapped in tortillas, "a heavy soggy imitation of a pancake made of corn enough to poison the stomach of an ostrich"—and inevitably contracted food poisoning; the fleas, gnats, ticks, and mosquitoes had evolved from a mild nuisance to a dreadful plague; and his initial admiration for the Hondurans' relaxed lifestyle had soured into a bilious contempt: "The natives are the lowest, laziest, most ignorant bunch of brainless bipeds that ever polluted a land and retarded its future. Until some just Fate grows weary of watching the gropings in the dark of these human maggots and exterminates them, until the Universe shakes these human lice from its sides, Honduras has no future, no hopes of being anything but what it is at present—a Siberia of the tropics."[61]

A revolution broke out in Honduras while O'Neill was there, but he reassured his parents that its combatants were "of the comic opera variety and only affect Americans in that they delay the mail." He begged them to send three pounds of Bull Durham tobacco and some magazines, then ended on a homesick note: "I never realized how much home and Father and Mother meant until I got so far away from them." O'Neill was bedridden with malaria during his last three weeks in Tegucigalpa. He was given a bed at the American consulate, since the hotels were booked up, and his chills from fever became so relentless that his caretakers draped old American flags over him on top of whatever blankets they could spare. "I looked," he said later, "just like George M. Cohan," the American song-and-dance man best known for his performances of "Yankee Doodle Dandy" and "You're a Grand Old Flag." Many years later, O'Neill tersely summed up the ill-fated expedition: "Much hardship, little romance, no gold."[62]

It had been a pleasant afternoon strolling along Fifth Avenue in that May 1910 when Ella O'Neill and a friend saw a nursemaid march by pushing a baby carriage carrying an adorable infant. Her friend instantly recognized the woman as an employee of O'Neill's mother-in-law, Kate Jenkins. "Did you see that little boy?" she asked, waiting until they'd passed. "That's your grandson!" O'Neill in fact returned from his exile in the "Siberia of the tropics" right on time for the embarrassingly public arrival of Eugene Jr., on May 5, 1910. Two days later, the *New York World* ran an article under the exuberant headline "The Birth of a Boy / Reveals Marriage of 'Gene' O'Neill / Young Man in Honduras, / Doesn't Know He Is Dad / May Not Hear News for Weeks / Working at Mine to Win / Fortune for Family." Another article on May 11 featured a photograph of Kathleen Jenkins with the accusatory caption, "Gene Home, / But Not with Wife." Kate Jenkins was undoubtedly the source. "It seems impossible," his mother-in-law was quoted as saying, "that 'Gene' is in town and has remained away from his wife and their baby. There must be some mistake, but if there is not, Eugene's attitude is inexcusable. He knows how we all feel toward him and that he could have come to this house to live any time since his marriage to my daughter. There would have been no 'mother-in-law' about it, either, and he knew that. I felt toward him as if he were my own son." Jenkins then insinuated, not without some basis of truth, that James O'Neill was responsible for keeping the young family apart.[63]

Kathleen Jenkins with Eugene O'Neill Jr.
(COURTESY OF SHEAFFER-O'NEILL COLLECTION, LINDA LEAR CENTER FOR SPECIAL
COLLECTIONS AND ARCHIVES, CONNECTICUT COLLEGE, NEW LONDON)

✳   ✳   ✳

With no game plan or prospects for employment in New York, O'Neill joined his father on a boondoggle to St. Louis, Missouri, for James's traveling production of *The White Sister*, another of his numerous though commonly forgotten departures from *Monte Cristo* over the years. O'Neill slogged along as an assistant manager and security man at the ticket counters; but when they arrived in Boston, he once again fled the country—this time as a passenger on the Norwegian bark *Charles Racine*, skippered by the highly competent Captain Gustav Waage and bound south for Buenos Aires. The voyage cost James O'Neill $75, no paltry sum given that the ship's crew earned between $13 and $14 a month.[64] Once under way, the *Charles Racine* sailed for weeks with no land in sight,[65] during which time O'Neill composed the poem "Free," his earliest known literary work. (Several years

after publishing it in the *Pleiades Club Year Book* in 1912, he admitted
to the club, a hail-fellow-well-met group of bohemian patrons and
dilettante practitioners of the arts, that the poem was "actually written on a deep-sea barque in the days of Real Romance.")[66] In the
poem, O'Neill acknowledges the deep remorse he felt over his desertion of Kathleen and Eugene Jr. while at the same time revealing a
profound spiritual release:

> I have had my dance with Folly, nor do I shirk the blame;
> I have sipped the so-called Wine of Life and paid the price
>   of shame;
> But I know that I shall find surcease, the rest of my spirit
>   craves,
> Where the rainbows play in the flying spray,
> 'Mid the keen salt kiss of the waves.[67]

Time spent with the crew aboard the *Charles Racine*—"At last to be
free, on the open sea, with the trade wind / in our hair"—would instill
a lifelong infatuation with a spiritual transcendence he would never
achieve again; and the impact of this seminal voyage would find its
most lyrical expression in Edmund Tyrone's monologue from *Long
Day's Journey Into Night*:

> When I was on the Squarehead square rigger, bound for Buenos
> Aires. Full moon in the Trades. The old hooker driving fourteen
> knots. I lay on the bowsprit, facing astern, with the water foaming
> into spume under me, the masts with every sail white in the
> moonlight, towering high above me. I became drunk with the
> beauty and singing rhythm of it, and for a moment I lost myself—
> actually lost my life. *I was set free!* I dissolved in the sea, became
> white sails and flying spray, became beauty and rhythm, became
> moonlight and the ship and the high dim-starred sky! I belonged,
> without past or future, within peace and unity and a wild joy,
> within something greater than my own life, or the life of Man, to
> Life itself! To God, if you want to put it that way. (*CP*3, 811–12;
> emphasis added)

The *Charles Racine* carried over a million feet of lumber below decks, and the overload was lashed to the upper decks and hatches with chains and wiring. The trip lasted sixty-five days, an exceptionally long haul for the heavily trafficked lumber route from Boston to Buenos Aires; if it exasperated the crew, for O'Neill the prolonged trip was a boon. Not only did he take in the stories of the men about their ports of call and commit traditional sea shanties to memory, the voyage also offered him a glimpse of the full range of extreme conditions at sea, without the stabilizing force of engine power, from the stillness of a ship becalmed to terrifying hurricane conditions.[68]

O'Neill greatly admired the sailors he met onboard, and he later broadened his respect for their straight-talking swagger to include the working classes as a whole: "They are more direct. In action and utterance. Thus more dramatic. Their lives and sufferings and personalities lend themselves more readily to dramatization. They have not been steeped in the evasions and superficialities which come with social life and intercourse. Their real selves are exposed. They are crude but honest. They are not handicapped by inhibitions."[69] "O'Neill was well-liked onboard," said one of the crew of the *Charles Racine*. "We thought him an interesting strange bird we all loved to talk to." "It's strange," O'Neill wistfully recalled decades later, as death approached, "but the time I spent at sea on a sailing ship was the *only* time I ever felt I had roots in any place."[70]

On the afternoon of July 24, 1910, a fierce hurricane pummeled the ship. Captain Waage, alarmed by his barometer's plummeting descent, noted in his log a "terrific heavy sea. . . . Some deck cargo—planks—washed over." From the relative safety of the forecastle alleyway, O'Neill looked on in awe while the crew members relieved one another to stand watch in the crow's nest. They would pause until a wall of water crashed down on deck, and then, when it had receded into the billowing swells, they sprinted across the slippery deck to the mainmast, while the previous man on watch would climb down and perform the same treacherous maneuver in reverse. The brutal winds had died down by morning only to rematerialize as "violent hurricane squalls" outside Buenos Aires at the mouth of

Crew of the S.S. *Charles Racine*.
(COURTESY OF SHEAFFER-O'NEILL COLLECTION, LINDA LEAR CENTER FOR SPECIAL
COLLECTIONS AND ARCHIVES, CONNECTICUT COLLEGE, NEW LONDON)

✳   ✳   ✳

the Rio de la Plata, the massive estuary separating Uruguay and
Argentina. After this, the deck boy, Osmund Christophersen, asked
O'Neill what he thought of the rough weather. "Very interesting," he
replied, "but I could have wished for less of it."[71]

Once the *Charles Racine* had docked safely at Buenos Aires in early
August, agents scrambled onboard from local bars and brothels to
pass around advertisement cards designed to entice sailors eager to
blow off steam after weeks of toil at sea: "Come up to my house,
plenty fun, perty girls, plenty dance, three men killed last night." In
due course, after O'Neill checked in at the deluxe Continental Hotel,
he trailed the swarm of thirsty seamen down Avenida Roque Sáenz

Peña toward Paseo de Julio. It wasn't long before O'Neill ran short of cash and had to swap the downy beds of the genteel Continental for the debauched thoroughfare's rigid public benches. The Argentine author Manuel Gálvez depicted the Paseo de Julio much as O'Neill must have first seen it for himself: "His artist's soul forgot for an instant the penury of his life. Because he found this street fantastic, with its high arcades; its cheap, foul shops; its kaleidoscopes with views of wars and exhibitions of monsters; the dark hotels that rented out dirty beds for occasional lovers; the sinister cellars that stunk of grime and where sailors reeking of booze sang; its whores, who were the dirtiest dregs of society; its vagabonds who slept under the columns of the arches; its sellers of obscene pictures; the nauseating stink of human dirt."[72]

For nine squalid months O'Neill worked odd jobs and lived hand-to-mouth, touring the city's brothels and attending the pornographic "moving pictures" playing in the suburb of Barracas. He ate little and drank all day; if he had enough money, his drink of choice was a jar of gin with a dash of vermouth and soda. If he didn't, he drank the local beer. "I wanted to be a he-man," O'Neill said. "To knock 'em cold and eat 'em alive." Much of his time was spent at a waterfront saloon called the Sailor's Opera. "It sure was a madhouse," he recalled. "Pickled sailors, sure-thing race-track touts, soused boiled white shirt déclassé Englishmen, underlings in the Diplomatic Service, boys darting around tables leaving pink and yellow cards directing one to red-plush paradises, and entangled in the racket was the melody of some ancient turkey-trot banged out by a sober pianist."[73]

After a month or so "on the beach" (sailor talk for being stuck in port), O'Neill reluctantly looked for more steady employment. He worked for a time as a longshoreman on another square-rigger, the *Timandra*, whose "old bucko of a first mate was too tough," he said, "the kind that would drop a marlin spike on your skull from a yard-arm." (The ship appears as the *Amindra* in *The Long Voyage Home*, O'Neill's 1917 one-act about a shanghaied sailor.) He worked brief stints at several other jobs, including at the Westinghouse Electrical Company, "the wool house of a packing plant" at La Plata, and as a repairman for the Singer Sewing Machine Company. La Plata was the worst of them; the worst job, in fact, he would ever have. O'Neill was assigned the odious task of sorting raw hides, while the noxious fumes of the carcasses permeated his hair, clothing, nose, eyes, and mouth. He was about to relinquish his post when a warehouse fire saved him the trouble, and the fetid compound burned to the ground. ("I didn't do it," he said, "but it was a good idea.")[74] Working for Singer Sewing Machine was only slightly less demoralizing. "Do you know how many different models Singer makes?" the boss asked him at the job interview. "Fifty?" "Fifty! Five hundred and fifty! You'll have to learn to take each one apart and put it together again." O'Neill couldn't bear the mechanical drudgery for long, and he quit. "And then I hadn't any job at all," he recollected, "and was down on the beach— 'down,' if not precisely 'out.' "[75]

One day a man of O'Neill's tastes, a socialist and freelance reporter for the *Buenos Aires Herald* named Charles Ashleigh, walked into a seaman's café, probably the Sailor's Opera, and, seeing there wasn't a vacant table, "picked one where but a single customer was sitting—a rather morose, dark young American." Ashleigh ordered a schooner of beer and sat quietly listening to a mulatto piano player "pounding out popular tunes." But after ordering a second schooner, he threw caution to the wind and blurted out, "Good Lord, I'm sick of this. I haven't talked with a soul all day." "Nor have I," replied O'Neill. "Have another drink?" That night they stayed up for hours "talking, talking, talking," said Ashleigh, about "sailing ships and steamships, Conrad and Yeats, the mountains and ports of South America, politics and the theater." They also exchanged drafts of each other's verse "across the sloppy table, read, discussed, criticized."[76]

For decades scholars believed that none of O'Neill's writing from Argentina had survived. But in the spring of 1917 at a saloon in Greenwich Village, O'Neill showed Robert Carlton Brown, a fiction writer and editor at the *Masses*, a poem he said he'd written in Buenos Aires entitled "Ashes of Orchids."[77] Unpublished before now, here is the earliest version of this poem, which O'Neill later revised in the summer of 1917 with the new title "The Bridegroom Weeps!":

There are so many tears
In my eyes
Burning, unshed:
There are so many ashes
In my mouth
Ashes of orchids:
There are so many corpses
In my brain
Of decomposing dreams—

And Columbine, also,
Decomposes![78]

"The Bridegroom Weeps!" is O'Neill's second known literary effort after "Free." No doubt the poem, like "Free," was partially inspired by Kathleen Jenkins, but his guilt over her and Eugene Jr. was now combined with his hopelessly dissolute life in Argentina. O'Neill often recycled his own phrasing from the past, and the title would later inform those of his biblical mask play *Lazarus Laughed* (1926) and, more important, his late masterwork *The Iceman Cometh* (1939).

A more substantial literary legacy from Buenos Aires materialized in the figure of a young Englishman at the Sailor's Opera, a man the future playwright later mirrored in Smitty, the antihero of his 1917 one-acts *The Moon of the Caribbees* and *In the Zone*. O'Neill regularly observed his future inspiration "sopping up all the liquor in sight, and between drunks he'd drink to sober up. He almost caused an alcoholic drought in Buenos Ayres."[79] In his midtwenties, blond, and "extraordinarily handsome," Smitty was, O'Neill said, "almost too beautiful . . . very like Oscar Wilde's description of Dorian Gray. Even his name was flowery." O'Neill describes him in *The Moon* as "a young Englishman with a blonde mustache" who speaks to other sailors "pompously" and exudes an attitude of unearned entitlement (*CP1*, 528, 538); the actual Smitty was similarly an aristocratic, college-educated, former member of a "crack British regiment," according to O'Neill, who "suddenly messed up his life—pretty conspicuously."[80]

Smitty had escaped to Buenos Aires to evade a scandal at home, and though armed with letters from British dignitaries to Argentine counterparts, he was deathly afraid that someone might offer him a job, so he kept the letters to himself.[81] One drama critic quipped that O'Neill's fictional character was "an uninteresting young man," but this was precisely O'Neill's point.[82] The true hero of *The Moon of the Caribbees*, chronologically the first of his S.S. *Glencairn* series of one-act sea plays, was not Smitty, O'Neill clarified, but rather "the spirit of the sea—a big thing." Smitty went to sea to forget his past, and he drinks to forget it too. But everything the sea offers in the play—the drink, the music, the local women, the moonlight—combines to become a potent reminder of a life half lived. Oblivious to the beauty of the sea and the other sailors' unselfconscious revelry, Smitty's "silhouetted gestures of self-pity are reduced to their proper insignificance." For O'Neill, he's a hollow "insect" ineffectually buzzing amid the wonder of nature's "eternal sadness." Smitty lives his life "much more out of harmony with truth, much less in tune with beauty, than the honest vulgarity of his mates."[83] With the notable exception of Smitty, O'Neill's maritime plays express nothing but admiration for the seamen he encountered. "I hated a life ruled by the conventions and traditions of society," O'Neill said. "Discipline on a sailing vessel was not a thing that was imposed on the crew by superior authority. It was essentially voluntary. The motive behind it was loyalty to the ship!"[84]

In due course, O'Neill became fed up with the vagabond lifestyle of a penniless beachcomber, "sleeping on park benches, hanging around waterfront dives, and absolutely alone." At one point, he was tempted to partner up with an out-of-work railroad man to hold up a currency exchange at gunpoint. O'Neill considered the proposal seriously but turned the hopeless robber down. "He was sent to prison," he said, "and, for all I know, he died there." The capture of his would-be accomplice served the future playwright as a keen reminder of life's fragility in the hands of pitiless circumstance: "There are times now when I feel sure I would have been [a writer], no matter what happened, but when I remember Buenos Aires, and the fellow down there who wanted me to be a bandit, I'm not so sure."[85]

Exorcism in New York

O'Neill shipped out of Buenos Aires aboard the tramp steamer S.S. *Ikala* in March 1911, but this time as a seaman, not a passenger. After a brief stopover at Port of Spain, Trinidad (the harbor of which inspired the mise-en-scène for *The Moon of the Caribbees*), the *Ikala* docked in New York on April 15. As his poems "Free" and "The Bridegroom Weeps!" indicate, O'Neill's guilty feelings still lingered over Kathleen Jenkins and Eugene Jr., and by telephone he arranged with Jenkins to stop by and visit his one-year-old namesake. The reunion between husband and wife was civil but awkward; of the few words spoken by O'Neill, none of them justified his behavior over the last year and a half. After a brief stay, he left in silence. O'Neill wouldn't see Eugene Jr. for more than a decade, and Jenkins he never saw again.[86]

Given his time in Buenos Aires, O'Neill was far more at home among the denizens of Manhattan's Lower West Side waterfront district than the respectable uptown neighborhoods his parents and brother inhabited in New York. So he checked in at a boardinghouse and saloon near the docks at 252 Fulton Street, around the corner from where he'd worked as a supply clerk. The other boarders referred to the bar as Jimmy the Priest's (and a few years later Jimmy's Place), though officially it was listed as Jimmy's Hotel and Café.[87] Such a name for a low saloon like Jimmy's was doubtlessly intended to boost the perception among the municipal authorities that Jimmy's was a compliant Raines Law hotel. New York's Raines Law provided a loophole for serving liquor after hours and on Sundays at establishments located on the ground floor of tenement buildings, but only if they offered rooms for rent on the upper floors and served food. The Raines Law was signed in 1896 as a measure to curb working-class drinking habits and deviancy, but for the most part it had the opposite effect. By requiring that there were rooms that could be used for sleeping off a drunk or conducting illicit assignations, the moral-reform legislation had inadvertently enabled in equal measure binge drinking and prostitution.

James J. Condon, the eponymous proprietor, was a reserved but very tough Irishman. A ship chandler who worked in the building next door recalled that "Jimmy feared nothing. In most bars if a customer turned nasty, the bartender would first try to calm him down, but not Jimmy. The moment he smelled trouble, he'd grab the man, no matter how big he was—Jimmy was tall but thin—and give him the bum's rush through the swinging doors. He did it so fast he bowled over the toughest characters. There were two steps at the entrance, high stone ones, and sometimes the man would stumble and land flat in the street, yet Jimmy never looked over the doors to see if he was hurt or anything. He'd just return behind the bar, looking as cool as ever—he was a real poker face. I never heard him raise his voice, but you could tell when he had his Irish up." O'Neill portrayed Condon as a character in *"Anna Christie"* in similar terms, as a "personage of the waterfront [who], with his pale, thin, clean-shaven face, mild blue eyes and white hair, a cassock would seem more suited to him than the apron he wears. . . . But beneath all his mildness one senses the man behind the mask—cynical, callous, hard as nails" (*CP1*, 959).

O'Neill described Jimmy the Priest's as "a saloon of the lowest kind of grog shop." To rent a bed upstairs cost $3 a month, which O'Neill paid for out of a dollar-a-day allowance from his father, and the saloon on the first floor served free soup for lodgers and a shot of whiskey or a schooner of beer for a nickel.[88] Condon's signage was a yellow painted glass of beer on the window out front with the words "SCHOONER—5¢." "I lived there for a time," O'Neill told a reporter. "You lived down there while you gathered atmosphere?" he was asked. "Hell no," O'Neill replied. "I was flat."[89]

Jimmy Condon and his bar did provide the future playwright with an abundance of material, however. O'Neill soaked up Jimmy's dissolute world the way Jack London had earlier the San Francisco waterfront saloons, as immortalized in one of O'Neill's favorite books, London's chronicle of alcoholic despair *John Barleycorn: "Alcoholic Memoirs"* (1913). O'Neill's autobiographical character Edmund Tyrone in *Long Day's Journey Into Night* mentions Jimmy's by name, and the bar also served as the setting of his short story "Tomorrow" (1916) and his plays *Chris Christophersen* (1919), *Exorcism* (1919), *"Anna Christie,"* (1920) and, along with two other bars in New York, *The*

Iceman Cometh. In an early poem, "Ballad[e] of the Seamy Side" (1912), O'Neill rhapsodizes over the freewheeling mode of living at Jimmy's and its neighboring dives and dance halls:

> Where is the lure of the life you sing?
>   Let us consider the seamy side. . . .
> Think of the dives on the waterfront
>   And the low drunken brutes in dungaree,
> Of the low dance halls where the harpies hunt
>   And the maudlin seaman so carelessly
> Squanders the wages of a month at sea
>   And maybe is killed in a bar room brawl;
> The spell of these things explain to me—
>   "They're part of the game and I loved it all."[90]

By and large, the men at Jimmy's and those loafing and working around the docks nearby were a "hard lot," as O'Neill remembered them: "Every type; sailors on shore leave or stranded; longshoremen, waterfront riffraff, gangsters, down and outers, drifters from the ends of the earth." But O'Neill developed a deep respect for these men: "They were sincere, loyal and generous. In some queer way they carried on. I learned at Jimmy the Priest's not to sit in judgment on people."

In less than a year, at least two of the men at Jimmy's would save his life.[91]

Upon returning to the Unique Book Shop that spring, O'Neill learned of the anarchist Emma Goldman's journal *Mother Earth*, and Goldman, along with her chief editor, Bayard Boyesen, agreed to print O'Neill's first published work, "American Sovereign." That May, the Supreme Court had ruled that John D. Rockefeller's Standard Oil Company was in violation of the Antitrust Act, and the title of O'Neill's poem refers to a phrase from a speech made by the "muckraker" Lincoln Steffens, one of the first of a dauntless cohort of fire-eating journalists who in the early decades of the twentieth

Jimmy the Priest's, 252 Fulton Street in New York City, where O'Neill
attempted suicide in late 1911. Its official name was Jimmy's Hotel and
Café.

*   *   *

century denounced the nation's wealthiest classes and corrupt politicians. The previous December in Greenwich, Connecticut, ironically
one of the wealthiest towns in the United States, Steffens asserted the
muckraker doctrine that "American sovereignty has passed from our
political establishment to the national organization of money, credit,
and centralized business." In "American Sovereign," O'Neill addresses the vexing riddle of why working-class Americans vote for politicians with only upper-class interests in mind: "This is all the Working
Class has reaped—Their efforts help their leaders get the Dough."[92]

On July 22, 1911, O'Neill again put his literary aspirations on hold
and signed onto an American Line passenger steamer, the S.S. *New
York*. But as with his time on the S.S. *Ikala*, the transatlantic voyage

on the *New York* offered none of the high romance O'Neill had experienced on the sailing ship *Charles Racine*, and he later characterized the berth as an "ugly, tedious job, and no place for a man who wanted to call his soul his own. ... There was about as much 'sea glamor' in working aboard a passenger steamship as there would have been in working in a summer hotel. I washed enough deck area to cover a good-sized town."[93] The *New York* arrived in Southampton, England, to find that dock laborers and transportation workers had gone on a nationwide strike. O'Neill's early full-length *The Personal Equation* depicts the anarchist movement's involvement in this strike, which was supported by the American labor union the Industrial Workers of the World, better known as "the Wobblies." Coal stokers and seamen, in an unusual show of solidarity, rose up to support the workers in a brief but reverberating protest that would be remembered by posterity as the Great Labor Strike of 1911.

Stokers and seamen didn't generally fraternize in this way; in fact, a shipboard class division existed between the two groups that created strains of bitter animosity. And their clash of temperaments as well as job status informed O'Neill's lifelong conviction about the dehumanizing pitfalls of modern industrialization. In O'Neill's *The Hairy Ape* (1921), for instance, which explores this rift among modern-day seaman, an Irishman named Paddy contrasts a sailor's life in the sail-powered past to the demoralizing slavery of the industrial present:

> Oh to be scudding south again wid the power of the Trade Wind
> driving her on steady through the nights and days! Full sail on her!
> ... 'Twas them days men belonged to ships, not now. 'Twas them
> days a ship was part of the sea, and a man was part of a ship, and
> the sea joined all together and made it one. (*Scornfully*) Is it one
> wid this you'd be, Yank—black smoke from the funnels smudging
> the sea, smudging the decks—the bloody engines pounding and
> shaking—wid devil a sight of sun or a breath of clean air—choking
> our lungs with coal dust—breaking our backs and hearts in the hell
> of the stokehole—feeding the bloody furnace—feeding our lives
> along with the coal, I'm thinking—caged in by steel from a sight
> of the sky like bloody apes in the Zoo! (*CP*2, 127)

Once engine designers had introduced triple-expansion engines, shipping costs lowered, and the steamships were three times faster than sail-powered ships. But like Paddy, O'Neill believed that in the days of sail—in contrast to the thankless toil on steamships like the *Ikala*, the *New York*, and the ship he took on his return to the United States, the American Line's S.S. *Philadelphia*—sailors valued "the spirit of craftsmanship, of giving one's heart as well as one's hands to one's work, of doing it for the inner satisfaction of carrying out one's own ideals, not merely as obedience of orders. So far as I can see, the gain is over-balanced by the loss."[94]

By the time of O'Neill's return voyage to New York on August 26, he'd earned the rank of able seaman, or AB, an achievement that, though his tenure as a working seaman was little more than six weeks total, filled him with pride for the remainder of his life. "Do you want to see something I prize very highly?" O'Neill asked a friend years later. "Wait. I'll show you." Shoving aside two gold Pulitzer Prize

S.S. *Ikala*.
(COURTESY OF THE PEABODY ESSEX MUSEUM, SALEM, MASS.)

* * *

medals, he produced a tattered AB certificate. "Here it is."[95] Another cherished possession from his days at sea was his blue American Line sweater, an item of memorabilia he saved and wore proudly in the years to come as a reminder of a happier, more liberated time.

Back at Jimmy the Priest's, O'Neill plunged headlong into a self-described cycle of "great down-and-outness." He took another room above the bar, this time with a hardened Irish sailor named Driscoll. Driscoll was an American Line "fireman," or coal stoker, who had served with O'Neill on the S.S. *Philadelphia*, and he'd appear as the Irishman Driscoll in his S.S. *Glencairn* series, Lyons in the short story "Tomorrow" and, most notably, as the Irish American antihero Robert "Yank" Smith in *The Hairy Ape*. "I shouldn't have known the stokers if I hadn't happened to scrape an acquaintance with one of our own furnace-room gang at Jimmy the Priest's," O'Neill said. "His name was Driscoll, and he was a Liverpool Irishman. It seems that years ago some Irish families settled in Liverpool. Most of them followed the sea, and they were a hard lot. To sailors all over the world, a 'Liverpool Irishman' is the synonym for a tough customer."[96]

Driscoll occupied a grandiose place in O'Neill's imagination: "a giant of a man, and absurdly strong. He thought a whole lot of himself, was a determined individualist. He was very proud of his strength, his capacity for grueling work. It seemed to give him mental poise to be able to dominate the stokehole, do more work than any of his mates."[97] Not much has been uncovered about Driscoll's past; even his first name has remained a mystery. A few clues have surfaced, however: the initial of Driscoll's first name was J, and he was five feet seven. He was born in Ireland, not Liverpool, in 1878, and he moved to New York, where he gained American citizenship.[98] The only Driscoll that passed through Ellis Island and fits this profile is John Driscoll, who arrived in New York in 1899 from Cromore Village in Northern Ireland. Politically, this makes a good deal of sense, given that Yank Smith regards his Protestant Northern Irish engineer on the steamship as a "Catholic moiderin' [murdering] bastard" (*CP2*, 137). John Driscoll also had a sister living at 44 Broad

Street in New London, O'Neill's hometown, which might have
served as a handy conversation piece between the men at the bar.[99]

No one was more shocked than O'Neill when he heard a few
years later at Jimmy's that on August 12, 1915, at age thirty-seven,
Driscoll leapt overboard into the middle of the North Atlantic while
bound west as leading fireman on the S.S. *St. Louis* on one of its regular round-trip crossings from Liverpool to New York. (This route
might explain the confusion about Driscoll being a "Liverpool Irishman.") Driscoll's suicide inspired O'Neill to write a short story in
1917 titled "The Hairy Ape," since lost; and he later revisited the idea
in his 1921 play of the same title, this time replacing Driscoll's actual
Irish, a brogue we find in the *Glencairn* plays, with the accent of a
Brooklyn man of the waterfront.[100]

O'Neill's next important roommate at Jimmy's after Driscoll had
gone back to sea was a former press agent of James O'Neill's, James
"Jimmy" Findlater Byth. The forty-four-year-old newspaperman and
O'Neill had formed a close friendship while drinking at the Garden
Hotel bar around 1907, when James first hired Byth, who at the time
was working in New York as a Coney Island amusement park operator. A recurrent figure in the O'Neill canon, Jimmy Byth would
serve as the model for James "Jimmy" Anderson in "Tomorrow," the
drunken roommate Jimmy in *Exorcism*, and, most famously, as James
"Jimmy Tomorrow" Cameron in *The Iceman Cometh* (O'Neill's first
title for this much later play was also "Tomorrow").

Byth's character in "Tomorrow" lived in a "dream of tomorrows,"
while *Iceman*'s "Foolosopher," Larry Slade (based on the Irish anarchist Terry Carlin), refers to Jimmy as "the leader of our Tomorrow
Movement" (*CP3*, 584). In his stage directions for *Iceman*, O'Neill
describes Byth as having a face "like an old well-bred, gentle blood-
hound's. . . . His eyes are intelligent and there once was a competent
ability about him. His speech is educated, with a ghost of a Scotch
rhythm in it. His manners are those of a gentleman. There is a quality
about him of a prim, Victorian old maid, and at the same time of a lik-
able, affectionate boy who has never grown up" (*CP3*, 567). Byth was
a hack writer as well as press agent who shared O'Neill's predilection
for drink but none of his literary ambition, though he did manage

to publish a reminiscence during this period, "Cecil Rhodes," which recounts his time as a correspondent during South Africa's Boer War (1899–1902).

Those just looking for a quiet drink who sat down on a barstool next to Byth would be regaled with tales of his adventures as a war reporter embedded with the Boers (Dutch colonialists). Indeed, Byth had friends on both sides in the conflict, and he worked with them closely in the Great Boer War Spectacle. The show premiered at the 1904 St. Louis World Fair, where Byth's job title was vice president and amusement manager, then traveled to Coney Island the following year. The Great Boer War Spectacle was a spectacularly elaborate battle reenactment that, like Buffalo Bill's Wild West, which featured actual cowboys and Indians, included veterans who'd fought viciously against one another in South Africa. The New York press release for the show is attributable to Byth, who wrote that the Boer War Company integrated "1,000 men, including 200 Kafirs, Zulus, Matabeles, and representatives of other South African tribes," and 600 horses trained to feign death. Because of his close friendship with Byth, O'Neill considered South Africa "a country I have always had a strong yen for because in the distant past I was pals with so many of its people, both British Africanders and Boers and really know a lot about it for one who has never been there." Two of Byth's associates from the Spectacle, the Boer general Piet Cronjé and the British captain A. W. Lewis, the general manager of the Spectacle, would appear as Piet Wetjoen and Cecil Lewis in *The Iceman Cometh*.[101]

By the spring of 1912, O'Neill and Byth had both managed to find their way into print with "Free" and "Cecil Rhodes" in the yearbook of the Pleiades Club, and their contributions are separated, appropriately enough, by the music and lyrics of the "Pleiades Drinking Song." Two poems in the same collection appear to have influenced *The Iceman Cometh*. The first, "To-day's the Time" by William Johnston, warns its readers against languid procrastination:

> ONCE YESTERDAY's gone, it's mighty
>   far off,
> And TO-MORROW's still further away.

So whatever there is you want to be doing,
You might as well do it TO-DAY.[102]

Another poem, "Beside the Road" by Madison Cawein, which
directly follows Byth's reminiscence in the book, concludes,

Of hope, whose light makes bright the road,
And beautifies the lonely hours,
And turns the sorrow of our load
To thoughts, like shining flowers."[103]

Thus from this volume and from Byth's tales of the Boer War and his
Spectacle, O'Neill absorbed much of the rich thematic material that
informs *The Iceman Cometh* and represents the most prominent dramatic motif of his career: the hopeless hope for a better tomorrow.[104]

Byth and O'Neill's room at Jimmy the Priest's was adorned with piles
of books and was "filthy," as O'Neill remembers it in his stage directions for *Exorcism:* "The walls and low ceiling, white-washed in some
remote past, are spotted with the greasy imprints of groping hands
and fingers. The plaster has scaled off in places showing the lathes beneath. The floor is carpeted with an accumulation of old newspapers,
cigarette butts, ashes, burnt matches, etc."[105] Next to them lived a retired telegrapher nicknamed "the Lunger," a disparaging epithet for
someone suffering from tuberculosis; the Lunger appears in O'Neill's
story "Tomorrow," his one-act *Warnings* (1913), and his novella *S.O.S.*
(1917). The man would die of the disease, but not before attempting
to teach O'Neill the International Code for wireless communication.
O'Neill was always too drunk during their sessions, however, and by
morning had forgotten everything he learned.[106]

O'Neill hadn't always been belly-up at the bar at Jimmy's over his
cycle of "great down-and-outness." He had a lover for a time named
Maude Williams. Most of the information about her comes from
Kathleen Jenkins, who testified in court the following year that Williams lived at 123 West Forty-Seventh Street and that Jenkins pos-

sessed "information" confirming that O'Neill had "committed adultery" with Williams "at divers times during the months of June, July,
August, and September, 1911."[107] Williams was most likely a small-
time actress in musical theater by that name who's listed in several
trade columns as having performed in the variety show *A Knight for a
Day* that past April and in the summer for the "beauty chorus" of the
musical farce *The Countess Coquette*.[108]

Late in December 1911, O'Neill attended a performance of the
famed Irish Players from Dublin's Abbey Theatre. Produced by his
father's former advance man George C. Tyler, the historic tour included plays by John Millington Synge, William Butler Yeats, T. C. Murray,
Lady Augusta Gregory, Lennox Robinson, and George Bernard Shaw,
among others. For O'Neill, the Irish Players were a revelation: "[The
Irish Players] first opened my eyes to the existence of a real theatre," he
said, "as opposed to the unreal—and to me then—hateful theatre of my
father, in whose atmosphere I had been brought up." "As a boy I saw
so much of the old, ranting, artificial, romantic stage stuff that I always
had a sort of contempt for the theatre. It was seeing the Irish players for
the first time that gave me a glimpse of my opportunity."[109]

O'Neill also attended political lectures and raucous beer parties
hosted by the avant-garde Ferrer School, one of the "Modern Schools"
of the prewar period named for Spanish educator Francisco Ferrer.
Over the school's short-lived existence, 1911 to 1915 (when it was
shut down for vocally opposing America's entry into World War I), its
advisory board consisted of some of the era's most notorious political
firebrands—Jack London, Hutchins Hapgood, Upton Sinclair, and
Emma Goldman, to name a few. The Ferrer was first housed at 6 St.
Mark's Place in the East Village, where it conducted evening and Sunday classes for students aged fifteen to twenty. Tuition was 15¢ a week; if
you couldn't afford that, it was free of charge. The school's philosophy, according to its director Bayard Boyesen, was that "different
natures develop differently." Contrary to their reputation as dangerous socialists and anarchists, its teachers refused to enforce any "ism."
Instead, they encouraged their students' intellectual self-discovery in
their own time, at their own pace. "Our radicalism finds expression

in our modes of teaching, not in imposing any doctrines on the children," Boyesen told a reporter for the *New York Times*. "However, I must say that I will be disappointed if any child, after having the facts set before him, does not revolt against the iniquity of the system of government in this and every other country."[110]

Like O'Neill, Boyesen was a philosophical anarchist. He had been ousted from his post as a Columbia professor for radicalism, which had earned him the status of a minor celebrity. In a speech given at the Ferrer School in the spring of 1912, he'd pointedly made mention of similar academic careers notoriously cut short: Percy Bysshe Shelley had been expelled from Oxford, Edgar Allan Poe from Virginia, James Russell Lowell from Harvard, James Fenimore Cooper from Yale, and so on. (He might later have added Eugene O'Neill from Princeton.) Boyesen declared that "art above all is unrespectable and unrespecting." He concluded with a glum appraisal of the state of the arts in the United States, a declaration prophetic of O'Neill's future as a perpetually banned playwright: "In pure creative art America is giving little or nothing to the world, and if an artist tries to do so it is as likely as not that he will turn some Anthony Comstock [a notoriously powerful moral reformer] loose on him to declare him and all his purposes special creations of the Evil One."[111]

O'Neill made lasting friendships among the Ferrer's habitués, including his later editor Manuel Komroff and future Provincetown Player Christine Ell, and he stopped in at the school regularly with buckets of beer to liven up the meetings. According to one attendee, Ell, who had worked as a prostitute in Denver, boasted at one gathering that a taxi driver tried to rape her on the way over.[112] She could well have been telling the truth. Ell later dated O'Neill's brother Jim, and she served as the model for the oversized female lead Josie Hogan in *A Moon for the Misbegotten*. O'Neill describes Josie as "five feet eleven in her stockings and weighs around one hundred and eighty," "so oversize for a woman that she is almost a freak" (*CP*3, 857).

To be granted a divorce in New York State required proof of adultery provided by witnesses. O'Neill obliged. His divorce trial, which he wasn't required to attend and did not, on June 10, 1912, in White Plains, New York, where Kathleen had relocated, included several testimonies to substantiate the charge of adultery. The following is a summary of the eyewitness accounts of O'Neill's infidelity: On the night of December 29, 1911, O'Neill met with the legal counsel of Kathleen's mother, James C. Warren, and his associates Edward Mullen and Frank Archibold, a friend of Archibold's named Mr. Reel, and O'Neill's friend the painter Edward Ireland. The co-conspirators gathered for dinner at Ireland's apartment at 126 West 104th Street, then commenced a bar crawl at the Campus tavern on the same block. Ireland returned home, and the rest headed to Midtown for more drinks at various watering holes. They eventually landed at a brothel around three a.m. at 140 West Forty-Fifth Street, across from the Lyceum Theatre, a couple of blocks up from where O'Neill was born, at which point Mr. Reel departed. After stalling "a short time" in the lobby, O'Neill selected "some girl there that attracted him," according to Mullen's testimony, and followed her upstairs.[113] Mullen, Warren, and Archibold waited in the lobby for two hours until O'Neill instructed a maid to call them up, whereupon they found O'Neill naked with the prostitute. They had a drink or two, and then, duties fulfilled, left at around half-past six or seven a.m.[114] End of testimony. End of marriage.

But on the next evening, December 30, after the events related in the testimony, or possibly it was New Year's Eve, 1911, James Byth and another boarder at Jimmy the Priest's, Major Adams, discovered O'Neill half dead in his room. He'd attempted to kill himself with an overdose of the barbiturate veronal. In October 1919, O'Neill recorded the traumatic experience in his one-act play *Exorcism*. A prequel of sorts to *Long Day's Journey Into Night*, *Exorcism* opens in a room at a downtown boardinghouse (Jimmy the Priest's) with Ned Malloy, O'Neill's autobiographical protagonist, possessed by demons after committing an odious act. Having just returned from a brothel, Ned recounts to his roommate Jimmy (Byth) a degrading experience he had with a prostitute, whom he'd visited to provide grounds for divorcing his estranged wife. "You know the law in New York," Ned mutters. "There's only one ground that goes."[115]

"We arrived in the small hours and I was very drunk," Ned tells Jimmy. "I must have fallen asleep—almost immediately. When I awoke the room was strange to me. It wasn't dawn, it was mid-day, but it appeared like dawn, with faint streaks of light shedding from the edges of the green shades and the whole room in a sort of dead half-darkness. . . . The whole thing was no new experience—but I was afraid!" This depiction of a gray dawn spent with a prostitute recalls similar stories associated with O'Neill's brother Jim, most vividly in *A Moon for the Misbegotten*, with Jim Tyrone as the protagonist. Both Ned and Jim describe prostitutes as "pigs," and Ned awakes to a gray light coming in the windows, just as Jim does.[116] "I've seen too God-damned many dawns creeping grayly over too many dirty windows," Jim tells Josie in *Moon* (*CP3*, 919).

Once alone, Ned swallows a handful of pills, lies down in a fetal position, and mutters, "Well, that's over." Several hours later, Jimmy and Major Andrews (Major Adams) find him unconscious and call a doctor. His stomach is pumped, and he's ordered to walk around the block to revive himself. Ned's father arrives (though in real life James O'Neill was on tour at the time) and pleads with him to go to a rest cure sanatorium. Surprisingly, Ned agrees and decides that after a period of healing, he'll move out west to Minnesota. "My sins are for-given me!" Ned declares. "God judges by our intentions, they say, and my intentions last night were of the best. He evidently wants to retain my services here below—for what I don't know yet but I'm going to find out—and I feel of use already!" Ned has thus been resurrected from an ignominious end, his demons "exorcised."[117]

The discovery of *Exorcism* in 2011 revealed something buried in *Long Day's Journey Into Night*—what's been missing in Edmund Tyrone, culpability, is all too apparent in Ned Malloy. Ned, a nickname for Edmund, is as autobiographical as Edmund but with considerable dif-ferences: Ned is bitter, spiteful, self-absorbed, an emotional bully to friends and family, and insensitive to their deep concern for his well-being. In this way he's redolent of another close avatar of O'Neill's, Dion Anthony in *The Great God Brown* (1925). (Ned's wife is called Margaret, not coincidentally the name O'Neill later gives Dion's long-suffering spouse.) Ned, like Jamie Tyrone, uses the word "rotten" to capture the depths of his self-loathing: "Everything I had ever done, my whole life—all life—had become too rotten! My head had been pushed under, I was drowning and the thick slime of loathing poured down my throat—strangling me!"[118] Ned, Edmund, Dion, and Jamie Tyrone Jr. in *Long Day's Journey* epitomize the O'Neillian archetype of a wounded soul, men so utterly disappointed with themselves and life in general that they take it out on those who love them most—suicide, in Ned and Edmund's case by pills, in Dion and Jamie's by alcohol, providing the maximum pain one can inflict upon caring survivors.[119] In short, with *Exorcism*, we are offered a glimpse into the true personality defects of Edmund Tyrone, and thus of O'Neill himself.

For many decades, before the lost script of *Exorcism* came to light, the only surviving accounts of O'Neill's actual suicide attempt were those of his friend George Jean Nathan and O'Neill's second wife, Agnes Boulton. Neither has been taken seriously. Their stories are embellished with details of raucous drunken behavior, and both conclude with O'Neill being escorted by drunks at the bar to Manhattan's Bellevue Hospital. Boulton's account, when placed beside *Exorcism*, appears the more legitimate. She quotes O'Neill telling her that upon arriving back from the brothel to Jimmy the Priest's on the morning of December 30, he'd hoped to find a check from his father. The absent check not only deprived him of the cash he needed to keep his room (and to keep drinking), it also signaled a complete abandonment by his parents—"of this he was sure now." Boulton adds that O'Neill was troubled that Jim wasn't there "to talk things over with," that "he couldn't stand his thoughts anymore," that he was disgusted by his night with the prostitute, and that he was regretful for having gotten involved with Jenkins, "who seemed like himself just another pawn of fate."[120] For a man with suicidal tendencies, any of these torments might have nudged him over the edge into attempting to reach the serene finality of death. Combined, they were more than sufficient.

O'Neill told Boulton that he spent what money he had (two drinks' worth) on veronal tablets from several pharmacies in the neighborhood around Jimmy's. Then he locked the door to his room with a flimsy hook, swallowed the tablets with "a glass of dirty water," and passed out cold. "I must have been there twenty-four hours, maybe longer," he said. "I vaguely remembered coming to, hearing a knocking on the door, then silence. . . . This happened a number of times, but I paid no attention to it. It didn't occur to me that I was alive—after all those pills! At first I probably thought I was still on my way, not dead yet, but getting there. Perhaps I didn't think at all, just felt resentful that the veronal hadn't yet completely put me out and that I could hear the knocks. . . . Then a horrible thought came to me—*I was dead, of course, and death was nothing but a continuation of life as it had been when one left it!* A wheel that turned endlessly round and round back to the same old situation!"[121]

Ned Malloy in *Exorcism* tells his roommate Jimmy that he went directly from the brothel to Battery Park and remained there six hours. This would validate the date of his actual attempt as December 30 or 31, 1911 (though the play is set in March, the gateway month to spring and thus rebirth). James O'Neill's check arrived while Eugene was unconscious, and after the rent had been deducted, "drinks were on the house . . . *Wow!* What a celebration."[122] Boulton's and Nathan's stories both conclude with a drunken celebration among O'Neill and his saviors, an anticlimactic if joyful tableau that ends both *Exorcism* (which was subtitled "A Play of Anti-Climax" at the time of its production in 1920) and *The Iceman Cometh*.

Kathleen Jenkins never appeared to hold a grudge after the divorce. As O'Neill remarked to his third wife, Carlotta Monterey, "The woman I gave the most trouble to has given me the least."[123] But no one document verifies that admittance more than the script of *Exorcism*. "I wouldn't forgive or forget the fact that I despise her," Ned says, to which Jimmy responds, "But didn't you—don't you care for her at all?" "Not a damn!" Ned snaps back. "Not a single, solitary, infinitesimal tinker's damn! I never did! Body—that was what I wanted in her and she in me. And I married her for an obsolete reason—a gentleman's reason, you'd call it. . . . That's all it was, so help me—a silly gesture of honor—and a stunt!" Jimmy then asks if his wife, Margaret, truly wants a divorce. "Of course," Ned replies acidly. "She's rich. She'll be married again within a year. [It would be three years before Jenkins remarried.] Her pinhead won't even retain a memory of what happened to her two years ago." And along with the "silly gesture" of marrying her for "honor"—because she was pregnant—he sourly admits that he'd gotten hitched merely "because a perverse devil whispered in my ear that marriage was one of those few things I hadn't done." Ned's then told that Margaret went "out of her mind with grief," presuming he attempted suicide because she's suing him for divorce. "Aha!" Ned says, even after his "rebirth." "So that's what she thinks! The devil!"[124] Ned's abusive portrayal of Margaret throughout the play, and thus O'Neill's of Jenkins, must have played a key role—*the* key role, perhaps—in O'Neill's resolution to destroy the play. In the distant future, he would discreetly, if also self-servingly, omit Jenkins and his son from *Long Day's Journey Into Night*.[125]

Return to Monte Cristo

On January 20, 1912, O'Neill was served his divorce summons from Jenkins's attorney. Then he hopped a train for the Deep South. At the station in New Orleans, he stumbled onto the platform, in his words, "broke on the tail end of a bust which terminated in that city."[126] O'Neill claimed he'd won some money at faro cards, went on a bender with a few pals from Jimmy the Priest's, blacked out, and awoke, startled, to find himself on a train heading south. Actors in his father's company remember a different story: James had wired money to Eugene in New York, they felt sure, in response to a telegram that read, "To eat or not to eat, that is the question."[127] Whatever the case, O'Neill's first stop in New Orleans was the city docks to drum up a berth back to New York. He had the papers on him to prove he was a qualified able-bodied seaman, but no ship sailing for New York had an opening. Only then did he contact his family.[128]

James, Ella, and Jim were in New Orleans on a tour that had started the previous fall. Tormented by the prospect of financial insolvency in his elder years, James held his nose and cobbled together a tabloid version of *Monte Cristo* with a stage time of forty-

one minutes (whittled down from its usual three hours). The touring company's bill included, among others, a perky ragtime songster
named Rae Samuels, a.k.a. "the Blue Streak of Ragtime," a tram-
poline stunt team, and "the Juggling Burkes," a two-man act that
juggled "Indian clubs." But James O'Neill as the Count of Monte
Cristo was, of course, the main attraction. Jim was billed as "one of
the foremost of the younger generation of leading men," a short-
lived reputation based chiefly on his ephemeral 1909 success in *The
Travelling Salesman*. Eugene later described Jim's choice of acting
for a living as a "line of least resistance." Jim had performed onstage
throughout the previous decade, including several tours with his
father, and in this vaudeville tour of *Monte Cristo*, he played a number
of roles, one of which, in an inescapable irony, was that of Edmund
Dantès's financial benefactor Abbé Faria.[129]

The tour had arrived in Memphis, Tennessee, when James was
first informed of Eugene's attempt on his life. At that time, it was
"whispered around" among the actors that the elder O'Neill's son had
"suffered some kind of misfortune." James refused Eugene the money
for a return ticket from New Orleans but offered him a job for $25 a
week. "It was a case of act or walk home," O'Neill remembered, "so I
acted for the rest of the tour over the Orpheum Circuit." O'Neill was
cast as a jailer and a gendarme; while playing the gendarme, he wore
a mustache wired to his nostrils to distinguish one character from the
other. "That cut-down version was wonderful," O'Neill joked to a
reporter years later. "Characters came on that didn't seem to belong
there and did things that made no sense and said things that sounded
insane. The Old Man had been playing Cristo so long he'd almost
forgotten it, so he ad-libbed and improvised and never gave anybody
a cue. You knew when your turn came when he stopped talking."[130]

"The tabloid presentation of 'Monte Cristo,' " a Salt Lake City
drama critic neatly summed up its reception, "is rather pitiful, all
things considered, when one remembers past performances." (Rae
Samuels stole each evening with hoots of laughter and applause. In
October 1920, Agnes Boulton would see Samuels perform the musical
comedy *The Tooting Tooties* in order to glimpse, as she wrote O'Neill,
"the eyes that smiled on your mad youth!")[131]

From New Orleans, the company rode the Overland Limited rail line up to Ogden, Utah, and points north and west—Salt Lake City, Denver, and St. Paul, Minnesota (not coincidentally, the state to which Ned Malloy will head at the end of *Exorcism*).[132] The O'Neills kept relations with the company cordial but aloof, sequestering themselves between towns in their own train car. When they arrived at a destination, Jim would drink heartily with the other actors but assume a haughty reserve if they got too chummy. An actor in the production, Charlie Webster, remembered Jim's intoxicated face as "an alcoholic mask, reddish, glazed expression, or rather no expression." And Jim wasn't holding up his end onstage. "Imagine an actor who can't fence!" James groused during rehearsals. On their afternoons off, he tried to coach his son in swordsmanship but finally gave up, simplifying the finale so that Jim merely had to strike James's raised weapon once.[133]

One grainy image of this production still exists. Taken at the Orpheum Theatre in Ogden, the photograph (too obscured by age to reproduce here) appeared in the *Salt Lake City Evening Tribune*. It was taken Friday night, February 2, the first time Eugene O'Neill had ever acted on the professional stage.[134] The photo shows James glaring down at the corrupt police chief Villefort—who, with the same aquiline nose and jutting chin, must be Jim—dead on the floor of the inn Pont du Gard. Eugene can just be made out upstage right, with his fake pointy mustache, hiding behind more expressive gendarmes. (Eleven people were advertised as having roles in the production, and ten are onstage; the missing cast member is whoever was playing the scoundrel Danglars.) Webster's sketchy description matches James in the photo to a fault: "He was very graceful, used his hands eloquently. As Monte Cristo, wore black satin knee breeches, a white wig. His body had thickened but was still graceful. . . . Production had good costumes, came from his regular production."[135]

Despite the vaudeville circuit's lowbrow reputation, its standards of behavior were notoriously strict. You couldn't swear in public (signs forbade you even to say "damn"), and drunkenness and unruly behavior were forbidden. Jim respected this and played it relatively safe while still trying his father's patience with crude practical jokes.

Charlie Webster, playing Edmund Dantès's son Albert, had a line challenging a villain to a duel, pronouncing it his "duty to repress calumny." One night before the show, Jim cautioned Webster not to slip up and say "calomel" (a laxative). Sure enough, he uttered "calomel" instead of "calumny," and James, playing opposite Webster, grunted, "Hmph," as he generally did after such gaffes, but the audience didn't appear to notice. On another night after the performance, Jim exited the theater out the stage door and into the alleyway singing at the top of his lungs, his baritone voice echoing off the building walls; but he was cut short when a bucket of water was dropped on his head.[136]

Webster described the elder James's magnetism among the troupe in nothing but admiring terms: he was like "a priest, quiet; he never raised his voice; he had a spiritual quality." Frustrated as James was with his boys, he occasionally revealed a deep paternal affection for them. Once, when a group of reporters was interviewing James and the other players, Eugene walked in the front entrance and hopped up onstage to join them. "He's a handsome chap," one reporter said. "Takes after his father." James waved off the compliment. "I was never as good looking as he is." He expressed less parental satisfaction in private, once taking Eugene aside and reproaching him with cool reserve. "I am not satisfied with your performance, sir," he said. "I am not satisfied with your play, sir," Eugene retorted.[137]

William Lee, an electrician at the Olympic Theatre in St. Louis, where the company played in late February, remembered Eugene as a conspicuously dreadful addition to what he considered an otherwise "grand" production. "I can't understand," scoffed Pat Short, a stagehand at the Olympic, "how a fine actor and a smart man like James O'Neill can have a son so dumb." Lee remembered overhearing James and Eugene in a testy backstage exchange: "You never could act," James fumed. "You can't act. And you never will." "What of it?" his son shrugged.[138]

Eugene rarely greeted the doorman with so much as a hello when he arrived at the theater, nor did he chat with the other actors while waiting for his cue. "He never had a word to say to anybody," Lee recalled.[139] He also suffered terribly from stage fright (an affliction he

would never overcome), and like so many of O'Neill's future companions and theatrical associates, Webster found his anxiety infectious.
Once during the Château d'If scene, for instance, just before the set
change for James's climactic proclamation that the world is his, a trembling O'Neill, playing a jailer, looked down at the body of Abbé Faria
and spluttered out a line he'd rehearsed at least a dozen times: "What
has happened here?" Webster, affected by O'Neill's halting delivery,
responded with a clipped, "Yes, he is dead."[140] The audience howled
with laughter. O'Neill and Webster heard James from the wings thun-
dering, "What happened? What did they do? Why are they laughing? . . . Where are they? I'll kill those boys." They made a hasty exit
and clambered up into the fly lofts.[141] Even so, James rarely raised
his renowned cello-toned voice in anger, even when enraged by his
children's drunken behavior; instead, he'd slip into an Irish brogue.[142]

"I had a small part," O'Neill remarked in hindsight, "but I couldn't
have been worse if I'd been playing Hamlet." He later boasted that
throughout the tour neither he nor Jim had drawn "a sober breath."
Full-blown alcoholics by this time, the two made a habit of down-
ing several whiskeys before each performance. "The least said about
those acting days the better," O'Neill said. "The alcoholic content
was as high as the acting was low. They graduated me from the Orpheum Circuit with degree of Lousy Cum Laude. If the tour lasted
a month longer I would also have won my D.T. [delirium tremens].
The one remorseful thought . . . is that I didn't warn audiences in advance about my performance so they could all get drunk, too. It must
have been a terrible thing to witness sober." Nonetheless, O'Neill
recalled his brief time on the circuit fondly: "My brother and I had
one grand time of it," he said, "and I look back on it as one of the
merriest periods of my life."[143] But the experience as a whole spoiled
his enjoyment of attending the theater, as he couldn't keep his mind
off the actors: "I can't help seeing with the relentless eye of heredity,
upbringing, and personal experience, every little trick they pull."[144]

James O'Neill, in fairness, had reason to grumble over these few
months on tour with his family: Eugene had just attempted suicide;
Jim was weak willed, a lush, and failing as an actor, the one profession

that might have allowed him to survive on his own steam; and James's reputation as a has-been among the press corps had expanded to intolerable levels. Even his hometown paper had admitted a few years earlier that, proud as everyone was that James was a Cincinnati boy, " 'Monte Cristo,' one might say, ruined James O'Neill . . . his success was such that he has never been able to entirely break away from the part or persuade the public to abate its demands for its continuance." Adding financial insult to domestic and professional injury, James also lost nearly $40,000 when two firms he'd invested in went belly-up.[145]

Then there was Ella O'Neill—lost to "the poison" again. Ella was rarely glimpsed by the rest of the company, except when she slipped in and out of her husband's dressing room. Webster's impression, though he observed her only from a distance, closely resembles that of Ella's counterpart in Long Day's Journey Into Night: "Someone remote. . . . Frail, unsteady . . . very sensitive, quiet, someone who had been well born, floating, wore clothes very feminine. . . . On train always hidden, like a wraith." The O'Neill men treated her with the utmost care and deference, like some kind of purified essence that might be "contaminated," he said, by a stranger's touch. Ella had also begun behaving erratically after Eugene joined the tour. In one disquieting incident, she edged her way toward the stage while James roared his line, "Revenge is mine, Fernand—I hold thy heart in my hand!" Glancing over and seeing her approach from the wings, he nearly signaled for the curtain when a stagehand stopped her before she could reveal herself to the audience. Ella attempted this several more times, prompting James to check the wings each time he performed the scene.[146] No one but the three O'Neill men could have known that Ella was on morphine, that her otherworldly demeanor was a result of the drug's effect rather than her ordinary temperament.

Long Day's Journey, the play that allowed O'Neill to come to terms with his mother's drug addiction, is set that following summer. But O'Neill only hints that it might have been his suicide attempt and presence on the tour afterward that instigated Ella's relapse, rather than the more blameless diagnosis of tuberculosis that the work implies.

The O'Neills returned to New York by early March 1912, and though Eugene's subsequent movements remain a mystery, there was one place he undeniably wasn't: his divorce proceedings. Not legally obliged to attend the June 10 trial in White Plains, O'Neill was spared the depositions about his night with the prostitute as well as exchanges between the presiding judge, Joseph Morschauser, and Kathleen like this one: "Have you voluntarily cohabitated with [the defendant] since he committed these adulteries?" the judge asked. "No." "Have you forgiven him?" "No."[147] Kathleen was granted "exclusive care, custody and control" of Eugene Jr., and O'Neill was absolved, presumably to ensure an unmitigated dissociation from her and Eugene, of child support and alimony. The interlocutory judgment was filed July 8 and, since O'Neill made no attempt to challenge it, the final judgment on default was handed down on October 11. It's unknown whether O'Neill ever read this second document, but the judge who wrote it, Isaac N. Mills, made it clear that he believed O'Neill unfit for marriage: "It shall not be lawful," he ruled, "for the defendant to marry any person other than the plaintiff in the lifetime of the plaintiff."[148]

Back in New London that summer, O'Neill spent long, lazy days drifting nude in a rowboat on the Thames River and enjoying frequent swims off the Scott family dock across the road. He also swam a mile across the Thames, and the *Day* newspaper reported that he made "good time." At night he visited the Bradley Street brothels and drank with his friends Art McGinley, Ed Keefe, Hutch Collins, and "Ice" Casey. "Gene O'Neill and I tried to drink America dry," McGinley liked to say, "and nearly succeeded." Many evenings they played cards and read poetry at Dr. Joseph "Doc" Ganey's "Second Story Club," where a cohort of like-minded intellectuals congregated at the physician's apartment on Main Street (now Eugene O'Neill Drive).[149]

When his father's harangues about working for a living could no longer be ignored, O'Neill took a job for $10 a week at the *New London Telegraph*, a liberal-minded newspaper then struggling to stay afloat. Upon receiving one of O'Neill's first filings from the police court, city editor Malcolm "Mal" Mollan called him into his office. "The smell of the rooms is made convincing," Mollan began, with

barely concealed sarcasm, "The amount of blood on the floor is precisely measured; you have drawn a nice picture of the squalor and
stupidity and degradation of that household." Then the editor lowered the boom: "But would you mind finding out the name of the
gentleman who carved the lady and whether the dame is his wife or
daughter or who? And phone the hospital for a hint as to whether
she is dead or discharged or what? Then put the facts into a hundred
and fifty words—and send this literary batik to the picture framers."
On another assignment, the Harvard/Yale rowing regatta, O'Neill's
prose dripped with pretentious alliteration—"bronze and brawny
backs bent against the oars" and so on. The editors, having read a few
sentences into the piece, demanded to know at what point the reporter might deign to inform his readers which crew team had won the
race. O'Neill regularly showed up drunk at the news desk, and after
he'd done so once too often, Mollan warned him he'd be dismissed;
but the business manager, Charles Thompson, took the editor aside.
"Hell," he said. "You can't do that. His father is paying his salary."[150]

The *Telegraph*'s editor in chief, Frederick P. Latimer, a former
judge and friend of James's, allowed O'Neill some latitude by publishing his poetry in the newspaper's "Laconics" column, even though
Latimer believed that given O'Neill's stylistic flourishes in his prose
reporting, he would "eventually abandon the poetic medium and
become a novelist." (As late as the mid-1920s, Latimer maintained his
belief that O'Neill should have been a novelist, and so did O'Neill.)[151]

O'Neill's talents proved better suited to writing poetry than reporting, in fact, but not by much. He wrote sophomoric, propagandizing verse consisting mainly of barbs at Standard Oil and other
business interests and backhanded brickbats at politicians such as
presidential rivals Teddy Roosevelt and Howard Taft:

> Our Teddy opens wide his mouth,
>   N'runs around n'yells all day,
> N'calls some people naughty names,
>   N'says things that he shouldn't say.
> N'when he's nothing else to do

He swells up like he'd like to bust,
N'pounds on something with his fist
    N'tells us 'bout some wicked trust.
I always wondered why that was—
        I guess it's 'cause
        Taft never does.[152]

Most of O'Neill's poems at the *Telegraph* consisted of stylistic
send-ups of popular rhymesters like Kipling, Robert Burns, and
Robert W. Service with topics alluding to local events, political figures, and wealthy citizens. O'Neill's verse, Latimer wrote, would
"make us choke with wrath at the queer wildness of his ideas, so different from those of other folks and hard to comprehend." Frustrating as their debates were while rowing together on the Thames or
smoking in a back room at the paper, the editor nonetheless retained
a "dim, small notion" that this upstart had a touch of the poet in
him. O'Neill's estimation of these propagandistic verses once he'd
matured as a writer is plain enough: by 1923, he admitted that
although they marked the true start of his writing career, the work
was "junk of a low order." "I was trying to write popular humorous
journalistic verse for a small town paper," he said in 1929, "and the
stuff should be judged—nearly all of it—by that intent." Later still, in
1936, he scolded a publisher interested in reprinting this early poetry
as a collection: "Frankly ... I'm all against it. It would be a shame
to waste good type on such nonsense. If those small-town jingles of
my well-misspent youth were amusingly bad, I would have no objection, for their republication might hand someone a laugh, at least.
But they're not. They are merely very dull stuff indeed—and so my
decision must be to let them lie suitably defunct." Even so, O'Neill's
consistent refrain in the offices of the *Telegraph* must have sounded
laughably conceited at the time—that one day James O'Neill would
be remembered chiefly for being Eugene O'Neill's father.[153]

After a few months at the *Telegraph*, however, O'Neill had convinced
himself that the humble pursuit of small-town journalism was to be

his true calling. If nothing else, it might provide the requisite financial stability to marry his eighteen-year-old girlfriend, Maibelle Scott. Scott lived with her sister Arlene and her husband, who had moved into a property of his father's known as the Pink House, where the O'Neills lived before moving into Monte Cristo Cottage two doors down. Maibelle and Arlene were the daughters of John Scott, a grocer who lived a block away, and Eugene had known the family for years. But to reintroduce himself in a more romantic light, he arranged to cover a wedding Scott was attending for the *Telegraph*. Pretentiously donning one of his father's black capes, he bowed before her and spluttered with inept gallantry, "At last we meet!" Later that night, at eleven o'clock, the tranquility of the Scott household was disturbed by the jangling of the telephone. It was Eugene O'Neill. Could he speak to Scott to ask her out for a date?[154] Maibelle would later be the model for the fifteen-year-old Muriel McComber in his 1933 comedy *Ah, Wilderness!* (though the play takes place in 1906, not 1912). Richard Miller, O'Neill's loosely based fictional counterpart, sends Muriel love letters and racy poetry, just as his creator did Scott. O'Neill gave her the original manuscript of his poem "Free" and wrote her over two hundred love letters, a unique store of material from this period in his life that calamitously, for posterity, Scott burned after she'd become engaged to another man a few years later.[155]

O'Neill and Scott met each other secretively on and off for the rest of the fall, as neither of their mothers was pleased to hear of the liaison. One night, after O'Neill saw her home after a showing of *The Bohemian Girl* at the Lyceum Theatre, Scott's mother informed her that she would "shoot him" if he ever showed his face there again. For her part, Ella warned another local girl on the phone, wrongly assuming it was Scott, "You'd better stay away from him. He isn't a good influence for you or any other girl." Mary Tyrone, Ella's fictional double, similarly chides her son, "No respectable parents will let their daughters be seen with you" (*CP3*, 739). But Ella's disapproval of Eugene's behavior was equaled by her disapproval of Scott as a match for him—she had little enthusiasm for her handsome young son's marrying a grocer's daughter.[156]

Maibelle Scott was perplexed by Eugene's reputation in town as an unseemly roustabout. "He was always a gentleman around me, never drunk or anything like that," she recalled, "and I couldn't understand why people talked against him, including his own parents. I felt that he was very much misunderstood." She was nevertheless surprised to see him ill at ease at parties and other public gatherings, exhibiting an all-too-commonly reported "sad streak in him, a what's-the-use sort of attitude." She later acknowledged that this depressive attitude prevented her from truly falling in love with O'Neill. "When I met my husband, I realized the feeling was different. I knew then that I had never loved Eugene but had only been fascinated."[157]

As well as conducting Romeo and Juliet–style romances, O'Neill and Richard Miller from *Ah, Wilderness!* also shared left-wing views considered unsuitable for consumption by respectable young women. Like his creator, Richard disdains the Fourth of July as a "stupid farce": "I'll celebrate the day the people bring out the guillotine again and I see Pierpont Morgan being driven by in a tumbrel!" "Son," responds his tolerant father, Nat Miller, a character recognizable to New Londoners as O'Neill's editor Frederick Latimer, "if I didn't know it was you talking, I'd think we had Emma Goldman with us" (*CP*3, 13).

Notwithstanding his father's relative wealth and celebrity, O'Neill experienced anti-Irish bigotry firsthand in New London, and his Irish characters would lay bare their creator's emotional and political affiliation with "shanty" or "bogtrotter" Irish against the capitalist classes, Puritan morality, and the hypocrisy of the socially ambitious "lace-curtain" Irish. "The one thing that explains more than anything about me is the fact that I'm Irish," O'Neill would later say. "And, strangely enough, it is something that all the writers who have attempted to explain me and my work have overlooked."[158] The ethnic tensions in New London and across New England between defiant Irish Catholics and establishment Yankee Protestants left O'Neill with a profound sympathy for America's disenfranchised populations writ large. When he voted in the presidential election, he cast his very first ballot for the socialist Eugene V. Debs, who'd run his campaign from a jail cell, despite O'Neill's belief that American party politics was "the acme of futility." "I voted for Debs," he glibly remarked, "because I dislike John D. Rockefeller's bald head."[159]

O'Neill openly and enduringly despised the Yankee families who represented the New London elite. The Chappell family, for instance, would later appear as the offstage Chatfields in *Long Day's Journey Into Night*, and he portrays Mary Tyrone as harboring a deep-seated jealousy of this clan whose lives appear somehow more meaningful than those of her own Irish Catholic family. In one scene, Mary peers out a window and notices her older son Jamie ducking behind a hedge he's trimming as the Chatfields drive by. Jamie is embarrassed to be seen engaged in menial work, while casually dressed James Tyrone bows with dignity to the passing car. The episode sparks a revealing conversation between Edmund and Mary about the town: Edmund likes it "well enough. I suppose because it's the only home we've had." "Jamie's a fool to care about the Chatfields," he scoffs. "For Pete's sake, who ever heard of them outside this hick burg?" Mary agrees: "Big frogs in a small puddle." "Still, the Chatfields and people like them stand for something," she says. "Not that I want anything to do with them. I've always hated this town and everyone in it" (*CP3*, 738).

More widely known targets of O'Neill's Irish begrudgery were Edward C. Hammond, a wealthy member of the local gentry, and Edward S. Harkness, whose father had been a partner in John D. Rockefeller's Standard Oil empire. These men were more crocodiles than big frogs in that small puddle. O'Neill lampooned Harkness later as the stuffy millionaire T. Stedman Harder in *A Moon for the Misbegotten*: "Not unpleasant . . . he is simply immature, naturally lethargic, a bit stupid . . . deliberate in his speech, slow on the uptake, and has no sense of humor" (*CP3*, 884) and offstage as Harker in *Long Day's Journey Into Night*. But O'Neill's characterization was perhaps more accurate of Hammond than of Harkness. The latter, over the course of a generously philanthropic life and later through bequests, donated hundreds of millions of dollars to various universities and museums, including $1 million to establish Yale University's celebrated Theatre Department. (In an ironic twist, it was through that department's influence that Yale chose O'Neill for an honorary doctorate in 1926. Edward C.

Hammond's former estate also became the current location of another renowned theatrical organization—the Tony Award–winning Eugene O'Neill Theater Center.) O'Neill nevertheless immortalized Harkness, from the playwright's earliest years as a scribbling reporter to the last play he ever completed, *A Moon for the Misbegotten*, as the archetype of the well-heeled but vapid Protestant oppressor.[160]

The Harkness and Hammond properties were adjacent to one another, just west of New London on Long Island Sound. Between these two massive estates lay a strip of land owned by James O'Neill and rented by an Irish-born tenant named John Dolan. Dolan made a lasting impression on Eugene in 1912, and he would straggle on as a tenant of the O'Neill family's into the 1920s. Nicknamed "Dirty" in reference to the permanent state of his feet, Dolan would appear as the offstage Shaughnessy in *Long Day's Journey*, then as Phil Hogan in *A Moon for the Misbegotten*. In fact, O'Neill first conceived of *A Moon for the Misbegotten* as his "Dolan play" before his brother Jim took it over. O'Neill describes Dolan as fifty-five years old, short in stature, thick-necked and muscular, with a voice that was "high-pitched with a pronounced brogue" (*CP*3, 862). Phil Hogan's quick-witted sense of humor—grounded in laughing off life's difficulties, rapid tone reversals, and word play—is all Irish. His other traits associated with Irishness, however (pugilistic, drunken, conspiratorial), badly offended "lace-curtain" Irish audience members when *A Moon for the Misbegotten* was first produced in 1947.

Edmund Tyrone shares a story with his family in the opening scene of *Long Day's Journey* that their tenant Shaughnessy (Dolan) had told him the previous night at a local inn. Offering a comic parable of the tensions between the Irish and the Yankees, Shaughnessy delights Edmund with his triumph over the Standard Oil magnate: Harker had accused Shaughnessy of tearing down the fence that separates their land in order for the farmer's pigs to bathe in his ice pond. The Irishman retorted that it was Harker who was tampering with *his* fence, thus nefariously exposing his unsuspecting pigs to pneumonia and cholera. "He was King of Ireland, if he had his rights," Edmund laughs, "and scum was scum to him no matter how much money it had stolen from the poor." Shaughnessy then ordered the millionaire off his land and threatened legal action for Harker's vandalism. James chuckles at the joke on the recognized sachem of the Protestant gentry, then abruptly resumes the role of an outraged landlord—"The dirty blackguard!" Fearful of trouble arising from the harassment of one of the town's leading citizens, James attacks Edmund for his "damned Socialist anarchist sentiments" against Standard Oil; but the whole family knows that deep down, as Edmund says, James is "tickled to death over the great Irish victory" (CP3, 726).[161]

The (Love) Sick Apprentice

At first O'Neill felt as if he just had a nasty cold that October of 1912, a wretchedness he'd foolishly exacerbated by bicycling to his job at the *Telegraph* in a rainstorm. Then the family physician, Dr. Harold Heyer, concluded that he had pleurisy, but by November, he'd upgraded his diagnosis: tuberculosis.[162] The lung disease, commonly referred to as "the Great White Plague," was perceived at the time as more of a moral than a physical affliction, because it appeared to originate in the congested urban slums. (O'Neill blamed his contracting the disease on Jimmy the Priest's, where he'd shared quarters with "the Lunger.") Ella also relapsed that fall back into her own morally charged affliction, having poisoned her system with so much morphine that she too required medical attention. This confluence enabled Mabel Reynolds, a young nurse in training whom Dr. Heyer first assigned to the family, a rare window into life at Monte Cristo Cottage.

When Reynolds arrived at the door, she heard male voices shouting back and forth inside. She was already frightened of Jim, whom New Londoners spoke of as "a problem, always in some kind of scrape." Someone eventually heard her knocking and ordered her in. The three O'Neill men were hunched over a round table in the living room with a whiskey bottle and glasses. No one got up to greet her; they simply waved her upstairs. What she found there horrified her. "[Ella O'Neill] was in bed and looked terrible," Reynolds remembered. "She looked— this is a horrible expression but it will give you the idea—she looked like a witch, with her white hair and large dark eyes. She was rocking back and forth, wringing her hands. 'My son, my son,' she kept repeating, and tears were running down her face."[163]

The dreadful commotion of the O'Neill men shouting downstairs never let up, and Reynolds must have heard Ella sob, "My son, my son," a hundred times, though it wasn't clear whether she meant Eugene or her dead child Edmund. It especially shocked her that Ella, such a proper lady in public, could behave this way. It took hours to calm her, during which time Reynolds gave her an alcohol rub, exposing the track marks on her arm. None of the men came upstairs, and they were gone the next morning when Reynolds left for home. Her impression was that "they were terribly upset that [Ella] had gone back to the addiction." "No," Reynolds told her interviewer, "I never went back."[164]

Dr. Heyer then dispatched Olive Evans, whose experiences were less nightmarish than Reynolds's. She did hear Ella crying as she rocked in her chair. "It was a whimpering sound, like a kitten. I once said to Eugene, 'Shouldn't I go downstairs and see about your mother?' He told me not to; he was very insistent about it, and said I was never to go unless invited. I never was." Ella later dressed Evans down for delivering messages between Eugene and Maibelle Scott: "I know what's been happening. There are many reasons why we don't want this affair to go on, and religion is the principal reason." Evans further recollected that O'Neill wanted nothing to do with his father James, referring to him acidly as "the Irish peasant." "Oh, please, Geney, don't call Papa that," Ella would plead hopelessly. Once, when James poked his head into his son's room to ask how he was feeling, O'Neill hardly looked up from bed.[165]

On December 9, 1912, O'Neill endured a painful aspiration procedure to relieve the fluid in his thoracic cavity.[166] He was then accompanied by Olive Evans to New Haven, where they were met by James, who'd been in New York overseeing legal issues regarding a film version of *Monte Cristo*. (James's film was released the following year, but not before a rival company had dampened moviegoers' interest by releasing its own adaptation.)[167] For the paltry sum of $4 a week,

Monte Cristo Cottage at 325 Pequot Avenue in New London. The small
addition at the left is where the complete action of *Long Day's Journey Into
Night* takes place.
(COURTESY OF SHEAFFER-O'NEILL COLLECTION, LINDA LEAR CENTER FOR SPECIAL
COLLECTIONS AND ARCHIVES, CONNECTICUT COLLEGE, NEW LONDON)

✳   ✳   ✳

James checked his son into the Fairfield County Home for the Care
and Treatment of Persons Suffering from Tuberculosis in Shelton,
Connecticut, a state-run sanatorium that, in contrast to its grandiose
title, consisted of a farmhouse and two shacks that served as makeshift
infirmaries. (This is the scorned institution reffered to in *Long Day's
Journey Into Night*).

James O'Neill, like most Irishmen before the discovery of antibiotics, regarded tuberculosis as nothing short of a death sentence. "If
Edmund was a lousy acre of land you wanted, the sky would be the
limit!" Jamie Tyrone pillories his father in *Long Day's Journey*: "What
I'm afraid of is, with your Irish bog-trotter idea that consumption is
fatal, you'll figure it would be a waste of money to spend any more

than you can help." "I have every hope Edmund will be cured," James retorts. "And keep your dirty tongue off Ireland! You're a fine one to sneer, with the map of it on your face!" (*CP3*, 730, 761).

Eugene checked himself out of the Fairfield County Home after only two days and took a train straight to New York to confront his father about paying for a better facility. James then consulted with several New York specialists, one of whom, Dr. James Alexander Miller, encouraged him to send Eugene to Gaylord Farm Sanatorium in Wallingford, Connecticut. Gaylord Farm was a well-funded treatment center, one that at the time, though it cost only $7 a week, had an exemplary reputation (as it still does to this day).

O'Neill was admitted on the first day he was notified that there was a vacancy: Christmas Eve, 1912. Explaining later that the medical staff considered him "an uninteresting case, there was so little the matter," O'Neill insisted that the only element of heroism to be found in his tale of woe was that he'd checked in on Christmas Eve— "at least, some folks thought it so, not knowing that to an actor's son, whose father had been on tour nearly every winter, Christmas meant less than nothing." In fact, O'Neill had never experienced the disenchantment many children feel after discovering that their beloved Kris Kringle is just a holiday myth; he'd never had reason to believe in Santa Claus from the start.[168]

Gaylord Farm, it turned out, offered a profound respite from the chaos of the last several years within its nurturing walls. O'Neill hit it off with several patients and nurses there, but he also discovered a replacement father figure in his attending physician, the sanatorium's superintendent, Dr. David Russell Lyman. O'Neill affectionately describes his character based on Dr. Lyman, Doctor Stanton in *The Straw* (1919), as speaking with a slight southern accent; he is "a handsome man of forty-five or so with a grave, care-lined, studious face lightened by a kindly, humorous smile. His gray eyes, saddened by the suffering they have witnessed, have the sympathetic quality of real understanding" (*CP1*, 747). O'Neill and Lyman corresponded for years after his case was deemed arrested, and their letters reveal the kind of mutual respect and intimacy one might associate with a

devoted father and adoring son rather than a physician and his patient. More than a year after his release, O'Neill wrote Dr. Lyman,
"If, as they say, it is sweet to visit the place one was born in, then it
will be doubly sweet for me to visit the place I was reborn in—for my
second birth was the only one which had my full approval."[169]

Thanks to the warm-hearted atmosphere cultivated by Lyman
and the head nurse of his infirmary, Mary Clark, O'Neill indeed experienced a transformative intellectual and psychological "second birth"
at Gaylord Farm. Ten years later, though, he gently corrected a
reporter who referenced the growing legend that O'Neill had
decided to become a writer while convalescing there. No, he said,
he'd discovered his vocation while writing for the *Telegraph*. However,
he added, "It was at Gaylord that my mind got a chance to establish itself, to digest and valuate the impressions of many past years in
which one experience had crowded on another with never a second's
reflection. At Gaylord I really *thought about* my life for the first time,
about past and future. Undoubtedly the inactivity forced upon me by
the life at a san forced me to mental activity, especially as I had always
been high-strung and nervous temperamentally."[170]

O'Neill's convalescence had less to do with physical health, given
that he only had a mild case of tuberculosis, and more to do with
mental and artistic health, as if Gaylord Farm had been a writers'
retreat like Yaddo in upstate New York or the MacDowell Colony in
New Hampshire. It was there that O'Neill chose to pursue drama,
acknowledging to himself that his experiences touring with his father
would prove invaluable for the genre. O'Neill began reading many
of the playwrights who were to become his greatest influences—Irish
writers like Synge, Yeats, Lady Gregory, and Shaw as well as Ibsen,
the Elizabethans, and the Greeks and, perhaps most important, the
Swedish dramatist August Strindberg. He read the *Rubáiyát of Omar
Khayyam*, Dostoevsky's *The Idiot*, and Francis Thompson's *The Hound
of Heaven*, an epic poem that an Irish Catholic nurse presented to
him in the hopes that it might revive the young apostate's faith.[171]
Attracted by the poem's portrayal of the modernist presentiment of
continual flight—from society, from God, from the self—he learned

it by heart and later recited it when well soused and deep in reflective thought to friends and lovers in Greenwich Village.

O'Neill's 1919 play *The Straw*, based on the friendships he'd made among Gaylord's patients and staff, also portrays a fleeting romance with a fellow Irish American patient, Catherine "Kitty" MacKay. Like the play's female lead, Eileen Carmody, MacKay was from a large Irish family (her parents had raised ten children) in Waterbury, Connecticut; her father was as heartless, miserly, and self-pitying as Eileen's father, Bill Carmody; and Eileen falls in love with the darkly handsome patient Stephen Murray, who like his creator boasts of his literary aspirations and prides himself on his deeply cynical view of life. O'Neill's portrayal of Eileen in his stage directions faithfully describes the actual MacKay: "Her wavy mass of dark hair is parted in the middle and combed low on her forehead, covering her ears, to a knot at the back of her head. The oval of her face is spoiled by a long, rather heavy, Irish jaw contrasting with the delicacy of her other features," and her shape is "slight and undeveloped" (*CP*1, 729). Upon his departure from Gaylord, O'Neill kissed MacKay, promising that one day she would see herself onstage in one of his plays.[172] She never would. MacKay died of the disease in 1915, and *The Straw* wouldn't premiere for another six years.

O'Neill and MacKay's relationship ignited an acute preoc- cupation in the budding dramatist about the devastating results of uneducated working-class women pairing up with educated men from wealthy families. In each case, what the women want—stability, the romantic ideal of the artist—and what they get—volatility, alcohol- ism, and unwanted exposure to existentialist angst—are devastatingly at odds. O'Neill presents working-class women in his plays as less morally compromised than their male counterparts, as in this sonnet he wrote for MacKay after his return to New London:

Smile on my passionate plea abrupt,
   On bended (so to speak) knee I sue
Doubtless my morals are most corrupt,
   There is an elegant chance for you.
Why not reform my life? Thru and thru,

    Scour and cleanse my soul of the mire,
  (A regular Christian thing to do)
    Oh come to my Land of Heart's Desire.

Further on in the love poem, O'Neill refers to tuberculosis as "punishment full and dire. . . . Penance for sins we've paid in advance."[173] He later equated battling the disease with the challenge of life as a whole. "And the harder the patient's fight has been," he said, "the more this applies, I should think. After having conquered T.B. by a long grind of a struggle, one's confidence in coming out on top in other battles ought to be increased ten-fold."[174]

Each of O'Neill's so-called physical and social inadequacies up to that point, the ones that his parents reminded him of—his shyness, his constitutional depression, his stammering speech, his alcoholism, his reputation as a dissolute Irishman among the New London establishment (thus giving beloved Ireland a bad name), his accusations of abandonment by his family, his suicidal tendencies, his loss of Catholic faith—all combined in O'Neill's imagination in the form of tuberculosis. Determined to make good, his natural impulse would be to overcompensate. "Someday I won't be known as his son. He will be known as my father," he boasted at the *Telegraph*.[175] Then it was only bluster, perhaps; but now he'd gained the confidence to make good on the pledge.

The American writer William Saroyan wrote in 1939, at a time when American heroes were sorely needed, that "only the weak and unsure perform the heroic. They've *got* to."[176] A year later, Dr. Louis E. Bisch, one of O'Neill's psychoanalysts, likened his patient's widely perceived "human defects" to Conrad's belated arrival to the English language at age twenty, Beethoven's deafness, and Paderewski's frail fingers, among so many other remarkable instances in which overcompensation breeds inspiration: "Shyness, inferiority feelings and self-consciousness, as well as physical handicaps, have served as spring-boards which catapulted individuals to success far greater— in many cases—than they might have achieved otherwise." "It is the overcompensation that does it," Bisch said. "Eugene O'Neill did not set out to become a dramatist. The son of actors, he was inclined to resist all things connected with the stage." But then came his tuberculosis, a disease closely associated in American society with his other "defects," and "thus was he started on the road to winning the Nobel Prize."[177] O'Neill's literary idol Friedrich Nietzsche more broadly established this proposition when he wrote, "Out of thy poisons brewedst thou balsam for thyself. . . . Of all that is written, I love only what a person hath written with his blood. Write with blood, and thou wilt find that blood is spirit. . . . Creating—that is the great salvation from suffering, and life's alleviation. But for the creator to appear, suffering itself is needed, and much transformation."[178]

O'Neill had been born to a race of overcompensators. At that very moment in history, the Irish Players of the Abbey Theatre, the vanguard of the Irish Renaissance, had ensured that what had been an abject fantasy in Ireland for eight hundred long years would grow into an undeniable reality in but one generation: retribution. This scheme for retribution, though most pronouncedly carried out by the singular talents of James Joyce, was not only long-sought independence from British rule but a literary counterattack fought with the very language they'd been mandated to speak as their fiercest weapon. The Irish would transform, utterly, the despised, compulsory tongue of their British colonizers into a new and terrible beauty. While at Gaylord, O'Neill, however unwittingly, was formulating a similar plot. He would also strike back against the language he deplored: that of the tawdry, hateful popular theater of his father, the overwhelmingly powerful institution that had denied him his family. But he required a motivational push, which Bisch would quite rightly identify. "It took T.B.," O'Neill wrote after years of punishing insecurities, "to blast me loose" (*CP1*, 742).

Within a week of O'Neill's release from Gaylord Farm on June 3, 1913, he learned of his friend James Byth's untimely death. On June 5, Byth had plunged from his bedroom window on the third floor of Jimmy the Priest's down to the paved courtyard below. He was discovered alive but unconscious, with both legs broken and a fractured skull; without regaining consciousness, Byth died in the hospital the following day. The New York Health Bureau listed the death as a suicide, and O'Neill resolutely believed it was.[179] Byth, like Driscoll before him, would hold an abiding place in O'Neill's imagination for the rest of his life: "Always my friend—at least always when he had several jolts of liquor—saw a turn in the road tomorrow. He was going to get himself together and get back to work. Well, he did get a job and got fired. Then he realized that this tomorrow never would come. He solved everything by jumping to his death from the bedroom at Jimmy's."[180] Subsequently, the British pressman became one of O'Neill's most significant case studies in self-delusion. In the last scene of his story "Tomorrow," Jimmy is haunted by his failures as a husband and as a war correspondent in Cape Town; from within "Tommy the Priest's" bar, the O'Neill character, named Art, hears "a swish, a sickish thud as of a heavy rock dropping into thick mud." A group of the men rush outside to find Jimmy's body shattered on the flagstones in a black pool of blood. "The sky was pale with the light of dawn," the story concludes. "Tomorrow had come" (*CP3*, 966–67).

O'Neill's low standing among New Londoners as a drunken misanthrope only worsened over that summer, doubly so in his father's eyes. James implored his New London friend Clayton "Ham" Hamilton, one of the best-known theater critics of the day, to have a serious talk with his wayward son about his future. Hamilton and O'Neill's first meeting ended badly. Hamilton saw in O'Neill a young man suffering from "a habit of silence, and an evident disease of shyness." He remembered O'Neill as a more interesting creature to look at, with his "very large and dreamy eyes," than to listen to: "His speech was rather hesitant and he never said very much." Having gathered no useful feedback from Hamilton, James stowed his son away for the winter months in New London at the Packard, a riverfront boardinghouse run by the Rippin family at 416 Pequot Avenue just down the street from Monte Cristo Cottage. Hamilton, who frequently boarded with the Rippins, recalled that the exasperated paterfamilias dropped Eugene off, ordered his son "to behave himself," then skipped town.[181]

Back in New London late in that spring of 1914, Hamilton was astonished to discover that O'Neill had been writing at a breakneck pace over the winter months, having already composed five plays—*A Wife for a Life*, *The Web*, *Thirst*, *Recklessness*, and *Warnings*—a clutch of maladroit yet promising one-acts that O'Neill later referred to as the "first five Stations of the Cross in my Plod up Parnassus."[182] The last four, along with *Fog*, were published the following year in his first book, *Thirst and Other One-Act Plays*, for the American Dramatists Series of the Gorham Press of Boston (a volume financed with a $450 payment from his father). O'Neill was still exasperated by the mystifying process he'd devoted himself to and bluntly asked the seasoned critic, "How are plays written?" "Never mind how plays are written," Hamilton snapped. "Write down what you know about the sea, and about the men who sail before the mast. This has been done in the novel; it has been done in the short story; it has not been done in the drama. Keep your eye on life,—on life as you have seen it; and to hell with the rest!"[183]

Hamilton pointed out that writers of poetry and fiction like John Masefield, Jack London, and Joseph Conrad, each of whom O'Neill read avidly, had enjoyed enormous critical and popular success with their sea tales. But up to then no American playwright had adopted the sea as a subject. Eugene's time on the *Charles Racine*, the *Ikala*, the *New York*, and the *Philadelphia*, combined with his theatrical know-how accumulated over the years touring with his father, made the aspiring playwright a superlative candidate to exploit such a national literary deficit.

O'Neill was way ahead of him: *Thirst*, *Warnings*, and *Fog* all take place either during or just after a shipwreck, and O'Neill's readership, small as it was, couldn't have helped recalling the horrific doom of the thousand-foot transatlantic liner *Titanic* in 1912. One of the many tragic ironies of the *Titanic* catastrophe was that the steamer *Californian* was within twenty miles of the foundering vessel before it sank; but the *Californian* didn't hear the other ship's call for help because no wireless operator had been on duty. After the sinking, in which 1,503 souls had drowned, legislation was passed requiring that large ships post a radio operator on duty at all times. *Warnings*, based in part on Joseph Conrad's "The End of the Tether," tells the story of a ship's wireless operator who goes deaf, misses a warning signal, and commits suicide from guilt after his disability causes the destruction of the ship.

Thirst takes place on a life raft with three survivors: a dancer, a businessman, and a West Indian mulatto sailor. The first two are racists and become convinced the mulatto is withholding water. The dancer dies of thirst, but not before devolving into insanity. When the sailor insists that they must cannibalize her to save their own lives, the businessman heaves her remains overboard. The sailor turns on him next, and in the struggle, they fall into the water and are devoured by sharks. *Fog* is set on a lifeboat adrift off the Grand Banks of Newfoundland, where the *Titanic* hit the iceberg and where the playwright himself had kept watch while returning to New York on the *Philadelphia*.[184]

At the Packard that spring, O'Neill composed another sea play, the *Children of the Sea*, based on his time on the *Ikala* and later titled *Bound East for Cardiff*, and a one-act, *The Movie Man*, a satire about the Mexican Revolution. He also completed two full-length plays, *Bread and Butter*, which contrasts small-town life in New London with his time in the Manhattan art studio scene in 1909, and *Servitude*, a boorish domestic comedy about sacrifices, primarily made by women, for a successful marriage. That spring, he left the Packard for Monte Cristo Cottage after his father returned to New London and was, O'Neill explained to young Jessica Rippin, so "lonely [he] had to solace himself with the comforting presence of his younger mistake."[185] While there, he published a political poem, "Fratricide," on May 17 in the socialist paper the *New York Call* and penned another one-act, *Abortion*, about a superstar college man who impregnates a local girl while attending a school resembling Princeton (which can't help but bring to mind his actual affair with the Trenton girl), pays for her abortion, then commits suicide after hearing that she'd died during the surgery. When James read these plays, he threw up his hands. "My God! Where did you get such thoughts?"[186]

Clayton Hamilton, on the other hand, convinced James that his son would do well to attend Professor George Pierce Baker's renowned English 47 playwriting seminar at Harvard University.

That June in New London, a passionate courtship took place between O'Neill and a local nineteen-year-old named Beatrice Ashe.

If Maibelle Scott had been his first true romance (his marital tryst with Kathleen was anything but romantic), "Bee" Ashe—my "Bumble Bee," as he called her—was his first true love. The depth of his passion has been preserved in more than eighty letters and over a dozen love poems dedicated to her, with titles such as "Just a Little Love, a Little Kiss," "Just Me n' You," and "Ballade of the Two of Us." One of these, "Speaking, to the Shade of Dante, of Beatrices," was published in the *New York Tribune* in July 1915. The poem's early title indicates O'Neill's rakish competitiveness with the Italian bard's adoration of his own great love, " 'My Beatrice' (Being a few words with that guy Dante who wrote so much junk about his Beatrice)":

> Dante, your damozel was tall
>   And lean and sad—I've seen her face
> On many a best-parlor wall—
>   I don't think she was such an ace.
> She doesn't class with mine at all.[187]

Beatrice Ashe and Eugene O'Neill at Ocean Beach, New London, 1914.
(COURTESY OF SHEAFFER-O'NEILL COLLECTION, LINDA LEAR CENTER FOR SPECIAL
COLLECTIONS AND ARCHIVES, CONNECTICUT COLLEGE, NEW LONDON)

* * *

O'Neill gave Beatrice a scarab bracelet as a sign of his deep commitment and told her that he wished he could buy her an ankle-length sable coat and a silk bathing suit as well. (Maibelle Scott remembered Ashe as "breathtaking in a bathing suit.") Ashe never agreed to marry him, though he asked her often and, according to her, "carried a wedding ring for two years hoping I'd change my mind." Like Maibelle Scott before her, Ashe was devoted to O'Neill but soon came to recognize unresolvable personality conflicts. For one thing, he was ill at ease around children: "He had a sweet, gentle smile," she said, "the sort he should have had for children but didn't." And though he pontificated ad nauseum about being true to yourself in the philosophical anarchist tradition, she felt it was only to his writing career that he hoped she would be true. Ashe was the soloist soprano at the Congregational church across the Thames, but O'Neill never respected her dream to sing professionally. Eventually, he recognized her frustration over his chauvinism and told her, in reference to Ibsen's famous play about women's subjugation to male power, *A Doll's House* (1879), "You are no Doll Girl nor shall our house be a Doll's House."[188] Unlike Scott, Ashe saved the scores of poems and letters he wrote her, hoping they would offer a window into the inner world of the loving young man whom she knew, "that some one sometime will recognize that sensitive, kind, patient, understanding man who asked so little of God . . . the Eugene O'Neill I knew and loved—but not enough."[189]

Thirst's sales were paltry, and Clayton Hamilton published the only important review the book received (the others include one in the *Baltimore Sun* and a few glorifying notices in the New London papers). His critique reads much like thousands of reviews of O'Neill's later work: "This writer's favorite mood is that of horror. He deals with grim and ghastly situations that would become intolerable if they were protracted beyond the limits of a single sudden act. . . . He shows a keen sense of the reactions of character under stress of violent emotion; and his dialogue is almost brutal in its power." In the years to come, after O'Neill's celebrity had soared, early efforts like *Thirst* became immensely valuable, and O'Neill pointed out the irony that *Thirst*, "the A-1 collector's item of all my stuff . . . has sold [for] as much as $150 a copy . . . the publisher at one time offered me all the remainder of the edition (and that was practically all the edition, for few copies were sold) at 30 cents a copy! With the usual financial acumen of an author, I scorned his offer as a waste of good money on my lousy drama!"[190]

O'Neill's gratitude for Hamilton's review was effusive, long-lasting, and sincere: "Do you know that your review was the only one that poor volume ever received? And, if brief, it was favorable! You can't imagine what it meant, coming from you. It held out a hope at a very hopeless time. It *did* send me to the hatters. It made me believe I was arriving with a bang; and at that period I very much needed someone whose authority I respected to admit I was getting somewhere."[191] He considered this one of two "boons" Hamilton had conferred upon him in that crucial first year of serious writing from 1913 to 1914; the other was an "unvarnished truth" Hamilton had ruthlessly imparted upon meeting him by chance at New London's Union Station.

One morning in late summer, O'Neill left Monte Cristo Cottage and went to the train station to mail two scripts to George C. Tyler, his father's former advance man but now a top theater producer.[192] Arriving early to ensure that his package would go out with the first pickup, he bumped into Clayton Hamilton and buoyantly explained what he was up to.[193] O'Neill naively expected Tyler to give his plays "an immediate personal reading and reply within a week—possibly an acceptance," and he asked Hamilton what sort of timeline one might typically expect for a reply. Hamilton responded with a stinging reality check: "When you send off a play remember there is not one chance in a thousand it will ever be read; not one chance in a million of its ever being accepted—(and if accepted it will probably never be produced); but if it is accepted and produced, say to yourself it's a miracle which can never happen again."[194] Sure enough, George Tyler wrote in his memoir about the plays sent O'Neill to him that morning that he'd "take them in and forget about them, for a while—maybe read a little, but I wouldn't take an oath I did that often, and I'm certain that I can't remember at all what they were like."[195] In point of fact, when

O'Neill requested the scripts back after Tyler's Liebler and Company fell into bankruptcy, he received them still sealed in the original envelopes.[196]

O'Neill later recalled having felt so self-assured and hopeful just before his ego-deflating tough-love encounter with Hamilton that afterward he'd "wandered off a bit sick." In hindsight, however, he considered the wake-up call formative for his philosophy as a playwright—from that moment on, he steeled himself for the inevitable defeats of a working dramatist and vowed to "hew to the line without thought of commercial stage production." "Yes, of all the help you were in those years," he wrote Hamilton, "I think that bit ranks brightest in memory. It was a bitter dose to swallow that day but it sure proved a vital shock-absorbing tonic in the long run. It taught me to 'take it'—and God knows that's the first thing most apprentice playwrights need to learn if they are not to turn into chronic whiners against fate or quitters before their good break comes." Nearing the end of his life, Hamilton dedicated the last of his books on drama criticism "to Eugene O'Neill, who began his career as one of my apprentices and is now fulfilling it as one of my masters."[197]

It Takes a Village

James O'Neill gravely doubted his son's ability to succeed in George Baker's seminar at Harvard, especially after the disastrous year at Princeton. But he also had great respect for Baker's renowned skill for cultivating talent. O'Neill himself was thrilled, and going to Harvard would also, with impassioned apologies to Beatrice, have the added advantage of getting him out of New London.[198] Hamilton sent a letter of recommendation to Baker but urged his twenty-five-year-old protégé to write a formal letter to ask permission to enter the course, which he did. "Less than a year ago," O'Neill wrote the Harvard professor, "I seriously determined to become a dramatist. With my present training I might hope to become a mediocre journey-man playwright. It is just because I do not wish to become one, because I want to be an artist or nothing, that I am writing you."[199]

Under separate cover, O'Neill sent Baker two one-acts, most likely *Children of the Sea* (*Bound East for Cardiff*) and *Abortion*, "from which," O'Neill said, "you will be able to form a judgment as to my suitability for taking your course."[200] Baker accepted him, and by October, after a brief stint in New York trying to market his plays, O'Neill took the train to Cambridge and installed himself as a boarder on the ground floor of a German-speaking Mennonite home.[201] To O'Neill's annoyance, his host family held Bible readings every morning after breakfast and asked the new boarder if he would like to join in. "Imagine it!" O'Neill groaned. "I begged to be excused." An invitation to join them at Revere Beach was also turned down. "When I found out the children were to be taken along I backed out," he wrote Ashe. "A long trolley ride with a couple of playful brats is my idea of one of the tortures Dante forgot to mention in the Inferno."[202]

During the fall semester of 1914, O'Neill wrote two comedies, *Dear Doctor* and *The Knock on the Door*, and he collaborated with classmate Colin Ford on a full-length play called *Belshazzar*, about the fall of Babylon. (None of these plays has survived.) He then began a second play on the topic of abortion, this time full length. Professor Baker insisted that no respectable theater company would take on such a hot-button issue and persuaded O'Neill to select a less incendiary theme.[203] O'Neill relented, in a way, if one considers violent anarchist revolutionaries combating wage slavery less incendiary.

That November, while he "mapped out a tentative scenario," O'Neill boasted that "if it is ever produced—and it never could be in this country—the authorities will cast me into the deepest dungeon of the jail and throw away the key." Indeed, at Harvard, O'Neill's political voice had reached a high radical pitch. One classmate in Baker's seminar described him as "intellectually . . . a philosophical anarchist; politically, a philosophical socialist."[204] (The latter, of course, would fade away, as philosophical anarchism concerned itself more with inner well-being than the socialist's creed of effecting change from without.)

O'Neill's *The Personal Equation*, initially titled "The Second Engineer," was completed that spring. The play contains much of O'Neill's early social philosophy—his despair over materialism, his belief in the destructive influence of Victorian propriety, and his sympathy for the working class. In the mode of outspoken socialist playwrights of the 1930s like Mike Gold and Clifford Odets, *The Personal Equation* mostly reads like agitprop, a form of literature O'Neill would come to denounce. (The play was later rejected by the Provincetown Players and never produced in his lifetime.) His most accomplished work from his days at Harvard, *The Sniper*, won honorable mention in Baker's one-act play competition. The winning three plays were produced by the Harvard Dramatic Club, and he wrote Beatrice that it was just as well he'd lost: "Those amateur butchers on the Dramat. [Dramatic Club] would murder *The Sniper*." Additionally, the three winners were all written by women, and O'Neill quipped with self-conscious envy that the "Harvard spirit and taste runs to the sort of clever plays women usually write. (Sorehead!)"[205]

The Sniper takes place in the Belgian countryside, when Germany's Schlieffen Plan of the previous August 1914 called for an attack on France through Belgium and Luxembourg. Belgium refused to grant permission, so Germany disregarded the threat of international censure and entered the country by force. Few understood what this "Great War" was being fought over, but the "Rape of Belgium," as it was called, outraged Americans, most of whom were otherwise oblivious to European affairs. "The sniper" of the title is a Belgian villager and expert shot with a rifle named Rougon, whose wife, son, and son's fiancée are all killed. Rougon demands of the local priest how God could allow the killing of innocents. "God knows," the priest replies. "Our poor country is a lamb among wolves" (*CP1*, 298). But he makes Rougon vow not to fight and promises to officiate at his son's burial the following night. The two kneel beside the boy's body to pray, but the meaningless words of the rite—"Almighty God," "merciful," "infinite justice"— incense Rougon, and he explodes in a fit of grief-stricken rage. When the Germans approach his cottage, Rougon opens fire and kills two men. He's eventually detained, and the German captain orders his execution. Asked if he wishes to pray, Rougon disavows God and dies before the priest can administer a benediction.

Baker applauded *The Sniper*'s well-wrought structure, timely sub-ject matter, and dramatic power. In fact, he believed it was the best play submitted for the competition; he didn't "think it judicious," however, for Harvard to "put on a war play" during actual wartime.[206] O'Neill then showed *The Sniper* to his father, who shopped it around the vaudeville circuit in March 1915. O'Neill proudly wrote Beatrice that the play "has made a big hit with all the people he has had read it," but James was told that censors would quash the play unless O'Neill "omitted all reference to Prussians, French, Belgians, etc." Holbrook Blinn, a well-known vaudevillian, did "seriously con-sider" performing it, but again, only after the war had ended.[207]

Over that year, O'Neill's male classmates looked on with envy as the women of Cambridge vied with one another for O'Neill's attentions. "There was something apparently irresistible," recalled one green-eyed student, "in his strange combination of cruelty (around the mouth), intelligence (in his eyes) and sympathy (in his voice). . . . From shop girl to 'sassiety' queen, they all seemed to develop certain tendencies in his presence."[208] O'Neill was immune to their advances and determined to stay true to Beatrice Ashe, "My Own Little Wife." Though he returned to New London on weekends and holidays, he still mailed her a gush of treacly love letters ("Ah My Own, My Own, how I love you, and how the relentless hours drag their leaden feet when I am not with you!"), many containing love poems dedicated to her. He even sent her a photo of himself in his underwear taken by a Cambridge artist practicing studies in the nude, and he teased her over her refusal to have sex with him. His male biology, he said, ensured that they had done so in his dreams anyway: "Nature has foiled you in your effort to put restraint on the 'Irish Luck Kid.' It simply kinnot be did! I can't keep your picture from my brain."[209]

In the seminar, O'Neill's manner was largely off-putting. One classmate remembered that "he would writhe and squirm in his chair, scowling and muttering in a mezzo-voce fearful imprecations and protests." He mostly intimidated his fellow students at first, and "did not invite approach." Politically, his "savage radicalism" was discon-certing, and his critiques were often terse and unexpected. Once he

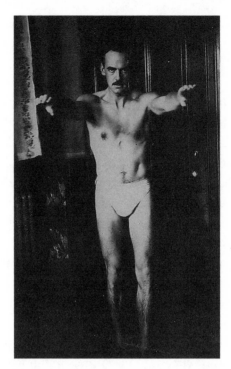

Eugene O'Neill posing for an art student at Harvard University, 1914. He
gave this photo as an unconventional gift to his girlfriend Beatrice Ashe.
(COURTESY OF THE YALE COLLECTION OF AMERICAN LITERATURE, BEINECKE RARE BOOK
AND MANUSCRIPT LIBRARY, NEW HAVEN)

* * *

stormed out after discovering the lesson involved diagramming a play.
He loathed Sundays and remained in his room, unspeakably bored,
while the other students attended church: "Damn Sunday, say I, for
the thousandth separate time." But they all recognized O'Neill as
the most talented among them, remarking to one another with more
than a whiff of jealousy, "Well, I wonder how long it will be before
he is the country's greatest playwright?"[210]

"He rarely contributed to the discussion," a student said of
O'Neill's input in class, "but when he delivered himself of a remark, it
was impressive. We felt that Gene had things to write about because
he had lived—Greenwich Village, the sea, South America—while the

rest of us had led sheltered lives."[211] O'Neill met with Baker regularly to discuss his progress, and one night they even spent hours in the plush study of the professor's Cambridge home smoking his gold-tipped cigarettes late into the evening ("almost unprecedented to give up a whole evening to one student," O'Neill boasted to Ashe). Baker asked him if "his preference for grim and depressing subjects was not something of a pose." O'Neill responded that it wasn't, that to him "life looked that way" after his years as a sailor and down and out in Buenos Aires and New York. O'Neill told Ashe that Baker had plied him for tales of his "adventures along the Ragged Edge," and O'Neill "saw that even he was forced to acknowledge that I have knocked about a bit."[212]

In the end, Baker concluded that his pupil demonstrated great promise but also that his skills to "manage the longer forms" required fine-tuning. O'Neill's trouble lay not so much in creating plausible characters but rather in his tendency to place them amid the entanglements of a melodramatic plot.[213] When Charlie Webster, the actor from the tabloid *Monte Cristo* tour, ran into O'Neill in New York, he asked him whether he'd learned anything from Baker and received an unequivocal *no*. But by the mid-1930s, O'Neill remarked that Baker had been teaching his playwriting seminar "back in the dark ages when the American theater was still, for playwrights, the closed-shop, star-system, amusement racket." Only Baker's students, he contended, could "know what a profound influence Baker exerted toward the encouragement and birth of modern American drama. It is difficult these days ... to realize that in that benighted period a play of any imagination, originality or integrity by an American was almost automatically barred from a hearing in our theater. ... The most vital thing for us, as possible future artists and creators, to learn at that time (Good God! For any one to learn anywhere at any time) was to believe in our work and to keep on believing. And to hope. He helped us to hope."[214]

Back in New London, Beatrice Ashe was ill with a fever through most of the summer of 1915. This was just as well, as her desire for O'Neill had been steadily cooling. And aside from submitting a few treatments for screenplays (without luck), his writing was going nowhere, and he never returned to Harvard. Baker heard that O'Neill's "means...made this impossible," and James O'Neill was in fact out of work, though the New London press made it sound as if producers were knocking down his door. His popular appearances at the Crocker House bar and the exclusive Thames Club never let up, and a few local politicians even tried to convince him to run for mayor. James demurred with his characteristic Irish charm: "Every politician seeking office aspires to the Presidency of the United States. If I were to enter politics, I should want to make that my goal and I can't be President because I was born in Ireland, God bless it!"[215]

That fall, James and Ella checked into the lavish Prince George Hotel on Twenty-Eighth Street, while Jim and Eugene preferred the low-rent Garden Hotel around the block at 63 Madison Avenue on the corner of Twenty-Seventh Street.[216] Scandal alluringly permeated the hotel's atmosphere. America's preeminent architect Stanford White, designer of the old Madison Square Garden just across the street, was sharing a room there with Evelyn Thaw in 1906, when Thaw's millionaire husband, Harry Thaw, in one of the nation's most sensational crimes of passion, unflinchingly shot White three times in the face at a rooftop party at the Garden across the street.[217]

The Garden Hotel's barroom sold 5¢ beers, and during their many extended benders there, the brothers O'Neill made the acquaintance of a colorful gallery of characters, several of whom, like James Byth and his South African associates before this, would resurface as characters in O'Neill's plays. "There was good food at the Garden, and it was a good place," O'Neill said. "The circus men who stayed there I knew very well. Not only the circus men, but the poultry men, the horse breeders and all others who displayed their wares at the old Madison Square Garden. Used to meet them all in the bar. One of my old chums was Volo, the Volitant, a bicycle rider whose specialty was in precipitating himself down a steep incline and turning a loop or so in the air. Volo is now a megaphone man on one of the Broadway sightseeing buses. Billy Clark is his real name. Jack Croak was

The Garden Hotel (center) and the old Madison Square Garden.

✳   ✳   ✳

another. He used to work on the ticket wagon of the Willard Shows."[218] O'Neill became an avid fan of the grueling six-day bicycle races at Madison Square Garden's indoor track, a spectacle of physical and mental endurance that into his later years remained, along with base-ball, football, and prizefighting, one of his favorite lifetime diversions.

O'Neill also drank at O'Connor's Pub at Sixth Avenue and Eighth Street, a Greenwich Village hangout patrons called the Working Girls' Home, best known for its former bartender, the future poet laureate of England John Masefield. O'Neill reconnected with his old friend Lou Holladay too, who by that time was running a bar called the Sixty Club, after its address at 60 Washington Square. Sixty competed with his sister Polly Holladay's restaurant for being the epicenter of the Village bohemian scene; but on December 29, Sixty was shut down, and Holladay spent several months in jail for operat-ing without a liquor license. After the marshals had served Holladay with a "dispossess" and took him into custody, the *New York Tribune* ran a piece titled " 'Sixty' Is Dead; Long Live Polly's!" (Holladay was to be sentenced that day, but the *Tribune* reported that his impending incarceration hadn't prevented his sister Polly and her friends from planning a festive New Year's Eve costume party at Webster Hall.)[219]

Greenwich Village, the storied Manhattan neighborhood south of Fourteenth Street and north of Houston, is best known for its red- and brown-brick townhouses, its picturesque alleyways and side streets, and its closely packed clusters of cafés, restaurants, and sa-loons. The Enlightenment-era urban planning of Manhattan's grid pattern, designed in 1811, falls away south and west of Washington Square, where the streets descend back to the cow-pathed chaos of New Amsterdam. By 1915, the Village's bohemian culture, then thriv-ing among the area's German, Italian, and Irish immigrants and for which the Village has been legendary for well over a century, had reached its maximum romantic allure. "Some said in those days," the avant-garde writer Djuna Barnes recalled in the mid-1910s, "that you could not get any nearer to original sin than renting a studio anywhere below Fourteenth Street."[220]

In retrospect, then, it's just as well O'Neill hadn't returned to Harvard that fall. His time in the Village was not about writing, per se (though he did submit *Thirst* and *Bound East for Cardiff* to the Washington Square Players, an ambitious new drama group that summarily rejected both)—rather, it was more about abandoning the child-self that had possessed him for too long. In a pleading letter to Beatrice Ashe the previous March, when she had threatened to break up with him for another man, O'Neill referred to himself as "your tearful little boy." And when a couple of weeks later she expressed mother love for him as opposed to romantic passion, he said, "Why not? . . . I promise to always be your child. Where you are concerned, like Peter Pan, I shall never grow up."[221] But that winter, the Village would teach Pan to believe in himself before he could learn to fly.

O'Neill soon became a regular at the Golden Swan Café on the southeast corner of West Fourth Street and Sixth Avenue, a dive bar its patrons referred to as the Hell Hole. In the back room, gaslights "flickered wanly, both startling and inadequate," as one observer put it, and out front, a moth-eaten stuffed swan on painted lily pads collected dust in a glass display case. Food was ordered and retrieved through a jagged hole in the wall—the sandwich or bowl of spaghetti or stewed tomatoes you could get were all pretty good, considering the orifice they had come out of. Leftover scraps were dispatched to a pig that the bar's Irish American proprietor Tom Wallace kept in the basement for garbage disposal. To order a beer, customers had to buzz a bell about a half dozen times until they heard one of the bartenders roar Wallace's name, at which point they could be sure their order was on its way.[222] Women were required to use a discreet "family entrance" on Fourth Street, but they did so under a glare of scowling disapproval from Wallace's two bouncers, Lefty Louie and John Bull, who didn't like women in the bar; believing they "brought trouble and police." Louie and Bull would appear in O'Neill's late masterwork *The Iceman Cometh* as Chuck Morello and Rocky Pioggi, and Wallace himself would be immortalized as Harry Hope, the local

The Golden Swan Café, a.k.a. "the Hell Hole," at Sixth Avenue and
Fourth Street, circa 1900. The Hell Hole was razed in 1928 and is now site
of the Golden Swan Garden.
(PHOTO BY ROBERT L. BRACKLOW. COURTESY OF THE NEW-YORK HISTORICAL SOCIETY)

*   *   *

Tammany politician and owner of Harry Hope's Bar, where O'Neill's
epic tragedy takes place.[223]

"Much of [O'Neill's] best work came from the time when he was
bumming around," wrote O'Neill's friend and future collaborator the
labor journalist Mary Heaton Vorse. "When he was the companion
of sailors and when he sat in the Hell Hole with a bunch of bums.
. . . He liked the people from the lower depths." "There was a smoky
quality," she remarked of the Hell Hole's interior, "Something at
once alive and deadly." At the bar in front, truckers often bragged
to O'Neill about crates of contraband they'd "pinched," and he
befriended Joe Smith, a professional gambler and the black crime
boss of "Cocaine Alley" around Cornelia Street. Mary Vorse remembered Smith with admiration as "a chieftain though a small man
and shabby. Not bothering to be flashy but about him was the

authentic air of a ruler." Agnes Boulton, soon to meet O'Neill at the Hell Hole and become his second wife, described Smith as "the boss of the Negro underworld near the Village . . . [whose] tales were startling." Smith's white spouse would often be seated next to him, and the pair were gracious to outsiders. Smith, a Village native, first ran a gambling house, then became legit with a day job as an auctioneer for the Wise Auction Company.[224] But it was for his close friendship with and influence upon O'Neill that he'd be remembered best, and he'd later be portrayed in *Iceman* as the good-hearted gambler Joe Mott.

It was also at the Hell Hole that winter that O'Neill befriended the Hudson Dusters, an infamous West Side Irish gang that claimed the bar as its headquarters. The Dusters included the likes of "Knock-Em-Dead" Bolan, "Big" Kennedy, and "The Rabbit" Crosby, a revolver-toting mob of "cocaine crazed young men," as one journalist labeled them, whose exploits were scrutinized closely by the police and sensationally covered in the New York press. According to Agnes Boulton, the Dusters thought highly of O'Neill as "a two-fisted drinker, one of their own kind," and Mary Vorse recalled that the gangsters "all accepted him as an equal and didn't question him."[225] O'Neill recited poetry to the Dusters at the Hell Hole, typically *The Hound of Heaven*, and they became so devoted to the aspiring writer that they once offered to steal a coat for him when he was cold. All they needed was his size. He politely declined.

"One remembers the Hudson Dusters," wrote the New York writer Harry Golden in a satiric sketch of the organization's rise and fall, as "a gang of toughs who hung out in Greenwich Village. The Dusters terrified the Bronx. They were the scourge of the Palisades. The police precincts always had their eye out for the appearance of the Dusters. What happened to the Dusters was that the Bohemians began to move into Greenwich Village. These poets and artists and writers thought the Dusters were charming fellows. The Bohemians used to recite their poetry aloud at Duster meetings whether the Dusters wanted to hear or not. Eugene O'Neill found their conversation stimulating. . . . When the Dusters realized none of these painters and writers and poets were afraid of them, sullenly the gang broke up and the Dusters all found gainful employment." As comical as this association between gangsters and bohemians must have seemed to an astute observer like Golden, the Dusters were a public menace. "In spite of the Rabelaisian quality of Wallace and his companions," Vorse said, "the Hell Hole was sinister. It was as if the combined soul of New York flowed underground and this was one of its vents."[226]

Wanting to live closer to the crowd at the Hell Hole, O'Neill moved from the Garden Hotel into a boardinghouse at 38 Washington Square West. He was soon kicked out for not paying his rent, however, and the landlady retained his trunk of extra clothes and books as collateral until he returned with the $46 he owed. That spring, after countless nights spent with heads down on a table in the Hell Hole's back room, O'Neill and a new friend, an older Irishman named Terry Carlin, found an apartment just down the block from the Hell Hole, which they shared with the journalist Jack Druilard and affectionately dubbed "the Garbage Flat." (Druilard, O'Neill said, "was momentarily—and miraculously—'in the bucks,'" so he could pay the first month's rent.) Decades later, O'Neill remembered the Garbage Flat "fondly and vividly. . . . It continued to be unfurnished except for piles of sacking as beds, newspapers as bed linen, and packing boxes for chairs and tables. . . . Toward the end of our tenancy, there was a nice even carpet of cigarette butts, reminding one of the snow scene in an old melodrama."[227]

Terry Carlin wasn't a writer (that involved too much exertion), but he was a world-class talker steeped in philosophy. Jack London knew Carlin well from their early days as activists in California, and he thought of Carlin as a kind of mystic, as did many of the anarchist contingent in America at the time, though just as many others thought of him as a laughable crank. O'Neill and Carlin whiled away their hours drinking and smoking and reading Friedrich Nietzsche and volumes of Eastern philosophy that Carlin recommended, like Mabel Collins's *Light on the Path* (1885); but time and again O'Neill found himself too swamped in the miasma of drink and its aftereffects to do any serious writing. "After I'd had a quart and a half of bourbon," he told a reporter in 1946, "I could walk straight and talk rationally, but my brain was nuts. If anybody suggested that I climb up the Woolworth Building, I'd be tickled to death to do it." Instead, he took advantage of this nearly year-long hiatus in playwriting to methodically train his mind to think like a dramatist, first in dialogue, then scene changes, then acts, based on the scores of plays he'd read by this time—Strindberg, Ibsen, the Greeks, even romances and melodrama.[228]

O'Neill did muster enough wherewithal to volunteer for *Revolt*, an anarchist weekly helmed by another Hell Hole associate, Hippolyte Havel. The paper had offices in the basement of the soon to be defunct Ferrer School, but it was shut down after three months, along with the Ferrer, for its vocal opposition to World War I. O'Neill reveled in the romance of political rebellion, bragging to Ashe about his abbreviated tenure at *Revolt* that he was "one of the group that helped get the paper out every week. We all narrowly escaped getting a bit to do in the Federal pen."[229] Meanwhile, Terry Carlin had attracted big trouble from the opposite direction—the anarchists themselves. Carlin had been falsely accused of colluding with the federal government, informing agents of the whereabouts of the anarchist group that had bombed the Los Angeles Times Building in 1910, taking twenty-five lives in the process. The actual snitch, Donald Vose Meserve, was Carlin's friend, and evidence had been found in Meserve's apartment pointing to the connection between them.[230]

The whirl of accusations against Carlin from the nation's radicals prompted author and journalist Hutchins "Hutch" Hapgood to publish an impassioned plea in *Revolt* that February titled "The Case of Terry." Hapgood was a respected authority on such matters: over the previous two decades, he'd penned sketches and book-length studies on anarchists, socialists, labor unionists, immigrants, bohemians, free-love advocates, prostitutes, and thieves. He'd published a book back in 1909 chronicling Terry and his ex-girlfriend Marie's vagabond life together called *An Anarchist Woman*, which became something of a bohemian manifesto and solidified Carlin's legacy as an anarchist folk hero. Eventually counting among his cohort the philosophers William James and George Santayana; painters Pablo Picasso and

Henri Matisse; fiction writers Theodore Dreiser, John Dos Passos, Gertrude Stein, and Ernest Hemingway; political activists, John Reed, "Big Bill" Haywood, and Emma Goldman; and, of course, O'Neill himself, Hapgood appears, Zelig-like, on the ground floor of nearly every major intellectual achievement of the modern era. (In 1920, after cavorting together for several years, Hapgood and O'Neill found themselves together on an overnight train; O'Neill reported that the pair of them "sat up in a deck stateroom and theorized the universe to sleep until about midnight. I have grown to love Hutch. He's a peach!")[231]

Despite Hapgood's best efforts, however, Carlin continued to be hounded over his damning association with Meserve. "When Donald was suspected," Hapgood wrote, "but before his guilt appeared openly by his testimony on the witness stand, Terry clung to the idea of the boy's innocence. It was a terrible shock to him. His faithful soul would not suspect, until the definite proof came." Carlin's alleged collusion with the Feds would harass him and taint his reputation, such as it was, to his death; as Hapgood remarked of the accusations, "The human mind tends to harbor a doubt once suggested. Such is the terrible character of suspicion."[232] The controversy over Carlin and Meserve would later serve as the models for the tormented relationship between Larry Slade and Donald Parritt in *The Iceman Cometh*.

For his part, O'Neill had reached a dead end finding a theater group to produce his plays in New York; and writing while living hand-to-mouth and perpetually drunk in the Garbage Flat and at the Hell Hole had proved impossible. It was time for a change.

Hapgood rented a summerhouse in Provincetown, Massachusetts, where he headed with his family that May. As well as Hapgood and his wife, the writer Neith Boyce, the journalist Jack Reed, and Hippolyte Havel were planning to go there that summer. Reed had met with a few of the former Washington Square Players, including George "Jig" Cook, at the Working Girls' Home that winter. Together, Reed and Cook intended to carry on with an experimental drama group launched in Provincetown the previous summer.[233] That's where O'Neill and Carlin would go.

*   *   *

"Now that I look back on it," Eugene O'Neill mused in 1923, "I realize that I couldn't have done better for myself [as a playwright] if I had deliberately charted out my life." Indeed, O'Neill's experiences in New York, New London, at sea, and on the vaudeville circuit shaped his future ideas, plots, and characters, and thus equipped him, along with his determination to "hew to the line," to forge a modern American drama. Whether college dropouts, prostitutes, war veterans, vagabond sailors, has-been revolutionaries, or members of O'Neill's own family, these ghosts at the stage door brought philosophical and psychological depths that even the most open-minded American theatergoers might never have believed possible.

Before O'Neill, producers had been painfully slow to accept such characters as these on the stage, given their hidebound view of theater as a profit-making industry, what O'Neill disgustedly referred to as "the closed-shop, star-system, amusement racket." Few American plays had yet to transcend the Victorian tastes of the era—historical romance and melodrama. And the most powerful commercial force of the time was the contract and booking duopoly run by the Theatrical Syndicate and the Shubert Brothers.

Managed by booker Charles Frohman, the Syndicate reflected the growing industrial order by standardizing plays based solely on profit potential, privileging melodramatic plots that pit good against evil, with good always winning out. The understood requirement for booking a production through Frohman was, above all else, a happy ending. The Syndicate, also known as the "Trust," was founded in 1896, and for more than a decade it often stymied the impassioned efforts of playwrights like Clyde Fitch, James A. Herne, Percy MacKaye, Rachel Crothers, and even the theatrical giant David Belasco, to produce a lasting American drama. The Shubert Brothers, according to one observer, "aimed at and almost succeeded in controlling the American theatre by coercion, bribing critics, boycotting newspapers, blackballing actors, and hogtying managers and owners of theatres." Finding themselves "debarred" time after time at venues across the country, theater professionals "finally succumbed one by one, the playwrights listened to their commercial dictators, managers of minor theatres became their henchmen." In this way, the majority of American plays between the Civil War and World War I were written and produced with moneymaking stars in mind, and playwrights were viewed as hired guns rather than artists, much as screenwriters were soon to be regarded during the reign of the Hollywood studio system.

By the 1910s, what became known as the "Little Theatre Movement" boldly answered the modern call for a distinctly American drama, confronting head-on the cultural and political debates then roiling in both smaller communities and the nation at large. Baltimore's Vagabond Theatre, Manhattan's Neighborhood Playhouse and Comedy Theatre, the Chicago Little Theatre, and the Boston Toy Theatre soon inspired copycat venues throughout the United States in truly off-off-off Broadway locales like Ohio, Indiana, and even South Dakota. Then, in the fall of 1916, after two summers in Provincetown, Massachusetts, the members of the experimental theater group known as the Provincetown Players introduced Greenwich Village, and soon the world, to their two greatest dramatic discoveries: Eugene O'Neill and Susan Glaspell. The Players' defiant mission was "to establish a stage where playwrights of sincere, poetic, literary and dramatic purpose could see their plays in action and superintend their production without submitting to the commercial manager's interpretation of public taste."

✳   ✳   ✳

ACT II: "To Be an Artist or Nothing"

The stupidity of our theater at the present time, with but little qualification, is of an excellence so signal and arresting that it is certain to reawaken the latent interest in the playhouse. By virtue of its very astounding magnitude it is certain to attract again to the theater such erstwhile rebels as, exasperated by merely mediocre plays and merely mediocre mummering, until now have remained steadfastly away.

—GEORGE JEAN NATHAN, 1916

The great hope of the future lies in the fertilization of the large by the little theater, of Broadway by Provincetown ... in the region of Washington Square and Greenwich Village—or ultimately among the sand dunes of Cape Cod—we must look for the real birthplace of the New American Drama.

—WILLIAM ARCHER, 1923

Washed Ashore at Land's End

O'NEILL AND TERRY CARLIN stepped down off the *Dorothy Bradford*'s gangplank onto Provincetown's Railroad Wharf in late June of 1916. Slick with seagull droppings and cod guts and strewn with tangled nets, the Railroad Wharf functioned as a fish-wagon railway stretching at least one hundred meters out into Provincetown Harbor. Fishing was the town's only cash source, and the briny fumes of the daily catch steamed up off the harbor's more than fifty wharves.

The *Dorothy Bradford*, named for a *Mayflower* passenger who, in the winter of 1620, toppled overboard into the black maw of Provincetown Harbor and drowned, was a four-tiered iron ferry that carried up to 1,650 passengers daily from Boston's Rowe's Wharf to Railroad Wharf.[1] The heartrending tale of the vessel's namesake mirrors much of O'Neill's thematic territory: the horror of an untimely death, the legacy of Puritan New England, the treacherous nature of life at sea, and, in terms of the ferry itself, the soul-destroying transition from the sail power of old to the factory-like steam engines of the modern age. The *Mayflower*'s crew had estimated, before setting sail for Plymouth Rock, that within the protected water of the Province-town Harbor "a thousand sails may safely ride." A more accurate estimation, from 1875, was three times that.[2]

The two Irish "wash ashores" scored $10 from Hutch Hapgood, then moved into a sailmaker's loft overlooking the harbor on the "East End" of the main thoroughfare, Commercial Street. The vacant space was usually inhabited by Bayard Boyesen of the Ferrer School. Hapgood was a friend of Boyesen's, as he was of all anarchists, and O'Neill and Carlin had known him from the Ferrer. (He'd also been a contributing editor at Emma Goldman's *Mother Earth* magazine when O'Neill published his first poem, "American Sovereign," in May 1911.)[3] The loft's owner, John Francis, was a portly man whose mother was Irish and whose father was a Portuguese fisherman "with rings in his ears."[4] Francis didn't drink or smoke himself but was a tolerant, generous host to impoverished bohemians, like O'Neill and Carlin, who did a great deal of both. "Twenty-five dollars till the snow flies," Francis told his tenants at 377 Commercial Street, known as Francis's Flats. "This loft won't be warm in winter."[5]

John Francis ran a general store on the ground floor of his apart-ment building, and a sign out front entreated his customers, "Please loaf in the rear!"[6] Followers of this edict would find a wood stove set up in a back room around which they could warm up after a swim or a walk and converse. One visitor described the shop as "a great hulking place, heaped high with the miscellany common to old time village shops where one can purchase everything from candy sticks to kerosene." The welcoming ambiance Francis nurtured for his tenants is immortalized by Provincetown's "Poet of the Dunes," Harry Kemp, in a eulogy written after Francis's death:

> With that slow speech not slow in apt reply,
> With that smile that was too kind to be sly,

> He will surprise us, rising from his chair
> To greet us with his fostering friendship there![7]

O'Neill felt equally tender about the landlord. When Francis's obituary in 1937 highlighted his friendship with O'Neill, the recent Nobel laureate was sincerely touched: "I feel a genuine sorrow. He was a fine person—and a unique character. I am glad the article speaks of him as my friend. He was all of that, and I know he knew my gratitude, for I often expressed it."[8]

Hutch Hapgood's wife, Neith Boyce, had cobbled together an amateur theater group the previous summer in Provincetown with Hapgood, the director George "Jig" Cram Cook and his wife Susan Glaspell, an emergent playwright, along with about twenty other writers and artists.[9] Their goal was to outshine the Washington Square Players, a thriving but to their mind overly cautious theater group that they themselves had helped found in 1914. Their plays were initially performed at Hapgood and Boyce's house, the Pinehurst, at 621 Commercial Street. On the first evening, they read Boyce's one-act *Constancy*, a farce based on a burning romance between Jack Reed and the Greenwich Village doyen Mabel Dodge. The designer of the set was Robert Edmond Jones, Jack Reed's roommate from Harvard who was, like O'Neill, a former student of George Pierce Baker. The space was so cramped that the front deck of the house served as a makeshift stage while the audience watched through the living room's picture windows. For their second play of the evening, *Suppressed Desires*, Cook and Glaspell's send-up of faddish bohemian life, the audience sat outside while the players performed within. But as their ambition swelled, the group demanded more space.

In August 1915, for $2,200, the writer Mary Heaton Vorse, who'd first brought the Hapgoods to Provincetown back in 1911, bought a fish house on Lewis Wharf, a broken-down Grand Banks cod-fishing pier several blocks down from her and her husband Joe O'Brien's place. The group soon christened it the Wharf Theatre and adopted the name "The Provincetown Players at the Wharf." The wooden structure was twenty-four to twenty-six feet tall and wide and thirty-four to thirty-six feet long; once they'd cleared out the discarded nets, rusty anchors, and rotted oars and dinghies, it was ideal for a makeshift theater. Carpenters installed a ten-by-twelve-foot stage, and there was a massive rolling door at the back that could be opened if a play warranted the harbor as a backdrop. Scores of wooden planks were set across kegs and sawhorses, for a seating capacity of about a hundred. Before electricity was installed, a few members operated lamps and lanterns with tin reflectors as footlights that projected a flickering glow upon the stage. But with its darkly weathered walls, cracked floorboards, and perpetual draft, the theater was a firetrap; as a precaution, the Players posted sentries during productions with shovels and buckets of sand. Financially, after Vorse's initial payment, the space was a boon. No production in the summers of 1915 and 1916 ran over $13 in expenses.[10]

"Terry," Susan Glaspell asked Carlin on a stroll along Commercial Street that June of 1916, "haven't you a play to read us?" "No," he replied. "I don't write, I just think. And sometimes talk. But Mr. O'Neill has got a whole trunk full of plays."[11] Terry was hyperbolizing; O'Neill had actually brought with him a copy of *Thirst* and a wooden box just big enough to carry a half dozen or so manuscripts. On the top of the box were stamped the words "Magic Yeast."[12]

On July 1, Hutch Hapgood sent word to Mabel Dodge, who also spent her summers in Provincetown but decided to remain in New York for a few more weeks, that "Terry Carlin and O'Neill (son of James O'Neill) have taken Bayard's studio." "The play fever is on," he declared, and O'Neill was one of the most "enthusiastic in our circle."[13] Of course, they'd all heard of his father James, the celebrated "Monte Cristo," but few had made the acquaintance of his young son Eugene. Dodge clearly hadn't, and, as Jack Reed's close confidante and ex-lover, she'd made it her business to keep abreast of all the movers and shakers of Greenwich Village.

The same day Hapgood established that Eugene O'Neill had become a member of the Provincetown group, July 1, the Players' famed precursors, the Irish Players of Dublin's Abbey Theatre, had temporarily foundered. Actors were threatening to disband as a

The Wharf Theatre, Provincetown, where O'Neill premiered as a playwright in the summer of 1916.
(COURTESY OF SHEAFFER-O'NEILL COLLECTION, LINDA LEAR CENTER FOR SPECIAL COLLECTIONS AND ARCHIVES, CONNECTICUT COLLEGE, NEW LONDON)

* * *

response to the high-handed attitude of their more professional-minded stage manager, the playwright St. John Ervine. "Rebellion is in the air in Ireland," the drama tabloid *New York Review* reported, referring to the Easter Rising of the previous April during which Sean Connolly, an actor for the Players, had been the first rebel to die, "and it is not strange that The Irish Players should have become infected with it." The *Review* continued that Lady Gregory, playwright and patroness for the Abbey Theatre, was feeling "very much grieved over the collapse of the company."[14]

Across the Atlantic, meanwhile, the members of the Provincetown group were just beginning to creatively and socially cohere. Together, they sprawled on the beaches and swam in the ocean, congregated at one another's houses for dinner and drinks and hunkered together at local bars like the Atlantic House—all the while, Susan Glaspell recalled, "talking about plays—every one writing, or acting, or producing. Life was all of a piece, work not separated from play." The painter Marsden Hartley dubbed this period "The Great Provincetown Summer," a time in which O'Neill wrote drama, fiction, and poetry, drank lots of whiskey, took long swims in the harbor, and practiced various forms of stagecraft along with playwriting, including his least favorite—acting. He embraced Jig Cook's idea that "the art of the theatre cannot be pure, in fact cannot be an art at all, unless its various elements—play-writing, acting, setting, costuming, and lighting are by some means fused into unity." For the Players, the term "amateur" wasn't a condescending slur; rather, it signaled a break from the "professional" theater, which connoted a witless adhesion to outdated rules of drama that hampered self-expression and artistic innovation. O'Neill's advice for aspiring playwrights, offered thirty years later, was a pared-down description of what he'd learned from his own humble beginnings in Provincetown: "Take some wood and canvas and nails and things. Build yourself a theater, a stage; light it, learn about it. When you've done that you will probably know how to write a play . . . if you can."[15]

During rehearsals at the Wharf, they would dive into the harbor to cool off, with O'Neill always plunging in ahead of the pack.

Mary Vorse compared his swimming prowess to that of "a South Sea Islander." Reed showed off to his fiancée, the flamboyant political journalist Louise Bryant, by diving forty feet into the water off the peak of the fish house. (Such a stunt could only be safely accomplished during high tide, a lesson Max Eastman, the visiting *Masses* editor, discovered later that same afternoon—the hard way.)[16]

Jack Reed, as Marsden Hartley aptly phrased it, was "one of those rare specimens who crashed through Harvard and came out on the other side 'alive.' "[17] Louise Bryant had just that January left her husband, the dentist Paul Trullinger, in Portland, Oregon, to run off with the radical reporter. Also an Oregonian, Reed had been visiting family in Portland for the holiday season, after which he lured Bryant back to Greenwich Village and then out to Provincetown. A dark-haired enchantress with melancholy eyes and a wistful smile, she was instantly enamored with the taciturn Irishman. He was younger than she by several years, but who could ignore those scorching, soul-piercing black eyes? She also shared O'Neill's pride in being an Irish American for whom a nonconformist lifestyle had replaced religious faith.

Reed and Bryant occupied 592 Commercial Street, down the block from Hapgood and Boyce, and they'd hired Hippolyte Havel, the *Revolt* editor, as their "chief cook and bottle washer." Max Eastman, who lived across the street, remembered Havel as a "long-haired, owl-eyed, irrepressibly intellectual, and conscientiously irresponsible anarchist." Terry Carlin, he said, loafed "with the determination of a Navajo brave," while Havel "outwitted work instead of attacking it head-on." As a result, given Reed and Bryant's equal disdain for housework, their home was "barnlike in its physical aspect," bare of furniture and other amenities. Nonetheless, Reed, Bryant, and Havel always had plenty of food and beds available for guests to sleep off a night's debauch. "Don't have anything to do with those two bums," Havel grumbled when O'Neill and Carlin first arrived at the house, drunk as lords. "You'll be sorry if you do."[18] Ignoring Havel's admonition, Bryant ordered him to serve O'Neill and Carlin coffee, but O'Neill's hands shook so that he could barely keep the cup level. Bryant helped steady it to his mouth and asked where he planned to stay.[19] "He said he wanted to get a place where he could live simply," Bryant recalled later, since he and Carlin had to live on about $20 a month from O'Neill's father. Bryant suggested they abandon Boyesen's studio and set up camp for free at a fisherman's shack on the beach right across Commercial Street from her and Reed.[20]

Marsden Hartley, who'd just arrived from Paris and was in town as a summer guest of Reed and Bryant's, remembered that O'Neill and Carlin lived in their net-strewn fisherman's shack "like sailors, slept in hammocks and lived most of the time out-of-doors, with their door open to the sea." Hartley never forgot the image of hoary-headed Carlin standing for hours at his misshapen doorway. "How clearly I see his gnarled profile against the ruffled sea," he wrote, "ruminating over what indescribable pasts, stroking the surfaces of life with a prophet's tenderness, gnawed too persistently with hungers rich in emotions, thoughts, and the wiser way of knowing things, earned at what terrible cost." A sign above O'Neill and Carlin's door welcomed visitors with three words: "Go to Hell."[21]

"Terry understood me," O'Neill mused about his time with the affable old anarchist. "He was always the same. If I was bored it didn't affect him, he didn't get bored and unhappy too. If I felt like a few drinks, he felt like a few drinks too." Carlin could also handle his friend's black Irish doldrums better than anyone. "Cheer up, Gene," he'd brusquely declaim, "the worst is yet to come!" Susan Glaspell was so taken by their friendship that she jotted down a play idea titled "Misfits": "Terry's philosophy on Gene 'Every soul is alone. No one in the world understands my slightest impulse.' 'Then you don't understand the slightest impulse of anyone else.' "[22]

O'Neill's choice of *The Movie Man*, his one-act play about actual Hollywood filmmakers' cynical gold digging during the Mexican Revolution, as his tryout at Jack Reed and Louise Bryant's wound up being an unfortunate lapse of judgment. It was a a misfire that he would attempt in the years to follow to wipe from historical memory.[23] His decision was surely meant to impress Jack Reed, who in the fall of 1913 had reported as a war correspondent during the Mexican

Terry Carlin in Provincetown.
(COURTESY OF SHEAFFER-O'NEILL COLLECTION, LINDA LEAR CENTER FOR SPECIAL
COLLECTIONS AND ARCHIVES, CONNECTICUT COLLEGE, NEW LONDON)

* * *

war in a widely hailed series for *Metropolitan* magazine. O'Neill based
his protagonist Jack Hill in *The Movie Man* on the actor/directors
Christy Cabanne and Raoul Walsh, backed by producers Harry E.
Aitken and Frank N. Thayer of the Mutual Film Corporation, who
filmed Pancho Villa's exploits across Chihuahua, Mexico, in the spring
of 1914. The studio brokered a lucrative deal for Villa: The general
was granted 20 percent of the film's revenue to allow cameramen to be
embedded with his troops on rebel raids against loyalist forces.[24] "To
make sure that the business venture will be a success," the *New York
Times* reported two days after Villa accepted the deal, "Mr. [Harry E.]
Aitken dispatched to General Villa's camp last Saturday a squad of

four moving picture men with apparatus designed especially to take pictures on battlefields."[25] It's an absurd fiction, however, reported as fact by the press and perpetuated by O'Neill, that Villa agreed to restrict his battles to camera-friendly daylight or that he reenacted battle scenes to accommodate the American camera crews. Titled *The Life of General Villa*, Aitken's silent film—part fiction, part gruesome reality—was released on May 9, 1914, just a month before O'Neill dashed off his first and only surviving draft of *The Movie Man*.

The Players rejected *The Movie Man* outright, understandably enough, and O'Neill most likely destroyed this revised draft soon after. But if a long-term lesson had begun to sink in, along with the Players' subsequent refusal to put on *The Personal Equation*, it was O'Neill's ultimate recognition that propaganda had no place in his dramas. Jack Reed was a radical; agitprop was his stock-in-trade. O'Neill was an artist, and he learned that political avowals like the anti-interventionism of his revised *Movie Man*, however satiric the intent, leave audiences feeling emotionally empty and their views unchanged. Political arrows, he came to realize in the years that followed, kept sharpest when left in their quiver.

But then, at Cook and Glaspell's house only a few days after *The Movie Man* fiasco, July 16 or 17, O'Neill read them *Bound East for Cardiff*.[26] The one-act sea play takes place on a steamship and depicts the round-robin from port to sea and back to port again, where the crew's meager wages are blown on prostitutes and whiskey. Most of the dialogue concerns a sailor dying in his bunk named Yank, who confides his final thoughts to his long-time shipmate and best friend Driscoll, an Irishman. Yank confesses that he'd always secretly wished that he and Driscoll could start a farm together in Canada or Argentina but had never admitted this to his companion for fear of being made fun of. "Laugh at you, is ut?" Driscoll responds. "When I'm havin' the same thoughts myself, toime afther toime" (*CP1*, 196). The relationship conveys strong homoerotic overtones, and in a moment of touching remembrance, Driscoll reminisces about adventures they shared at exotic ports of call: Buenos Aires, Singapore, Port Saïd, Sydney, Cape Town. O'Neill's word choice "bound" for the title (which he'd changed from "Children of the Sea") indicates more than their route across the Atlantic to Wales; these sailors are "bound" to the sea without hope of escape. This script the Players accepted unanimously.

On July 28, 1916, *Bound East for Cardiff* opened on a double bill with Louise Bryant's morality play *The Game*. *The Game* was nearly turned down, but set designers William and Marguerite Zorach improved upon Bryant's pedestrian work by devising an Egyptian-style set. O'Neill directed *Bound East* and, in spite of his stage fright, took a one-line part as the second mate who steps into the forecastle and asks, "Isn't this your watch on deck, Driscoll?" (*CP1*, 194).

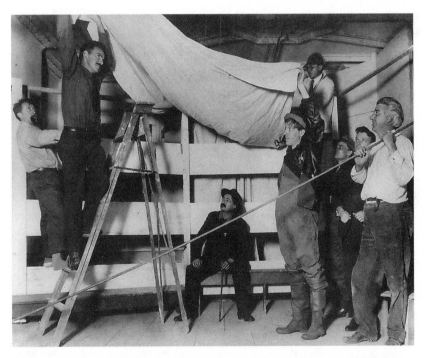

Setting up for *Bound East for Cardiff* at the Wharf Theatre in July 1916. O'Neill is on the stepladder, Hippolyte Havel is seated at center, and George "Jig" Cram Cook is at right with the pole.
(COURTESY OF THE MUSEUM OF THE CITY OF NEW YORK)

✳   ✳   ✳

Jig Cook was cast as the dying sailor Yank. Seated among the rapt audience, Susan Glaspell remembered the evening well: "There was a fog, just as the script demanded, fog bell in the harbor. The tide was in, and it washed under us and around, spraying through the holes in the floor, giving us the rhythm and the flavor of the sea while the big dying sailor talked to his friend Drisc of the life he had always wanted deep in the land, where you'd never see a ship or smell the sea. . . . It is not merely figurative language to say the old wharf shook with applause."[27]

Adele Nathan of the Baltimore little theater group the Vagabond Players (who'd rejected *Bound East for Cardiff* the previous winter) was there at the Provincetown opening. She asked O'Neill for a copy of the play and found that the "rehearsals had been conducted from a single working script, and that was in sad condition." O'Neill offered to type up a fresh copy for her but warned her apologetically that he was a terrible typist, and the process would take a while. Nathan gave O'Neill $15 for the retype and the play was produced in Baltimore that fall; given that O'Neill never earned any royalties from *Thirst*, this paltry sum was notably the first money he received as a working dramatist. It was a fitting play for such an initiation. *Bound East for Cardiff*, O'Neill said later, was "very important from my point of view. [In] it can be seen, or felt, the germ of the spirit, life attitude, etc., of all my more important future work."[28]

Then it was Susan Glaspell's turn. Within ten days, she completed *Trifles*, now a hallmark of modern drama, and the Players produced the one-act on August 8. In the years to come, Mary Vorse placed their achievements that summer among the top innovations of the era: the architecture of Frank Lloyd Wright and the inventions of Alexander Graham Bell; the first flight of the Wright brothers and Henry Ford's creation of the Model T; Sigmund Freud's breakthroughs in psychoanalysis and the achievements of the moguls of the budding Hollywood filmmaking industry.[29] Millennia before, Seneca of Rome, a fellow dramatist, had classified "luck" as what happens when preparation meets opportunity. The Provincetown Players, above all the most ambitious of them, O'Neill and Glaspell, now had both.

Cook and Glaspell owned a modest whitewashed house at 564 Commercial Street across from the Wharf Theatre, which they inhabited with their cat, Carnal Copulation, or "Copycat" for short. Each day, Cook labored away in the front yard constructing theater props and household improvements while Susan tapped out their living on the typewriter within. Max Eastman characterized the couple's lifestyle as an old-fashioned tableau of American domesticity, "an atmosphere of Christian conservatism, a quiet piety" in which Cook was the "husky, brown-skinned farmer" and Glaspell "an overtired but sweetly conscientious farmer's wife."[30]

Honest-spoken and hardworking to a fault, Cook and Glaspell were typical midwesterners in temperament but with eastern-style intellectual bravado. A larger-than-life personality among the Players, Cook was a modernist thinker who worshiped the Greeks. (He'd translated Sappho and often thought in Greek.) But he was keenly aware that writing wasn't his strong suit. It wasn't a lack of ability so much as a lack of self-discipline. Cook's zeal for "social creativeness" and the commitment of his volcanic energy to O'Neill's and Glaspell's work, Eastman observed, might best be explained "by his abstract wish to be a genius combined with an inability to retire into a lonely corner and get down to concrete work."[31]

In contrast to Cook, and most of the other Players, O'Neill excelled at locking himself away to write for days on end. "O'Neill was quite savage in his determination to find solitude," said Harry Kemp, who like Cook preferred communal activity to writing. "No early Christian martyr sought his hilltop remote from men, in order to be with his God, with greater zest than O'Neill, solitude to be alone with his work."[32]

Cook's impassioned speeches commanded a room with the grandiloquence of an orator in the ancient tradition of Cicero. When he spoke, pipe jutting from his mouth, jaw clenched, everyone listened. If he demanded total silence, he got it. A more festive atmosphere? He got that too. When O'Neill spoke, a rarity in itself, he mumbled out of the side of his mouth. He avoided eye contact, Kemp recalled, but instead "looked straight through those in his presence." If he didn't want to talk with you, which was generally the case, he just turned and walked away without a word.[33] One day, the usually gregarious Kemp tested O'Neill's taciturn nature by walking past him with a simple "Hello." Sure enough, though O'Neill resented intrusive small talk, he found Kemp's off-handed dismissal of him even more upsetting. As Kemp strode away, he heard "this pat-pat-pat like a big St. Bernard dog" behind him. "You know," O'Neill said, "I'd have liked to be a prizefighter . . . but I got a blow once that loosened all my teeth."[34]

Jealousy was not an issue with Cook, not publicly at least, and his management and leadership skills were indispensable to the group's success. Cook had "all the resources of the University" at his mental disposal, according to Hapgood, but he was no academic snob or well-heeled layabout.[35] Back in Iowa he'd run a truck farm and taught English at the University of Iowa, where he studied as an undergraduate before moving on to Stanford University. (By the time Cook was finished with theater and had moved to Greece in 1922, after a falling-out in which the Players became too professional for his taste, he left behind an impressive record: he had cultivated as many as fifty writers and ushered over one hundred plays onto the boards.)

Cook was the indisputable "big man" among the Players, O'Neill said later, "always enthusiastic, vital, impatient with everything that smacked of falsity or compromise, he represented the spirit of revolt against the old worn-out traditions, the commercial theater, the tawdry artificialities of the stage."[36] In his autobiography, Hutch Hapgood neatly sums up Cook's critical role in O'Neill's career: "Eugene O'Neill might never have been heard of in the theatre, certainly not for long after this [summer], had it not been for the work of George Cram Cook. Every writer needs a sympathetic background; that background was entirely absent from Broadway at the time and, as far as O'Neill's personality was concerned, it was absent everywhere. The man who felt O'Neill's personality vividly and who created, not only the social enthusiasm for it, but the definite mechanical body and setting, was George Cram Cook."[37]

Cook, like his new protégé O'Neill, was also a passionate devotee of the bottle. At Provincetown soirees, he christened wine casks with names like Bacchus, Aeschylus, and Sophocles, and he invented "Fish House Punch": four parts three-star Hennessey brandy, two parts rum, two parts peach brandy, two parts lemon juice, and a heap of sugar poured into a bowl over a giant block of ice.[38] At Cook's gatherings, O'Neill would squat on the floor apart from the others and hold his tongue until he'd gotten thoroughly intoxicated. Agnes Boulton explained later that for O'Neill, especially among this cohort of boisterous thespians, drinking whiskey "seemed a needed prop to meet the situation, rather than an escape from it. . . . In more important things, alcohol enabled him to do what he wanted to do—*not* what was expected of him, or was the conventional thing to do." Harry Kemp similarly recalled that "in the midst of a party he kept that aura of being apart. When he spoke it was hesitatingly and haltingly. It was only when he drank that he expressed himself fluently. Then he was worth listening to."[39]

Mabel Dodge arrived late that July and looked on as the Players habitually got inebriated, though not, to her mind, in an obnoxious way: "Everyone drank a good deal, but it was of a very superior kind of excess that stimulated the kindliness of hearts and brought out all the pleasure of these people. Eugene's unhappy young face had desperate dark eyes staring out of it and drink must have eased him. Terry of course was always drunk. A handsome skeleton, I thought. Jig Cook was often tippling along with genial Hutch. The women worked quite regularly, even when they, too, drank; and I envied them their ease and ran away from it."[40]

Hutch Hapgood laid down his own unapologetic love of alcohol in his memoir "Memories of a Determined Drinker; or, Forty Years of Drink," for which he failed, unsurprisingly, to find a publisher. The title might reassure a prospective editor that the book was yet another temperance memoir warning readers against the "demon rum." Nothing could be further from the truth. "Without the glass Cook's genius would never have been," Hapgood wrote, and then linked O'Neill's debt to whiskey to its inevitable conclusion: "It is fair to say that without Cook the Provincetown Players would never have existed. His was not the original idea, but his was the complex activities which made it possible. . . . Without him O'Neill's talent would not, at any rate for many years, have found a means of putting itself over."[41] By the time Hapgood wrote this exhortation, 1932, O'Neill was in his judgment "our only important American playwright," and without the Players' drinking habits in Provincetown that summer, he said, the state of American theater as we had come to know it would not exist.[42]

One of the despised rules of nature, of course, is that heavy whiskey drinking invariably leads to its less delightful result: the hangover. And O'Neill's hangovers were epic. "There was no such darkness as Gene's after a hangover," Mary Vorse recalled. "He would sit silent and suffering and in darkness. You could have taken the air he breathed and carved a statue of despair of it."[43] O'Neill's New London friend Art McGinley, who later came to visit O'Neill in Provincetown, described his mercurial friend's drinking habits this way: "Gene was a periodic drinker, and once started wouldn't stop—I guess he couldn't stop—until he was really sick. He was the most trying morning-after drinker I've ever known. He would gloom up and not say a word, or else talk of suicide, he was so disgusted with himself. But when he stopped drinking, he would work around the clock. I never knew anyone who had so much self-discipline."[44]

O'Neill wrote prolifically that summer despite his hangovers. Along with revising *The Movie Man*, he turned out the one-act *Before Breakfast*, the short story "Tomorrow," and a full-length comedy about pretentious bohemianism entitled *Now I Ask You*. The story of an upper-middle-class young woman with a studied affectation of Greenwich Village radicalism, *Now I Ask You* echoes the Players' mordant view of affluent would-be radicals who disingenuously promoted revolutionary politics and free love merely as an outlet to escape bourgeois ennui. And along with Cook and Glaspell's *Suppressed Desires*, Neith Boyce and Jack Reed wrote similar satires on the subject, *Constancy* and *The Eternal Quadrangle*. As a *Boston Post* reporter noted, "The Provincetown Players are so modern that they not only write about modern things, but satirize them."[45]

That July, O'Neill plunged into an affair with a determined *non*-drinker, Louise Bryant. Bryant's father had been a severe alcoholic, and for a long time she disdained people who drank to excess. (In her later years, however, she fell to drinking so heavily that her second husband, the wealthy diplomat and a close friend of Reed's from Harvard, William C. Bullitt, would win custody of their daughter Anne on the grounds that she was an incompetent mother.)[46] O'Neill's fruitful summer of writing was attributable in part to Bryant, as she helped him control his whiskey intake just enough to work. Reed knew about the affair, of course, but his one-act play *The Eternal Quadrangle* suggests that extramarital affairs bothered him little, and he himself had been recently involved in a long-standing and public romance with the married Mabel Dodge.[47]

A rare photograph of O'Neill and Bryant together, the only known portrait of them offstage, captures the two lovers languidly sunning on a cottage's front steps. In this picture, published here for the first time, Bryant poses for the photographer with a fetching if somewhat strained smile. O'Neill is gripping an uncooperative cat and appears more hungover than haunted. Reed, as it happens, is seated off camera over O'Neill's left shoulder; a highly circulated photograph of O'Neill and Reed from that afternoon, this time with Bryant off camera to O'Neill's right, confirms that the three were relaxed and happy in each other's company.[48]

Placed side by side, the two images produce an almost cinematic quality. One can imagine that Reed had just snapped his friend out of a dark mood with a wisecrack. O'Neill is also, fittingly enough, separating the couple. Of the two, a stranger might think it was O'Neill, not Reed, who would soon marry the coy-looking young woman beside him.[49] (The three-way romance was later dramatized for the big screen in the 1981 film *Reds* with Diane Keaton as Bryant, Jack Nicholson as O'Neill, and Warren Beatty as Reed.) Bryant, who was often seen following O'Neill around in Provincetown, initiated her romance with the playwright on the Fourth of July with a love poem:

Dark eyes
you stir my soul
Ineffably.
You scatter
All my peace.
Dark eyes,
What shall I do?

The sentiment was entirely mutual. "When that girl touches me with the tip of her little finger," O'Neill told Carlin, "it's like a flame."[50] Two days later, he sent her this impassioned, only recently found reply:

Blue eyes.

You stir my soul
Ineffably.
You scatter all my peace.
Blue eyes,
What shall I do? . . .

I dream
In a great wide space
Where horizons meet
And the unattainable is possessed.

Blue eyes.
The sky is blue,
I dare not look at it
Because my soul is lonely.

Don't you know then
Why,
Blue eyes?[51]

Terry Carlin arrived at his and O'Neill's shack one day delivering a pleading note from Bryant: "I must see you alone. I have to explain something, for my sake and Jack's. You have to understand."

Louise Bryant and Eugene
O'Neill in the summer of 1916,
Provincetown.
(COURTESY OF HENRY W. AND ALBERT A.
BERG COLLECTION OF ENGLISH AND
AMERICAN LITERATURE, NEW YORK PUBLIC
LIBRARY)

Eugene O'Neill and John
Reed in the summer of 1916,
Provincetown.
(COURTESY OF SHEAFFER-O'NEILL
COLLECTION, LINDA LEAR CENTER FOR
SPECIAL COLLECTIONS AND ARCHIVES,
CONNECTICUT COLLEGE, NEW LONDON)

✳   ✳   ✳

At the ensuing liaison, Bryant informed O'Neill that she and Reed
weren't sexually active, that they lived like siblings because of a kidney ailment he suffered from that required surgery. It was true about
the kidney at least (he would have surgery that fall), and O'Neill and
Bryant's affair began in earnest; it would last, on and off, for nearly
two years. In theory, O'Neill was still involved with Beatrice Ashe. In
one of his last letters to her, sent on July 25, he implored Ashe to visit
him on the Cape, as he didn't have the money for a ticket to New
London; but he understood that by then she'd been mulling over her
future, and he had no place in it.

The Players as a group neither liked nor respected Bryant. Most of
the men considered her a "bitch," a "nymphomaniac," and a "whore";

the women resented her preferential treatment at the theater as exclusively the result of her relationships with Reed and O'Neill.[52] "Just because someone is sleeping with somebody," one of them scoffed when Bryant's *The Game* was accepted for the double bill with *Bound East for Cardiff*, "is no reason we should do her play."[53] "Bryant was not really a playwright," another quipped, "she only slept with one."[54] News of the affair quickly spread to New York, and Mabel Dodge had gone to Provincetown to see if, under the circumstances, she might win Reed back: "I thought Reed would be glad to see me if things were like that between him and Louise—but he wasn't."[55]

In an unpublished memoir, Bryant offers a telling anecdote about Reed's reaction to her sexual relations with O'Neill. Reed had a friend, Fred Boyd, whom he'd rescued from prison after Boyd was arrested at the Paterson Silk Strike of 1913. From that point on, Boyd was loyal as a hound. According to Bryant, when Boyd found out about the romance brewing between O'Neill and Bryant, he showed up drunk at Reed and Bryant's house at four o'clock in the morning and demanded $40. When Reed asked what the money was for, Boyd told him it was to buy a gun to murder O'Neill. Reed responded by kissing his fiancée tenderly and telling Boyd to go home and sleep it off. Later that morning, he went to O'Neill's shack and warned him, "Boyd was drunk last night and shooting his face off around town. If you hear any stories don't pay any attention to them. And I wish you and Terry Carlin would take all your meals with us for a while."[56] For most of their friends, as *Suppressed Desires* and *Now I Ask You* satirize, the belief in free love was so much bohemian posing. On this matter, Louise Bryant and Jack Reed were no posers.

By the end of the summer, the Players were desperate to schedule plays for a final bill and thus premiered a second O'Neill play, *Thirst*, on September 1. Unlike the storied premiere of *Bound East*, this bill, which included a revival of Cook and Glaspell's *Suppressed Desires*, wasn't the Players' finest hour. O'Neill, darkly tanned and lithe from swims in the harbor, took the role of the mulatto sailor, the largest role of his truncated acting career, while Cook played the gentleman and Bryant the erotic dancer. During rehearsals, the Zorachs had fashioned as symbolic a set for *Thirst* as they had with Bryant's *The Game*, but O'Neill wanted the production to seem as realistic as possible and refused them; thus, instead of a symbolic ocean, the water was represented by long yards of "sea cloth with someone wriggling around underneath it."[57] Bryant wanted to bare her breasts in the final scene, since O'Neill's stage directions called for the dancer, driven insane by thirst, to tear off her bodice, but the Players opted for discretion. (Bryant was indeed comfortable in her own skin. Along with nude sunbathing in Provincetown, William Carlos Williams said that at his first encounter with her in New York that fall, she wore "a heavy, very heavy white silk skirt so woven that it hung over the curve of her buttocks like the strands of a glistening waterfall. . . . There could have been nothing under it, for it followed the very crease between the buttocks in its fall.")[58]

Though no formal review of *Thirst*'s premiere exists, a *Boston Sunday Post* article entitled "Many Literary Lights among the Provincetown Players," announced in September, less than a week after the Players had officially incorporated on the fourth, that "the Provincetown Players, like the Irish Players, are trying to get away from stage

A performance of *Thirst* at the Wharf Theatre in August 1916. From left, Louise Bryant appears as the dancer, George Cram "Jig" Cook as the gentleman, and Eugene O'Neill as the mulatto sailor.
(COURTESY OF THE YALE COLLECTION OF AMERICAN LITERATURE, BEINECKE RARE BOOK AND MANUSCRIPT LIBRARY, NEW HAVEN)

✳   ✳   ✳

convention, to act naturally and simply, to be on the stage much as they are off the stage. . . . It begins to look as if the American drama may be richer for the fun and the work of the Provincetown Players this summer. They have put on two plays by Eugene O'Neil [sic], a young dramatist whose work was heretofore unproduced and who, they are confident, is going to be heard from in places less remote than Provincetown."[59]

Jig Cook didn't need a reporter to tell him what he already knew. When his friend Edna Kenton, a founding member of the feminist group Heterodoxy, arrived for a visit in early September, Cook immediately ushered her out to the Wharf Theatre. Kenton remembered the tides rolling beneath the wide, sand-strewn planks while she gazed about at the "net-hung, shell-hung, seaweed-fronded walls." Then Jig thrust open the backdrop to "let in the sparkling sea." "You don't know Gene yet," he told her. "You don't know his plays. But you will. All the world will know Gene's plays some day. . . . Gene's plays aren't the plays of Broadway; he's got to have the sort of stage we're going to found in New York."[60]

Below Washington Square

On the train ride back to New York early that October 1916, after his triumphant premiere in Provincetown, O'Neill stopped over at New London for a brief visit with his parents. Never one to let go of a bad idea, O'Neill rewrote *The Movie Man* that week in New London as the short story "The Screenews of War."[61] Bryant joined him there, and the elder O'Neills approved of her if only because she'd evidently curtailed O'Neill's drinking.[62] O'Neill's friend Jessica Rippin remembered Bryant wandering around New London barefoot wearing a pair of O'Neill's trousers. "After the way he'd raved about her," Rippin said, "I expected something special, but she was a mess, she looked like a Greenwich Village character who needed a bath."[63]

By the time O'Neill was back in New York, Jig Cook had located the Provincetown Players' next stage: 139 Macdougal Street, an 1840 brownstone for $50 a month just south of Washington Square.

O'Neill proposed naming it the Playwrights' Theatre, to which the Players voted a resounding "yea," to highlight the new role of playwrights as controlling artists rather than Broadway lackeys. The cramped auditorium was built in the first floor parlor, with only a couple of feet left behind the stage for scenery changes. Because of fire laws, there was no box office, so ticket revenue could be collected only through seasonal subscriptions. The second floor housed dressing rooms, a lounge, an office, and a restaurant run by Christine Ell.[64]

O'Neill, with Lou Holladay and the freelance journalist, restaurant worker, and future speakeasy proprietor Barney Gallant, rented for $3 a month an unfurnished flat at 38 Washington Square, which reeked of horse dung from a nearby stable.[65] Gallant, like so many others, felt on edge around O'Neill, but understood over time that whenever O'Neill shared a tale from his past, "he was already shaping his plays; he was like a painter trying to fix a scene in his mind. He would watch us closely, gauging the effect his stories were having on us—we were, you might say, the audience."[66]

Over their six seasons of operation, the Provincetown Players produced works by an astonishing lineup of literary lights: along with O'Neill and Glaspell, Theodore Dreiser, Djuna Barnes, Mike Gold, Floyd Dell, Edna St. Vincent Millay, and other writers who were prepared to face off against the moral certitude of the American genteel tradition, with its stifling and arbitrary censorship laws, and the Theatrical Syndicate and Shubert Brothers' systematic commercialization of Broadway. For this reason, they intentionally discouraged reviewers from attending their performances and sloughed off the age-old convention of offering them complimentary tickets.

"People drifted down to Macdougal Street because it was something of a lark," Clayton Hamilton told an audience of three hundred at Columbia University in 1924; the makeshift venue was "a sort of intellectual substitute for going slumming." "To go to the New Amsterdam Theatre and see 'The Follies' was mainly an expense," he said, "but to go down to Macdougal Street and see the Provincetown Players was not an expense but an adventure."[67] During one performance, for instance, a gang of Italian kids threw open the stage door, shouted "Go fuck yourselves!" and ran off down the block. The actor Charles Ellis, watching from the edge of the stage as perplexed audience members got to their feet, refused to allow his show to be so easily interrupted. Holding a shovel, a prop that his part required, high above his head, he broke the "fourth wall" and bellowed, "If anybody makes a move, you don't listen to me, I'll bury you all!"[68]

For a clubhouse to hold meetings and gather after performances, the Players appropriated Nani Bailey's Samovar, a renowned Village café around the corner in a second-floor loft space and former art studio above a junk shop at 148 West Fourth Street. They painted the tables and chairs an assortment of colors and the crumbling brick walls and enormous rafters a rose red. The center of the restaurant featured an enormous working samovar to tap glasses of tea and wash down Bailey's famously savory cheese sandwiches.[69] O'Neill's frequent absence was a frustration. "Someone's got to go and rake Gene out of the Hell Hole!" one of the Players would yell. "But it happened often," Mary Vorse recalled, "that whoever went 'to rake Gene out' himself also had to get raked." One Player after the other would go to the Hell Hole, just two doors down on Sixth Avenue, until the whole troupe had transferred to the bar.[70]

The long stretches of time Jig Cook spent with his protégé O'Neill were often tense, even when the encounters were generously lubricated with beakers of Fish House Punch or quarts of Old Taylor bourbon, O'Neill's preferred blend. O'Neill's perpetual uneasiness, especially when sober, had a grating effect on Cook. In a letter to Glaspell that October, he grumbled that O'Neill's temperament was irritably contagious: "O'Neill's nervous tension is a thing that I feel instantly when I see him. I mean that I instantly catch it from him—I feel it myself in myself. Sort of anxiety complex. He likes to be with me since he discovered that I feel what he feels. But it isn't good for me."[71]

Cook also came to interpret O'Neill's painful self-consciousness as a form of narcissism. "You're the most conceited man I've ever known," he said as he observed O'Neill staring, once again, at his reflection. "No," O'Neill replied, "I just want to be sure I'm here."[72]

O'Neill's unique skill as a playwright, in fact, was in large part due to his ability to drive people, both onstage and off, into the shadows of his own psychic torment, and he used it to advantage in his next play, *Before Breakfast*. An American version of August Strindberg's *The Stronger, Before Breakfast* involves alcoholism, suicide, an extramarital affair, two illegitimate pregnancies, a miscarriage, and a housewife who quite literally nags her husband to death. "O'Neill didn't care about the success of the play," Provincetowner Edna Kenton said. "He cared only about the reaction of the audience to monologue, trick shocks, trick relief. It was a deliberate experiment for a definite result—the endurance of the audience." "How much are they going to stand of this sort of thing," O'Neill wondered before the December 1 opening, "before they begin to break?" O'Neill himself played the offstage hand of Alfred Rowland, a bohemian artist from a well-to-do family who reaches through the bathroom door for his shaving cream and then slits his throat. Having seen O'Neill in his biggest part, the mulatto sailor in *Thirst*, Harry Kemp joked that the playwright "was fonder of his part in 'Before Breakfast.'" "The audience sees only the hand, which according to the script is long-fingered, sensitive, slender. Later a groan is heard. There's a part that calls for delicacy, restraint and finish. To coordinate the hand and the groan. . . . Well, O'Neill did the hand and the groan, and a fine performance it was."[73] (This would be the last time O'Neill, or any part of his anatomy, would appear onstage.)

"My son," O'Neill's father James implored, "why don't you write more pleasant plays?"[74] James had begun taking an active interest in his younger son's budding theatrical career, and he stopped by to view a rehearsal or two of *Before Breakfast*. A resplendent contrast to the frayed white and gray woolens and cotton garments the Players wore, James conspicuously sported a fur-collared coat, a gold-headed cane, and an outsized sparkling diamond ring. Eugene was deferential to his father and consulted him, reported a bystander, William Carlos Williams, "when there was some point they had to solve about the play itself or its presentation."[75] James interrupted the Irish beauty Mary Pyne, who starred as the sole onstage character, to coach her, "with the voice and gesture of Monte Cristo," in his old-fashioned methods of acting. As the actor departed the theater that night, a few of the Players complimented him on his son's "gifts and promise." "Yes, yes," James responded. "I think the boy has something in him."[76]

Before John Reed's kidney operation that fall, Bryant left O'Neill behind in the village and traveled with Reed to Innisfree, a cottage they'd found in Croton-on-Hudson, New York. After her departure, even Jim O'Neill began to worry about his brother's excessive drinking, and he contacted Bryant to help talk him down off the ledge. Bryant tracked him down at the Hell Hole, looking filthier and more steeped in booze than she'd ever seen him, and coaxed him onto a bus to dry out with his parents. The elder O'Neills were staying at the Hotel St. George in Brooklyn Heights instead of their usual suite at the Prince George in Manhattan. They were most likely seeking the assistance of the Sisters of Charity convent nearby, where Ella had kicked her morphine habit in 1914. (In the fall of 1918, Ella would undergo a mastectomy, an experience that resulted in her temporarily returning to the drug.)[77]

Reed and Bryant married in secrecy in Peekskill, New York, before Reed traveled alone to Johns Hopkins University in Baltimore on November 12 to have his kidney removed. During Reed's convalescence, O'Neill and Bryant occupied his apartment on Washington Square. Bryant became unwell that November, and the gossips among the Villagers postulated that her illness was due to complications that had resulted from aborting O'Neill's child. She relied upon the freethinking Village doctor Harry Lorber, who was known to treat such delicate matters as abortions, venereal diseases, and even the odd drug overdose with discretion.[78] Bryant and Reed both recuperated after a few weeks, but she carried on with her passionate affair with O'Neill.

The Players next put on O'Neill's one-act *Fog* on January 5, 1917. Composed a year after the *Titanic*'s disastrous voyage in 1912, *Fog* is set on an oarless lifeboat lost off the Grand Banks. The principals, a poet and a man of business, argue over the poet's assertion that success (material or otherwise), survival, and happiness can only be obtained when less fortunate souls are subjected to their opposite. O'Neill's stage directions were highly ambitious for a theater as small as theirs—the play requires fog, a rising sun, falling ice, rolling swells, and two boats, among other special effects. *The Sniper*, O'Neill's drama of World War I, was then staged on February 16, two weeks after the United States broke diplomatic ties with Germany. The Players put on *The Sniper* for precisely the same reason that Professor Baker and his father's vaudeville friends had rejected it two years earlier, because of its timely subject matter, and they advertised *The Sniper* and two other antiwar plays as their "war bill."[79]

The Players' self-assured and capable new director, Nina Moise, first met O'Neill at the Samovar while O'Neill was talking to a few people about *The Sniper*. Moise was unimpressed: "He was so inarticulate I wondered how he ever thought he could write a play." "Then I read 'The Sniper,' which was not," she recalled in hindsight, "a very good play, but even so I remember my thrill when I read it—it had such vitality." Though O'Neill found it nearly impossible to articulate his ideas to actors at this time, for directors, Moise said, "his scripts are fool-proof. The director can follow his stage direction and never go wrong."[80] (For the 1917–18 season, Moise would direct his one-acts *The Long Voyage Home* and *Ile* in the fall and *The Rope* that spring.)

That March 1917, O'Neill stole himself away from the heady distractions of Greenwich Village and returned to Provincetown to write in peace. He was joined by the hard-drinking pulp fiction writer Harold de Polo, and they took a room at the Atlantic House while John Francis refurbished a suite of rooms for them in his apartment building. O'Neill had met de Polo at Lou Holladay's bar Sixty in 1915, before it was shut down and Holladay went to jail. O'Neill had overheard de Polo scoff with some others at the bar that the bohemian Village crowd was a bunch of out-of-town exhibitionists. O'Neill interrupted to counter defensively that he was born on Broadway, and the ensuing conversation marked the start of an intimate bond with de Polo that would last for well over a decade. (They became such fast friends that de Polo was one of the few to whom O'Neill admitted that his mother's aloofness was the result of her morphine addiction.)[81]

During this stay at the Atlantic House, where the owners hung a sign on the veranda, "Dogs and Artists Not Allowed!," O'Neill completed what was to become his first hit play for a wider audience: *In the Zone*. Cashing in on a rampant fear of German invasion, the one-act takes place on the British tramp steamer *Glencairn*, the setting of *Bound East for Cardiff* but now loaded down with stores of dynamite and ammunition as it passes through a German U-boat zone. The paranoid crew, discovering that one of the seamen, Smitty, had stowed a black box in the forecastle, suspects it is a bomb and that he is a German spy with designs to destroy the ship.

It was thus an uncanny coincidence that O'Neill and de Polo were themselves arrested and charged with espionage on March 27. The local Provincetowners, whose wariness matched that of O'Neill's fictional crewmen, had grown suspicious after observing O'Neill and de Polo taking long, meandering walks on the beaches and through alleyways of their village. Convinced the strangers were scoping possible German landing sites, a few residents reported them to the authorities, noting that one of them carried a mysterious black box (possibly O'Neill's "Magic Yeast" box or a typewriter case). Officer Reuben R. Kelley soon arrested them at gunpoint while they were eating dinner at the New Central Hotel. "What for?" de Polo asked. "You know what for!" Kelly shouted back. They'd been seen "prowling around" the radio station in the nearby town of North Truro, he said, and, though the initial charge was vagrancy, they were suspected of espionage. Secret Service agent Fred Weyand of the Department of Justice was then called in from Boston to interrogate them in the Town Hall lockup. They were held for over twenty-four hours without access to a lawyer, but O'Neill's identity as the son of James O'Neill was soon verified, and the young men were released. (The reaction among the locals wasn't merely the result of unfounded wartime paranoia; a German U-boat was in fact spotted and fired at after it breached off Provincetown's shoreline the following summer, 1918.)[82]

O'Neill, unaccustomed to demoralizing interrogations, left the station in equal parts infuriated and scared. Two of the detectives assigned to the case were staying at the Atlantic House as well, and they'd been tasked with monitoring O'Neill's mail. "Well," one of them would goad O'Neill at breakfast, "you got a letter from your mother, Gene, but your girl's forgot you today, but someone sent you a knitted tie just the same."[83] The incident as a whole was later revisited by the Bureau of Investigation in 1924, while it was investigating O'Neill for treasonous political activity.

This story so closely approximates the plot of *In the Zone* it was nearly impossible to believe that O'Neill wrote the play prior to his discomfiting experience; nevertheless, O'Neill and de Polo insisted that it had already been written by the time of their arrest. O'Neill's likely source for the play was a story printed in the *New London Telegraph* on September 9, 1912, when he was on staff there. Entitled "Box Mystery Alarms Many until Solved," the article reports that an Italian shopkeeper in New London grew suspicious about a black box left in his care. Believing it might belong to the Black Hand terrorist organization, he notified the police. Upon inspection, the box was found to contain some men's clothing and was duly retrieved by its owner.[84] Much later, in O'Neill's 1940 work diary, he sketched out the plot of a comedy, "The Visit of Malatesta," based on the life of Italian anarchist Enrico Malatesta. In it, Malatesta visits a fictional version of New London. Although Italian Americans in the play consider him a regicidal hero, the mastermind behind the assassination of Umberto I in 1900 (actually killed by the anarchist Gaetano Bresci), the character, O'Neill writes, "denies he had anything to do with [the assassination]— terrorist group fanatics—true anarchism never justifies bloodshed."[85]

Wartime intrigues aside, O'Neill's stay at the Atlantic House was one of the most industrious periods of his career. Along with *In the Zone*, he completed *Ile* and two more *Glencairn* plays, *The Long Voyage Home* and *The Moon of the Caribbees*. *Ile* is the story of a whaling captain's wife who's driven to insanity by her husband's myopic pursuit of oil (the "ile" of the title). Based on the actual 1903 polar expedition of Captain John A. Cook and his wife, Viola Fish Cook, the fictional couple in *Ile*, David and Annie Keeney, are also clear stand-ins for James and Ella O'Neill. *The Moon of the Caribbees*, though, was O'Neill's unrivaled darling of the group. First titled "The Moon at Trinidad," the play takes place off the coast of Port of Spain, where his ship the *Ikala* had anchored en route to New York from Buenos Aires. With virtually no plot, more than twenty speaking roles, and no melodramatic elements that might have made for a box office hit, *The Moon of the Caribbees* was a radical departure even for O'Neill. "No one else in the world," O'Neill told Nina Moise, "could have written that one."[86]

O'Neill appeared "thunderstruck," according to Louise Bryant, when she surprised him with an unannounced visit in mid-May. Jack Reed had been in Washington, D.C., conducting antiwar protests—and, it turned out, the occasional affair. Bryant, enraged in spite of her own blatant infidelity and claims of adherence to the free love movement, chose this as her breakout moment but only stayed with O'Neill for a week. Back in New York, she attained her journalistic credentials, with Reed's help, just as the United States decided to join the weakened alliance of Great Britain, France, and Russia against the German war machine. Now a certified, if untested, war correspondent, Bryant sailed to France under constant threat of U-boat attacks.[87]

O'Neill wasn't as keen for a firsthand observation of the Great War as Bryant or many other American writers of the time, such as Reed, John Dos Passos, Ernest Hemingway, E. E. Cummings, and Edith Wharton, to name a few. Once the draft was in place, he attempted to join the navy but was turned down for "minor defects which will not count in the draft." He then sent a letter to Dr. Lyman at Gaylord Farm asking for a medical excuse to avoid the draft, given that "conditions in the camps and at the front are the worst possible for one susceptible to T.B. Is this so?" "I want to serve my country," he said, "but it seems silly to commit suicide for it."[88]

That summer O'Neill submitted *The Long Voyage Home* and *The Moon of the Caribbees* to the *Smart Set*, a journal that advertised itself as dedicated to "enlightened skepticism" and was run by H. L. Mencken, the notorious enfant terrible of American letters. "I want these plays," O'Neill wrote Mencken, "which to me are *real*, to pass through your acid test because I know your acid is 'good medicine.' "

Mencken published *The Long Voyage Home* in October 1917; he also accepted *Ile* that winter and published it the following May. Another prominent literary journal, the *Seven Arts*, published O'Neill's short story "Tomorrow" in June, whetting O'Neill's appetite to continue writing fiction as well as drama. The journal's editor Waldo Frank didn't like the story, although he published it at Louise Bryant's behest (nor did he like O'Neill's poem "I Am a Louse on the Body of Society," since lost, which Bryant also passed along to him). He insisted upon significant changes, including the elimination of a melodramatic postscript. O'Neill envisioned "Tomorrow" as the first of a series of short stories based entirely on his life at Jimmy the Priest's, "yarns in which the story-teller was to hog most of the limelight—a sort of Conrad's Marlow." But he couldn't find a sustainable plotline, so he abandoned the series altogether.[89] (He would return to the concept decades later, in dramatic form, as *The Iceman Cometh*.)

Terry Carlin arrived in Provincetown to join O'Neill that spring, and the two moved into another "Garbage Flat," as they again named their quarters, this time at John Francis's. O'Neill hung a sign on their door for passersby, "May wild jackasses desecrate the grave of your grandmother if you disturb me."[90] On the rafters, he and Carlin etched their own adaptation of the guiding tenets of Mabel Collins's book of mystical thought *Light on the Path:*

> Before the eyes can see, they must be incapable of tears!
> Before the ear can hear, it must have lost it's sensitiveness!
> Before the voice can speak, it must have lost the power to wound!
> Before the soul can fly, it's wings must be washed in the blood of the heart![91]

Once settled into the new Garbage Flat, O'Neill wrote at a breakneck pace, completing his one-act comedy *The G.A.N.* (a reference to Henry James's waggish pet name for the ever-elusive "Great American Novel"), which he later destroyed, his short story "The Hairy Ape," and the novella *S.O.S.* (based on his 1913 one-act play *Warnings*). "Sent my long story ['The Hairy Ape'] to the Saturday

Evening Post Monday," he wrote a friend in September. "They might really take it and if they do it will mean some honest-to-Guard money. I'm pretty sure it will sell some place any way in the long run." He'd written his most mature dramas to date over the previous months in Provincetown, but still sought the quick cash of popular fiction. "Here's hoping!" he said just before sending off *S.O.S.*, "I can certainly use a little money, divil a lie av ut!"[92]

O'Neill evidently had a minor fling that summer with Elaine Freeman, a painter associated with Independent Artists, the avant-garde cohort that included Man Ray, Marcel Duchamp, John Sloan, and Helene Iungerich, one of Freeman's roommates in Provincetown. "Living in the Big Town on an author's shoe-string, and a beggar's mite extracted from a reluctant Pater," he complained to Freeman about the prospects of another winter in New York, "is not my dream of the Perfect Life. It's sure hell to nourish the instincts of a real artist in these degenerate days. The Coast, moreover, is a long step nearer the South Seas of my Visioning." O'Neill gave Freeman an autograph manuscript of his Buenos Aires poem "The Bridegroom Weeps!" and wrote her several letters after her departure in September. In these unpublished letters, he details the state of his health (strong), his economic condition (weak), and the progress of his work (solid, but fiction, so ultimately futile). Lou Holladay had invited him to an apple orchard in Oregon owned by his fiancée, Louise Norton, who suggested he go out there to work and dry out if he wanted to marry her, and de Polo was hunting for a place for them to "bunk" in the New England countryside as well. Both propositions had their "charms," he told Freeman, "as [de Polo] and I are lenient toward each other's sins—as I and Lou are for that matter—and get along like real pals." O'Neill also dreamed of moving to the South Sea islands and playing, for the rest of his life, on his "spiritual fiddle while modern civilization is destroyed by flames."[93] Instead, he plunged back into the roiling conflagration of Greenwich Village.

Upon Louise Bryant's arrival back from Europe on August 13, Jack Reed, wearing a white shantung suit and Panama hat to shield himself from the sweltering sun of a terrific heat wave, met her as she disembarked at the pier in New York. They had four days, he informed her, to pack before they steamed back across the Atlantic. The signs all indicated that a socialist revolution in Russia was a near certainty, and they were going to cover it. Bryant's sojourn in France had largely been an uneventful disappointment, so she eagerly agreed to return.

O'Neill was devastated by the blow, but Bryant assured him that she could never stop loving him even while she was as far away as Russia. He promised to stay true to her, but that he would only remain so until November. Bryant wouldn't return until March. O'Neill wired her cable after lovesick cable, but she rarely responded; when she did, her tone struck him as "cold and indefinite." He began drinking more than ever, "all I could," he informed her. "I refused to endure the ache, and drink drugged me to an indifferent apathy." He conducted numerous one-night stands, he said, "in a spirit of revenge, against you, all women, myself for being heartbroken, and life in general."[94]

It wasn't long before O'Neill eased his yearning for Bryant with a strikingly beautiful, intellectually precocious nineteen-year-old political activist named Dorothy Day.[95] A recent college dropout, Day had just begun writing about labor issues for the *Masses* and the socialist newspaper the *New York Call*. O'Neill admired Day's ability to drink with the best of them, sing "Frankie and Johnny" and, as she said later, quoting the nineteenth-century English poet Ernest Dowson, "fling roses riotously with the throng." (But she denied the writer Malcolm Cowley's future claim that she could drink longshoremen under the table. Cowley meant this a compliment, but Day considered it a malicious bit of libel that dogged her throughout her career.) The left-wing novelist and playwright Mike Gold, to whom Day was briefly engaged, had introduced her to O'Neill that fall, 1917, and regretted it immediately. Gold likened Day's adoration of the burgeoning playwright to an adolescent's crush on the high school rebel. She wanted more than anything to be a writer, and O'Neill was one of the Village's most radiant new literary lights. Moreover, his evident love for Bryant made him all the more attractive to women in their circle. Still, though captivated by his intellect, Day felt he was not "really physically exciting." She claimed they never slept together, that he never even tried to kiss her. Sometimes he would ask, "Don't you want to lose your virginity?" but appeared glad when she rebuffed him.[96]

Rehearsals and performances at the Playwrights' Theatre that season reliably concluded with the cast and crew trotting around the corner to the Hell Hole. "No one ever wanted to go to bed," Day wrote of those autumn months, "and no one ever wished to be alone."[97] By this time, the Hell Hole's back room was as saturated with talk of Dostoevsky, Baudelaire, Strindberg, Nietzsche, and Francis Thompson as it was tobacco smoke and the sour stench of stale beer. O'Neill could recite Thompson's epic poem *The Hound of Heaven* by heart, all 182 lines of it:

> I fled Him, down the nights and down the days;
> I fled Him, down the arches of years;
> I fled Him, down the labyrinthine ways
> Of my own mind; and in the midst of tears

Day had never heard the poem before, and she would stare at O'Neill enraptured while he sat with "his elbows resting on the table, chin cupped in hand, eyes looking inward and seeing none of us listening."[98] She noted that he placed particular emphasis on a line that spoke to his doomed obsession with Bryant: "And now my heart is as a broken fount, wherein tear drippings stagnate."[99] O'Neill delivered the poem "in his grating, monotonous voice, his mouth grim, his eyes sad," she wrote in her autobiography, and his recitations, she added in an unpublished reminiscence, "Told in Context," galvanized "an intensification of the religious sense that was in me."[100] The spiritual awakening that followed inspired Day to begin attending St. Joseph's Church in the Village.[101] (Subsequently, she became a renowned leader of the Catholic Worker Movement, and her name has since been mentioned at the Holy See for canonization.)

Day recalled that by this time O'Neill was "surrounded by admirers." "He was beginning to feel his powers," she said, "and exult in them." "One of the fine things about Gene was that he took people seriously, more seriously than the rest of us did," Day remembered. "He took Terry Carlin seriously. He took Hippolyte Havel seriously, and almost no one else did. . . . Hip would get up in the center of the room, when he'd been drinking, and whirl around in exuberance. . . . We laughed at him, but not Gene." Havel, for instance, was smitten with a lesbian named Rick Hornsby and used to chirp in his goofy way, "I'm her little doggie," but O'Neill berated anyone who sneered at Havel's oddball behavior. "This man has been in every prison in Europe. He's suffered." "We were revolutionaries," Day said, "and were supposed to sympathize with the unfortunate, and we did *en masse*. Gene was very responsive to people who suffered."[102]

Maxwell Bodenheim, "the King of Greenwich Village Bohemians" and a contributing playwright for the Provincetown Players that season, quoted O'Neill intoning his political credo that fall in the Hell Hole while flanked by two Hudson Dusters: "If the proletariat and the intellectuals and artists would only get together, they could rule the world. I mean the real ones—not the fake slobs on either side. The gangsters, gunmen, and stokers, joined to the few, important rebels among artists and writers, would make a hot proposition. . . . They're all aristocrats in a different way, and they're all outcasts from the upper worlds of society; and if their eyes ever open up to these resemblances, well, it'll be goodnight government and middle classes! . . . This world will always be ruled by somebody, and the only trouble is that the sharpest minds and the strongest fists have never come together to polish off the job."[103]

"Turn Back the Universe"

The uptown production of *In the Zone*, O'Neill's second *Glencairn* play, was greeted with high praise by almost everyone but its creator. Too much the mainstream thriller for the Playwrights' Theatre, the one-act was accepted by the Washington Square Players, whose premiere on October 31, 1917, at the Comedy Theatre received a flood of glowing reviews. While the Provincetowners actively discouraged critics from attending performances, the Washington Square Players just as actively encouraged them, and *In the Zone* was the play that, according to Edna Kenton, "sprang [O'Neill] into the Broadway lime-light." Among other notices, it roused the *New York Times* to run a fea-ture story with the tantalizing headline, "Who Is Eugene O'Neill?"[104]

The *Times* story celebrated the arrival of O'Neill, just as his early mentor Clayton Hamilton had predicted only a few years before, as the Jack London and Joseph Conrad of American theater: "He knows the haunts of the men when they are on shore, and he swaps yarns with them, not as an outsider but as one of themselves." Although there were four short plays performed back-to-back at the Comedy Theatre, *In the Zone* took up three-quarters of the *New York Times*'s review of the evening, and the *Globe and Commercial Advertiser* gushed over the audacious newcomer as well: "I don't know where this young man got his knowledge of the speech, character, and characteristics of seafaring men, but this is the second play he has written about them with remarkable power and penetration. He makes the sailors in the forecastle of a tramp steamer passing through the submarine zone live for you with a vividness that is quite astonishing. Not only that, but the thing is at various times intensely exciting, thrilling, pathetic, and ironical. . . . A young man who can write such a piece has a marvelous gift."[105]

O'Neill initially rejected a deal for a vaudeville tour, on the grounds of artistic integrity, but then decided that he couldn't afford to turn down the $200 advance and $70 royalty a week (which he split with the Washington Square Players). They were the first royalties of his career and nicely supplemented the weekly $15 allowance he con-tinued to collect from his father. The tour lasted thirty-four weeks but ended as the market for war stories wound down with the war it-self, along with the rise of the 1918 flu pandemic.[106] (The flu claimed three times more lives worldwide than the war, with a death toll of 50 million, and the Provincetown Players weren't immune; among the 675,000 Americans who succumbed to it were Hapgood and Boyce's son Harry in 1918 and O'Neill's New London pal and Provincetown leading man Hutch Collins the following year, 1919.) *Seven Arts* also paid O'Neill $50 for the script. Though the journal folded before it could appear, he still got paid the money, enough to keep him and

Carlin well marinated at the Hell Hole and afford the down payment on one of John Francis's flats in Provincetown summer.[107]

That fall, 1917, an Ohio State University graduate, James "Jimmy" Light, a handsome, blond twenty-two-year old with a dashing mustache and self-satisfied way of tilting his hat, had been accepted on scholarship into a master's program in English at Columbia University and moved in with Charles Ellis above the theater at 139 Macdougal Street. As Light began to unpack, he heard hammering below and went downstairs. There he discovered three men shooting craps while a fourth hammered away at a shoddily built set of wood benches. One of the players was O'Neill, his dark eyes following the dice as they jounced across the floor. When Light criticized the workmanship of the benches, a saw was thrust into his hand. "I started sawing immediately," he said. Then, as he was walking up to his flat with a load of books, the Players "tapped" him for the role of the English instructor in Susan Glaspell's newest play *Close the Book*. Light was a quick study; by 1925, he had acted in thirty-four plays with the Players and had directed, reported the *New York Times*, "more plays by Eugene O'Neill than anyone else in America."[108]

Close the Book appeared on the same bill as O'Neill's *The Long Voyage Home* (just three days after *In the Zone*), a one-act play that's set in a waterfront dive in London and dramatizes the perilous fate of sailors on shore leave. (James Oppenheimer's *Night* concluded the evening.) The *New York Tribune*'s drama critic arrived too late on opening night to be admitted. Standing outside on Macdougal Street, he heard a ruckus within, "consisting chiefly of breaking tableware, punctuated at intervals by guttural male tones and the strident shrieking of a woman." Inside the house was the *Boston Evening Transcript*'s reviewer, who averred of *The Long Voyage Home*, "The substance is the merest penny-dreadful tale, and if it did not carry clear illusion of reality it would be thrown into the rubbish-heap as melodramatic bosh." "Even the hardened newspaper man," he wrote, "is not likely to know that there are so many distinct and individual kinds of drunkenness as are here disclosed." The inevitable result of this kind of sordid talk was that the Players' subscription requests expanded to such an extent they had to begin performing seven nights a week. O'Neill's sea play *Ile* opened next, on November 30, and once again, theater critics hailed O'Neill as American drama's answer to Conrad and for exuding, like Jack London, a refreshingly masculine literary voice, but for the stage, a medium that up to then overwhelmingly catered to a female audience: "This writer, a son of the noted actor, James O'Neil [*sic*], has the faculty of writing 'man stuff' drama that, while gray in tint, is tense and gripping."[109]

O'Neill exulted in his notoriety at first, but became weary of it before long. "It's like everything else, I guess," his character Stephen Murray in *The Straw* remarks of newfound literary success. "When you've got it, you find you don't want it" (*CP1*, 783). Similarly, a few years later, O'Neill responded to Maxwell Bodenheim's letter of congratulations by explaining his avoidance of Bodenheim's beloved Greenwich Village scene: "Well, the saddest part of the 'acclaim' you mention is not that I take it seriously but that other people do, one way or another. Some hate me for it, or envy me, or like me, or use me, or flatter me—all for it—while they seem absolutely unable to see the me they knew ever again. Yet I'm sure I'm still that 'me,' and that I'm lonely, and that it is these stupid folk who change me by their suspicions into a suspicious one. Not that I don't realize all this is inevitable—but it's distressing and I've learned for my sensitive skin's sake to duck and dodge." O'Neill went on to Bodenheim that as his fame grew, he felt punished for it, always "eternally apologetic and self-consciously cringing, seeming to say: forgive me, good people, for having had my name five times in the Evening Journal."[110]

Even worse than the jealousy stewing among the Village "branch of swine," he complained to Louise Bryant, was the chattering, "serpent-tongued" innuendo of what he referred to as the " 'How is Jack' tribe": "How is Jack?" "Have you heard from Louise?" "Are they married yet?" "Is it true they married here before they left?" He could play their pretentious games, expertly when necessary, he told Bryant, but he'd come to loathe the "Tarantulas of the Village." Most of the damning gossip involving O'Neill's romantic conquests Bryant had heard was true, however. "Occasionally," he admitted, "just to show I could and romance their thread-bare souls a bit—hence my reputation for indiscriminate love-making. Love? Great God, what a title you give it! You reminded me of the fact that we are both Irish, and yet you cannot be lenient to—blarney!"[111]

Jim O'Neill swore that his little brother Gene was wasting his talent by not working on Broadway; but this didn't prevent him from enjoying such rewards of downtown life as Christine Ell's beguiling company. Hutch Hapgood considered Ell, with her great height and carrot-colored hair, a character out of Dostoevsky (the Players' unrivaled literary idol) and described her as "the Perfect Lioness." Ell was married to the stagehand and amateur actor Louis Ell, who one night in late November 1917, stormed into the Hell Hole. Not finding Christine there, he shouted that he would divorce her, then marched out, slamming the door behind him. When Ell finally arrived at the bar, she announced that she was there to meet her latest lover—Jim O'Neill.

At around 10:30 that night, a twenty-five-year-old beauty named Agnes Ruby Boulton stepped into the Hell Hole's back room to join Ell for a drink. Boulton, already a well-published fiction writer, had just moved to Greenwich Village from Cornwall Bridge, Connecticut, where she'd been struggling to manage a dairy farm with her parents and two-year-old daughter, Barbara "Cookie" Burton. The ostensible child of Boulton's first husband, James Burton, who she claimed had died under mysterious circumstances in Europe, Cookie had been left in the care of Boulton's parents. Boulton was good friends with Harry Kemp and Mary Pyne, who'd visited her farm the previous summer and no doubt gave her the lowdown on recent happenings in the Village.[112] Once in New York, she checked into the Brevoort Hotel, hoping to land a factory job to earn some quick money and, perhaps, collect material to write about the inner lives of factory girls.

The Players gathered at the Hell Hole that night were struck speechless by how eerily Agnes Boulton resembled Louise Bryant. She was a more classic beauty than Bryant, but otherwise a dead ringer. O'Neill was paralyzed, gaping at her from his dark corner. By now his "type" was clear: slim of build (Boulton was five feet four and just over one hundred pounds), long of neck, dark of hair, high of cheekbone. Boulton remembered catching O'Neill staring at her in those first few moments in the back room as if "he had once known me somewhere."[113]

Jim O'Neill swept in soon enough, flamboyantly dressed like a Broadway dandy with his signature black-and-white checked suit, bowler hat, manicured nails—even a carnation was securely inserted into the buttonhole of his jacket. He was drunk, as usual. "What Ho!" he roared into the murk of the Hell Hole's back room. "Late? Yes! I got lost in the subway, looking for a big blonde with bad breath!" (After a glimpse at Boulton, Jim thought, "High cheek bones—she'll get him.")[114] The two things that impressed Boulton most about Eugene O'Neill were, in her words, "that he was Irish" and "that he was a revolutionary." She was also vaguely disturbed by what so many others had felt before her: the man projected an unnerving, contagious vulnerability, "that of being himself—an awareness on the part of others of his being always intensely aware of himself. . . . This would account for his shyness or whatever it was—which was really an intense self-consciousness." "I want to spend every night of my life from now on with *you*," O'Neill told her after escorting her back to the Brevoort that night. "I mean this. *Every night of my life*."[115]

O'Neill and Boulton's next encounter took place soon after at a party at Christine Ell's Village apartment. For a long time, it wasn't certain whether O'Neill would show. "Where is he now?" Ell shouted. "At the Hell Hole, drunk. Big guy among the gangsters!" When O'Neill did finally arrive, he refused to acknowledge Boulton. She took this as a challenge rather than a snub, and for a time pretended to be "quiet and uninterested." After a while, she couldn't stand it any longer. "Hello!" she said, looking him in the eye, "Remember me?" His response was polite but distant; a few minutes later, he stepped into the next room, took a pint bottle of whiskey from his coat pocket, drained it, and swayed back into the crowd. "With a violent, sardonic, and loud laugh," Boulton recounted, he dragged a chair up to the mantelpiece where a large clock was ticking, stood upon it as if back in his Princeton days, and chanted,

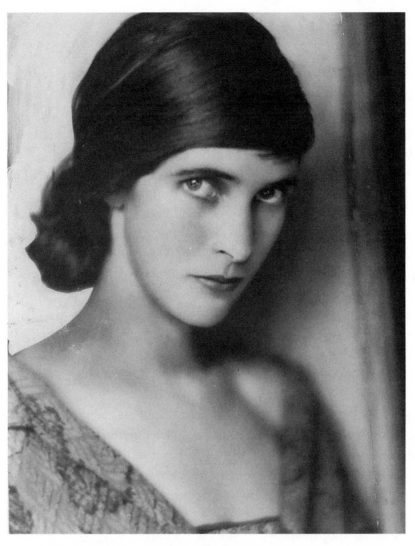

Agnes Boulton.

*   *   *

"Turn back the universe,
And give me yesterday.
TURN BACK"—

O'Neill then opened the glass face of the clock and pried the big hand counterclockwise, his eyes fixed on the little hand as it followed along behind. After this strange communion with the clock, he made a bee-line for Nina Moise. Those who knew him doubtlessly saw his odd behavior at Ell's party as a call for Bryant's return; but he confessed to Boulton afterward that he'd been trying to conceal his overwhelming desire for her. Either way, in the days to follow, O'Neill and Doro-thy Day started to double date with de Polo and Boulton. De Polo, who was married, soon dropped out of the picture, and the remaining three, to use Boulton's term, formed a ménage à trois.[116]

"*I am more beautiful than Dorothy, even though I can't keep a tune!*" Boulton beseeched O'Neill inwardly. "*Please look at me?*"[117] She accused Day of being envious of O'Neill's attraction to her, a charge Day later denied. In fact, the reverse was true. For her part, Day thought Boulton was "much better-looking than Louise ... but without Louise's brains and sophistication." Boulton had nothing to fear from Day, as O'Neill increasingly focused his attention on her; and Day, although she loved him as a friend and admired him as a writer, claims to have been more worried for Boulton than jealous. She believed he'd fallen in love with Bryant because Reed loved her, not for her own sake. "Gene needed a hopeless love," Day said. "Jack was more in love with Louise than Gene was or could ever be. All Gene's experiences were 'copy' to him. So I watched the Agnes-Gene asso-ciation and hoped she would not be too hurt."[118]

Day's fears were justified, as time would bear out, but it was too late. O'Neill convinced Boulton, if not yet himself, that he'd fallen in love with her. Though he felt anguished through the opening weeks of their relationship by the flux of his "painful ardor" for and "bitter-ness" toward Bryant, he was honest to Boulton about his feelings; but he also told her he was unsure Bryant would still be in love with him after the excitement of her exploits in wartorn Russia.[119]

Boulton soon developed misgivings of her own about O'Neill, whose behavior was unaccountably erratic: he had frightening mood swings, made drunken pronouncements of love and hate, and exhibited a paradoxical combination of "contemptuous self-pity" and overweening narcissism. She heard him make "ironic and unkind comments about supposed friends—people to whom he was charming when face to face." And she realized, as had Beatrice Ashe before her, that he did not like children. "I don't understand children," he told her, "they make me uneasy, and I don't know how to act with them." Finally, his views on women were problematic, to say the least. Once he remarked to her, "mockingly perhaps," she admitted, that his ideal woman would be one who performed the composite roles of "mistress, wife, mother, and valet."[120]

What outweighed these concerns for Boulton was his stance as an Irish revolutionary. One night at Sheridan Square, for instance, O'Neill spoke of himself as cut from the same cloth as the great Irish martyrs of the Easter Rising of less than two years before—Patrick Pearse, James Connolly, The O'Rahilly—and he assured her that when the revolution came to America at long last, no matter his belief in nonviolent anarchism, he would take up a machine gun alongside his comrades and mow down the establishment forces. He pointed to one of the square's triangular structures and made an oath that the building would live through the ages as a memorial of American freedom, just as Dublin's General Post Office would for the Irish.[121]

That January 1918, word spread through the Village that Lou Holladay was returning from his trip to Oregon a sober man. On the day of his arrival, Tuesday, January 22, 1918, festivities were set to take place at Christine Ell's restaurant. His friends all swore to respect his sobriety and not offer him a drink, so O'Neill spent the day at the Hell Hole to get ahead of the drinking curve before reuniting with Holladay. Boulton came in, followed by the painters Charles Demuth and Edward Fisk, and they all walked down the block to Christine's, where they met up with Dorothy Day and a few others. When Holladay entered, everyone approvingly remarked upon his physical vigor. "I have never seen anyone so at the peak of his life," Boulton recalled, "so confident and happy. He had conquered. He had come through—and tonight he was going to see his love again and this coming week they were to be married."[122]

It was late at the Hell Hole when Holladay's fiancée, Louise Norton, finally joined the group. The revelers watched uneasily as the two had a tense exchange of words. Then Norton abruptly walked out. She had found someone else in Holladay's absence. That he'd gone to Oregon to sober up as a condition of their marriage made the betrayal sting all the more, and he headed for the bar.

O'Neill escorted Boulton back to her new apartment on Waverly Place, then returned to the Hell Hole to help console his jilted friend. But O'Neill surprised Boulton by returning much earlier than she'd expected. Without saying a word, he curled up beside her in bed fully clothed and grasped her hand like a child. Dorothy Day came over soon after, looking pale and expressionless. "Louis is dead," she murmured. "I knew he would die." She pleaded with O'Neill to return with her to Romany Marie's restaurant at 133 Washington Place, where Holladay's corpse still occupied a table. The coroner had arrived, Day told them, and the police were questioning people. According to Boulton, Day then removed a bag of white powder from her coat pocket, the evidence of what had caused Holladay's heart to fail—heroin. All the while, O'Neill was "fumbling at the edge of horror, refusing to be aware of it."[123]

On the way back to the restaurant, O'Neill stopped abruptly at a street corner and said, in a strained tone of defiance, "I'm going back to the Hell Hole. I'll see you later." Police officers met Boulton and Day at the entrance to Romany Marie's but left them alone. There, the two women stared down at Holladay's propped-up corpse, Boulton remembered, "while a wind from an open window ruffled his hair, and his empty eyes stared into space—those eyes that had been so sure and joyous on his return the afternoon before."[124]

Dawn was just beginning to break, and no one answered Day's knock on the door at the Hell Hole, so they retreated to a nearby café. They were soon joined by a friend of Holladay's and O'Neill's, probably Robert Allerton Parker, who recounted the events of the early morning. After Louise Norton had left, Holladay had begun buying drinks for the house with money he'd saved for his marriage. Later that night he'd somehow got his hands on a vial or two of heroin, though from whom remained unclear. A "shifty character" at the Hell Hole? A restaurant waiter on Prince Street? Terry Carlin?[125] Holladay, Parker, and Charles Demuth got high immediately sniffing it off the back of their hands. (O'Neill, no stranger to altered states of consciousness, always refused hard drugs, the result, no doubt, of growing up the son of an addict.) When the Hell Hole closed, this group and O'Neill went to Romany Marie's restaurant, where they were joined by Day. Once seated at a table, Holladay "half-smiled" at O'Neill and looked over at Day, as if he thought they might understand, then swallowed a huge dose of the drug straight from the vial. Leaning on Day's shoulder, he quietly died. Aside from Demuth and the proprietor Romany Marie (Marie Marchand), all the others made themselves scarce, O'Neill included.[126]

Questions remain whether Holladay intended to commit suicide or whether the overdose was accidental (though in 1944 O'Neill told his third wife, Carlotta Monterey, that he believed it was definitely a suicide).[127] Either way, he'd been drinking alcohol on top of heroin, a lethal combination. When the Hell Hole reopened its doors that morning, Boulton and Day found O'Neill at a table too drunk to speak, with a half-finished pint of Old Taylor bourbon in front of him. As the bar began to fill and excited whispers swirled around Holladay's death, his sister Polly suddenly appeared in the doorway, "sinister and cold," Boulton remembered, "and stood staring around in search of something that she did not find, and went out again, without a word, and without even looking at Gene," one of Holladay's oldest friends and one of the few witnesses to his death.[128]

After several days of oblivion with Jim at the Garden Hotel, O'Neill returned to Boulton and beseeched her to marry him. She told him they should wait, but O'Neill, determined to quit drinking and find long-term happiness with Boulton, bought them both tickets for Provincetown. Faced with the impending return of her rival, Louise

Bryant, Boulton agreed to go. As the Fall River boat pulled away from the pier, O'Neill produced a hidden pint of Old Taylor. Hands shaking uncontrollably, he gulped down a deep swig.[129] Holladay's probable suicide was the first time he'd witnessed a loved one's death, but the next one, tragically, wasn't far off.

Louise Bryant returned to New York in early March 1918 and fired off a bruising letter to O'Neill in Provincetown accusing Agnes Boulton, from what she'd heard in the Village, of enabling his alcoholism. She also demanded to know if he still loved her. O'Neill responded that Boulton accepted him "at my worst—and [she] didn't love me for what she thought I ought to be." "Whether I love her in a deep sense or not," he went on, "I do not yet know. For the past half-year 'love' has seemed like some word in a foreign language of which I do not know the meaning. It dazes me." Bryant also accused O'Neill of having "affairs" with Nina Moise and Elaine Freeman. He denied both but called her out on her hypocrisy: "For over a year and a half I loved you. During most of that time you lived with another man. That is undeniable. What does it matter if physically you were faithful to me—especially considering the circumstances."[130] O'Neill still regarded his passion for her as straight from Irish legend: "And Ailell said to her: 'My desire was a desire that was as long as a year; but it was love given to an echo, the spending of grief on a wave, a lonely fight with a shadow, that is what my love and my desire have been to me.' "[131] "It is more than probable," he told Bryant in this final letter to her, "that you have burned yourself so deep into my soul that the wound will never heal and I stand condemned to love you forever—and hate you for what you have done to my life."[132]

John Francis met O'Neill and Boulton at the Provincetown railroad station and settled them into a temporary studio with a writing loft. When the weather warmed and Francis finished some renovations, they would move into the flat O'Neill and Carlin had occupied the previous summer. "That Gene is a wonderful fellow—a real genius," Francis told Boulton as he showed her around. "I never seen anybody work like he does—when he's working."[133]

O'Neill took full advantage of their idyllic winter at Francis's Flats, completing two one-act plays, *Shell Shock* and *The Rope*. *Shell Shock*, alternately titled "Butts," "A Smoke," and "At Jesus's Feet," was O'Neill's third attempt to dramatize the horrors of World War I. Whereas his first, *The Sniper*, takes place in Belgium, with Belgian and Prussian characters, and the second, *In the Zone*, on a steamship passing through the German U-boat "zone," *Shell Shock* is set on the home front, in a student grill at Harvard University. (Unlike the other two plays, *Shell Shock* was never produced in O'Neill's lifetime.)

The Rope is a cynical inversion of the biblical tale of the prodigal or "lost" son (Luke 15:11–32). A young man named "Luke" Bentley claims his inheritance before his father's death and squanders the money. He's an unrepentant wastrel who unmistakably resembles Jim O'Neill, with his "good-natured, half-foolish grin, his hearty laugh, his curly dark hair, a certain devil-may-care recklessness and irresponsible youth in voice and gesture" (*CP1*, 556). (In 1909, Jim had played the title character in the popular play *The Prodigal Son*.)[134] Luke is also a stand-in for O'Neill himself: "You country jays oughter wake up and see what's goin' on," Luke tells his brother-in-law. "Look at me. I was green as grass when I left here, but bummin' round the world, and bein' in cities, and meetin' all kinds, and keepin' your two eyes open—that's what'll learn yuh a cute trick or two" (*CP2*, 561–62). Though O'Neill had lived a dissolute vagabond's existence, he'd become even more of a prodigal in the theater world. Indeed, if his father James's plays were meant to offer uplift with redemption and reconciliation, O'Neill's spiteful Luke never redeems himself. Far from it. Luke's experiences abroad do little but confirm his contempt for his family and its small-town parochialism.[135]

The Players accepted *The Rope* for that April, though O'Neill and Nina Moise argued over the script. O'Neill respected Moise's directing, but she wanted to cut most of the exposition in the first scene, while he insisted that "if the thing is acted naturally all that exposition will come right out of the characters themselves. *Make them act!*"[136] Moise capitulated, and the play opened to strong reviews, despite her concerns, on April 26 at the Playwrights' Theatre.

Toward the end of this same letter to Moise, O'Neill informed her, almost offhandedly, that he'd gotten married two days earlier, April 12, in the "best parlor" of the local parsonage. The clergyman, one Reverend William L. Johnson, was "the most delightful, feeble-minded Godhelpus, mincing Methodist minister that ever prayed through his nose." "I don't mean to sneer, really," he added. "The worthy divine is an utterly lovable old idiot, and the ceremony gained a strange, unique simplicity from his sweet, childlike sincerity. I caught myself wishing I could believe in the same gentle God he seemed so sure of. This seems like sentimentality but it isn't."[137]

After Boulton had agreed to marry him, they'd decided to delay the nuptials until April. They did so for a couple of reasons: she didn't trust that O'Neill was over Bryant (their sole witness at the ceremony, Alice Woods Ullman, overheard Boulton berate O'Neill, "You still love Louise as much as ever"), and he worried over the "detail and personal exposure that it would put him through."[138] One rather alarming "detail" has eluded scholars, personal friends, and family members alike about O'Neill's marriage to Boulton: either their marriage was legally invalid or, at the very least, O'Neill was in contempt of court. The judge who wrote the interlocutory judgment of O'Neill's divorce from Kathleen Jenkins, had decreed that O'Neill could not remarry "without the express permission" of the White Plains court, which O'Neill did not receive to marry Boulton. The final judgment on default, filed on October 11, 1912, and only open to the public one hundred years and a day later, gave Jenkins the right to marry again "in like manner as if the defendant [O'Neill] were dead." But as for O'Neill, the second judge assigned the case had ruled unambiguously that "it shall not be lawful for the defendant to marry any person other than the plaintiff in the lifetime of the plaintiff."[139]

O'Neill received a copy of this final judgment, but the philosophical anarchist in him evidently chose to ignore it.[140] He didn't even inform Boulton that he'd been married or had a child until that August. When he broke this news, he claimed that "any consequences such as divorce, money or anything else—I never thought of it. I guess . . . I just didn't consider myself a married man. I left everything to Papa. He was grim-lipped and said nothing about anything."

O'Neill's contravention of the judge's order aside, Kathleen Jenkins, who at one point admitted she'd been "deeply in love" with him, had little reason to contest her ex-husband's marriage. She'd married George Pitt-Smith in 1915, and the two were raising Eugene Jr., who was almost eight, in Little Neck, Long Island. They'd even changed the boy's name to Richard Pitt-Smith. "No," Jenkins recalled, "we never saw each other again [after O'Neill's return from Buenos Aires]. Why should we? We were two people ignoring one another's existence."[141]

During the previous summer in Provincetown, 1917, O'Neill chanced upon the title for his first mature full-length play. One evening while he was perched on a dock awaiting the arrival of a local fishing boat, a slow-minded local boy named Howard Slade sat down beside him.[142] "What's beyond the ocean?" Slade asked. "Europe." "What's beyond Europe?" the boy persisted. "The horizon," O'Neill said. "What's beyond the horizon?"[143]

O'Neill completed his tragedy *Beyond the Horizon* in his and Boulton's studio that spring of 1918 and dedicated it to Boulton. Robert Mayo, the play's autobiographical protagonist, lives with his parents and older brother Andrew on a New England farm. But Robert dreams of experiencing life "beyond the horizon," a metaphor he repeatedly invokes. His wanderlust is quashed by the more powerful drive to explore a romantic relationship with a local girl, Ruth Atkins, whom everyone had assumed would marry his more practical brother Andrew, an able farmer. In this way, Robert condemns himself to an ironic fate in that he pursues the life of rural domesticity meant for his brother; and Robert's decision to marry Ruth and remain on the farm goads Andrew into taking his brother's place at sea. Andrew's fate is thus also tragic—by following Robert's path, he falls into a materialist trap bereft of the spiritual meaning he once knew on the farm. The draw of sex and the power of jealousy impel both brothers to enact a role reversal that ends, fatalistically, in love lost for Ruth (who discovers she loved Andrew after all), the death of their child, Mary, emotional and financial bankruptcy for Andrew, and the release of death for Robert.

O'Neill conceived this plot while recalling a Norwegian sailor from his time aboard the *Charles Racine* who pined for his family farm and cursed the day he first signed on to a ship (the character Olson in *The Long Voyage Home* is also based on him). O'Neill sensed that the Norwegian's complaints were disingenuous, since in his twenty years at sea, he'd not once returned to Norway. O'Neill asked himself, "What if he had stayed on the farm, with his instincts? What would have happened?"[144] "But I realized at once he never would have stayed. . . . And from that point I started to think of a more intellectual, civilized type . . . a man who would have my Norwegian's inborn craving for the sea's unrest, only in him it would be conscious, too conscious, intellectually diluted into a vague, intangible, romantic wanderlust. His powers of resistance, both moral and physical, would also probably be correspondingly watered. He would throw away his instinctive dream and accept the thralldom of the farm for— why, for almost any nice little poetical craving—the romance of sex, say."[145]

Fortuitously, O'Neill sent the script to the well-connected *Smart Set* editors H. L. Mencken and George Jean Nathan. Nathan, the celebrated "father of American drama criticism," forwarded it on to the powerful Broadway producer John D. Williams. Williams loved it. It was precisely the kind of script he'd been searching for—an authentically American tragedy—and he wrote O'Neill a check to option the play for six months. "I have been trying to get [Joseph] Conrad to do a play for me," Williams affirmed. "His stories of the sea are so marvelous, but he simply cannot write a play. I wanted something with a feeling of the sea, without the sea scenes. . . . In *Beyond the Horizon* the farm is played against the sea, and is the adventuring spirit of the latter. It is the most honest tragedy I have ever seen. . . . It is utterly devoid of 'stage English,' and is the only play by an American author I have ever seen which is."[146]

O'Neill and Boulton were in a festive mood and decided to spend their recent windfall on an informal honeymoon in New York. It was there, with Jim at the Garden Hotel, that Boulton witnessed for the first time the true severity of her husband's alcohol problem.

O'Neill oversaw rehearsals of *The Rope* but otherwise avoided the Village "tarantulas." (Louise Bryant, not incidentally, was sighted at the Hell Hole dressed in a flashy embroidered red jacket and high black boots from Russia demanding to know where he was.) O'Neill was also determined to stay sober: "I will never, or never have written anything good when I am drinking," he told Boulton, "or even when the miasma of drink is left." He'd also grown "terrified" about the damage alcohol was inflicting on his brain. A doctor told him that the brain had the texture of raw egg white, and alcohol "toughened" the tissue like it was cooked.[147] Nevertheless, if O'Neill wasn't writing, he was drinking, especially when Jim was around.

From New York, Boulton took the train down to New Jersey, where her family had returned after leaving the farm in Connecticut. Her father needed help with the upkeep of their family home, known to the Boultons as the Old House, where she had grown up, about seventy miles south of the city in West Point Pleasant. When she returned to New York, her husband had finished his work on *The Rope* with the Provincetown Players and, to her delight, had remained sober. Not wishing to tempt fate, they planned to leave for Provincetown the following day. When the next day came, however, he accepted a drink from Jim, a backslide that began innocently enough with a pull from a bottle of Old Taylor. That pull stranded them in their hotel room for over a week. "What I did not know then," Boulton said, "was that after one drink the cycle must be fulfilled."[148]

The brothers drank pint after pint of Old Taylor, starting from when they awoke late in the morning to when they passed out in the early hours of the following day. Jim ate his meals at a nearby restaurant, but O'Neill never left his room and survived on soup and brandy-laced milkshakes from the bar downstairs. After a few days, only the milkshakes would stay down. Boulton repeatedly traveled uptown to Grand Central Station to buy tickets back to Massachusetts; and just as repeatedly, O'Neill would wake up, initiate the day's souse with what he called a "hooker," or a large shot, emptying whatever was left in the bottle from the previous night. He mulishly ignored her pleas to leave, but eventually she got him onto a train, this time with

Jim conspicuously in tow. At the transfer in Boston, Jim wandered off and reappeared with a flea-bitten mongrel he named Bowser, arguing with the conductor until the dog was allowed to travel in the luggage car. For the length of the journey, Jim swayed up and down the corridors obstreperously demanding the company of a "big blonde with bad breath."[149]

Upon their return to Provincetown, O'Neill and Boulton moved into O'Neill and Carlin's old apartment in Francis's Flats, where the rafters still heralded their mantra from *Light on the Path*, and Jim was installed in a room down the hall.[150] The Provincetown arts crowd was now in awe of the rising theatrical star. In less than two years' time, he'd written over twenty plays, eight of which, after *The Rope* opened that April, had already been produced in New York. The fact that O'Neill rarely appeared at cocktail parties and didn't join any social clubs only added to his mystique; he'd also developed a reputation for being one of the hardest-working artists in the bohemian beach community, where loafing was the accepted summer pastime. He routinely ended his work day by crossing Commercial Street and spending long hours in deep consultation with Susan Glaspell, exchanging playwriting ideas (a ritual that deeply incensed Boulton).[151] Glaspell's handwritten notes for a talk she'd give later about her time working with O'Neill in Provincetown convey briefly but tellingly O'Neill's unique style in the years to come: "Hands himself everything—sea—fate—God—murder—suicide—incest—insanity. Always the search for new forms. Because necessary to what he would express."[152]

O'Neill and his brother's bender at the Garden Hotel that spring made O'Neill's first couple of weeks in Provincetown a torturous exercise in self-control; but once he'd succeeded in "tapering off" and shedding the "miasma" of drink altogether, he worked at a feverish pace. He began with a daring one-act called *The Dreamy Kid*, a dialect play about the early years of black migration and one of his first of several forays into the African American experience. Prior to his and Boulton's hard-won departure from Manhattan, O'Neill had reunited with a cadre of drinking cronies at the Garden who were unaffected by the venom of the Village gossips. Joe Smith from the Hell Hole was there, and he told O'Neill about a black gangster in New York with the street moniker "Dreamy." O'Neill spoke the name lovingly. "Dreamy," he laughed. "A Negro gangster named Dreamy. . . . *Why* Dreamy?"[153] (The Players rejected *The Dreamy Kid* for the fall season but would produce it the following year, a white company with an all-black cast, making it yet another first.)

O'Neill had also decided that spring, in his words, to "cut loose from paternal aid," the $10 a week from his father, "not in anger but in confidence of independence which is liable to prove premature."[154] This last point was true enough: when Harold de Polo and his wife, Helen, arrived in Provincetown in May, they found that the O'Neills had left for New York. (De Polo later claimed that they'd gone for Boulton to obtain an abortion.)[155] De Polo soon received a wire from Fall River, Massachusetts, begging for $25 for a return ticket to Provincetown, as O'Neill had drunk away their money for the connecting train. De Polo wired the cash, then received another frantic wire from Boulton: Gene was "dying." De Polo didn't take this seriously; he knew Boulton wasn't yet savvy about O'Neill's drinking habits. But he acknowledged that his friend was "probably a damned sick lad due to his custom of refusing to eat when drinking heavily."[156]

When de Polo embarked on his rescue mission, a lonely stranger took the seat next to him, though the train was nearly empty. He apologized but said he "just *had* to talk." This was the writer Sinclair Lewis, then laboring on his breakout novel, *Main Street*. Lewis joined de Polo when they got off at Fall River, and the two men discovered O'Neill and Boulton at the Hotel Mellen. As de Polo had suspected, O'Neill was "gloriously and happily drunk." They went out for three more pints of "bottled-in-bond bourbon" and stayed up drinking and talking until five in the morning, de Polo said, "a particularly wonderful time, with great conversation being had by all."[157] Lewis then spared them the ticket price and drove them back to Provincetown in his car.

"I was at a snooty temperamental stage of souse," O'Neill told the playwright Sidney Howard years later, "where I'd be damned if I'd descend to travelling on a dirt plebian railroad train." Lewis, he added, "rescued me from a week's binge in Fall River . . . and volunteered to bear the remains to Provincetown." O'Neill wrote this just prior to winning the Nobel Prize in Literature, the second American do to so after Lewis himself. When Howard threatened, in fun, to publish this letter, O'Neill replied, "As for your dire threat to ruin Nobel majesty with my letter about Lewis's rescue work in Fall River, all I can say is, go to it with my grateful blessing! This being Eminent, even if it's only for a few days, is a most godforsaken pain in the neck."[158]

Safely back in Provincetown, O'Neill and Boulton were still tormented by their shortage of funds. They both acknowledged that fiction was the most reliable moneymaker, so de Polo shopped around O'Neill's story "The Screenews of War," which he'd written in New London back in 1916, at a couple of "smooth-paper magazines." "It didn't, alas, sell," de Polo admitted, "hanged if I know why." O'Neill grinned after the second rejection notice and told him, "To hell with it. Throw it away if you want." (De Polo didn't share O'Neill's predilection for destroying literary work, whatever the quality, and "The Screenews of War" was brought to light in 2007.)[159]

Boulton, an accomplished fiction writer, was herself struggling over several pieces that summer, including a short story she entitled "The Captain's Walk": "Old Captain Curtis . . . cannot let go, in spite of his age, his uselessness. The sight and sound of the sea awake in him a passionate longing for something more tangible. His lost ship on which his thoughts dwell becomes the symbol of all this. . . . After prowling for a while through the silent house he always winds up by going up to the walk and keeping watch there for the boat that does not return." O'Neill read the piece with interest, but bluntly informed her it wasn't dramatic enough. Boulton explained that she meant it as "a story of atmosphere and obsession," like *The Moon of the Caribbees*, but O'Neill co-opted the project and titled it *Where the Cross Is Made*. In the spirit of exchange, he offered her his full-length satire *Now I Ask You* to rewrite. "It's not my sort of stuff," he said, "but it's a damn good idea for a popular success." He suggested she make it a novel or improve the play, but instead she turned her attention to a new story of hers titled "The Letter."[160]

Time and again to clear their heads after a morning's work, O'Neill and Boulton found themselves rambling on long hikes through the pine forests and sand dunes to Peaked Hill Bar, a converted life-saving station on the peninsula's northern shore. Locals called the region "the outside," as Glaspell documented in her play by that title, "an arm that bends to make a harbor—where men are safe . . . [where] dunes meet woods and woods hold dunes from a town that's shore to a harbor." The station had been sold to the financier and art collector Sam Lewisohn by the U.S. Life-Saving Service, and Mabel Dodge supervised its renovation into a picturesque summer bungalow. "This is the house you and I should have!" O'Neill proclaimed to his new wife. "We would live like sea gulls, two sea gulls coming home at night to our home."[161]

For their next New York season, 1918–19, the Provincetown Players removed themselves to a larger space at 133 Macdougal Street, an old horse and carriage stable called Claflin's three doors down from the Playwrights' Theatre. Once again, they were hard up for cash; but a theater "angel," Dr. Albert Coombs Barnes (best known for popularizing Argyrol, a treatment for gonorrhea), offered the Players $1,000 to renovate the building if they could raise enough to match the gift. They did so, thanks to their new secretary M. [Mary] Eleanor Fitzgerald, known as "Fitzie," a political activist associated with Emma Goldman and Alexander Berkman who had an unparalleled flair for down-to-the-last-minute fund-raising. The Players now had a box office and dressing rooms in the basement, and the house seated nearly 200, up from 150. Christine Ell's restaurant went with them, though the odor of cooking from the second floor intermingled, audience members complained, with the former stable's "faint, pungent aroma of horses and manure."[162]

Jack Reed's passion for the theater of dissent never subsided while he covered the Russian Revolution. Just after his return, he regaled his friends at the Harvard Club with tales of the political theater he'd attended: "You know, right behind the lines, they're doing a production of *Hamlet*—and you ought to see it, it's the greatest production of *Hamlet* I've ever seen. And it's announced as *Hamlet: A Study in*

Danish Imperialism!"[163] Reed insisted that the Players keep an old cross tie ring screwed firmly into the auditorium's right wall. This would remind them, he said, of their populist roots. About the ring, one of the Players' designers, Donald Corley, painted in striking letters a rousing motto for their new playhouse: "Here Pegasus was Hitched."[164]

The meaning and provenance of that inscription has remained a mystery over the years. But a lighthearted exposé penned by the illustrator and hack writer W. Livingston Larned had circulated in the popular theater tabloid, the *New York Review*, just after the Players had transferred to Greenwich Village in November 1916. In this droll account, "Below Washington Square," Larned pokes fun at the epidemic of idleness among the Village's bohemian crowd:

> It goes with poetry and sich,
>   To loaf around the flowing bowl;
> A genius, somehow, hates to hitch
>   Pegasus up—th' lazy soul.
> Bring on another jug of wine;
>   Th' garlic's running fine, tonight.
> "Say . . . read this little jig of mine;
>   And . . . won't you buy a chap a bite?"

(Larned credited these lines to *A Merchant of Venice*, act 4, scene 3. There is no act 4, scene 3 in Shakespeare's play.) "Look 'em over," Larned said of the Village gadabouts, "these young folks, sooner or later, awake to the wastefulness of their funny Bohemia and climb out and up to safety. While they're wading around in the dregs, however, they're interesting."[165]

The Players debunked such stereotypes by hitching Pegasus up at 133 Macdougal with unbounded creative energy and personal sacrifice. Once the proper permits had been acquired from the Tenement House and Building Department, the Players—galvanized by Jig Cook, who slept on the stage after working hours—constructed an inclined auditorium floor to maximize the audience's view and fashioned comfortable seating with padded cushions and backs. They painted the walls a "rich tawny orange," the ceilings a "deep blue," and the proscenium a "dark smoke gray." Houselights and a control board were installed, and the new curtain opened and closed with silky effortlessness. Lacking the advantage of fly lofts above the stage, brawny stagehands would extract and replace the sets, without pulleys, through a slot in the floor that led to their basement set-construction shop. Although the name wouldn't be official for a couple of years, Cook began "The Provincetown Players Fund," and they hung a painted shingle out front that read simply, "Provincetown Playhouse." [166]

"The Town Is Yours"

The Players celebrated O'Neill's return to New York with a homecoming party and embraced Boulton as one of their own. After that, O'Neill and Boulton went to a restaurant with actor Teddy Ballantine and his wife, Stella, O'Neill's friend Saxe Commins's sister. O'Neill's

The Provincetown Playhouse at 133 Macdougal Street, New York City.
(PHOTO BY BERENICE ABBOT. © BERENICE ABBOTT/COMMERCE GRAPHICS)

✳   ✳   ✳

thirst for liquor was particularly overpowering. His mother had just been diagnosed with breast cancer that fall, which resulted in a successful, if terrifying, mastectomy procedure (and a brief relapse of her drug addiction). O'Neill knew that if he wanted not to get too "tight," he should drink whiskey with a lot of water. He did so and tolerated the teasing good-humoredly; but a whiskey bottle was inevitably passed around, and O'Neill helped himself to a straight drink. Spotting this, Boulton whispered that maybe they should leave. He pushed her backward and then, "his mouth distorted with an ironic grin," slapped her hard across the face with the back of his hand. Boulton, in a state of shock, was hastily led out by Stella Ballantine. "It means nothing, my dear, nothing!" Stella tried to reassure her. "Genius is like that, my dear! Genius must have its outlet!" Late that night, Boulton said, O'Neill pitifully returned to his wife, "a sick man."[167]

Jimmy Light, who was cast as the captain's son in the upcoming production of *Where the Cross Is Made*, showed up at O'Neill's hotel a few days later. O'Neill had avoided Macdougal Street after his loutish behavior, but his presence was required at the dress rehearsal. Among the actors, according to Edna Kenton, the play had given rise to "one prolonged argument, to give it no more brutal name."[168] Hutch Collins, playing the psychotic captain, and Ida Rauh, who both directed and played the female lead, tried to convince O'Neill that a group of ghosts he called for in the final scene should be imagined rather than played by actors. Ghosts, they argued, do not tread their feet on floorboards, and the audience might find such an incongruity more hilarious than terrifying. The Players were reluctant to take such a gamble, particularly on the opening night of the season.

What was left unspoken was their mutual fear of a new adversary—the critic. Although they retained their policy of making critics pay for their own tickets, opening night at the new theater was sure to attract a fair number of scoop mongers willing to pay out of pocket. "We begged Gene, as if it were a favor to the dying, to cut the ghosts," Kenton recalled.[169] "No," he said after watching the scene rehearsed. "They're rotten, but they won't be so bad tomorrow night, beyond the first twenty rows anyway. This play presumes that every-body is mad but the girl, that everybody sees the ghosts but the girl. Everybody but the girl means everybody in this house but the girl. I want to see whether it's possible to make an audience go mad too."[170]

O'Neill was right: when the houselights went green and the ghosts appeared, Heywood Broun, writing for the *New York Tribune* and one of the few willing to pay the ticket price, had been seated too close to appreciate the "visual illusion," he said, "but the sweep of the story and the exceptional skill with which the scene of the delusion is written made us distinctly fearful of the silent dead men who walked across the stage."[171] In spite of the play's relative success, O'Neill had never taken it seriously. "It was great fun to write," he said, "theatri-cally very thrilling, an amusing experiment in treating the audience as insane—that is all it means or ever meant to me."[172]

Conversely, on December 20, the Players staged for their sec-ond bill a play O'Neill took very seriously indeed: *The Moon of the Caribbees*. Set on the forward deck of the fictional *Glencairn* at anchor off Port of Spain, Trinidad, *The Moon of the Caribbees* features a mélange of over twenty seamen drinking rum, brawling, and whoring; the men cavort with West Indian "bumboat" women as Old Tom, the "Donkeyman" (or engineer), looks on in toler-ant amusement and listens patiently as Smitty, based on O'Neill's actual Buenos Aires acquaintance, recounts memories of his lost love back home. The West Indian dirge ethereally drifting over the gunnels from the island was performed by poet Edna St. Vincent Millay, her two sisters, and their mother.[173] "It was a mood play, and the Millay family provided the background music, which set the mood," Jimmy Light's wife, Susan Jenkins Brown, remembered. "It was all swooping vocal harmonies—they weren't seen, and . . . well, it was unearthly."[174]

O'Neill avowed that *The Moon of the Caribbees* signaled his most conscious revolt against the "conventional construction of the theatre as it is." Indeed, one of the two mystified critics in attendance consid-ered the "mood play" "just an interlude of a drama, with prelude and afterlude left to the imagination of the spectators." O'Neill ignored such gainsayers and in hindsight contended with immense satisfaction that *The Moon* "was my first real break with theatrical traditions. Once I had taken this initial step the other plays followed logically."[175]

On the night before *Where the Cross Is Made* had opened, O'Neill and Boulton fled to her ancestral home, the Old House, in West Point Pleasant, New Jersey. Life there proved as rustic and uneventful as O'Neill could have hoped for; and he remained mostly sober, aside from the occasional drunken excursion to monitor the Players' progress with *The Moon of the Caribbees*. He and Boulton were amused to discover that a rumor had spread around town that O'Neill was a drug addict. "Doesn't your husband take drugs?" a wary local woman asked. "Those walks—those long walks! It ain't natural, a man walking like that. . . . I've passed him looking so quiet, you could tell he wasn't drinking, so I calculated he must have been taking drugs."[176]

Boulton's family had moved back to West Point Pleasant from Connecticut, but O'Neill and Boulton had the place to themselves. Prior to their arrival, Boulton's father Teddy, an accomplished artist himself, had amiably agreed to remove the family so his son-in-law could work in peace. Over the bitterly cold winter months at the Old House, O'Neill completed two plays he'd sketched out in Provincetown the summer before: *The Straw*, about his convalescence at Gaylord Farm, and *Chris Christophersen*, about his friend of that name from Jimmy the Priest's. He checked the mail obsessively, but still no word arrived from John Williams about a production schedule for *Beyond the Horizon*, and Williams's frustrating reticence spurred O'Neill to hire his first (and lifelong) agent, Richard J. Madden of the American Play Company.

Boulton visited her daughter at her family's provisional house nearby, but "only for a few minutes," she recalled. "Cookie," as Barbara was nicknamed, "appeared astonished and detached" when she received a hug, but was "mildly pleased" by her present of a glass angel figure adorned with a bouquet of flowers.[177] Boulton didn't tell O'Neill about the visit, or even that her family was in the vicinity; but he found out from neighbors. "What's the idea of not telling me your family was here?" he demanded.[178] But she knew her husband well enough—the first time her sisters Margery and Barbara visited the Old House, he hid in a closet. Eventually, though, he found the Boultons enjoyable company, particularly her free-thinking grandmother and Teddy, who'd been friends with Algernon Swinburne, one of O'Neill's favorite poets.[179] The sentiment proved mutual, which was fortunate, given that Boulton would discover that winter that she was pregnant.

Back in Provincetown in May 1919, rather than moving back into Francis's Flats as usual, O'Neill and Boulton moved into a home of their own—Peaked Hill Bar, the renovated life-saving station nestled among the dunes on the uninhabited, weather-exposed northern shore. Ella O'Neill, though she'd frowned upon her son's marriage to "the Irish servant girl," had persuaded James to purchase them this spectacular, if belated, wedding present on Provincetown's "outside."[180]

"Peaked Hill Bar." The name alone brought to mind the sea in all its romance, danger and, for O'Neill, solace. "The Atlantic for a front lawn, miles of sand dunes for a back yard," he rhapsodized. "No need to wear clothes—no vestige of the unrefined refinements of civilization." The wooden rafters were strung with wire to prevent high winds from blowing the roof into the sea, and Mabel Dodge had modernized the kitchen with state-of-the-art appliances; enlisting expert aid from the artist Maurice Sterne and set designer Robert Edmond Jones, she'd also "fitted it up inside" with coat upon coat of white and blue paint, giving the light-drenched interior a celestial ambiance. Stepping into the house from the beach, the effect was that one hadn't left the outside, but rather that the rooms had been merged with the sand and sky and ocean.[181]

O'Neill had a knack for outlining his sets for designers in his stage directions and often sketched out his own designs; in a 1921 interview, he described the interior of his breathtaking new estate as if composing a new play: "The interiors of the buildings ... still preserve their old sea flavor. The stairs are like companionways of a ship. There are lockers everywhere. An immense open fireplace. The big boat room, now our living room, still has the steel fixtures in the ceiling from which one of the boats was slung. The lookout station on the roof is the same as when the coast guards spent their eternal two-hour vigils there. The exteriors of the buildings are as weather-beaten as the bulwarks of a derelict. The glass in the windows is ground frosty by the flying sands of the winter storms. . . . The place has come to mean a tremendous lot to me. I feel a true kinship and harmony with life out there."[182]

O'Neill's writing studio was set up on the second floor, where the sand-scraped windows overlooked the North Atlantic. The room was fitted with a captain's chair and a desk constructed from driftwood; and he adorned his walls, like his room at Princeton (if without the women's undergarments and used condoms), with fishing nets and old floats. When O'Neill was struggling over a difficult bit of dia-logue, he'd step onto the look-out platform and, in blissful solitude, take in his private view of the open sea. Other than the odd fishing or life-saving boat, no sign of civilization disrupted the panoramic coastal scenery for miles in any direction.

Most of his first summer there was spent revising *Chris Christo-phersen* while awaiting the birth of his and Boulton's first child. The actual Christopherson from Jimmy the Priest's, like his fictional coun-terpart, inveighed repeatedly against "dat ole davil, sea."[183] "When I knew him," O'Neill told a reporter, "he was on the beach, a real down-and-outer. He wouldn't ship out, although it was the only work he knew, and he spent his time getting drunk and cursing the sea. 'Dat ole davil,' he called it. Finally he got a job as captain of a coal barge." O'Neill reported that in 1917, Christopherson "got terribly drunk down at Jimmy's . . . and reeled off at about two o'clock in the morn-ing for his barge. On Christmas morning he was found in the river, frozen to death."[184] In fact, the old barge skipper had accidentally fallen into New York Harbor on October 15, 1917, and his remains were found a week later floating off Liberty Island.[185]

O'Neill wrote each morning after breakfast and ended his work-day around one o'clock with a sandwich and a nap. In the afternoons he took long swims, sunbathed nude among the dunes, or strolled along the coastline with Boulton. Together they broke up flocks of

Peaked Hill Bar in Provincetown.

* * *

sandpipers that gathered at the water's edge and analyzed horseshoe crabs; for exercise, especially if it rained, O'Neill pounded away at a punching bag he'd installed in the back room. Most evenings he read in his white Morris chair until eleven or so, then went to bed at midnight. "Gene was beautiful that summer," Boulton recalled, "tall and brown and tender and smiling, working all morning, lying for hours in the sun, absorbing life and courage and hope from the sea."[186]

Over time, however, Peaked Hill Bar's remoteness proved as much a curse as a blessing. O'Neill and Boulton's volatile personalities had steadily begun to chafe against each other. Any trip to town required an onerous slog across dunes and pine forests, and socializing was reserved for summer guests who braved the three-mile tramp out. No road led to the site, and their mail and supplies had to be delivered by horse-drawn carts. They rarely went into town more than once a week, where they would visit with Susan Glaspell and Jig Cook, Mary Vorse, Hutch Hapgood and Neith Boyce, and Teddy and Stella Ballantine, among others on the East End.

That September, they rented a small cottage called Happy Home behind Cook and Glaspell's house on Commercial Street so Boulton would be closer to their doctor and supplies for the baby, who was due in October. Boulton's mother and nineteen-year-old sister Margery came to stay with her as the birth approached. On September 10, Boulton and her family bunked with the Ballantines while Happy Home was prepped and sterilized. O'Neill worked at Peaked Hill Bar but made frequent trips to town. He was surprised to discover, given his lifelong aversion to children, that he looked forward to the child's arrival. As the due date loomed closer, he rented another cottage across from Happy Home. It was there that he wrote his one-act *Exorcism*, the narrative of his suicide attempt that ends on an exultant note of rebirth, while the actual birth of his son was about to take place a stone's throw away.[187] He gave the corrected typescript to Boulton, either for her to type up a clean script for the Players or as a present—probably both. (O'Neill's motivation for treating his first wife, Kathleen Jenkins, so shabbily in the play might be in part explained by Boulton's ardent jealousy.) "[God] evidently wants to retain my services here below," Ned/O'Neill says after surviving the attempt on his life, "for what I don't know yet but I'm going to find out—and I feel of use already!"[188]

O'Neill stood at Boulton's bedside as Shane Rudraighe O'Neill was born on October 30. He was named for the sixteenth-century Irish chieftain Séan an Díomais Ó Néill, known to the ages as "Shane the Proud." "Shane the Loud!" O'Neill chuckled, gazing down at the howling newborn. "It'll be *us* still from now on," he said. "Us—alone—but the three of us. . . . A sort of Holy Trinity, eh, Shane?" Ella O'Neill, the elated new grandmother, wrote a warm (if backhandedly malicious) congratulatory note to her son: "I am one of the happiest old ladies in New York tonight to know I have such a wonderful grandson but no more wonderful than you were when you were born and weighed *eleven* pounds and no *nerves* at that time. I am enclosing a picture of you taken at three months. Hope your *boy* will be as *good looking*."[189]

The Dreamy Kid premiered at Macdougal Street the day after Shane's birth. Jig Cook had taken a leave of absence to write his full-length play *The Spring* in Provincetown, and Jimmy Light took the helm of the Provincetown Playhouse. Under his directorship, the Players doubled down on their revolutionary methods by flouting the long-standing tradition of white companies using white actors in blackface and instead hired an all-black cast. O'Neill's future associate and close friend Kenneth Macgowan, though he was a stranger at the time, raved that *The Dreamy Kid* was "short, sharp, and incisive. Its people live. Its story moves. It is full of 'punch.' "[190]

During his last month in Provincetown, before returning to New York, O'Neill preoccupied himself, along with fathering his newborn, with trying to sell *The Straw* either to the Washington Square Players, who'd recently renamed themselves the Theatre Guild, or to George C. Tyler, once his father's advance man from the old days of *Monte Cristo* but now a major Broadway producer. O'Neill admitted to Tyler, who did eventually buy it, that he was "in the devil of a hurry . . . because it is my pet play and I am anxious to hug to my heart the certainty that it *is* going to be done."[191]

For $6 a week, the O'Neills hired the French-born widow of a Provincetown sea captain named Fifine Clark (soon nicknamed "Gaga") as a nanny for Shane and general "dame of all work."[192] Once Boulton was settled, with Terry Carlin left behind to sponge from her in the name of domestic assistance, O'Neill hopped the train to New York with Jig Cook and Hutch Hapgood. The tasks at hand were threefold: he would find a producer for *The Straw*, get straight answers from George Tyler about *Chris Christophersen*, and ascertain at long last John Williams's plans for *Beyond the Horizon*.

O'Neill resolved to steer clear of the Macdougal Street crowd while in New York and took a room down the hall from his parents at the Prince George Hotel. But the reunion was less than cheerful: his father had been diagnosed with intestinal cancer, he reported back, "so serious that Mama was going to summon the priest and wire for Jim and me at one time."[193] Instead of a priest, they summoned Dr. John Aspell, the oncologist who'd performed Ella's mastectomy in 1918. Dr. Aspell stabilized him for the time being, but the prognosis was not good.

O'Neill got down to business nevertheless; now armed with an agent, Richard Madden, he felt that he'd reached a level of professionalism requiring a semblance of decorum. So he went shopping with his mother at Lord & Taylor's for more reputable attire for his meetings with Tyler and Williams. The meetings went well. Tyler bought *Chris Christophersen*, shortened to *Chris*, and Williams assured O'Neill that *Beyond the Horizon* was slotted for February. He'd also made another important connection the previous spring, one that would result in one of his closest friendships and gain him a powerful defender for the remainder of his career—*Smart Set* editor and drama critic George Jean Nathan. O'Neill and Nathan were a perfect fit, both professionally and personally, and at the time of their second meeting, at the Royalton Hotel, Nathan was "gratified" to find O'Neill "as proficient at drinking cocktails as at concocting dramas."[194]

By the late fall of 1919, though, the Eighteenth Amendment and the Volstead Act had made liquor a frustratingly scarce commodity in New York. "Believe me," O'Neill complained to Boulton,

"Prohibition is very much of a *fact*." Even the Garden Hotel was "dry as dry."[195] At Jimmy the Priest's, James Condon's tolerance for drunkenness at all costs had gotten the better of him: on December 27, 1919, just a few weeks before Prohibition began that January 1920, Condon, then fifty-five, was forced to shut down the bar after four men died while drinking there. One was found dead in the back room, another upstairs in his bed; and two more, one of whom was found on the street outside in a coma, were taken to Bellevue Hospital, where they couldn't be helped. When the conscious man admitted that he'd been drinking at "Jimmy's Place" before he died, Condon and his bartender William Nolan were arrested for homicide. They were charged with allegedly serving "coroner's cocktails," a wood alcohol moonshine responsible for scores of deaths on the East Coast (and one of Terry Carlin's favorite beverages through Prohibition).[196] Condon and Nolan were taken to Manhattan's notorious Tombs prison; though they were each released on $1,000 bail after a few days, Jimmy's Hotel and Café was to be shut down for good. (In 1966, the neighborhood would be razed to make way for the World Trade Center.)

At the same time, the Provincetown Players had begun hosting "John Barleycorn parties," which O'Neill attended for the drinks if not the company. Boulton wrote to express her disapproval over his getting drunk with the Players: "The whole crowd is more or less envious and only too glad to drag you down somehow into the dirt. . . . You know, as well as I do, the shape you get into after much drinking! . . . You should have had guts enough *not* to go, at this time when so *very* much hangs in the balance." "No more lecture letters, please!" he retorted. "You never used to be a moralist, and I've never in my life stood for that stuff, even from my Mother."[197]

Far more satisfying was a night at the Hell Hole when Tom Wallace, Lefty Louie, Joe Smith, and a few prostitutes hanging around got O'Neill loaded on sherry; even without hard liquor it was a gretime, free of the suffocating Village crowd. Louie was delighted that his song "My Josephine," which he'd long ago concocted for a "tough Wop cabaret," would be featured in *Chris*. "This little incident of the song seems to me quite touching in a way," O'Neill wrote Boulton recounting the edifying night with his old friends, "and I think all the hours seemingly wasted in the H.H. [Hell Hole] would be justified if they had resulted in only this."[198] (Louie's song would be made far more popular by O'Neill's revision of *Chris*, *"Anna Christie."*)

O'Neill's otherwise bad fortune tracking down hooch in "Dry New York" took another turn after meeting Richard Bennett, the future star and unofficial director of *Beyond the Horizon*. The two met at John Williams's office, then retired to Bennett's Greenwich Village apartment. Bennett's wife prepared them a dinner of scrambled eggs, then went off to bed, at which point Bennett asked the playwright, "Do you like absinthe?" "Yes," he replied, putting aside his disastrous initiation to the "green fairies" at Princeton with Lou Holladay, "but what good does a liking do me?" Bennett announced that he had fifty cases of the hallucinogenic liquor. "I knew I was going to like you from the first moment we met," O'Neill said, and they drank absinthe until seven thirty in the morning while reading the script together line by line.

Back at his hotel room, O'Neill, still affected by "the subtle fireworks from the queer poison of absinthe," wrote a prose poem while "the whole world was shot through with White Logic."[199] ("White Logic" was Jack London's term for the existential angst that drunkenness incurs while paradoxically also making it endurable.) O'Neill's prose poem testifies to what happens to a mind affected by absinthe: "The golden oranges in the patio dream of the Hesperides. The earth is a sun-struck bee, its wings sodden with golden pollen, sifted dust of sunbeams. . . . Green parrots in the green of the orange trees gossiping like deaf people—a discord rasps saw-teeth in the keen blue blade of silence," and so forth. But it eventually concludes with a passionate cry of eternal devotion to Boulton in life and in death.[200]

Meanwhile, over the holiday season of 1919–20, the worldwide flu epidemic was claiming thousands of lives and New York residents were brought low for months by one of the worst blizzard seasons in the city's history. Tempers had also begun to flare at rehearsals for *Beyond the Horizon*. At one point Bennett and O'Neill "went to the mat," Bennett said, over the climactic scene in which Robert calls Ruth a "slut." When Robert finds out that Ruth loves his brother, he responds as O'Neill might have when Bryant broke with him in favor of Reed: "God! It wasn't that I haven't guessed how mean and small you are—but I've kept on telling myself that I must be wrong—like a fool!—like a damned fool! . . . You—you slut!" (*CP1*, 616). John Williams didn't like the use of the word either. O'Neill refused to back down, even face-to-face with such intimidating professionals. (He was invariably drunk during Macdougal Street rehearsals, but not for these.) "Will you be responsible for the failure of this scene if we play it your way?" Bennett asked O'Neill. The dramatist replied in the affirmative. Bennett finished the scene, then shouted, "By God, you're right! Let's have a few more fights and this play'll pick up 100%."[201]

Such on-the-job anxiety, vitriolic letters from home, and his father's declining health triggered a paralyzing insomnia, and O'Neill barely made it to rehearsals. At one point he felt compelled to take the sleep aid veronal, the drug he'd used in his suicide attempt. Above all, he feared low attendance at *Beyond the Horizon*, insisting that Cook and Glaspell release the Players' subscription list in order to "paper" the house with respectable numbers. Glaspell was agitated by the request and chastised Boulton that lists were "sacred things—*secret things*." "Jig feels as I do," she said. "Gene should have use of the list, but it should not be let out of the office."[202]

But in spite of the feuds and hangovers, his father's cancer, and the blizzards, his flu, and the insomnia that plagued him through the season, working on Broadway afforded a priceless education for the budding playwright. "I've learned a tremendous lot that I wouldn't miss for worlds," he told Boulton, "knowledge that will be of *real* worth hereafter. . . . This whole experience has been invaluable to me as an artist who ought to know his medium from top to bottom."[203]

Beyond the Horizon's world premiere, and thus O'Neill's debut as a commercially viable playwright, took place on the afternoon of February 2, 1920, just north of the Bronx at the Warburton Theatre in Yonkers, New York. This trial performance at the Warburton, a small-time venue that lived up to its self-styled repute as "The Theatre of Constant Surprises" by hosting the first full-length Eugene O'Neill play ever to appear onstage, was a bargain at 50¢ a seat. O'Neill, distressed by several days of poor rehearsals, excused himself from attending, using his incipient flu symptoms as a weak pretext. O'Neill may have had his doubts, but the local *Yonkers Statesman* reviewed the matinee enthusiastically, if briefly, reporting that "the audience, although not large, was a representative one and liberal with applause."[204]

O'Neill's Broadway debut took place the following afternoon, February 3, at the Morosco Theatre. James and Ella reserved box seats, while O'Neill was dismayed to find himself seated next to his producer John Williams. He squirmed through all three acts, disgusted with the play and with what he believed, wrongly it would turn out, was a distinct lack of emotional response from the audience. "I suffered tortures," he wrote Boulton. "I went out convinced that *Beyond* was a flivver artistically and every other way." His father wept openly through the performance, though tempered his judgment after the show. "It's all right, if that's what you want to do," he told his son outside on the street, "but people come to the theater to forget their troubles, not to be reminded of them. What are you trying to do—send them home to commit suicide?"[205]

That night, O'Neill received a congratulatory wire from Boulton at the theater: "Three cheers for you and *Beyond* and much love, Agnes." Otherwise, isolated on the Cape, she was in no mood to commiserate over his disappointing evening. Earlier that day, she'd written him, "Frankly—you don't mind my being frank, do you?—it is *hell* for me that you are not coming—that you are not here now." Another letter written the same day describes her failed attempt to rein in her fury in his upstairs office: "There I was, staring at the silly, stupid wall paper, and two hundred miles away, *Beyond* was having its premiere. Well—if a year ago, when we were down in Pt. P. [Point Pleasant] someone had told me I'd be in that room—in Provincetown—alone—and you and *Beyond* in N.Y.—I suppose I should have rebelled! Certainly, I'd never have believed it—I'd have said—'I'll get there *somehow*!'" "What is the matter?" she persisted over his lackluster responses to her earlier love letters. "Has Louise [Bryant] been writing you—congratulations?"[206] Miserable throughout O'Neill's absence that winter, having been left alone with Shane, Gaga, and Terry Carlin, she still managed to revise *Now I Ask You* and complete two short stories, "The Hater of Mediocrity" and "The Snob," both of which would be accepted at the *Smart Set.*

Back at the Prince George after the opening, O'Neill collapsed into bed, too dejected to write Boulton. Then, the next morning, the papers arrived. "Lo and behold, in spite of all the handicaps of a rotten first performance, *Beyond* had won," he wrote her. "You never saw such notices!" The *New York Times* hailed it as "an absorbing, significant, and memorable tragedy, so full of meat that it makes most of the remaining fare seem like the merest meringue." Those left behind in Provincetown received an exultant telegram from Jimmy Light: "Just saw Gene's play, a great great play. I am wildly excited, dawn of a new day. Superb acting audience enthusiastic, hurrah . . . !" The only sustained criticism by seasoned theatergoers was over the play's alternating scene changes from interior to exterior, which many considered amateurish and distracting. O'Neill fumed to Barrett Clark over the critics' accusations that the playwright showed "ignorance of conventional every day technique—I, a Baker 47 alumnus!" (Baker had in fact read *Beyond the Horizon*, he said, and was "delighted with and proud of it.")[207] Such relatively minor complaints aside, few critics failed to point out the great promise of this young dramatist.

"I felt sure when I saw the woebegone faces of the audience on the opening day that it was a rank failure," O'Neill told a reporter, "and no one was more surprised than was I when I saw the morning papers and came to the conclusion that the sad expressions on the playgoers' faces were caused by their feeling the tragedy I had written." That July 1920, George Jean Nathan described O'Neill in a *Smart Set* article entitled "The American Playwright" as "the one writer for the native stage who gives promise of achieving a sound position for himself." After expressing his heartfelt gratitude, O'Neill agreed with Nathan's estimation that he was still wet behind the ears: "God stiffen it, I *am* young yet and I mean to grow! And in this faith I live: That if I have the 'guts' to ignore the megaphone men and what goes with them, to follow the dream and live for that alone, then my

real significant bit of truth and the ability to express it, will be conquered in time—not tomorrow nor the next day nor any near, easily-
attained period but after the struggle has been long enough and hard
enough to merit victory."[208]

Boulton was openly envious of her husband's New York adventure
and the great triumphs celebrated in her absence. She'd begun to feel
abandoned sexually too. "Gene—your little Miss P[ussy] is meowing,
and howling and behaving like a perfect devil," she said. (O'Neill and
Boulton referred to his penis, incidentally, as "The Nightingale," a
sobriquet they'd appropriated from Boccaccio's *Decameron*.) During
the week that followed opening night, they exchanged a burst of acrimonious letters, which only intensified in rancor over those collective-
ly wretched February days. Her mood grew increasingly gloomy, while
his more obstinate and defiant. "Your letter was gall when I prayed
for wine," he wrote. If the bickering didn't stop, he warned, "my only
remaining hope is that the 'Flu,' or some other material cause, will
speedily save me the decision which would inevitably have to come at
my own instance. If you and I are but another dream that passes, then I
desire nothing further from the Great Sickness but release."[209]

John Williams at first restricted *Beyond the Horizon*'s run to "special
matinees," given the blizzards and the flu epidemic, which made even
the most devoted theatergoers wary of an auditorium's congested air.
But once the reviews arrived, Williams deftly transferred the production to the Criterion Theatre, then arranged for a standard engagement at the Little Theatre. Williams had tried to persuade either Jack
or Lee Shubert to take it on; but whichever of the two theatrical power brokers it was, he jerked his cigar from one corner of his mouth to
the other and barked, "Nothin' doin! It's got great notices but nix on
the tragedy stuff until you show us the old box-office returns." After
111 performances, the play wound up generating a small fortune in
returns: $117,071. "I'm sure you'll be pleased to know," O'Neill wrote
Nina Moise, "that I am not compromising but 'hewing to the line,'
and not trying to get too wealthy although, as you can imagine, the
opportunities to sell myself have not been lacking of late."[210]

By the spring of 1920, when O'Neill was only thirty-one, his name had appeared in every major newspaper from Boston to Philadelphia. The conservative Irish dramatist and critic St. John Ervine wrote O'Neill that *Beyond the Horizon* was the first play he'd attended in America, and that he was "proud to think that so beautiful a thing was made by a man with Irish blood."[211] *Theatre Magazine* profiled O'Neill that April, noting that he even looked the part of the "literary genius." When the reporter, Alta M. Coleman, said good-bye after their interview, she admitted her worry about feeling disappointed with him after seeing his plays. "But I'm not!" she said. "They're all there—in your eyes." "So be prepared to read of my 'great sad eyes,' " he wrote Boulton after Coleman left him "to cough in peace."[212] Sure enough: "Though not striking in appearance," Coleman wrote, "Eugene O'Neill is not the usual type. Lack of robustness gives his five-feet ten inches added heighth [O'Neill was five feet eleven]; his clothes, which hang loosely upon his well-proportioned frame, suggest neither dapperness nor the conscious carelessness of the artist. Hands well-manicured and white from a winter indoors; but his face retains a tinge of summer tan. His forehead high and rounded calls to mind pictures of Edgar Allan Poe; it narrows at the temples where his crisp black hair is tinged with white. . . . Chin and nose are well defined though not aggressive; a narrow black moustache marks his upper lip but cannot hide the extreme sensitiveness of his mouth—a sensitiveness that is intensified in his large brilliant eyes, the whites of an opaque clearness contrasting with the rich glowing brown of the iris. These eyes have seen both the sunshine and suffering of the world—they say 'Life is a tragedy—hurrah!' "[213]

O'Neill's slow-budding flu symptoms blossomed to full strength after the premiere; what he glimpsed in the mirror looked like a corpse "dug out of the grave by mistake." His temperature hovered just over a hundred degrees for a full week, and his weight dropped to about 125 pounds. "Stripped, I look like a medical student's chart, every muscle outlined and every bone and bit of sinew." Boulton warned him to avoid the infected trains, whose close quarters were known to spread the disease, and be careful in the blizzard—there had been many cases, she reminded him, of the effects of freezing weather lethally compounding flu with pneumonia. Much worse than O'Neill's flu was that his father James, already wasting away from intestinal cancer, had just suffered a stroke. "Papa, it seems, is doomed," O'Neill told Boulton. "To have this happen just at the time when the Old Man and I were getting to be such good pals! . . . I'm all broken up and begin to cry every time the meaning of it all dawns on me."[214]

Far and away the most significant result of this rapprochement for O'Neill was James's heartfelt confession to his son about the play that had made his fortune and reputation. *Monte Cristo*, James intoned repeatedly, had been his "curse," O'Neill wrote of their conversation: "He had fallen for the lure of easy popularity and easy money." James believed that overall, with his neglected potential and failed investments, "he had made a bad bargain. The money was thrown away, squandered in wild speculations, lost. . . . The treasures of *Monte Cristo* are buried deep again—in prairie dog gold mines, in unlubricated wells, in fuelless coal lands—the modern Castles in Spain of pure romance." "How keenly he felt this in the last years," O'Neill told George Tyler, "I think I am the only one who knows, the only one he confided in."[215] Before this, of course, James had made this confession to a great many people over his career, including to the tabloid press. But for his son it was a revelation. James's anguish over his choice inspired O'Neill to write a profoundly illuminating monologue in *Long Day's Journey Into Night* wherein James Tyrone divulges his self-loathing to his son Edmund: "I've never admitted this to anyone before, lad, but tonight I'm so heartsick I feel at the end of everything, and what's the use of fake pride and pretense. That God-damned play I bought for a song and made such a great success in—a great money success—it ruined me with its promise of an easy fortune" (*CP*3, 809). "What the hell was it I wanted to buy, I wonder," James asks in somber reflection, "that was worth—" (*CP*3, 810).

George Tyler's production of *Chris* was scheduled to open on March 8 at Nixon's Apollo Theatre in Atlantic City, but O'Neill decided to return to his wife and son in Provincetown a few days earlier. Tyler pleaded with O'Neill to come back to New York and help him at the rehearsals, but was flatly refused. *Chris* opened to a horde of "tango lovers and chewing gum sweethearts," O'Neill griped after reading the bad reviews, and it then moved to Philadelphia, where its equally lukewarm reception squelched any hopes for a New York run. O'Neill wasn't in the least surprised; he recognized that "the last scene is weak and that the love affair in the play is piffling and undramatic." He accepted most of the responsibility and informed Tyler that he'd "write a completely new script" and advised him to "throw the present play in the ashbarrel."[216]

O'Neill had delivered his one-act *Exorcism* to the Players the previous December,and it opened the same month as *Chris*, on March 26, at the Provincetown Playhouse for a standard two-week run.[217] The Players' program listed the perversely autobiographical one-act depicting O'Neill's suicide attempt as "A Play of Anti-Climax"—and so it was.[218] Jasper Deeter, who played Ned Malloy, recalled that O'Neill "wrote both 'Exorcism' and 'Diff'rent' [the following year] as exercises in anti-climax, experiments, not exercises, because so much in our lives is anti-climax, and he wanted to put it into the theatre." M. A. McAteer, who played Jimmy, remembered that O'Neill, justifiably, appeared "more than normally worried about the play during rehearsal."[219] "When the curtains opened on the second scene," Deeter said, "I felt like this: Here we are trying to do something impossible for a man who thought that nothing was impossible. 'Let's go.' "[220]

After *Exorcism*'s final appearance in April, O'Neill contacted Eleanor "Fitzi" Fitzgerald, now the Players' dependable business manager, to request all copies of the script. He destroyed them upon receipt, presumably more sickened over his treatment of Jenkins than proud of his redemption with Shane. After that, there was little remaining evidence of the play's existence—a page of notes, a playbill, a couple of interviews with actors, and a handful of reviews running the gamut from the near rhapsodic (*New York Times*) to the patently disappointed (*New York Tribune*).[221] In 1922, when Frank Shay, Greenwich Village bookstore owner and publisher of the Provincetown Players' plays, inquired whether O'Neill would be interested in publishing *Exorcism*, O'Neill replied, " 'Exorcism' has been destroyed . . . and the sooner all memory of it dies the better."[222] (Memory of it refused to die, however: the script was found more than ninety years later, in 2011, among the papers of the Academy Award–winning Hollywood screenwriter Philip Yordan. It was a Christmas gift from Boulton and her subsequent husband, Morris "Mac" Kaufman. The accompanying greeting card reads, "Something-you-said-you'd-like-to-have Agnes + Mac.")

O'Neill's prolonged absence that winter ruptured his bond with Boulton irreparably. "I just feel as if I don't really know anything about you or your plays anymore," Boulton wrote him. And she resented his victory—or at least her peripheral role in it. Just as the stellar notices for *Beyond the Horizon* had begun to roll off the presses, Boulton admitted that she could hardly write him at all: "I'd start—write a few stupid words. Then a curious rage—resentment, something that—yes, really!—made me *tremble*, would overcome me. Against all the circumstances that keep us apart now, just when we should be together! . . . For, oh Beloved, I have been with you when you were suffering, when despair and loneliness were upon you, and I needed to be with you triumphant! . . . I wanted to see you happy, proud, elated, secretly *intoxicated* with this success, which so soon—for such are *you!*—I'll see you drop as an empty bauble." Her prophecy came true soon enough. When John Williams sent a get-well note to O'Neill that cheered exultantly, "The Town is yours," O'Neill replied acidly, "They can keep it. Success has meant to me the meaningless futility I always knew it would—only more so."[223]

O'Neill had never heard of the Pulitzer Prize, a national honor first awarded just two years before in 1918, and accepted the news that he'd won it with a Bronx cheer. "Oh, God, a damn medal! And one of those presentation ceremonies! I won't accept it."[224] Back in Provincetown, his tune changed when he heard that it came with $1,000, at which point he sprinted down the beach swirling his arms with joy.

Clayton Hamilton had served on the Pulitzer committee that season and championed *Beyond the Horizon*, thwarting the opposition of novelist and literary lion Hamlin Garland. Garland argued that to reward O'Neill for his "violent and turgid" style, his "ruthlessness for the sake of ruthlessness," would merely cheapen the award's gravitas.[225]

Eugene O'Neill running down the Provincetown beach in 1920 after hearing he won $1,000 for the Pulitzer Prize for Drama.
(COURTESY OF SHEAFFER-O'NEILL COLLECTION, LINDA LEAR CENTER FOR SPECIAL COLLECTIONS AND ARCHIVES, CONNECTICUT COLLEGE, NEW LONDON)

* * *

George Jean Nathan and H. L. Mencken, aware of O'Neill's un-quenchable thirst for liquor, summoned him to the offices of the *Smart Set* for a "surprise." When he arrived with Jimmy Light during a brief visit to New York, Nathan and Mencken presented him with a cheap medal to honor his Pulitzer, complete with an outsized safety pin to attach it to his lapel. A bottle of Napoleon brandy and four glasses were placed enticingly on a tray atop a table in the center of the room. When O'Neill grabbed for the bottle, it wouldn't budge. They'd glued it and the glasses to the tray, which was itself glued to the table. "We have to be going," they said, straight-faced, then walked out.[226]

Upon receiving word that his son had won the award, James O'Neill boasted to his friend Clayton Hamilton, "My boy ... Eugene; I always knew he had it in him! Remember how I always used to say that he would do something big some day? People told me he was wild and good-for-nothing; but I always knew he had it in him,—didn't I?" Hamilton laughed, well remembering what James had really said: "The boy would never amount to anything."[227]

On June 10, 1920, James, whose condition had declined pre-cipitously, transferred from a New York hospital to Lawrence and Memorial Hospital in New London. O'Neill took the train down from Provincetown and wrote Agnes from his father's deathbed. "The situation is frightful! Just a few moments ago he groaned in anguish and cried pitifully: 'Oh God, why don't You take me! Why don't You take me!'" During long hours at his bedside, O'Neill found his seventy-six-year-old father, by then speechless with agonizing pain, a "very pitiful, cruelly ironic thing . . . [since] all through his life his greatest pride has been in his splendid voice and clear articulation!" "He seems to me a *good* man, in the best sense of the word," O'Neill said, "and about the only one I have ever known." But then he acknowledged the mor-dant irony that the last words he'd heard his father utter sounded "like a dying dialogue in a play I might have written." "Glad to go, boy," James told his son, "a better sort of life—another sort—somewhere. . . . This sort of life—froth!—rotten!—all of it—no good!," words that impressed his son as "a warning from the Beyond to remain true to the best that is in me though the heavens fall."[228]

James O'Neill died on August 10, 1920, at four fifteen in the morning. "Helluva time for the old man to die," Jim grumbled after he'd dutifully supported his mother in the wretched days before and after his father's death (aside from the occasional drinking jag with Eugene and old friends in downtown New London). James O'Neill's funeral was a monumental affair for the residents of New London, as they watched crowds of theater people, members of the Knights of Columbus (a fraternal organization in which James had long been a member), various Irish American notables, and community leaders file into St. Joseph's Roman Catholic Church to say good-bye to their city's most famous, if not always most respected, citizen.[229]

O'Neill found no consolation in the new family he'd created. Upon his return to Peaked Hill Bar, O'Neill, who'd fawned over Shane at first, now considered the child an obstacle to healing his ruptured relationship with Boulton as well as disruptive to his work. O'Neill had never demonstrated any interest in fatherhood before Shane, nor did he pretend to. He complained that the "old sea flavor" of their home had been replaced by the stench of dirty diapers and milk. He put the blame that Boulton hadn't been with him in New York to celebrate his success and nurse him during his bout of flu squarely on the baby. "It would all be so simple," he'd written her, "if Shane were not in our midst, or if you only had him weaned."[230]

O'Neill turned violent that summer too. Boulton, though no shrinking violet, characterized him during such episodes as "more like a madman than anything else—a strange being who was not the real Gene at all." She realized that there were moments, all of them alcohol related, of "sudden and rather dreadful outbursts of violence, and others of bitter nastiness and malevolence."[231] Boulton's thickly applied makeup didn't fool anyone in Provincetown. O'Neill had been hitting her. "The promiscuities and the experimental narcotics didn't interest him," wrote Provincetown native Hazel Hawthorne of O'Neill at the time. "His sins were not the little ones but the savage ones of hard drinking and wife beating."[232]

Perhaps it's no coincidence, then, that during this period O'Neill worked up a treatment for his play *The First Man*, the story of a workaholic anthropologist who revolts against his wife's longing for a child. But he then turned to his revision of *Chris*, now retitled "The Ole Davil," in which he transformed Anna, at Boulton's suggestion, from a prim English typist to a sexually abused, streetwise prostitute; and he'd already put the finishing touches on *Gold*, the full-length version of *Where the Cross Is Made*. With two unproduced plays ready to send off, O'Neill was moved to turn out something unexpected, something unique to American theater. He had just the thing.

Back in O'Neill's days at the Garden Hotel, the "old circus man" Jack Croak (the model for Ed Mosher in *The Iceman Cometh*) had returned from a boondoggle in Haiti and told O'Neill the story of the murderous dictator Vilbrun Guillaume Sam. He'd duped the Haitian people by spreading a legend, O'Neill said, "to the effect that Sam had said they'd never get him with a lead bullet; that he would get himself first with a silver one," and he promptly jotted down the "story current in Hayti." Croak also gave him a Haitian coin stamped with Sam's visage, a talisman O'Neill carried in his pocket as a reminder of the idea's inception.[233]

O'Neill at first titled the eight-scene drama "The Silver Bullet" after the Haitian dictator's scam, but settled on *The Emperor Jones*. A portrait of one man's horrifying descent into his racial past, *Jones*, along with its bold elevation of a black protagonist, signaled a radical departure in American theater: rather than showing life "as it is," this play would dramatize the stripping away of society's false trappings and expose humanity at its most primal.[234]

Civilization Unmasked

By early October 1920, O'Neill had completed *The Emperor Jones*, the first play to open American audience's eyes to European expressionist theater.[235] Characterized by grotesque exaggerations of character and setting and the enactment of distorted psychological fantasies, expressionistic dramas project their heroes' inner conflicts not only through dialogue but through the scenery as well. "King Lear is given a storm to rant in," Jimmy Light explained, whereas "the Expressionist hero in anger walks on a street, and all the perspectives of the walls, windows and doors are awry and tortured."[236] For O'Neill, at least, expressionism wasn't meant simply to entertain or edify; it was meant to induce in his audiences an altered state of consciousness.

O'Neill's title character, Brutus Jones, is a former porter on the Pullman passenger trains, a convicted murderer, and a fugitive from the law. Jones escapes prison and flees to a Caribbean island, only to betray his race (hence the name "Brutus") by adopting the role of a white colonialist. An assassination attempt on Jones by a gunman hired by his political rival, the island native "Old Lem," fails when the gun misfires. After Jones shoots the assassin dead, he declares to the bewildered crowd—made up of those Jones considers "low-flung, bush niggers," as a white colonialist would—that only a silver bullet can kill him. Jones has a silver bullet crafted for him, proclaiming to the natives, "I'm de on'y man in de world big enuff to git me" (*CP1*, 1036). He then crowns himself emperor and enacts self-serving, punitive laws that raise taxes from his impoverished subjects. Perched eagerly at his side is a small-time British crook named Smithers, a ferretlike white man whom Jones treats with open disdain. Smithers is greedy, treacherous, and lazy, not coincidentally, in O'Neill's reversal of the widely held racial beliefs of his time, the characteristics associated with blackness by American white supremacists. Smithers informs Jones what an old native woman has told him—that a rebellion led by Old Lem is brewing in the hills above the palace. The faraway sound of tom-toms softly fills the air. Jones knows his game is up.

Having foreseen a coup against his reign, Jones had memorized the island's labyrinthine jungle paths, stored caches of food along the way, and made plans to evade the rebel band by escaping to Martinique in a French gunboat. Once informed of the impending revolt, he makes his getaway. "So long, white man," he bids Smithers farewell, and plunges into the jungle forest (*CP1*, 1041). During his flight through the jungle, Jones encounters a series of phantasmagoric apparitions that start off as "Formless Little Fears," then grow more specific to African American oppression—chain gangs, slave auctions, the horrifying "Middle Passage" of slaves crossing the Atlantic, and lastly the banks of the Congo, where Jones meets his reckoning in the form of a crocodile god conjured by an African witch doctor. In the final scene, Jones has been tracked down by island natives who gun him down offstage with specially prepared silver bullets.[237]

O'Neill's early schooling in philosophical anarchism with Benjamin Tucker dictates the play's moral logic. The philosophy's founding father, Max Stirner, had denied the existence of good or evil, since murder and other crimes are acceptable so long as the state deems them legal. "According to our theories of penal law," Stirner wrote, "they want to punish men for this or that 'inhumanity'; and therein they make the silliness of these theories especially plain by their consistency, *hanging the little thieves and letting the big ones run.*"[238] O'Neill adopts precisely this language to describe the criminal life Brutus Jones embraced after a decade working on the Pullman trains "listenin' to de white quality talk": "Ain't I de Emperor?" he asks Smithers. "De laws don't go for him. . . . Dere's little stealin' . . . and dere's big stealin'. . . . For de little stealin' dey gits you in jail soon or late. For de big stealin' dey makes you Emperor and puts you in de Hall o' Fame when you croaks" (*CP*1, 1035). (The 1933 Hollywood film retains Stirner's language: "Dere's little stealin' like you does, and dere's big stealin' like I does." But the suggestion that it was white businessmen on the trains who taught Jones how to steal "big" was, predictably, omitted.)

The play also unmasked an escalating political fiasco: the American government's disastrous involvement in Haiti. In the fall of 1919, when O'Neill decided to write up Croak's "story current in Hayti" as a play, the U.S. Marines had just crushed a guerrilla uprising against the protracted American occupation there (1915–34). By the end of the rebellion, approximately three thousand Haitian men, women, and children lay dead. (This was the My Lai Massacre of its time.) As such, O'Neill's preface to *The Emperor Jones* coyly identifies the setting as "an island in the West Indies as yet not self-determined by White Marines," a sarcastic taunt aimed at the absurd legality of "big stealin' " by American business interests abroad (*CP*1, 1030, 1035).

The Emperor Jones therefore takes place just prior to 1915, a tumultuous political phase for Haiti when four "emperors" ruled its people in as many years before the U.S. Marines took control of the island. Before completing the first year of his dictatorship in 1915, the Haitian dictator Sam, like Jones, was hunted down by insurgents and executed (Jones gets gunned down in the jungle; Sam was torn apart limb from limb in the streets of Port-au-Prince). Sam held close ties with American financial interests, specifically the National City Bank of New York. Thus on the afternoon of the insurgency and Sam's execution, July 28, 1915, President Woodrow Wilson ordered the Marines, then patrolling the coast in a warship, to seize the country by force. O'Neill's original draft, "The Silver Bullet," specifies that Brutus's island is "as yet self-determined by the U.S. Marines," a detail changed to the less explicit "White Marines" in the final play. In so doing, O'Neill partially disguised his politically charged setting.[239]

In late winter 1920, the NAACP dispatched the African American writer and diplomat James Weldon Johnson to Haiti to investigate the military occupation from a black perspective. Given the lack of reporting in the white press about Haiti and its majority-black citizenry, the American public's response up to then had been largely indifferent. From August 28 to September 25, 1920, Johnson published a series of four articles in the left-wing journal the *Nation*, which O'Neill and Boulton read often in Provincetown, wherein Johnson reported in gruesome detail on the atrocities perpetrated by the Marines against the Haitian people.[240] With this series, if only for a brief time, Johnson single-handedly placed the otherwise ignored occupation of Haiti on the front pages of newspapers nationwide. The title of the series, "Self-Determining Haiti," substantiates the connection with O'Neill's West Indian island "as yet not self-determined by White Marines," and O'Neill wrote *The Emperor Jones* from late September to October 3, 1920, one week after the final installation of Johnson's exposé had appeared.

By then, O'Neill fully recognized that open propaganda should have no place in his work, as it counterproductively weakened a play's message. A few years later, he told the *New York Herald Tribune*, "As soon as an author slips propaganda into a play every one feels it and the play becomes simply an argument"; following that, he advised Mike Gold, a sharply political writer who was looking for feedback on his play *Hoboken Blues* (1929), "My quarrel with propaganda in the theatre is that it's such damned unconvincing propaganda—whereas, if you will restrain the propaganda purpose to the selection of the life to be portrayed and then let that life live itself without comment, it does your trick."[241] Mentioning the "White Marines" was even less restrained than O'Neill would later become; but if he'd said "the U.S. Marines," the play might have been mistaken for propaganda and thus prove "damned unconvincing."[242]

The Provincetown Players welcomed *The Emperor Jones* with near-fanatical zeal, and Jig Cook chose himself to direct it. Cook was profoundly moved by O'Neill's script, and he seized the opportunity to breathe new life into an idea he and set designer Robert Edmond Jones had been mulling over for some time. They would construct a dome, or "cyclorama"—a *Kuppelhorizont*, as the Germans called it—for their stage at 133 Macdougal. It would be the first of its kind in the United States. The theater group's executive committee balked at the scale of the dome project, however, citing a lack of funds for the estimated $500 construction cost. Hearing this, Cook began acting like "a madman," Edna Kenton said. Each time he broached the subject, the Players said it was impossible, and he'd pick up his hat and storm out. Before long he'd return and declare, "We *have* to do this." Impossible. And off he'd march on "another restless tramp."[243]

Days of frustrating denials goaded Cook into designing the dome without the committee's approval. He next bought bags of cement and other construction materials and slept on the stage at night to save money. The Players relented and emptied their bank account for the project.[244] When Cook finished the installation, each of the Players signed the dome as if indelibly marking a child's plaster cast.[245] Cook's dome allowed them to create lighting effects that gave the illusion of unbounded height and distance, thus enhancing O'Neill's hallucinatory mise-en-scène. Once the installation was complete,

Jimmy Light was awestruck by the dome's "almost unlimited capacity for suggesting mood, even weather, by means of lighting."[246]

Subsequently, Light furnished an explanatory article for *Bulletin* magazine at the time of *The Emperor Jones*'s production that remains the most vivid existing description of the dome's design, assembly, and ultimate purpose: "The dome in the Provincetown Playhouse is made of rigid iron and concrete construction. . . . The constant rate of change in direction of the surface of the dome in the elliptic and circular form is what gives the sense of infinity. The light rays strike along this curve and are reflected in millions of directions. Every light ray as it strikes the small particles of sand finish casts its shadow as a complementary color. The mingling of a colored light with its complementary color shadow produces, with the constant curve of the surface, the effect of distance and makes the dome appear what it in reality is—a source of light. By varying the lights thrown into the dome one can control the effects emerging from the dome. . . . There is a parallel between the methods of using the dome and those of Monet in producing atmospheric effects on canvas. In one case light, and the other case color, are placed in juxtaposition as ingredients of a tone which finally arrive at the eye. This tone has the brilliancy of daylight. . . . When we have installed material and apparatus to take every advantage of the new construction there is absolutely no atmospheric or lighting effect that we cannot achieve."[247]

For the play's sound effects, O'Neill had happened upon an idea while reading about "religious feasts in the Congo." Tribal members would beat a tom-tom at the normal pulse of the human heart, seventy-two to seventy-five beats per minute; the rhythm then "slowly intensified until the heartbeat of everyone present corresponds to the frenzied beat of the drum." "There was an idea and an experiment," O'Neill mused. "How would this sort of thing work on an audience in the theater?"[248] O'Neill's stage directions specify that near the end of the first scene, the tom-tom begins at seventy-two beats per minute, then "continues at a gradually accelerating rate from [the end of scene 1] uninterruptedly to the very end of the play" (*CP1*, 1041). The drumbeat continues to quicken, even through intermission, as

the rebels close in and Jones's nightmares become increasingly horrific. The desired effect was that the audience members' hearts would
start beating along with the tom-tom. "Each succeeding scene left
that audience more excited, more keyed up than the previous one,"
actress Kyra Markham recalled of the opening. "No play is written
for only one performance, but that night was colossal."[249]

Provincetown Player Chuck Ellis, a white man, had been the
Players' first choice to play Jones—in blackface. Despite their
prior success casting black actors for *The Dreamy Kid*, they didn't
yet trust that white audiences would come to see a "colored" leading
man supported by a white cast. But Ida Rauh held firm. "This isn't
a burlesque," she said, "this is a serious play."[250] They all assented,
but then there was the challenge of finding a black actor who might
agree to play a part written in black dialect by a white playwright
using the word "nigger." Jazz guitarist Opal Cooper's name was
floated, but he was out of town for a six-month engagement in Paris.
Next, they approached a twenty-two-year-old unknown named Paul
Robeson.

At the time, Robeson had only performed in one amateur production, Ridgely Torrence's *Simon the Cyerian* at the Harlem YMCA
(which O'Neill had reportedly attended). Though untrained as an
actor, Robeson was no ordinary performer. He'd been an academic
and athletic superstar at Rutgers University: the captain of the debate
team; a member of the academic honors society Phi Beta Kappa
before his senior year; a "three-letter man" in track, football, and
basketball, and picked for the All-American football team; and his
soon-legendary baritone voice made him the featured performer in
the glee club.[251] By the time the Players had decided to approach him
for the role of Brutus Jones in the fall of 1920, Robeson was studying
law at Columbia University while working off his tuition there as an
assistant football coach.

Jasper Deeter, who was to play Smithers, had been tasked with
recruiting Robeson for the part, and he visited the law student at
his Harlem flat. "Yes, what can I do for you?" Robeson asked him
at the door. "We'd like you to be in a play by Eugene O'Neill," said

Deeter. "Never heard of him." But Robeson allowed Deeter inside to read him the script out loud. Before long, Robeson grew so infuriated according to him, that he "couldn't breathe." "The more he read me that terrible character," he recalled, "the angrier I got." A giant of a man, he could have picked Deeter up and effortlessly hurled him out his window; he said later that he nearly did.[252]

Deeter returned to Macdougal in one piece, but without his emperor. A future "little dictator" did show up in these first days of planning, however: the silent film impresario Charlie Chaplin, wearing a disguise and giving his name as Charles Spencer (his middle name). For reasons known only to himself, the thirty-one-year old celebrity badly wanted a part in the play. The Players happily welcomed him at first, but Hutch Hapgood warned, "Is that a good idea? Do you know what will happen if word gets around that Chaplin's going to be in it? The theatre won't be large enough to hold everybody who'll want to come, and this will throw Gene's play right out the window."[253] The point was well taken, and Chaplin was politely dismissed.

After Ellis, Cooper, and Robeson, the Players' fourth choice for Brutus Jones was the veteran actor Charles S. Gilpin, one of the founders of the Lafayette Players, Harlem's first stock company. No stranger to white theater, Gilpin had performed admirably the previous season in John Drinkwater's hit play *Abraham Lincoln* as a Frederick Douglass–like emissary on a visit to the sixteenth president. When O'Neill and Light observed Gilpin for the first time, through the box office window from the street outside the playhouse, they both uttered simultaneously, "There he is."[254]

Gilpin had led a vagabond life and worked a string of low-paying jobs: barber, printer, elevator operator, janitor, minstrel show performer, boxing trainer and, like the fictional Jones, Pullman porter. Gilpin was also as burly, arrogant, and practiced at the art of survival as his fictional counterpart. "You may know this kind of person," Robeson had fumed to Jasper Deeter that day in his apartment, "and Mr. O'Neill may know this kind of person, but I don't." Gilpin knew him well. "I take my characters out of the street and study them," he told a *New York Tribune* reporter. "I have seen 'The Emperor Jones.' I have watched his braggadocio and I have seen him delirious with fear. I play him as he really is in life, with very little exaggeration."[255]

When O'Neill returned to New York after several sober months of writing in Provincetown, he felt like a sailor again "making port" and summarily embarked upon an "anti-Volstead orgy" with the city's "poison masquerading as whiskey." Though for the most part he avoided rehearsals, when he did turn up, he was "deeply excited and gaudily indifferent all at once," Edna Kenton recalled. He remained largely silent during the final dress rehearsal, but he did correct Gilpin on one point: "Charlie, don't play the emperor—play the Pullman porter from 137 Street." This was at eleven thirty at night, two days before opening night, and Gilpin turned to Cook and Light and asked for another run-through. This time, he nailed it. "That was the performance everybody saw," Light said. "Gene had a great gift as a director. He wouldn't say much but what he said would go right to the heart of a character. He gave an actor the key."[256]

Problems arose between O'Neill and Gilpin over time, however, especially when Gilpin refused to say the word "nigger," replacing it with euphemisms like "negro" and "colored man." First, O'Neill threatened him with bodily harm: "If you change the lines again, I'll beat the hell out of you!" Unfazed, Gilpin still didn't comply. O'Neill then demanded his dismissal, but that was out of the question. Gilpin was too perfect for the role to lose over a few line changes. O'Neill also castigated the actor for relying on "cheap theatrical tricks," but he admitted decades later that his personal response to Gilpin had little to do with his performance: "As I look back now on all my work, I can honestly say there was only one actor who carried out every notion of a character I had in mind. That actor was Charles Gilpin as the Pullman porter in *The Emperor Jones*."[257]

"[Gilpin] is a man," Jig Cook reflected on the actor's success with the role, "who for years had within himself the power to mount to the top of the ladder, and there has been no ladder, none upon which circumstances permitted a man of his race to set foot." "Eugene O'Neill made the ladder," he said, adding that he couldn't have done it without the Players' philosophy of collaborative theater. Their innovations in lighting and sound, Cook said, combined with designer Cleon Throckmorton's primordial sets, amplified Gilpin's tour de force performance and O'Neill's groundbreaking script: "Had O'Neill not been a member of a group which he knows to be ready to attempt the untried—ready to make any interesting new departure— he would have no incentive to write 'The Emperor Jones.' " O'Neill concurred. Together, he remarked a month into the production, the Players had formed "a new ingenuity and creative collaboration on the part of the producer—a new system of staging of extreme simplicity and flexibility which, combined with art in lighting, [permitted] many scenes and instantaneous changes, a combination of the scope of the movies with all that is best of the spoken drama."[258]

On the night of November 1, 1920, the crowded line to the box office for the premiere of *The Emperor Jones* stretched up the block to Washington Square. "You cannot see it unless you are a subscriber or the guest of a subscriber," the *New York Sun* alerted its readers. "So subscribe now and avoid the rush. Telephone Spring 8363 and secure your reservations." At $7.15 a subscription, the Players added a thousand members to their "sacred list" in the first week, for a total of fifteen hundred. They also expanded their performances to Sundays, though since there was a prohibition against Sunday performances in New York, admission was limited to "membership ticket only or by guest ticket purchased through a member." The New York Sabbath Committee still contacted the police. Cook and Light, with their lawyer Harry Weinberger, battled the charge of "violating the law against Sunday theatricals" in court and won on the grounds that 133 Macdougal was a private clubhouse, not a professional theater.[259]

Among the throng at Macdougal Street on one of those nights was James Weldon Johnson, author of "Self-Determining Haiti," who'd recently been elected the first black president of the NAACP. Johnson noted that *The Emperor Jones* wasn't the first American play to rise above the grotesque distortions of black-faced minstrelsy, the hugely popular variety shows that caricatured "happy darkies." Ridgely

Torrence's three one-act plays with the Coloured Players at Madison Square Garden in 1917, he said (also designed by Robert Edmond Jones), deserved that distinction. But *The Emperor Jones* starred a black man supported by a white cast and, Johnson observed, "No previous effort on the stage with African American actors and themes, so far as the Negro is concerned, evoked more than favorable comment." Thanks in large part to Gilpin's operatic interpretation of the role, he said, "another important page in the history of the Negro in the the-atre was written. . . . By his work in *The Emperor Jones* Gilpin reached the highest point of achievement on the legitimate stage that had yet been attained by a Negro in America."[260]

The Emperor Jones ran for an extended run of seven weeks before it moved uptown on December 27 to the Selwyn Theater. "They didn't really understand what I was writing," O'Neill recalled bitterly about the droves of fashionable New Yorkers in attendance. "They merely said to themselves, 'Oh look, the ape can talk!' "[261] Still, the produc-tion moved on to the Princess, the Majestic in Brooklyn, and the Shubert Brothers' Riviera Theatre; after 490 performances around New York, it spun off on a thirty-five-week national tour.[262] By 1928, even as sophisticated a theatergoer as the novelist Edith Wharton, who respected O'Neill as "our only real playwright," quipped to a friend, with a racist reference to the trend *The Emperor Jones* had start-ed, "No one knows how long a play without murderers or niggers will be able to hold the public."[263]

The company understood that the tour in the South wouldn't be without its perils. But the Players couldn't have foreseen how hostile the pushback would be from white supremacists. After an engage-ment before thousands of students at the traditionally black Howard University in Washington, D.C., the play moved on to Norfolk and Richmond, Virginia (Gilpin's hometown), where it was so well received it attracted the ire of the Ku Klux Klan. The "Ku Klux jackasses," as O'Neill called them after hearing about the incident, sent a letter to Gilpin's hotel warning the actor not to travel below the Mason-Dixon line. The warning was heeded, and the company redirected the tour to Ohio. They never went further south than Richmond.[264]

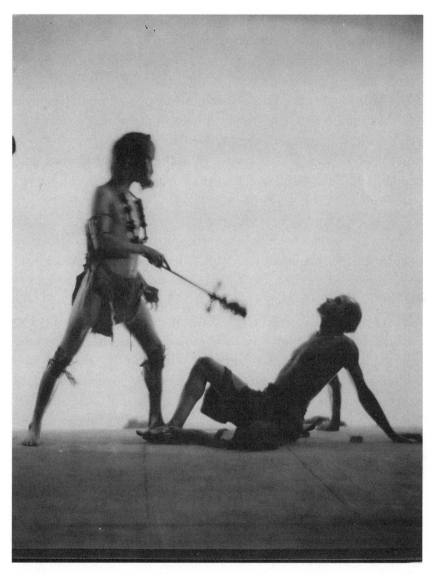

Charles S. Gilpin (right) as Brutus Jones with the African witch doctor,
performed by Japanese Noh dancer Michio Itow, in O'Neill's *The Emperor
Jones* at the Provincetown Playhouse, November 1, 1920. The brilliant
lighting effect is generated by George "Jig" Cook's dome.

✳   ✳   ✳

The Emperor Jones infuriated many within the African American community as well; the portrayal of Jones "does not elevate the negro," they contended.[265] And it wasn't just O'Neill's use of the "N-word" (though that didn't help, nor did the minstrel-sounding dialect). Rather, it was the more odious perpetuation of the stereotype of black Americans as innately superstitious. As the white *Brooklyn Daily Eagle* critic ignorantly wrote of O'Neill's antihero, "Jones is shrewd and stupid, remorseless and genial, far-seeing and superstitious, uniting in himself the racial qualities which make the American negro a problem and a delight."[266]

By portraying blacks as susceptible to irrational fears, O'Neill was in fact walking the same perilous tightrope that Mark Twain had several decades before him. Yet both O'Neill and Twain shared the belief that Christianity was no less superstitious than any other supernatural faith. From the beginning of Twain's *The Adventures of Huckleberry Finn* (1885), Huck Finn sees little difference between his friends Tom Sawyer and the slave Jim's rites involving dead cats and Irish potatoes and the Sunday School he's forced to attend; in *The Emperor Jones*, O'Neill pits even more "primitive" superstitions against the white-sanctified superstition of Christianity. Preparing to sacrifice himself to the crocodile god, Jones cries out for mercy for "dis po' sinner" and prays to "Lawd Jesus" to save him, contrasting the god of the enslavers with the pagan god of his African ancestry (*CP1*, 1058, 1059). (O'Neill had been conscious of his use of racial superstition with *The Dreamy Kid*, too, but had regrettably disregarded what would later be made evident in *Jones*: when Agnes Boulton read Dreamy's resolution to wait by his grandmother's deathbed in spite of the danger of the police, Boulton mistakenly assumed it was love that made him stay. "No," O'Neill replied, then slowly read out Mammy's threat and Dreamy's terrified response: "'If yo' leave me now yo' ain't goin' to get no bit of luck so long as yo' live, I tell yo' dat!' . . . 'Don't yo' hear de curse she puts on me if I does?'")[267]

Back in the winter of 1915–16, O'Neill had written little of consequence and spent most of his time at the Hell Hole getting stewed with Terry Carlin; but he did manage to commit a key poem to paper, a few lines that both look forward to *The Emperor Jones* and tackle the apparent human need, even for atheists like himself, for superstition of any kind. This untitled work contains, like *Jones*, the relentless beat of a tom-tom drum, the primal rhythms of the African jungle and the Congo, the existential terror of recognizing one's pointlessness in an indifferent universe, and then, most significantly, a futile last-minute plea to a higher power. The final stanza reads:

> And here we sit!
> You and I—
> In the Congo of the soul
> All the reverberating tom-toms
> Of everlasting infancy
> Are drumming out the boom-boom-boom—
> (The presence of God in one's ear-drums)
> Until one's atheism
> Shrieks in the Dark
> And cowers on a heap of dung
> To pray![268]

Not all African American critics decried O'Neill's approach. When the West Indian American "father of Harlem radicalism" Hubert Henry Harrison reviewed *The Emperor Jones* for the Black Nationalist leader Marcus Garvey's *Negro World*, he noted regretfully that when Boni and Liveright published the book that April (with *Diff'rent* and *The Straw*), the publisher had foolishly advertised the play as "a study of the psychology of fear and of race superstition." "A censorious critic might cavil at the propriety of the last four words," Harrison admitted, "but the rest of the statement is quite correct. It is pre-eminently a psychological study." Singling out Gilpin's performance in particular as "a work of genius ... [that] stands on its own feet and justifies itself," Harrison countered what he otherwise thought a "commendable racial pride" from other black critics: "Mr. O'Neill, in portraying the soul of an ignorant and superstitious person of any race could not be so silly as to put in that person's mouth the language of a different sort of person. He did the best he could—and he did it very well." "The fault, dear Brutus," he said, quoting Shakespeare while alluding to O'Neill's protagonist, "is not in our stars, but in ourselves."[269] Harrison would later compare Marcus Garvey's demagoguery to Brutus Jones's after Garvey had been convicted in 1923 for, Harrison noted in his diary, "using the mails to defraud his 'fellow-men of the negro race.' "[270] "He gave them what they wanted," Harrison wrote in a damning critique of Garvey and his followers. "And at this point I am reminded of 'The Emperor Jones'—a fine picture of the whole psychology of the Garvey movement."[271]

On June 9, a few days after Harrison's review of *The Emperor Jones* was published, O'Neill responded to its author with deep gratitude for his interpretation, "one of the very few intelligent criticisms of the piece that have come to my notice."[272] In this unpublished letter, O'Neill expressed his desire that Gilpin's talent might inspire black playwrights, and he again argued that propaganda meant to "elevate" the disenfranchised doesn't "strike home": "I am glad to see you remonstrate with those of your people who find fault with the play because it does not 'elevate.' Such folk do not realize that the only propaganda that ever strikes home is the truth about the human soul, black or white. Intentional uplift plays never amount to a damn— especially as uplift. To portray a human being, that is all that counts. ... And, by the way, that same criticism of 'Jones' which you protest against is a very common one made by a similar class of white people about my other plays—they don't 'elevate' them. So you see!"[273]

"I am hoping in the time between now and the end of the play's career," O'Neill continued, "to write another Negro play which I have in mind—in which case my association with Mr. Gilpin, always a pleasant one from the very start, may be continued and his 'Where do I go from here?' may find a solution to his liking. He is a wonderful actor and should not go playless." The other "Negro play" O'Neill had in mind, about his friend Joe Smith from the Hell Hole, was going to be titled either "White" or "Honest Honey Boy." His 1921 work diary reads: " 'Joe'—tragic-comedy of negro gambler (Joe Smith)—8 scenes—4 in N.Y. of his heyday—4 in present N.Y. of Prohibition times, his decline."[274] (His next "Negro play," also related to Joe

Smith's life, would be *All God's Chillun Got Wings*, produced in 1924, but the original idea would be more fully realized as the background for Joe Mott in *The Iceman Cometh*.)

O'Neill nevertheless recognized that he was writing as an outsider and saw the need for the black experience to be written from within. "Don't you think the writers among your people should be encouraged—and urged—to try and write plays for [Gilpin]?" O'Neill wrote to Harrison. "Something very fine for the Negro in general might evolve from such an attempt." Indeed, black writers, artists, and musicians were just then emerging from Harlem, and for them Brutus Jones's white tyranny might also be read as a cautionary tale: while serving as a judge for a Harlem playwriting contest, O'Neill counseled its participants to ignore white literary authority. "Be yourselves," he advised. "Don't reach out for our stuff which we call good!"[275]

By the close of the 1920–21 season, Charles Gilpin had become the first African American listed by the Drama League of New York as one of the top ten people who had done the most that year for American theater. The League traditionally honors its chosen few at its annual gala; but a public outcry erupted over the invitation of a black man to the exclusive gathering, and the Drama League hastily, if contritely, withdrew Gilpin's invitation. In spite of a growing dislike for his leading man, O'Neill, also on the list, was revolted by the League's pandering to its racist membership, and he and the critic Kenneth Macgowan, the League's former director with whom O'Neill had developed close ties during *Beyond the Horizon*'s run, together petitioned the other recipients to turn down their invitations—which they all did. Gilpin's invitation was promptly reinstated and the event was a great success. A decade later, James Weldon Johnson wrote that the affair had already taken on "an archaic character. It is doubtful if a similar incident today could provide such a degree of asininity."[276]

Gilpin originally thought he'd make an appearance at the gala of "about four minutes." He proudly admitted that after his

performances he wouldn't go "hobnobbing" with the white theater crowd either, instead returning to his "little circle of friends" in
Harlem, "where I belong." But after receiving the night's longest
standing ovation, he said, "I stayed for four hours and had the time
of my life. No, it didn't take much nerve to go and face the crowd. I
could count on the artists treating me fairly, and I didn't care a hang
about the others. They could sit there and stare at me as though I
were some kind of a prize monkey and it wouldn't disturb me at all."[277]

The NAACP awarded Gilpin the Spingarn Medal in 1921 for "the
highest or noblest achievement by an American Negro during the
preceding year or years," and President Warren Harding invited him
to dine with him at the White House. But O'Neill said in April of that
year that Gilpin was ultimately edged out of the production in early
1922 because of "the effect of too much alcohol and actor's swell head
[egotism]." At one point in New York, he'd reasoned with Gilpin, one
alcoholic to another: "Charlie, if you won't keep a bottle in your dressing room, we'll let you have a drink after each scene." Gilpin accepted
the terms, and the Players served the actor a shot after each scene,
making it seven shots total before the last scene, when Jones's lifeless body is carried onstage by the natives who'd gunned him down.
Whether because of or in spite of such measures, Gilpin's drinking
problem continued to spiral out of control, and Paul Robeson agreed
to replace Gilpin for the London production in 1923. Robeson by
then had come to see Brutus Jones as a "great part" and the play "a
true classic of the drama, American or otherwise." O'Neill was equally
impressed with Robeson, who became a cherished compatriot in the
years to come. From the first, O'Neill thought the actor a "wonderful
presence & voice, full of ambition and a damn fine man personally
with real brains—not a 'ham' "—like Gilpin.[278]

Though after this humiliating dismissal, Gilpin was hired for the
occasional role, including several revivals as Brutus Jones, his acting
career never fully rebounded. In 1930, he died in poverty on a chicken
farm in New Jersey at age fifty-one. His death notice in the black
press lamented that after his breakout performance in *The Emperor*

Jones, Gilpin had been "the envy of the theatrical world. If America had been a fully civilized country, he would have gone on to greater fame—he would have electrified the stage as Othello. But the chance never came, and one of America's great actors was left to die broken-hearted."[279]

The Emperor Jones marked the beginning of the end for the Provincetown Players, too, at the same time, paradoxically, it had launched them into the public eye. "Values had shifted overnight, astonishingly," Edna Kenton later wrote. After the notoriety of *The Emperor Jones*, most of the Players would no longer settle for less than Broadway greatness: "To go uptown with our first success was higher honor than to stay down town with our experiments. It was human; it was natural . . . we were a little drunk with the wine of applause and we lost our balance and fell." Kenton believed that their only savior from ruin was Jack Reed; but then the tragic news arrived. Reed had died of typhus in Russia, with Bryant at his side, less than two weeks before the opening night of *Jones*, and he lay buried, after a Soviet hero's funeral, inside the Kremlin walls. "If Jack could have risen from his grave in the Red Square at Moscow and come back to us for just one night—that night," Kenton said, "when we decided to go uptown with *The Emperor Jones*. . . . But Jack was lying in his tomb at Moscow and Jig was an old prophet, saying over and over again familiar words that held no meaning any more for most of us. He knew it."[280]

In truth, Cook's ideas, however inspiring, were often incomprehensible to the other Players. "It was a kind of drunkenness that is beyond recall," the writer and Provincetowner Djuna Barnes reminisced over Cook's heady notions of community theater. "Jig who could inspire divergent minds to work together for one idea, an ideal that was never quite clear to him, or if clear to him, one that he could not make clear to me nor to a number of others, sent his actors on a scent of no man's rabbit. It was, I think, Jig's rabbit, Jig's conjuring trick; he knew the passes, he spoke the formula, he had the hat, but— was he too proud, or was he too wise, or was he too limited to produce the hare? Who knows?—but it made good hunting."[281]

The Theatre F(r)eud

By the time O'Neill sent *The Emperor Jones* off to Macdougal Street the previous October of 1920, he'd already completed his next play, *Diff'rent*. The Players opened the two-act on December 27, the day *The Emperor Jones* moved uptown. *Diff'rent*, like its predecessor, also moved to several uptown theaters (the Selwyn, the Times Square, the Princess); but unlike its predecessor, it received a tepid critical response. Kenneth Macgowan applauded O'Neill's gifts but lamented that "the unescapable impression of anyone who remembers 'The Emperor Jones' and its fine imaginative quality, its color, and its spiritual power, and compares it with 'Diff'rent,' must be that the newer play is a step backward for its author." Barrett Clark joked the play was a box office flop, "even with the help of the censor who tried to stop it." Following his enormous successes with *Beyond the Horizon* and *The Emperor Jones*, O'Neill shrugged off the failure: "Well, this is rather reassuring. I had begun to think I was too popular to be honest."[282]

Based loosely on a story Fifine Clark told O'Neill about a local Provincetown woman, *Diff'rent* portrays a repressed middle-aged woman who seeks a degenerate younger man's sexual attention in a coastal New England town. The posters stapled on the billboards around Manhattan thus announced the play lasciviously as a "daring study of a sex-starved woman."[283] As a consequence, O'Neill grumbled, the play "aroused the ire of all the feminists against me."[284] He forcefully denied their accusations that his heroine, Emma Crosby, was meant to reflect all women: "She is universal only in the sense that she reacts definitely to a definite sex-suppression, as every woman might. The form her reaction takes is absolutely governed by her environment and her own character. Let the captious be sure they know their Emmas as well as I do before they tell me how she would act."[285]

Worse yet, the news media forged an intellectual pairing that would hound O'Neill to his grave: Sigmund Freud, the celebrated German psychologist, had gained a wide following in the United States, and many critics believed O'Neill was peddling bandwagon psychoanalysis. The *New York Sun* fired a warning shot: "There is a tendency among the Provincetown Players to present plays that turn their stage into a Freudian clinic. This inclination should not be overplayed unless these ambitious and successful players desire their little Macdougal street playhouse to become known as the Theatre Freud."[286]

The *New York Tribune*'s drama critic Heywood Broun, a member of the famed Algonquin Round Table, who generally thought of O'Neill as punching above his intellectual weight, also happened to be the husband of feminist writer Ruth Hale. Glaspell warned O'Neill that Hale "objected strongly" to the play's sexist implications and gave him the impression that Broun was prepared to publish his wife's review of *Diff'rent* under his own byline.[287] Whichever of them did write it, the notice took the other criticisms a step farther. Not only had O'Neill written a trendy Freudian play, he also didn't know what he was talking about: "O'Neill seems ill informed of the more searching theories of sex psychology. He does not understand that repressed instincts tend to burrow deeper and deeper and without some adequate explanation the sudden impulse of the heroine to translate into actuality the desires which she has long suppressed, or perhaps sublimated, is not convincing."[288] Within two weeks, the *Tribune* printed a self-restrained but pointed riposte by O'Neill. Any channeling of Freud's work into his own was incidental, he insisted. As far back as the Greeks, Freud's postulations had been available to anyone "intuitive" enough to grasp them.[289] "What has influenced my plays," he said, "is my knowledge of the drama of all time—particularly Greek tragedy—and not any books on psychology."[290]

In fact, in 1920 his reading of Freud was limited to *Totem and Taboo* (1913).[291] (He would later read *Beyond the Pleasure Principle* in 1925 to assist in his effort to quit drinking.)[292] He'd also read Carl Jung's *Psychology of the Unconscious* (1912) after it was translated to English in 1916. "If I have been influenced unconsciously," he admitted later, "it must have been by [Jung's] book more than any other psychological work."[293] "The Freudian brethren and sisteren seem quite set up about it and, after reading astonishing complexes between the lines of my simplicities, claim it for their own. Well, so some of them did with 'Emperor Jones.' They are hard to shake!"[294] "Whether it is psychoanalytically exact or not," he said, "I will leave more dogmatic students of Freud and Jung than myself (or than Freud and Jung) to decide. It is life, nevertheless. I stick out for that—life that swallows all formulas."[295]

That winter, O'Neill swore a "New Year's oath" to quit drinking and went back to work on *The First Man*. If he'd felt cowed by the feminist or Freudian backlash caused by *Diff'rent*, this play didn't show it. In what itself might have been read as a four-act Freudian slip, *The First Man* exposes O'Neill's actual hostility toward the whole-cloth demands and limitations of family life. His marriage to Boulton doesn't appear to have been the problem, at least not yet. On April 12, 1921, he'd arranged for friends in New York to buy and ship a longed-for kimono for their third anniversary, and he missed her terribly whenever events conspired to separate them—for the first few days, at least.[296]

In late April, the chronically bad state of O'Neill's teeth induced him to travel up to his friend Saxe Commins's new dental practice in Rochester, New York. (Commins's first name is pronounced like the instrument, but O'Neill referred to him as "Sox.")[297] O'Neill had met Commins, Stella Ballantine's brother, back when the Players produced Commins's play *The Obituary* in 1916 during their first season in New York. Both reticent men among outgoing thespians, they'd bonded over their quiet ways; but after this trip to Rochester, a friendship was forged that would endure through O'Neill's final years.

But after more than a week of excruciating root canals and extractions, O'Neill longed to be back with his wife: "God, how I wish you were here! I love you so! It is truly love that passeth all bounds, beyond which there is nothing. I am You. So take care of the real me whilst this poor ghost is haunting dental parlors!"[298] The flurry of love letters back and forth tapered off after a week or so, however, replaced by the commonplace matters of domestic and professional life—Shane's health, bills, Provincetown gossip, Terry Carlin's drunken antics, production schedules, the condition of Peaked Hill, and so on. Later that summer O'Neill felt miserable and neglected as he labored on his writing while Boulton went off for the month of August on a whirlwind tour to visit friends in Boston, Jim and Ella

O'Neill in New London, members of her own family in Litchfield, Connecticut, then down to West Point Pleasant and back up to New York and Westchester County to hunt for a winter residence.

While she was gone, he'd finished *The First Man* and revisited his "Fountain of Youth" play, *The Fountain*, about Juan Ponce de León's quest for eternal life in the New World. "If I really believed that *The Fountain* were as rotten as it seems to me now I'd hang the script out on the hook in the toilet," O'Neill wrote to Boulton. "Either it is a dead thing or I am. . . . Come home and bring my life back! These days crawl sufferingly like futile purgatories."[299]

After a frustrating week of false starts and delays, O'Neill's four-act *Gold* opened at New York's Frazee Theater on June 1, 1921. Once he'd attended rehearsals with its notoriously histrionic star, Willard Mack, O'Neill knew it would be a catastrophic failure. Several rehearsals in, he recused himself and "got good and 'pickled' to chase the memory of it away." Having absorbed toxic amounts of Prohibition rotgut, O'Neill made his way back to Provincetown in order, he said, "to regain sanity and await the crash."[300] Boulton went down on her own to oversee the final rehearsals and report back on the opening night. O'Neill remained at Peaked Hill to lick his wounds and continue work on *The Fountain*, but was soon buoyed by news that producer Arthur Hopkins had optioned *"Anna Christie,"* his revised version of *Chris*, for production that fall.

John D. Williams, the financial muscle behind *Beyond the Horizon* and now *Gold*, was an alcoholic in his own right, and he might have been more "pickled" than usual when he approved *Gold*'s press release: "Eugene O'Neill's greatest drama . . . the greatest dramatic event of the year!!"[301] The absurd hyperbole of this statement was laid conspicuously bare on opening night. "Talky, balky, tiresome and impossible," brayed *Variety*.[302] The *Nation* accused O'Neill of beginning to sound like a broken record—another charge, like Freud and misogyny, that has withstood the test of history: "We cannot rid ourselves of the feeling that we have heard all this before."[303] When George Jean Nathan told O'Neill that he actually liked aspects of *Gold*, even its author responded with terse finality, "You're wrong. It's a bad play. I'm telling you."[304]

Heywood Broun was goaded by the play into calling for a moratorium on the "great-great-grandchildren of Ophelia." "Madness, to be sure," he wrote, "is a stage convention much abused. Ophelia can hardly have died in any such untimely manner as Shakespeare pretends. She has left too many grandchildren to the dramatists of all succeeding centuries." In a later review, Broun added, "Ophelia really ought to have heeded the advice of Hamlet and got her to a nunnery. She has bequeathed a tiresome strain to the theater. The defective drama is too much with us."[305] After this, O'Neill's low opinion of Broun curdled into a rancid hatred. To the playwright, Broun was now "a proper yellow son of a bitch. . . . A faker and liar, envious, etc."[306]

O'Neill hadn't yet admitted it to himself, but Broun wasn't far off the mark. He denied Freud's influence to the very end; but he did feel shackled by the constraints of dramatic realism, which concealed what he called "the submerged mountain" that shaped human behavior. The realist movement, thanks for the most part to Henrik Ibsen, had mercifully given the vaudevillian hook to the cheap romances and tawdry melodramas of James O'Neill's generation; but it had also dragged the soliloquy offstage along with them. This was the problem he had to contend with as a dramatist. Up to then, the only solution to match the depth of the soliloquy or the novel that had presented itself, in Jimmy Light's words, was "psychopathic raving," which was "still realism and not passé dramaturgy if the heroine is psychotic and the lines do make literal sense."[307] Susan Glaspell had also employed mentally unhinged women in her one-acts *Trifles* (1916) and *The Outside* (1917) as well as in *The Verge*, a full-length the Players would produce that November 1921, but Glaspell's women had conveyed a deeper understanding at work. "And that is called sanity. And made a virtue—to lock one in," her protagonist Claire Archer in *The Verge* says to her husband, then declares, "No, I'm not mad. I'm—too sane!" Or perhaps, Claire reflects, Emily Dickinson–like, "Madness . . . is the only chance for sanity."[308] Though *Diff'rent* and *Gold* were critical failures because of their purposeful use of psychic malfunction, O'Neill would revisit Ophelia's descendants over the years with a racist white woman driven to madness by her marriage to an ambitious black man in *All God's*

Chillun Got Wings; a fantastical treatment of the Oedipal complex in *More Stately Mansions;* and, most poignantly and self-consciously, his drugged mother in *Long Day's Journey Into Night*. "The Mad Scene," Jamie Tyrone scoffs when Mary descends the stairs in a morphine-induced haze. "Enter Ophelia!" (*CP3*, 824).

The First Man, which O'Neill copyrighted that October 1921, on the same day as *The Fountain*, was originally conceived as a modern re-counting of Jason and the Argonauts' quest for the Golden Fleece (the protagonist's surname is "Jayson"). Instead, the play wound up being O'Neill's first intentional foray into the gender wars. He'd complained about feminists giving him a hard time after *Diff'rent*, "as if the same theme could have been woven with equal truth about a man, with a different reaction, of course."[309] This time, he had his female counterpart in the form of Susan Glaspell, who was writing her own gender play, *The Verge*, that same summer in Provincetown.

Glaspell's Claire Archer offers a singular window into the literary cross-pollination between Glaspell and O'Neill. Like O'Neill's protagonist Curtis Jayson, Claire also balks at the constraints of parenting in favor of self-actuation. In the final scene, she rejects her conformist daughter and husband and murders her lover, all of whom she views as symbols of social and psychological entropy. O'Neill, in his early play *Servitude*, had written a neglectful father and husband in David Roylston, a character who would have gotten under a female audience's skin had it been produced; with *The First Man*, likely emboldened by Glaspell's work in progress, nakedly exposed his jaundiced view of domestic living.

What appears to have inspired *The First Man* more than his marriage was the imprisonment of fatherhood. O'Neill's protagonist Curtis Jayson is an ambitious anthropologist searching the globe for evidence of "the first man." He and his wife, Martha, have lost two children to pneumonia before the action of the play, a tragedy that brings about a ten-year world tour and a compact between them to have no more children. When Curtis turns on Martha for getting pregnant without his permission and defends their child-free existence, he sounds eerily like O'Neill at the time he was courting Agnes Boulton:

CURTIS: Haven't we been sufficient, you and I together? Isn't that a more difficult, beautiful happiness to achieve than—children? Doesn't it mean anything to you that I need you so terribly—for myself, for my work—for everything that is best and worthiest in me?[310]

O'NEILL: You [Boulton] had seemed to me alone and virginal and somehow—with nothing but yourself. I wanted you alone . . . in an aloneness broken by nothing. Not even by children of our own.[311]

BOULTON: To be alone with me—that was what he wanted; we had everything—work, love and companionship. Never, *never* let anything interfere with work or love![312]

Martha Jayson dies in childbirth in a tragic final scene, complete with blood-curdling shrieks of agony offstage that would appall audiences when it eventually opened in March of 1922. Martha's infant survives to be raised by nurses until Curtis returns from his expedition.

Late that summer, Boulton felt certain she'd become pregnant again and took, she said, "strong medicine" to end the pregnancy. In mid-August, during her visit to Litchfield, she wrote O'Neill assuring him that she was monitoring her periods closely (September 11 being her next "Red-letter day"). "The joke of it is," she told him, "I came sick on the day which was O.K. according to my *second* set of calculations—so there wasn't much chance of anything being wrong. Hereafter, let's hang a calendar in the bedroom! (*You'd* enjoy that!)"[313]

"Anna Christie" opened on November 2, 1921, at the Vanderbilt Theatre, the day before *The Straw*'s out-of-town New London premiere. Nearly everyone loved it, aside from, as was the case with *In the Zone*, its creator. (A predictable exception to the general acclaim was Heywood Broun: "After seeing 'Anna Christie' we cannot escape feeling that Eugene O'Neill has not yet lifted himself out of being 'the most promising playwright in America.' ")[314] The curtain opened to reveal Robert Edmond Jones's much praised rendering of the interior of Johnny "the Priest's," a bar based on O'Neill's old hangout Jimmy the Priest's. In the stage directions, O'Neill describes the

bar in minute detail, and his dialogue re-creates the common slang and defiant attitudes of the waterfront figures he knew intimately. Anna Christopherson, a young prostitute, has arrived in town to reunite with her seafaring father, Chris Christopherson (O'Neill's friend from Jimmy's), and Anna agrees to sail with him on his barge from New York to Boston. Trapped in a fog bank off the Massachusetts coast, they rescue a shipwrecked, Driscoll-like Irish sailor named Mat Burke, and he and Anna fall in love. Chris doesn't approve of the union, as he believes that the sea, embodied for him by the Irishman, is an "ole davil" responsible for annihilating his family back in Sweden. Now his daughter has fallen under its spell.

"Anna Christie" garnered even larger box office returns than *Beyond the Horizon* or *The Emperor Jones*. The drama critic James Whittaker proclaimed, with more than a hint of sarcasm, that with *"Anna Christie,"* "Eugene O'Neill has turned New York into what is known in stage vernacular as a 'dog town.' " ("Dog town" was theater argot for smaller cities where tryouts are held before a play moves to New York.) "He has bewitched those flinty mercenaries, the managers," he wrote in mock disbelief. "For him all the vulgar preliminaries to production are dispensed with. . . . He does not have to peddle script on the Broadway curb. He does not have to have a letter from a Senator to pass through doors. And he does not have to travel to Wilmington, Del., to see his play staged in secret, and lend a humiliated hand to its stealthy rewriting."[315] Tongue-in-cheek as Whittaker's pronouncement sounds, the truth behind it was undeniable. Clayton Hamilton's warning at the New London station that when a dramatist submitted a script there was "not one chance in a thousand it will ever be read; not one chance in a million of its ever being accepted" was a rule that no longer applied to Eugene O'Neill.

Audiences confounded O'Neill by cheering the notoriously gloomy playwright's "happy-ever-after," and very few critics departed *"Anna Christie"* with the sense of tragic fate he'd intended. When George Jean Nathan read the four-act play the previous winter, Nathan prophetically warned his friend that the final scene would be regarded as a "happy ending," whereas O'Neill, he knew, wished to evoke the sea's "conquest of Anna." O'Neill insisted that the moment when Mat discovers Anna is non-Catholic—not religious at all, in fact—the integrity of her "oath" to forget the past and never return to prostitution is slippery at best. But the "weak-minded" arm of the press had latched on so firmly to the idea of the happy ending that he was moved to publish a denial in the *New York Times*: "In this type of naturalistic play, which attempts to translate life into its own terms, I am a denier of all endings. Things happen in life, run their course as the incidental, accidental, the fated, then pause to give their inevitable consequences time to mobilize for the next attack. . . . The curtain falls. Behind it their lives go on." "Lastly," he concluded, "to those who think I deliberately distorted my last act because a 'happy ending' would be calculated to make the play more of a popular success I have only this to say: The sad truth is that you have precedents enough to spare in the history of our drama for such a suspicion. But, on the other hand, you have every reason not to believe it of me."[316]

O'Neill wrote the final scene of *"Anna Christie"* to act as a figurative "comma at the end of a gaudy introductory clause, with the body of the sentence still unwritten." At one point, he even toyed with naming it *Comma*.[317] But almost no one got this. Burns Mantle, for instance, summed it up in his *Evening Mail* review: "When the record of his playwriting achievements is written, 'Anna Christie' will likely be pointed to as the first Eugene O'Neill play in which the morbid young genius compromised with the happy ending all true artists of the higher drama so generously despise." Nathan railed against such critics who "snicker self-satisfiedly that he has arbitrarily stuck a theatrical happy ending onto his play. In them the poison of the showshop has worked so long that it is simply impossible for them to consider him as an autonomous artist." Among the critics, Alexander Woollcott of the *New York Times* was a notable exception: "O'Neill seems to be suggesting to the departing playgoers that they can regard this as a happy ending if they are short-sighted enough to believe it and weak-minded enough to crave it."[318]

That American audiences would applaud a respectable marriage as a happy ending for a "girl gone bad" was a remarkable development nevertheless.[319] Even the quotation marks around the name (rarely respected as part of his title) are meant to accentuate that "Anna Christie" is a prostitute's street name. Beyond that, the play contained unmistakably feminist overtones: when Anna's father and lover argue over who will control her future, she stops them, delivering what can only be read as a feminist's decree: "Gawd, you'd think I was a piece of furniture! . . . I'll do what I please and no man, I don't give a hoot who he is, can tell me what to do! I ain't askin' either of you for a living. I can make it myself—one way or other" (*CP1*, 1007).

Kenneth Macgowan crowed that with this play O'Neill had made "dramatic history": "It is hard to think of any American play that is the superior of Eugene O'Neill's newest work in truth of life or in dramatic force."[320] O'Neill himself soon publicly renounced it, not only for the widespread belief in its happy ending but for its "naturalism," which he defined simply as drama that's "true to life."[321] "Naturalism is too easy," he told a reporter. "It would, for instance, be a perfect cinch to go on writing *Anna Christie*s all my life. I could always be sure of the rent then. . . . Because you can say practically nothing at all of our lives since 1914 through that form. The naturalistic play is really less natural than a romantic or expressionistic play. That is, shoving a lot of human beings on a stage and letting them say the identical things in a theatre they would say in a drawing room or a saloon does not necessarily make for naturalness." "It's what those men and women do not say," O'Neill said, "that usually is most interesting."[322]

O'Neill's *The Straw* premiered at the Lyceum Theatre in New London on November 3, then moved to the Greenwich Village Theatre a week later. *The Straw*, about his time at Gaylord Farm, would always remain one of O'Neill's personal favorites. As he told George Tyler, its producer, he considered it "the best play I have written—better even than *Beyond the Horizon*." Most critics dismissed it, however, as decent in quality of dialogue but grimly clinical in theme and setting. One reviewer described it as "the most lugubrious and depressing play that could possibly be encountered within theatre walls." "We wish Mr. O'Neill would stick to the sea as his background," said another.

"His salt water dramas never make us seasick, but this play sort of makes us landsick, as it were. . . . This particular sanitarium may cure a patient when there is the straw of love and hope to cling to, but it is likely to kill the audience." Yet another chided O'Neill for his "tuberculosis Romeo and Juliet," suggesting that the dramatist "will probably write a musical comedy around cancer later on." When Jimmy Light had first read it, he'd found the love story impossible to believe. O'Neill replied, "Something like that happened to me once."[323]

O'Neill's tragic heroine Eileen Carmody dies from her disease, just as Kitty MacKay, O'Neill's "kitten," had two years after O'Neill's release from Gaylord Farm; but the tragedy doesn't shake O'Neill's faith in the bobbing "straw" of hopefulness that might rescue him and the other drowning souls he'd met. "It is for this reason," Barrett Clark wrote of *The Straw*, "that I have always considered O'Neill at bottom an optimist. He never leaves us feeling that life is not worth living. If he were as pessimistic as he is often said to be, in the first place he would not have gone to the trouble of trying to prove the futility of existence."[324] When Ed Keefe, O'Neill's friend from New London, wrote to say how much he enjoyed the play in New London, and O'Neill responded that he'd hoped to make the opening but hadn't been able to: "It was a rather hectic, nerve-wracking time for me," he said, though he thought it amusing that *The Straw* opened in New London since "there is so much autobiographical stuff in it connected with that town."[325] What O'Neill failed to say was that the concurrent productions weren't the only issues wracking his nerves that fall.

The previous August 1921, Kathleen Jenkins's lawyer had notified O'Neill that she expected him to finance their son's education. O'Neill agreed to pay $800 the first year, $900 the next, and then $1,000 each year thereafter until Eugene Jr. turned twenty-one. After eleven years, Jenkins also believed that Eugene was old enough to reveal to him the identity of his true father—the famous playwright Eugene O'Neill. Hearing this, the boy desperately wanted to meet him. O'Neill was apprehensive, though not averse to the idea (no diapers, less milk). As he'd written at the time in *The First Man*, Curtis

Jayson (O'Neill) would be able to embrace fatherhood only once the newborn is "old enough to know and love a big, free life" (*CP2*, 116).

That fall, Kathleen's mother Kate accompanied Eugene Jr. to the lobby of O'Neill's apartment building at 36 West Thirty-Fifth Street. Kenneth Macgowan stood at O'Neill's side to help out if the meeting took an awkward turn. In fact, according to Jenkins afterward, "They hit it off so well" she felt she was losing her son's allegiance to her ex-husband.[326] Father and son were both great baseball fans and connected strongly with that, most likely discussing the relative merits of the New York Yankees and the Brooklyn Dodgers. (O'Neill, it must be said, was a Yankees fan.)[327]

Surprisingly, O'Neill and Jenkins appear to have gotten back in touch much earlier than has previously been thought. On January 14, 1919, when O'Neill was commuting from West Point Pleasant to Macdougal Street and back, he sent his ex-wife a lengthy, amiable letter from New York. Written in pencil and warmly signed "Gene," a sign-off reserved only for his closest friends and relations, this tightly written eight-page communiqué is now presumably secure in private hands. Sotheby Parke-Bernet, a highly reputable auction house, sold this missing document to an unknown buyer in 1977. Its catalogue of sales describes the letter in startling terms, especially given it's been widely assumed they'd cut off all correspondence: "Unusually fine long early letter, full of information on his activities in the theater, the last page on social and family matters, with a loving conclusion."[328] (Jenkins's later discretion over the letter's existence in some ways parallels Boulton's decades later regarding *Exorcism*.) At the time O'Neill wrote this, he'd achieved neither fame nor fortune. But by the summer of 1921, when Jenkins requested money, he had both. O'Neill agreed to pay for Eugene's education, was granted visitation rights, and invited his son out to Peaked Hill for the following summer.

"Better luck next time!" O'Neill yawped in a letter to George Tyler after learning that *The Straw* had closed in New York after less than three weeks; but he expressed his abiding appreciation for Tyler's courage in backing his "hopeless hope." He wrote Saxe

Commins that he wasn't sure why *The Straw* had shut down before Saxe had time to attend it: "Everyone was afraid they'd catch T.B. by entering the theatre, I guess."³²⁹ But again, O'Neill brushed aside the failure. In a 1948 interview with the *New Yorker*, he borrows a line from *The Straw* from three decades earlier: "When *everybody* likes something, watch out!"³³⁰ In the play, Eileen Carmody tells Stephen Murray that "everybody" at the sanatorium has read his stories and "thinks they're fine." "Then [the stories] must be rotten," he replies with a smile (*CP1*, 784).

Over the holiday season, 1921–22, O'Neill granted an interview to Malcolm Mollan, the city desk editor from his *New London Telegraph* days, now a struggling freelancer, who'd threatened to fire him if he showed up drunk again. "Are you our foremost apostle of woe?" Mollan asked mischievously. "Many say you are." O'Neill grinned. "Oh, I don't know," he said, "there's Volstead." "You'll grant, I suppose," Mollan went on, "that there are interesting situations in life, even dramatic situations, out of which genuine happiness sometimes ensues?" "Sure, I'll write about happiness," came the reply, "if I ever happen to meet up with that luxury, and find it sufficiently dramatic and in harmony with any deep rhythm of life. But happiness is a word. What does it mean? Exaltation: an intensified feeling of the significant worth of man's being and becoming? Well, if it means that—and not a mere smirking contentment with one's lot—I know there is more of it in one real tragedy than in all the happy-ending plays ever written."³³¹

Mollan pressed O'Neill to clarify his apparent attempt to reform American society through drama. "I am not a propagandist," he responded, "not consciously, at any rate—in any sense of the word. . . . I have tried to keep my work free from all moral attitudinizing. To me there are no good people or bad people, just people. The same with deeds. 'Good' and 'evil' are stupidities, as misleading and out-worn fetishes as Brutus Jones's silver bullet."³³² Much of this outlook was derived from Max Stirner, who proposed that good and evil are mere fantasies, since one can murder freely so long as it's sanctioned by the state, which makes "morality nothing else than *loyalty*." O'Neill's views on morality, what would be called "moral relativism" today, also came from August Strindberg, who argued that to compose a believable fictional character demands roundness not just of personality, the simpler definition of strong characterization, but also of morality: "There is no such thing as absolute evil," Strindberg wrote, "the summary judgments that authors pass on people—this one is stupid, that one brutal, this one jealous, that one mean—ought to be challenged by naturalists, who know how richly complicated the soul is, and who are aware that 'vice' has a reverse side, which is very much like virtue."[333] In kind, O'Neill never considered himself or his plays as "immoral," he said, but rather "unmoral."[334]

A later friend of O'Neill's, the drama critic Sophus Winther, called this in 1934 a "naturalistic ethics" (also akin to the moral relativism of today). "If no one is to blame," he wrote of O'Neill's plays, "then moral certainty cannot exist." Naturalistic ethics are therefore untethered by the petty notions of good and evil one finds in melodrama; rather, they give the lie to society's ever-changing standards of morality. As early as 1914, in *Abortion*, O'Neill had already spelled out this worldview: "Some impulses are stronger than we are," his protagonist Jack Townshend says to his father, "have proved themselves so throughout our world's history. Is it not rather our ideals of conduct, of Right and Wrong, our ethics, which are unnatural and monstrously distorted? Is society not suffering from a case of the evil eye which sees evil where there is none?" (*CP1*, 213). Winther concludes by noting that O'Neill thus pushed society's laws "even further in that he condemns a fixed standard as destructive of life, holding that in the last analysis it will lead to false pride, arrogant and cruel behavior, hypocrisy and a destructive fanaticism."[335]

In 1957, Tennessee Williams echoed this with his own naturalistic ethics: "I don't believe in 'original sin,' " he wrote. "I don't believe in 'guilt.' I don't believe in villains or heroes—only right or wrong ways that individuals have taken, not by choice but by necessity or by certain still-uncomprehended influences in themselves, their circumstances, and their antecedents." In simpler terms, as O'Neill's third wife, Carlotta Monterey, later remarked on this same point, "Gene was never shocked at *what* people did. He was only interested in *why* they did it."[336]

After ten days of shepherding *"Anna Christie"* and *The Straw* onto up-town stages, O'Neill's artistic muse had withered out of commission, and he returned to Provincetown for a an indefinite period of recovery from "the after-effects of much bad booze." "After all the worry and bustle of rehearsals, openings, I'm all in—very much of a nervous wreck—and glad to be back up here where no one can talk theatre to me. For the nonce, I'm fed up on that subject."[337]

"I am in one of my periods of uncreative doldrums," he told Arthur Hopkins's press agent Oliver M. Sayler. "Read only the papers and the Saturday Evening Post, think not at all, walk much, and for emotional reaction have only a great and self-blighting loathing for the world in general. But these moods of the great loathing never last very long with me when the dunes are within walking distance, and I hope to report to you in my next that I am fully resurrected."[338]

Less than a week later, O'Neill reported that his "creative *élan*" had been "fully resurrected," and he'd begun writing his next play, *The Hairy Ape*, "with a mad rush": "Think I have got the swing of what I want to catch and, if I have, I ought to tear through it like a dose of salts. It is one of those plays where the word 'inspiration' has some point—that is, you either have the rhythm or you haven't, and if you have you can ride it, and if not, you're dead." *The Hairy Ape*'s protagonist Robert "Yank" Smith is also, like Driscoll in the *Glencairn* plays, based on O'Neill's old drinking partner and fellow sailor on the S.S. *Philadelphia*. Driscoll, O'Neill said, "committed suicide by jumping overboard in mid-ocean." Why would such a "tough customer" do something like that? "It was the *why* of Driscoll's suicide that gave me the germ of the idea." The rough draft was done in three weeks, "without interruption save for writer's cramp."[339]

The First Man was scheduled to open at the Neighborhood Playhouse on March 4, five days before *The Hairy Ape* at the Provincetown Playhouse. This was just as well. O'Neill admitted that he wished he'd destroyed *The First Man*, and *The Hairy Ape* offered diverting cover. Even George Jean Nathan tore *The First Man* apart: "Eugene O'Neill's new drama, 'The First Man,' " Nathan wrote, "is the poorest full-length play that he has written. While not without certain minor merits, it discloses its distinguished author in a tedious and profitless vein, with all of his most obvious faults magnified and with his sardonic point of view trembling perilously at the brink of burlesque."[340] "You let it down too easy," O'Neill told him. "It is no good."[341]

The Hairy Ape, on the other hand, was a masterwork of avant-garde theater. O'Neill wrote a gushing note about the play to Kenneth Macgowan immediately upon completing it in early January 1922: "I don't think the play as a whole can be fitted into any of the current 'isms.' It seems to run the whole gamut from extreme naturalism to extreme expressionism—with more of the latter than the former. I have tried to dig deep in it, to probe in the shadows of the soul of man bewildered by the disharmony of his primitive pride and individualism at war with the mechanistic development of society. And the man in the case is not an Irishman, as I at first intended, but, more fittingly, an American—a New York tough of the toughs, a product of the waterfront turned stoker—a type of mind, if you could call it that, which I know extremely well. . . . Suffice it for me to add, the treatment of all the sets should be expressionistic, I think." O'Neill's patchwork of dialects, his unique blending of "isms," his terrifying indictment of the industrial world order, made *The Hairy Ape* seem to many as if it had been written a century ahead of schedule. *The Hairy Ape*, Macgowan declared after witnessing its opening night that March at the Provincetown Playhouse, "leaps out at you from the future."[342]

* * *

From the Provincetown Players' earliest stage, Hutchins Hapgood and Neith Boyce's cottage during the summer of 1915, to their breakup at the Macdougal Street theater in 1922, the amateur drama group produced an astonishing ninety-seven original plays by forty-six playwrights, all but two of them American. The foundation had been set for serious American drama on a mass scale. The triumph of The Emperor Jones *and* The Hairy Ape *in 1922 and the Pulitzer Prize awarded to* "Anna Christie" *that same year would galvanize, just as the Players predicted, a theatrical revolution in the United States. Although the majority of the many hundreds of new American plays to follow replicated the naturalism of* "Anna Christie," *it was* The Hairy Ape, *with its groundbreaking blend of naturalism and expressionism, what O'Neill called "super-naturalism," that would prove to have the longest lasting impact.*

"The greatest day of the Provincetown Players was between 1919 and 1922," Mary Heaton Vorse declared. "A great contribution was made then to the American stage." The pioneering novelist John Dos Passos agreed: in his provocative 1925 essay "Is the 'Realistic' Theatre Obsolete?" Dos Passos warned that if theater was to survive as an art form, it must progress in the ways O'Neill had shown in The Emperor Jones *and* The Hairy Ape. *Dos Passos declared that "the throb of the drum in* The Emperor Jones *cleared many a pair of ears that had been until that time tuned only to suburban comedy. The chesty roar of* The Hairy Ape *made several people forget to read how The Well Dressed Man would wear his cravat."*

A year after the Players' historic finale in 1922, O'Neill would join forces with Kenneth Macgowan and Robert Edmond Jones to form a new production team: the Experimental Theatre, Inc. At the same time, the American Laboratory Theatre was established, producing such theatrical luminaries as Harold Clurman and Lee Strasburg. (Strasburg's Group Theatre would subsequently introduce "method acting" to the American stage in 1931.) By the mid-1920s, moreover, "The Great

White Way" was no longer the enemy of serious drama. The number of new Broadway productions had more than doubled since the 1915–16 season, just one year before the opening of the Playwrights' Theatre and the New York debuts of O'Neill and Glaspell. To this day, the 1925–26 season remains the historical peak of Broadway activity, with a staggering 255 new productions. (The 2013–14 Broadway season, in comparison, had 44.) The previously despised Shubert Brothers—the owners, in fact, of the Plymouth Theatre, where The Hairy Ape would achieve its success—were no longer reviled out of hand as lording over a greedy syndicate of philistines and knaves working at cross-purposes with risky innovation. Now they were behind-the-scenes allies striving, in their fashion, to help usher in this increasingly sought after New American Drama.

O'Neill and the Theatre Guild, formerly the Washington Square Players, even got over their mutual aversion in time. The Guild had begun to produce cutting-edge American dramatists like Elmer Rice, John Howard Lawson, Sidney Howard, DuBose Heyward, and others, and in 1928, it accepted its first O'Neill plays, Marco Millions and Strange Interlude; the latter would earn O'Neill his third Pulitzer Prize. O'Neill's most accomplished work of this period, Desire Under the Elms (1924), Strange Interlude (1927), and Mourning Becomes Electra (1931), embodied the blend of naturalism and expressionism that came to dominate twentieth-century drama, what has since become known as the "American Style."

* * *

ACT III: The Broadway Show Shop

It is too soon yet to be committed about O'Neill, though young as he is, he is already a quantity to make one wonder at the truth of the above assertion.

—WILLIAM FAULKNER, 1922

I question the moon above Broadway, "Where do I get off at? Where do I fit in?"

—EUGENE O'NEILL, 1926

Prometheus Unbound

WHEN O'NEILL read *The Hairy Ape* out loud to the Players gathered at the Macdougal Street theater, he did so without performance or embellishment. After the last line, though, he stood up, faced the group, and shouted, "This is one the bastards [uptown] can't do!" The Players, stunned by the play's bold originality, cheered in agreement. What they didn't yet know was that O'Neill had already begun courting the uptown producer Arthur Hopkins to produce it before the script was even ready for the Players. He sent copies to both in the same mail—a detail the press agent Oliver M. Sayler publicized, to O'Neill's embarrassment, in the *New York World*. "Oliver, as a friend I love you as a brother," O'Neill berated him gently, "but as a publicity man . . . you must know what an utterly depraved, conscienceless character you are in that role."[1]

The Emperor Jones's breakout success signaled both the overture of experimental American drama and the coda for the Provincetown Players. Back when Saxe Commins had been drilling and bridging and extracting away inside O'Neill's mouth, in April 1921, Boulton, in a chat with Jig Cook in Provincetown, learned of his intention to build a theater exclusively for O'Neill, Glaspell, and a couple of others he'd cultivated. She reminded him that new O'Neill plays now had uptown draw. "If we have this theater," Cook rejoined, "will Gene want *any* of his work done uptown? I think Gene sees by this time that the uptown commercial game is no good. . . . I think Gene *will* want us to do *all* his plays." "Now," Boulton wrote her husband that same day, "do you, or don't you, think it rather presumptuous on Jig's part to feel that when they have this new theatre, which will seat 299 people, that they can count on the pick of your work?"[2]

Boulton's response to the exasperated Cook might have struck him as Lady Macbeth–like, but he knew it was well founded: O'Neill's move uptown was an inevitability. That February 1922, O'Neill, Cook, Glaspell, Fitzie Fitzgerald, Cleon Throckmorton, and Edna Kenton convened a secret meeting with their attorney Harry Weinberger to decide, once and for all, whether to disband. The vote was unanimous: "We would call in some outside director and new actors from somewhere, and call it the end," Kenton said. "All this we did."[3] On February 24, they legally incorporated the Provincetown Players, holding onto the name and the theater but with no plan for the future. They wouldn't make the announcement of their breakup until season's end, until after they'd produced what they all knew would be their crowning achievement, O'Neill's *The Hairy Ape*.

The Hairy Ape consists, like its precursor *The Emperor Jones*, of eight scenes. The first four take place on an ocean liner and the second four in Manhattan while the protagonist, Robert "Yank" Smith, a coal stoker on the steamship, is on shore leave. Yank proclaims that industrial technology is the future, where he "belongs," a word, with variations for parts of speech, used over forty times in the play. O'Neill's subtitle, "A Comedy of Ancient and Modern Life," accurately describes the play insofar as "ancient" refers, in part, to Greek tragedy: Yank is a "tragic hero" figure of the Greek tradition, doomed by hubris, or unwarranted and excessive pride. The subtitle also harks back to our Darwinian ancestry, just three years before the infamous Scopes "Monkey" trial in which a Tennessee high school teacher would be indicted for teaching the theory of evolution. That O'Neill regards *The Hairy Ape* as a "comedy" seems like morbid irony; its meaning, however, can be found in the "happy ending" of Yank's doom, since death provides his sole escape from the cages thrown up around him by modern times.

Yank's overblown sense of belonging rapidly deflates when a wealthy young woman slumming in the stokehole, Mildred Douglas, faints after witnessing his grotesque behavior. Before losing consciousness, Mildred utters, "Filthy beast," though Yank's shipmates remember it later as "hairy ape," an insult that tears Yank's confidence apart. He then embarks on an existential quest to "belong" that ends at the gorilla cage of the city zoo. At first Yank feels as if, with this caged primate, he might at last have found a place where he belongs; recognizing his mistake, he says to the gorilla, "I ain't on oith and I ain't in heaven, get me? I'm in the middle tryin' to separate 'em, takin' all de woist punches from bot' of 'em. Maybe dat's what dey call hell, huh? But you, yuh're at de bottom. You belong! Sure! Yuh're de on'y one in de woild dat does, yuh lucky stiff!" (*CP2*, 162). Yank mistakes the gorilla's alternating growls, roars, and cage rattling for fraternal sympathy and jimmies open the lock, whereupon the great ape slowly exits his cage. Yank holds out his hand to shake on their allegiance, but the gorilla lunges and crushes him with a "murderous hug." He then flings Yank's body into the cage, shuts the door, and wanders off. "Perhaps," O'Neill writes in the final line of his stage directions, it's only in death that "the Hairy Ape at last belongs" (*CP2*, 163).

The Hairy Ape's premiere on March 9, 1922, was a widely hailed victory in the press, most amusingly wrought by critic Arthur Pollock in his rhapsodic write-up for the *Brooklyn Daily Eagle:* "We didn't learn anything at all in high school, but the only thing we regret not having learned is a knowledge of how to make ear-splitting noises with two fingers in the mouth. . . . The accomplishment would have been so useful a thing the other night at the opening of Eugene G. O'Neill's 'The Hairy Ape.' . . . It was the best play by an American we have ever seen. The audience shouted at the end. Some of the auditors whistled.

But they weren't very good at it. We wanted to try the two finger noise, tried it and failed. Which was humiliating. And there wasn't a critic present who could do it. Critics are a limited crew."[4] Notices like these poured in, though not all were as unequivocal as Pollock's. Much of the chatter revolved around the style of the play and its origins. The critics had heard of European expressionism, but not many had actually witnessed it aside from *The Emperor Jones* (which few at the time identified as expressionism) and the Hungarian playwright Ferenc Molnár's *Liliom* (1909), which had just been translated into English and produced by the Theatre Guild the previous summer.

"It isn't Expressionism," O'Neill explained. "It isn't Naturalism. It is a blend—and, as far as my knowledge goes—a uniquely successful one." O'Neill was thus moved to invented an "ism" of his own, "super-naturalism," or rather, he co-opted the term from Theodore Dreiser's *Plays of the Natural and Supernatural* (1916), a collection meant to reveal, in the novelist's words, "the inscrutability of life and its forces and its accidents."[5] O'Neill would also come to borrow this language from Dreiser several years later in his explanation to his first biographer, Barrett Clark, telling him that his overall goal was to reveal through writing the "inscrutable forces behind life."[6]

O'Neill had nevertheless instructed the Players that the set designs "must be in the Expressionistic method," and Bobby Jones and Cleon Throckmorton accepted his challenge with extraordinary ingenuity. For one thing, they made Cook's dome once again earn its keep: Alexander Woollcott, writing for the *New York Times*, applauded the designers of what he considered (although he was frequently critical of O'Neill's plays) "one of the real events of the year." They'd transformed, he said, by means of the dome "that preposterous little theatre . . . one of the most cramped stages New York has ever known [and created] the illusion of vast spaces and endless perspectives." "In that tiny space," wrote Robert Benchley in *Life*, "are produced scenic effects which make those of up-town theatres appear like something you might do in the barn." Benchley advised his readers "to see 'The Hairy Ape' before it moves up-town (as it unquestionably must), for Jones and Throckmorton have achieved a focus with their effects on this miniature stage which may be lost or diffused in a larger and more commercial theatre."[7]

The casting for Yank Smith had been critical to the play's success, of course. Yank is arguably the most demanding role in O'Neill's repertoire: his emotional transitions are erratic; his monologues numerous and lengthy and must be performed with a pitch-perfect Brooklyn accent; his appearance is that of a Neanderthal, though he's capable of projecting deep introspection (he's often required to pose in the seated position of Auguste Rodin's *The Thinker*). The choice was simple: before O'Neill had written a word of the play, he'd already pegged Louis Wolheim, known to friends as "Wolly," a close friend and associate of the celebrated actors John and Lionel Barrymore. O'Neill took one look at this hulking ex-football player, most likely for the first time at one of the Barrymores' legendary parties, with a face that looked as if it had been pulverized with a croquet mallet and knew immediately that he'd found his leading man.[8]

Wolheim's moving portrayal of Yank, like Charles Gilpin's of Brutus Jones, catapulted the actor from near obscurity into the limelight. Wolheim was a natural for the part because, again like Gilpin with Jones, he regularly associated with people like Yank and could handily reproduce the Brooklyn workingman's persona. The strong box office returns were attributable as much to theatergoers wishing to see Wolheim as Yank Smith as to see the acclaimed new play by Eugene O'Neill. Mary Blair, on the other hand, who'd played the leads in *Before Breakfast* and *Diff'rent*, was a dubious choice for Mildred; from the outset it was clear that the otherwise brilliant actress was the production's weakest link. Mildred must be an anemic, artificial-looking by-product of wealth. Blair, Arthur Hopkins said, was too vibrant a personality to render this effectively.[9] When the Players moved uptown, Blair was replaced by a far better choice, Carlotta Monterey, an older but stunningly beautiful performer with a natural hauteur that embodied the part. (O'Neill ignored her at their first meeting, a slight he wouldn't live down when they met again four years later.)

One night after a performance, O'Neill, Wolheim, Light, Fitzgerald, and a few others met at the Samovar for an after party.

Carlotta Monterey and Louis Wolheim in the 1922 Broadway production
of *The Hairy Ape*.
(COURTESY OF SHEAFFER-O'NEILL COLLECTION, LINDA LEAR CENTER FOR SPECIAL
COLLECTIONS AND ARCHIVES, CONNECTICUT COLLEGE, NEW LONDON)

＊   ＊   ＊

They spoke with elation about each of their roles in the production
but also about the theatrical revolution *The Hairy Ape* was sure to
set in motion. Wolheim pronounced that Yank Smith's lines were
not just dialogue but real poetry, especially in that one scene. "What
scene?" O'Neill asked. And there was Yank, conjured from the air
and sprawled out on the restaurant floor, roaring out his final lines
at the zoo in Brooklynese. Someone at an adjoining table snickered,
and Wolheim fell silent. Then Yank was back, leaping at the offender
with a roar—the Hairy Ape in the flesh, unencumbered by the stage.
Just as instantly, Wolheim was "Wolly" once again and calmly returned to the table. The Players often retold this anecdote to friends
and colleagues, seeing in it, they would say, "an instant of unlimited
possibilities."[10]

Wolheim's loutish stage presence belied a fact about the actor
that might have surprised his uptown audiences: along with his acting

ability, he was endowed with a keen intellect. An avid bibliophile, Wolheim had graduated from Cornell University, where he'd received an undergraduate degree and a Ph.D. in mathematics, and he was nearly fluent in French, German, Spanish, and Yiddish. As such, Wolheim found himself beleaguered by the same question from those who knew him about *The Hairy Ape:* "What does it mean?" "People are always trying to find hidden meanings," he averred, "when the truth is knocking at their door." "An individual throws himself headlong against an impregnable system, and in the struggle inevitably and dramatically perishes. The system carries on unchanged. . . . A man attacks a false god. He fights with mighty strength, with bitter fury. Again and again with despair in his rudimentary soul he throws himself on the image. At last he lies a broken mass at the feet of the god. He has beaten his life out. The god is unchanged."[11]

As a dramatist, Wolheim declared, O'Neill "has no axe to grind, no propaganda to promote, no psychoanalysis complex to unravel"; but each of his characters nonetheless "express[es] a deep resentment against our present civilization." In this way, he said, the playwright "resembles Tolstoy, but he is without the latter's naïve religious faith. A fighting Tolstoy—that is O'Neill." O'Neill must be welcomed, he concluded, as "the Prometheus of modern drama." "Prometheus stole fire from the gods and bestowed it on man. For this offense the gods had him chained to a rock and an eagle tortured him with beak and talons. . . . The mantle of Prometheus has fallen on Eugene O'Neill."[12] A couple of years on, O'Neill made it clear that he shared Wolheim's analogy about himself, though he replaced Prometheus's eagle with a flock of mangling vultures:

> My vultures are still flapping around, thank God, hungry and
> undismayed; and I am very proud of them for they are my test and
> my self-justification. I would feel a success and a total loss if they
> should ever desert me to gorge themselves fat and comforted on
> what the newspaper boys naively call fame. But luckily they are
> birds that fly from the great dark behind and inside and not from
> the bright lights without. Each visit they wax stranger and more
> pitiless—which is, naturally, a matter of boast between them and
> me!—and I look forward to some last visit when their wings will

blot out the sky and they'll wrench the last of my liver out; and
then I predict they'll turn out to be angels of some God or other
who have given me in exchange the germ of a soul.[13]

O'Neill had been in no mood to celebrate *The Hairy Ape*'s opening
night on March 9 with a "John Barleycorn party" at Christine Ell's
restaurant. He didn't go to Macdougal Street that night at all. Back in
December 1921, he'd been told that Ella and Jim O'Neill were traveling to California for six months to sort out some real estate hold-
ings of James's outside Los Angeles. Ella had remained socially aloof
after conquering her addiction; but after James's death, she discovered that she was adept at managing her deceased husband's financial
affairs. Also thanks to Ella, her son Jim had, remarkably, stayed on the
wagon for a year and a half. O'Neill felt obligated to spend Christmas
in New York with them, though he'd been in the midst of writing
The Hairy Ape and grumbled about the "risk of breaking this mood
up."[14] If he made the trip, and there's some doubt about whether he
did, he kept his presence in New York a close secret. One hopes he
did visit Ella, as this would have been his last opportunity to see his
mother alive.

Ella was hospitalized with a stroke that February, and Jim wired
O'Neill, pleading with his brother to take a train out. O'Neill replied
that a specialist had warned that he'd surely have a "nervous collapse"
if he undertook such a journey in his "present condition." (O'Neill
was actually in reasonable health but was in the process of directing the most ambitious play of his life.) "Be fair. . . . Would not help
Mother or you? Also you wire she is unconscious, will not know me.
Want to help in any possible way. Everything I have at your command.
Wire me what and how. . . . My plans depend on health. Would leave
immediately if able. You must accept truth. I am in terrible shape."[15]

Ella O'Neill died eight days later, on February 28, 1922.

The First Man premiered at the Neighborhood Playhouse on
the sleety, bitter-cold night of March 4, 1922. Earlier that same day,
Jim climbed aboard the eastbound train toting ten bottles of whiskey
to escort Ella's remains back to New York.[16] Jim arrived at Grand

Central Station with Ella's casket on the day of *The Hairy Ape*'s premiere, and he was definitively off the wagon—this time for good.

O'Neill received Jim's wire from Los Angeles on March 4 that
he and Ella's body would arrive in New York by train five days
later. He then contacted his father's friend and longtime advance man
William Connor to accompany him to the station and help make
arrangements for Ella's casket and funeral. But, at the last minute,
O'Neill backed out, just as he had on the street corner while heading
with Boulton and Dorothy Day to Lou Holladay's body at the Samovar. Perhaps the horror of watching first his friend and then his father
die had convinced O'Neill that he was unfit for the emotional hell that
direct exposure to a loved one's death entails. Whatever his state of
mind, he phoned Connor to say he wasn't going.

Connor received this news with disgust but reluctantly enlisted his
nephew, Frank Wilder, to replace the absentee son. At Grand Central,
Connor and Wilder oversaw the porters' removal of Ella's casket and
placement on a luggage cart on the platform. Jim was nowhere to be
seen, but they eventually tracked him down in his compartment, inco-
herent and surrounded by empty whiskey bottles. They loaded Jim into
a taxi and checked him into a Times Square hotel, then Connor phoned
O'Neill at his suite at the Netherland Hotel on Fifth Avenue across from
Central Park. O'Neill had shamefully failed in his duty to his mother,
and Connor let him know it.[17]

A few minutes before midnight, Boulton and Commins returned to
the Netherland after attending the premiere of *The Hairy Ape*. According to Commins, he called O'Neill's room from the lobby to let him
know they were coming up but was told to wait downstairs. Stepping
off the elevator, O'Neill looked terrible: his face was ashen gray and
his lips "two lines of blue." "A tremor shook his body and he seemed to
have lost control of his hands." He could barely speak, as if his words
"scraped past a rough lump in his throat."[18] Too humiliated to admit the
truth, O'Neill lied by omission, leaving the impression that he'd been
to Grand Central for his mother. He asked Boulton to go up to the
suite without him and left with Commins for a walk, first around the
back of the Metropolitan Museum of Art and then across Central Park.

For a half hour O'Neill didn't utter a word while Commins prattled on about *The Hairy Ape*'s triumphant debut: when the final curtain fell just an hour before, he said, the audience members leapt to their feet. Wolheim got a standing ovation, and the packed auditorium echoed with cries of "Author! Author!" Their shouts carried on after the lights went up; but once they'd begun to realize that O'Neill was not going to appear, they slowly headed for the exit, glancing over their shoulders in eagerness for a last-minute entrance of the ingenious creator of this remarkable new play. "For Christ's sake, cut it!" O'Neill snapped. "I don't give a damn."[19]

Commins pressed on, bursting to relive the experience, if only for himself. He described the audience's gasps of astonishment when actual fire burst out of Jones and Throckmorton's furnaces in the stokehole scene, the innumerable curtain calls for the cast members, the praise he and Boulton overheard from audience members between scenes and outside on Macdougal Street after the show. "I might have been talking to myself," he later recalled. "If he had heard anything I had been saying, it meant as little to him as the other night noises in the park."[20]

"It doesn't mean anything," O'Neill said, though not, Commins realized, in response to what he'd been telling him about the premiere. "It doesn't mean anything," O'Neill repeated. Then he started talking about his family. He began incoherently, stammering with his usual stand-alone words and half-finished sentences. He talked about his mother, her convent school days in Indiana and, in Commins's words, her "sheltered, innocent" life before joining the vagabond lifestyle of her husband, "the antithesis of everything she had ever known." He talked about how *Monte Cristo* had been "the dominant factor in their lives; they were chained to it"; about how his mother endured, year after year, "the agonies of one-night stands, the shabby accommodations and the improvised food of theatrical hotels"; about how their summers in New London provided her with much-needed but unsatisfying breathing space between tours; about how his father had frittered away the family's aggregate wealth with "wildcat mine stocks and even wilder real-estate gambles."

"Imagine!" O'Neill said of James's role as Edmund Dantès. "He played that part more than six thousand times, no wonder it made an addict out of her."[21]

The air was frigid and damp in Central Park, and Ella's funeral had been scheduled for the next morning. Commins broke O'Neill's trancelike state several times, urging that they return to their hotels and get to bed. "Stay with me," O'Neill responded each time. His soliloquy then turned to Jim, or rather on Jim, and his incredible potential, squandered on booze and prostitutes and gambling—the climax of his tragic existence being the disgraceful night of drunkenness at the train station earlier that day. By then, Commins remembered, his halting speech had disappeared: "Jim could have been a fine writer, a poet and certainly a barbed satirist or a romantic actor in the best tradition or even, highest in Gene's esteem, a clear and persuasive thinker. But no, Jim was too bedazzled by Broadway, by round-heeled women, by his autointoxication with his own boasting while his sycophants urged him on. . . . If only he, Gene, had Jim's gifts, then perhaps the O'Neills might be redeemed from the father who allowed himself to be trapped by success. The old man was a Sisyphus and *Monte Cristo* was the stone he was condemned to push uphill into hell."[22]

Back at the hotel around four in the morning, the two men exchanged an awkward embrace, and Commins left O'Neill alone in the lobby. As well as helping his friend through this difficult night, Commins had also, though neither of them could have known it at the time, listened to O'Neill sketch out the thematic contours of what would become, two decades later, *Long Day's Journey Into Night* and *A Moon for the Misbegotten*.

Ella's funeral service was held a few hours later at St. Leo's Church, where Ella had attended Mass when she'd stayed at the Prince George Hotel. O'Neill and Boulton were at the service, which was conducted by Father Fogarty, a classmate of O'Neill's from St. Aloysius. His childhood nurse Sarah Sandy was there too, but he avoided her, though this was the last time they would see each other.[23] Later that afternoon, O'Neill and Boulton took a train up to New London to bury his mother in the family plot with James and

Edmund in St. Mary's Cemetery. Jim, no longer the loyal presence he'd been when James passed, hadn't shown up for any of it.

On the night of *The Hairy Ape*'s opening at the Shubert Brothers' Plymouth Theatre on April 17, the first thing the rowdy crew of Hudson Dusters would have seen was their friend's name glowing in electric lights on the marquee. This must have impressed them. That's where the star's name usually went, rarely if ever the playwright's.[24] O'Neill had invited them himself, and once they'd taken their balcony seats, they started feeling rambunctious and would soon let loose during the pivotal third scene, when Mildred encounters Yank in the stokehole.

Jones and Throckmorton's set design for scene 3 stunningly evoked the volcanic representation of Dante's inferno that O'Neill specifies in his stage directions: "The fiery light floods over their shoulders as they bend round for the coal. Rivulets of sooty sweat have traced maps on their backs. The enlarged muscles form bunches of high light and shadow" (*CP2*, 135–36). The firemen work in unison, savagely, ritualistically. Now and then a whistle sounds, signaling the men to shovel faster so the engines can pick up steam. Yank goads the workers to follow his own backbreaking pace. Mildred enters behind him, just at the moment when the whistle blows once too often, and Yank "brandishes his shovel murderously over his head in one hand, pounding on his chest gorilla-like," and roars at the top of his lungs, "Come down outa dere, yuh yellow, brass-buttoned, Belfast bum, yuh! Come down and I'll knock yer brains out! Yuh lousy, stinkin,' yellow mut of a Catholic moiderin' bastard!" (*CP2*, 137).

The Hudson Dusters went wild in the balcony, erupting into hoots and whistles and cheers, shocking the respectable uptown audience in the orchestra seats below.[25] Along with a propensity for two-fisted drinking, the gangsters shared O'Neill's Irish pride, and scene 3 in the play has the distinction of being the only one in which, before his encounter with Mildred, Yank allies himself with a group: the Catholics of Belfast. Belfast was the steamship-building capital of the world, where the *Titanic* was built. To Yank, the officers are Protestant,

"Catholic moiderin' bastards," and the Dusters may well have received their tickets from the playwright the night before as they celebrated the anniversary of the Easter Rising of April 16, 1916.

On December 6, 1921, the Irish Free State was formed, ending the two-year Irish War of Independence—the very week O'Neill recovered his "creative *élan*" and had begun composing *The Hairy Ape* "with a mad rush." Of course, six of Ireland's traditional thirty-two counties had remained part of Great Britain, as Northern Ireland, and many irredentist Catholics and Protestants loyal to Great Britain alike ignored the ceasefire and continued fighting through the spring of 1922, the violence mostly concentrated in the north. Given the torrent of dialogue that gushes from Yank's mouth over the first three scenes, it's more than likely O'Neill had tipped the Dusters off ahead of time to listen for the line—even more, perhaps, for the satisfaction of disrupting an evening at an uptown theater than the desire to make a political statement.

O'Neill also dedicated a scene to the Industrial Workers of the World (IWW) or "Wobblies," as the radical labor union members were then called, and a number of them attended the play as well. O'Neill portrays the Wobblies at their waterfront headquarters at 9 South Street as staid and bureaucratic, juxtaposed against Yank's imposing ferociousness. In the previous scene, scene 6, Yank had overheard the union men described as a "devil's brew of rascals, jailbirds, murderers and cutthroats" (*CP2*, 152). Since the American press had already printed this overblown portrait of the labor organization, O'Neill counters the accepted stereotype by making the IWW scene, paradoxically for middle-class audience members at the time, the only realistic scene in the play. (In fact, the play's original iteration, the short story "The Hairy Ape," though rejected by *Metropolitan* magazine in 1918, had ended with Yank joining the IWW.)[26]

"[O'Neill] has found a cause and he has become a propagandist," smirked Heywood Broun, now unrivaled among O'Neill's most adversarial critics. This time Mike Gold stood up to defend O'Neill against Broun's attacks. With *The Hairy Ape*, Gold said, O'Neill had ushered onto the boards "that deep spirit of revolt that burns even in the American working-man, even in the callous-handed citizens of the richest country in the world."[27]

The Wobblies, like the Dusters with the reference to Ireland's troubles, greeted *The Hairy Ape* with cheers for attempting, they said, to "explode the popular misconception of the I.W.W. as a bomb-throwing organization—an idea especially prevalent among the limousine class of theatergoers, who are now having it dislodged from their minds." "[O'Neill] understands us," wrote a port delegate of the Wobblies' New York division. "Even the spies that the detective agencies sometimes got into the organization," said another, "know better than to think that the I.W.W. preaches violence." The delegate wrote a review for the union-run *Marine Worker* applauding the play's veracity: "Most books and plays of the sea leave the real seaman with a bad taste in his mouth and much disgust in his heart. *Very* different is 'The Hairy Ape,' written by an old time seaman Eugene O'Neill. . . . This play, which every seaman should attend, catches the exact spirit of . . . the forecastle and spreads a flow of language which takes the breath away from the wearers of dress satin and evening gowns. The throb of the engines, the whir of the propeller, the whistle of the wind through the rigging, and the choicest kind of cursing are all there and true to the life of the sea." "It's good to hear from someone who knows what he is talking about that my 'Hairy Ape' rings true," O'Neill responded in a letter to the *Marine Worker*. "I wish there were more of the critics who were familiar enough with the life and background of the play to be able to give it a hearing for what it is, and not what they guess it is."[28]

That June 1922, O'Neill and every member of *The Hairy Ape* cast and crew signed a petition to President Harding urging him to free, without the humiliation required for individual pardons, ninety-six IWW prisoners at Leavenworth Penitentiary who'd been arrested under the Espionage Act for conspiring to obstruct America's entry into World War I.[29] (Harding paroled three of the political prisoners on the condition that he could send them back at his discretion. In August 1923, Harding died suddenly in office, and by Christmas, his successor, Calvin Coolidge, had granted amnesty to them all.) This heated political climate had earlier gotten the Players into the same trouble with Sunday performances as they'd had with *The Emperor Jones*. "For a performance or two," said Kenneth Macgowan, "getting by the plain clothes men at the door was harder than getting a passport."[30] It was a female undercover cop, Officer Anna Green, who paid for a membership to attend the show on Sunday evening, March 12.

New York's prosecuting attorney argued that the idea of the playhouse as a private club was "merely a subterfuge for the sale of tickets in violation" of the penal code forbidding Sunday theatricals. After hearing the testimonies of Fitzie Fitzgerald and O'Neill's lawyer Harry Weinberger, Magistrate Simpson publicly disagreed. While approvingly reading an article quoting Simpson, O'Neill took out his pencil and underlined what he considered the key points: "The Provincetown Players is an organization that *is a credit to the community*. It has encouraged native drama and has the support and approval of influential citizens. *It would be a calamity to interfere with or hamper* the work of this club. It is a boon to those practicing the art of the drama and acting who have no other place to turn to for original experiments."[31]

But the New York Police Department wasn't yet finished with the thirty-three-year-old playwright. A Lieutenant Duffy attended *The Hairy Ape* at the Plymouth that May, then submitted a report to Chief Magistrate William McAdoo confirming that the drama was "obscene, indecent and impure." McAdoo then requested a copy of the script from Arthur Hopkins's office. After giving it a once-over, he sent it back with no comment. McAdoo believed (not unjustifiably) that Hopkins had sent a bogus "concerned citizen" to police headquarters to file a complaint that the play was "immoral and unfit for the eyes and ears of New York theatre-goers" in hopes of boosting sales and publicity. Within the week, O'Neill noted with satisfaction, the bid for suppression had worked against itself: "As for the attempt to suppress 'The Hairy Ape,' it simply reacted against the people who started it, as the sale of seats to the play went up with a bang. And, in another way, it has been a very good thing—I feel that it has dealt a decided blow at state censorship." The next night, in fact, the performance sold out and advance sales skyrocketed. The *New York World* telegrammed O'Neill in Provincetown for comment: "Such an idiotic attempt at suppression," he responded with brusque finality, "will bring only ridicule on the poor dolts who started it."[32]

New York Herald critic Lawrence Reamer caviled that by scene 4 of *The Hairy Ape*, "the air is growing pretty thick with blasphemy." He looked forward to its print publication so he might count precisely how many times O'Neill used the word "Christ" in vain (it's eight). But the play's relatively mild language—"Christ," "tart," "boob," "damn," "tripe," and so on—was inconsequential, argued David Karsner, a left-wing columnist for the socialist newspaper the *New York Call*, compared to O'Neill's blistering critique of the American way of life. Karsner insisted it wasn't "the choicest kind of cursing" that attracted the censors, as the more priggish critics assumed and the police at first charged. *The Hairy Ape* hit audiences on a deeper level than that: "It carries a text and a message that is outlawed in this country, and it proclaims an abiding and everlasting hatred and contempt for the law as it is made and enforced, for the church as it apologizes for the greed of its rich patrons, for the press as it lies and misrepresents, for the state as it censors and suppress-es the natural impulses of clean beings, and for all other manifold evidences of hypocrisy and cant with which our people are so sweetly and securely endowed.... And through this medley of derision those in that part of the audience who believe in things as they are are made to feel somewhat insecure in the permanency of their faith."[33] Two years later, on April 22, 1924, when J. Edgar Hoover took over as acting director of the Bureau of Investigation, he heard O'Neill's subversive dog whistle against the "American way" loud and clear. The Bureau's memorandum on O'Neill shows that he was now under investigation for treason, and it warned that *The Hairy Ape* "possesses inferential grounds for radical theories."[34]

That May 1922, Columbia University announced that *"Anna Christie"* had won O'Neill his second Pulitzer Prize. The selection once again met with a churlish response from his detractors in the press, and for the same objection raised two years earlier with *Beyond the Horizon*: the Pulitzer was meant for the play "best representing the educational value of the stage in raising the standards of good morals, good taste and good manners." "[Anna Christie] goes over her training period in a brothel," fumed *Billboard* critic Patterson James. "She swallows drink after drink and smokes cigaret after cigaret. All in the interest of good morals?"³⁵ O'Neill reveled in this surge of notoriety, one that invariably follows when the world of fine arts and the world of law enforcement reflexively operate in tandem—the former with a mix of applause and outrage, the latter with ham-fisted investigations and threats of obscenity charges. "Yes, I seem to be becoming the Prize Pup of Playwrighting, the Hot Dog of the Drama," he laughed. "When the Police Dept. isn't pinning the Obscenity Medal on my Hairy Ape chest, why then it's Columbia adorning the brazen bosom of Anna with the Cross of Purity."³⁶

Meanwhile, amid the commotion over O'Neill's latest triumph, an unyielding wedge had been driven between Cook's "way of the group" philosophy of theater and the expansive ambitions of other Provincetown Players like O'Neill, Fitzie Fitzgerald, Bobby Jones, Cleon Throckmorton, and Jimmy Light. Cook's grandiloquence had, quite simply, lost its inspirational appeal on the heels of their uptown success. "Our playwrights outgrew the home nest," Fitzgerald said, making instant enemies of Kenton and Glaspell, who after this pegged her as a traitor. But Fitzgerald responded to the disbandment of the Players with assurances that their revolutionary mission would carry on to the commercial stage: "Their plays demanded better stages, better productions, than we could give them. Both plays and actors needed the advantages of larger audiences than the faithful old stable could house."³⁷

Glaspell and Cook departed for Greece in early March, the week before *The Hairy Ape*'s opening night. *The Hairy Ape*'s playbill lists Cook as director, apparently as a parting gesture of respect, though he and Glaspell were halfway across the Atlantic before the dress rehearsals had even begun. Consternation had spread over who would direct if not Cook; but by mid-February, O'Neill wrote Saxe Commins that he'd been doing "most of the directing." Light was listed as the play's stage manager, and he sat devotedly at O'Neill's side during rehearsals as well. (Anticipating the move uptown, Arthur Hopkins also offered directorial advice and financing when necessary.)³⁸ Glaspell's *Chains of Dew* followed *The Hairy Ape* on the next bill. This three-act comedy, Kenton admitted, "was not good—none knew it better than [Glaspell].

But we foresaw that *The Ape* would go uptown, taking with it most of our players. Certainly by now it had become an honor higher to go than to stay." (Glaspell would go on to win the 1931 Pulitzer Prize for her play *Alison's House*.) Cook and O'Neill each thought the other had let them down. "Our richest, like our poorest," Cook opined, "have desired not to give life but to have it given to them," while O'Neill wrote Fitzgerald that "primarily, as you undoubtedly will agree, it is all Jig's fault. As I look back on it now, I can see where he drove all our best talent, that we had developed, away from the theatre for daring to disagree with him—this in a supposed group democracy! Then beat it to Greece leaving a hollow shell as a monument to his egotism."[39] Cook would never return to New York. He succumbed to typhus at Delphi less than two years later and was buried in a tomb respectfully adorned with a stone from the Temple of Apollo.

Over the summer of 1922, Cook mailed off several drunken letters denouncing his former associates for selling out to the "quicksand of commercial New York." "I do not see how Gene could possibly permit this," he wrote to Kenton. "Edna, I vomit."[40] Just after Cook cabled to agree to the legal termination of the Players, a personal letter arrived at the theater lamenting what he regarded as a collective defeat: "I am forced to confess that our attempt to build up, by our own life and death, in an alien sea, a coral island of our own, has failed. . . . What one who loved it wishes for it now is euthanasia—a swift and painless death. We keep our promise; we give this theatre we love good death. The Provincetown Players end their story here."[41]

Draining Bitter Cups

Eugene O'Neill Jr., now twelve years old, was scheduled to visit Provincetown in the summer of 1922. "I want to have an opportunity to get to know him," O'Neill told Kathleen Jenkins, "to convince him that I am his friend as well as his father." Eugene arrived early that August and stayed for three weeks of sunbathing and picnicking in the dunes, splashing in the surf with his little half brother, Shane, and generally making a fine impression for his newfound family. Even Jim O'Neill, by this time determined to drink himself into oblivion, trekked out to Cape Cod to make the acquaintance of his nephew. O'Neill admired the boy's precocious intelligence and was secretly pleased that he was a troublemaker at school, just as he himself had been.[42] That summer, father and son forged a genuine and lasting bond, a mutual admiration that would carry over into Eugene's adulthood, and that Shane, much as he longed to, would never achieve.

When Eugene Jr. left to go back to his mother, O'Neill gave himself entirely over to drink. His behavior that summer was outrageous, and he was, by most accounts, a nasty drunk. One night he showed up at a costume party, darkly tanned as usual, wearing nothing but a leopard-skin loincloth and an orange fright wig. A Boston journalist, believing his tan was makeup, wiped a piece of paper against his arm, hoping to take the illustrious smudge back home as a unique souvenir of the playwright. O'Neill glared down at her, then dealt a merciless blow that sent her flying across the room. Bobby Jones, who visited that summer, informed Mabel Dodge that both O'Neill and Boulton had been "rendered entirely will-less by liquor." Not much of a drinker himself, Jones witnessed some of his colleague's worst binges yet. One night when Terry Carlin was present, O'Neill urinated into a bottle of whiskey and then drank from it. "I worship the O'Neills," Jones admitted, despite the crass behavior. "They are the noblest spirits there are . . . [but] they know nothing about anything except suffering and hell generally."[43]

That November O'Neill and Boulton packed up Shane and Fifine Clark, or "Gaga," as Shane had come to call his stalwart nanny, and relocated the family to a thirty-acre estate known as Brook Farm in Ridgefield, Connecticut. The property consisted of acres of woodland, an old apple orchard, two ponds, and an expansive lawn dotted with elms and maples. Ridgefield was an easier commute to New York than Provincetown, but the manor house that came with the property was ill suited to the O'Neills. Terry Carlin inhabited the attic for a time, and O'Neill felt more at ease up there jawing with the old anarchist than anywhere else in the house.[44] Brook Farm's twelve rooms lacked furniture and other amenities, making its enormity doubly daunting and expensive. More to the point, its stately grandeur reflected the kind of complacent, gentrified existence that,

Eugene O'Neill adorned with seaweed outside Peaked Hill Bar.
(MARGERY BOULTON COLLECTION, COURTESY OF DALLAS CLINE AND THE SHEAFFER-
O'NEILL COLLECTION, LINDA LEAR CENTER FOR SPECIAL COLLECTIONS AND ARCHIVES,
CONNECTICUT COLLEGE, NEW LONDON)

✳   ✳   ✳

philosophically at least, O'Neill and Boulton abhorred. O'Neill ratio-
nalized its expense as a worthy investment, and it spared them from
living in hotels, the demoralizing theatrical lifestyle of his itinerant
father and mother. When guests arrived, the O'Neills were determined to make it seem, if only in outward appearance, that they had
a real home.[45]

Nine original O'Neill plays had appeared on Broadway in just
two years, an astonishing run. He also received a gold medal from
the National Institute of Arts and Letters that winter, and his plays
were becoming known in Europe. Macgowan and Jones had gone to
Germany the previous summer to drum up producers for O'Neill's
plays, and they'd induced one in Berlin to put on *"Anna Christie."*
(This was postwar Germany, a defeated nation in financial ruin;
for the rights to his play, O'Neill received 7,840,000,000 marks, or
$1.39.) By February O'Neill had completed his three-act play *Welded*,

Brook Farm in 1922.

* * *

a histrionic account of his tumultuous marriage to Boulton. It was a good time to take stock of their relationship. "You know," he told Kenneth Macgowan during one of his visits to Brook Farm, "I don't really like Agnes." Macgowan winced. "That seemed to me stronger somehow," he said afterward, "than if he'd said he hated her."[46]

The couple's frequent skirmishes that winter, 1922–23, escalated into outright warfare. O'Neill began accusing Boulton of having or at the very least desiring to have affairs. It was the indisputable nadir of O'Neill's decades-long battle with alcoholism, and in the aftermath of his most abusive episodes, O'Neill would guiltily confess to his wife, according to her, that he'd come to believe that "marriage is a gotdamn thing. You become part of another person, the two of you become one person, and it's frightening. When you realize that you start trying to beat your way out." "Then the horrible thing happened," reported Boulton's would-be chronicler Max Wylie about an episode she would relate to him personally. "After a lot of unprovoked abuse, [O'Neill] suddenly snatched up a large stack of papers and flung them into the fire. And she knew what he was doing to her: he was burning up her novel! She fought and screamed, but he was too strong for her. He held her until it seemed quite consumed. Then he left."[47]

On another occasion, O'Neill cut up photographs of Boulton, then proceeded to maul irreparably what Boulton considered her "greatest treasure"—a portrait of her father, Teddy Boulton, by the renowned painter, and Teddy's mentor at the Arts Students' League of Philadelphia, Thomas Eakins. (Teddy and Eakins, among other collaborations, had cast Walt Whitman's death mask in 1892.) An early snow had just begun to fall that November 1922, as Boulton and Shane were returning home.[48] As the two of them proceeded up the walk, Boulton told Wylie, O'Neill "burst out the front door in a rage, full of his seafaring profanity." He was obviously drunk, so she ignored him; but while putting Shane to bed, she heard from downstairs "the most awful clattering and banging, and a chair turned over." Then the front door slammed, and from Shane's window Boulton saw her husband "rubbing something in the snow."

I was still upstairs when a horrifying thought struck me. I couldn't credit my own suspicion. I whirled down the stairs, looking up over the mantel. Father's portrait was not there. Gene was trying to smear off the face in the snow. I ran out but it was too late. The paint was so hard set it wouldn't smear, and on this fence post he was mercilessly shredding the canvas, banging it up and down till it was a mass of tattered ribbons. . . . Gene knew I loved this portrait more than anything we'd ever had in our home. . . . Gene knew how to hurt me. He knew how to hurt everybody. I think he was hurting so much inside himself, that periodically he *had* to lash out. After such enormities, he was so contrite, he was embarrassing to be around. . . . If he hadn't had his plays in which to play out his principal hatreds, I feel very sure he'd have found his way to an asylum before he was thirty.[49]

Boulton's telling of this ghastly "enormity" has been met with deserved skepticism.[50] Wylie, who related the incident, has elsewhere been proven unreliable; Boulton also contradicted the account in a different interview, saying that O'Neill destroyed the portrait while she was away on a visit to New York.[51] It's therefore been an open question whether Eakins had painted a portrait of Boulton's father at all. In terms of its existence and destruction, Boulton wasn't confabulating.

Thomas Eakins's painting was a small, ten-by-fourteen-inch portrait of Teddy's head. Teddy's friend Frances J. Ziegler, also a student of Eakins's, recalled that Teddy adored the portrait, refusing to sell it even though he was very poor.[52] Agnes Boulton held onto the savaged remnants until at least 1931, at which time she informed Eakins's biographer Lloyd Goodrich that the picture was "badly injured, so much so that I doubt it can ever be restored."[53] Another Eakins portrait of Teddy has survived (and for the first time is published here).[54]

The stranglehold that alcoholism had taken over O'Neill by the early 1920s is nearly impossible to overstate. Though it's often been said that once O'Neill finished a play, he would go on a binge, during this period it was precisely the reverse: O'Neill would stop binging just

A sketch of Theodore "Teddy" Boulton by Thomas Eakins. Another
portrait of Teddy Boulton by Eakins was destroyed by O'Neill in a drunken
rage at Brook Farm.
(COURTESY OF THE WILLIAM INNES HOMER PAPERS, UNIVERSITY OF DELAWARE, NEWARK)

* * *

long enough to write a play.[55] During this first winter at Brook Farm,
O'Neill became so unwound that he appears to have even broken his
rule to abstain from drink while writing. "I don't think anything worth
reading was ever written by anyone who was drunk or even half-drunk
when he wrote it," he told Barrett Clark. "The legend that I wrote my
plays when I was drunk is absurd," he went on. "It was when I was not
writing that I drank. I'd drink for a month and then go out and snap
out of it by myself. It was during these periods that I wrote." *Welded*
was almost certainly an exception; but either way, drunk or sober, the
script reveals two profoundly fragile egos, and Boulton verified that
its fictional marriage was a "carbon copy" of their own.[56]

Welded, in O'Neill's words, depicts "a man and woman, lovers and
married, [who] enact their spiritual struggle to possess one the other.
I wanted to give the impression of the world shut out, just of two
human beings struggling to break through an inner darkness."[57] The
principals are Michael Cape, a playwright, and his wife, Eleanor, an
actress. The couple has been married, like O'Neill and Boulton, for
five years. Eleanor looks just like Boulton: tall, with high cheekbones
and a mass of dark hair.[58] Michael is nothing less than his creator's
reflection; this is, revealingly, O'Neill on O'Neill: "His unusual face
is a harrowed battlefield of super-sensitiveness, the features at war

with one another—the forehead of a thinker, the eyes of a dreamer, the nose and mouth of a sensualist. One feels a powerful imagination tinged with somber sadness—a driving force which can be sympathetic and cruel at the same time. There is something tortured about him—a passionate tension, a self-protecting, arrogant defiance of life and his own weakness, a deep need for love as a faith in which to relax" (*CP2*, 235).

Over the course of the play, Michael arrives at the revelation that a perfect union is an unreasonable goal, that love and strife go hand in hand, particularly when embodied by two such passionate, artistic-minded individuals as himself and Eleanor. Michael receives this life-altering vision on life and love from a highly improbable source, a streetwalker channeling the marital advice of Friedrich Nietzsche: "You got to laugh, ain't you?" the prostitute advises Michael about his life's seemingly intolerable agonies. "You got to loin to like it!" (*CP2*, 267).

O'Neill derived many of his views on women from Nietzsche's *Thus Spake Zarathustra*, a cult classic of early existentialist thought. "This book," Boulton said, "had more influence on Gene than any other single book he ever read. It was a sort of Bible to him, and he kept it by his bedside in later years as others might that sacred book." Nietzsche, she added, "at the time moved his emotion rather than his mind."[59] O'Neill's destitute emotional health that winter, and the play it gave impetus to, points to one of Nietzsche's chapters in particular: "Child and Marriage." The individualist "Superman" Zarathustra preaches to a spellbound acolyte that "even your best love is only an enraptured simile and a painful ardor. It is a torch to light you to loftier paths for you. Over and beyond yourselves you shall love one day. Thus *learn* first to love. And for that you had to drain the bitter cup of your love. Bitterness is in the cup even of the best love: thus doth it cause longing for the Superman."[60] O'Neill doubtless took *Welded*'s working title, "Made in Heaven" (as in "a match made in heaven") from this chapter as well, since it's there we find Zarathustra sneering at the treacly cliché.[61] After his evening with the prostitute, Michael returns home to Eleanor, and his monologue indicates that O'Neill himself had accepted Nietzsche's dictum that no marriage is made in heaven. But he adds the intrinsically sadomasochistic line that in the coming years, "we'll torture and tear, and clutch for each other's souls!—fight—fail and hate again . . . but!—fail *with pride*—with joy!" (*CP2*, 275).

O'Neill and Boulton did strive to keep their marriage intact over the coming years, and would have another child; but their efforts ultimately failed with neither pride nor joy. The rest of O'Neill's prophecy held true. In his heartrending breakup letter to Boulton, he told her that their bond had been hopelessly undermined by "moments of a very horrible hate [that] have been more and more apparent, a poisonous bitterness and resentment, a cruel desire to wound, rage and frustration and revenge. This has killed our chance for happiness together. There have been too many insults to pride and self-respect, too many torturing scenes that one may forgive but which something in one cannot forget." Known as O'Neill's "I love you, I hate you" play, *Welded* is built upon these "torturing scenes." O'Neill inscribed Boulton's copy with Michael Cape's closing plea to Eleanor: "I love you! Forgive me all I've ever done, all I'll ever do."[62]

Moving in with his brother's family at Brook Farm was never an option for Jim O'Neill. His famous sibling could neither write nor maintain any semblance of sobriety with him around. Jim had also come to detest Boulton, believing that she'd turned his brother against him. (Boulton, he thought, resented him after he'd been bequeathed sole ownership of some property James had owned in Glendale, California.) Harold de Polo invited him to stay at his house in nearby Darien, Connecticut, a favor that de Polo and his wife Helen almost immediately came to regret. "He had the wittiest, most ruthless tongue I ever knew," de Polo remembered of Jim's insufferable disposition when drunk. "He'd find out your weaknesses and play on them all night. The next morning he couldn't remember what he'd done and would ask, 'Was I terrible?' 'Yes, you were.' 'Christ! It's the old spirit of the perverse in me again.' " Jim's ruthless tongue wasn't his only threat to their peace of mind. One night when de Polo was out of town, Jim was smoking a cigarette in bed and accidentally set his mattress on fire; but as he was too inebriated to do anything about it, Helen de Polo had to drag the burning hulk outside herself.[63]

O'Neill had just added the finishing touches on *Welded* when he was informed that his brother had been nearly arrested, on February 16, 1923, in Stamford, Connecticut, at a performance of *"Anna Christie."* "Stinko profundo," as usual, Jim had abruptly leapt to his feet in mid-performance and bellowed, "Why shouldn't my brother, the author, know all about whores!" The actors fell silent and peered out into the dark auditorium. As if trying to steal the limelight while his younger brother Gene was—yet again—the center of attention, Jim then screamed that Agnes Boulton was a whore and, turning to Helen de Polo, rounded off his trade by calling her one too. De Polo put an end to Jim's outburst by roughly escorting him out of the theater and onto a train to New London. After O'Neill got off the phone with de Polo, O'Neill wired the family's estate attorney, C. Hadley Hull, about his brother's "most disgraceful scene" at Stamford: "Any measures however drastic you see fit to take to restrain him in New London will have my full approval."[64]

The O'Neills returned to Peaked Hill Bar that summer just before Jim checked into a mental asylum in Norwich, Connecticut. Word around New London had it that he'd been forcibly hauled off in a straitjacket. By August, O'Neill wrote Saxe Commins from Provincetown that although his older brother had been released from the asylum, he soon after went "nuts complete" and was now incarcerated in another sanitarium. This was Riverlawn in Paterson, New Jersey, where Jim regained his sanity but wallowed in the throes of "alcoholic neuritis." He'd also gone nearly blind from the Prohibition rotgut he'd been swilling by the gallon, and the Riverlawn doctors informed O'Neill that Jim would be lucky to recover 50 percent of his eyesight. "What the hell can be done about him is more than I can figure," O'Neill wrote Commins. "He'll only get drunk again, I guess, after he gets out and then he'll be all blind."[65]

Jim had fouled up their family estate too while under the sway of a notorious pair of gamblers he hung around with in New London. Hadley Hull had warned O'Neill about Jim's association with the swindlers back in mid-November. At first, O'Neill ignored the lawyer's pleas to intervene; when he responded a month later, he made some petty excuses, then gave up and confessed, "I don't know what to say ... It seems there is nothing I can do about it. The last I heard of him he was in pretty bad shape. In New York, he phoned to me, but I have not seen him. ... And I have learned by experience that the more I should urge him toward one course of action, the more obstinate and determined he will be to do the opposite. So what can I do?"[66]

James O'Neill Jr. died from alcoholism on November 8, 1923, at first with a stroke, then arteriosclerosis and cerebral apoplexy. As a result, O'Neill inherited $140,000, the lion's share of which was caught up in devalued real estate and outstanding legal and administrative fees.[67] But on the same day Jim had died, his "Frankenstein," as Jamie Tyrone calls his brother Edmund in *Long Day's Journey Into Night*, had embarked on a serious bender of his own.

O'Neill's latest spree was instigated by a weekend visit from the writer Malcolm Cowley, his wife, Peggy Baird, and the poet Hart Crane. O'Neill and Cowley knew each other peripherally from the Village, when Cowley had played a black ghost in *The Emperor Jones* and a white ghost in a revival of *Where the Cross Is Made*. "Then Gene stopped writing plays with ghosts in them and my stage career came to an end," Cowley joked later. "It was a minor example of how his decisions affected all of us."[68] O'Neill was deeply interested in Crane's poetry and invited him to Brook Farm after meeting him in New York the week before. (Crane wouldn't find out until later that O'Neill considered him at the time the finest poet in America.)[69] O'Neill was only thirty-five, though his dark hair had a premature fringe of gray around the ears; yet Cowley already thought of himself and Crane as emissaries to the old guard from the upcoming literary generation.

Cowley's party was met at the train station by the O'Neills' chauffeur, Vincent Bedini. Arriving at Brook Farm, they were greeted at the door by a Japanese butler named Kawa and Finn Mac Cool, a massive Irish wolfhound "the size of a three-month-old calf," that O'Neill had named for a warrior of Irish legend.[70] O'Neill was on the wagon, and to the disappointment of his parched young guests, no alcohol was served at dinner. He explained that he was working on a play about New England (*Desire Under the Elms*) but didn't want to discuss it further until he was finished.

On Saturday night, O'Neill ushered Cowley and Crane down to the cellar, "the only part of the house," Cowley thought to himself, "that seems to arouse his pride of ownership." The playwright motioned into the darkness at a rack of three fifty-gallon casks of cider that Bedini had distilled using apples from their private orchard: hard cider, "the Wine of the Puritans." "Let's broach a cask," Crane suggested. At this, O'Neill became visibly agitated and said he was worried Bedini wouldn't approve because the cider hadn't properly fermented. Cowley knew something about cider distillation and convinced his host that early batches often turn out best. Stripped of resolve, O'Neill mounted the stairs to the kitchen and returned to the cellar with a pitcher and three glasses. "Gene takes a sip of cider," Cowley remembered, "holds it in his mouth apprehensively, gives his glass a gloomy look, then empties the glass in two nervous swallows."[71]

The next day, Boulton drove off with Cowley, Baird, and Crane to a friend's house in Woodstock, New York, and by the time she'd returned, O'Neill was gone. A week's time passed after his first glass of cider before she found him in a room above the Hell Hole and there informed him of Jim's death. Though Jim had turned sour toward Boulton, she'd dutifully made the arrangements for his casket, funeral service, and burial. Pleading a hangover, just as Jim had with their mother's funeral the year before, O'Neill refused to make an appearance at his brother's sparsely attended funeral on Twenty-Eighth Street. Nor was he present when Jim was buried beside their father, mother, and brother in the family plot.

"It was a shame," O'Neill wrote a schoolmate later. "[Jim] and I were terribly close to each other, but after my mother's death in 1922 he gave up all hold on life and simply wanted to die as soon as possible. He had never found his place. He had never belonged. I hope like my 'Hairy Ape' he does now." In this way, Jim's death led to a kind of catharsis; but it also left O'Neill feeling terribly alone: "I have lost my

Father, Mother and only brother within the past four years," he wrote his Gaylord Farm nurse Mary Clark. "Now I'm the only O'Neill of our branch left. But I've two sons to 'carry on.' However, neither of them will be pure Irish, so I must consider myself the real last one."[72]

Back in the spring of 1922, after the Provincetown Players had silently disbanded, O'Neill, Kenneth Macgowan, and Robert Edmond Jones resolved to form a new kind of experimental theater. For one thing, O'Neill insisted that the old model of a communal theater should be thrown out entirely. Macgowan, he said, "ought to be absolute head with an absolute veto. To hell with democracy!" Bobby Jones would design the sets and direct, and O'Neill would write plays, supervise the productions, and make artistic policy. Fitzie Fitzgerald was hired as their business manager,[73] Jimmy Light as stage manager, and Cleon Throckmorton would continue his work alongside Jones as technical director.[74] They signed the lease to take over the Mac-dougal Street theater, now officially the Provincetown Playhouse, in the summer of 1923, but only with incontrovertible assurance that the Players never reorganize. Macgowan wanted to co-opt the name Provincetown Players, but O'Neill stridently rebuffed the idea. "I won't be mixed up in any organization which has to straddle the old and new," he warned his friend. "Make it an entirely fresh effort! To hell with the old name! Any name will do if you've got the stuff."[75]

The unexpected death of Jig Cook on January 14, 1924, was followed closely by an acrimonious letter from Susan Glaspell to Macdougal Street demanding that the name "Provincetown Playhouse" be replaced. The internecine war among the former Players had already been ignited in the summer of 1922 by Cook, who considered the hangers-on a voracious flock of "carrion crows after the sweet stink of that carcass." "Bide time on Gene," he'd instructed Kenton. "His mood toward us was bad. It is up to him to come to us again—if he needs us. He ought sometime to see a light about [Arthur] Hopkins and us—but he may never see."[76]

After hearing of Glaspell's appeal to preserve the Provincetown name for Cook's legacy alone, O'Neill informed Kenton that he'd argued for that but was outvoted; he then wrote a separate letter to Glaspell, one of the few women among the Greenwich Village crowd whom he considered "a real person":⁷⁷ "When I heard of [Jig's] death, Susan, I felt suddenly that I had lost one of the best friends I had ever had or ever would have. . . . I'm sure if Jig can look into the hearts and minds of Bobby, Kenneth, and me he sees an integrity toward the creation of beauty in this theatre with which he can be content." In an unexpected but welcome letter from Greece, Glaspell reassured him that she understood his good intentions for the theater. Her onetime protégé responded with elation that he and Boulton "read and reread" her letter. "It made us feel close to you," O'Neill wrote with sincere gratitude, "and we love you so much Susan."⁷⁸ Fitzie Fitzgerald, on the other hand, received another sort of letter from Glaspell, this one defending Kenton for fighting to preserve the name for Cook's legacy, and she ended with bitter certitude: "Fitzie, and all of you, for this letter is for all of you, from very deep down, I am through."⁷⁹

Over the following decades, O'Neill time and again acknowledged the "tremendous lot" he owed the Provincetown Players, if with some qualifications. "I can't honestly say I would not have gone on writing plays if it hadn't been for them," he said. "I had already gone too far ever to quit." Edna Kenton agreed, but only in hindsight and with a sternly worded but indisputable codicil: "There is no doubt at all that had he not had our Playwrights' Theatre and our experimental stage to use always precisely as he wished to use them, he would have reached Broadway by quite another road and with quite other plays. . . . No other American playwright has ever had such prolonged preliminary freedom with stage and audience alike."⁸⁰

On January 3, 1924, the Provincetown Playhouse reopened its old stable doors, with a fresh coat of paint, an enlarged stage, and newly built proscenium entrances. Their manifesto, written by O'Neill and published in their first playbill, declared that "the difficult is properly our special task—or we have no reason for existing. Truth, in theatre as in life, is eternally difficult, just as the easy is the everlasting lie." The newly formed Provincetown group would maintain a strict code of artistic integrity, but Jig Cook's days of idealistic amateurism, O'Neill now decreed, were over.

Instead, the spirit of professionalism had taken hold: they now welcomed critics and hired a press agent, Stella Hanau. "The premières had some of the glitter of uptown openings," Hanau said, "and those who remembered the early days eyed the limousines and the top hats with amazement faintly touched with disapproval."[81] Though most of them used the metonymy "the Provincetown," they still didn't have an official name. "We are just a theatre," O'Neill said. "Beyond that, let what we do give us a name." O'Neill, Macgowan, and Jones soon adopted one based on an article by Boulton in *Theatre Arts* magazine that announced their arrival and defined their mission with two unambiguous words: "Experimental Theatre." Thus when the three men incorporated, they called the group the Experimental Theatre, Inc. (ETI). In due course, the press conferred a more portentous label: "The Triumvirate of Greenwich Village."[82]

O'Neill had suggested August Strindberg's *The Spook Sonata* (1907) for their debut. The Swedish dramatist, O'Neill contended in his program note, "remains the most modern of moderns, the greatest interpreter in the theatre of the characteristic spiritual conflicts which constitute the drama—the blood—of our lives today." Also at O'Neill's behest, they chose to reinterpret Strindberg's "chamber play" (a three-act work with minimal cast and props) using self-crafted masks. O'Neill had deployed masks before in *The Emperor Jones* and *The Hairy Ape*; but in *Jones* it was just the African mask for the witch doctor, and in *The Hairy Ape* the costume designer Blanche Hays had thrown together masks at the last minute for background characters. Jimmy Light, who designed the masks for *Spook Sonata*, boasted that before this landmark production, "no one had used the mask" in modern drama "as the focus of dramatic action."[83]

Light explained that prior to this, the mask in modern theater had "disappeared along with other fundamental tools of the theatre, such as the aside, the soliloquy, the prologue, and the epilogue." In his profoundly illuminating but as yet unpublished reminiscence of his time with O'Neill, "The Parade of Masks," he stresses that *Spook Sonata*'s qualified success was less important to the playwright than its "demonstration of the possibilities of the mask." "It was 'Expressionism,' though not pushed to the point at which the physical setting," in the mode of *The Emperor Jones* and *The Hairy Ape*, "takes on the anthropomorphical shape of the dramatic conflict." O'Neill realized that the mask, rather than merely "an archaeological feature of classical theatre," as it had been widely regarded, could be a powerful "tool for the exposition of emotional conflict in plays dealing with man as he is today." "However, the actor has no manner or means by which he could change the rigid places and lines of the mask. It is we, the spectators, who living the past experience of the character and undergoing the immediate agony, place kinesthetically, our emotions on the face of the mask. They are *our* emotions."[84]

O'Neill's dramatic arrangement of Coleridge's *Rime of the Ancient Mariner* opened at the Provincetown Playhouse on April 6, 1924. For this play O'Neill was determined, as he'd been from the start, to heighten his audience's sense of "identification," a term that Light defined as the "memory and emotional resources of the spectator" informing a character's inner self. Once audience members ceased to rely on the personality-tainted expressions of an actor (particularly those of the "hams" of the day), they might encounter a far more intimate and interactive theater than the superficial, passive entertainment they were accustomed to.[85] Even revivals of classics like *Hamlet*, O'Neill argued as late as 1932, would do well to make use of masks: "Masks would liberate [*Hamlet*] from its present confining status as exclusively a 'star vehicle.' We would be able . . . to identify ourselves with the figure of Hamlet as a symbolic projection of a fate that is in each of us, instead of merely watching a star giving us his version of a great acting role." "From the standpoint of future American culture," O'Neill wrote, "I am hoping for added imaginative scope for the audience, a chance for a public I know is growing yearly more numerous and more hungry in its spiritual need to participate in imaginative interpretations of life rather than merely identify itself with faithful surface resemblances of living."[86]

Heywood Broun regarded Jimmy Light's mask designs as "cadaverous and ghastly" and the experiment on the whole an "abject failure ... a cracked test tube in the Provincetown laboratory." Other reviewers were on less sure footing, and most agreed that Teddy Ballantine's haunting recitation of Coleridge was magnificent. Even a mystified Broun reported that when the curtain fell, the little theater shook with applause. "Special students of the stage will find in new productions of the Provincetown Playhouse much to study and discuss," wrote critic Robert Gilbert Welsh. "The ideas expressed are not likely to appeal to the general public—yet!"[87]

O'Neill's first original play in nearly two years, *Welded*, premiered uptown at the Thirty-Ninth Street Theatre a few weeks earlier on March 17. The play was directed by Stark Young but overseen by the Triumvirate and designed by Bobby Jones. Its run was a meager twenty-four nights, and the reviews were abysmal, often derisively so: "Climax after climax goes by," scoffed E. W. Osborn of the *New York Evening World*, "at each of which one can imagine a well-trained curtain fairly aching to drop." "Indeed, if the program had not indicated positively that the whole action of the play transpires within a six-hour period," groaned Arthur Pollock in the *Brooklyn Daily Eagle*, "the audience would have been justified in regarding it as much longer."[88]

At one performance, the actress Doris Keane, who starred as Eleanor Cape, overheard an audience member grumble about Jacob Ben-Ami, who played Michael, "If that fellow says ['I love you'] again, I'll throw a chair at him." The audience was also laughing at inappropriate times, at first guiltily, then uproariously, and the *Billboard's* critic guessed why: "It is an axiom that repetition, if continued long enough, will result in laughter. A well-known example is that of the old vaudeville gag, 'I'm going away—but before I go I have something to say. I'm going away—but before I go I have something to say.' Repeat this long enough and the audience will laugh, tho there is nothing intrinsically funny in the words or thought themselves. Mr. O'Neill has his couple alternating between the themes of 'I love you' and 'I hate you' far too long." Edna Kenton, enjoying a moment of schadenfreude, gossiped to novelist and critic Carl Van Vechten that she'd overheard a friend of O'Neill's sigh over the humiliating laughter made worse by the excruciatingly personal dialogue. "He has torn out his heart and put it on his sleeve for stupid peckers to peck at," the person said. "I suppose it was something he MUST do."[89]

After the bad notices began pouring in, O'Neill complained privately to its director, Stark Young, about the distinction between the modern actors of the 1920s and the romantic actors of his father's generation: "Here's just the difference: the actors those days would not have understood my play but they could act it; now they understand it but can't act it." In public, however, O'Neill and Macgowan admitted a major blunder they'd recognized during rehearsals but too late to do anything about it: Jones's set of the Capes' Manhattan duplex was magnificently rendered but far too realistic for a "supernatural" play. "The creative mind does not always see clearly what it is doing," Macgowan said in a *Vogue* "review" that really amounted to a public apology. "It would have been far better if he had provided nothing but dark curtains and stabbing shafts of light and a few chairs." It should only have been done at Macdougal Street in the experimental way, he concluded. "It was our error—O'Neill's and Jones's and mine—that we chose to mount it on Broadway." "I wanted to give the impression of the world shut out, just of two human beings struggling to break through an inner darkness," O'Neill told the *New York Times*. "But the sets which I described in my stage directions were so 'natural' that they inevitably conjured up all the unimportant paraphernalia of daily living, daily existence, to stand between the life of my characters and the lives in the audience."[90]

Meanwhile, in the lead-up to the May 15 premiere of O'Neill's next Macdougal Street production, *All God's Chillun Got Wings*, the playwright inadvertently found himself at the center of a racially charged firestorm of his own making. First commissioned as a one-act by George Jean Nathan for his *American Mercury* magazine, *All God's Chillun* swelled into a two-act, seven-scene play that expressionistically delves into the torments of a mixed-race marriage. Macgowan reported that over the weeks after its publication, the mailman nearly broke his back lugging shoeboxes overflowing with press clippings to the upstairs office. The clipping bureau also nearly broke the theater's bank, since the price for the service was $50 per one thousand clippings. (The clippings, he complained, wound up costing them more than the scenery.) "What with the weekly syndicate letters and dispatches from Cape Town, Sydney, and Calcutta," Macgowan said, "it is no risk at all to say that 'All God's Chillun' received more publicity before production than any play in the history of the American theatre, possibly of the world."[91]

Note to the Ku Klux Klan

Alarmed citizens from all walks of life, racist, religious, and progressive reformers alike, discharged an unending flood of rage upon the Provincetown Playhouse in the late winter and early spring of 1924. Every book club, college library, and gardening society printed diatribes about *All God's Chillun Got Wings*. "It seemed for a time there," O'Neill told a classmate about the indignation that the news of the production inflamed, "as if all the feeble-witted both in and out of the K.K.K. were hurling newspaper bricks in my direction, not to speak of the anonymous letters which ranged from those of infuriated Irish Catholics who threatened to pull my ears off as a disgrace to their race and religion, to those of equally infuriated Nordic Kluxers who knew that I had Negro blood, or else was a Jewish pervert masquerading under a Christian name in order to do subversive propaganda for the Pope! This sounds like burlesque but the letters were more so."[92]

The NAACP also received letters about the pending production in Greenwich Village, from those sympathetic to O'Neill to those prepared to drive African Americans off the continent if it were to appear: "The furor of intolerance that is being raised against O'Neill's play is so absurd," wrote one of the former. "White and colored people do occasionally get married, so why should not a serious dramatist use that phase of our national life as material for a big play." Another, scribbled in black crayon, is addressed to "Nigger Johnson" (an allusion to the African American boxing champion Jack Johnson, who had married a white woman) and signed "white man." The play, "white man" wrote, was exclusively designed to "help the black bastards to get what was in their rotten hearts for years." He alleged that the leading lady Mary Blair was a mulatto, "not white," and that for race relations in America, "this play is going to spoil everything. America is not for niggers—you shines belong in Africa. Bring on the Riot—that's what we want."[93]

Jimmy Light, who was directing the play, told a reporter that he'd been "accused of being a Jew hiding under an English Christian name, and O'Neill was called a dirty Irish Mick." Another of their correspondents considered O'Neill "so low he'd have to take a stepladder to get up to a cockroach." Light neglected to mention the masses of Victorian ladies, one hundred thousand in number, who, through their representatives in the City Federation of Women's Clubs of New York, unanimously passed a resolution condemning the playwright for inflicting upon New York "this unwholesome, revolting and disgusting exhibition of what Mr. O'Neill regards as art."[94]

The main cause of this uproar? The press had made a shocking discovery, circulated nationwide, that in the upcoming O'Neill production on Macdougal Street, a white actress, Mary Blair, would kiss the hand of her black leading man, Paul Robeson, live on stage.

All God's Chillun Got Wings treats the unlikely relationship between an educated African American man, Jim Harris, and a working-class Irish American woman, Ella Downey, from their preadolescent days as childhood sweethearts to their tumultuous marriage. Through the course of the play, Jim, a hardworking student, attempts to pass the American Bar Association exam; but he repeatedly fails it as a result of his low self-esteem, which he attributes to being intimidated by the white test takers in the examination room. His failure is also due in large part to the fact that Ella, at first incongruously, makes every effort to thwart his dream. This interracial union, divisive for both black and white audiences of the early twentieth century, ultimately destroys Jim's professional ambitions and sends Ella spiraling into murderous racist pathology.

The idea had been percolating for a couple of years: in O'Neill's 1922 work diary, following the triumphant reception of *The Emperor Jones*, he'd jotted down, "Play of Johnny T.—negro who married white woman—base play on his experiences *as I have seen it intimately*—but no reproduction, see it only as man's." The only mixed-race marriage O'Neill saw "intimately" was that of his close friend Joe Smith from the Hell Hole and his wife, Miss Viola. The week Smith died at age fifty-six in 1929, the African American *New York Amsterdam News* ran an obituary headlined, "Village Man Who Helped Famous Playwright Dies." The death notice's opening line didn't identify Smith as the gangster, auctioneer, or Greenwich Village personality that he was but rather as the man "whose knowledge of the relations of Negroes and whites and his vivid imagination enabled Eugene O'Neill, noted white playwright, to write 'All God's Chillun Got Wings.' " (Indeed, Smith must have been more engaged in the actual production than formerly known, since his granddaughter, Alice Nelson, was cast as one of the girls for its opening street scene.)[95]

O'Neill was touring around France in 1929 when he received a despondent letter from his old crony from the Hell Hole. In his plaintive letter, written just before his death, Smith told O'Neill that he'd given up trying to make it in the world. O'Neill responded with a check and words of encouragement that simultaneously look back on O'Neill's anguished protagonist in *All God's Chillun* and forward to Smith's later appearance as the black gambler Joe Mott in *The Iceman Cometh:* "You know you've always got my best wishes and that I am your friend and will always do anything I can to help you. I haven't forgotten the old days and your loyal friendship for me. . . . Buck up, Joe! You're not going to confess the game has licked you, are you? That isn't like you! Get a new grip on yourself and you can knock it dead!"[96]

Along with Smith, the story of Etta Johnson, the boxing sensation Jack Johnson's white wife, was another likely source for the play. News of her suicide, a highly publicized consequence of antimiscegenation feelings on both sides of the racial line, appeared in the pages of the New London *Day* on September 12, 1912, while O'Neill was in town working for the *Telegraph*, with the headline, "Mrs. Jack

Johnson Could Not Endure Ostracism: Champion Pugilist's Wife Killed Herself with Bullet After Saying Everyone Shunned Her Because She Had Married a Negro." Etta Johnson's suicide note read, "I am a white woman and am tired of being a social outcast. I deserve all of my misery for marrying a black man. Even the negroes don't respect me; they hate me. I intend to end it all."[97] If members of the public hadn't made this connection with O'Neill's play on their own, William Randolph Hearst's *New York American* drama critic made it for them: "It seems that negroes would be the first to resent this thing. When the negro pugilist, Jack Johnson, was parading his ownership of white womanhood, no one showered him with 'bravos.' That was in real life, too, but hardly a thing to form the basis of a play."[98]

O'Neill conspicuously co-opted his protagonists' first names, Jim and Ella, from his recently departed parents. And the parallels between the actual couple and the fictional couple don't end there. Jim's desire to "pass" the bar exam is analogous in the play to "passing," if only psychologically, as white, a dual goal that he ultimately fails to achieve as a result of his racist wife's mental sabotage. (In a noteworthy coincidence, Paul Robeson was forced to put off his own bar exam in order to devote himself to the rehearsals of the play.)[99] Jim fails to achieve his dream of success, just as James O'Neill had failed to attain real stature as a Shakespearean actor. Both Jim and James are also thwarted by the needs of their troubled wives—in the final scenes, Ella Harris is driven back to angelic childhood by her own racism and Mary Tyrone in *Long Day's Journey Into Night* to her Catholic schoolgirl days through the power of morphine. Still, along with his parents' names, the characters also share the two best-known slave names in all of American fiction: the slave Jim from Mark Twain's *Adventures of Huckleberry Finn* (1884) and Eliza Harris from Harriet Beecher Stowe's *Uncle Tom's Cabin* (1852).

O'Neill completed *All God's Chillun* in October of 1923, and the play appeared in George Jean Nathan's *American Mercury* that February 1924, at which time the Provincetown Playhouse announced they would put it on that spring.[100] To print such a tale in a literary journal

read by a handful of downtown literati was one thing; but to show a
white actress kissing the hand of a black man *live* on a public stage was
quite another. Simply put, O'Neill was accused of promoting miscegenation. It was then reported that Helen MacKellar, who'd starred
as Ruth Atkins in *Beyond the Horizon*, turned down the role with "outraged hauteur" after hearing that the leading man wasn't to be played
by a white man in blackface. O'Neill denied this and made a public
statement that he'd meant the part for Mary Blair from the beginning.
The press then circulated a follow-up story with a picture of Blair
captioned, "The play requires that the white girl kiss the negro's hand
on stage,"[101] which circulated in papers across the country.

At the end of a day-long interview at Brook Farm with the
New York Times, O'Neill admitted to the incendiary nature of the
material while at the same time maintaining his rejection of open
propagandizing: "Of course, the struggle between [Jim and Ella] is
primarily the result of the difference in their racial heritage, but it
is their characters, the gap between them and their struggle to
bridge it which interests me as a dramatist, nothing else. I didn't
create the gap, this cleavage—it exists. And members of both races
do struggle to bridge it with love. Whether they should or not
isn't in my play." Thematically, he said, the plot would still hold true
if Jim had been Japanese and Ella white, "or if Harris had been a
German, and the play produced in France. Or an Armenian in Tur-
key. Or a Jew and a Gentile."[102] But they weren't. He was black and
she was white, in America, and that seemed to matter a great deal to
a lot of people.

If O'Neill's hoped-for effect was for race relations to come across
as "incidental" in *All God's Chillun*, he couldn't have failed more di-
sastrously. But he remained obstinate. "I know I am right," he said. "I
know that all the irresponsible gabble of the sensation-mongers and
notoriety hounds is wrong. They are the ones who are trying to rouse
ill feeling [between the races] and they should be held responsible. . . .
All we ask is a square deal."[103] "Prejudice born of an entire ignorance
of the subject," he said in a follow-up press release, "is the last word
in injustice and absurdity. The Provincetown Playhouse has ignored

all criticism not founded on a knowledge of the play and will continue to ignore it."[104] In the weeks leading up to the production, however, some criticism would prove impossible to ignore.

"Gentlemen!" roared Professor George Odell of Columbia University, thumping his fist on a table, "Eugene O'Neill is responsible for the profanity and insanity on the American stage today!"[105] Countless voices rose up to join Odell's cry: the Society for the Prevention of Vice and Crime, Hearst's *New York American* newspaper, the Ku Klux Klan, the United Daughters of the Confederacy, the Authors' League of America, the Salvation Army, the New York Board of Education, and New York City Hall all united against the production on Macdougal Street.

When asked in the spirit of compromise to take out the hand-kissing scene, O'Neill flatly refused: "The play will stand as it is. That would weaken the entire last scene. It is the climax on which the entire play is built."[106] This only exacerbated matters, of course. The Provincetown Playhouse was next harassed with poison-pen letters, bomb threats, and warnings of race riots. The Long Island chapter of the Ku Klux Klan threatened to blow up the theater on opening night. "If you open this play," it warned, "the theater will be bombed, and you will be responsible for all the people killed." In retrospect, Paul Robeson considered the whole affair pretty laughable, but the situation was worse than he ever knew. O'Neill and Jimmy Light purposefully hid the vilest letters from their actors. "A great many," Light recalled later, "were obscene or threatening or both, but Mary and Paul didn't see the largest part because we began holding them back. I remember one in particular to Mary, really filthy, pathological."[107]

The worst was addressed to O'Neill from the Georgia Klan's Grand Kleagle. The letter began reasonably, more of a form letter than a threat, but then got to the point: "You have a son [Shane]. If your play goes on, don't expect to see him again." Without hesitation, Light said, O'Neill scrawled across it in bold letters, "Go FUCK YOURSELF!" signed it "Gene Tyrone O'Neill," and fired it back to the Klansman by return mail.[108] (O'Neill's actual middle name was Gladstone, named for the nineteenth-century British prime minister who favored home rule for Ireland. Tyrone is the county from which the O'Neill tribe originated and the name O'Neill would give the family in *Long Day's Journey Into Night*. It's probable that by signing his letter this way, he was defiantly identifying himself as Irish Catholic, another group hated by the Klan.)

George Jean Nathan noted in *American Mercury* that Colonel Billy Mayfield "of the Protective Order of the Ku Klux Klan, Texas Lodge" wrote an editorial in the Klan's newsletter *The Fiery Cross* demanding "the immediate dispatch of [O'Neill] on the ground that he is a Catholic and hence doubtless trying to stir up the Negroes to arm, march on Washington, and burn down the Nordic White House." *The Fiery Cross* responded with an equally sarcastic item of its own: "Art is fast approaching its highest pinnacle in America. We are to be congratulated. ... It will be interesting to watch the success of the production. ... Its uplift will be tremendous and do much toward bringing about 'universal brotherhood,' of which we now hear so much."[109]

This wasn't the criminalized white supremacist outfit of later years. The Klan by the mid-1920s had a national membership of around 5 million. Thus O'Neill wasn't facing just the condemnation of racists and the press but a reigning moral stance of the times. Miscegenation, after all, was illegal in thirty of the forty-eight United States. (This number would remain steady until 1948 and wouldn't arrive at zero until 1967.) Augustus Thomas, one of the most highly respected American playwrights of the time, publicly stated that he thought O'Neill was treading on thin societal ice. "In the first place," Thomas wrote, "I should never have written the play, and in the second place, if I had I should be willing to do what is usually done in such cases, to permit a white man to play the part of the negro. The present arrangement, I think, has a tendency to break down social barriers which are better left untouched." The choice to cast Robeson instead of a white actor, Thomas said, appealing to the literary angle, was an "unnecessary concession to realism." (When Thomas was a guest lecturer at Baker's English 47 seminar during O'Neill's time there, he'd encouraged the students to write their plays as vehicles for actors; O'Neill refused to attend.)[110]

Several prominent literary figures, on the other hand, black and white, rallied to support O'Neill. On the latter side, these included two rising men of letters, Edmund Wilson and the poet T. S. Eliot. Eliot wrote that in his estimation, the dramatist "not only understands one aspect of the 'negro problem,' but he succeeds in giving this problem universality, in implying wider application." Wilson, in his *New Republic* review, hailed the play as "one of the best things yet written about the race problem and among the best of O'Neill's plays."[111]

New York's black audiences were just as divided over the play as whites. Alain Locke and W. E. B. Du Bois, two of the era's most respected black intellectuals, defended it. Locke dubbed it, along with *The Emperor Jones*, a work of "fine craftsmanship" by a "clairvoyant genius," while Du Bois wrote an impassioned program note for the Experimental Theatre's playbill: "Any mention of Negro blood or Negro life in America for a century has been occasion for an ugly picture, a dirty allusion, a nasty comment or a pessimistic forecast. The result is that the Negro today fears any attempt of the artist to paint Negroes. He is not satisfied unless everything is perfect and proper and beautiful and joyful and hopeful. He is afraid to be painted as he is, lest his human foibles and shortcomings be seized by his enemies for the purposes of the ancient and hateful propaganda. . . . Eugene O'Neill is bursting through. He has my sympathy, for his soul must be lame with the blows rained upon him. But it is work that must be done."[112]

Others responded with open hostility. O'Neill had made one of the country's most feared taboos, mixed-race marriage, even more inflammatory by choosing to unite an upright African American man with an ignorant Irish American woman. It was demeaning, they contended, that Ella was intellectually and morally beneath Jim. In the *Nation* review, proving their point, a white critic wrote, "Why mate a first-rate Negro with a third-rate white woman? Because those are the facts. . . . Only this woman would have married a Negro in America today."[113]

William H. Lewis, the son of Virginia slaves and the first African American to hold many essential government posts, including U.S. attorney general, had become a political leader in Boston and declared that O'Neill's play would be banned not only in Boston but across New England—and justifiably so: "Every negro in New England," he said, "will engage in this battle against this insidious effort at propaganda that insults the intelligence and self-respect of every negro in this country." Religious leaders from the black community also joined in the protest. Macgowan related in a satiric *New York Times* article that the controversy had "stirred up the racial feelings of the Rev. Dr. Squiddlebottom"—that is, Rev. Adam Clayton Powell, pastor of the Abyssinian Baptist Church in Harlem and father of the future political leader of the same name. Powell asserted that *All God's Chillun* would place racial equality in jeopardy because the play "intimates that we [black men] are desirous of marrying white women. . . . The kissing of a white woman by a big, strapping negro is bound to cause bad feelings. . . . For myself and my congregation, the largest colored Baptist Church in the city, I want to go on record as being opposed to Mr. O'Neill's play." Rev. J. W. Brown, pastor of Mother Africa Methodist Episcopal Zion Church agreed: "This play is most unfortunate as it portrays the negro in the wrong light. No thinking colored man desired to marry outside of his own race."[114]

Paul Robeson, soon one of the most revered African American performers in history, was twenty-six when he published his essay on the matter entitled "Reflections on O'Neill's Plays." This moving reminiscence of his experience working with O'Neill and Jimmy Light was published, six months after the run, in the Urban League's journal *Opportunity*—one of the most influential organs of the Harlem Renaissance. "The reactions to [*Jones* and *All God's Chillun*] among Negroes," he wrote, "but point out one of the most serious drawbacks to the development of a true Negro dramatic literature. We are too self-conscious, too afraid of showing all phases of our life—especially those phases which are of greatest dramatic value. The great mass of our group discourage any member who has the courage to fight these petty prejudices." "If there ever was a broad, liberal-minded man," Robeson said of O'Neill, "he is one. He has had Negro friends and appreciated them for their true worth. He would be the last to cast any slur on the colored people." He admits to having been a neophyte to the stage less than a year earlier but states that his opportunity to act in "two of the finest plays of America's most distinguished playwright" had transformed him permanently into a dedicated man of the theater.[115]

Nearly a decade later, in 1933, when Robeson's film version of *The Emperor Jones* was released, the reaction in Harlem was divided once again: "I can't see how a man in Mr. Robeson's standing would be a parrot just to make a few bucks," an audience member wrote to Harlem's *Amsterdam News*. "I am a man that loves my race and am willing to stand up and fight to the end any day for it." The article goes on to describe a standing-room-only screening at Harlem's Roosevelt Theatre: in spite of protests over the word "nigger," "which aroused more heated discussion, and in some quarters more indignation, than any other incident in the last decade . . . the audience—or the major part of it—fairly worshipped [Jones]."[116] Still, as the audience gathered on the street out front, a man was overheard remarking, "I got my opinion of a nigger who would stoop that low and use that word on the screen for the white folks."[117]

Jimmy Light directed *All God's Chillun Got Wings*, and he'd initially hoped to get out in front of the escalating hullabaloo and release the production as early as possible; but then he delayed it for the season's final bill. In part, this was because when the *American Mercury* first commissioned the play, O'Neill's contract stipulated that it not go on until at least three weeks after publication. On top of this, when rehearsals began, Mary Blair came down with pleurisy and was hospitalized for nearly a month. Macgowan conceded that to blame a leading lady's illness for a delay, given the theater world's unbending "the show must go on" tradition, was the "lamest excuse in the world." Buoyed by an approval rate of about 85 percent from their subscribers, the Provincetown Playhouse moved ahead with rehearsals.[118]

Given these setbacks, Light and the Triumvirate concocted a shrewd tactical move that would draw the press away from the *All God's Chillun* scandal, which they saw only exacerbated with time: they would revive *The Emperor Jones*, with Robeson playing that role as well, ten days before the scheduled opening of *All God's Chillun* on May 15, 1924. This decision had the favorable effect of taking the spotlight off the escalating scandal and onto the comparative talents of the Provincetown's newest African American star against Gilpin's by then legendary performance.[119] Although Robeson had at first rejected the role of Brutus Jones as at best unseemly and at worst racist, he then he heard about Gilpin. "I remember vividly picking up the paper one morning at breakfast, and reading the printed eulogies," Robeson said. "I could not help wondering if I too should have been so acclaimed if, when my chance came, I had accepted it."[120]

The Emperor Jones's revival allowed cast and crew to blow off steam beforehand as well, in the calm eye of this unrelenting storm of public hysteria. One night after a performance, Jimmy Light discovered O'Neill pounding the tom-tom drum onstage. He never stopped drumming, even as he and Light climbed the stairs to attend the party in Cleon Throckmorton's apartment. At one point, Light, Robeson, and Throckmorton removed their shirts to compare physiques. Boulton, with connubial pride, induced O'Neill to show off his. He did so, revealing his own well-muscled torso, then continued on with his drumming. Boom—boom—boom—the noise reverberated up and down Macdougal Street, attracting the attention of a cop on the beat. The officer also happened to be one of their bootleggers, and he agreed to let the party relocate to O'Neill's old roommate Barney Gallant's basement-level speakeasy, Club Gallant, at 40 Washington Square South. There O'Neill continued his shirtless communion with the tom-tom late into the night.[121]

Heywood Broun arrived at the theater on *All God's Chillun*'s opening with a holstered Colt .45. Hart Crane stepped into the building armed, in his words, with a "cane for cudgeling the unruly."[122] James "Slim" Martin, a steelworker associated with Terry Carlin, had rounded up a gang of roughnecks to protect the actors and the theater. Two of these were assigned to Robeson as bodyguards—staring six inches upward at the former football all-star, they snorted at the ludicrous prospect that he needed protecting and strode off to look after weaker targets. (O'Neill was, naturally, back at Brook Farm on opening night, pleading an unspecified illness.)[123]

Manhattan district attorney Joab H. Banton, a Texan, had sworn he'd "get" O'Neill, and he had one last possibility do so: he would refuse to allow children to perform in the play. Black and white children are featured in the opening scene, before they lose their angels' wings and age into racist adults. The theater knew the law requiring a permit to employ child actors; but that was largely a formality of the Gerry Society, which had already granted them permission. Then, late in the night before the opening, the playhouse received a call from Mayor John F. Hylan's "Chief Magistrate," reported the *Herald Tribune*, that "revoked the Gerry Society's permission for children to appear in the performance. . . . It is evidently believed by the officials that the small actors of both races would be hurt by contact with one another in the theater, though not in the public schools and elsewhere." (One white father did send a telegram from Georgia refusing to allow his preteen son to perform onstage with black children.)[124]

Hylan submitted his legal grounds a few days later, when the damage had already been done: the children were too young to act on a professional stage. This didn't hold up, since the eight child actors were aged eleven to seventeen, within acceptable bounds; in addition, a Broadway show was granted a permit to hire an eight-year-old the following week, a clear indication that the city simply wished to put an end to the O'Neill production. Harry Weinberger, the Experimental Theatre's attorney, hiked down to city hall the day after the premiere. Hylan refused him an audience, but his executive secretary listened to the arguments in silence. When Weinberger had finished his case, the secretary responded by asking if he'd ever seen such a long spring. Weinberger then invited the mayor or his secretary to attend the play gratis and see it for themselves but was declined.[125]

When Jimmy Light stepped out from a proscenium entrance on opening night to explain the mandate from city hall, he was welcomed with cheers and whistles. Light asked if he should read the children's dialogue out loud, to which the audience chanted, "Read! Read!"[126]

The audience that evening was racially mixed, and to ward off a riot, or even an isolated scuffle, no one was permitted to watch the

Paul Robeson and Mary Blair in the Provincetown Playhouse production
of *All God's Chillun Got Wings*, spring 1924.
(COURTESY OF JEFF KENNEDY)

✳   ✳   ✳

play standing. Seated to the left of Kelcey Allen, the drama critic for *Women's Wear Daily*, Allen reported, was "one of the best poets of the negro race in America, a man who probably understands the strivings of his people as few others do." (Allen kept him anonymous, though in all likelihood this was Claude McKay, a vanguard poet of the Harlem Renaissance who'd just arrived back from Paris that January. As a former editor of Max Eastman's radical magazine the *Liberator*, he often appeared at Village happenings like this one.) "Such a man," Allen wrote, "possessing the delicate emotional sensitiveness of a poet, would be likely to sense the most intangible slight or slur against his race. But it was evident that he found nothing in the play that is degrading and everything that is ennobling."[127]

Another reviewer, hostile to "the little reds, pinks, radicals and general nuts of Greenwich Village nutdom," thought the play "miscegenation propaganda" and wrote that "an agitated patroness, who sat next to me did not keep her thoughts secret by any means. She confided to me that she was from the South and regarded the whole affair as worthy of the attention of the Ku Klux Klan. She was heartily seconded by half a dozen who sat around us."[128] The only interruption of the night was a drunk who stumbled into the theater in midperformance and took a seat; he muttered that he didn't understand the play, then said, "Where the hell am I?" and stumbled out. Aside from this unrehearsed bit of comedy, O'Neill said later, "nothing at all happened, not even a single senile egg." The only evidence of potential foul play was a yellow pamphlet left behind on a seat entitled "The Ku Klux Klan."[129] By the end of the performance most critics had felt "cheated," O'Neill said, "that there hadn't been at least one murder that first night." Even the scene when Blair kissed Robeson's hand, noted one disappointed critic, "caused no more than a tremor of resentment and was, so far as any demonstration is concerned, completely unnoticed by the audience." Robert Benchley of *Life* pronounced drily that the production, "long dreaded by the champions of Nordic supremacy and the guardians of the honor of white womanhood, has taken place, and, at a late hour last night, white women were still as safe on the streets of New York as they ever were and the banner of purity still floated from the ramparts of our own Caucasian stronghold."[130]

Paul Robeson played the roles of Brutus Jones and Jim Harris back-to-back from May 5 to October 10, then played Jones again that December.[131] The racial attacks persisted on all sides over the role of Jim Harris, Robeson wrote in his *Opportunity* piece, but never from people who had either read or attended the play. "Audiences that came to scoff," he said, "went away in tears."[132] "Robeson adds to his extraordinary physique a shrewd, rich understanding of the role," the *New York Sun* raved, "and a voice that is unmatched in the American theater. This dusky giant unleashed in a great play, provides the kind of evening in the theater that you remember all your life."[133]

All God's Chillun lasted one hundred performances, with a break to transfer to the Greenwich Village Theatre in Sheridan Square that August. However, the last-minute solution to the problem of casting children, according to O'Neill, "enraged the police authorities" so badly that it "stirred up trouble" for his next highly contentious play, *Desire Under the Elms*.

"God's Hard, Not Easy"

That August 1924, O'Neill, to his irritation, was browbeaten into attending a performance of his S.S. *Glencairn* plays. It was held at Provincetown's local Barn Theatre, and he'd been "expecting to be bored stiff," he told Kenneth Macgowan afterward, but found himself utterly charmed by the production. He was most impressed by the way its director, his Provincetown friend and Greenwich Village bookstore owner Frank Shay, had combined the independent one-acts (minus *In the Zone*) into a seamless "single-complete play about sailors." But the old tales of his time with his shipmates at sea also made him "homesick for homelessness and irresponsibility," he admitted, "and I believe—philosophically, at any rate—that I was a sucker ever to go in for playwrighting, mating and begetting sons, houses and lots, and all the similar snares of the 'property game' for securing spots in the sun which become spots on the sun."[134]

O'Neill's urge toward possessiveness, a trait he'd always decried in his father, had gotten the better of him, and he was now broke. *Welded* hadn't even made enough to pay his income taxes for the year, his family's estate continued "quiescently in probate," and the $1,000 to Kathleen Jenkins for Eugene was causing his financial back to "creak under the strain." He needed a quick infusion of cash, and after seeing the *Glencairn* plays produced together in Provincetown, he believed that they would make a hit in New York and proposed that the Triumvirate put them on themselves. *All God's Chillun* had also reopened at the Greenwich Village Theatre that August, and to boost ticket sales he suggested that Macgowan hire a "foxy press-agent" to stir up ticket sales with controversy by goading Mayor Hylan into attempting to shut the production down again.[135]

O'Neill had begun a new play, *Marco Millions*, and was hunting for a new uptown producer. *Marco Millions* required an enormous cast and complex scenery changes that, he knew, couldn't be performed adequately downtown. In an attempt to entice the backing of theater giant David Belasco, he explained in a letter to the wary producer that although it takes place in the thirteenth century, the play was in reality a "*comedy satire by an American* of our life & ideals." The usually dependable Arthur Hopkins had also left him hanging on his decision regarding *The Fountain*, which led O'Neill to regard Hopkins as "not the right sort of Santa Claus for me to believe in."[136] At the end of the day, his financial hopes rested on his full-length tragedy *Desire Under the Elms*, which the Triumvirate scheduled to follow S.S. *Glencairn*.[137]

By the time the S.S. *Glencairn* plays opened at the Provincetown Playhouse on November 3, 1924, O'Neill's work could no longer be dismissed as an aberration of the times. His celebrity had grown all out of proportion to what anyone could have expected from an American playwright. His plays were also making headway in Europe, with productions scheduled in Italy, Germany, Czechoslovakia, and Russia. Quite a few drama critics attended the *Glencairn* one-acts when they'd premiered singly on Macdougal Street; but given the Provincetown Players' hostility to reviewers, only a handful had actually reviewed them (*In the Zone*, staged by the Washington Square Players, excepted). When the *Glencairn* plays appeared as one bill that fall, 1924, the notices reflected a wistful nostalgia for O'Neill's sea plays of the 1910s after the high-pitched clamor of the last four years. Their respite from controversy lasted for about a week.

Desire Under the Elms opened on November 11 at the Greenwich Village Theatre on nearby Sheridan Square. The Experimental Theatre, Inc., had taken over the space for its second season to expand its audience base while still running plays at the Provincetown Playhouse. The critics diverged wildly over O'Neill's new full-length: the more conservative-minded among them viewed the play as a needlessly sordid and pessimistic tableau; others praised it ardently, while still recognizing its flaws. "I don't wish to pretend that 'Desire Under the Elms' is a good play simply because O'Neill happens to be the author of it," wrote George Jean Nathan. "But it is far and away so much better than most of the plays being written by anyone else who hangs around here that one gratefully passes over even its obvious deficiencies. It doesn't matter much if a beautiful and amiable and engaging woman tucks in her napkin at her chin or not."[138]

O'Neill acknowledged the clear "line of development" from *The Emperor Jones* to *The Hairy Ape* to *All God's Chillun* to this latest creation.[139] But his expressionistic-naturalistic portrayal of New England culture, which takes place in 1850 at a Connecticut farmhouse, was also a by-product of nineteenth-century realism's local-color tradition. Before the action of the play, Ephraim Cabot, a farmer in his seventies, believes that God ordered him to find a new wife, and he does—a much younger woman named Abbie Putnam. (As an inside joke to his Provincetown friends, O'Neill named Abbie after a librarian there who'd once refused O'Neill a library card and thrown him out for drunkenness.) Ephraim's son Eben believes that their farm is rightfully his, as his deceased mother had a claim on its ownership. At first Eben hates Abbie for presuming the farm is now hers; but in spite of her greed, Abbie and Eben fall in love, and she gives birth to a son. Ephraim believes the new heir is his own and convinces Eben that Abbie's been playing him for a fool. After Eben confronts her, she murders their infant in his crib as proof to Eben (and to a large extent the audience, given her earlier manipulations) that she loves him alone. At first, Eben is horrified by the news and notifies the authorities. But he returns crestfallen over his betrayal and, throwing off his previous possessiveness over the farm as she'd thrown off her own, takes shared responsibility for the crime. In the final scene, the lovers pledge their love to one another and admire the sunrise as the sheriff's men lead them to their punishment—most likely the gallows. Ephraim resigns himself to living out his final years alone on the farm.

By this time, Robert Edmond Jones, who directed and designed the play's sets, was the recognized "father" of American scenic design. After a decade of perfecting his methods with, among others, Arthur Hopkins, the Provincetown Players, the Theatre Guild, and now the Experimental Theatre, Inc., Jones had effectively imported from Europe what became known as the "new stagecraft"—the use of colorful backdrops and lighting to complement each play's plot and characters rather than the traditional scenery that was merely functional or ornamental. For *Desire Under the Elms*, only the rooms of the Cabot house in which action is taking place were meant to be visible at any given time, making the four chambers of the two-story structure intimate the systole and diastole of the human heart. Two massive elms loom over each side, their branches hanging down over a battered roof and emitting a green glow in contrast to the house's gray exterior. O'Neill describes these elms in gendered terms: "There is a sinister maternity in their aspect, a crushing, jealous absorption. They have developed from their intimate contact with the life of man in the house an appalling humaneness. . . . They are like exhausted women resting their sagging breasts and hands and hair on its roof, and when it rains their tears trickle down monotonously and rot on the shingles" (*CP2*, 318).[140]

At an early rehearsal in that fall of 1924, the three members of the Triumvirate convened the entire cast and crew of the Experimental Theatre, Inc., at the Greenwich Village Theatre. They were preparing to open the season with Stark Young's *The Saint*, and Bobby Jones, who was directing that too, solemnly addressed the troupe: "Recently I heard the story of a blind child on whom a successful operation had been performed. When the bandages were finally removed from its eyes, the child looked around in ecstasy and murmured, 'What is this thing called light?' To me, the theatre is like a light that blind people are made to see for the first time. The theatre is a dream that the audience comes to behold. The theatre is revelation. That is what I want to tell you."[141] Jones then silently walked up the aisle and out of the theater. Macgowan turned to O'Neill and asked if he had anything to add. He said no, and the performers were dismissed.

Jones had been raised in New Hampshire, and he understood that O'Neill wanted the New England setting and Puritan attributes to equal in importance O'Neill's plot and characterization. Tough-minded "New England granite" culture was to be symbolized by a permanent fieldstone wall in front of a shabby gray farmhouse. New England Puritans believed that God was a jealous, pitiless, and wrathful being, a vision Jonathan Edwards immortalized in his blood-and-thunder sermon "Sinners in the Hands of an Angry God." Edwards's theology guides the play's devout protagonist Ephraim Cabot's worldview: "God's hard, not easy! . . . I kin feel I be in the palm o' His hand, His fingers guidin' me. . . . God's hard an' lonesome!" (CP2, 377). Outside of intellectual circles in the 1920s, Puritans were widely admired in the United States, as one reviewer wrote, "for their courage, their rugged persistency, their industry, their narrow adherence to narrow standards. . . . [But] we have begun to wonder," she said after attending the play, "if England had not something on her side when she ejected the Puritans."[142]

For all of O'Neill's own atheism and bohemian living, he still regarded the hellfire-and-brimstone Puritan farmer Ephraim as "so autobiographical." When O'Neill hired a man to type up the script, he invited him on a series of three-mile walks through the woods, always pointing out crumbling fieldstone walls, quoting from his play, "Stones atop o' stones—year atop o' year." "What I think everyone missed in *Desire*," he said that March, "is the quality in it I set most store by—the attempt to give an epic tinge to New England's inhibited life-lust, to make its inexpressiveness poetically expressive, to release it."[143] Such a release, of course, sends his characters to their doom. But he deplored the "sneering contentment" of soft thinking, if not always in practice, and he thus equated a "happy ending" for the audience with unearned success. Tragedy was hard and therefore earned. For O'Neill, the notion of a tragic ending as "unhappy" was a "mere present-day judgment," and he pointed out that the Greeks and Elizabethans had recognized the elevating attributes of tragedies like *Desire Under the Elms*. "Truth," he said, "in the theatre as in life, is eternally difficult just as the easy is the everlasting lie."[144]

The shadow of Sigmund Freud once again descended upon the talk over O'Neill's dramatic vision. Ephraim's son Eben fixates on his mother's memory, hates his father, and conducts a heated sexual affair with his stepmother, which is technically incest though they are not blood related. Most critics were thus aroused to single out Freud's influence, especially the "Oedipal complex," or the subconscious desire among men to kill their father in order to marry their mother, rather than Greek mythology itself, as the guiding source for *Desire Under the Elms*. (Since Eben adores both his mother and stepmother, critic Gilbert W. Gabriel wryly asked a doctor in the lobby whether this might be diagnosed as an "Oedipus duplex.") O'Neill was yet again moved to write a public denial: "To me, Freud only means uncertain conjectures and explanations about the truths of the emotional past of mankind that every dramatist has clearly sensed since real drama began. . . . I respect Freud's work tremendously— but I'm not an addict! Whatever Freudianism is in *Desire* must have walked right in 'through my unconscious.' "[145]

After two successful months in Greenwich Village, *Desire Under the Elms* transferred to the Earl Carroll Theater for its Broadway run. Prior to this, producers assumed that no tragedy, that is, a play without a happy ending, no matter how tantalizing, could last more than twenty weeks uptown. It ran for nine months, 420 performances total, making it the longest-running tragedy yet in American theater history. And once it had moved uptown, the Triumvirate required no "foxy press-agent" to manufacture controversy. That would come free of charge.

*　*　*

Over the summer of 1924, O'Neill had resolutely steered clear of alcohol, with but one exception—a cruel trick orchestrated by "dat ole davil, sea." One morning at Peaked Hill Bar, Boulton notified Harold de Polo that a ten-gallon drum of "200 % pure alcohol" had been "left up on our doorstep by the sea!" O'Neill's bender lasted only a couple of days, she said. (This was reassuring but false: She later told a doctor he was off the wagon for nearly two weeks.)[146] On November 12, the day after *Desire Under the Elms* opened, O'Neill returned to the bottle and continued drinking, around the clock, through December.[147] Quitting in Ridgefield proved impossible. Not only was it close to New York, a city he could now tolerate only when drunk, but Brook Farm itself, he wrote Theatre Guild producer Lawrence Langner in hindsight, "always drove me to hard cider, acidosis, and the Old Testament in the weepy, muddy, slush-and-snow days."[148] O'Neill desperately wanted out of New England, preferably to a warmer climate.

At Peaked Hill Bar that previous summer, O'Neill and Boulton hosted Mary Blair, following her ordeal with *All God's Chillun Got Wings*, and Juliet Brenon, Cleon Throckmorton's fiancée. Brenon had just returned from Bermuda and gushed over the island's tropical climate. O'Neill remembered when Susan Glaspell and Jig Cook mentioned back in 1920 how, after he'd finished with *Beyond the Horizon* and *Chris*, they should go down to visit the writer Wilbur Daniel Steele, who'd sent them "entrancing letters" from Bermuda.[149] They hadn't, but now he needed no further persuasion—that's where they would escape the punishing New England winter.[150] *Desire Under the Elms*, along with the two-volume *The Complete Works of Eugene O'Neill*, forthcoming that December through his publishers Boni and Liveright, promised enough in royalties for them to sail to Bermuda in late November for an indefinite stay.[151]

The voyage from New York to Bermuda took two days on the S.S. *Fort St. George*, a steamer that weekly ferried passengers the seven hundred miles out to the British island. O'Neill and Boulton disembarked in Hamilton, the capital, on December 1, with Shane, Gaga, Cookie Burton, Finn Mac Cool, and a new bull terrier named Bowser after his brother's story. The famed couple made a spectacle as they extracted themselves, their entourage, and their dogs from customs to the New Windsor Hotel. Oleander and hibiscus were in bloom, dappling the colonial town in pink and scarlet. In 1925, Bermuda's population was twenty-four thousand, about the same as New London's, and no automobiles were allowed on the island. Bermudians traveled exclusively about the countryside in surreys with a fringe on top, traps, and other horse-drawn vehicles.[152]

The O'Neills rented two bungalows, Campsea and Crow's Nest, perched high upon the cliffs overlooking the pink-hued beach and south shore of Paget parish (a site since occupied by the Coral Beach Club). The flowers and sultry air notwithstanding, the first weeks did not go well. Boulton had announced that she was pregnant, and the idea of a third "heir" exacerbated O'Neill's drinking. Mentally, he felt "depressed and slushy ... miserably disorganized" from booze, and he suffered from insomnia.[153] Devoid of inspiration, not even for a swim in the azure sea, he was capable only of sifting through a pile of *Saturday Evening Posts*. For him, the weekly offered an intellectual vacation. "Talk about narcotics!" he wrote in his diary. "My favorite!"[154]

By January 4, O'Neill had begun to taper off drinking and recorded in his diary how many drinks he consumed each day—one before lunch, three before dinner, and so on.[155] After a week, he was back on the wagon, with only the occasional ale with lunch, and he even quit smoking. (Aside from such intermittent pulmonary holidays, O'Neill was at least a pack-a-day smoker for life.) He was finally able to settle down and cut *Marco Millions* down to a performable size. Within a few weeks he sent it off to Dario Belasco, who'd expressed interest in producing it. He also read Freud's *Beyond the Pleasure Principle* ("interesting stuff but damn dryly written") and a book-length issue of the medical journal *Practitioner* on alcoholism ("very interesting + applicable to me"). On January 31, while reading David Seabury's *Unmasking Our Minds* ("too primary school"), he'd begun his latest and most ambitious work yet, a mask play entitled *The Great God Brown*.[156]

O'Neill's abstinence might well have eased marital tensions had whiskey not been promptly replaced by another source of conflict by

the name of Alice Cuthbert. Cuthbert was vacationing at the nearby
Elbow Beach Club with her sister Charlotte "Tottie" Barbour, who
worked in publishing and was acquainted with a few of the Provincetown Players.[157] Upon their first meeting on the beach, O'Neill
thought Cuthbert "a peach! Athletic swimmer's figure—out-of-door
girl—simple (perhaps too) + unspoiled."[158] He told an increasingly
jealous Boulton that the young woman exuded "a rare & beautiful
quality," and she soon heard a rumor of their holding hands while
swimming together. O'Neill denied this and swore they were merely "swimming in tandem."[159] Growing more and more enraged by
the number of trysts between her husband and Cuthbert, Boulton
reached a breaking point in early February, and O'Neill ruefully noted in his diary, "fight over Alice." This time, if perhaps she had in the
past, Boulton wasn't overreacting; a love poem O'Neill wrote that
winter titled "To Alice" longingly begins and ends,

> The sun
> And you
> Two things in life
> Are true. . . .
> You, the sun, & sea,
> Trinity!
> Sweet spirit, pass on
> Keep the dream
> Beauty
> Into infinity.

Still, Boulton recognized that her compulsive husband had neither
the time nor the emotional wherewithal for extramarital affairs—not
of a sexual nature, she felt certain, at least not yet.[160]

"Dirty day!" O'Neill groaned on February 21, 1925. "Wild cable from Madden." Their production of *Desire Under the Elms* was
about "to be indicted. Can't believe." " 'D' played to 13,500 last week,
fancy that! Helped by scandal, damn it! M. [Richard Madden, his
agent] says 'situation favorable'—jury trial Wednesday likely. Damned

nonsense! . . . Wire from Kenneth saying no indictment, that 'D' has been referred to play jury. This is good news. Old [District Attorney Joab] Banton seems to be beaten again, the bloody ass! . . . Much talk of Banton's calling me 'damned fool.' Ha-ha! Business booming. It's an ill wind! But it attracts wrong audience, damn it!"[161]

The play's moral "distresses," reported the *Herald Tribune*, "range from unholy lust to infanticide, and they include drinking, cursing, vengeance, and something approaching incest." Once it moved uptown, District Attorney Banton again played right into the Triumvirate's hands. The play was "too thoroughly bad," said Banton, who charged the theater group with promoting "salacity and indecency."[162] As a public relations ploy, Macgowan was the one who suggested they invite a "citizens' play-jury" to sit in on a performance, which they did on March 13. The play was duly exonerated, but the word was already out among New York's theatergoing public. The Triumvirate looked on in delight as thousands ignored the scathing reviews, of which there were quite a few, and stampeded the box office. Gross ticket sales shot up from $10,000 or $12,000, which O'Neill already considered a "miracle," to an astonishing $16,000 a week.[163]

"The *Desire* censorship mess has been amusing, what?" he wrote George Jean Nathan after Banton's rancorous attacks. "It has a background of real melodramatic plot—the revenge of Banton's enraged Southern Nordic sensibilities on the author of *All God's Chillun*." Similarly, while paying off his dentist in New York, Dr. J. O. Lief, O'Neill noted the same delicious irony: "But don't thank me, thank that so-amiable District Attorney!" "Seriously though," he went on to Lief, "his press-agent work is bad in the long run. It attracts the low-minded, looking for smut, and they are highly disappointed or else laugh wherever they imagine double-meanings. Banton is a vindictive Southern jackass. This was all an attempted revenge on me for 'All God's Chillun' which he tried so hard—and unsuccessfully!—to stop last season."[164]

Law enforcement officials fought the production in cities across the United States, and the furor spread across the Atlantic to Great Britain. (The Lord Chamberlain succeeded in delaying the play's

London premiere until 1940). Upon hearing that the entire cast of the touring company had been arrested in Los Angeles, O'Neill wrote the novelist Upton Sinclair, "I hear they have 'pinched' my play 'Desire Under the Elms' in your Holy City, Los Angeles. Well, well, and so many of the pioneers are said to have come from New England! Boston has also barred it."[165] A Los Angeles police sergeant, Officer Taylor, arrested the entire cast after attending a performance on behalf of L.A.'s wary Board of Education; he then testified in court, "I was painfully shocked, I blushed" during the scene in which Abbie Putnam is wearing a full-length flannel nightgown. "I sat there so embarrassed that I feared for the time when the act would end and the lights would again be turned on. After I left that place I couldn't look the world in the face for hours." Pressed by the judge, Taylor added that his "feelings were hurt, terribly hurt." The *New York Times* reported that "snickers and giggles" could be heard from the gallery of the courtroom, "punctuated by the sharp crack of the bailiff's gavel swung vigorously in a futile effort to preserve decorum."[166] "And so you object to flannel nightgowns, do you?" the defense attorney queried. "Yes, sir," he replied, and the gallery burst out laughing.[167]

After the judge ordered the cast to perform scenes in the courtroom, the actors were released from custody.[168] Such an absurd courtroom drama might have come straight from O'Neill's hand. Nearly all of O'Neill's law enforcement officials are satirically drawn, and many plays—*The Web, The Dreamy Kid, The Hairy Ape, Desire Under the Elms, The Great God Brown, A Touch of the Poet*, and *The Iceman Cometh*—conclude with policemen ineptly confronting his tragic heroes and heroines. These scenes depict the legal system as hopelessly petty when compared to the laws of nature and desire. "The injustice of Justice," O'Neill said, "it's big. It's fundamental. Too much can't be said about the farcicality of man-made laws."[169] The last line of *Desire Under the Elms* is spoken by the arresting officer, providing an absurd blindness to the tragic heights reached before his arrival: Abbie and Eben kiss and then are led off to face their punishment, while the sheriff gazes about Ephraim's farm and mutters enviously, "It's a jim-dandy farm, no denyin'. Wished I owned it!" (*CP2*, 378).

O'Neill was soon confronted with a less amusing legal issue, however: rather too obvious similarities were inferred between *Desire Under the Elms* and Sidney Howard's *They Knew What They Wanted*, which the Theatre Guild produced and which beat out *Desire* for the 1924 Pulitzer Prize. Howard's play, though a comedy, resembles O'Neill's triangular romance to such an extent that he was accused of plagiarism. Howard had, in fact, sent his script to the Triumvirate before O'Neill began working on his own play, which he completed in June, so the possibility was real. Malcolm Cowley noted of his visit to Brook Farm in November 1923 that when O'Neill informed him about his New England play, he repeatedly used the word "easy" as his "strongest expression of disapproval," as Ephraim does; but O'Neill informed Walter Huston, who played the lead as Ephraim Cabot in the premiere, that he dreamed the entire plot one night between Christmas and New Year's Eve, 1923. Kenneth Macgowan admitted later that he'd lent the Howard script to O'Neill, who then came to him in early 1924 with the astonishing news that the play had come to him in his sleep. At the time, Macgowan secretly believed that O'Neill's borrowing was probably a case of cryptomnesia, what he called "unconscious plagiarism." Howard, in the end, brought the matter graciously to a close by writing in his preface to the book version of his work that "no two plays could possibly bear less resemblance to each other than this simple comedy of mine and [O'Neill's] glorious tragedy."[170]

The Novelist behind the Mask

After his legal battles had been resolved, O'Neill exulted in the quietude of life in Bermuda: "There's absolutely nothing interesting to do, and the German bottled beer and English bottled ale are both excellent," he wrote George Jean Nathan, hoping to get him out for a visit. "The frost and hard cider of too many successive New England winters are slowly being rendered out of my system." Along with the year-round swimming, "which I do above everything," the lifestyle permitted him, by March 22, 1925, to complete his four-act mask play *The Great God Brown*. "Finish 'B' in tears!" his diary

entry reads for that day. "Couldn't help myself! . . . I think it really marks my 'ceiling' so far." A few days later, he'd finished reading
Friedrich Nietzsche's *The Birth of Tragedy* (1872), which left him in
awe: "Most stimulating book on drama ever written!"[171]

On March 30, Eugene Jr. arrived for a weeklong visit, and he
and his father enjoyed another grand reunion, clothes shopping in
Hamilton, taking long swims, and lounging on the beach. On April
10, after seeing Eugene off, the O'Neills moved into a large, coral
stone house called Southcote. Having completed *Brown*, O'Neill fell
right back off the wagon and consequently neglected to sign the lease,
a crime in Bermuda. When the landlady, Aunt Lilla Smith, arrived at
their doorstep, for the second time, she was furious to be told, again,
that Mr. O'Neill was sleeping. "You don't seem to realize who my
husband is," Boulton said. "I don't care who he is," Smith snapped
back. "I shall be back in the morning and if he doesn't sign you can
all get out." When morning arrived, Smith was finally compelled,
if with a sniff of haughty disapproval, to accept Boulton's signature
instead. (After attending a production of *Desire Under the Elms*, Smith
was appalled the O'Neills had occupied her house at all.)[172]

Jimmy Light arrived from New York on April 17 and stayed at
Southcote with the O'Neills for nine days. His visit wasn't without its
tensions. After a disappointing season, Light was worried that the Triumvirate were shortchanging the Provincetown Playhouse to the advantage of the Greenwich Village Theatre (which they were). He'd also
been annoyed that after he managed the uproar over *All God's Chillun*, O'Neill promised him the director's job for *Desire Under the Elms*
but then reassigned the play to Bobby Jones just before rehearsals. At
the time, O'Neill asked Light to take a walk with him and was visibly
agitated, the sweat pouring down his face and neck. He informed him,
albeit contritely, that he was offering the position to Jones because Jones
was a New Hampshire native and understood the New England dialect better than Light, a Midwesterner. (It was the "because" that had
rankled Light. He might as well have been disqualified from directing
the Glencairn cycle "because" he'd never gone to sea.) Most likely as a
result of these disputes, O'Neill declined to show his new "mask play" to

one of the few people who might readily have comprehended it. Light would again be passed up for director in favor of Jones for *The Great God Brown*, but when he read the script later in New York, he greeted O'Neill's concept for the masks with such eagerness that he was tasked with their design. O'Neill, Light wrote later in "The Parade of Masks," had contrived to build on their earlier deployment of masks in *Spook Sonata* and *Ancient Mariner* and "violate" the millennia-old tradition of immutability. The masks in *The Great God Brown* would expose a character's duality by their removal but also change hands and even transform over time. In this way, they would reveal the development of the characters' exterior as well as interior selves. "The violation of the use of the mask," Light said, "enabled O'Neill to dramatize the change of character in the protagonist and the antagonist in revealing their opposite developments by the removal by the actor of the mask. The actors' make-up behind the mask, showed the new state of the character's soul. Thus, there were two masks—one, the actor changed, and one the mask maker changed."[173]

The play would also address what Friedrich Nietzsche in *The Birth of Tragedy* identified as the central crisis of Western drama. Nietzsche compared the tensions that exist between internal desire and external reason with the conflict between the antithetical Greek gods Dionysus, the god of wine and fertility, and Apollo, the sun god. As Greek tragedy developed from the openly imaginative work of Sophocles, Nietzsche contended, to the more temperamentally realistic and practical plays of Euripides, the Dionysian elements began to wane. Nietzsche thus argued for a rebalancing of the ecstatic beauty and structural moderation represented by Dionysus and Apollo, respectively. O'Neill would answer this call with *The Great God Brown*.

Dion Anthony, another O'Neill protagonist with strong autobiographical overtones, represents in name and personality the Dionysian side of Nietzsche's duality, that of instinct and sensuality. Behind his mask, Dion's actual face is, O'Neill writes, "dark, spiritual, poetic, passionately supersensitive, helplessly unprotected in its childlike, religious faith in life" (*CP2*, 475). O'Neill regarded this type of ascetic, moral face (his own) as requiring a mask's cynical protection from outside view (also his own)—hence the last name, evoking the "masochistic, life-denying spirit of Christianity as represented by St. Anthony."[174] Dion's friend, the straitlaced architect William Brown, with his lackluster name and professional ambition, represents Apollonian restraint and reason.

Elizabeth Shepley Sergeant, in a later profile for the *New Republic*, praised O'Neill's innovative use of the mask for the stage, but also for what it reveals to us about the playwright's own inner battle with the world: the mask, she wrote, "signifies to him more than a stage trick, or a screen interposed between the crucial self and the bleary public eye. It is an integral part of his character as an artist. For, as he once said, the world is not only blind to Dion, the man beneath the mask, it also condemns the mask of Pan. O'Neill has known and feared the world's sneer. He responded for long by giving back to life a lurid and caustic picture of itself. A picture whose distortions—like those of the Chamber of Horrors—are never those of illusion; whose dreams are nightmares. But gradually, through a deepening of his own currents, the warfare between himself and life grew sterile. All his slings and arrows had not altered the duality of the world. All the slings and arrows of the world had not altered the duality of O'Neill."[175]

Dion in the play marries a woman named Margaret, who wears the mask of a wholesome American "good girl." As with her namesake, Marguerite from *Faust*, which O'Neill had also read that spring, Margaret is so blinded by her desire to bear children that she encourages her husband's transformation into a hardened misanthrope—the type of man that is materially and emotionally equipped to prosper in a cynical world. (Only a prostitute named Cybel accepts Dion's unmasked persona.) They have three sons, but Dion's lack of artistic success on his own terms, in contrast to his corporate triumphs as an architect at Brown's firm, leads him to sink deeply into alcoholism. Over time, Dion's Pan-god mask transforms into a twisted Mephistophelean leer, and he dies of alcoholism. Brown, who has secretly loved Margaret, claps on Dion's mask and passes as his friend. But the mask proves too tormenting for Brown's earthly inner self. After Brown's first mask is mistaken for the murdered body of Brown himself, he's gunned down by the police who, because of the mask exchange, believe he's Brown's alleged murderer Dion. Jimmy Light understood that the way in which Dion's mask becomes, as O'Neill specified, "distorted by morality from Pan to Satan," and is then climactically transferred to Brown, would make for an incredible theatrical accomplishment.[176] The only question was whether they could make it work.

On the day Oona O'Neill was born, May 14, 1925, Kenneth Macgowan received a tongue-in-cheek notification: "It's a goil. Allah be merciful. According to indications will be first lady announcer at Polo Grounds. Predict great future grand opera. Agnes and baby all serene."[177] Macgowan sailed to Bermuda with Jones early that June, and O'Neill met them at the gangplank. After a swim at the beach below Southcote, O'Neill read them the opening scenes of *The Great God Brown*, noting in his diary that both were "much impressed."[178] When Macgowan and Jones sailed for New York a week later with a typed copy of the script in hand, O'Neill felt emboldened, if only for a few days, to begin the scenario for an even grander departure. He'd first come up with an idea in 1923 of a woman obsessing over the loss of her husband, an aviator in World War I. At the time, O'Neill called it "Godfather," but then gave it a new title, *Strange Interlude*.[179]

On June 29, the O'Neills sailed back to New York on the *Fort St. George*, a contraband copy of James for obscenity, Joyce's novel *Ulysses*, which had been banned in the United States for obscenity, buried deep in their luggage. Boulton then took Oona, Shane, and Gaga for the summer to the resort island of Nantucket off the coast of Massachusetts; "Peaked Hill," Boulton wrote Harold de Polo, "is a little too primitive for the baby."[180] O'Neill stayed behind in New York at the Hotel Lafayette for a month of hobnobbing and hard drinking with friends and theater associates.

Paul Robeson, well aware of O'Neill's taste for hot jazz, invited the playwright up to Harlem to swill liquor and take in the speakeasies with him and Experimental Theatre, Inc., member Harold McGee. It was the height of the Harlem Renaissance, and Robeson and McGee were in a celebratory mood. They were heading off that August for the London revival of *The Emperor Jones* with Robeson playing Jones, McGee managing the stage, and Jimmy Light directing. They caroused the Harlem clubs all night, and O'Neill wouldn't climb into bed at the Lafayette until ten a.m. Head pounding with a hangover, he noted in his diary, "Up all night. Disaster."[181] (A couple of months later, O'Neill received something of a consolation prize, if one needs such a thing after clubbing in Harlem with Paul Robeson in 1925: Jimmy Light cabled from London on September 11 that *The Emperor Jones* was a "big hit.")[182]

O'Neill reunited with his family in Nantucket that August for a month of ostensible reform. After a week in the modest clapboard cottage at 5 Mill Street, his diary reads, "On the wagon," then a few days of nothing until, "Off! But not serious."[183] He'd found it impossible to work in New York, but Nantucket wasn't much better. Ed Keefe arrived from New London only to discover that Boulton had no idea where her husband was. Keefe eventually hunted him down and brought him to a friend's schooner where they sat up drinking all night. Keefe fell asleep but was startled awake by a sailor shouting that a man had fallen overboard. They fished O'Neill out of the harbor, drenched and flailing helplessly. After he'd slept it off, Boulton arrived in a rowboat and paddled him home.[184] Despite such relapses, O'Neill was able to revise *The Fountain*, which he'd started in 1922, and expand his scenario for *Strange Interlude*.

On his way back to New York in early October, O'Neill took off on another "bust" during a stopover in New London. He'd first looked in on Monte Cristo Cottage, sorrowfully describing the scene: "Decay + ruin—sad."[185] Wanting to get drunk, he met up with Art McGinley's brother Tom, Ed Keefe, Doc Ganey, "and the rest of the corrupt herd" for lunch at the Thames Club on State Street. It was a reunion of sorts of the old Second Story Club, and from there they "embarked on a debauch" through the night, "everyone blotto," that wrapped up at Doc Ganey's, where O'Neill passed out cold. ("They are much too swift for me in New London these days," he joked to Art McGinley a couple of years later. "I am glad to have moved to a clime [Bermuda] where they take things easier.")[186] "You know," O'Neill told

Doc Ganey before losing consciousness, "I always wanted to make money. My motive was to be able, someday, to hire a tally-ho and fill it full of painted whores, load each whore with a bushel of dimes and let them throw the money to the rabble on a Saturday afternoon; we'd ride down State Street and toss money to people like the Chappells. Now that I've made as much as I need, I've lost interest."[187]

O'Neill temporarily placed *Strange Interlude* on the shelf that autumn at Brook Farm. Instead, he worked on a new play, *Lazarus Laughed*, and cleaned up *The Fountain* for its mid-December premiere. He drank heavily on the nights when he attended rehearsals for *The Fountain* in New York. By then, he'd become sickened by the play, by the whole business of playwriting, in fact. On the night of November 23, 1925, he drowned his misery on yet another "bust," this time with Mary Blair and her husband, Edmund Wilson. The Experimental Theatre, Inc., had produced Wilson's play *The Crime in the Whistler Room* the previous season as a favor to Blair, who starred in it; after that O'Neill didn't encourage "Bunny," as the literary critic was known, to go any further with playwriting. Wilson could be critical of O'Neill's work too, even if his wife was then considered "*the* O'Neill actress," but he still admired his talent for "drawing music from humble people."[188]

O'Neill stayed on at their place until four a.m., emptying the apartment of Scotch and rambling on about topics ranging from the plays of Sophocles to the louche behavior of the actresses of his father's generation to the homosexual tendencies of sailors. "O'Neill had a peculiar point of view on the homosexual activities of the sailors he'd known on shipboard," Wilson recalled of their conversation that night: "He thought that in degrading themselves by submitting to the demands of other sailors, they were always trying to atone for some wrong which was on their conscience." (At the time, in fact, O'Neill was planning to write a play about what he'd witnessed firsthand of sailors' homosexual relations during his time with the merchant marine, but only have it printed for private consumption; as far as is known, he abandoned the idea.)[189]

The next day, dog-tired and profoundly hungover, O'Neill stumbled into the Greenwich Village Theatre for yet another dismal *Fountain* rehearsal. This time, he left so "disgusted" that he traveled uptown to commiserate with Jimmy Light at his flat on East Seventy-Eighth Street.[190] Light was then designing the masks for *The Great God Brown* production at the Greenwich Village Theatre while at the same time trying to keep the Provincetown Playhouse afloat with Fitzie Fitzgerald. (The Triumvirate had found it too unwieldy to run two theaters at once, so they'd gratefully handed over the reins to their colleagues.)

Light welcomed O'Neill into his home that afternoon, he remembered, as "a friend with whom he could say what he wanted and needed to say."[191] O'Neill hadn't written a word in nearly two weeks, and he made a startling admission: after striving as a dramatist for more than a decade, he was through. He would become a novelist. "Crowding a drama into a play," he told Light, "is like getting an elephant to dance in a tub."[192] The analogy must have brought to Light's mind the time when Walter Huston was overacting as Ephraim Cabot at rehearsals for *Desire Under the Elms*; O'Neill had, with his typical breviloquence, instructed the seasoned performer, "Walter, don't help the elephant to walk."[193] (This metaphor would also come back to taunt O'Neill when the writer Mary McCarthy, in her devastating takedown of *The Iceman Cometh*, compared him with other contemporary American writers such as Theodore Dreiser and James T. Farrell, whose works "can find no reason for stopping, but go on and on, like elephants pacing in a zoo.")[194]

O'Neill's dissatisfaction with drama wasn't news to Light. He'd generally written his plays to be read like novels anyway; how they'd appear in print was oftentimes more important to him than how they'd appear in front of the footlight. But his determination to write novels instead of plays was news, and it raised questions about why he wished to and how it would affect his writing in the years to come. Of course, he'd already tried to blend drama and fiction with *Beyond the Horizon* and *Chris*: the latter, O'Neill said just after its production, "was a special play, a technical experiment by which I tried to compress the theme for a novel into play form without losing the flavor of the novel. The attempt failed." And while writing *Beyond the Horizon*, he said, "I dreamed of wedding the theme for a novel to the play form in a way that would still leave the play master of the house. I still dream of it." O'Neill wondered at the time if "such a bastard form deserved to fail," whether he'd been "attempting the impossible."[195] Light transcribed this conversation as an addendum to his unpublished essay "The Parade of Masks," a previously unknown document that illuminates O'Neill's otherwise shadowed motives for abandoning plays; it is, therefore, invaluable for understanding nearly all his work from *The Great God Brown* onward.[196]

Not one of his plays up to then, he told Light, had given him any real sense of satisfaction by the time it went into production. "When I first have the idea," he said, "it is a blazing fire. When I have written it, it is glowing coals. When it is rehearsed and acted, it is warm embers. When an audience sees it, it is ashes."[197] Gone were the days of the Greeks, of Shakespeare, of the romanticists. The dramatist's job now was merely "getting his character onto the stage and letting him unpack his trunk."[198] O'Neill's bottom line was that modern realism had rendered soliloquies obsolete; the soliloquy was now considered a worn-out throwback that made characters seem like mere symbols rather than actual human beings. What theatrical device, then, was left to express true conflict, the psychic pain and inner language of the speaker? O'Neill's imagination was ill served by "kitchen sink" realism because its most vital edict is the "fourth-wall illusion"—the idea that characters must disregard the audience as if there were a fourth wall standing between them. Hence the soliloquy was consigned to Shakespeare and hack melodrama. No sane person looks off into the distance and bares his soul, just as actual people don't randomly break into song and dance as they do in musical theater. To make a connection with the audience, the dialogue must be "natural." Light neatly summed up O'Neill's grounds for reverting to the novel this way:

> The arena of vital action, the island of immediacy the dramatist
> certainly has, but the submerged mountain holding it up to the
> present remains submerged. To disclose this submerged foundation,

the dramatist only has the soliloquy. But the *soliloquy* is in the
dramatic warehouse relegated there by modern realism. . . . The
novelist as God, as reporter, as surrogate for the hero has both
exterior and interior command of his work. The dramatist has
only exterior command[;] what interior life of his characters he
can reveal to his audience must flash through the palings of the
stockade enclosing him. Providing he remains true to his theme and
his character, the choice open to the novelist is wide. Philosophy,
social comment, descriptions of nature, human moods, satire, even
dramatics, all and almost everyone, are allowable in a novelist's
medium. Though he has as deep and inevitable insight, as revealing
an interpretation of the human condition as the novelist, the
dramatist's effect is achieved by song-and-echo, blow-and-impact,
fight-and-victory, whereas with the same human material the novelist
has built a cathedral or at least a chapel of the understanding.[199]

O'Neill had already written four works of fiction—"Tomorrow," "The
Screenews of War," *S.O.S.*, and the lost "The Hairy Ape." But aside
from "Tomorrow," the others were meant as moneymakers, not truth
seekers. Even "Tomorrow" struck O'Neill as "inferior stuff not worth
republishing" when Boni and Liveright asked permission to rerelease
it.[200] Therein lay the problem: O'Neill knew he was a bad hand at
writing fiction, as bad as Mark Twain was at drama. Probably worse.
(Agnes Boulton could write fiction well, which must partly explain
why, subconsciously at least, he'd tossed her manuscript into the fire at
Brook Farm—envy.) Now genreless for a time, a creative standstill
ensued that would last for over eighty days. After *The Great God
Brown*, a new O'Neill play wouldn't be staged for two years. But in
the years to follow O'Neill's abiding wish to converge fiction with
drama would come to define his unique dramatic voice.[201]

At Brook Farm that fall, 1925, O'Neill mostly read, chopped
wood, trimmed trees, and took long hikes through the woods with
Boulton in a mutually desired but doomed attempt to repair their
widening rift. Nothing lightened his mood. "Too bored," he wrote
in his diary, "R'field is no home for me! Dull as hell." He even got

bored with his diary: "Read. Worked in woods ... Ditto ... Ditto ... Ditto ... Ditto ..." These lackadaisical notations are only interrupted on December 10, the day *The Fountain* opened at the Greenwich Village Theatre, "Alas!" "Refused to look at any [*Fountain*] notices," he entered the next day. "I know how bad they must be."[202]

The Fountain charts the ill-fated expedition of the Spanish co-lonialist Juan Ponce de León after he'd signed on with Christopher Columbus for the famed explorer's second voyage to the New World. Robert Edmond Jones designed breathtaking sets for the exotic lo-cales and engineered a series of equally arresting sound and lighting effects. Given *The Fountain*'s extravagant time shifts (stretching over a twenty-year period), enormous cast, and demanding scene changes— Moorish and Spanish courtyards in Spain and Puerto Rico, a Florida beach and jungle, and a monastery in Cuba—Jones's accomplishment, if not necessarily O'Neill's, was extraordinary.

Although O'Neill refused to look at reviews of *The Fountain*, he might've been surprised that more than a few were appreciative; the bulk of them nevertheless echoed the sentiments of Gilbert W. Gabriel of the *Sun*, who wrote, "Ponce de Leon and his coming to Florida, that land which has passed from the Spanish brethren to the Marx Brothers, are merely pegs on which to drape the pity of man's everlasting legend of a spring of eternal youth. They are voluminous drapes and they draggle." No reviewer, however, came close to abhor-ring the play as much as O'Neill himself. By the time of its opening, he'd lost interest in anything to do with the production and turned his full attention to *The Great God Brown*, a play that, he promised, was "worth a dozen *Fountains*."[203]

On December 27, O'Neill was offered "a ray of hope amid general sick despair." Kenneth Macgowan, after a Scotch-soaked evening at Brook Farm, had intervened in his friend's debilitating alcohol problem by scheduling him an appointment with a top psychiatrist, Dr. Gilbert V. Hamilton. The morning after his night with Macgowan, during which he'd polished off no less than a full bottle of Scotch, O'Neill again began his method of tapering off—five drinks the first day, then three, then one. On New Year's Eve, 1925, he wrote, "On wagon. Good'bye—without regret—1925 (except for a few mos. In Bermuda)." His diary entry for New Year's Day, 1926, greets the year with the hopeful exhortation, "Welcome in a new dawn, & pray!"[204]

To get a handle on the severity of his new patient's condition, Dr. Hamilton asked Boulton to jot down a summary of O'Neill's drinking patterns over the past year and a half. (The resulting document, incidentally, plainly shows that her husband had lied to her about the extent of his drinking over the fall and early winter on his visits to New York.) O'Neill and Boulton also agreed to take part in an ambitious study on marriage the psychiatrist had been conducting. In the book that resulted from dozens of similar interviews, *A Research in Marriage* (1929), which also includes data samples from Macgowan and his wife, Edna, Hamilton distilled his conclusions from anonymous statistical data, so it's difficult to parse what O'Neill and Boulton contributed to the study themselves (though in the column "Sources of [Marital] Friction for Which Mothers Were Blamed," only one participant listed "Mother's drug habit").[205] Hamilton burrowed deeper into the cause of O'Neill's alcoholism than anyone had before, at one point asking him to pencil out his psychoanalytic diagram of his childhood development. O'Neill obliged, and the diagram clearly shows his resentment of his mother's emotional absence, his loss of admiration for his father, the trauma of his nanny Sarah Sandy's horror stories, and his feelings of abandonment at having been thrust into boarding school before his seventh birthday.

Hamilton's final diagnosis for O'Neill wasn't especially enlightening: an acute Oedipus complex. "Why, all he had to do was read my plays," O'Neill deadpanned.[206] Perhaps less obvious, though a clear undercurrent in his dramas, was the verdict of psychiatrist Dr. Louis E. Bisch, a neighbor in Bermuda. Over the previous summer O'Neill had consulted with Dr. Bisch, who prescribed him veronal, seemingly unaware of his patient's history with the drug, to help counter his alcohol-induced insomnia. On O'Neill's thirty-seventh birthday, October 16, 1925, Bisch trundled out to Brook Farm for a visit, during which, O'Neill noted, they shared "much talk about divorce."[207] After meeting with him several times, Bisch concluded that "O'Neill had an unconscious homosexual attraction toward his father, which he carried over to some of his friendships for men. His antagonism toward his mother carried over to his relationships with women; because his mother had failed him, all women would fail him, and he had to take revenge on them. All women had to be punished."[208]

That he was Irish didn't help with the drinking either. By the mid-twentieth century, the Irish in America were statistically proven to be twenty-five times more likely to succumb to alcoholism than any other American group; as one priest described it, aptly for O'Neill, "The characteristic Irish alcoholic syndrome is of the compulsive perfectionist who feels that he has never been loved for who he is but only for what he can do."[209]

The degree of Hamilton's helpfulness to O'Neill was probably negligible. "Gene liked Hamilton personally," Boulton said later, while debunking the doctor's presumed success, "but was not helped by him in his drinking problem."[210] Whatever credit Hamilton deserves or doesn't, O'Neill knew he'd arrived at a physical and emotional impasse. His cycle of drunkenness, elevation, violence, and despair would cease only when he'd "convinced" himself, as his Provincetown friend Harry Kemp put it, "that alcohol is no friend to creative writing—is nobody's friend and soon a bad master."[211] O'Neill could dedicate his adult years to whiskey, as his brother had, or to writing, as he'd tried to do, but together they were unsustainable. And on that New Year's Eve, he believed he had, at long last, conquered his seemingly unconquerable illness.

The Great God Brown opened at the Greenwich Village Theatre on January 23, 1926, and the Triumvirate took preemptive action on what they were certain would be a hard-nosed critical response to the enigmatic play: on the day of the premiere, they rushed the script to a team of transcribers, then forwarded the newly typed pages to key reviewers so they'd have a copy in hand while mulling over their critiques; additionally, they chose a Saturday night for the opening to allow the reviewers all day Sunday without the usual pressure of a tight deadline. Many scenes in *Brown* equally confounded the actors; and even their *metteur en scène*, Bobby Jones, betrayed a lack

of comprehension about O'Neill's intent with the play. Leona Hogarth, who played Margaret Anthony, complained that Jones had failed
to make the roles "intelligible" to his cast, saying that "there was so
much talk of overtones and subtle meanings that the cast was tied up
tight as knots." The scene where Dion and William's masks change
hands, Hogarth said, "was always obscure and the more Jones tried to
explain it the more clouded it grew."[212]

In the days that followed *Brown*'s premiere, the inevitable public
confusion led O'Neill to "put himself on the dock" once again and print
an explanation: the play, he wrote, represents a "mystical pattern which
manifests itself as an overtone . . . dimly behind and beyond the words."
"[William] Brown," he continued, "is the visionless demi-god of our
new materialistic myth—a Success—building his life of exterior things,
inwardly empty and resourceless, an uncreative creature of superficial
preordained social grooves, a by-product forced aside into slack
waters by the deep main current of life-desire. . . . Brown has always
envied the creative life force in Dion—what he himself lacks."[213] Immediately after its release, O'Neill wondered if he should write "an
explanation regarding this explanation." But it wasn't necessary. The
consensus was that O'Neill had overreached with this oddity, but
brilliantly. The *Post* regarded *Brown* as "a superb failure. . . . He has
poured into it more than the stage can hold. His imagination has
soared on wax wings too near the sun of dramatic illusion and, though
he comes tumbling from the skies, it is a brilliant and thrilling fall,
since he has dared greater heights than any other." Brooks Atkinson,
the *Times*'s new critic, agreed but added that O'Neill "puts a responsibility upon his audience too great and far too flattering."[214]

O'Neill was heartened by the notices on the whole, but it irked
him that so many critics designated him as "high brow," an elitist label
he loathed. "I write from the back wall of the theatre," he protested.
"I'm not high brow." But for all the masks and expressionism, symbolism and philosophy, theology and psychology, *The Great God Brown*
was a tremendous popular success and moved uptown, first to the
Garrick Theatre, and then to the Klaw Theatre, for a total of eight
months in New York—an incredible run for an experimental play. "I

shall always regard this as the one miracle that ever happened in New York theatre!" O'Neill said, as he looked back in wonder nearly two decades later.[215] Indeed, a rumor circulated around Broadway that two shopgirls were overheard commenting on *Brown* in the lobby: the first turned to her companion and said, "Gee, it's awful artistic, ain't it?" The other replied, "Yes, but it's good all the same."[216]

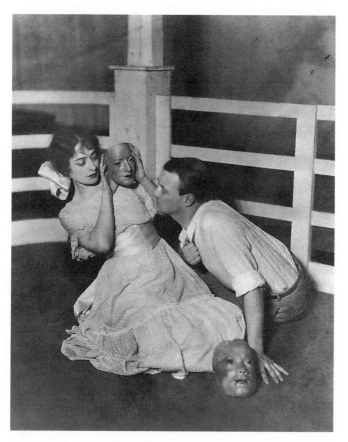

Leona Hogarth and Robert Keith as Margaret and Dion Anthony in the Triumvirate's 1926 premiere of *The Great God Brown*.
(COURTESY OF THE MUSEUM OF THE CITY OF NEW YORK.)

* * *

"Old Doc" at Loon Lodge

The O'Neills again left "dull as hell" Brook Farm behind them and returned to Bermuda in February of 1926. The first home they rented was a stately eighteenth-century manor called Bellevue, a hilarious irony, O'Neill thought, given its namesake, the world-renowned psychiatric hospital in New York, where he felt he and his family *really* belonged.[217] Located in blissful isolation on the south shore of Paget East, the newly constructed mansion featured wraparound columned porches on both levels and lush tropical grounds that sloped down to Grape Bay beach. The O'Neills wanted to lease it for several years, but that fell through, and they soon found a waterfront property for sale named Spithead in Warwick Parish. Spithead, a fortress-like pink stone sanctuary with a panoramic view of Hamilton Harbour and twenty-five acres of land, was built around 1780 by the British privateer Hezekiah Frith. The current owner hadn't been to the house since before the war, and the neglect showed. Its stone wharf was crumbling, and the ceilings between floors were cracked and rotted through. But after obtaining the Bermudan government's permission, the O'Neills made an offer of about $17,000, which was duly accepted.[218]

O'Neill returned to writing for the first time in months, invigorated with a renewed hope to push through *Lazarus Laughed*, which he completed at Bellevue that spring. *Strange Interlude* was next. (Other ideas had begun knocking around in his head as well; one of these, another mask play, which he never finished, was to be a condemnation of America's mob mentality with a protagonist named Mob, "a Jones but *white*.")[219] He also received the proofs of Barrett Clark's biography.

At first, the prospect of Clark writing the earliest chronicle of his life had thrilled him, but the final product was dispiriting. The book was sketchy and incomplete, and yet at the same time too long. Clark read his plays well, but he seemed incapable of writing "a more concise and interest-catching" tale about his life. Worst of all, O'Neill didn't see the least resemblance between himself and the man described: "It isn't I. And the truth would make such a much more interesting—and incredible!—legend. That is what makes me melancholy. But I see no

Spithead, O'Neill's home in Bermuda.
(COURTESY OF SHEAFFER-O'NEILL COLLECTION, LINDA LEAR CENTER FOR SPECIAL
COLLECTIONS AND ARCHIVES, CONNECTICUT COLLEGE, NEW LONDON)

✳   ✳   ✳

hope for this except someday to shame the devil myself, if I ever can
muster the requisite interest—and nerve—simultaneously!"[220]

By June the island climate had again lifted his spirits. "It's getting pretty hot down here now but the bathing is the most wonderful
you can imagine," he wrote his father-in-law Teddy Boulton, who was
then convalescing from an advanced case of tuberculosis at Shelton
(the public-funded sanatorium where O'Neill was briefly treated in
December 1912). "The water is so warm and the air so soft that you
can sport around in the water and on the beach in the moonlight as
pleasurably as in sunlight. Shane is in the water all the time and Oona
wades about in it." "I've found Bermuda hits me better than any spot
heretofore," he wrote Hart Crane. "I can relax . . . get rid of nerves,
be more free myself—and still keep from losing the needful pep."[221]

Once he'd turned his complete attention to *Strange Interlude*, O'Neill started to problem-solve yet again over what must be done to compensate for demise of the soliloquy. He was especially inspired by Theodore Dreiser's recent *An American Tragedy* (1925), America's most talked-about literary event of the year; Dreiser's epic novel revolved, O'Neill said, around an "unexceptional man," whereas he would compose a "novel in dramatic form of an exceptional woman."[222] This idea would make for a play of "revolutionary" length—perhaps the longest play in modern memory—which would approach in dramatic form "a novel's comprehensiveness."[223] Having accepted, since his evening with Jimmy Light, that fiction was not his métier, O'Neill still groped for a theatrical equivalent for the novelist's access to inner thoughts. This would ultimately come through best, in the years to come, by making his characters drunk, high on drugs, or very hungover—the "in vino veritas" that informs the inner voices of his late plays *A Touch of the Poet*, *The Iceman Cometh*, *Long Day's Journey*, *Hughie*, and *A Moon for the Misbegotten*.[224] But other methods were tried first.

With Spithead undergoing renovations, O'Neill knew that he would require an anonymous summer retreat to write *Strange Interlude* and, just as important, retain his hard-won sobriety. Provincetown was out of the question. Carlin, Harry Kemp, Frank Shay, and other hardcore inebriates were still there and swilling more rotgut than ever. "Not that I'm afraid anymore," he told Macgowan, "but it's no use making it harder for oneself."[225] On the recommendation of Richard Madden's partner, the theatrical agent Elizabeth "Bess" Marbury, the O'Neills settled on Belgrade Lakes, Maine, and on June 15, they sailed back to New York, then headed north to New England.

On June 23 in New Haven, Connecticut, at Yale University's commencement ceremony, "Gene" O'Neill, the college dropout, became Dr. Eugene Gladstone O'Neill. He'd been awarded an honorary doctorate of literature. "Old Doc," he mused. "O'Neill, the Yale grad." (The honor, he joked, was likely a gesture of retroactive gratitude from the hallowed university for his decision to attend Princeton and Harvard instead of Yale.)[226] Yale's press release for the event stated that O'Neill had been chosen for his role "as a creative contributor of new and moving forms to one of the oldest of arts, as the first American playwright to receive both wide and serious recognition upon the stage of Europe."[227] But O'Neill also knew what, or more precisely who, was the motivating force behind the pick.

The year before, 1925, his old playwriting professor George Pierce Baker had left Harvard to head Yale's Department of Theatre, and one of his first acts in office was to lobby for O'Neill to be granted the award. "Eugene O'Neill today," Baker asserted in the *Yale Review*, "is the best known in other countries of all our dramatists. Vienna, Prague, Dresden, Berlin, Paris, London, Rome—all capitals of Europe have seen his finest plays."[228] (O'Neill was convinced at the time that his soaring popularity across the Atlantic was largely because the Europeans believed he was actually from Ireland.)[229] "Coming from Yale," O'Neill had replied to the university's offer in May, "I appreciate that this [degree] is a *true* honor ... and hope that this recognition of my work really should have a genuine significance for all those who are trying, as I am, to do original, imaginative work for the theater."[230]

O'Neill was seated near a fellow honoree, the secretary of the treasury and billionaire industrialist Andrew W. Mellon. O'Neill glanced over at Mellon and saw, he said, "the epitome of the cold banker. You couldn't read anything there. What a cold face, what cold piercing eyes!" In his introductory remarks, Professor William Lyon Phelps pronounced that O'Neill was "the only American dramatist who has produced a deep impression on European drama and European thought. ... He has redeemed the American theater from commonplaceness and triviality." When O'Neill rose from his seat to accept the award, he looked across the lawn in astonishment as the newly minted graduates exploded into a "tremendous ovation."[231]

After the post-ceremony formalities, O'Neill drove his family in their Packard touring car along the Connecticut coastline fifty miles northeast to New London. While there he watched the long-venerated Harvard-Yale regatta on the Thames and rooted for the blue-shirted oarsmen of his new alma mater. In a thrilling win, Yale's varsity eight-man crew crossed the line ahead of Harvard's crimson-shirted heavyweights by a boat length (a hairsbreadth distance over the brutal four-mile course). O'Neill had covered "Boat Day" back in 1912 when he was a reporter for the *Telegraph*, but he decided then that the venerated regatta, the longest-running rowing race in the nation, would be the ideal setting for the final scene of *Strange Interlude*.

O'Neill left Boulton at the hotel with the children and steered the Packard, "very slowly and reminiscently," he wrote Jessica Rippin afterward, down to 325 Pequot Avenue. Grimly looking up the hill at the dilapidated Monte Cristo Cottage, he kept driving. The Rippin house looked dark, so he continued on for the mile or so to Ocean Beach. This too was a pitiful sight. The town had decided to imitate the flash of Coney Island, and the "atrocities committed at the beach," as far as he was concerned, had cheapened the beloved haunt of his youth.[232]

On July 1, O'Neill maneuvered the Packard through the pines, farmland, and blueberry hills of inland Maine and down into the village of Belgrade Lakes. Their first stop was a real estate office and general store run by Ervin Bean (brother of clothing magnate L. L. Bean) and a local named Ken Bartlett to inquire about a summer residence. Few of the Belgrade locals had ever heard of Eugene O'Neill; if they had, Bartlett said later, "It wouldn't have mattered anyway." The O'Neills considered the first cottages Bean showed them "dumps" and much too small for the family's extended stay.[233] Finally Bean located a suitable rental on Rupus Lane, less than a mile down the road from the village. A two-story rustic log cabin, spacious inside but perpetually dark from the surrounding pines, Loon Lodge, as it's still known, occupies a shadowy lot on the western shore of Great Pond. *Loon* Lodge, O'Neill, joked, perfect: "This, after living in 'Bellevue' all winter, makes me suspect that God is becoming a symbolist or something!" But after a week, despite the cabin's ironic association with madness, "I remain not only sane but also sober."[234]

Sobriety was as trying as ever. Each time O'Neill went on the wagon, he rediscovered the chief reason he ever really drank in the first place: the effects of alcohol, even during the worst of his almighty hangovers, simply made him feel less alone. Drunkenness had been his closest companion for over twenty years, he told Macgowan, and although he didn't "feel any desire to drink whatever," his clear-headedness deepened his feeling of isolation: "I rather feel the void left by those companionable or (even when most horrible) intensely dramatic phantoms and obsessions, which, with caressing claws in my heart and brain, used to lead me for weeks at a time, otherwise lonely, down the ever-changing vistas of that No-Mans-Land lying between the D.T.s and Reality as we suppose it. But I reckon that, having now been 'on the wagon' for a longer time—a good deal—than ever before since I started drinking at 15, I have a vague feeling of maladjustment to this 'cleaner, greener land' some-where inside me. . . . One feels so normal with so little to be normal about. One misses playing solitaire with one's scales."[235]

O'Neill's cavernous feelings of self-alienation weren't lost on the two New York reporters granted permission to drive up and interview him. David Karsner, the *Call* columnist who'd championed the politics of *The Hairy Ape*, interviewed him that summer for a *Herald Tribune* feature story in which Karsner admitted that, while they talked on the wide porch overlooking Great Pond, the "playwright . . . did not dis-turb me at all, but the man disturbed me much. It was what gave those eyes of his their burning luster and what contributed to his intense, almost jerky exterior that mattered."[236] Elizabeth Shepley Sergeant, who interviewed him for her *New Republic* profile, concluded her piece, "When O'Neill steps lightly along some pagan shore with Shane, he walks a little behind, a tall figure, in a bathing-suit, with limbs burnt to a pagan blackness; and on his face the look, not of a 'father,' but of some trusting elder child who has grown up into a strange world." Sergeant further considered the effect this personality had on his work: "Always thus hiding, always thus revealing himself, this Irish-American mystic, with his strange duality of being, has made his plays a projec-tion of his struggles with the unmanageable universe. Their power and their tension of his taut spirit, which are ever trying, like a pair of acrobats, to transcend themselves. Even the plays that fail to convince have a way of piercing the spectator in the ribs with some blade of vital truth. Those who are looking for diversion in the theatre cannot endure O'Neill's stark and desperate revelations."[237] (That March and April 1927, Shepley would spend six weeks at Spithead recovering from an automobile accident; this was just after her article appeared, and O'Neill told her it was "the best thing ever done about me. The others have been pretty dull and lame. Yours is the only one!")[238]

"You don't like me, do you?" O'Neill remarked that July 15 to the shadowy-eyed woman accompanying him down to Bess Marbury's bathhouse. "You're the rudest man I've ever met," came an icy reply from the actress Carlotta Monterey. "When I went into that play of yours [*The Hairy Ape*], I didn't want to. I had just finished one thing and wanted to go out to California and see my mother and daughter. But Hoppy [Arthur Hopkins] kept after me, so I did, with hardly a rehearsal, and you never had the decency to thank me." (Monterey had every reason to feel this way; O'Neill, after being introduced to her by Jimmy Light, turned to him and said, "What a dumb bitch she is.")[239] Only a couple of months younger than O'Neill, Monterey was no longer the ingénue of eighteen when she'd become 1907's Miss California and a Miss America runner-up. But her great beauty made an impression at Belgrade Lakes, especially in her bathing suit. (Boulton's daughter Barbara recalled her wearing a "boyish white wool bathing suit with no overskirt such as suits usually had," which revealed far more of her anatomy than just her legs.)[240]

The previous spring, Monterey, née Hazel Neilson Tharsing (a change from her Danish name to accentuate her Spanish-style allure), had married and then promptly divorced the man-about-town *New Yorker* caricaturist Ralph Barton. She believed that Barton, her third husband, was a drunkard who'd wasted his talent cavorting with celebrities and hosting all-night parties. Her first husband, the Scottish lawyer and California mining speculator John Moffat, was nine years older than she; her second, the law student Melvin C. Chapman, was seven years younger. Moffat lost access to his fortune when World War I shut down the banks in England, and Monterey claimed that he'd almost fired a gun at her and once threatened to commit suicide by jumping from their hotel window. Chapman she'd only married, she informed him soon after their breakup, to get pregnant. They did have a child, Cynthia Jane Chapman, in 1917, but Monterey left her in California in the care of her mother, Nellie Tharsing, and moved to New York to pursue her career on the stage. Meanwhile, Monterey conducted a long-standing affair with a hoary Wall Street banker named James Speyer. Speyer, whom she referred to as "Papa," worshiped Monterey, and though their relationship had apparently ceased being sexual, he ensured her financial security with a trust that would supply her with a $14,000 annuity for the rest of her life.[241]

After Monterey's divorce from Ralph Barton had been finalized that spring, she'd been invited for the summer to Bess Marbury's residence on Upper Long Pond, about a mile from Loon Lodge. Making up in ambition what she might have lacked in talent, Monterey considered time spent with the illustrious theatrical agent a professional coup that might get her back on the stage. Marbury was a portly seventy-year-old woman with a list of renowned clientele, past and present, including Oscar Wilde and George Bernard Shaw. (The talk of Broadway had it that Marbury preferred the company of her own sex. According to Boulton, O'Neill at first thought that Monterey was Marbury's lover; when Boulton said she didn't think so, he responded, "You're so naïve.")[242] Marbury's household was thus a step up for a second-tier actress like Monterey. Nevertheless, she'd resolved to welcome "the Great O'Neill" with a stony silence.

Agnes Boulton stepped out of the Packard with O'Neill and straightaway inquired about Monterey's sex life. "I *have* no sex life," Monterey replied, offended. "I've just been divorced." "Oh, but you must have a lover! Don't you have a lover?" No.

Boulton and Marbury dominated the conversation that afternoon, with O'Neill and Monterey deathly silent. After a time, Marbury took note of the awkwardness between them and instructed Monterey to accompany the playwright to the boathouse and find him a swimsuit. Monterey herself had an intense phobia of water from the time that her father, Christian Tharsing, had thrown her headlong into the glacially cold Pacific in a bungled attempt at teaching her to swim. Her hauteur softened a bit when she beheld O'Neill emerge from the bathhouse clad in an ill-fitting woman's suit, then lunge, unselfconsciously, into Long Pond. Her icy demeanor thawed yet more after O'Neill apologized about their "moment's introduction" at the Plymouth Theatre in 1922; he'd been overwhelmed with grief, he explained, over his mother's recent death.[243] Monterey may not have shared his love of water, but they both—O'Neill feeling as lost without alcohol's "phantoms and obsessions" as Monterey did after her recent divorce from Ralph Barton—felt very alone.

O'Neill's favorite activity that summer was paddling his canoe over to the majestic home of the actress Florence Reed and her

Shane O'Neill, Eugene O'Neill, and Carlotta Monterey at Belgrade Lakes, Maine, in the summer of 1926.
(COURTESY OF THE YALE COLLECTION OF AMERICAN LITERATURE, BEINECKE RARE BOOK AND MANUSCRIPT LIBRARY, NEW HAVEN)

* * *

husband, Malcolm Williams, a half mile north along Great Pond's edge from Loon Lodge. Their property included a wide lakefront lawn and dock area where he could relax, sip tea, and enjoy hours of genial conversation, uninterrupted by shouting children, the smell of cooking, and other domestic annoyances. He was desperate for male companionship, and he and Malcolm Williams swiftly became friends. When Monterey was visiting their home with Bess Marbury and discovered O'Neill there, she "accidentally" left her scarf behind. Reed was about to ask her maid to return it, when Williams said, "Don't bother, she won't thank you for it. She'll be back for it herself tomorrow, when Gene's here."[244]

Monterey soon visited him and his family at Loon Lodge and occasionally went canoeing with O'Neill. Reed remembered that the O'Neills' lodge smelled of "diapers and lamb stew," to the disgust of Monterey, who always made it a point to keep her living spaces, including Bess Marbury's that summer, utterly immaculate.[245] Boulton ignored such trifles on the whole and recalled more generally of Monterey's advances on her husband, "I didn't worry about him because she didn't seem smart enough for him. It seemed to me he was more amused by her than anything else." But then again, she added musingly, O'Neill did say that Monterey had eyes just like his mother's.[246]

O'Neill, to combat his post-alcohol doldrums, took advantage of every diversion that drew tourists to Belgrade Lakes each summer by the thousands—swimming, boating, fishing, and aimlessly driving through the countryside. "The Lakes are fine," he wrote Macgowan, "and we have a good camp, good rowboat & canoe and fish abound. . . . Eugene is here & Barbara so we're a fat family." He took swims several times a day, often across from Loon Lodge to Abena Point and back. Eugene Jr., who was then sixteen, and Barbara Burton, eleven, were there for July and much of August. During this time Barbara plunged "madly in love" with her stepfather's good-looking namesake, "so dashing and handsome and full of exuberance."[247]

Eugene, Barbara, and Shane held competitions to see how many perch they could catch; the withdrawn six-year-old Shane, happy to sit alone and wait patiently for a bite, usually won. Eugene, now an honor student at the prestigious Horace Mann School in the Bronx, dreamed of attending Yale. While at Loon Lodge, he befriended an equally well-read boy of his age named Frank Meyer, who was surprised to find himself discussing life and literature with the likes of Eugene O'Neill. "I found him very kind and gentle," Meyer recalled. "What I especially liked was that he talked to you as an equal, none of that talking down because you were a kid." At one point, he said, "we talked about Freud. I remember in particular our discussing puns and slips of the tongue in connection with the unconscious."[248]

Shane and Oona's clamoring needs, on the other hand, though they were no different from other children their age, had become nearly intolerable to O'Neill. "Perhaps I could do with less progeny about," O'Neill said, "for I was never cut out, seemingly, for a pater familias and children in squads, even when indubitably my own, tend to 'get my goat.' "[249] To offer her husband a semblance of privacy, Boulton arranged for local builders to construct a makeshift shack close to the water's edge.[250] After several morning hours of frustratingly slow progress on *Strange Interlude*, he'd emerge from his shack and, unable to face the racket in the main house, plunge into Great Pond for a long swim. Only afterward could he relax and enjoy lunch with his family.

Harold de Polo rented a cottage in Maine about a hundred miles away at Lake Kezar, and O'Neill invited him over in early September to teach him bass fishing. "Come on along, kid," he wrote his old friend, "and show me something about bass." O'Neill, de Polo, and Boulton went night fishing off an island across from Loon Lodge, and O'Neill was a determined student, ignoring the sparkling northern lights that left Boulton and de Polo entranced. Time spent with O'Neill always reminded de Polo of a popular cartoon: two British youths are looking at Mont Blanc in the Swiss Alps. "Not bad," one mumbles. "Don't be so demmed enthusiastic," the other yawns. "Purty?" de Polo asked, quoting from *Desire Under the Elms*. "Ay-eh," O'Neill responded, also from the script, then he struck a bass. "How about it," de Polo asked, "ain't it the grandest sport in the world? . . . Ain't it got all the thrills—" "Yeah," O'Neill said and cast his rod again.[251]

De Polo was still drinking a good deal but admired his friend's resolve to quit. He later remembered that instead of bourbon, their usual, they drank glasses of milk while warming up at the fireplace and ate can after can of "exceptionally sweet figs in syrup which Gene seemed very much to like." When the O'Neills agreed to try their luck fishing at Lake Kezar, de Polo phoned Helen and told her to stock up on figs. During the O'Neills' visit, while they sat around the fireplace and the two men tucked into their milk and figs, Boulton burst out laughing: "Two old topers drinking *milk* and eating figs in sweet syrup! My God, what would the boys in the Hell-Hole say?"[252] O'Neill smiled wanly, then reached behind him for a copy of *The Great God Brown*, signed it, handed it to his friend, and told him to read it out loud, which he did: "To Harold de Polo—My friend of 'those days' and these—'The Donkeyman—I done my share o' drinkin' in my time. (Regretfully) Then was good times, those days! Can't hold up under drink no more. Doctor told me I'd got to stop or die. (He spits contentedly) So I stops!' Gene—The Moon of the Caribbees."[253]

Strange Interlude had proved "damn difficult" to get through in spite of O'Neill's abstinence. During the first few weeks, all he could do was revise the second scene over and over; after a while, however, he admitted that although it was "coming forth more slowly than usual," he was confident it was progressing well.[254] By August he'd completed five acts, but again felt "sour . . . on life generally." Then the Triumvirate decided to call it quits, and he needed a producer. "Seriously, I honestly am getting awfully fed up with the eternal show-shop from which nothing ever seems to emerge except more show-shop," he complained to George Jean Nathan over the trouble of drumming up a financial backer. David Belasco had, for a time, optioned *Marco Millions* and promised the whopping sum of $200,000 for its production costs (including a research trip for Bobby Jones to study Chinese set designs firsthand); but he eventually passed on the play, as did Arthur Hopkins and several other producers after him. Macgowan proposed that they join forces with the Actors' Theater company to offset *Marco*'s expenses, but O'Neill argued that signing with such a "show-shop" outfit would be demeaning after what they'd accomplished: "It cheapens us both and it cheapens the plays in the minds of cheap people." "It's a most humiliating game for an artist," he said. "Novelists have the best of it."[255]

On October 13, 1926, while Boulton stayed behind in Maine to decamp from Loon Lodge, O'Neill took an overnight train back to New York—and back to the beautiful Carlotta Monterey.

The Soliloquy Is Dead! Long Live—What?

To celebrate his thirty-eighth birthday, O'Neill was invited as an honored guest to the Yale-Dartmouth football game, which he attended with George Pierce Baker and Kenneth Macgowan. In New York, he dropped in on Paul Robeson backstage at the Comedy Theatre, where Robeson was starring in *Black Boy*, a play based loosely on Jack Johnson that closed after only three weeks. Robeson admitted to O'Neill that he was as fed up with acting in dramas as O'Neill had been with writing them and decided to exclusively pursue a career as a singer. O'Neill also met with prospective producers for *Marco Millions* and *Lazarus Laughed*, conducted several sessions with Dr. Hamilton, and attended rehearsals for the Triumvirate's final production as a team—a revival of *Beyond the Horizon*, in conjunction with the Actors' Theater, on November 20. Boulton arrived for a ten-day "honeymoon," but then left him to his devices.[256] Most of his energy after his wife's departure was spent wooing and decisively falling in love with Monterey.

"He came up on three afternoons," she recalled. "I hardly knew the man . . . and he paid no more attention to me than if I were that chair, and he began to talk about his early life—that he had no real home, that he had no mother in the real sense, no father in the real sense, no one to treat him as a child should be treated . . . those three afternoons I sat and listened to this man—at first I was a little worried, and then I was deeply unhappy."[257] It's true that O'Neill and Monterey had met on only six occasions at Belgrade Lakes.[258] What isn't entirely true is that she "hardly knew the man" when they reunited in New York, as several pictures of them in Maine make clear. Indeed, O'Neill's work diary indicates that rather than "three afternoons" at her apartment, as the ever-decorous Monterey wished posterity to believe, they met every chance they had through late October and November.

They shared meals together, went shopping at Abercrombie & Fitch and Macy's, attended the Philharmonic, and even, on November 22, had their portraits taken by the celebrated photographer Nickolas Muray. During his last five days in New York, they were inseparable. O'Neill was with her at her flat at 20 East Sixty-Seventh Street until two thirty on the morning he sailed back to Bermuda.[259]

Boulton had traveled with the children to Connecticut from Belgrade Lakes to look in on Brook Farm and visit her family. From there, she departed for Bermuda, only crossing her husband's path once during a few days' visit from him at Brook Farm, which they'd put up for sale to cover the cost of buying and renovating Spithead. Again O'Neill felt abandoned, and he soon blamed Boulton's disregard for his relationship with Monterey: "It was partly your never sending me any word," he wrote to her that spring after having confessed, and bitterly argued over, his love affair. "When you went to Bermuda and left me alone in New York that helped me to forget myself."[260]

Back in Bermuda, Boulton rented a small house near Spithead called Belmere, which the family inhabited for the entire winter because of endless snags with Spithead's renovations. Boulton wanted a new kitchen and O'Neill wanted a tennis court; the enormous water tank in the side yard, constructed by the privateer to hold seven thousand gallons of water to supply his ships, required an electric pump for indoor plumbing. A section of the stone wharf had been pulverized by a devastating hurricane that summer with winds up to 114 miles per hour and now also needed repair. Boulton hadn't expected the work to be completed by the time she arrived, but she'd expected that *something* would have been done. The colossal project was overseen by Frederick Hill, the architect of James and Ella O'Neill's longtime residence, the Prince George Hotel in New York. That October Boulton had written O'Neill from Loon Lodge complaining that Hill was too cryptic in his responses to her: "Another futile letter from Hill—too stupid. No info. at all. He *is* an ass." After such insults were trained at him personally, Frederick Hill offered to resign from the job but, lacking an alternative, they kept him on.[261]

O'Neill arrived in Bermuda in late November, thinking of little but Monterey. He wrote her long, passionate letters pledging his devotion, but not to her alone. "As soon as I reached here I told Agnes exactly how I felt about leaving you," he told her. "I said I loved you. I also said, and with equal truth, that I loved her. Does this sound idiotic to you? I hope not! I hope you will understand. . . . It is possible to love like that." (Carlotta, at this point ambivalent about their future, pleaded with O'Neill to destroy their letters, insisting that anyone who saved their mail "ought to be shot," yet she judiciously saved his to her.)[262]

In December 1926, O'Neill dedicated himself to preparing *Marco Millions* for his publisher Horace Liveright and readying *Lazarus Laughed* for the stage, "cutting loose ends, concentrating, clarifying."[263] (*Lazarus* required a cast of 120 and would cost $50,000 or more; Macgowan warned that such an undertaking "doesn't slip onto the American stage very quickly or easily.")[264] O'Neill celebrated his one-year anniversary of sobriety, December 31, by sending off *Marco* and arranging for the anarchist Alexander Berkman, then in exile in Russia, to translate *Lazarus* for a Moscow production. He could finally resume work on *Strange Interlude*, "in which," he told Berkman, "I attempt to do in a play all that can be done in a novel."[265]

O'Neill labored over the sprawling nine-act script through the winter, completing a first draft in early March. Including the three months at Loon Lodge, the play had taken no fewer than three hundred creative workdays to complete. "It does all I hoped it would do, I think," he told George Jean Nathan, "and seems to me a successful adventure along a new technique that offers limitless new possibilities." Jimmy Light again visited Bermuda that summer, but this time O'Neill explained the play to his discerning friend. In Light's concluding paragraph of "The Parade of Masks," he writes, "O'Neill neither gave up writing plays nor did he write a novel. He did, however, write 'Strange Interlude.' In this play, he again used the mask but this time not the physical mask. In this play he used the novelist's prerogative of inner revelation. The means by which he accomplished both artistic ends was the soliloquy used forthrightly and continuously as no other playwright before him has dared to use it. By the insight furnished by the soliloquies we as audience, can project the emotions, the true not the apparent ones onto the face of the characters as he presents a facade to the rest of the world. It is the mask returned, making possible two levels of dramatic action."[266]

Just after finishing *Strange Interlude*, O'Neill roughly sketched out an autobiographical series with the working title "The Sea-Mother's Son," an idea he would return to years later. The autograph manuscript of this work was discovered among Boulton's papers after her death in 1968, and it was most likely written on March 8, 1927.[267] The working title became "The Sea Mother's Son: The Story of the Birth of a Soul."[268] Again his idea was to blur the genre lines between the novel and the play: as he wrote George Jean Nathan the following year, "This [Grand Opus] is to be neither play nor novel although there will be many plays in it and it will have greater scope than any novel I know of. Its form will be altogether its own and my own."[269]

His original notes from 1927 read, in part: "M—Lonely life—spoiled before marriage (husband friend of father's—father his great admirer—drinking companions)—fashionable convent girl—religious & naive—talent for music—physical beauty—ostracism after marriage due to husband's profession—lonely life after marriage—no contact with husband's friends—husband man's man—heavy drinker—out with men until small hours every night—slept late—little time with her—stingy about money due to his childhood experience with grinding poverty after his father deserted family to return to Ireland to spend last days."[270] By 1935, he returned to the idea and envisioned nine plays, "a notion I had years ago for a combination autobiographical novel in play form for publication in book, not production on stage."[271]

By 1939, he'd boil these ideas down to a single tragedy to take place over a single day: *Long Day's Journey Into Night*.

O'Neill's infatuation with Monterey slowly began to diminish after months of steady work. He continued writing her, but the letters, as in the past when he'd separated from Boulton, became more matter-of-fact and emotionally distant in tone, and Monterey decided to head to a spa in Baden-Baden, Germany, that June, in part to stamp out (or put to the test) their lingering desire for one another. When Boulton left the island in mid-April to visit her dying father at Shelton, O'Neill's letter to her betrays a guilt-ridden and desperately needy conscience. After dropping her off at the ship, "I drove right back to Our Home. *Our Home!*" he said. "The thought of the place is indissolubly intermingled with my love for you, with our nine years

Shane, Agnes, Oona, and Eugene O'Neill in Bermuda, 1926.
(COURTESY OF SHEAFFER-O'NEILL COLLECTION, LINDA LEAR CENTER FOR SPECIAL
COLLECTIONS AND ARCHIVES, CONNECTICUT COLLEGE, NEW LONDON)

*   *   *

of marriage that, after much struggle, have finally won to this haven, this ultimate island where we may rest and live toward our dreams with a sense of permanence and security that here we do belong. 'And, perhaps, the Hairy Ape at last belongs.' " Boulton wasn't over his affair, he knew. "I was never in love with her. That was nonsense. . . . I love you and only you, now and forever."[272]

Lawrence Langner, the managing director of the Theatre Guild, paid a visit to O'Neill at Spithead that March. Aside from Langner, O'Neill never liked the Guild's board of directors; they were an infamous assortment of difficult personalities but by then the most respected producers of serious drama in the country, having produced such breakout American plays as Elmer Rice's *The Adding Machine* in 1923, Sidney Howard's *They Knew What They Wanted* in 1924, which won the Pulitzer Prize, and S. N. Behrman's *The Second Man* in 1927.

The acrimony between O'Neill and the Guild had a long history. From the time O'Neill had first submitted *Thirst* to the Washington Square Players in 1915, before they'd become the Theatre Guild, to the end of the Provincetown Players in 1922, O'Neill and the Guild's executive committee simply didn't see eye to eye: "In rejecting my work you have a clear lead [in numbers] over any other management," he wrote Langner in 1922. "All this without any trace of hard feelings on my part," he said. "It is merely a question of unprejudiced disagreement, but I am afraid the evidence indicates that your Com. [committee] & I are doomed forever to disagree."[273] Of course, the one play of O'Neill's the Guild had produced, as the Washington Square Players, was *In the Zone*, which he thought of as a lesser work.

The Guild had rejected *"Anna Christie"* in 1921, but Langner pleaded with the committee to reconsider its approach to the playwright. O'Neill had outlined what he believed to be a series of slights against him by the Guild and its management to Langner, who forwarded the letter to his fellow producer Theresa Helburn with a note to be read out loud to the committee: "The trouble with you people is that you don't understand O'Neill's temperament. O'Neill is perfectly easy to get along with if you treat him as a friend. If your relations are *impersonal*, you'll get nowhere. (Why [don't we] get up a booze party for him?)"²⁷⁴ By the spring of 1927, O'Neill was willing to swallow his pride and accept the Guild's (to his mind paltry) option because "it is all going out and nothing coming in with me at present and I direly need all the cash I can grab." But the Guild must reciprocate his own "eagerness" by committing themselves to an "actual production at the earliest possible date."²⁷⁵ He was especially concerned that the method of *Strange Interlude* would be leaked and that someone else might steal the idea and produce a play before his appeared.

Langner read *Marco Millions* during his stay in Bermuda, and it intrigued him; but *Strange Interlude* was a revelation. He read the script in one night in his hotel room. A tropical storm had descended on the island, and as the storm grew louder and more menacing, the action of the play grew correspondingly more thrilling. He read until four o'clock in the morning, and by the time he'd reached the sixth act, he said, "I judged it one of the greatest plays of all time."²⁷⁶ The next day O'Neill celebrated Langner's eulogies over *Strange Interlude* with a swim, while Langner filmed him with his cine-Kodak movie camera. "He was built like an athlete," Langner said, "his deep black eyes set in a sunburnt Irish face, as handsome as one could hope to see anywhere, and the skin of his lean body was the color and texture of mahogany with underlying muscles of whipcord. At no time before or since have I seen him in such good health."²⁷⁷ (When Langner later informed George Bernard Shaw that O'Neill was done with alcohol, the Irish playwright wryly responded, "He'll probably never write a good play again.")²⁷⁸

O'Neill already had made it clear to Langner before he'd arrived that for the Guild to option his plays would require a binding agreement to produce both *Marco* and *Strange Interlude* for its next season. Langner agreed and convinced him to return to New York to strategize for the ambitious productions.

On May 15, less than three weeks after Boulton's return from Connecticut, O'Neill sailed back to New York with Harold de Polo, who'd rented a house near Spithead, and stayed at Lawrence

Langner's apartment in New York. On six out of the eight nights he was there, Langner remembered, O'Neill left his apartment for Monterey's. "He told me he had fallen in love with her," Langner recounted of O'Neill's stay. "He said one reason he got on so well with her was that she was such a good manager; she was able to organize the material side of his life—arranging for railroad tickets, and so forth. Agnes, he said, could seldom plan ahead; she was easygoing and helpless, and needed to be looked after by *him*."[279]

By the time O'Neill returned to Spithead, the property no longer appeared as the "haven" he'd envisioned when Boulton was absent. "Perhaps it is my mood," he wrote Monterey, "but the weather has seemed intolerably oppressive and I've found little zest in anything I used to take pleasure in. Even the sea has failed me. It is such a tepid, lukewarm ocean now, there is no life or sting to it, the only reaction one gets is lassitude. I would never spend another summer down here on a bet. It really is just too boring! . . . My visit to New York in May was far too short!" He and Boulton had a summer of "nervous bickerings and misunderstandings," during which time he'd been either sick with the Bermuda flu or working zealously on cutting the action of *Strange Interlude* to one night, down from the multiple nights its cumbersome original length would require.[280]

O'Neill traveled back to New York late that August to convince the Theatre Guild to stop delaying, with its convoluted options and paltry advances, and produce *Marco Millions* and *Strange Interlude* that season. Boulton also believed that, given the breakdown of their relationship that summer, it would be good for him to be away from the family. This solo trip to New York amounted to a trial separation.

Once aboard the *Fort St. George*, O'Neill wired Agnes Boulton with a bawdy reference to their last night together. But he longed to see Carlotta Monterey, who'd just returned from a restorative couple of months luxuriating in Baden-Baden. On September 9, they reunited for the first time since May, at which point he reported back to Boulton that he was bored and lonely ("the alcoholic days were much pleasanter!"); he was spending time with Monterey, he told her, but their relationship was platonic.[281] He would remain in New York until mid-October.

During this separation, the correspondence between O'Neill and Boulton oscillated between mutual pledges of freedom from their conjugal vows and strident accusations of betrayal. "Please do anything you want to do," Boulton wrote, "anything that will make you happy, or give you pleasure." Then, a few days later, "Goodbye. I'm glad Carlotta's nerves are gone. Do you think she would be interested in taking charge of Spithead? If so, tell her I've given up the job. She is certainly more beautiful than I am." "What sort of game is this you're playing, Agnes?" he demanded, after accusing her of having an affair. "Either I'm crazy or you are! Probably I am, anyway. Or, at any rate, I wish to Christ I could escape from this obscene and snaily creeping tedium of dull days, and empty hours like nervous yawns, into some madness—of love or lust or drink or anything else!"[282]

"Oh, you've gone and done it!" Monterey moaned helplessly to O'Neill before he departed once more for Bermuda. "I love you, damn it!"[283]

O'Neill arrived at Spithead on October 21, his marriage of over nine years effectively, and mutually, sabotaged. O'Neill had arranged for Macgowan to keep Monterey showered in roses and addressed his love letters to "Shadow Eyes," his pet name for her. When he returned to New York in mid-November, his letters to Boulton became either guardedly accusatory or all business. Planning for his second divorce, he knew that any correspondence could be used against him in court. He requested that Boulton send him every item of manuscript material that was stored at Spithead, giving the only partially true justification that he planned to sell it to a rare books dealer to avoid financial catastrophe. At Christmastime, after she'd sent him the majority of the material (minus his 1925 diary, his autograph manuscript outlining "The Sea Mother's Son," and *Exorcism*, among other valuable items), he broke up with her permanently. "You don't love me any more," he wrote. "We don't love each other. . . . I love someone else. Most deeply. . . . And the someone loves me."[284]

The Theatre Guild at long last scheduled *Marco Millions* and *Strange Interlude* to open in January 1928, but most of his attention was

Carlotta Monterey. An inscription by Monterey reads,
"This was Gene's favorite photograph of me."
(PHOTO BY MARCIA STEIN. COURTESY OF SHEAFFER-O'NEILL COLLECTION, LINDA
LEAR CENTER FOR SPECIAL COLLECTIONS AND ARCHIVES, CONNECTICUT COLLEGE, NEW
LONDON)

✳   ✳   ✳

focused on extracting himself from his marriage and attaching himself more firmly to the future Mrs. Eugene O'Neill. Boulton, however, ignored O'Neill's entreaties for her to keep away until after the dual openings. Leaving the children behind, she sailed to New York and checked into a room at the Hotel Wentworth, where O'Neill was staying.[285] Monterey wasn't amused. "She calls me every day to get that bitch out of the room," O'Neill complained to Harold de Polo.[286]

On January 14, Boulton ordered a sunlamp in her hotel room to battle a cold before heading back to Bermuda. Sprawling naked and miserable under the heat, she heard a knock. Thinking it was her sister, she opened the door en dishabille, and there was O'Neill. They fell into each other's arms. It was, Boulton later recalled of the spontaneous tryst, "like two ghosts sleeping together."[287] This was the last night they made love and, unless by accident before her return to Bermuda, the last time they would encounter one another for more than a decade.

Then came an unexpected triumph. After several years of fiendishly annoying rewrites, compromises, and disappointments, *Marco Millions* premiered on January 9 at the Guild Theatre and was a box office hit. O'Neill's only accomplished satire, *Marco* tracks the legendary journey of the thirteenth-century Venetian trader Marco Polo. Determined to return home a millionaire, Marco cavalierly spreads materialism across the Far and Middle East. The script demands terrifically complex scene changes and a gigantic cast—thirty-one speaking roles as well as "People of Persia, India, Mongolia, Cathay, courtiers, nobles, ladies, wives, warriors of Kublai Kahn's court, musicians, dancers, Chorus of mourners" (*CP2*, 382). Casting this show wasn't easy, even for the nonspeaking roles. Nearly every scene includes music, poetry, dancing, and chanting, and the dialogue must come across as satiric one minute and transcendent the next.

O'Neill always bore an abiding fascination with the Far East. "Europe somehow means nothing to me," he said to Boulton when she'd expressed her longing to transplant to Europe. "Either the South

Seas or China, say I." He read Kate Buss's *Studies in the Chinese Drama* (1922), which informed his medley of styles; for plot and characterization, he consulted Marco Polo's *Il milione*, or "The Million," the first narrative of Marco's expedition in 1271–95. This alleged travelogue, actually written by a romance writer named Rusticello da Pisa, remained the only source for the West's imaginings of the Far East until the seventeenth century, and most of it was based on lies. (Polo's reports of dog-faced natives, unicorns, and parakeets lifting elephants to the sky are a few indications that the Venetian's account was to a great extent bogus.) O'Neill's notes from the scholarly edition of *The Book of Ser Marco Polo* reveal that O'Neill quoted the editor's description of Marco Polo verbatim—"a practical man, brave, shrewd, prudent, keen in affairs, and never losing interest in mercantile details, very fond of the chase, sparing of speech," after which he scrawled, "The American Ideal!" His own dialogue made him "guffaw as I write . . . and not bitter humor either although it's all satirical. I actually grow to love my American pillars of society, Polo Brothers & Son." Yet he still wanted the nation to acknowledge "the true valuation of all our triumphant brass band materialism; [the country] should see the cost—and the result in terms of eternal verities. What a colossal, ironic, one hundred percent American tragedy that would be—what?"[288]

O'Neill's comical anachronism (the Venetians in the play speak in 1920s American slang) was a frontal assault on the excesses of American cultural imperialism. Allusions to contemporary American society in the stage directions are pronounced. He likens Marco's comportment to that of a southern senator who wants a constitutional amendment, referring to Texas's notorious anti-immigration stance and denial of the theory of evolution, to prohibit "the migration of non-Nordic birds into Texas, or . . . the practice of the laws of biology within the twelve-mile limit" (*CP2*, 424). When Marco's uncle mulls over their prospects in the Middle East, he reads the notes from a previous voyage: "There's one kingdom called Mosul [now the second-largest city in Iraq] and in it a district of Baku where there's a great fountain of oil. There's a growing demand for it. (*then speaking*) Make a mental note of that" (*CP2*, 401).

O'Neill was plainly at risk here of betraying his own doctrine that propaganda doesn't "strike home." The critics split both ways: liberals, the choir to whom O'Neill preached, applauded *Marco Millions* for "poking fun at American philistinism, American money-grubbing and money-wallowing," while conservatives denounced it as scurrilous opinionating. Many parallels were made between O'Neill's play and Sinclair Lewis's novel *Babbitt*, a popular satire of the spiritual bankruptcy both authors believed American capitalism had spawned. (*Babbitt* was published in 1922, the year O'Neill began *Marco*.) George Jean Nathan referred to his friend's play as "the sourest and most magnificent poke in the jaw that American big business and the American business man have ever got." The *Wall Street News* review, on the other hand, was O'Neill's worst fear of propaganda realized: "By many sterile devices, O'Neill drives home his sledgehammer points until the play takes on some of the dull witlessness of the Babbittish business man he is so intent on impaling."[289] But for all of *Marco Millions*' notoriety, it would be overshadowed by O'Neill's next production, *Strange Interlude*, three weeks later.

On January 30, O'Neill avoided the premiere of what he knew would be either his greatest theatrical sensation or, given its unconventional themes and stage techniques, merely an ambitious failure. He strolled aimlessly around the city for the first couple of hours of the play's opening and bumped into an old crony from his seafaring days. "Gene O'Neill!" he heard the aged sailor call out on the street. "What the hell are you doing these days?" ("At that very minute," mused a publisher O'Neill told this to years later, "his greatest hit was being played on Broadway!")[290] After this brief encounter, O'Neill went back to the Wentworth to meet Kenneth Macgowan and his wife, Edna, who were attending the play, for dinner during intermission. The curtain rose at five fifteen instead of eight thirty, New York's usual curtain time. After a ninety-minute dinner break at seven forty, they were to reconvene at nine o'clock, with a final curtain at eleven.[291] Macgowan informed his apprehensive friend that the publicity was so hyped up around the theater district, a Broadway drugstore was selling "Strange Interlude" sandwiches to the theatergoers. "I know what that is," O'Neill replied. "It's a four-decker with nothing but ham!"[292]

Strange Interlude premiered at Broadway's John Golden Theatre and was largely hailed as O'Neill's first true tour de force; with its groundbreaking "thought asides" and timely themes, the play signaled its author's complete maturation as an artist.

O'Neill's self-described "woman play," *Strange Interlude* revolves around the convoluted relationships of Nina Leeds, one of his most deeply wrought female characters. Nina has built a myth of perfection around her deceased fiancé, Gordon Shaw, a World War I aviator shot down two days before the armistice. She surrounds herself with four men who individually cannot satisfy her needs but together comprise her ideal man—lover, provider, father, and son. (The father figure, Charlie Marsden, the combined names of O'Neill friends Charles Demuth and Marsden Hartley, is the only demonstrably bisexual character in his canon.)[293] Along with meeting Nina's essential desires, they also represent the forces shaping the nation: her dead fiancé American "schoolboy ideals," her lover scientific advancement, her provider venture capitalism, her father figure Puritan morality, and her son Gordon a false sense of national innocence. Since none of these are compatible, the nation (Nina) defaults to the protective and stable, if morally restraining, realm of the puritanical.[294]

Strange Interlude, O'Neill said, was an "attempt at the new masked psychological drama . . . without masks—a successful attempt, perhaps, in so far as it concerns only surfaces and their immediate subsurfaces, but not where, occasionally, it tries to probe deeper."[295] Writing from inside O'Neill's head, George Jean Nathan, in his arch 1929 sketch "Eugene O'Neill as a Character in Fiction," sets down a prolonged, playfully satiric dialogue in O'Neill's voice that must have, at least partially, originated in a conversation: "The truth about soliloquies and asides as I employ them is that, while they are cunningly announced by me to represent my characters' unspoken thoughts—I'm a shrewd hand at concealing the obvious and artfully masking it in a way to make the impressionables gabble—they are actually nothing more than straight dramatic speeches."[296]

In this way, O'Neill's method united Elizabethan soliloquy with twentieth-century psychology: the alternatively called "spoken thoughts, inner monologues, thought asides, double dialogue, poetry of the unconscious, Freudian chorus, and silences out loud,"[297] the asides embedded in the dialogue recall the psychological theories and "stream of consciousness" concepts found in William James, Freud, Carl Jung, Alfred Adler, Marcel Proust, and James Joyce. Yet O'Neill wrote one of the play's reviewers that "these same ideas are age-old to the artist and ... any artist who was a good psychologist and had had a varied and sensitive experience with life and all sorts of people could have written S[trange]. I[nterlude]. without ever having heard of Freud, Jung, Adler & Co."[298]

That the characters' thoughts are conscious, rather than windows into their subconscious, amplifies the dramatic irony, the point at which the audience knows what some characters do not. And while tension builds on the stage, the audience members become more and more aware that their own lives, even in their most intimate relationships, are all too often based on the very same types of falsehoods. Everyday speech takes up less than a third of the script; the remainder consists of inner monologues masked by the superficiality of public speech, and the stage directions are so intricate that the script reads, intentionally, more like a novel than a play. (During rehearsal O'Neill groused to Lawrence Langner that "if the actors weren't so dumb, they wouldn't need asides; they'd be able to express the meaning without them.")[299] These thought asides presented a daunting challenge for the director, Philip Moeller, however: just how, precisely, were actors supposed to represent conscious thought without the audience confusing their asides with actual speech? Spotlighting? Voice-overs? Then one day while Moeller was on a train, the conductor pulled the emergency brake. Moeller instinctively clenched, and he looked around to see the other passengers had frozen up too. He'd stumbled on his solution: when an actor delivered an inner monologue, the others must freeze in "arrested motion" or "physical quiet."[300]

*　*　*

The critics, once again, put up their gloves. The majority considered *Strange Interlude* "the most significant contribution any American has made to the stage" and "a monument in the history of American dramaturgy." Nearly everyone understood that it was a novel for the stage; and most agreed didn't all agree with *New York World* critic Dudley Nichols's assessment of the result: "It would seem that he has not only written a great American play but the great American novel as well. This is a psychological novel of tremendous power and depth put into the theatre instead of between the covers of a book. It is a great novel without any of the novelist's padding."[301]

Naysayers were still legion, and the disputes often turned personal. When St. John Ervine accused O'Neill's asides of being "either an attempt to prevent actors from acting or a sign of laziness in the author," George Jean Nathan shot back, "With all due respect to friend Ervine, I have the honor to believe that on this occasion he has pulled what may politely be described as a boner." While one critic asserted that "nine acts of psychopathic fury may weary, but when Mr. O'Neill is the black magician they do not bore," another fumed, "There were NINE acts and one intermission of one hour, during which we craved for chloroform, but got only—soup. Some of those present wore evening dress in the afternoon and others wore afternoon dress in the evening, and neither mattered. The only thing that did matter was the excessive and glutinous boredom of the thing and its bombastic pretence." Heywood Broun scoffed that the play's angel Otto Kahn, the Wall Street millionaire and early backer of the Provincetown Players (whom O'Neill jokingly referred to as "Otto the Magnificent, the Great Kahn"), was a "sucker" for financing it.[302]

Theater professionals often think it best to ignore reviews of their plays, good or bad, when the show is still in production. Not O'Neill. He pored over his notices with a vigilance that bordered on the pathological, then collected them in enormous scrapbooks.[303] Richard Watts Jr. of the *New York Herald Tribune* reported this fact in what he described as a casual conversation with O'Neill after *Strange Interlude* premiered: "Among the notable things about Eugene O'Neill is the fact that he is one playwright who does not pretend that he never sees the notices of his plays. He reads them and is interested in them and, heaven knows, he has his likes and dislikes among the local critics. It is only fair to everybody to add that these judgments of his are not necessarily based on the degree of enthusiasm expressed for his works, even though he would object to being used as a sort of injured Belgium in a war between rival viewers."[304]

World War I, in fact, was a fitting metaphor for the rousing war of words fought in the press over *Strange Interlude*, and the critics ran afoul of one another as Germany had with the Allies over Belgium. In Europe alliances and counter-alliances redrew the map the way O'Neill redrew the map of American theater. (The appearance of *Long Day's Journey Into Night* in 1956, three years after O'Neill's death, might be regarded as the Treaty of Versailles, simultaneously ending and renewing the age-old battles over O'Neill's legacy.) "I'm getting awfully callous to the braying, for and against," O'Neill wrote a few years later to Nathan. "When they knock me, what the devil!, they're really boosting me with their wholesale condemnations, for the reaction against such nonsense will come soon enough. These tea-pot turmoils at least keep me shaken up and convinced I'm on my way to something."[305]

By this time, 1928, O'Neill had divided his critics into three classes: "Play Reporters," "Professional Funny Men," and "the men with proper background or real knowledge of the theater of all time to entitle them to be critics": "The play reporters just happen to be people who have the job of reporting what happens during the evening, the story of the play and who played the parts. I have always found that these people reported the stories of my plays fairly accurately. The Professional Funny Men are beneath contempt. What they say is only of importance to their own strutting vanities. From the real critics I have always had the feeling that they saw what I was trying to do and whether they praised or blamed, they caught the point."[306]

O'Neill made it a habit to contact "real critics" after encountering what he considered a particularly keen insight into his plays. Joseph Wood Krutch, for instance, placed O'Neill's melding of the novel and the drama within the broader context of history: "The drama has always seemed the form of expression best suited to an heroic age and the novel the form best suited to a complex and baffled one, since a certain simplicity of presentation has been inseparable from playwriting. . . . The stage has seemed destined to remain, perforce, content with simple outlines. It has been, in short, a place where only major chords could be struck even though existing in an age which had lost the power to be moved by any but the subtlest and most difficult harmonies."[307] O'Neill wrote Krutch that his remarks had been "deeply gratifying" to him, "especially that you found that there was something of a novel's comprehensiveness in [*Strange Interlude*]. What you say about slightness of even the best modern plays is exactly the way I feel. To me they are all totally lacking in all true power and imagination."[308] But by then he'd relinquished his vow to quit the drama for the novel. "No," he told Krutch, "I think the novelists are worse than the playwrights—they waste more of one's time!"[309]

The play's inclusion of sexual promiscuity, infidelity, contraception, prostitution, abortion, atheism, near polyandry, and incest provided a bounty of red meat for censors as well as the critics. Manhattan's ever-faithful attorney general Joab Banton got back in the game; but he found the Theatre Guild far more accommodating than the Triumvirate had been when it came to such bowdlerizing as replacing the word "abortion" with "operation," which they did.[310]

Mayor Malcolm Nichols of Boston banned a long-planned production in his city, labeling the script a "disgusting spectacle of immorality and advocacy of atheism, of domestic infidelity and the destruction of unborn human life." To allow the play to be produced in Boston, Langner and Helburn again revised the play, this time without O'Neill's knowledge and far more drastically. "The deletion of a few pages from a great play cannot destroy the whole," Langner told the *Boston Post*. "The play does not depend upon mere words for its effect," Helburn added, "and we can easily cut out every one of the words that the Mayor wishes deleted." Publicly, Nichols stood firm that regardless of any deletions or revisions "the play in any version glorifies an indefensible standard of conduct and an abject code of morals." (Langner later accused the mayor of rejecting it because he'd failed to shake them down for $10,000.)[311]

Mayor Thomas McGrath of Quincy, a Boston suburb, volunteered his city as an alternative. (Near the theater was a local restaurant owned by one Howard Deering Johnson, as yet unknown among Boston's elite, who sold enough meals to begin expanding his business into the nation's largest hotel and restaurant chain, Howard Johnson's.) When McGrath entered the theater on opening night, September 30, 1929, he was greeted with a grateful ovation from the "ninety-nine and some tenths percent pure Bostonian" audience.[312] After the five-and-a-half-hour performance (with a break for dinner at Howard Johnson's), the cast received fourteen curtain calls. Mayor McGrath was then bombarded for his opinion of the play. Though a citizens' jury had also attended that night, its judgment was irrelevant. McGrath proclaimed that what he'd learned watching *Strange Interlude* was "worth a hundred sermons."[313]

Langner and Helburn left in many of the cuts they'd made for Boston, nevertheless, and made further cuts for Philadelphia and elsewhere.[314] Providence still banned the play that April 1930 under its "Chastity and Morality" law, a prohibition on theatricals that a committee of locals believed might corrupt the city's youth.[315]

Overall, the "ayes" had won it for *Strange Interlude* from the start. Performances of its first run sold out so quickly that for months, in an unventilated theater of about nine hundred seats in record-breaking heat, theatergoers chose to stand in back rather than miss out on what had been billed as the must-see cultural event of the season. O'Neill had suspected that *Strange Interlude* would be his "big bacon-bringer," but he never anticipated this. "That trends on fanaticism it seems to me," he mused that April after hearing there were still standees at the performances. "Myself, I wouldn't stand up 4 1/2 hours to see the original production of the Crucifixion!"[316]

Strange Interlude's Broadway run alone lasted seventeen months and 432 performances, then more in the multiple touring productions that followed, and the book version topped the best-seller list. The play also enjoyed two successful national tours, and, in 1932, was made into an MGM film starring Clark Gable and Norma Shearer. O'Neill's pioneering play-as-novel ultimately made him $250,000 richer and won him his third Pulitzer Prize (the prize money was promptly donated to the Authors' League Fund).[317] After this, O'Neill was no longer spoken of as merely "America's greatest playwright," a rather unimpressive title at the time, but now as one of the world's greatest living writers; over the following year, the Nobel Prize committee on literature, eager to place an American on its roster by the late 1920s, added him to their short list.

On February 7, O'Neill wrote Boulton to say good-bye. He admitted that the triumph of *Strange Interlude* had passed him by just as the arrival of his mother's casket from California had deprived him of reveling in the success of *The Hairy Ape:* "The trouble with my triumphs is that there's always so much of my own living on my mind at the time I haven't got any interest left for plays," he wrote. " 'So ist das Leben,' I guess. Or at least my 'leben.' The power & the glory always pass over—or under—my head." He was resolute that they "must not see each other again for a long time," but ended on a conciliatory note: "All my loving friendship to you always!"[318]

Boulton had already written him from Bermuda a few days before receiving this. "I am very much in the dark," she said. "I received a cable from the N.Y. *Times* saying you had just left for Europe. . . . I know nothing."[319] Sure enough, without notifying anyone but a solemnly sworn few, and leaving no trace of their destination behind for Boulton, his children, or the press, O'Neill and Monterey had clandestinely sailed for Europe. Their flight to avoid the combustible reactions of his wife's acrimony and that of the scandal-mongering press would last for more than three years.

By the late 1920s and well into the 1930s, American dramatists could claim a leading role in world theater. They'd largely surpassed Europeans in experimental and socially conscious plays, with the singular exceptions of George Bernard Shaw and Sean O'Casey. But two major forces held them back: the Great Depression and Hollywood. Over seventy theaters were built in the Broadway theater district by the late 1920s. But when the economic crash of 1929 dammed the flood of box office sales and drowned out real estate values, many producers shut their doors and resigned themselves to bankruptcy. At the same time audiences, broke as they were, crowded the movie houses for a soothing, relatively inexpensive retreat from reality.

While many American playwrights did venture west to Southern California, tempted by lucrative contracts with Hollywood studios, the more independent minded of them arose from the Depression and produced socially conscious theater companies such as the Group Theatre, the Theatre Union, and the Actors' Repertory Company. And given that so many of the financial backers of the 1920s had lost their fortunes in the wake of the market crash, after the election of 1932, at the urging of the new first lady Eleanor Roosevelt, government subsidies had begun to fill the void.

A New Deal initiative called the Federal Theatre Project was established, importantly creating a separate unit, the Negro Theatre Project. For a time, O'Neill disparaged much of this work as charging willy-nilly through "blind alleys—theatre for sociology's sake, partisan politics' sake, provincial patriotism's sake, etc."; but later, especially after the outbreak of World War II, he'd begun to respect the dramas produced by the project tremendously.

Throughout most of the Depression and Word War II, O'Neill cloistered himself outside the glare of the public eye for twelve long years, from 1934 to 1946. "There is something to be said for the Mad Twenties," he wistfully declared in 1941. "They were sometimes crazy in the right way." O'Neill won the Nobel Prize in Literature in 1936, a time when, astonishingly, he hadn't yet reached his highest *level of artistic achievement. Meanwhile, during O'Neill's long interlude of silence, the younger generation—Clifford Odets, Sidney Kingsley, William Saroyan, Lillian Hellman, Thornton Wilder, Maxwell Anderson—had started to unleash, if in fits and starts, new methods and perspectives onto the American stage.*

O'Neill's "Mad Twenties" rejection of naturalistic plays as "too easy" turned out to be short-lived, as what he chose to write (or at least complete) through the 1930s and early 1940s belongs in that tradition, while also building upon the psychological turn of 1920s "high modernism." In response to the Depression and World War II, American drama as a whole increasingly coupled the social torments of the era with their damaging psychological effects. By the 1940s, given O'Neill's pioneering work and innovations in the fields of physiology, sociology, and psychology, American playwrights rejected the false dichotomies of good and evil, hero and villain, right and wrong—a moral and artistic repudiation O'Neill had always embodied, and one that has pervaded American drama well into the twenty-first century.

Tennessee Williams's breakout play The Glass Menagerie *was produced in 1944, and sophisticated theatergoers, especially those of the younger generation, cried out for more. Williams, to whom O'Neill wrote a congratulatory note after* A Streetcar Named Desire *appeared in 1948, would speak of O'Neill, even after the ascendancy of such dramatic talents as Thornton Wilder and Arthur Miller, as his only true American superior. "O'Neill gave birth to American theatre," Williams said, "and died for it."*

*   *   *

ACT IV: Full Fathom Five

It was a great mistake, my being born a man, I would have been made much
more successful as a seagull or a fish. As it is, I will always be a stranger who
never feels at home, who does not really want and is not really wanted, who
can never belong, who must always be a little in love with death!

—EDMUND TYRONE IN *Long Day's Journey Into Night*

Uncharted Seas

Once aboard the S.S. *Berengaria*, Neill and Monterey never exited their
cabin over the rough transatlantic crossing, his first voyage to Europe
since 1911. After scanning the passenger list, O'Neill noted that there
were several people onboard who might recognize him; and though
he'd already made the precaution of signing on under an assumed
name, he still badly wanted to avoid the press. Gazing out the porthole
of his cabin, he began to cry uncontrollably, then spoke his thoughts
aloud to Monterey, as if enacting a scene from *Strange Interlude:* "It's a
terrible thing," he said, "to leave behind so many you love, everything
that means anything to you." "Well, Carlotta," she thought to herself as
he wept, "you've let yourself in for it this time."[1]

Safely ashore in Great Britain and as yet undetected, they checked
into the Berkeley, a five-star hotel in London. O'Neill reveled in the
anonymity far from the "frazzle of New York." "When we'll return
to U.S. I don't know," he reported back to Kenneth Macgowan, "and
somehow I can't seem to care." After years of uncertainty and despair,
O'Neill roamed about the British capital with Monterey on his arm,
"foolish and goggle-eyed with joy in a honeymoon that is a thousand
times more poignant and sweet and ecstatic because it comes at an
age when one's past—particularly a past such as mine—gives one the

power to appreciate what happiness means and how rare it is and how humbly grateful one should be for it." He now felt a cosmic love for Monterey, "sappy" as he knew it sounded, as if some mystical God had taken pity and was repaying him for the cruel practical jokes of his past.[2] "It is all deeply beautiful, this—the dream come true!" he wrote Elizabeth Shepley Sergeant. "The Hairy Ape at last 'belongs.' That this should come about through the love of the woman who took the part of the girl in that play whose meeting with our hero first jolted him out of himself is a coincidence with an amusing reverse-english, what?"[3]

O'Neill and Monterey ferried to France in March; but they were spotted during a stopover in Paris and so, with reporters from the *International Herald* nipping at their heels, they abandoned plans to tour the celebrated hub of modern culture, rented a touring car, and motored out of town. First they meandered through the château district of the Loire Valley, stopping at "Chambord, Amboise, Loches, etc.—the most beautiful and dramatic places I have ever seen," he reported back. They then headed southward down the Atlantic coast in search of a villa to rent for an indefinite stay. This they ultimately found in Guéthary, a historic whaling village like New London that overlooked the Basque coast on the border of Spain. O'Neill felt at home there, especially once he heard that Basques "come from the same stock as the original Black Irish to which I obviously belong."[4] For a summer residence, they rented the Villa Marguerite, an old beachfront property just outside the village. And from there O'Neill initiated his negotiations for his divorce from Agnes Boulton.

Boulton indicated that she wished their marriage to dissolve quietly. And she'd made a solemn vow at the hotel to grant him freedom. "I wish you happiness," she wrote him from Bermuda, if with a wistful, slightly ominous tone: "Think of me sometimes when you see the Europe I so longed, once, for us to see together." O'Neill mostly trusted Boulton as "fine and sound at bottom"; but he worried about advice she might gather from the "Philadelphia Social Register bunch," a faction she'd befriended in Bermuda that O'Neill considered "about as far removed from fundamental human beingism as one

could get—and [Boulton] is easily swayed by the rich and the social."
To ward off such threats, he promised her she could stay indefinitely
at Spithead and that he'd provide anything for the children, including
his stepchild Barbara—within reason, of course.[5]

Meanwhile, more than five thousand miles away from his villa at
Guéthary, O'Neill's play *Lazarus Laughed* premiered on April 4, 1928,
at the Pasadena Community Playhouse in California. O'Neill had
subtitled the work "A Play Performed for an Imaginative Theatre,"
but given its outlandish set design and casting demands, even beyond
Marco Millions, his chronicler Barrett Clark remarked that he "might
more appropriately have said an Imaginary Theater."[6]

The Pasadena Playhouse enlisted a cast of 16 speaking roles plus
159 amateur actors doubling in over 400 roles as Lazarus's guests,
orthodox Jews, Nazarenes, followers of Lazarus, Greeks, Roman
soldiers, Roman legionnaires, Roman senators, a crowd of Roman
courtiers, a chorus of children, a chorus of senile old men, and even a
dying lion. For more than six weeks they designed over 400 costumes
and 325 masks depicting various ages, sexes, classes, religions, and
races, each with matching wigs and headdresses, thanks to students
and faculty of stagecraft from the University of California, Los Angeles.[7] Tickets sold out twenty-eight nights in a row, then the company
moved on to the Hollywood Music Box theater. Under the expert
direction of Gilmor Brown, this West Coast production was a stu-
pendously bold achievement—not simply for O'Neill but for the possibilities of community art theater in the United States as a whole.

The title *Lazarus Laughed* signals a mood reversal from O'Neill's
early poem of despair "The Bridegroom Weeps!" It conflates the
Gospel of Matthew, "At midnight there was a great cry made, behold, the bridegroom cometh!" with the Gospel of John, when "Jesus
wept" upon first being told that he'd arrived too late to save his fol-
lower Lazarus from death, and then miraculously rose him from the
grave. In the Bible, the "bridegroom" is Jesus Christ, offering salvation and humankind's triumph over death. But O'Neill's experimental
mask play takes up where the Bible leaves off, speculating on Lazarus's

future after Christ's miracle. (*Lazarus Laughed* therefore represents, as Kenneth Macgowan pointed out even before it had found a producer, "the first time in all his score of plays Eugene O'Neill puts a Jew upon the stage as the central figure.")[8] Lazarus becomes a figure of worship himself by preaching life over death—"yes" over "no"—across the Roman Empire. When questioned about the afterlife, Lazarus responds, "O Curious Greedy Ones, is not one world in which you know not how to live enough for you?" (*CP2*, 546).

O'Neill had known early on that the play's biggest stumbling block, even more than its necessarily enormous cast size, was finding an actor to pull off Lazarus's celestial laugh. Lazarus's laugh has the power to relieve the fear of death, having a spellbinding effect on the masked characters on the stage (Lazarus is the only character who does not wear a mask) but also on the audience itself. After seeing Paul Robeson sing spirituals at a dinner party in New York the previous September, O'Neill seriously considered casting him as Lazarus, in white face. "Don't laugh," he'd written Boulton. "White folks make up to play negroes and there's no reason why the reverse shouldn't be practiced. He's the only actor who can do the laughter, that's the important point. It would be good showmanship, too—no end to the publicity it would attract."[9]

Luckily the members of the California regional group didn't find it necessary to resort to this. They knew exactly the right man for the part: Irving Pichel. Critics were unanimously moved by Pichel's performance, many of them awestruck: "The laughter," wrote George C. Warren for the *New York Times*, "which at one time runs without cessation for four minutes, calls for absolute repose and poise, and Pichel's splendid and resonant voice carried him to a triumph." The *Los Angeles Times* was equally impressed, congratulating the actor for conjuring "the Dionysian laughter of the eternal cosmos." "Long I expect to be haunted by that laughter," the *Pasadena Evening Post* marveled over Pichel, "and to think I see, as it reverberates in memory, the glowing countenance of Lazarus, and the luminous garments in which, with face uncovered, he moved in a world of masks."[10] O'Neill had always admired the man's "brains, ability and imagination," and back in 1923 he'd hoped to recruit him for the Ex-

perimental Theatre, Inc. At one point he'd told Pichel he was going
to try to make it for opening night, and local newspapers reported
he would attend the performance but lose himself among the audience and conceal his identity. "O'Neill had been expected, but was not
present, report asserting he was in the South of France," wrote a
well-informed newsman, blowing O'Neill's cover, "and there was
a feeling of disappointment because of his nonappearance, but the
splendor of the production, the vital and thrilling performance, and
the poetic beauty of the play itself made up for his absence."[11]

Yet the "power & the glory" of victory evaded O'Neill once again, as
his elation over *Lazarus's* triumph was offset by a consternating letter
from Boulton. Earlier that year, on January 27, Boulton had found
out that she was pregnant and wrote O'Neill in April claiming the
unborn child was conceived that day at the Hotel Wentworth.
O'Neill refused to believe it, and he was right not to. In her first letter about this "indiscretion," the dates of her pregnancy didn't add
up, since they'd been together on January 14, the day she left for
Bermuda; O'Neill was thus armed with "proof positive of adultery
in your own handwriting." "You have the unscrupulous effrontery
to attempt to lay this thing at my door! You must have changed, by
God, and hardly for the better spiritually—when you can do such a
thing!"[12] Boulton soon recognized the futility of protesting further
and traveled to New York that May to have an abortion at the home
of Mary Blair.

   Since her days as a leading lady for O'Neill's plays, Blair had
become Boulton's intimate confidante. After Boulton arrived at her
apartment, the actress stormed back and forth in front of her shak-
en guest. "He will never write another play—I spit!" she said, and
spat on her floor. Blair had just been divorced from Edmund Wilson,
and was a dedicated supporter of women through such trying times.
Boulton remembered back in March 1922, for instance, when Blair
was playing Mildred in *The Hairy Ape*, she'd met F. Scott Fitzgerald's then twenty-one-year-old wife, Zelda, at Blair's flat. Boulton
and Zelda went to Pennsylvania Station together, and while they
were passing a flask back and forth, the chic young woman dropped

unconscious on the station floor. She'd just had an abortion that morning.[13] (Fitzgerald noted bitterly in his ledger for that month, "Zelda and her abortionist." In a letter to him outlining the events leading up to her first institutionalization, Zelda listed "pills and Dr. Lackin.")[14]

Boulton's unborn child was likely fathered by a dock builder at Spithead named John Johnson (or possibly Johnston), whom Gaga had caught with Boulton in flagrante delicto that fall. This breach of privacy was the last straw for Boulton, and she sent the nursemaid packing back to Provincetown. From there Gaga wrote several letters to O'Neill, evidently informing him of Boulton's love affair and that her mistress had been drinking heavily and had "gone to pieces." (In a letter to Boulton, O'Neill quoted his anonymous informant as saying, "Such a shame for my poor dear little children.") Gaga pleaded with him to convince Boulton to reinstate her. He then wrote Boulton, who'd figured out Gaga's duplicity, contending that she "can't hold her idiotic gossip against her when it's a case of wounding an old woman who has been a good friend to us, if there ever was one. . . . It's on my conscience and I feel like hell about it." Boulton did re-hire Gaga that summer after moving back to the Old House in West Point Pleasant; but Gaga died the following year on July 6, 1929.[15]

"I've taken a motor trip—invitation—to Prague since I last saw you," O'Neill lied in a letter to Boulton, trying to get her off his scent." "I'm going to stick on and do some work here—not in the city but in a remote suburb in a home on the river—a quiet lovely spot." He told the same story to Harold de Polo, while at the same time calling him "an old friend in whom one can really trust through the good breaks and the bad," since he knew de Polo had remained close with Boulton. He informed Shane that he'd been in Germany on the Baltic Sea, where he'd arranged for postcards to be sent.[16]

Only members of a trusted group, Harry Weinberger, Kenneth Macgowan, Saxe Commins, and a few Theatre Guild members, were notified of his true location. "Don't let anyone know the above address," he wrote Commins from Guéthary. "I have left here a long time ago as far as anyone knows. But it will be a favor if you will advertize it that you have heard from me from Berlin or Vienna or Prague or any other town provided it isn't France. . . . The fair Aggie's broken heart was transformed over night into a gaping money greed." The whole affair, he said, was the kind of legalized blackmail "one might expect from a chorus girl wife." "But what the hell?" O'Neill wrote Macgowan with finality. "She is so damn dead for me now that it doesn't matter—and she realizes this and it infuriates her more than anything else because she knows now that her power to hurt is gone."[17]

O'Neill's agent Richard Madden warned his client that if Boulton went public about his affair with Monterey, it would blow up in the tabloids on the scale of Charlie Chaplin's disgracing scandals. "He's a damn fool," O'Neill wrote Weinberger, regarding Chaplin as a base comparison. "Chaplin's wife had charged him with ruining young girls, with every form of perversion—and he was guilty as everyone knows. There was every form of dirt to it."[18] (Oona O'Neill, Chaplin's future wife, had not yet celebrated her third birthday.) O'Neill preferred the story of Sinclair Lewis, who'd also fled to Europe and whose divorce "came off without scandal and with dignity" because he and Grace Hegger announced their divorce, and the story died.[19]

For leverage, O'Neill hired a law firm in London to investigate Boulton's alleged marriage to a James Burton; the firm found no record of this, so he next instructed Weinberger to investigate who Barbara Burton's father might have been and whether Boulton was guilty of bigamy.[20] He was pleading with Boulton to go to Reno, as Sinclair Lewis's ex-wife had done, where women could establish residency in three months then be granted an unfussy divorce. What was then known as a "Reno divorce" could be done with charges of "desertion," whereas in Connecticut a divorce would necessitate proving "intolerable cruelty."[21] (Presumably it would have been in neither party's interest for O'Neill to reveal the final judgment on his divorce from Kathleen Jenkins, if O'Neill had even read it, indicating that his marriage to Boulton had never been lawful in the first place.)[22] "Speaking of my own end of it," O'Neill wrote de Polo, "as long as I could embark on a brain-drowning drunk once in a while the things one can't forget didn't pile up on me to any unbearable extent. I swallowed them with old J.B. [John Barleycorn] for a chaser of memory. But when I reformed they began to pile up into obtrusive prison walls."[23]

In May 1928, O'Neill's prison walls crashed down around him and Monterey when a journalist and former shack mate of Terry Carlin's in Provincetown, Louis Kalonyme (a.k.a. Louis Kantor) stopped in to visit O'Neill at the Villa Marguerite. The instant Monterey overheard O'Neill laughing loudly with Kalonyme behind closed doors, she knew he'd been drinking—for the first time in over two years. She then packed her bags and got as far as the train station before turning around. Back at the villa she found the men passed out, with black coffee splashed "all over the blue satin walls of the salon."[24] "So, this is genius—this is love!" she thought. "God help us!"[25]

"Remember to forget that incident in May!" O'Neill wrote Kalonyme later. "It had no meaning and was really a damned good thing in its effect on my future, by the way of a final K.O. to an old mistake. But how A[gnes] & Co. would love to get hold of it!"[26]

O'Neill's next project, *Dynamo*, gushed out of him that summer at the Villa Marguerite. The previous fall, on September 31, 1927, O'Neill had traveled up from New York to General Electric's hydroelectric plant in Stevenson, Connecticut. He'd arranged for a private tour of the facility, during which he was, he said, "taken all over and shown everything from roof to cellar. Quite an experience!"[27] (By 1928, when O'Neill had begun sketching out scenarios for *Dynamo*, Mike Gold had contacted him about resuscitating the radical journal the *Masses*, which became the *New Masses*, but for a time he considered calling it *Dynamo*, O'Neill's likely inspiration for the title.)[28] O'Neill's notes in his work diary read: "Play of Dynamos—the despairing philosopher—poet who falls in love with balance equilibrium of energy—his personification of it—his final marriage with it—the consummation ending with his destruction."[29] He wanted the philosopher-poet's struggle to evoke in audiences "the general theme of American life in back of the play, America being the land of the mother complex."[30] He wrote Mike Gold in mid-August that *Dynamo* was, like so many of his plays, "another attempt at a biography of a section of the American soul."[31]

Dynamo's protagonist Reuben Light was the latest iteration of O'Neill's modern-day prodigal sons. After a year at college, Reuben returns to his puritanical New England home with a messianic desire to replace the Christian God of his pastor father, the Reverend Hutchins Light, with the modern god of electricity. Reuben's mother has died, heightening his desperation to have his new God reveal to him some tangible form of enlightenment. He attempts to find this at an actual dynamo nearby and imagines he'll become the next savior of the human race. Reuben feels that he betrayed his mother by having sexual relations with his girlfriend Ada Fife, thus preventing the miracle he'd hoped for. In desperation, he kills Ada, then grabs hold of live carbon brushes at the humming dynamo, renounces his quest, and electrocutes himself to reunite with his mother.

In mid-August 1928, O'Neill sent off a handwritten manuscript of *Dynamo* to Saxe Commins to type up for the Theatre Guild. Commins had given up his dental practice by this time and decided to spend the year in France with his wife, Dorothy Berliner, an accomplished concert pianist whom he'd married the year before. O'Neill included instructions on which he scrawled, "Suggestions, Instructions, Advice, along with sundry snooty remarks and animadversions as to the modern theatre." This treatise, never published in its entirety, stresses the importance of getting the sound effects right so the generator wouldn't sound "obviously like a vacuum cleaner"; it also includes O'Neill's thoughts on modernizing stage effects in modern theater writ large: "Looking back on my plays," he wrote, "in which significant mechanical sound and not music is called for . . . I can say none of them has ever really been thoroughly done in the *modern theatre* although they were written for it. Someday I hope they will be—and people are due to be surprised by the added dramatic value—*modern* values, they will take on."[32] He also suggested, in a separate letter to the Guild's Theresa Helburn, that for the dynamo's hum the Guild should hire a General Electric specialist to consult on "the continual metallic nasal purr of the generators—if you've ever spent a short time in a power house you know how essentially symbolic and mysterious and moving this sound [is] (which is like no other sound but itself)."[33]

O'Neill envisioned *Dynamo* as the first of a planned trilogy of plays he was alternately calling "Myth Plays for the God-forsaken" or "God Is Dead! Long Live—What?" that combined would "dig at the roots," O'Neill said, "of the sickness of today as I feel it—the death of an old God and the failure of Science and Materialism to give any satisfying new One for the surviving primitive religious instinct to find a meaning for life in, and to comfort its fears of death with."[34]

Monterey's fastidiousness in domestic management was perfectly suited to O'Neill's hermetic lifestyle. She took care of the house, wrote most of their letters, planned engagements, shopped for clothes. She took no interest in socializing or the life of a celebrity. In short, she excelled at the very things that interested Boulton least about her marriage with O'Neill. Monterey's previous husband, the celebrated caricaturist Ralph Barton, who still pined for her, and Charlie Chaplin, with whom Barton was close friends, intuited that Monterey's chief aim had always been to attach herself to "a man of genius, to cut him off from everybody and minister to his genius, while she herself shone in reflected glory."[35] Barton knew he'd failed to appreciate this; then O'Neill appeared, and it was too late.

For Monterey, the play her lover was writing at the Villa Marguerite, *Dynamo*, would be the first work of O'Neill's that she could claim as theirs alone, the way Boulton had with *Beyond the Horizon* ("our play," Boulton called it). "I—too—am alive with 'Dynamo,' " Monterey wrote Commins, "but Gene at the stage of wondering if it is *rotten* or *what not!* . . . I understand & soothe—! This Lover of mine is also my child—& living beside him thro' Fire & Beauty has greatly developed & enriched the inner me."[36] Even with such rapturous support, O'Neill's mind was besieged by hideous attacks of rage, guilt, and fear—the divorce negotiations with Boulton, his worry over the children, and a "snotty" interview Boulton had given the *New York World* with the unsettling headline, "O'Neill Divorce Rumors Scouted."[37] Flouting O'Neill's wish, at the outset, to end the marriage with dignity, Boulton whetted the press's appetite for a good scandal by denying there was any talk of divorce. Another interview appeared late that June in the *New York Daily News* with the more egregious title, "Wife Will Grant O'Neill His 'Illusion' of Freedom."

Once *Dynamo* had been sent off to the Theatre Guild, O'Neill induced Monterey to join him on an expedition that would further remove them from the public eye and consummate his fascination with the Far East. On October 3, 1928, two days before sailing for Hong Kong, O'Neill sent Boulton one last piece of correspondence. It was a postcard, on the back of which he penned a backhanded well-wish: "This is a marvelous château! You must visit it when you come to France. Kiss Shane & Oona for me. Love. Gene." The front of the postcard showed a picture of an old tomb with a caption that reads, in part, "Tombeau d'Agnès" (the tomb of Agnes).[38]

On their guard against further scandal, O'Neill and Monterey booked separate cabins, and Monterey brought along her masseuse Tuva Drew to serve as nurse, maid, and secretary. O'Neill noticed the wire from New York on the bed in his cabin only after their packet ship *André-Lebon* had already sailed from Marseille. It was the Theatre Guild's verdict: a unanimous acceptance of *Dynamo* and a "Bon Voyage" wish. Monterey wept uncontrollably with relief. "It was such a divine send off," she wrote Saxe Commins, "& Gene is resting & relaxing & is his dear *un*-worried self!"[39] They spent his fortieth birthday, October 16, 1928, docked in the Yemeni seaport Aden. En route to Singapore they passed through the Red Sea, stopping in Djibouti before continuing on to the Indian Ocean and British Ceylon. Each morning for nearly two weeks, O'Neill worked on "It Cannot Be Mad," a play about the rise of an automotive billionaire; as with *Dynamo*, the theme was "the general spiritual futility of the substitute-God search."[40] This time in his planned trilogy the substitute-God would be wealth; but he couldn't contrive a sustainable dramatic structure, and once they'd sailed east of the Suez Canal, he abandoned writing entirely.

In Singapore O'Neill caught a dire case of sunstroke after he insisted on taking a swim in the furnacelike noonday heat. He'd also chosen a lake, Monterey fumed in her diary, in which "*the* CITY SEW-ER *empties right into the place where Gene is swimming!*" The next port was

Saigon, the capital of French Indochina, where he caught a bad flu, "a nasty combine in sickeningly hot tropic weather," though he found the city "fascinating in a queer sinister way." All of the exoticism of Indochina ignited O'Neill's imagination as much as it revolted Monterey's. On a tour of Cholon, a Chinese city there, she felt a "strange 'thing' in the air as we motored along the swamp highway. Breathless, quiet—the clang of cymbals—all seemed decadent—There was death, decay—to me it was frightening and something I don't like." O'Neill again dove headlong into unsanitary waters, in "a literal mudhole," Monterey wrote, exasperated, "a privy by it!"[41]

Firmly resolved that Monterey wouldn't control him, O'Neill found a "swell gambling joint" where he spent long hours frittering away hundreds, possibly thousands, of dollars at the roulette wheel. Too run down to disembark at Hong Kong, O'Neill stayed aboard until, on November 9, they arrived at British-controlled Shanghai. They checked in to the Palace Hotel and on the first day enlisted the service of hotel physician Dr. Alexander Renner, a Hungarian nerve specialist, who prescribed him daily with "nerve tonic" injections.[42]

It was inevitable that O'Neill would be recognized on the streets of Shanghai. "Eugene O'Neill tramping it through the Far East," noted a stateside newshound, "will have to do it to the accompaniment of the telegraph wires' drumbeat recording his advance."[43] But luckily the first journalist to spot him was a pal from Greenwich Village, Alfred Batson, who was then reporting for the *North China Herald*. "Do me a favor," O'Neill said, "just keep me out of the paper." In the longed-for company of another man, and with Monterey either off shopping with Dr. Renner's wife, another Théres, or prostrate from fatigue in her hotel room, O'Neill once again dropped off the wagon. In between drinks, Batson delighted in guiding him through the less frequented sights. "The place that interested Gene most," Batson remembered, "was the crime museum at police headquarters, a room full of murder weapons, mementoes of outstanding crimes, torture devices, and so forth." One of these devices was "Death of a Thousand Cuts": "The bandits would double-track wire all over a person's body, bunching the flesh, and then slice off the skin—the one thousand cuts."[44] On a separate drunken outing O'Neill found himself helplessly ensnared at another "Wheel palace," gambling through the night until his credit ran out, then cabling for more money. "I must have that Jim [O'Neill] strain in me after all," he confessed in a letter to de Polo while denying that alcohol had anything to do with it. "Can you beat it? Me!"[45]

On November 21, at about one in the morning, after drinking all night with Afred Batson, "Gene comes into the sitting room," Monterey wrote, "sees me—& weaves over to me (*filthy*, Black-Irish drunk) & says 'What the h—— are you doing here?' Horrified at the sight of him, Monterey told him she'd just been worried. He stepped back a moment, she wrote in her diary the next morning, then turned on her and shouted, "No —— —— —— is going to keep tables on me! . . . and he knocked me flat!"[46] (Much later she quoted him as saying, evidently leaving out a choice descriptor, "I'm not going to have an old whore telling me what to do!")[47]

By the time O'Neill awoke the next morning, Monterey had disappeared. When Batson showed up at the hotel, O'Neill admitted to hitting her but was remorseless: "I took a poke at Carlotta, and she's gone. She's going home, I guess, but I don't give a damn." Her absence only made him more defiant, and that night Batson took him on a tour of the city's late-night scene. After an evening's bar crawl, they stopped at the St. George Dance Hall to cavort with the Chinese "taxi dancers," or paid dancing partners. There weren't many customers in the place, and O'Neill felt sorry for the bored dancers lined up against the wall and bought them each a bottle of champagne. In the men's room, he asked the attendant, "Why do you do this kind of work?" But the man, unable to speak English, didn't respond. "Good for you!" O'Neill barked. "To hell with the capitalists!" "Take it easy," Batson said, retrieving what looked like about $1,000 O'Neill had stuffed into the attendant's hand. Outside the St. George, O'Neill dropped to the curb and started to sob. Across the street several Sikh policemen began laughing at him. "Did I ever tell you," he asked Batson, his eyes filled with tears, "what a son of a bitch I've been to Agnes?"[48]

*   *   *

Dr. Renner admitted O'Neill into a hospital the following day and told Monterey, as she reported in her diary, that he'd "drank himself into a coma or somesuch!" Wracked by delirium tremens, O'Neill later described his state of mind as "teetering on the verge of a nervous breakdown and lying awake nights listening to the night-target practice of a Welsh regiment whose garrison was two blocks away, and to the beating of Chinese gongs keeping the devils away from a birth or a bride of a corpse or something devils like. It nearly had me climbing the walls of my room and gibbering a bit." Renner inveigled Monterey to accompany him to the hospital. With her at his bedside glaring at the repugnant sight of him, O'Neill, Monterey wrote that night, turned on "all the Irish charm & looks *terrible!!* . . . He is so full of guile and soft speech—it's the Irish—I will never feel for him as I have. I do not trust him!"[49]

Dispatches were wired back to the United States that Eugene O'Neill was dying. After leaving the hospital, with newsmen on his trail, O'Neill checked into the Astor House, where Monterey was staying; then, on December 12, they both disappeared. Renner booked cabins for O'Neill, Monterey, and Monterey's nurse Tuva Drew on the S.S. *Coblenz*, a German liner heading for Manila and points westward, and accompanied O'Neill onboard to get him settled in his cabin. Then he played along with his patient's ruse to sidetrack the press. "I don't understand O'Neill," he told a group of reporters a day or two later, "Apparently he dislikes my services. He had a right to dismiss me, but he shows no appreciation for my kindness, and his actions are most unethical." (He then also told them that O'Neill had suffered from tonsillitis and a nervous breakdown.) The Astor House's staff played along, too, claiming O'Neill was still registered there after the *Coblenz* was well under way.[50] O'Neill had written a letter for Renner to share with the press which stated that he'd come to China, "seeking peace and quiet and hoping that here . . . people would mind their own business and allow me to mind mine. But I have found more snoops and gossips per square inch than there is in any New England town of 1,000 inhabitants. . . . At any rate, I will find peace and solitude to work in if I have to go to the South Pole."[51]

O'Neill signed on the *Coblenz* passenger list under the alias James O'Brien and Monterey as "Miss Drew," passing herself off as Tuva Drew's daughter. (Newspapers reported that he'd traveled as "the Reverend Mr. William O'Brien"; but after his return, he wrote Eugene that he regretted to say that this was "hilariously amusing" but "untrue.") The press was still attempting to track him down in Shanghai when O'Neill resurfaced in Manila and amiably came clean after a Filipino newspaperman who'd been carrying his picture confronted him onboard the ship. O'Neill had been up all night from the racket of longshoremen unloading the ship's cargo and "looked haggard," according to a reporter. But he laughed when shown a recent dispatch claiming he was still in Shanghai. It was common for Westerners traveling in the Far East to pose as celebrities in order to receive preferential treatment and, suspicious he might be an imposter, the Filipino reporter asked for identification. O'Neill looked at him and smiled, "Why not let me admit my name is O'Brien and not O'Neill? . . . Since I am endeavoring to travel quietly, it would be gunning my own game if I offered proof I really was O'Neill." Then he reached into his pocket for his passport, showed letters addressed to him and his bankbook, and opened his jacket to reveal his name printed inside and pointed out the name on his luggage.[52]

On Christmas Eve O'Neill and Monterey arrived in Singapore, where he received a frantic cable from Lawrence Langner, who'd read in the papers about the hospitalization of the Guild's most prized dramatists. "Feel well now," O'Neill responded. "Much idiotic publicity in Shanghai, Manila. My discovery, disappearance, kidnapped, bandits, death, etc. Merry Christmas to all."[53]

On the voyage west, O'Neill held off his alcohol craving with the psychosis-inducing prescription drugs allonal and bromide. But while docked in Hong Kong he ordered a Scotch at lunch. Then, after Manila, he befriended a newspaperman named Theo Rogers, whose cabin was next door to Monterey's and whose drunken antics kept her up all night. When the ship's doctor introduced them to Rogers, Monterey described him as "a vulgar man," "an obvious shanty Irish type!" "Gene is off again," she said after a reasonably pleasant Christmas onboard, "and it won't be pretty this time.... If I had the guts I'd kill myself." Rogers and O'Neill went on a several-day bender, which included them banging on her wall from Rogers's cabin. "How this would please A[gnes] and well it might," Monterey wrote. "She wins! ... *We are what we are!*"[54]

On New Year's Day, 1929, Monterey abandoned ship at Ceylon. She checked into a hotel overlooking the harbor, ordered a pot of tea, and watched from her balcony as the *Coblenz* slowly disappeared from view. She then booked a return trip to France on the S.S. *James Monroe*. After two lonely weeks at sea and desperate cables sent back and forth, O'Neill and Monterey arranged to meet in Port Saïd. The second officer of the ship witnessed firsthand the outrageous lovers' quarrel and then the surprising truce that ensued: "Their reunion on the *Monroe* was a combination of name-calling, insults, jumping up and down, screeching, hair-pulling, stamping feet, wrestling and finally winding up in a passionate embrace smothering each other with kisses and hugs. From then on they were like a couple of lovebirds."[55]

For O'Neill, the voyage across the Far East, with its maladies, drunkenness, heavy gambling losses, and vicious warfare with Monterey, was, in the end, a great success. "The fact that I was weakened by illness and nerves really helped in a funny way," he wrote Eugene. "It got me into such a highly sensitized state that every impression hit me with all it had and registered with full force. Everything seemed to be revealing itself for my benefit."[56] "I met all kinds of people of all nationalities," he said, "and I got the feeling from the East that I was after that made it real and living to me instead of something in a book. I'm full to the brim with all sorts of vivid impressions of sound, color, faces, atmosphere, queer experiences that pursued me."[57] He even came up with a play idea that would take place on the *André-Lebon* titled "Uncharted Sea." The play, which he abandoned, would involve a "half-caste" woman and "the American Poet, the drunkard who flies from reality to the negative acceptance of the East." And it would take to task, like *Marco Millions*, the arrogance of American cultural imperialism. "The conflict of races on board, the trend of the races of the world struggle today, the essential characteristics, the awakening of the East to the West, the growing dominance of the American idea."[58]

For Monterey, the voyage had been nothing less than a nightmare. Throughout the trip, she'd been exhausted, prostrate with nerves, struck down by flu or a cold, or the prey of her drunken lout of a lover. Just as Agnes Boulton had in the early days of her marriage to O'Neill, Monterey learned over four and a half trying months, in the hardest of ways, what it meant to be initiated into the life of a severe alcoholic who was miserably obsessed with the past. "Why drink," Monterey wondered, "when you know you are not sane with alcohol in you. Literally not sane! . . . It's *dangerous.*"[59]

O'Neill's eyes had also been opened about Monterey. First off, she was a snob, a fact borne out by the way she treated hotel staff, shop clerks, and ships' crews. She fancied herself an *actress* and demanded obsequiousness; any disturbance, no matter how slight, was treated as a personal affront. Onboard the *James Monroe* the crew referred to her as "Queen Mary," and she openly treated the gracious, self-abnegating Tuva Drew like a servant. She was also materialistic: after they'd returned to France, Saxe and Dorothy Commins arrived to greet them, and Dorothy was dumbstruck by what she found in Monterey's brimming boudoir. "Showing me around one day," she recalled, "[Monterey] opened drawer after drawer of exquisite handmade lingerie, some of it from Shanghai; then a large closet with more than thirty pairs of shoes. Her jewels, her clothes, everything was out of the ordinary. When I complimented her on the fit of her clothes, she said she didn't have to go to Paris until the final fittings, as Poiret and Mainbocher had made mannequins of her exact figure." Worst of all, for O'Neill, Monterey was controlling: Theo Rogers later said that aboard the *Coblenz* Rogers's cabin had "provided a refuge where Eugene was safe from Carlotta's nagging. He was one of the gentlest persons I've ever met, while she was the domineering sort, possessive, and wanted him all to herself."[60]

O'Neill also importantly learned, however, over his weeks of solitude on the *Coblenz,* "half mad with utter loneliness," how dependent on her he'd become. Monterey was precisely the type of person he needed to keep sober and writing. This was her apparent mission in life, even surpassing, at times, his desire to maintain a life of security and hard work. She would listen in rapt attention when he shared his drafts, while Boulton had become less interested in their last years, once even falling asleep while he was reading.[61] Before their reunion at Port Saïd, Monterey had already noted in her diary, "I gained (re-gained) my faith in Gene." Convinced their relationship was salvageable after their reunion, she gave him a ring symbolizing her dedication. "He *is* the man I've loved—and *always will love!*"[62]

L'Aeschylus du Plessis

O'Neill and Monterey landed back in Europe at Genoa, Italy, on January 21, 1929. Both weary of travel, they headed straight for the French border. Within a week they settled in Cap-d'Ail, just outside Monte Carlo on the French Riviera, and rented the Villa Les Mimosas, which had a beautiful garden and a spectacular view of the Mediterranean. Monterey wrote Saxe Commins in rapture over their new location, "The sea for my darling Gene & a garden for me!—*I have found peace!* . . . Gene is lovelier than ever & an angel to me! . . . I sit back & admire & adore! What happier lot for a woman?!"[63] Their interlude of blissful tranquillity would be short-lived.

News soon arrived from the Theatre Guild about *Dynamo*, and it was again unanimous: the play's February 11, 1929, premiere had been a crushing defeat, and the blague among jealous competitors, sneering critics, and jilted colleagues was heard up and down Broadway. Edna Kenton, still resentful over the Provincetown Players' unceremonious end, was one of many gleeful observers of O'Neill's fall from grace. "75 years from now," Kenton chuckled, "[*Dynamo*] will be revived in some little Rialto theatre of some then Hoboken as a sample of what ancient Americans believed to be psychology, bitterness, and cynicism!! And how the audience will roar."[64]

Before *Dynamo*'s opening night, George Jean Nathan had published O'Neill's letter on his planned trilogy, without asking its author's permission, revealing that *Dynamo* was to be its first installment. "Throwing sand" in the critics' eyes like that, O'Neill complained to Nathan, led them to disregard the psychology of Reuben Light's tragic fall by focusing too closely on the trilogy's God-replacement theme.[65] Nearly every reviewer based their responses on Nathan's prerelease tell-all. But Reuben's conversion was also seen as too drastic, leading audiences to believe he'd gone insane as opposed to destroying himself out of self-contempt, feelings of betrayal, and mother longing. Not one critic, O'Neill protested, "got what I thought my play was about."[66]

O'Neill also blamed *Dynamo*'s failure on his "domestic brawling" with Boulton during its composition the previous summer, and on the fact that his absence at rehearsals had the unfortunate consequence of actors speaking lines that neither they nor their director, Philip Moeller, wholly understood. Not even George Jean Nathan stepped in to defend him. "His play is a dud," Nathan wrote in his *Judge* review, "extremely poor" and "miles below his better work."[67]

Smelling blood in the water, Heywood Broun joined in the frenzy without having seen or read the play. "No living American writer," Broun wrote, "has so consistently sailed under false colors as Eugene O'Neill. With the aid of curtains, lights and mass psychology it is possible for a man to palm himself off as a creative genius merely by pulling rabbits out of a silk hat. Indeed, O'Neill has been shrewd enough to vary the familiar trick by using vipers and scorpions instead of bunnies."[68] Though Nathan himself had panned it, he was still moved to print a condemnation of the attacks gleefully rolling off the presses: "The stranger from Mars, perusing the New York newspaper reviews of 'Dynamo,' would, estimating them from their ferocity, doubtless assume that Eugene O'Neill had not merely written a bad play but had also been guilty of stealing the reviewers' wives, murdering their children and setting fire to their houses." Nathan recognized a perverse national pastime exposing itself in the whole ugly affair: "It probably goes back to the characteristic delight of Americans in pulling their heroes off their pedestals. If there is one thing an American likes to do better than putting a man on a pedestal it is booting him off it. . . . O'Neill is the current goat. He will now have to write at least three plays worthy of Shakespeare at his best to get half-way up the old pedestal again."[69]

However well intentioned such defenses by Nathan and others might seem, O'Neill resented any kind of mollycoddling from his peers: "It is sickening to be treated with such doleful tenderness as if I were the Pope's toe—me that was born on Times Square and not in Greenwich Village, and that have heard dramatic critics called sons of bitches—and, speaking in general, believed it—ever since I was old enough to recognize the Count of Monte Cristo's voice! The greatest burden I have to bear after each flop is the well-meant condolence chorus. They never reflect that a kick in the pants—especially when one feels one doesn't deserve it—is a grand stimulant."[70]

In this case, the "grand stimulant" inspired him on to drastically revise *Dynamo* for its book version (the script used for the play's few revivals) throughout that spring and into the summer. "I like it better now—but not enough," O'Neill wrote the critic Joseph Wood Krutch. "I wish I'd never written it—really—and yet I feel it has its justified place in my work development. A puzzle. What disappoints me in it is that it marks a standing still, if not a backward move."[71]

That spring the debacle over *Dynamo* was offset for O'Neill by welcome news: Agnes Boulton had agreed to move to Nevada for several months and from there arrange for a "Reno divorce." She'd also accepted O'Neill's original offer of $6,000 a year, $10,000 if he made more than $40,000 in a given year. She would also receive $2,400 in child support, with shared custody and unrestricted visitation rights for O'Neill. After his return to France, O'Neill wrote Shane and Oona asking them to relay a message to their mother that, while he'd been convalescing in Shanghai, "all the bitterness got burned out of me and the future years will prove this."[72]

O'Neill's bitterness reignited, however, when he heard that she'd refused to accept a clause prohibiting her from writing about their marriage during his lifetime. He'd been told that a literary agent had already contacted her about the prospect, and he wrote Weinberger,

"I think you should have brought more pressure to bear, what with all the muck we have on her—and as far as the writing clause goes you can tell her for me before Driscoll that if she ever dares write a line about me, either outright or as thinly disguised autobiography, I will write the play—a damned good play it would make, too!—about her past and her family's that will blast them off the map!"[73]

Boulton acquiesced, and on March 11, she took a train to Nevada, leaving Barbara, Shane, and Oona in the care of her new partner, the journalist James Delaney. She took up residence at a ranch outside Reno that catered to would-be divorcées, and that May wrote de Polo a bit of gossip she could be sure would get back to her soon-to-be ex: "I have a violent suitor, Harold—you will die! He is 25, six feet three, wild and handsome, and the crack 'Bronk rider' of the west—that is he goes to all the rodeo's and rides for show money. . . . He wears high boots with red roses on them, a big black sombrero, blue jeans turned up at the boots—now don't tell mother!"[74]

Whatever Boulton might have written about their marriage, and about Monterey's seduction of O'Neill, could be spread, less publicly but to him just as harmfully, by word of mouth in New York. Subsequently, O'Neill and Monterey's truce at Port Saïd all but collapsed by late March at the Villa Les Mimosas. They'd been told that Boulton was circulating, he wrote de Polo, "rough lies" and "foul fairy tales" about him, and Monterey was livid that O'Neill was allowing her name to be dragged through the slush by his "so-called" friends in New York. Bitter accusations flew back and forth with such mounting hostility that Monterey fled temporarily to Paris. O'Neill coaxed her back, pleading with her "to end this present situation in which we are forced by the world into an intolerable impasse. . . . When peace is measurably within our grasp, are we going to take the side of the world against each other and ourselves work the ruin?"[75]

Soon after Monterey's return, they leased a regal estate, Le Château du Plessis, in the inland province of Touraine, approximately ten miles outside its capital city, Tours. A four-hour train ride from Paris, with thirty-five rooms, two vaulted eighteenth-century turrets, carved wooden furniture, and ancient tapestries draping the walls, the château was owned by three sisters born of provincial French aristocracy—the vicomtesse de Banville, the marquise de Verdun, and Madame de la Boissiere. The ladies were delighted to have a well-known American writer in residence, if somewhat scandalized by the content of his plays, and he sealed their good opinion by showing them his gold medal from the National Institute of Arts and Letters.[76]

Château du Plessis was preposterously cheap, even by the standards of rural postwar France: it cost just over $100 a month in rent, which O'Neill and Monterey split fifty-fifty. The château was surrounded by over six hundred acres of woods for hunting, a broad stream for fishing, and an expansive farm with cattle, sheep, poultry, wheat, and hay overseen by its proprietor. O'Neill took on the role of the country farmer with gusto, and when he raised a litter of pigs, he affectionately christened them with names like the Duc de Haut Sauterne, Jean Louis Hohenzollern, and Fifi D'Arc. The vicomtesse de Banville opposed modern "improvements" to the estate (as did O'Neill, if less vocally); but Monterey insisted on new electrical and plumbing systems, a roof garden, a gymnasium, and on damming up the stream to install a concrete swimming pool for O'Neill.[77]

O'Neill ordered stationery with the letterhead "Le Plessis," and he made it a point to refer to the château by that name.[78] This might well be interpreted as a ruse to shroud the opulence of his new estate; the word "château" means "castle," of course, a fact O'Neill didn't want to get back to Boulton or his more radical associates. "Don't say anything about my gorgeous Renault [car]—make it a small Renault," O'Neill instructed Commins to pass on to "all and sundry of my friends."[79] O'Neill's estrangement from his father's wealth and then his own reveals itself in the souls of most of his money-obsessed characters—Andrew Mayo, Brutus Jones, William Brown, James Tyrone—each of whom is soul-destroyed by the spiritual bankruptcy that it takes to amass riches. The wealthy characters who aren't affected, Mildred Douglas in *The Hairy Ape*, Marco Polo in *Marco Millions*, or Sam Evans in *Strange Interlude*, have no souls to destroy. (After O'Neill's death, Boulton observed that there was "a misconception in the mind

Carlotta Monterey at the Château du Plessis.
(COURTESY OF SHEAFFER-O'NEILL COLLECTION, LINDA LEAR CENTER FOR SPECIAL
COLLECTIONS AND ARCHIVES, CONNECTICUT COLLEGE, NEW LONDON)

* * *

of the public ... an idea that he was hard up, stopped in shoddy
hotels, etc, knew nothing about nice living until he married Carlotta,
who practically taught him how to use a napkin and to wipe his shoes
when he came in." Her ex-husband's persistent longing for a "big house,
servants, the best of everything that could be had ... showed some

split in his personality—and that split does show in his work. . . . It was certainly not the life that an artist would live, was it?")[80]

Monterey adopted the same tight-lipped attitude at first, writing to Commins, "Tell no one of our home, unless they insist—& then give them the *description* of a *peasant's* cottage!—"[81] But over time she grew more defiant. She was especially enraged by Kenneth Macgowan's audacity in publishing a "Talk of the Town" vignette in the *New Yorker*, which he'd charitably written to downplay their extravagant lifestyle but which she considered an "apologia." Macgowan's piece ran almost exactly one month before the day, October 29, 1929, that the Wall Street stock market collapsed, taking many of O'Neill's friends with it. "Flamboyant descriptions of the château [O'Neill] has rented in France have exaggerated its grandeur," Macgowan wrote. "It is not a show place, simply an old residence on an estate owned by three noble ladies who rented it to the O'Neills furnished, for about half of what a four-room apartment rents in New York."[82]

Two weeks after the crash, Monterey wrote Commins that she'd strongly censured Macgowan in a letter for his presumption, and that she refused to play ball any longer: "I need no apology to the public or Gene's friends or acquaintance whether I am living in 30 *rooms* or 3," she said. "I pay as I go—& it's nobody's damn business!"[83] In a follow-up letter to Macgowan, still nursing her grudge against him over a year later, Monterey seethed, "But—will you tell me *why*—in the name of Heaven—Gene & I should apologize to anyone in this world if we have *thirty* servants or *no* servants? Will you tell me *why* you get fussed because a lot of *failures, sore heads, drunks*, and *would-be artists* (in one line or another) thro' envy, disappointment and jealousy criticize a man because he lives in the manner that all middle class people (have they the money!) live? It is too absurd. . . . And I *beg* of you,—no matter *what* they say,—to never apologize for us. We *have* a huge château,— we *have* 10 servants,—we *have* a concrete swimming pool,—we *have* three cars! . . . This letter is vulgar—but the superb is vulgar!"[84]

Monterey wrote on like this for over eight much-italicized, hyper-punctuated pages: how she'd done her most to give O'Neill, "for the first time in his life, a decent home," how she'd introduced him to

Beethoven and Bach, taken him to the finest tailors, "done everything possible to make him forget the self conscious, uneasy, slovenly atmosphere in which he lived." He was a dog lover, so she provided him with one; but in contrast to the unruly Finn Mac Cool, she bought a wire-haired fox terrier named Billy (who promptly died of distemper), then a Gordon setter and, most important for the long-term, a high-bred Dalmatian shipped over from England that they named Silverdene Emblem O'Neill, or "Blemie" for short. For her efforts, she fumed at Macgowan, "I was crucified for eighteen months . . . being called a harlot & other cruel names." Soon she devised a new time scale for her husband's life, "B.C."—"Before Carlotta."[85]

O'Neill's divorce from Agnes Boulton was finalized, with the charge of desertion, on July 2, 1929. Boulton's filed complaint was anticlimactic for the press, which had been hoping for a public airing of "many allegations of incompatibility." The judge let reporters inspect the file before sealing it, but it was pitifully thin and lacked the intimate detail necessary for a juicy society piece, and the trial itself lasted about fifteen minutes.[86] O'Neill and Monterey, after signing a prenuptial agreement, got married in Paris on July 22. The ceremony was private, with only a few official witnesses present. O'Neill chose the engraving on his and Monterey's rings from the script of *Lazarus Laughed:* "I am your laughter—and you are mine!" (*CP2*, 586).

The newlyweds lavished their bounty on a number of guests at the Château du Plessis over the next two years—George Jean Nathan and the silent film actress Lillian Gish, Saxe and Dorothy Commins, the author Carl Van Vechten and his wife, the actress Fania Marinoff, Theresa Helburn and Helen Westley of the Theatre Guild, Walter Huston, Stark Young, and Eugene Jr. all visited. Thérèse Renner (who would become his Hungarian translator) even made the trek from Shanghai via the trans-Siberian railroad. Monterey was especially delighted, for the time being, with her new stepson Eugene; after meeting him briefly in Maine when he was a teenager, she was genuinely impressed by the well-mannered, highly intelligent six foot two Yale man who'd just spent the summer studying in Germany. "If my Cynthia is as fine a woman at nineteen—as he is a man," she wrote Commins the day after Eugene arrived, "I will be a very proud & happy mother." And she compliment-ed the unpretentious Kathleen Jenkins that her "example and care & love show in his manner—his thoughts—& his viewpoint of life!"[87]

Prospective visitors were vetted in terms of their "B.C." status before any invitations were granted, however. From her writing desk at Plessis, Monterey initiated a ferocious campaign to avenge herself against O'Neill's "so-called friends"—that is, those she be-lieved had taken sides with Boulton, especially his Provincetown and Greenwich Village associates. "I, personally feel," she told Commins, whom she had come to regard as an ally and confidant, "that men or women who go about tearing down other people's reputations—personal or otherwise—should be *publicly flogged!*—I have no 'God is Love & all is Divine' in my nature—. To me 'an eye for an eye & a tooth for a tooth.' . . . If people *got* what they *gave* this world would have fewer parasites and weaklings." Among their female ranks, these included Fitzie Fitzgerald, Mary Blair, and Juliet Throckmorton, all of whom, she said, "were very fluent in their conversation concerning me during a certain time—& said things not only stupidly untrue—but *ridiculous* had they *looked into things!*"[88]

Jimmy and Patti Light were personae non gratae in the O'Neill household as well. Light had won a Guggenheim fellowship that year to study stagecraft in Germany and Russia, and O'Neill told others that he very much wanted to see Light but believed he'd been evading him. According to Patti Light, their rift with Monterey was caused by a misunderstanding: Boulton would tell Patti horrible things about Monterey, she said, then deny it—and then it would get back to Monterey and O'Neill that Patti was the source.[89] Patti had tried to explain this to O'Neill during the Lights' visit to Paris in March 1930, but upon hearing that Patti had "forced herself upon" O'Neill, Mon-terey had had enough. (Virulently anti-Semitic, Monterey blamed Patti Light's impudence in large part on the fact that she was Jewish: "That is the Jew of it! The jews in N.Y. . . . even G.[ene]'s attorney [Harry Weinberger]—I never, in my long & varied experience, have come across such tactless, thick skinned, stupid people.—")[90]

Taken aback by the abrupt severing of connections by Monterey, Light remembered the irony of one night at a performance of *The Hairy Ape* back in 1922: Monterey and he were then on sociable terms, and they'd played a practical joke on the cast. Horsing around in Monterey's dressing room, they began crying out, "Oh! Oh! Kiss Me! Kiss Me!" Louis Wolheim and other actors took the bait and peeked in, only to find Monterey casually applying her makeup and Light reading a newspaper with equal nonchalance. Now, when he first addressed her as "Carlotta," she snapped, "I'd like you to call me Mrs. O'Neill." To visit O'Neill at Plessis that spring, Light concocted the excuse to Monterey that he needed to talk business with O'Neill. Grudgingly she'd permitted him, without Patti, to stay at the château for one night—but never again. This would be the last time O'Neill and Light would see each other for over two decades.[91]

Back in the United States, *Dynamo*'s inglorious flop and the gossip over O'Neill's divorce proceedings were compounded by a plagiarism suit filed against him over *Strange Interlude*. The novelist Gladys Lewis claimed that O'Neill had stolen from the plot of her novel, published under the penname George Lewys, *The Temple of Pallas-Athenæ* (or, as O'Neill called it, "The Crap-Can of Pallas-Athenae"). "And her fool book—which I haven't yet seen—was privately printed at that," he told Macgowan. "It's like accusing a drunkard of stealing marshmallow sundaes."[92] The presiding judge in the case agreed. "Absurdity could not rise to greater heights," he said in court. "The plaintiff cannot claim a copyright on words in the dictionary or on usual English idioms, or on ideas."[93]

The notoriety had still begun to wear thin on O'Neill: "Who wants this garbage bath they are pleased to call fame? I'd like to give it away. It has always been about as welcome to me as an attack of hives, anyway! I've wasted almost as much energy ducking its annoyances as I've put in my work. I feel as pawed over by the sweaty paws of the public as a 4-bit whore—and correspondingly defiled! ... But I am forgetting our old watchword of the Revolution—F——k 'em all!"[94]

Bluster aside, O'Neill was now an exposed nerve emotionally, a man truly desperate for a protector. Carlotta Monterey, for all her perceived faults, was ideally suited to this task. She was not passive aggressive in the usual mold of American celebrity culture; her aggression was proactive and unyielding. She vowed to shield O'Neill from the annoyances of life, public and private, and thus enable him to compose his greatest plays yet. Any discussion of the early years would be forbidden. She would construct a fortress around her husband that would repel his past associations, including *anyone* connected to Agnes Boulton, which soon came to include his children. "We're going to have trouble with these offspring," she wrote Commins later, "but (knowing how Gene takes all this) will try to be the buffer between them."[95] By the standards she'd set for her devotion to "a man of genius," as Charlie Chaplin put it, her crusade was an unmitigated success. And within a few years, O'Neill would sound off with equal vehemence against those "who gave me the double-cross when I went to Europe." "They owed me loyalty, after all I'd done for them," he told Richard Madden. "They pretended to be my friends, and as soon as my back was turned gave me the knife. They chose which side of the fence they were on, then! Let them stick to it—for my side is barred to them now! There are some things I will neither forget nor forgive!"[96]

Most theater critics stateside agreed that *Dynamo* had likely sounded the death knell for "America's First Dramatist." But although O'Neill's reputation might have been withering on the vine back in the United States, his plays were filling houses to capacity in Sweden, Denmark, Russia, Hungary, Germany, Czechoslovakia, England, and France. *Strange Interlude* was a sensation at Stockholm's Royal Theatre, *All God's Chillun Got Wings* was produced at Moscow's Kamerny Theatre, *Lazarus Laughed* at the Cambridge Festival Theatre, and a production of *The Hairy Ape* was mounted in Paris by the avant-garde company of Georges Pitoëff, among many others.

Europeans attacked O'Neill's plays too, of course, but O'Neill likened his reaction to that of boxing champ Jack Sharkey when asked how it felt in the ring when crowds booed him. Sharkey had replied,

"Fuck 'em, I'm getting their dough!"[97] O'Neill largely chalked up the bad press to cultural arrogance on the part of Europeans: "We mustn't dare infringe on Europe's private property, the Arts."[98] But behind closed doors, he was distressed by their lack of civility about American culture. "They are forced to see our industrialism swamping them and forcing them to bad imitations on every hand, and it poisons them," he wrote Nathan. "They are bound they'll die at the post rather than acknowledge an American has anything to show them in any line of writers and artists. It's amusing—and disgusting!—this clinging of theirs to their last superiority of the past!"[99]

Europe's supercilious attitude toward American art was actually on the wane. European dramatists—Gerhart Hauptmann and Ernst Toller of Germany, Hugo von Hofmannsthal and Stefan Zweig of Austria, George Bernard Shaw and Sean O'Casey of Ireland, Henri-René Lenormand of France, Maxim Gorky of Russia—all followed O'Neill's progress closely.[100] (The Russians were so enamored of *Desire Under the Elms* that they held a mock public trial for Abbie Putnam's infanticide. She was acquitted.) "Along with Shaw, Ibsen, Strindberg, Chekov and his great love, Shakespeare," Shivaun O'Casey has said of her father, Sean, "he would place Eugene O'Neill."[101] Shaw, in what has to be the most artfully crafted left-handed compliment O'Neill ever received, referred to him as a "Yankee Shakespeare peopling his Isle with Calibans."[102] James Joyce was noncommittal, though he conceded that O'Neill himself was "thoroughly Irish."[103] By 1932, in fact, Irish writers would claim him as one of their own: "I was asked to be a member of the Irish Academy," O'Neill wrote Eugene Jr. with obvious delight, "being organized by Shaw & Yeats & [Lennox] Robinson, etc.—and accepted. Of course, I'm 'associate' because not Irish born. But this I regard as an honor, whereas other Academies don't mean much to me. Anything with [W. B.] Yeats, Shaw, A.E., O'Casey, [Liam] Flaherty, Robinson in it is good enough for me. Joyce refused to join—hates Academies. . . . Still & all I think little Ireland will have an Academy that will compare favorably with any country's. At any rate, I'm pleased about all this."[104]

In Germany, the novelist Thomas Mann publicly declared that he considered *All God's Chillun Got Wings* "one of the most impressive plays that has ever been written." "O'Neill is absolutely new and different and a real dramatist," Mann said. "He is one of the great figures in the history of the theatre." "We are well aware of your [Americans'] Puritanism and the other difficulties under which [Americans] struggle," another German belletrist remarked of O'Neill's role as an American cultural emissary to Europe. "It is all very well for you to maintain your policy of splendid isolationism in international affairs that touch us only on the material side, but you can't prevent our joining you intellectually."[105] Thomas Mann won the Nobel Prize in Literature in 1929, but O'Neill, along with Sinclair Lewis and Theodore Dreiser, was already on the short list.[106] (Lewis would become the first American to win it the following year.)

Patience, a trait O'Neill demonstrably lacked up to then, was required to orchestrate a comeback in the United States. But he resolved to "let nothing or no one hurry or any consideration influence me to seek a production until I'm damn good and ready for it." "I've learned a lesson—," he wrote Fitzie Fitzgerald, "forty is the right age to begin to learn!"[107] For his next project, O'Neill revisited a Civil War–era drama that had been brewing in his imagination since 1926: "Use the plots from Greek tragedy in modern surroundings—the New England play of Agamemnon, Clytemnestra, Electra & Orestes—Oedipus," and that May 1929, he knew it would be a trilogy, to which he gave the title *Mourning Becomes Electra*.

During his two years at Plessis, O'Neill spent the bulk of his time alone in his study, located in one of his turrets, focusing intently on the new trilogy. Between November and August, he wrote steadily for 225 days.[108] Even when he and Monterey vacationed for a month in the Canary Islands to escape the "lifeless and depressing" French weather in March 1931, he concentrated on the writing.[109] Toiling through at least half a dozen drafts, he alternately experimented with masks, soliloquies, and asides for the fourteen-act trilogy, eventually abandoning the avant-garde techniques of his recent plays; but in so doing he found he'd written himself into a corner: "The unavoidable entire melodramatic action," O'Neill was convinced, "must be felt as working out of psychic fate from the past—thereby attaining tragic significance—or else!—a hell of a problem, a modern tragic interpretation of classic fate without benefit of gods . . . fate springing out of the family." And he grappled once again with the abiding predicament of how to replace the outmoded soliloquy. "Oh for a language to write drama in!" he wrote Joseph Wood Krutch. "For a speech that is dramatic and isn't just conversation! I'm so straight-jacketed by writing in terms of talk! I'm so fed up with the dodge-question of dialect! But where to find that language?"[110]

For a brief time, O'Neill was even convinced that talking pictures might provide the format he needed for a modern-day soliloquy. He watched his very first "talky," *The Broadway Melody*, with great interest in Paris in November 1929, and exited the theater bursting with ideas about the potential of multimedia: "a stage play combined with a screen talky background to make alive visually and vocally the memories, etc. in the minds of the characters" (a concept he would abandon but return to with his 1941 one-act tour de force *Hughie*). "Talkies," he believed, had the potential to be "a medium for real artists if they got a chance at it."[111] It was an ironic change of heart. The spring before, the billionaire industrialist Howard Hughes had offered him, through MGM, the astounding sum of $100,000 to write the screenplay for his film *Hell's Angels*. O'Neill responded to the offer by collect telegram, billed by the word with a maximum of twenty words: "No. No. No. No. No. No. No. No. No. No. No. No. No. No. No. No. No. No. No. O'Neill."[112]

But his envy of novelists lingered, and he concluded that dramatic language was best found when he'd written plays with their book form in mind rather than a staged performance. "Hereafter I write plays primarily as literature to be read—," he told Macgowan, "and the more simply they read, the better they will act, no matter what technique is used." After much deliberation, he'd made up his mind that neither the masks he deployed for symbolic effect in *The Great God Brown* and *Lazarus Laughed* nor the thought asides of *Strange*

Interlude and *Dynamo* would heighten his trilogy's tragic power. Instead he offered only the implication of masks, as "a visual symbol of [the protagonists'] separateness, the fated isolation of this family, the mark of their fate which makes them dramatically distinct from the rest of the world."[113] But each character's expression in repose would share a "strange, life-like mask impression" (*CP2*, 897).

O'Neill appropriated *Mourning Becomes Electra*'s plot and characters from Aeschylus's *Oresteia* and its later adaptations by Sophocles and Euripides. Together the plays, *The Homecoming*, *The Hunted*, and *The Haunted*, chronicle the decline of the Mannons, a prominent New England family, and O'Neill's shared plotline with the *Oresteia* is unmistakable: a beloved leader (King Agamemnon in Aeschylus, General Ezra Mannon in O'Neill) returns home victorious from a great war—the Trojan War in Aeschylus, the American Civil War in O'Neill—only to be murdered by his spiteful wife (Clytemnestra, Christine), who has had an affair with a romantic stranger (Aegisthus, Adam Brant) in her husband's absence; in turn, the wife is destroyed by her progeny (Electra, Lavinia). In both trilogies, daughters and sons seek revenge for their fathers' murder, though in O'Neill, their act of revenge intensifies rather than alleviates their suffering.

In Euripides' version, the son Orestes succumbs to insanity after his complicity in his mother's murder, as Orin Mannon does in O'Neill's modern adaptation. But O'Neill offers a sequel to the *Oresteia*, as he had for Lazarus, that presents the torments of Lavinia (Electra) after her mother's death. The Mannon family occupies a mansion in a Connecticut town (New London) with a "white temple front . . . like an incongruous mask fixed on the somber, stone house" (*CP2*, 928).[114] (In Aeschylus, this is the house of Atreus.) The mansion's gray stone behind the white columns represents a mask that conceals the "New England granite" behind, a flinty deliberateness that rejects the kind of sentimental weakness O'Neill embodied as a youth. Through Christine Mannon, O'Neill describes the mansion as having a "pagan temple front stuck like a mask on Puritan gray ugliness!" (*CP2*, 903–4). (O'Neill's architectural depiction closely resembles New London's Shaw Mansion, now a museum off Bank

Street and the headquarters of the New London County Historical Society. The Shaw family also, like the fictional Mannons, figured prominently in the American Revolutionary and Civil Wars.)

Some time later, though before its production, O'Neill shared his script with a select few preliminary readers, including the *Times*'s drama critic Brooks Atkinson, whose opinion he respected and who was one of the only critics to praise *Dynamo*. As so many reviewers had in the past, Atkinson critiqued it by evoking Freud and Jung and the Greeks. But O'Neill insisted to Barrett Clark that he knew "enough about men and women to have written *Mourning Becomes Electra* almost exactly as it is if I had never heard of Freud or Jung or the others. . . . None compared to what psychological writers of the past like Dostoevsky, etc. have had."[115]

Mourning Becomes Electra unmistakably parallels Dostoevsky's probings into the "Russian soul." But in O'Neill's play, New England Puritanism is the "soul" governing the Mannons—psychologically, historically, religiously, genetically—and shapes the playwright's modern interpretation of the mythic gods, fates, and furies of Greek mythology. "Beyond the general plot outline of the first two plays there is nothing of the Greek notion about it now," he said. "I have simplified it until all its Greek similarities are out—almost."[116] O'Neill declared, in fact, that he held the whole faddish presumption of so-called Greek universality in contempt: "What modern audience was ever purged by pity and terror by witnessing a Greek tragedy or what modern mind by reading one? It can't be done! We are too far away, we are in a world of different values! . . . We can admire while we pretend to understand—but our understanding is always a pretense! . . . Our tragedy is just that we have only ourselves, that there is nothing to be purged into except a belief in the guts of man, good or evil, who faces unflinchingly the black mystery of his own soul!"[117]

Given the disastrous leaks about *Dynamo* being part of a trilogy, O'Neill kept his new trilogy a careful secret before sending it that April to the Theatre Guild, which enthusiastically accepted it for the next season. This time O'Neill knew he would have to oversee

the rehearsals in New York personally. (Besides, his and Monterey's
regal life in France had become to both of them "dull beyond bearing.")[118] What their reception back home would be like was a terrifying uncertainty. The smear campaigns on both sides of the Atlantic
had inflamed tempers, destroyed friendships, and taken a toll on their
two years of marriage. The finest distillation of his abiding love for
Monterey over the course of their exile in France can be found in his
inscription to her of *Mourning Becomes Electra*, as a proxy for the failed
Dynamo, a work that "did not represent what you are to me":

> *To Carlotta*
> In memory of the interminable days of rain in which you bravely
> suffered in silence that this trilogy might be born—days when
> I had to work but you had nothing but household frets and a
> blank vista through the salon windows of the gray land of Le
> Plessis, with the wet black trees still and dripping, and the mist
> wraiths mourning over the drowned fields—days when you had
> the self-forgetting love to greet my lunchtime depressing, sunk
> preoccupations with a courageous cheering banter—days which
> for you were bitterly lonely, when I seemed far away and lost to
> you in a grim, savage gloomy country of my own—days which
> were for you like hateful boring inseparable enemies who nagged
> at nerves and spirit until an intolerable ennui and life-sickness
> poisoned your spirit—
>
> In short, days in which you collaborated, as only deep love can,
> in the writing of this trilogy of the damned! These scripts are
> rightly yours and my presenting them is a gift of what is half yours
> already. Let us hope what the trilogy may have in it will repay the
> travail we've gone through for its sake!
>
> I want these scripts to remind you that I have known your love
> with my love even when I have seemed not to know that I have
> seen it, even when I have appeared most blind; that I have felt it
> warmly around me always, (even in my study in the closing pages
> of an act!), sustaining and comforting, a warm secure sanctuary

for the man after the author's despairing solitudes and inevitable defeats, a victory of love-in-love,—mother, and wife and mistress and friend!—And collaborator!

Collaborator, I love you!

Gene

Le Plessis—April 23, 1931[119]

The Prodigal Returns

Once aboard the passenger liner *Statendam*, O'Neill cabled the Theatre Guild that he and Monterey would be landing on May 23, 1931. The ship was actually scheduled to dock six days earlier, but the ploy offered them a few days' peace after a stormy, fogbound crossing. There they could brace for the inevitable hullabaloo from the press, which had been alerted ahead of time by the Guild that the playwright was returning stateside to supervise the production of his latest magnum opus. Newspapers across the country printed the same barb: "When Eugene O'Neill returned from Europe he made a very dramatic arrival. Six of his trunks were filled with the manuscript of one play." O'Neill and Monterey's arrival was discovered several days earlier than planned, however; and the story landed, as anticipated, on the front page of all the papers. What wasn't anticipated was how the press had found out they were in New York.

Monterey's ex-husband Ralph Barton, at thirty-nine years old, had somehow received word (possibly through Carl Van Vechten, who'd remained friends with both Monterey and Barton) that she and O'Neill were at the Madison, a hotel only a few blocks away from his Upper East Side penthouse. A day or two later, on Tuesday, May 20, Barton fired his .25-caliber handgun into his right temple. His body was discovered the next morning by his maid, Mary Jefferson, and the sight made a gruesome tableau: Barton was splayed out in bed wearing silk pajamas, a half-smoked cigarette in his left hand and the pistol in his right; also on the bed was a copy of *Gray's Anatomy*, a staple for any artist's library, open to illustrations of the human heart.

Barton left \$35 and a letter of apology to Mary Jefferson along with a typed suicide note headed in red ink "OBIT." The note cites his reason for ending his life as "melancholia," which he'd suffered since childhood and had worsened as an adult into a "manic depressive insanity." "I did it," the note read, "because I am fed up with inventing devices for getting through twenty-four hours a day and with bridging over a few months periodically with some beautiful interest, such as a new gal who annoyed me to the point where I forgot my own troubles." "No one thing is responsible for this and no one person— except myself. If the gossips insist on something more definite and thrilling as a reason, let them choose my pending appointment with the dentist or the fact that I happened to be painfully short of cash at the moment."[120] If Barton's aim was to fend off "the gossips," however, he made a poor show of it.

Contradicting his own claim that "no one person" was responsible, Barton singled out Carlotta Monterey as the root cause of his despair: "In particular, my remorse is bitter over my failure to appreciate my beautiful lost angel, Carlotta, the only woman I ever loved and whom I respect and admire above all the rest of the human race. She is the one person who could have saved me had I been savable. She did her best. No one ever had a more devoted or more understanding wife. I do hope that she will understand what my malady was and forgive me a little." He'd told his brother, the actor Homer Barton, that he'd gone on a "friendly visit" to visit Monterey and O'Neill at the Madison, after which "the realization that he had lost her broke his heart." The suicide note was signed with seven X's and the line, "I kiss my dear children—and Carlotta."[121]

On the morning of his suicide, the O'Neills received a telephone call from *New Yorker* editor Harold Ross, Barton's employer. "Mrs. O'Neill," he said, "we want you to know that Ralph Barton has died and left a note about you."[122] Monterey was dumbfounded. Why would Barton, whom she hadn't been with for over five years, kill himself out of the blue, leaving behind a pledge of everlasting love for her? At lunch the O'Neills went over the details of the incident with Carl Van Vechten and Fania Marinoff. Van Vechten assured Monterey and

O'Neill that Barton had merely introduced her into his note to enhance the dramatic impact his stagy departure. "He resented her marrying someone more famous than himself," Van Vechten explained. More to the point, he'd run out of money to sustain his high-flying lifestyle; in the depths of the Great Depression, Barton was no longer appreciated for his sophisticated, offbeat caricatures, which now seemed mere relics of a bygone age. "The market for his stuff had shrunk," Van Vechten said, "and he could see only lean times ahead, so he decided to go out in a splash of publicity."[123]

Although the O'Neills successfully avoided the press on the afternoon the suicide was announced, the Theatre Guild had already scheduled a press conference for the following day—right in the center of the media conflagration. O'Neill knew he shouldn't forestall the inevitable, so he decided not to cancel the conference, but did change the ground rules: only one reporter was allowed to ask questions, an assignment that went to the *Daily News*'s John Chapman, while the others took notes; Chapman's line of inquiry, O'Neill insisted, was to adhere strictly to *Mourning Becomes Electra*—no questions related to the Barton suicide would be permitted.

At the interview, Chapman said, O'Neill "was pallid and shaking and sweating when he faced his lone inquisitor, and so was I."[124] "Do you feel that you've derived any benefit from living abroad," Chapman asked him, had he "been able to see America any more clearly, for example?" "I feel that is the greatest benefit I have derived from living abroad," O'Neill agreed. "It has enabled me to see America more clearly—also to appreciate it more. . . . Most people who travel abroad get the sort of snobbish idea that they are coming in contact with something superior. I don't feel that way. I have talked with a great many people in the theater over there—I don't mean the critics, but the people who are working in it. They feel that it is flat, tired out. They feel that we have something dynamic, and that if we can get their cultural background the rebirth of the theater is not going to happen over there—in Europe—but here. So do I."[125]

When the questioning turned to *Mourning Becomes Electra*, O'Neill responded that without the benefit of soliloquies or masks he'd "tried to get the idea of Fate into it. Not exactly the Greek idea, but Fate more from the point of view of modern psychology." "My personal interest in the theater is to see just how much can be done with it—not only for my sake, but for everybody's sake. The more it is pushed out, the more can be done with it. That is why I am interested in seeing how this play is received." Chapman asked him whether he really cared about its reception. "Of course I care," O'Neill shot back, raising his voice for the first time. "I've been working like a Trappist monk for a year and a half."[126]

After ninety minutes or so, Chapman noticed that O'Neill had begun to look like "a man repressing himself with a mighty effort. He flushed intermittently and his earnest eyes flashed. Once he seemed on the point of breaking into a rage. That was when reporters pressed him for news of his wife's whereabouts." O'Neill denied having ever met Barton himself, but the questioning over Monterey's current location became intolerable. Now visibly unhinged, O'Neill shouted, "This isn't fair!" at which point a Guild member called him out of the room. The playwright reappeared briefly to thank the journalists, then exited the building up and down its fire escapes and across the rooftops.[127]

In early June, O'Neill and Monterey checked out of the Madison and moved to Northport, Long Island, where they rented a cottage for the summer. The beachfront property they found on Long Island's North Shore was close enough to New York to commute to meetings with the Theatre Guild and for friends and family to visit, yet far enough away from the city's nonstop distractions for O'Neill to plan for his upcoming production and revise the galleys for the book publication of *Mourning Becomes Electra*.[128] Their isolation at Plessis had nonetheless convinced even this taciturn playwright that he and Monterey needed to socialize more, so they leased a duplex penthouse at 1095 Park Avenue once he'd completed his *Electra* revisions.

The couple chose not, despite their close relationship to Eugene Jr., now twenty-one years old, to attend Eugene's wedding on June 15 to a girl from Queens named Elizabeth "Betty" Green. The ceremony was to take place in nearby Long Island City, and O'Neill no doubt wished to avoid a demoralizing reunion with Kathleen Jenkins; but this explanation is incomplete. He and Monterey had expressed only admiration and respect for Jenkins to Eugene and Jenkins herself. More to the point, given his history with Jenkins and Boulton, O'Neill had little faith in rash marital unions, especially when families got involved: "Even in the case of marriage," he'd told Eugene after denying him a visit to Plessis with Betty Green in 1930, "you might have only to go back to your Mother and me. If families had been kept out of it we might have had a chance. I must confess, with the guy I was then, the chance was slim and she was probably well rid of me—but you never can tell how much family interference and prejudices had to do with it."[129] (Eugene Jr. and Betty Green would divorce, childless, six years later.)

Rehearsals started for *Mourning Becomes Electra* in early September. This time, with *Dynamo*'s failure still fresh in his mind, O'Neill had a firm hand in the casting, set design, and script changes. Philip Moeller, who once again directed, would ask him, "Don't you think we ought to cut that line?" or "Don't you think we need a line or two here?" After a short silence, O'Neill would curtly respond, "No."[130] "I don't feel that Lavinia could ever sit down and smack her lips over a good slice of roast beef," actress Alice Brady asked him of her character Lavinia Mannon. "Could she?" That's right, he said, she couldn't. And that was the end of it.[131]

"Few people realize the shock a playwright gets when he sees his work acted," O'Neill lamented about these rehearsals. "I saw a different work from the one I thought I had written." "After you've finished a play and it goes into rehearsal," he said, echoing his chat with Jimmy Light six years before, "it begins to go from you. No matter how good the production is, or how able the actors, something is lost—your own vision of the play, the way you saw it in your imagination."[132]

After an uncommonly long rehearsal time because of the play's length (starting the first of fourteen scenes at four o'clock and lasting, with intermission at six for dinner, five and a half hours), *Mourning Becomes Electra* premiered at the Guild Theatre on October 26, 1931.

Along with the usual suspects, Commins, Macgowan, Weinberger, and Madden, other notables in the audience included the satiric wordsmith Dorothy Parker, the recent Pulitzer Prize–winning playwright Elmer Rice, and the vaudeville impresario Martin Beck. When the curtain fell for the last time, the audience members leapt to their feet and erupted into boisterous cries of "Author, author!" As usual, no appearance was forthcoming. "While there was time to ransack most of the town for the author," wrote one reporter in attendance that night, "he could not be found."[133]

Mourning Becomes Electra ran for 150 performances in New York and, surpassing the laurels heaped on *Strange Interlude*, brought O'Neill the highest critical acclaim he would receive. "There is no niggling reservation or hedging about this one," John Anderson raved in the *New York Evening Journal*. "It is O'Neill's masterpiece, if the word has any meaning left, and it bears the mark of true and enduring greatness."[134] John Mason Brown of the *New York Post* concurred: *Mourning Becomes Electra*, he said, "towers above the scrubby output of our present-day theatre as the Empire State Building soars above the skyline of Manhattan." Brooks Atkinson, in his *New York Times* review, announced that the trilogy was "Mr. O'Neill's masterpiece. . . . In sustained thought and workmanship it is his finest tragedy," and George Jean Nathan began his review with "the simple fact first. In 'Mourning Becomes Electra' Eugene O'Neill has written one of the most important plays in the history of American Drama, most of the other few most important plays, incidentally, having also been written by him."[135]

O'Neill could always count on detractors, of course. Elizabeth Jordan, in a febrile notice for the Catholic weekly *America*, was one of the few left unimpressed: "The dead, the dying, the insane, the abnormal, filled the stage before us," she wrote. "To a cheery start-off of two murders [O'Neill] had added two suicides and tossed in a heavy seasoning of vengeance, insanity, adultery and incest." That O'Neill relinquished any veneer of catharsis was evident when a playgoer seated next to Jordan placed her wet handkerchief on her breast and remarked weakly to her escort, "I think I should have been happier if I had never seen this play." Theresa Helburn overheard someone in the lobby say, "Gosh, isn't it good to get back out into the depression again!" But these predictable reactions were the exception, not the rule. "Although most of us have been brought up to bow and genuflect before the majesty of Greek tragedy," Brooks Atkinson wrote in his *Times* review, "it has remained for Mr. O'Neill to show us why."[136]

That November 1931, O'Neill reconnected with his son Shane, who'd just turned twelve and had started attending Lawrenceville Academy, in New Jersey, and his daughter, Oona, now a bashful six-year-old. The reunion, their first in three years, was awkward and brief. First they had lunch at O'Neill's Park Avenue apartment and then took a tour around Central Park in his new Cadillac, during which Oona vomited her dinner of beef kidneys into her appalled stepmother's lap. "GOOD GOD CHILD!" Monterey roared. "Why didn't you SAY SOMETHING?! We could have stopped the car. You must have KNOWN you felt sick! The new car! Poor Shane!" "It's not her fault, she felt sick," she tried to calm herself, "but why didn't she SAY SOMETHING!"[137]

Also that fall, O'Neill made the acquaintance of his mother-in-law, Nellie Tharsing, and Cynthia Chapman, Monterey's teenage daughter from her second marriage. Tharsing had raised Cynthia for over a decade, but she hoped now to end her (rather longer than expected) tenure as surrogate mother. But Monterey was no more interested in motherhood than Tharsing, so Cynthia was sent away to a Connecticut boarding school. O'Neill took a great paternal interest in Cynthia, far more so than any he displayed with his own children. In time, he even felt close enough to send her progress reports on his writing and poke fun at her mother's "super-efficient home management," as seen from his eyes and those of their Dalmatian, Blemie: "Your Mama is sure a demon housekeeper! I expect any day that she's going to grab me absent-mindedly and have me varnished, vacuum-cleaned, and polished with floor wax before I have a chance to resist! Every time Blemie sees an ad for Sapolio or Dutch Cleanser he shudders with dread!"[138]

In mid-November, after several grueling months of rewrites and rehearsals, O'Neill and Monterey availed themselves of a vacation and drove southward through Charleston, South Carolina, on to Savannah and then Brunswick, Georgia. From there they ferried across to Sea Island, a remote paradisiacal outpost among the "Golden Isles" off the Georgia coast. It took only a few days' rest at a fashionable new resort, the Cloisters, before they'd contacted the Sea Island Company's real estate agent George Boll. Soon they bought a lush expanse of seaside property, on the far side of the island from the Cloisters, at the rock-bottom Depression-era price of $12,600. When the stock market dropped again just weeks after the sale, and their new neighbors were hit hard, O'Neill and Monterey bought another lot adjoining their property for $5,000. Boll then introduced them to the Georgian architect Francis Louis Abreu, whom they hired to construct a grand but tasteful villa in the then fashionable Mediterranean style.

George Jean Nathan had to laugh. Whatever idyllic locale O'Neill happened upon in his travels, his crow call would arrive in the mail: it was "ideal," "the place for me," "the best ever." Provincetown: "ideal, quiet and the only place I could ever work." Bermuda: "I've gotten more work done that in the corresponding season up North in many years." Belgrade Lakes: "A place to think and work if ever there was one! Ideal for me." London: "I've been happier here since I left New York than ever in my life before." Guéthary: "I've felt a deep sense of peace here, a real enjoyment in just living from day to day, that I've never known before." Saigon: "This is the place! There is nothing more beautiful and interesting in the world. It is grand!" Touraine: "This is the place for me! . . . Here is the ideal place to live and work!" Granada: "What a place to live and work in!" New York: "Why I ever left here, damned if I know. There's life and vitality here. It's the place for ideas! This is the spot for me and my work." And now, perhaps his most unlikely retreat yet, Sea Island, Georgia: "The best place to live and work I've ever found!"[139]

O'Neill's latest writer's paradise was unique, at least, insofar as he was going to have his home custom built this time; and he and Monterey hunkered down in New York during the bitterly cold winter of 1931–32 while the first phases of its construction got under way. Early that May, they returned to oversee the final stages of building and land-

scaping, the specifications of which Monterey had painstakingly directed by mail from New York. They also hired two full-time servants, a
Georgian man-of-all-work named Herbert Freeman, who would live
in an apartment above the garage, and a cook, Vera Massey. The villa
had two wings separated by a terracotta courtyard and connected to the
main entranceway of the house, with separate suites for O'Neill and
Monterey on the second floor. "The Great Room," below Monterey's
side, was designed to approximate a medieval theater, while O'Neill's
wing was built to resemble the stern leveling of an eighteenth-century
galleon. His office on the second floor was where the captain's quarters
would be. It had an iron spiral staircase winding up to a lookout, like at
Peaked Hill, with a wide vista of the Atlantic Ocean. On June 22 they
moved in, and five days later they christened the villa "Casa Genotta,"
a portmanteau of their union: "The House of Gene + Carlotta."

House & Garden published a feature-length spread on Casa
Genotta describing its architectural design as "a combination of the
early Majorcan peasant house of the 16th Century tinctured with a
flavor of the 15th Century monastery found in such houses in Sierra

Architectural drawing of Casa Genotta, 1931. Carlotta Monterey referred
to its architectural design as "bastard Spanish peasant style."

✳   ✳   ✳

de Cordova as the estate of the Marquesa del Merito." For the benefit of guests, Monterey boiled this down to more concise terminol-
ogy: "bastard Spanish peasant style."[140] The interior was decorated
with austerity; but several personal flourishes indicated that you were
in the sanctified residence of O'Neill and Monterey. Japanese Noh
masks glared at visitors as they stepped through the front entrance;
the guestroom door on the ground floor had been imported from
a Mexican brothel, with iron bars and a slot through which money
had passed. For Monterey, the walls were adorned with Catholic
iconography, making the general atmosphere inside more chapel
than brothel-like. Gothic niches were cut into the walls to accommodate statuettes of Jesus and Mary. Even the medicine cabinet above
Monterey's bathroom sink was cut in the shape of a gothic niche; its
door was a mirror, where her own face replaced the Holy Mother's.

On July 1, 1931, during a visit to New York, O'Neill and Monterey
took the long drive out to New London. O'Neill idled his Cadillac on
Pequot Avenue in front of Monte Cristo Cottage, though Monterey
had advised against it. "Don't do it, darling," she pleaded, "don't ever try
to go back." But he did, and the homestead struck him as much smaller
than he remembered. It was definitely shabbier, in complete disrepair,
actually, and the rear of the house had been demolished. Seeing it for
the first time, Monterey later averred, "I was thunderstruck when I saw
this quaint little birdcage of a house sitting there." "I shouldn't have
come," O'Neill said. "Well, never mind, you have come now," she replied, "let's get out of here." "Yes," he agreed, "let's get away."[141]

But over a year later, it turned out that their disquieting visit to
Monte Cristo Cottage hadn't been time wasted. On the morning of
September 1, 1932, O'Neill awoke from a dream at Casa Genotta
with the setting (Monte Cristo Cottage), plot, characters, themes, and
even the title of a four-act play "fully formed and ready to write."[142]
He'd been struggling over another God-replacement play when this
idea, a comedy, descended on him that morning: *Ah, Wilderness!*

Ah, Wilderness! takes place during New London's 1906 Fourth
of July celebration, at which time O'Neill was preparing to head off

to Princeton. The play is a sentimental portrait of the Miller family, a happy, middle-class New England clan of the kind that contrasted sharply with O'Neill's own family and which he acutely longed to have been born into: "That's the way I would have *liked* my boyhood to have been," he said. "It was a sort of wishing out loud."[143] Nevertheless, Richard Miller, the child poet character at the play's center, shares a great deal with his creator, and beneath the veneer of the Millers' innocence lies more than a touch of cynical reality. *Ah, Wilderness!* would compel audiences to face the social and economic realities of America in the 1930s in contrast with his dreamlike portrait of a happier, simpler age. At the conclusion of *Ah, Wilderness!* everything turns out as it should, the fixed definition of a "comedy"—that is, until you step back into the despair of the Great Depression and, as O'Neill phrased it, the "corrupting, disintegrating influences" of the last three decades.[144]

Not since *Desire Under the Elms* had a play sprung from his imagination so fully and effortlessly. It was, he told Eugene Jr., "more the capture of a mood, an evocation [of] the spirit of a time that is dead now with all its ideals and manners & codes—the period in which my middle 'teens were spent—a memory of the time of my youth—not of *my* youth but of the youth in which my generation spent youth."[145] (O'Neill dedicated *Ah, Wilderness!* to George Jean Nathan, "who also," he said, "once upon a time, in peg-top trousers went the pace that kills along the road to ruin.")[146]

After only three weeks, some days working in excess of twelve hours at a time, O'Neill had completed a first draft. "It simply gushed out of me," he told Saxe Commins, who was now his editor at Horace Liveright. "Evidently my unconscious had been rebelling for a long time against creation in the medium of the modern, involved, complicated, warped & self-poisoned psyche and demanded a counterstatement of simplicity and the peace that tragedy troubles but does not poison. The people in the play are of the class which I get least credit for knowing but which I really know better than any other— my whole background of New London childhood, boyhood, young manhood—the nearest approach to home I ever knew." He was proud of the script but wary of the critical response: "I feel a great affection for it, so great that I don't know whether I'll ever subject it to the humiliation of production or publication."[147]

O'Neill and Monterey had survived the first years of the Great Depression relatively unscathed financially, if only for the time being, while countless friends and associates were left destitute. Their mail piled up with pleas for cash from New London, New York, Provincetown, and California. Old business associates wrote asking for money, like George C. Tyler, who admitted that it was "humiliating" to prostrate himself. O'Neill assured Tyler that he understood but couldn't help. "In short," he wrote Tyler disingenuously, "my story is the story of everyone today."[148] Others, perhaps more deserving in O'Neill's eyes, received a check with apologies that it couldn't be more.

The O'Neills' stability had largely been thanks to the huge income from *Strange Interlude*; and after France, *Mourning Becomes Electra* filled the coffers and paid for the Sea Island property. But their solvency was also due to the fact that neither he nor Monterey, though they too lost a small fortune in stocks and bonds, had overly speculated. "All that trouble," Monterey wrote after the crash of 1929, "was caused by the *wise ones* using Wall Street as a roulette wheel to gamble on & further their get-rich quick schemes."[149] Some of O'Neill's hardest-hit friends began raising funds by selling items he'd given them. Boulton sold a first edition of *Beyond the Horizon* O'Neill inscribed to his parents (which he retrieved from a dealer for $200), and Harold de Polo wrote to ask if he might sell a scenario of *The Hairy Ape*.[150]

But soon enough they became "house poor." O'Neill's collected royalties from *Mourning Becomes Electra* had been sunk into Casa Genotta, and even the conservative stocks and bonds they'd invested in had suddenly turned worthless. Their geographical location had its advantages, though: "Georgia is a very good spot to spend the depression in—at least, this backward neck of it," he wrote the Guild's publicity man Robert Sisk. "The only depression they've caught up with is the one inaugurated by General Sherman and General Hookworm. . . . One thing I know, starving isn't on the cards for anyone down here no matter what happens. Fish, oysters, shrimps, clams, game are to be bagged even by the laziest. . . . Perhaps it was Providence that guides me here, having an eye to the future when I become too lazy and disgusted to bother the Drama further!"[151]

In early May 1933, it became clear to Saxe Commins that his employer, O'Neill's publisher Horace Liveright, was about to go bankrupt. While the publishing house was postponing the inevitable, Commins called a meeting with the principal stockholders and gave them an ultimatum: either they provided O'Neill with the balance of his royalties for *Mourning Becomes Electra* and other projects, in full and within twenty-four hours, or he'd print an announcement in book pages of the *New York Times* that O'Neill was signing with a competitor. The blackmail worked; a certified check for the total amount landed on Commins's desk that same afternoon. He then took a train down to Georgia and presented O'Neill with the check. After Liveright went belly up that month, every other writer on its list was paid a meager 5 percent of his or her royalties.[152] Commins's swift action on O'Neill's behalf meant that the playwright was not only his best friend and godfather of Commins's infant son, named Eugene after him, but indebted to him financially too.

Thus when Bennett Cerf of Random House arrived on Sea Island to discuss a contract, O'Neill, who trusted Cerf right away and was prepared to sign, insisted that Commins be granted a three-year trial to carry on as his editor. For his part, Cerf thought O'Neill was "the most beautiful man I ever met . . . to look at him was soul-satisfying. He looked just the way a great playwright ought to but practically never does."[153] He gladly accepted the terms. It was a good deal for Random House over time, Commins worked there closely with other illustrious authors, including William Faulkner, Theodore Dreiser, Sinclair Lewis, William Carlos Williams, W. H. Auden, Gertrude Stein, and Theodore Geisel (Dr. Seuss). The journalist Murray Kempton remarked that "no writer who ever had him for an editor would ever take another," and Cerf later affirmed that Commins turned out to be "almost more important to us than O'Neill."[154]

Eugene Jr. had returned to Germany as a graduate student at the University of Freiburg in the fall semester of 1932. Despite his high regard for German literature and culture, by spring he'd grown despondent over the rise of the Nazi Party. He wanted to come home but worried that his father, who was paying the bills, would think he'd wasted his money frivolously. On the contrary, O'Neill responded, "Do I think your plans denote incipient insanity in the family? Far from it! I approve in toto! . . . [I] was afraid you might have fallen under the youthfully enthusiastic spell of the Hitler hokum. My own opinion of the Nazi movement is that it is the prize clowning of this doleful era of moronic antics! The stupidity of it is simply beyond belief—the incredible misunderstanding of the psychology of other peoples and the boomerang effect of that blunder! Really, it's hard to have any patience with the Germans now. . . . Here, after years of effort by their sensible leaders—and helped by the miserly gluttony of France—the world was all set to think pro-German—and now, smash!" (O'Neill's opinions of Mussolini were as low as of Hitler: "May wild jackasses of the desert piss on the grave of his grandmother!")[155]

Monterey, who owned German bonds, was less discerning about the Nazis. After the composer Louis Gruenberg, a Lithuanian Jew who'd written an operatic version of *The Emperor Jones* for New York's Metropolitan Opera, publicly voiced disappointment that his efforts had gone unappreciated, Monterey raged, "I hope somebody puts Gruenberg in his place. But he can't be insulted—his skin's too thick. . . . Enough of him—may Hitler catch him!"[156]

In August 1933, O'Neill and Monterey escaped the clammy heat of the Golden Isles for a month of pike fishing, swimming, and canoeing at Big Wolf Lake Camp near the Adirondack town of Tupper Lake, New York.[157] From there they attended rehearsals for *Ah, Wilderness!* then flew down to see a September 25 matinee of the out-of-town run at Pittsburgh's Nixon Theater. The play's October 2 New York premiere at the Guild Theatre heralded a remarkable production, critically and financially, which would run for a staggering 289 performances.

O'Neill's turn toward nostalgic Americana beguiled audiences unused to the "black magician" working outside his notoriously tragic vein. During intermissions, the theater buzzed with conjecture, summed up in one audience member's interjection after the final curtain, "Whatever possessed O'Neill to write a play like this!" Elizabeth Jordan of *America* reported that the Broadway gossips suspected that his wife's influence explained the dramatic about-face; in which case, Jordan said, she "should receive the Pulitzer Prize, the Nobel award, and the honorary degree of Doctor of Letters from every American college and university."[158] The gossips weren't far off the mark. Monterey had indeed alleviated much of her husband's painful sense of alienation, if only temporarily, and his drama had evolved to match this fleeting mood of peace and salvation.

One disarmingly fitting choice for O'Neill's "Comedy of Recollection," as it was subtitled (the Theatre Guild advertised it as "An American Folk Play"), was the highly sought-after actor cast as Nat Miller, George M. Cohan. Nat Miller is O'Neill's ideal middle-class head of the household—a good provider, a natural leader, caring, intellectually open-minded when circumstances call for it, and ferociously protective of his family. George M. Cohan, an old friend of James O'Neill's and the most beloved song-and-dance man of the World War I era, had up to then been principally regarded as a purveyor of musical comedies. He was a popular composer too, having written such trademark ditties for the American stage as "Give My Regards to Broadway," "The Yankee Doodle Boy," and "You're a Grand Old Flag." The man was even born on the Fourth of July. Cohan's Yankee Doodle patriotism, surprisingly, didn't trouble O'Neill, who declared that the casting was spot on: "I really didn't mean the setting [of the Fourth of July] as a shrewd device to lure Mr. Cohan to a part I wanted him for," he said, "but I realize now he was amused at the connection the date has with his own career." (He later referred to Cohan more candidly as "a vaudevillian who tried to turn the play into a one-man show.")[159]

Most agreed with John Mason Brown's concise assessment of *Ah, Wilderness!* in the *New York Evening Post:* "Mr. O'Neill has laid aside his Tragic Mask. Forgetting about Freud, 'the stream of consciousness,' the conflict between science and religion, the purple melodramas of the Greeks, the multiple natures and obsessions of his fellow mortals, and the fierce struggles his men and women have waged for

years against merciless gods, he has written in 'Ah, Wilderness!' a comedy about 'sweet scented youth' which is unlike any other play that
has come from his pen."[160] Hollywood took note. Two weeks after the
premiere, MGM Studios, which had produced the tamed-down film
version of *Strange Interlude*, paid him $75,000 for the film rights.[161]

It was time to return to more serious work. The previous summer,
1932, George Jean Nathan offered O'Neill an ideal opportunity to
collect his thoughts on the use of masks in drama. Nathan had talked
O'Neill into serving on the editorial board of his new literary journal
the *American Spectator*, in which O'Neill's name would appear on the
masthead beside Nathan, Theodore Dreiser, Ernest Boyd, and James
Branch Cabell. As a favor to Nathan, O'Neill agreed, if reluctantly, and
the playwright's first assignment was to write an essay on modern theater for the inaugural issue. He accepted the challenge but found prose
writing as difficult as ever. (He would even procrastinate on replying
to letters until it became offensively late to write, then he'd wait a few
days, weeks, or months more.) He'd already backed out on writing the
introduction for a book of Hart Crane's poetry, *White Buildings* (1926;
Crane had, tragically, thrown himself off a steamship into the Gulf
of Mexico that April of 1932), though O'Neill had found it in him to
contribute the foreword for the polemicist, journalist, and poet Benjamin De Casseres's *Anathema! Litanies of Negation* in 1928; but he'd
warned De Casseres from the start that he was "an awful bum at such
writing."[162] (They'd befriended one another in August 1927, after De
Casseres published a piece on O'Neill in *Theatre Magazine* in which he
described O'Neill as a figure who "almost awed me . . . a grim, unsmil-
ing face taut with suffering, he seemed to say to me: 'Excuse me for not
being nice, but I've just returned from hell.' ")[163]

"My old bean simply can't seem to get started functioning on
such lines," O'Neill admitted to Nathan while writing his essay. "It's
the same as if I asked you to write a play."[164] Still, working through
his ideas on masks sufficiently appealed to him—"the only subject I
can get up enough interest in"—to spend a week cobbling together
his disjointed notes from over the years and produce a coherent, if
epigrammatic, treatise.[165] Divided into three installments, the essay

appeared in *American Spectator*'s first three issues.[166] Within this series, titled "Memoranda on Masks" and his only contribution in the *Spectator*'s short-lived existence, O'Neill distilled his "dogma for the new masked drama" into a single line, one that shows a logical extension of the philosophical anarchist's credo that social forces shape inauthentic lives from both society and ourselves: "One's outer life passes in a solitude haunted by the masks of others; one's inner life passes in a solitude hounded by the masks of oneself."[167]

"Memoranda on Masks" also hints at his next play, in which, he said, Goethe's *Faust* would "have Mephistopheles wearing the Mephistophelean mask of the face of Faust. For is not the whole of Goethe's truth *for our time* just that Mephistopheles and Faust are one and the same—*are* Faust?"[168]

O'Neill had struggled through seven drafts of this Faustian mask play from late 1931 to early 1934. "But that's all in the life of an author," he told his stepdaughter Cynthia about the difficulty of writing as a profession. "It's always that way. You puff and sweat and groan inwardly, and like yourself and hate yourself, and after a long time, just when you're reaching for the insect powder to take a good gob and put yourself out of your misery, the darn thing somehow gets finished and you realize you've really done something good and get quite fond of yourself again. Or you realize it's punk—and you start to rewrite the whole thing."[169]

A note to himself reads, "Again reach same old impasse—play always goes dead on me here where it needs to be most alive or I go dead on it—something fundamentally wrong."[170] But he did finish it, and after several iterations ("Ending of Days," "Without End of Days," "An End of Days") eventually nailed down its title, *Days Without End: A Modern Miracle Play*.[171]

"The Game Isn't Worth the Candle"

Days Without End was arguably the most abysmal failure of O'Neill's career. When the Theatre Guild moved its production from Boston to New York's Henry Miller's Theatre on January 8, 1934, the four-act play received dreadful reviews and barely survived six weeks. O'Neill's new production, as former New York governor Al Smith succinctly remarked, was a "hot potato."[172] The giant swell of goodwill O'Neill had recouped after *Ah, Wilderness!* receded into oblivion after its release, with notices rejecting the play as "heavy-handed and pretentious," "fakery preachment," "holy hokum," and "reactionary." Even critics who revered O'Neill as America's foremost playwright were taken aback by its heavy-handed piety. "Sometimes Mr. O'Neill tells his story as though he had never written a play before," Brooks Atkinson wrote in bewilderment. "In view of his acknowledged mastery of the theatre it is astonishing that his career can be so uneven." Not only was *Days Without End* condemned for plunging below O'Neill's talent, its Catholic message also outraged his usual fan base; the play, one critic noted, "is not modern enough, I fear, for moderns."[173]

Days Without End was originally conceived as a segment of his planned trilogy "God Is Dead! Long Live—What?" The action unfolds in the midst of a spiritual crisis by a freethinking novelist named John Loving. John has a masked doppelgänger named Loving, the Mephistopheles to John's Faust, who looms over him and scorns his incessant yearning for salvation. John's wife, Elsa, soon discovers that he has committed adultery with her best friend. At first she refuses to forgive him and attempts suicide by exposing herself, sick with the flu, to the cold and rain of the Manhattan streets. After Elsa has been retrieved and languishes near death in their apartment bedroom, John takes a long walk and wanders into a Catholic church. A brilliant wash of sunlight shines through the stained-glass windows, and the face of the crucified savior lights up. In the throes of a spiritual transformation, John is informed by his uncle, a priest, that his wife, Elsa, has revived. His doppelgänger Loving dies at his feet as he shouts in glory, "Loves lives forever. . . . Life laughs with God's love again! Life laughs with love!" The curtain falls (*CP*3, 180).

To O'Neill's great consternation, because of the play's evident religiosity, the Catholic community largely venerated *Days Without End;* it fared so well in Catholic-dominated Boston, in fact, that at its first showing on December 27, 1933, it received fifteen curtain calls.[174] The Nobel Prize–winning poet William Butler Yeats also produced

Stanley Ridges (left) as Loving and Earle Larimore as John in the final
scene of *Days Without End* at Henry Miller's Theatre, New York, 1934.
(COURTESY OF THE YALE COLLECTION OF AMERICAN LITERATURE, BEINECKE RARE BOOK
AND MANUSCRIPT LIBRARY, NEW HAVEN)

✳   ✳   ✳

the play successfully on April 16, 1934, at Dublin's Abbey Theatre to celebrate the anniversary of the Easter Rising. (*Days Without
End* was banned, unsurprisingly, in the atheist-run Soviet Union.)[175]
"Eugene O'Neill," wrote one pious admirer, "former Catholic, cynic
of cynics . . . delver into the dark and oppressive secrets of sex-crazed

New Englanders ... has written the great Catholic play of the age."
Another called O'Neill's jeering critics "the minions of the Anti-Christ
... pseudo-intellectuals who hide their ignorance under the misapprehension that faith is outmoded." Few were more pleasantly surprised
by the playwright's apparent return to God than Gerard B. Donnelly,
S.J., of *America* magazine. Father Donnelly decreed that *Days* had a
"profound significance" for "all who glory in the Christian name."[176]

Saxe Commins, when he first read the script, uttered evasively that
he appreciated O'Neill's innovative use of the mask; but Monterey was
certain he was holding something back. When Commins then admitted that the religious aspect of the final scene seemed overwrought,
she rebuked him with contempt: "Gene and I nearly had a fit when we
saw you had taken the end of the play quite from the wrong angle. It
has *nothing* to do with *Christianity* or *prayer* that brings Elsa back—it
is her *great & all consuming love for her husband!* Thro' her love she
senses that her husband is in danger & that *love* gives her the strength
to *come back* & live for him—We suppose *no one* will understand that
tho'—that you didn't!"[177] "I think Gene has forgotten," she wrote in
her diary, cutting both ways, "that Saxe is *very Jewish* + *very radical* + a
play about the Christian faith being important for the happiness of a
man—would seem to him both childish + a bore!" That summer, 1933,
when George Jean Nathan read the script, she noted again in her diary, "Geo. Jean won't like 'D.W.E.' because he can't tolerate any play
with religion playing an important part!"[178] She was correct, of course,
and Commins and Nathan were in the majority.

Benjamin De Casseres went so far as to pen a razor-sharp lampoon titled "Denial Without End," in which a winged demon whisks
the playwright away to confront an assortment of his characters:
Lazarus, Marco Polo, Yank, Brutus Jones, Nina Leeds, Sam Evans,
Charlie Marsden, Ponce de León, Chris Christopherson, Abbie Putnam, and Lavinia Mannon each mock him in turn for offering his
soul back to the Church and reprimand him for selling out. O'Neill's
stand-in, named John Loving in De Casseres's satire, responds fatuously (and here it genuinely gets cruel), "It was all right while I was
poor, neurotic and had no château in France, no swanky Park Avenue

apartment. It was first-rate stuff—and you were a great pal!—before I made my pile, found my Isolde-Juliet-Brunnhilde [Monterey] and changed Friend Swig for Friend Swank. But now, I tell you, I'm a gentleman! To hell with your spittle-spattle about artistic creation and its spiritual jim-jams. I'm saved!" Thinking it was all in good fun, De Casseres sent a copy to O'Neill. He didn't hear back, and they never spoke again.[179]

In the fall of 1933, the Catholic Writers Guild hounded Cerf to change Elsa from a divorcée to a widow for the book version—if, that is, he wanted it to appear on their White List (plays that a committee of laymen decides are appropriate for children).[180] O'Neill told Cerf, who welcomed any helpful publicity, that even if the play was "about a Catholic . . . it is also a psychological study," whatever the religious overtone. If Cerf ignored his wishes on this, he threatened, he'd be forced "to oil up the family automatic and surge forth and eliminate you from our midst! . . . *It is not Catholic propaganda!* If, after it comes out, the Church wants to set the seal of its approval on it, well that's up to them. But I don't give a damn whether they do or not—and I certainly will not make the slightest move to win that approval in advance."[181]

Despite his atheism, O'Neill had always been enticed by the promise of an afterlife, of moral and spiritual certainty, and of Catholicism's alleviation of guilt through confession. In a letter to Sophus Keith Winther, a scholar from the University of Washington who was hurrying to include *Days Without End* in his 1934 book-length study of the playwright, O'Neill clarified this as best he could: "But the end [of the play] hardly means that I have gone back to Catholicism. I haven't. But I would be a liar if I didn't admit that, for the sake of my soul's peace, I have often wished I could. And by Catholicism I don't mean the Catholic church as a politically-meddling, social-reactionary force. That repels me. I mean the mystic faith of Catholicism whose symbols seem to me to approach closer than any other symbols to the apprehension of a hidden spiritual significance in human life."[182]

Brooks Atkinson, in an attempt to come to grips with the play, quoted Henry David Thoreau, who, when asked if he'd made peace with God, replied, "We have never quarreled." In contrast, Atkinson said, O'Neill's quarrel with the Almighty had finally conquered his atheism, since nothing replaces God in the play but God himself. Similarly, Dorothy Day observed decades later in "Told in Context" that "Gene's relations with his God was a warfare in itself. He fought with God to the end of his days. He rebelled against man's fate. [crossed out:] He shook his fist at God." Other friends were convinced that Monterey's embrace of Catholicism had invidiously taken hold in her husband. Monterey's ecumenical prodding may have made his turn to religion more explicit in the case of *Days Without End;* but O'Neill had already envisaged his inner life as Catholic prior to her arrival—in spiritual sensibility if not in actual faith—such as with the maskless Dion Anthony (St. Anthony) in *The Great God Brown.* But another explanation might be found in the most important female figure of his life who, along with Monterey, had returned to the Church for its "mystic faith" that provided "soul's peace"—Ella O'Neill.[183]

Ella had been devastated by her son Eugene's resolve to snub the Church at fourteen, the age he learned of her drug addiction, and Catholicism in *Days Without End* saves through forgiveness and love, strongly suggesting his mother's experience in recovery. Ella had overcome her addiction by returning to a spiritual state of mind, one that only the Church could afford her. Starting in June 1914, she'd ended her over twenty-five-year habit by cloistering herself at a Brooklyn convent and attending Mass each Sunday. Even when faced with the pain and disfigurement of her mastectomy in 1918, she'd never returned to the drug for good. (For O'Neill, an end to the churning nightmare at the heart of *Long Day's Journey Into Night* must have seemed the true stuff of his earlier play's subtitle, "A Modern Miracle.") Ella, of course, is one letter off from Elsa, John Loving's wife. Hence, O'Neill was paying off an "old debt" to the Church, as he told Lawrence Langner, for saving his mother; at the same time he asserted that "any life-giving formula," no matter how archaic and restrictive, should be regarded "as fit a subject for drama as any other."[184]

O'Neill also clarified John Loving's saving grace through Catholicism in a revealing 1935 letter to his Argentine translator Leon Mirlas: "I chose Catholicism because it is the only Western religion which has the stature of a real Faith, because it is the religion of the old miracle plays and the Faustian legend which were the sources of my theme—and last and most simply because it happens to be the religion of my [Irish . . . background, tradition, and] early training and therefore the one I know most about."[185] But when pressed elsewhere as to whether he'd in point of fact rediscovered his Catholic faith, O'Neill responded bluntly, "Unfortunately, no."[186]

"What am I doing now?" O'Neill, recovering from defeat back at Casa Genotta, replied to a letter from Kenneth Macgowan in February of 1934. "Loafing determinedly. I feel as stale as a mousetrap cheese on the theatre. I won't start anything new for a long while. I'm fed up." O'Neill's doctors had ordered six months of "compulsory rest," but then another crisis came to a head.[187] Two years earlier, on March 18, 1932, the O'Neills were in a car accident that returned to torment them that April 1934: Herbert Freeman had been driving O'Neill and Monterey down the Hutchinson River Parkway in Westchester County when they collided into the car of a Bronx elevator operator named Louis Gans and his daughter Isabelle. The Ganses were suing for $28,000. Her husband conspicuously absent, Monterey appeared in front of a jury in a Bronx court on April 12, 1934; she testified that O'Neill was "unfit to work," "very nervous," and physically and mentally incapable of leaving his hotel room. (During the trial, her nerves gave out, and she was escorted by an attorney to a vacant courtroom. O'Neill's attorney, A. J. D'Auria, further explained, in a statement that appeared in the *New York Times*, that his client wasn't able to attend the trial himself because he was, at the time, in the throes of a nervous breakdown. The presiding judge ordered that the Ganses receive $3,200 in damages.)[188]

That April O'Neill declined an invitation to meet the novelist Sherwood Anderson, he apologized to Anderson, because "I've been teetering on the verge of a nervous crack-up recently—too long a stretch of work without any real period of rest, is the doctor's dope— and I'm to be under a strict regime of rest cure here at home for an indefinite period until I can 'come back.' The medicos put it to me cold and claim that either I take time out voluntarily now or go on a complete bust and be laid out for years."[189]

O'Neill's self-removal from the public gaze, at first meant as a six-month hiatus, extended into a near-absolute silence that would last for more than twelve years.

Safely back at her Sea Island redoubt, Monterey labored diligently, in every imaginable capacity, to protect and serve her husband. "I am wife, mistress, housekeeper, secretary, friend & nurse," she wrote Macgowan. "Am everything but his tailor!"[190]

In his first weeks of sequestration, O'Neill mailed off a succession of letters, lashing out at anyone requesting money or work related to the theater. When his agent Richard Madden informed him that several items of their correspondence had been stolen and then turned up in a book dealer's catalogue, O'Neill gave him no quarter: "The more I hear of this dishonorable affair, the sorer I'm getting—and I tell you frankly that the person I am principally sore at is you." When Shane requested a $400 outboard motor as a gift, he angrily responded, "I think you have a lot of nerve to ask for such an expensive present. . . . In short, you have got to prove to me in these coming years that you are not lazily expecting something for nothing but are willing to work for it. Otherwise, you will get nothing. Is that clear? And, believe me, you will find out I mean it!" "No I won't cut a single damned line," he wrote Lee Simonson of the Guild, who was hoping for cuts in its ongoing production of *Ah, Wilderness!* "That's final." "I take my theatre too personally, I guess—," he added, "so personally that before long I think I shall permanently resign from all production and confine my future work to plays in books for readers only. The game isn't worth the candle."[191]

On April 16, 1935, after their initial rebuff, Sherwood Anderson and his wife, Eleanor, were invited to lunch at Casa Genotta. Anderson, in his subsequent thank-you note, told O'Neill what a delight it had been to make the acquaintance of "a man I have looked up to as one of the few great figures of the time." He shared a more dismal tale to a friend, however: Monterey was "cold, calculating. Certainly

Eugene O'Neill and Carlotta Monterey at Casa Genotta in 1933.
(PHOTO BY CARL VAN VECHTEN. COURTESY OF THE CARL VAN VECHTEN ESTATE AND THE
MUSEUM OF THE CITY OF NEW YORK)

* * *

she is not one of the women who make a house warm." Though he'd
told O'Neill he was "delighted to find you at work again and in good
spirits," the other letter was more frank on this subject as well: "Gene
is a sick man. . . . He is a very very sweet fine man but I did feel death
in his big expensive house. He has drawn himself away, lives in that
solitary place, seeing practically no one. He needs his fellow men. I
felt him clinging to me rather pitifully."[192]

As O'Neill worked hard to remove himself from "the game,"
he'd become a trademark of American 1930s pop culture. "If I were
Eugene O'Neill I could tell you what I really think of you two,"
Groucho Marx informs two society ladies competing for his attention in the Marx Brothers' 1930 hit film *Animal Crackers*. "You know,"
he remarks to the jockeying pair, "you're really fortunate the Theatre
Guild isn't putting this on," then adds, "and so is the Guild." Marx excuses himself for a "strange interlude" and somberly faces the camera.

The society ladies freeze while he intones, thespian-like, "How happy I could be with either of these two if both of them just went away."[193]

O'Neill's handlers thought such antics were played at his expense, but the playwright was delighted with them. When comedian Jack Benny requested permission to parody *Ah, Wilderness!* in January 1935, O'Neill dismissed Weinberger's opposition: "GIVE BENNY MY CONSENT TO GO AHEAD WITHOUT CHARGE STOP DON'T AGREE WITH YOU THINK BENNY VERY AMUSING GUY AND BELIEVE KIDDING MY STUFF EVERY ONCE IN A WHILE HAS VERY HEALTHY EFFECT AND HELPS KEEP ME OUT OF DEAD SOLEMN ILLUSTRIOUS STUFFED SHIRT ACADEMICIAN CLASS = GENE"[194] When Al Jolson, the vaudevillian known for his (later notorious) black-faced minstrel routines, asked to produce a live radio version of *The Emperor Jones* in 1934, O'Neill wrote Madden good-naturedly, "I hope Brutus Jones won't burst into 'Mammy!' "[195]

At the same time, O'Neill's avidity for the "talkies" after viewing *Broadway Melody* had mostly subsided, and he took no part in the film adaptations of his plays. He did nudge Robert Sisk, who was attempting to sell *The Hairy Ape* to Hollywood, to adopt a film treatment he'd written in 1926: "Of course, my idea in the screen story, was to build up the attraction-repulsion, hate-lust thing between Yank and Mildred, to make her even more of a bitch."[196] He still hadn't viewed Greta Garbo's famous MGM "Garbo Talks!" version of *"Anna Christie"* in 1930. In her first scene, Garbo slumps down wearily at a table in the back room of Johnny the Priest's and orders a drink from the barman. Moviegoers then heard the starlet's voice for the very first time: "Gimme a whiskey—ginger ale on the side. And don't be stingy, baby." "Well, should I serve it in a pail?" the bartender wisecracks. "Ah," she replies wearily, "that suits me down to the ground."[197]

"I couldn't sit though it without getting the heebie-jeebies and wondering why the hell I ever wrote it," O'Neill said, "even if Joan of Arc came back to play 'Anna.' " But when Grace Rippin informed him that the film had been a hit in New London, he responded, "Yes, it sure would have done me proud" to glimpse his name up in lights on Bank Street. "But I imagine that the talky of *'Anna Christie'* is all to the Garbo and very little of the O'Neill left in it." He did see MGM's

1932 adaptation of *Strange Interlude* but regarded it as a "dreadful hash of attempted condensation and idiotic censorship." He had no desire to go to MGM's *Ah, Wilderness!* of 1935, nor had he seen Paul Robeson play Brutus Jones on the silver screen. O'Neill respected DuBose Heyward, who wrote the screenplay for *The Emperor Jones*, and Dudley Murphy, who directed the film for MGM; but he heard they'd "opened up" the story to include Jones's early years as a Pullman porter and spooned out some "Harlem hooey" for their slumming audiences. He told Macgowan that he'd been told that "in the last stages of the making, rumour has it that everybody concerned started stepping on everyone else—and the result a shoddy compromise." The slave auction and the Middle Passage had been dropped and replaced with, outrageously, an African American Baptist church service—thus brusquely removing the culpability of white America for Jones's betrayal of his race. "However," O'Neill said, "I wail not, I got my money." "They can buy 'em for Movies," he often quipped, "but they can't make me go & see them!"[198] (The great exception would arrive with John Ford's 1940 film *The Long Voyage Home*, based on the *Glencairn* plays, which O'Neill considered the finest picture adapted from his work.)

In 1933, the Eighteenth Amendment was repealed, ending America's fourteen-year prohibition on the sale and purchase of alcohol. And contrary to the perception of O'Neill as abstaining from booze after his calamitous trip to the Far East, Jack London's "White Logic" caught up with him at Sea Island. Even before the repeal, the open secret among locals was that O'Neill and the real estate agent George Boll had installed a distillery for corn whiskey in Herbert Freeman's apartment above the garage.[199] And he would find an ideal drinking companion in the form of a gift from Monterey.

For O'Neill's forty-fifth birthday, October 16, 1933, Monterey ordered a player piano from a defunct New Orleans brothel. Painted over in red roses and nude women, the piano was the finest present O'Neill could imagine, and he affectionately dubbed it Rosie. Rosie came with a box of old music rolls that included "Alexander's

Ragtime Band," "That Mysterious Rag," "All Alone," and "Waiting for the Robert E. Lee."[200] In December 1935, Monterey scolded George Jean Nathan after his Christmas present had arrived. It was a keg of the Brooklyn lager Edelbrau: "What you and Frau Edelbrau have done to our household is shocking," she said. "Casa Genotta is completely demoralized." After tapping Nathan's keg, O'Neill began drinking beer at lunch, beer at teatime, beer at dinner, and beer as a nightcap. "Rosie plays and the Edelbrau flows!" Monterey told Nathan. That week, O'Neill and Boll gathered round Rosie, swilled the lager, and sang along with uproarious abandon. "Gene had a great sense of humor and did his share of talking," Boll recalled of these times with the playwright. "I found him a very human and normal person, which is contrary, I know, to what many thought."[201]

Monterey took her husband's drinking in stride at first; it was only beer after all. But things took a turn for the worse at their Christmas Eve "fête." "We have a bottle of Champagne to drink to Christmas!" she wrote. "Boll + Gene are very gay, play Rosie, sing + dance! I notice Gene keeps going up stairs—finally I go up to see if he is ill—I find him *drinking out of a bottle of whiskey!!* I nearly wept. This is what I had suspected for weeks! He should never have had any beer or wine—it only leads to whiskey, + whiskey leads to the usual excess—sickness + God knows what! When he sees me he laughs + goes downstairs with the bottle. He and Boll finish *the night drinking*."[202]

O'Neill kept on drinking whiskey with abandon for weeks. Though he'd first hid it from Monterey, drinking only in his study, by late February 1935, he was defiantly swilling it right in front of her and straight from the bottle. That same winter, a maid at Casa Genotta overheard an argument erupt between her otherwise emotionally remote employers. O'Neill shouted something inaudible, then said, "There'll be a murder!" For the next two days, the distraught Monterey sat at the dining room table "but wouldn't eat, with the tears rolling down her face."[203]

On a trip to New York that winter, O'Neill hid bottles in several places in the bedroom, bathroom, and closet of his hotel room. On February 21, he was admitted by his physician, Dr. George Draper, to Doctors Hospital in New York for several days in order Draper bluntly informed Monterey, "to get the whiskey out of him." "I am a wreck, + ill," she wrote in her diary. "Haven't eaten all day + had no real rest for nights. Weeping + can't stop."[204] (After O'Neill's death, although only a few episodes can be verified, Monterey swore to a psychiatrist at Harvard Medical School that O'Neill never completely stopped drinking as people believed; rather, according to the psychiatrist, Dr. Albert Rothenberg, he "engaged in periodic alcoholic binges" to the end of his life.)[205]

That March 1935, O'Neill was back on the wagon at Casa Genotta; but he then began suffering from a series of illnesses, including gastritis, prostate problems, and steadily worsening hand tremors that made writing all but impossible. Marshaling his resolve nonetheless, he resumed work on *A Touch of the Poet*, a four-act play about an Irish-American immigrant family called the Melodys (a family name O'Neill borrowed from a black prizefighter from Boston, Honey Melody).[206] Over the next year and a half, he labored on scenarios and drafts for what he'd begun to call *A Tale of Possessors Self-Dispossessed*—an immensely ambitious Cycle (which he always spelled with a capital "C") of historical plays that would include *A Touch of the Poet*, but mainly follow the progress of a New England family, the Harfords, who intermarry with the Melodys. The guiding theme of *A Tale of Possessors Self-Dispossessed* originates from one line in the Bible, Matthew 16:26, which for O'Neill summed up the full sweep of American history: "For what will it profit a man if he gains the whole world and forfeits his soul?"

O'Neill fervently believed that "success" in the American idiom was merely another word for "possession." Through this possessiveness Americans had become dispossessed of their authentic selves, only to repeat the process in order to stamp out the painful disenchantment that follows. One draft of the final play, *The Hair of the Dog*, ends with lines that equate the drunkenness of financial success with actual drunkenness from whiskey: "That's right! A hair of the dog that bit you! ... and they're all the same dog, and his name is Greed of Living and when he bites you there's a fever comes and a great thirst and a great drinking to kill it, and a grand drunk, and a terrible hangover and headache and remorse of conscience—and a sick empty stomach without greed or appetite. But take a hair of the dog and the sun will rise again for you—and the appetite and the thirst will come back, and you can forget—and begin all over!"[207]

A Touch of the Poet, the only Cycle play O'Neill would complete to his satisfaction, takes place in 1828, the year Andrew Jackson defeated the incumbent presidential candidate John Quincy Adams. The race was culturally significant in that Jackson had been the son of a poor Irishman while Adams was born into one of the most prominent families in Massachusetts. Although O'Neill later stated that "the one thing that explains more than anything about me is the fact that I'm Irish," he appeared to contradict himself in declaring, on a separate occasion, that "the battle of moral forces in the New England scene is what I feel closest to as an artist."[208] *A Touch of the Poet* reconciles this presumable inconsistency more than any of his works.

Before the play's action, O'Neill's Irish antihero Con Melody has emigrated with his wife, Nora, and daughter Sara to Massachusetts. Melody, an alcoholic, bought a tavern on a plot of land that promised to serve the railroads; but the rails were never laid down and the tavern fell into disrepair. A former soldier for the British during the Peninsular War (1808–14), Melody proudly wears a military uniform to commemorate his feats of bravery at the Battle of Talavera and quotes poetry while bemoaning the treachery of those around him. He puts on aristocratic airs—a "con," since in fact he's the son of a swindling Irish "shebeen keeper," or unlicensed publican—and habitually poses erect before a large mirror reciting, as his creator might, lines from Byron's "Childe Harold" to bolster his wounded pride:

> I have not loved the World, nor the World me;
> I have not flattered its rank breath, nor bowed
> To its idolatries a patient knee,
> Nor coined my cheek to smiles,—nor cried aloud
> In worship of an echo: in the crowd
> They could not deem me one of such—I stood
> Among them, but not of them. (*CP*3, 203)

Years of acting the part of the landed gentry are shattered when the lawyer of a prominent member of the Yankee establishment named Henry Harford offers Melody a bribe to put an end to Sara Melody and his son Simon's engagement. Melody storms the Harford estate with a few Irish cronies to challenge Harford to a duel; when a donnybrook ensues, the police arrive, overpower him, and lock him up. Deborah Harford, Simon's mother, witnesses the brawl from an upstairs window. Just as Mildred Douglas destroys Yank Smith's inflated ego with the words "filthy beast," Deborah undermines Melody's pretense by merely viewing his unseemly behavior. Back at the tavern, Melody's pose has been stripped away, and he resigns himself to the role of a drunken Irish peasant. In the final scene, Sara, who'd secretly admired her father's pride in the face of hardship, remarks with dismay, "He's beaten at last and he wants to stay beaten" (*CP3*, 279).

By March 18, 1936, O'Neill had finished a complete draft of *A Touch of the Poet* but held off reworking it and added to other Cycle plays instead. He'd first envisioned his cycle as five plays, with *A Touch of the Poet* as the first, then he expanded it into seven, then eight, then nine, then finally eleven plays. With this Cycle, he wanted to mete out, in his words, "the development of psychological characterization in relation to changing times—what the railroads, what the panics did to change people's lives."[209] The time setting, 1775 to 1930, would cover America's evolution from the War of Independence to the Great Depression, and the Cycle as a whole would serve as an allegory of American greed. His scheme was to develop a "special repertoire company" to perform the plays at two per season for five and a half seasons. "Try a Cycle sometime," he wrote Lawrence Langner, "I advise you—that is, I would advise you to, if I hated you! A lady bearing quintuplets is having a debonair, carefree time of it by comparison."[210]

That June, after Eugene Jr. had completed his doctorate in classics at Yale University, which then offered him a teaching position, O'Neill wrote to congratulate his son but also apologize that he shouldn't expect further financial aid from him. "Whatever income I have from investments," he said, "is more than abolished by the alimony dole," and he knew his Cycle wouldn't improve the situation for several years. "You will also appreciate," he said, "that I have many low days of O'Neill heebie-jeebies when I feel very old and tired, and doubtful of myself and my work, and wonder why in hell something in me drove me on to undertake such a hellish job."[211]

O'Neill and Monterey, by the summer of 1936, were fed up with Georgia's climate: "A hell of a hot oppressive summer here," he wrote in mid-August. "Carlotta and I are neck and neck toward the Olympic and World's sweating record! We just continually drip and drop."[212] That month, Sophus Winther arrived at Casa Genotta with his wife, Eline. O'Neill deeply admired Winther's *Eugene O'Neill: A Critical Study* (1934), which he felt explained his work almost better than he could himself. "What particularly strikes me," he'd written Winther upon first reading the manuscript, "is that you have so illuminatingly revealed the relationship of the plays to the mental and spiritual background of their time, and shown that background as inseparable from the work—something no one else has so far troubled to do except sketchily, yet which is so essential to any true comprehension of what I have attempted to accomplish."[213]

Before their first day was out, the Winthers had convinced O'Neill and Monterey to abandon Casa Genotta for the cooler climate of their hometown, Seattle, Washington.[214] By October the Winthers found a rental, and after a short stop in New York, the O'Neills boarded the Twentieth-Century Limited westward. They arrived in Seattle on November 3 and moved into a house in Magnolia Bluff, a colony on the city's outskirts overlooking Puget Sound. Soon after they'd settled in, at seven thirty on the morning of November 12, Winther notified O'Neill by phone that he'd just become the second American, after Sinclair Lewis, to win the Nobel Prize in Literature. He was the first American dramatist, and the last to date, to be awarded the honor.

Pandora's Box

"The morning is a Bedlam!" Monterey exclaimed in her diary on the day of the announcement: "Associated Press, United Press, . . . International News all call for interviews + photographs—head of the Swedish newspaper—man phones from N.Y.—San Francisco—wires from Geo. Jean, Crouse, Madden, H.W., Cerf, Shane—radio man furious because Gene won't speak over radio! We are both worn out. It isn't easy to protect Gene from *all* these people!"[215] O'Neill briefly considered refusing the prize, in part because he feared that the world's greatest literary honor might lead to complacency and hamper his creativity. The anarchist in him feared a more terrifying prospect: the patina of being labeled an "establishment" writer.

"Don't wish the Nobel on me!" he wrote Harry Weinberger back in 1934, after the lawyer had informed him that he was still on the short list. "My strong personal hunch is that it's a jinx (except for old men), that it puts you on a spot, and that I've been made into a too-respectable, stuffed-shirt eminent literary personage already without the Nobel piled on it." O'Neill did accept it, of course, and with reasonable grace, but he relayed his anxiety over the prize to George Jean Nathan and appealed to his friend to persuade the New York Drama Critics' Circle not to ask him to appear at its ceremonies and thereby put him in the awkward position of declining. "I feel it's very punk stuff of me to appear as the Dean of Drama who lays on the hands and contributes the official blessing on the prize-giving. You know what I mean—the venerable Stuffed-Shirt, whom the mobs get to assume is dead because venerated. . . . [I] am by no means dead yet."[216]

"Naturally, I am happy," the forty-eight-year-old playwright said to one of dozens of reporters clamoring for an interview. "I feel like a horse that has just been given a blue ribbon." In a letter to Kenneth Macgowan, however, his equine analogy was applied more truthfully: "I'm like an ancient cab horse that has had a blue ribbon pinned on his tail—too physically weary to turn round and find out if it's good to eat, or what." O'Neill also geniunely believed the prize should have gone to Theodore Dreiser. When the announcement arrived, he told the *New York Times*, "I thought perhaps it would go to Dreiser. He deserves it."[217] Upon receiving a congratulatory note from Dreiser himself, his response was one of heartfelt thanks and a touch of contrition: "You are one of the very few I really wanted to hear from. . . . I can say to you with entire sincerity and truth, from my head and heart both, that I would take a great deal more satisfaction in this prize if you were among those who had had it before me. As it is, I have a sneaking feeling of guilt—as if I had pinched something which I know damned well should, in justice, be yours."[218]

After seven months of toil on the historical Cycle, O'Neill was too exhausted to attend the Nobel ceremony in December. Besides, he and Monterey had just made the transcontinental journey to the Pacific, and they refused to go through the ordeal in reverse, with a transatlantic crossing on top of that. "I am not physically or mentally up to the strain of being a guest of honor," he wrote the American embassy in Stockholm. "I would simply crack up badly."[219]

In his acceptance letter to the Nobel committee, O'Neill graciously asserted that the award spoke less about his own career than the evolution of American drama as a whole.[220] Though he did feel strongly that the new European acceptance of American playwrights was necessary for them to reach "adulthood," he also told the playwright Russel Crouse that this section of his letter was "replete with amiable phonus bolonus." With few exceptions, he said, none of his American colleagues gave him sufficient credit for "[busting] the old dogmas wide open and [leaving] them free to do anything they wanted in any way they wanted. . . . My U.S. colleagues are, speaking in general, cheap shit-heels!"[221] In fact, many top American playwrights did write to congratulate him, including, as well as Crouse, Edward Sheldon, S. N. Behrman, George Middleton, and Sidney Howard. The chief culprit O'Neill had in mind here was the Pulitzer Prize–winning Maxwell Anderson, who hadn't written, proving, to O'Neill at least, as he told George Jean Nathan, that "that guy is just another cheaply-envious shit-heel . . . a lousy sport."[222]

O'Neill's acceptance letter ends with a heartfelt dedication of the prize to his well-acknowledged "Master," the Swedish playwright August Strindberg. It was a sincere tribute, but had the unfortunate effect of reopening old wounds: his line that Strindberg was the "greatest genius of all modern dramatists" mainly served as an awkward reminder to the Nobel committee that it had never given the prize to its own country's brightest literary star.[223] Along with the Nobel gold medal, O'Neill was awarded $45,000, which was reportedly double what other recipients had received, since there had been no prize for literature awarded in 1935.[224]

Although the Nobel committee cited several of his plays, from *The Moon of the Caribbees* through *Days Without End*, it was *Mourning Becomes Electra* that had tipped the scales. The committee singled out the epic Civil War trilogy as "the author's grandest work . . . a masterly example of constructive ability and elaborate motivation of plot, and one that is surely without a counterpart in the whole range of latter-day drama." Though the trilogy had opened in the United States five years earlier, it had remained fresh in the minds of European audiences, running triumphantly in theaters across the continent throughout the 1930s (and then well into the war years). A Swedish production of *Mourning Becomes Electra* was even enacted at the Nobel ceremonies. Later, when Theresa Helburn excluded the trilogy from the list of the Guild's finest productions, O'Neill complained to her, "Why, Christ, compared to it, a lot of the plays on your list are, as far as fine drama is concerned, merely things to hang on a hook in a backwoods privy!"[225]

O'Neill and Monterey stayed in Seattle for only about a month before heading down to San Francisco, the city of Monterey's youth. For them, the Pacific Northwest had lived up to its reputation for rainy weather, refreshing though it might have been after Sea Island's suffocating heat. "Seattle *does* seem damp," he wrote Nathan. "I toured to a town, last week, where they usually have 180 inches of rain a year and the milkman frequently makes his rounds in a canoe."[226]

Once checked in at the Fairmont Hotel in San Francisco, O'Neill began suffering from severe abdominal pain, and on December 26 he was admitted for observation to the Merritt Hospital in Oakland. His appendix was removed three days later. "Lucky I didn't go to Sweden!" he said. "My appendix would probably have burst as I was making my speech at the Nobel banquet, and ruined the occasion." A swift recovery seemed assured, but then his condition plummeted unexpectedly, first from a prostate-kidney infection, then a burst abscess. The latter, O'Neill said, "so poisoned me that they had to inject everything but T.N.T. to keep me from passing out for good."[227]

Monterey, who'd taken the room next door, was herself struck down by flu and nearly caught pneumonia. During their convalescence at the hospital, they both took a shine to two of the nurses, Kathryne "Kaye" Albertoni and Maxine Edie Benedict; and the O'Neills hired both of them on and off over the following years. "If I was around him," Albertoni recalled, "I never said do this or do that. I'd always ask him, 'What would you like to do?' So I think he respected that. Don't push. Don't push. And in the mornings when we had breakfast if he didn't want to talk, it's okay. Don't talk. So maybe he had that respect for me. I think so."[228]

Monterey returned to Sea Island to oversee the sale of the house while O'Neill remained in the hospital. Taking advantage of his brief bachelorhood, he enticed Albertoni to free him from his hospital bed incarceration for a day and accompany him to Jack London's legendary old waterfront hangout in Oakland, Heinold's First and Last Chance Saloon.[229] When the doctors finally released him, he'd been in their care for two and a half months.[230] Once again, they ordered eight months to a year of compulsory rest. The Cycle would have to wait.

That spring and summer of 1937, the O'Neills rented two houses in the Bay Area, first in Berkeley, then in Lafayette, where O'Neill could convalesce in peace. Until the following fall he had to appear at the hospital for twice-weekly treatments to prevent further infections. In late spring, now determined to make California their permanent home, O'Neill and Monterey purchased over 150 acres of verdant farmland outside of the town of Danville. The property commanded an Edenic panorama overlooking the gently sloping grassy hills of the San Ramon Valley. There they would build their second house together. Once more insisting he'd found paradise, he wrote Nathan that his new home was "better than Casa Genotta—as you will agree when you visit."[231] Then he wrote Barrett Clark, "This is final home and harbor for me. I love California. Moreover, the climate is one I know I can work and keep healthy in."[232]

"Here we have a splendid climate," Monterey wrote Saxe Commins with typical candor: "No negroes, sand flies, hookworms or mosquitoes. All of which I dislike—in quantity."[233] Having sold the bulk of Casa Genotta's furnishings to the new owners, the Cluett family, Monterey adorned their new home in Danville almost exclusively with Chinese decor. She was furious with President Franklin Delano Roosevelt, whom she blamed for the cost of the unionized workers building their new house, designed to accommodate eight thousand books for O'Neill and three hundred pairs of shoes for her and which would ultimately cost them over $100,000.[234] (The cost of the property's upkeep forced O'Neill's hand, and he sold Hollywood the rights to make a pedestrian film adaptation of *The Hairy Ape* for $30,000.)[235] The new home did, in truth, offer the most fruitful creative environment of any of O'Neill's previous retreats, even finer than the Sphinx-like dunes of Peaked Hill Bar. O'Neill named their new home Tao House after the Chinese philosophy of Lao-tse. "Tao" translates roughly as "the right way," and O'Neill believed, George Jean Nathan's ribbing aside, that he'd found it at long last.

By the time O'Neill and Monterey had settled into Tao House, O'Neill viewed his two children with Agnes Boulton as "nothing to be proud of, or take pleasure in—unlike Eugene—and unless they change drastically, I am off them for life."[236] He sent them birthday and Christmas presents, but claimed that they hardly ever responded to thank him. Monterey, wary of any connection to his children, was intercepting their letters. Over the next couple of years, in fact, Oona O'Neill sent repeated requests to visit her father, but he claimed he never got them, and Monterey was the only one who made contact with her directly.[237] Whatever her rationale, these circumstances had consequences: O'Neill's paternal love was not unconditional. He accused Shane of ignoring his Nobel, which Shane had not—as Monterey's diary makes clear on the day they found out about the prize—and his hospitalization in Oakland (which he may have), and he threatened to cut his son from his life entirely if Shane didn't start giving as much as he took. Shane had dropped out of two schools, Lawrenceville and

Tao House.

*   *   *

the Florida Military Academy, and was now attending the Ralston Creek School in Colorado, from which he sent his father a carved walrus tusk for his forty-ninth birthday. O'Neill sent his thanks and forgave him, for the time being, but still brandished Eugene's academic achievements as a contrast to Shane's failures.

In May 1937, Eugene Jr. announced his divorce from Betty Green and his new marriage to the daughter of a mathematics professor at Yale, Janet Hunter Longley. But as well as telling his father about his new wife and his work as a classics professor at Yale, Eugene complained of an inexplicable tremor in his hands. O'Neill responded that it was a hereditary affliction, one that he had suffered from his whole life: "The whole matter of tremors seems to be something doctors know little about, judging from my experience. I have had mine ever since I can remember, long before I had even smoked my first cornsilk cigarette, let alone dissipated any, and my mother had suffered from the same complaint, and told me her father had had it too." The only advice O'Neill could offer was to "regard it as a heritage of God knows how long a line of people with high-strung nerves, and bear the embarrassing discomfort of it as best one may."[238]

The clinical term for their condition was "familial essential tremor," and O'Neill's was worsening. He'd also begun to show signs of a neurodegenerative disease that set new limits on his creative output. This brought terrible losses but also some gains: the disease, in the end, wouldn't merely dictate O'Neill's own professional course, but in substantial ways that of American theater history as a whole.

By January 1938, the O'Neills had occupied Tao House, with renewed hopes of domestic permanency. For several months, it throbbed with the syncopated percussion of carpenters' hammers accompanied by the scraping of the plasterers and the digging of the pool builders. It was not a productive time for O'Neill. The ongoing construction of their new residence, his persistent dental ailments, an angry case of hives, and a diagnosis of neuritis (a nerve condition that sent excruciating pain shooting through his writing arm for several months) ruled out anything but the most perfunctory work on his Cycle. He rebuffed the Theatre Guild's plea for a new play from its newly minted Nobel laureate; but once Tao House was completed that spring and his neuritis had stabilized (after the removal of five teeth, the apparent cause of the affliction), he reported that "the old bean is functioning better than it has in years."[239] Within a year, he'd completed drafts of the Cycle's first four plays: *Greed of the Meek*, *And Give Me Death*, *A Touch of the Poet*, and *More Stately Mansions*.[240]

That spring of 1938, he received visits from Shane, who planned to attend the University of Colorado in the fall, and Eugene, who'd just released an anthology, *The Complete Greek Drama*, coedited with Whitney J. Oates, through O'Neill's own publisher Random House. By winter, however, after learning that Shane (then experimenting with drugs and alcohol) had abandoned college plans for another year at Lawrenceville, he began thinking of the boy as "a parasitic slob of a Boulton" who "simply does not interest me as a human being."[241]

O'Neill hadn't seen his daughter, Oona, for eight years, but their reunion in late August 1939 proved a "bright spot" for the playwright. She'd been chaperoned on the flight to the West Coast by her mother, or "the invertebrate trollop," as he referred to Boulton. (He called his alimony and child support checks Boulton's "dole," the Irish term for welfare.) It was the first time Boulton and O'Neill had seen each other in more than a decade. Boulton was polite to O'Neill and Monterey, but she wasn't invited into Tao House and headed south.[242]

To the surprise of all parties concerned, Oona delighted her father and stepmother. "A charming girl," he beamed, "both in looks and manners."[243] O'Neill's nurse Kathryne Albertoni was on duty during Oona's visit and recalled Monterey's reaction: "She said she had good manners. . . . That [was] important to Carlotta, manners." After the visit was over, Monterey told Albertoni she'd been relieved to discover that, whatever her feelings toward Boulton, Oona "was brought up properly."[244] (She didn't share this opinion of her own daughter, Cynthia, whom she regarded as unrefined and unladylike, too much of a tomboy.)[245] Fourteen-year-old Oona enjoyed her stepmother's company too, though she'd later acknowledge she was mainly in awe of her.[246] Most of her time was spent with Monterey shopping, touring, and sunbathing. Each day O'Neill would work in his upstairs office, then appear in the afternoon for tea and a swim.

Monterey repeatedly lectured Oona about the importance of financial independence, though she herself had lived lavishly for years off her former lover James Speyer's bottomless trust fund established in her name. "Earn your own way and don't depend on your father," she said.[247] O'Neill imparted the same advice to Shane: "You must find yourself, and your own self," he warned his increasingly wayward son. "You've got to find the guts in yourself to take hold of your own life. No one can do it for you and no one can help you. You have got to go on alone, without help, or it won't mean anything to you."[248] O'Neill and Monterey were preparing these children, at the earliest possible age, not to expect financial support in adulthood.

During the war years, Monterey became, according to Bennett Cerf, "more of a jailer than a wife" for O'Neill, though Cerf was

Eugene and Oona O'Neill at Tao House, August 1939.
(COURTESY OF THE HAGEMAN COLLECTION, THE EUGENE O'NEILL FOUNDATION,
DANVILLE, CALIF.)

* * *

one of O'Neill's few associates who still had cordial relations
with her. Behind two sets of electric gates that Monterey had installed
at the approach to Tao House, "she could watch over the terrain
like an old feudal lord guarding against invading armies." "She just
threw [his Guild associates and old friends] out of his life," Cerf said,
"and took possession of him herself." Robert Edmond Jones went
to visit O'Neill at Tao House for three weeks but returned to New
York after only two. Afterward, he met Jimmy Light for dinner at the
Harvard Club where, though Jones usually didn't drink, he ordered
a Scotch. Then another. "I've been watching a slow case of murder,"
he said. Similarly, Russel Crouse, who'd replaced Robert Sisk as press
agent for the Guild, reported after visiting Tao House that "Gene
reminded me of the stories you read in newspapers about someone
who'd been chained up for years and fed in a closet or a tiny room,
until freed eventually. For a long while, every time we'd meet, Gene
would hold back like a wary animal; then he would warm up and start

to wag his tail." When Eugene Jr. arrived in August 1939 with his third wife, Sally Hayward, Monterey was appalled by the incursion. "He married a girl who looks like a Minnesota fullback," she scoffed. "They think they're going to stay for two weeks. Ha, ha, ha! I'll have them out of the house in four days." O'Neill himself found Sally "all right in her way—which is all-too-familiar Connecticut small city type—but, from my angle, a rather disappointing daughter-in-law."[249]

O'Neill's routine when composing a play was to sketch out a scenario of the story, then write a lengthy first draft, and then pare that down to its final length. For *More Stately Mansions*, near completion by 1939, he didn't think he'd "be able to cut length much."[250] At a minimum of ten hours of playing time, this script remains the longest in his canon by far. *More Stately Mansions*, the sequel to *A Touch of the Poet*, unfolds in Massachusetts from 1832 to 1841 and revolves around the Panic of 1837. As O'Neill's conflicted, mother-obsessed protagonist Simon Harford's wealth and power accumulate over the course of the play, his acquisitiveness gives way to the obsessive, property-driven, monopolizing instincts that had led American financiers to their doom from the Panic of 1837 to the market crash of 1929. O'Neill offers no solutions for Simon or for the nation; he simply sends his protagonist back to where he'd lived when he first met his wife, Sara Melody—an idyllic cabin in the woods. Here Simon, a defeated relic of capitalism, may find solace and peace in the love of his wife and children.

Once again, O'Neill bypassed the agitprop that had taken over American drama in the Depression era: "I suppose these lousy times make it inevitable that many authors get caught in the sociological propaganda mill," he said. "The hell of it seems to be, when an artist starts saving the world, he starts losing himself. I know, I have been bitten by the salvation bug myself at times."[251] He admitted envying authors with a belief in "salvation through any sociological idealism," but couldn't abide those movements or an appeal to God or any brand of social reform. "My true conviction," he said, "being that the one reform worth cheering for is the Second Flood."[252]

"With the world exploding into revolution," O'Neill discarded *More Stately Mansions* and ultimately the Cycle as a whole. Hitler, that "little maggot of a man," had already invaded Czechoslovakia and Poland and commenced a policy of genocide against Jews, Gypsies, and other populations of Europe; Great Britain and France had declared war on Germany; the United States was still caught in the quagmire of the Great Depression; and O'Neill's beloved Far East was plunged into its own gruesome conflict.[253] American involvement as an antidote offered him no solace whatsoever. The absence of any measurable "intelligence in our government," O'Neill grumbled in a letter to Bennett Cerf, made it clear to him that their country would be directly engaged in the global bloodletting soon enough: "Anyone who expects anything of government these days except colossal suicidal stupidity seems to me a moron of optimism," he told Cerf. "Tell Saxe I am rapidly becoming reconverted to a sterling Anarchism!"[254]

O'Neill's isolationist stance was especially true with regard to the German Luftwaffe's terror bombing campaign against England. The "O'Neill" in him, he wrote Eugene Jr., took the Battle of Britain "philosophically": "Remembering the Black and Tan atrocities committed by the British not so many years ago. . . . One might even call it justice." If Ireland were invaded, he said, "I shall probably volunteer at once." When asked to sign an open letter to Prime Minister Éamon de Valera of the Irish Free State urging the leader to join forces with the Allies against Germany, O'Neill flatly refused. "My final conviction is that we Irish Americans owe it to the Irish people not to attempt to influence their decision by any means whatsoever." "No dead hand from the past bothers me," he assured the petitioner, "although I was reared with a hymn of hate for England the predominant lullaby. It is simply a matter of conscience."[255]

After France's surrender, O'Neill wrote Lawrence Langner that he'd given up entirely on writing, though hoped to return to his Cycle when he was able. "To tell the truth," he told Langner, "like anyone else with any imagination, I have been absolutely sunk by this damned world debacle. The Cycle is on the shelf, and God knows if I can ever take it up again because I cannot foresee any future in this country or anywhere else to which it could spiritually belong."²⁵⁶ "People are too damned preoccupied with the tragedy of war now—as they should be—to want to face such plays," he wrote Theresa Helburn. "And I don't blame them. I'd rather spend an escapist evening with legs and music myself—or with pipe dreams that were treated as truth."²⁵⁷

O'Neill's notion of "pipe dreams that were treated as truth" helped to subdue his horrific, insomnia-inducing wartime nightmares and rekindle an old idea. Over the summer and fall of 1939, he completed a draft of his monumental four-act play *The Iceman Cometh*. But the prospect of the work ever reaching the stage, O'Neill remarked, was "secondary and incidental to me, and even, quite unimportant."²⁵⁸ In the earliest years of World War II, a time when O'Neill was desperate to quell his premonition of humanity's doom, *Iceman's* theme was closely akin to Pandora opening Zeus's forbidden box: all the world's evils had been released from it; but the last thing to emerge, without which humanity could never endure, was the specter of hope.²⁵⁹

The Iceman Cometh features a band of down-and-out regulars at Harry Hope's saloon, a rundown Raines Law hotel modeled mostly after Jimmy the Priest's, but also the downstairs bar at the Garden Hotel and the Hell Hole. Each of the characters in the play resembles, with little modification, a vital figure from O'Neill's heavy drinking days through the 1910s—James Byth, Terry Carlin, Hippolyte Havel, and Joe Smith, to name a few. (O'Neill had continued to support Carlin until his death from pneumonia in 1934.) Near the end of the first act, a salesman named Theodore "Hickey" Hickman arrives at the bar to celebrate the owner Harry Hope's birthday; but he comes with a Messianic agenda to strip his friends of their "pipe dreams." By doing so, he believes he can offer them salvation from their delusional, misbegotten lives. In fact the opposite is true: pipe dreams and whiskey are the only tools they have that make their lives bearable.

O'Neill first titled *The Iceman Cometh* "Tomorrow," the title of his 1916 short story. The next day, however, he came up with "The Iceman Cometh," "which I love," he wrote George Jean Nathan, "because it characteristically expresses so much of the outer and the inner spirit of the play."²⁶⁰ (In the past, there's been the impression that he gleaned the title from Waldo Frank's novel *The Bridegroom Cometh* [1939], though he'd had at least the idea of that title in mind since 1910–11 with his poem from Buenos Aires "The Bridegroom Weeps!") The play's eponymous gag, when Hickey tearfully produces a picture of his wife, then admits he left her in bed with the iceman, is based on a bawdy old joke: A man yells upstairs to his wife in the bedroom, "Has the iceman come yet?" His wife calls back, "No, but he's breathing hard!"[261] O'Neill wrote the dialogue, he said, "in exact lingo of place and 1912, as I remember it—with only the filth expletives omitted."[262]

But another meaning was behind the title as well: O'Neill's wistful remembrance of his early days at Jimmy the Priest's, the Garden Hotel, and the Hell Hole were in a way themselves "pipe dreams." The past requires a level of tampering, he was saying, particularly in one's later years when death—the iceman—approaches. As such, *The Iceman Cometh*, O'Neill warned a friend, was "a big kind of comedy that doesn't stay funny very long."[263]

"I really admire this opus," O'Neill told Nathan. "I think it's about as successful an attempt at accomplishing a thing comprehensively and completely in all aspects as I've ever made. And I feel there are moments in it that hit as deeply and truly into the farce and humor and pity and ironic tragedy of life as anything in modern drama." "The depth of tragedy," he then wrote Langner, lay in stripping away the self-delusional facade, however temporarily, and exposing the "secret soul of a man stark naked" once he was bereft of his pipe dreams.[264]

O'Neill insisted on delaying a production until the war's end. Only then, he predicted (wrongly, it turned out), would the hangover of postwar disillusionment fully take hold. Only then would audiences comprehend his play's thesis—that mankind requires life-sustaining pipe dreams to endure the terrifying realities of modern life: "No, *The Iceman Cometh* would be wrong now," he told Dudley Nichols. "A New York audience could neither see nor hear its meaning. The pity and tragedy of defensive pipe dreams would be deemed unpatriotic, and uninspired by the Atlantic Charter [Churchill and Roosevelt's vision of a postwar world order], even if the audience did catch that meaning. But after the war is over, I am afraid from present indications that American audiences will understand a lot of *The Iceman Cometh* only too well."[265]

O'Neill again lost his creative stride as Hitler's blitzkrieg sank him "deeper and deeper into a profound pessimistic lethargy." "The war news," he wrote Oona just after completing *Iceman*, "has affected my ability to concentrate on my job. With so much tragic drama happening in the world, it is hard to take theatre seriously." Two weeks later, however, he wrote Langner that he'd begun "working again on something . . . after a lapse of several months spent with an ear glued to the radio for war news. You can't keep a hop head off his dope for long!"[266] His first diary note for the play, June 1939, reads, "The Jimmy the P.—H. H.—Garden idea." Below that, he jotted, recalling a play idea from as far back as 1927, "and N.L. [New London] family one"—what was to become *Long Day's Journey Into Night*.[267]

Even while O'Neill surrendered himself to nostalgia with *The Iceman Cometh* and the "New London family" idea, he'd barred any of his children from a place in the New London family plot. "I am the last of this pure Irish branch of the o'NEILLs," he wrote Harry Weinberger. "My children are a weird mixture, racially speaking,—and I certainly would rather be thrown down the sewer than be planted in New London. I want to be buried wherever my home happens to be when I die." A new headstone that he'd ordered for his family was to list the names from top to bottom, from James to Ella's mother, Bridget Quinlan, following the "pattern of a cast of characters in a play, which is absolutely appropriate for an actor's family."[268]

Sadly, by necessity this time, O'Neill ordered another tombstone when, on December 17, 1940, Blemie, the O'Neills' beloved Dalmatian of thirteen years, who'd accompanied them from France to New York, Georgia to Seattle, and San Francisco to Danville, died a lingering, painful death at Tao House. For a very long time, O'Neill and Monterey were inconsolable.

Saxe Commins remembered the special attention heaped upon the dog during one of his stays at Casa Genotta: "A Dalmatian of aristocratic canine lineage, idolized and pampered by Carlotta and protected by Gene. Blemie's food was shipped from New York after consultation with animal dieticians. Special steel instruments were made for scaling tartar from his teeth. He slept in a made-to-order bed. ... Sheets on this bed were changed at frequent intervals and a monogrammed blanket was provided for his comfort." "Gene & I spoil him to no end," Monterey admitted to Commins' wife, Dorothy, "but always say he is the only one of our children who has not disillusioned us—& seemed always conscious (& *grateful*) of our effort to do all we could for his welfare & happiness!!"[269] Blemie's bed at Tao House had been upgraded to a four-poster with linens and blankets, and his own bathtub was installed in the basement. (The contractor said this was the most expensive item in the house, since it required its own plumbing system.)[270]

On December 26, O'Neill memorialized his adored pet with "The Last Will and Testament of Silverdene Emblem O'Neill," a poignant reflection on the distinctions between the inner world of dogs and that of human beings. Unlike humans, he wrote in Blemie's voice, dogs don't waste their lives hoarding material things and obsessing over their ownership; and rather than fearing death in the mode of humans, "as something alien and terrible which destroys life," dogs "accept it as part of life."[271] The Dalmatian's headstone on the hill above Tao House reads, "Sleep in Peace, Faithful Friend." Soon after Blemie died, O'Neill said, "Everything has gone wrong."[272]

The Tyranny of Time

His dog was dead; his hand tremors had worsened; his marriage was not going well; and his despair over the escalating world war had reached its lowest ebb. Together, these crises forced O'Neill to acknowledge to himself that he was running out of time. But to write effectively, he had to conquer his enduring malaise of creative spirit, in which "my only thought about the Art of the Drama is Fuckit!"[273]

"I cannot believe the Cycle matters a damn," he conceded before abandoning it altogether, "or could mean anything to any future I can foresee." "At this time," he said, "when perhaps there is so little time left for the free writer even in this country—it seems the only wisdom is to concentrate on what is most important and get as much as I can write written."[274] What turned out to be "most important" was obvious to him, a play idea about his family that had been haunting him at least since 1927, much earlier when one takes into account its echoes in virtually everything he'd written up to then.

By the summer of 1941, with the assistance of a custom-made back brace to steady him while he wrote, O'Neill completed his four-act autobiographical masterwork *Long Day's Journey Into Night*. "When he started *Long Day's Journey*," Monterey remembered of this distressing time, "it was a most strange experience to watch that man being tortured every day by his own writing. He would come out of his study at the end of a day gaunt and sometimes weeping. His eyes would be all red and he looked ten years older than when he went in in the morning."[275]

Long Day's Journey takes place over a single day in August 1912, in the living room of Monte Cristo Cottage in New London. The Tyrone family of the play, based on his actual family, James, Ella, James Jr., and himself, acts out an often vicious blame game, in spite of their mutual love, over the course of which an audience begins to recognize, as he wrote in his work diary, "shifting alliances in battle": "Father, two sons versus Mother; Mother, two sons versus Father; Father, younger son versus Mother, older son; Mother, younger son versus Father, older son; Father and Mother versus two sons; Brother versus brother; Father versus Mother."[276] The Tyrones habitually suppress their emotional pain by condemning the others; and when that fails, they turn to stimulants— Mary to morphine, James to real estate, Edmund to poetry written by "whoremongers and degenerates" (*CP*3, 799), Jamie to the comfort of overweight prostitutes, and all three men to whiskey. But then, once they realize the impotence of stimulants and sex to provide a refuge from their constant suffering, they return to their living room to do battle.

Each of the Tyrones betrays noticeable Irish characteristics—lyrical language; quick mood reversals; physical features ("Keep your dirty tongue off Ireland!" James Tyrone shouts at Jamie. "You're a fine one to sneer, with the map of it on your face!" [*CP*3, 732].); whiskey drinking; the sympathy with the tenant farmer Shaughnessy (based on John "Dirty" Dolan) over the Protestant Standard Oil magnate

Harker (Edward S. Harkness), and thus their struggle deciding between a "lace curtain" or "shanty" Irish identity; James's notion that
Edmund's "self-destruction" stems from his denial of "the one true
faith of the Catholic church" (*CP3*, 759); James's terror of tuberculosis as inevitably lethal and not worth facing poverty over; and Mary's
distinctive place as the center of it all, thereby making her accusations
the most hurtful.

Overarching everything in *Long Day's Journey* is the horrifying
surety of a wasted past. James and Mary, along with their dissipated elder son Jamie, present two selves—the selves that might have
achieved their potential and the selves they've been fated to endure.
As well as his tuberculosis, Edmund discovers his own tragic core
in the fact that he was ever "born a man": "I would have been much
more successful as a sea gull or a fish. As it is, I will always be a stranger who never feels at home, who does not really want and is not really
wanted, who can never belong, who must always be a little in love
with death!" (*CP3*, 812). "At the final curtain," O'Neill explained after its completion, "there they still are, trapped within each other by
the past, each guilty and at the same time innocent, scorning, loving,
pitying each other, understanding and yet not understanding at all,
forgiving but still doomed never to be able to forget."[277]

Only O'Neill's most trusted friends were permitted to read *Long
Day's Journey* during his lifetime. Sophus Winther and his wife, Eline,
read it while they were houseguests at Tao House in 1943. Stunned by
the power of the play and its astonishing personal revelations, Winther recalled that, after he'd finished reading, O'Neill descended the
stairs and said nothing to him at first. Then he gazed out the window
at Mount Diablo and slowly recited Mary Tyrone's, and the play's,
final lines: "That was the winter of senior year. Then in the spring
something happened to me. Yes, I remember. I fell in love with James
Tyrone and was so happy for a time." Then, after a prolonged silence,
O'Neill said, "I think that is the greatest scene I have ever written."[278]

In the fall of 1941, a twenty-six-year-old Swedish actress playing Anna
in a San Francisco production of *"Anna Christie"* was invited out to

Tao House for a visit with her character's maker. Monterey had seen her perform that August and approved: "[She] was excellent when she had to dig in and work," she said, "at all times, I felt her the *woman*, not an *actress* acting! . . . None of *these damned* silly affectations!"[279]

Ingrid Bergman, the actress playing Anna and soon to be regarded by legions of filmgoers as the most beautiful woman in the world, always remembered the first time she saw O'Neill: "He came toward me, and there was a silence about him that was so effective. It was the stillness that impressed me. One hardly dared to speak to him. Then, as he came closer, I saw those eyes. They were the most beautiful eyes I have seen in my whole life. They were like wells; you fell into them. You had the feeling that he looked straight through you."[280]

Under Monterey's disapproving glare, O'Neill led Bergman upstairs and showed her the Cycle laid out in piles. He told Bergman he wanted her to join the company that would perform all of the plays. With her heart set on the movies, Bergman refused. (That spring, 1942, Bergman began filming *Casablanca* with Humphrey Bogart.) "You're abandoning me," he said when she told him no. "Not really," she replied. "Perhaps some other time. Maybe later."[281]

A year and a half later, on February 21, 1943, O'Neill would destroy two longhand drafts of *More Stately Mansions*, along with drafts of other plays meant for the Cycle. The surviving typescript of *Mansions* includes a note: "Unfinished Work. This script to be destroyed in case of my death! [signed] Eugene O'Neill." But in fact Bergman did accept the role of Deborah Harford for its 1967 premiere, after the script was discovered and the play produced, against his expressed wish.

In 1951, O'Neill and Monterey inadvertently sent the existing typescript of *More Stately Mansions* to Yale with the rest of O'Neill's papers. Swedish director Karl Ragnar Gierow of the Royal Dramatic Theater in Stockholm became aware of the script in 1957, four years after O'Neill's death, and Monterey gave him permission to shorten the length from ten hours of playing time to four. Gierow produced its world premiere in Stockholm on November 9, 1962. That production received strong reviews, but the play's American

Eugene O'Neill at Tao House.

✳   ✳   ✳

premiere, directed by the future O'Neill impresario José Quintero with Bergman as Deborah and Colleen Dewhurst as Sara, at the Broadhurst Theatre on October 31, 1967, and then Los Angeles, was unreservedly panned: "In its unfinished, raw and tortured state," wrote Clive Barnes in the *New York Times*, "it does, in my view, O'Neill's memory a disservice. With friends like Mr. Quintero, the shade of O'Neill might think he needs no enemies, and being his own worst enemy was the privilege O'Neill always retained for himself."[282] Ingrid Bergman, then fifty-two, defended Quintero's decision to see the recovered work onto the boards. "I thought it was important that the play had been found and that we were producing it. After all, O'Neill is one of America's greatest playwrights. Even if *More Stately Mansions* is not his best play, it was written by a playwright who will go down in history as the greatest in America."[283]

"It is like acid always burning in my brain," O'Neill, furious over the war, wrote Eugene in June of 1942, "that the stupid butchering of the last war taught men nothing at all, that they sank back listlessly on the warm manure pile of the dead and went to sleep, indifferently bestowing custody on their future, their fate, into the hands of State departments, whose members are trained to be conspirators, card sharps, double-crossers and secret betrayers of their own people; into the hands of greedy capitalist ruling classes so stupid they could not even see when their own greed began devouring itself; into the hands of that most debased type of pimp, the politician, and that most craven of all lice and job-worshippers, the bureaucrats. . . . I could go on from there, extensively and eloquently, and give you an Anarchist diatribe against the State which, published, would earn me fifty years in Leavenworth—or deportation to Ireland!"[284]

Feeling acutely helpless, O'Neill sketched out a couple of scenarios for propaganda plays, if for no other reason than to vent his frustration over the atrocities taking place across the globe.[285] He asked Saxe Commins to send him a copy of Stirner's *The Ego and His Own* to revisit philosophical anarchism, which validated his belief that any state, including his own, was capable of the kind of fiendishness

Hitler was then inflicting on humanity. But he shelved these projects in deference to the war effort. "I censor myself," he said. Instead, over three weeks' time back in April 1941, he dashed off *Hughie*, a play "written more to be read than staged."[286]

Hughie, O'Neill's last one-act play and his first since *Exorcism* over two decades earlier, tells the sad tale of a washed-up gambler's affection for the recently deceased desk clerk of a dingy fourth-rate hotel in Manhattan's theater district. Set during what O'Neill refers to in his stage directions as "the Great Hollow Boom of the twenties" (*CP3*, 831), 1928, *Hughie* closely analyzes the inner and outer lives of the hotel's new night clerk, Charlie (the listener), and the small-time Broadway hustler, Erie Smith (the talker). Erie finds meager solace in gambling and alcohol, short-term solutions to the long-term problems of isolation, alienation, and disillusionment. "The Night Clerk character," he told George Jean Nathan, "is an essence of all the night clerks I've known in bum hotels—quite a few! 'Erie' is a type of Broadway sport I and my brother used to know by the dozen in far-off days. I didn't know many at the time the play is laid, 1928, but they never change. Only their lingo does."[287]

Hughie is the sole surviving installment of a planned series of one-acts titled "By Way of Obit." "In each," he told Nathan, "the main character talks about a person who has died to a person who does little but listen."[288] (O'Neill completed one other "By Way of Obit" play, involving an Irish chambermaid, but destroyed it on February 2, 1944, along with the scenarios for several others.)

For his next play, *A Moon for the Misbegotten*, another four-act tragedy, O'Neill journeyed back in his past to another wrenching episode in his own life, exorcising the haunting ghost of his older brother Jim once and for all. Originally, he'd intended the story as a full-length play about James O'Neill's tenant John "Dirty" Dolan. Jim O'Neill was, in fact, Dolan's landlord in October 1923, when the play takes place, a month before Jim would die of alcoholism in the New Jersey sanatorium. But the character Jim Tyrone, seemingly without his creator's permission, before long stole the dialogue away, though not entirely, from the poor Irish farmer and his daughter, Josie Hogan.

O'Neill's working title was "Moon of the Misbegotten," "a good title," he thought; but then he changed it to "A Moon for the Misbegotten," "much more to the point."[289] "Even in titles," O'Neill said, "I have tried for that double meaning—which explains why many people, without realizing the reason, find a lot of them so striking. They hit the subconscious as well as the conscious."[290] For the Greeks, the moon symbolized Diana, goddess of the moon and chastity, for Christians, the Virgin Mary. The moon in the play thus presents Josie Hogan, based in large part on Jim O'Neill's lover Christine Ell, as a harbinger of forgiveness and spiritual serenity for the misbegotten Jim Tyrone. O'Neill's use of "misbegotten" refers to tragic souls whose lives are so tormented that they experience life as a kind of living death, as Jim does, and long for the peace death brings while wishing never to have been born at all. The culminating scene of the third act ends with Jim passed out from booze in Josie's arms in an evocation of the Pietà. After a year of self-loathing following Jim's betrayal of his mother, his longing for the peace, security, and sense of belonging only a mother can provide has been fulfilled at long last.

O'Neill was laboring through the second act of *A Moon for the Misbegotten* when the Japanese attacked the Pearl Harbor naval base in Hawaii on December 7, 1941. "I had to drag myself through [the play] since Pearl Harbor," he said months later, "and it needs much revision—wanders all over the place."[291] By New Year's, 1942, he'd completed a draft; he finished it, as well as his tremor permitted, the following year. It was the last play O'Neill would ever write.

Along with millions of other Americans, O'Neill and Monterey sat by their radio for long, excruciating hours, stony-faced and despondent, as the war coverage poisoned the very air of their living room with news of the horrors of World War II. "The world drama you hear over the radio every day, or read in the papers," he wrote George Jean Nathan, "is the one important drama of the moment, and one can't write anything significant about that because it's too close and the best one could do wouldn't be half as effective as a good war correspondent's story of the front line."[292]

In December 1942, Shane O'Neill signed on as a seaman in the merchant marine and served on multiple voyages across the Atlantic to England and North Africa under constant attack from German submarines. On an unknown number of occasions, he looked on as Allied vessels were torpedoed, and his own ships had been hit over half a dozen times. The memories of men burning and drowning at sea were so tormenting that he required psychological treatment after his return. But O'Neill heard little, if anything, of his son's exploits, since all correspondence went through Monterey. "Who does she think she is—St. Peter, opening and closing the gates?" Shane's girlfriend Margaret Stark demanded after Monterey had rebuffed a letter from her updating them on Shane's whereabouts. "Why does your father allow such a thing to happen? You are his son. Doesn't he have any feelings of responsibility to you? Does she open all his mail?"[293]

Eugene Jr. increasingly resented his tethered identity as the son of a major celebrity. In 1948, he wrote an article for *Collier's* magazine, which never went to print, titled "The Last Name Is Not Junior." The unfair and paradoxical position he describes in the piece was one his father, living in the shadow of James O'Neill, had known all too well: "Who does that conceited ass think he is anyhow?" Eugene would overhear people say about him at parties. "Even if you had the chance to make the obvious answer, 'Only what people have done their best to make me think I am,' " he said, "you would be talking to deaf ears. . . . People have got you coming and going." As for the younger son, Shane (though Eugene doesn't name him), "he has . . . run away from it, and has become a really tragic figure. He looks hunted and he acts hunted. He takes jobs that are far below his natural abilities. His associates are inferior persons. He drinks too much, and you have reason to believe that he has committed petty crimes. His whole life is aimless, a complete waste. Those who know him say, 'A nice guy, but . . .' That word 'but' contains a world of sadness."[294]

Meanwhile, their sister, Oona, according to a spate of tabloid articles, was having the time of her young life during the war years. Oona seemed able to make the most of her father's world-famous last name, apparently with her mother's blessings, while still cultivating her own public identity. After spending her first two years of high school at the Warrenton Country School in Virginia, Oona attended Manhattan's elite Brearley School from 1940 to 1942. There she befriended teen socialites Gloria Vanderbilt and Carol Marcus. Together the three classmates formed a much-sought-after debutante trio. Oona dated many young men in Manhattan, including an aspiring young writer named J. D. Salinger, whose idea for a young adult novel, *A Catcher in the Rye* (1951), had just begun to percolate. He was "crazy about" Oona, he told a friend, and "would marry [her] tomorrow if she would have me." His love for the debutante only deepened after he'd gone off to fight in World War II; while overseas, where he saw some of the worst fighting of the war, he sent dozens of finely crafted love letters to her, some of them ten to fifteen pages long. Though he once quipped that "little Oona's hopelessly in love with little Oona," Salinger never fully recovered from the heartbreak after she'd stopped replying to his letters from the front.[295]

In April 1942, sixteen-year-old Oona was named New York's ultra-fashionable Stork Club's "No. 1 Debutante" of 1942–43. The *New York Post*'s headline read, "Gene O'Neill Should See Daughter Now," accompanied by a photograph of the newly minted Glamour Girl beaming and cradling a bouquet of roses, her raven hair flowing past her high forehead under a broad-rimmed hat. Under the snapshot was the caption, "Put me down as shanty Irish"—her response to a reporter who inquired whether she considered herself shanty or lace-curtain Irish. How will your father react? he asked. "I don't think he's going to be wild about it." What did she think about world affairs? "It would seem very funny for me," she demurred with girlish innocence, "to sit in the Stork Club and express my opinion of world affairs."[296] She was right on both counts. O'Neill found her behavior utterly shameful: "Riding on my name!" he fumed.[297] "If she goes to Hollywood" to try her hand at acting, as she seemed ready to do, he wrote Weinberger, "it will be absolutely against my wishes. So much so, that if she does, I will never write to her or see her again as long as I live! . . . If Hollywood is in, then I'm out—*forever!*"[298]

That November O'Neill received a letter from Omaha, Nebraska. Oona was touring by train to the West Coast with Carol Marcus, who paid for the trip. They'd made plans to meet Marcus's fiancé, the thirty-five-year-old playwright William Saroyan, in Sacramento, California, where he was in basic training. Oona was hoping to stop in and see her father at Tao House but hadn't given a return address and called him from Sacramento. After answering the phone, Monterey pretended to discuss the visit with O'Neill, then told Oona her father said he didn't want to see her. Oona drove with Carol Marcus to Tao House anyway, but Monterey refused to let her in.[299] Desperate for an audience, she tried again with a follow-up letter. "All I know of what you have become since you blossomed into the night club racket," he responded, "is derived from newspaper clippings of your interviews. From those, you appear to have developed into a vain seventeen year old nitwit, without manners, good taste, self-respect, or pride—or any awareness that you are living in a gigantic world upheaval, which affects the lives and work and ambitions and future of everyone, including you—and me."[300]

The tabloid news portrayed a headless girl, O'Neill raged, a daughter heading willy-nilly toward the life of a "second-rate movie actress of the floosie—the sort who have their pictures in the papers for a couple of years and then sink back into the obscurity of their naturally silly, talentless lives. . . . One interview with a girl working in an airplane factory, or training to be a Red Cross nurse, is worth ten million of the glamour kind now." (Monterey had suggested that Oona study to be a nurse when she visited them last in the summer of 1941.) On top of his anger, O'Neill gave other excuses for her not to come: the O'Neills' loyal handyman Herbert Freeman had joined the Marines, he said, and the other drivers and domestic help had also left to join the armed services or otherwise aid the war effort, so there's "no one to wait on you." His tremors had gotten so bad he couldn't get a driver's license if he wanted to, he went on, and Monterey couldn't drive. "So we are marooned, more or less, and, considering all the above, our answer to any prospective guest is NO." He hoped she'd "grow out of the callow stage," he told her, then ended his letter with gruff finality: "Au revoir."[301] Although his feelings toward her would soften in later years, this was the last communiqué Oona would ever receive from her father.

Hollywood cared little about O'Neill's blessing or lack thereof, and welcomed his Glamour Girl daughter's company in inverse proportion to his disdainful rejection of it. Still seventeen, Oona began dating some of the most colorful personalities then gallivanting around at Tinsel Town's high-flying parties and swank nightclubs. One of these, the brilliant twenty-six-year-old filmmaker and actor Orson Welles, offered to read her palm at a nightclub. The Boy Genius had given up trying to seduce her as he glared down at her palm lines. She would marry a much older man, he told her in his renowned baritone voice, and soon. Moreover, astonishingly, he could name who the venerable groom would be: Charlie Chaplin.[302]

In a bid to steer Chaplin's gaze in Oona's direction, her agent, Minna Wallis, arranged for the two to meet, hoping Oona's gleaming smile and sultry Irish looks might entice Chaplin to hire her for his next project, a film based on Paul Vincent Carroll's play *Shadow and Substance* (1937). Chaplin, unimpressed by her pedigree, asked Wallis, "Can she act?" Wallis suggested they all convene at her house for dinner so he could see for himself if the young starlet had promise. When Chaplin first saw her, he wrote later, "I became aware of a luminous beauty with a sequestered charm and a gentleness that was most appealing." Afterward, Oona ended a note to Carol Marcus with an excited postscript: "*P.S. I just met Charlie Chaplin!*"[303]

On June 16, 1943, Oona O'Neill, just one month after her eighteenth birthday, eloped with the fifty-four-year-old filmmaker and movie star. She was his fourth wife (the third he'd married while they were still in their teens) and his last. After Chaplin was exiled from the United States in 1952 for alleged Communist sympathies, the celebrity couple went on to enjoy a contented family life in Switzerland. There they raised eight children together;four were born in Beverly Hills, before Chaplin's exile, but O'Neill never met any of them.[304] Oona wrote dozens of letters apprising him of his grandchildren's development, but Monterey had intercepted them all. "I never mentioned it," O'Neill's nurse Kaye Albertoni remembered of Oona's marriage. "Nobody mentioned it. He had absolutely nothing to do with Oona." But contrary to the assumed narrative, that it was Oona's marriage to

Oona and Charlie Chaplin in their first public appearance after their
marriage in 1943.
(COURTESY OF CULVER PICTURES)

* * *

a man as old as himself that ended their relationship, O'Neill told
Saxe Commins, "I had severed relations before this, for many other
reasons." "She's gone," he said to Albertoni. "She's gone."[305]

Three physicians had separately diagnosed O'Neill's incapacitating
tremor as Parkinson's disease; three others admitted frankly that they
had no idea what was wrong with him. O'Neill himself believed, inac-
curately it turned out, that it was his familial tremor combined with
years of heavy drinking.[306] Lawrence Langner presented O'Neill with
a "Sound Scriber" to try recording his plays orally; but after a good
faith effort, O'Neill realized he just couldn't write by dictation.[307]
The tremors weren't the only obstruction to his writing; in fact, they

weren't yet even the main problem. Rather, it was a persistent and inescapable apathy that had given way to an almost existential self-loathing. "My creative energy just balked," he told Elizabeth Shepley Sergeant: " 'All is vanity, including your plays, past and present, and I am fed up with you and your woes, so good bye and kindly scatter my ashes down the nearest drain.' Then it died."[308]

Monterey, with the aid of Kaye Albertoni, faced her husband's advancing illness with unwavering diligence: she monitored his steady ingestion of a dizzying array of sedatives, barbiturates, antibiotics, diuretics, opium suppositories, decongestants, and homeopathic remedies; she kept a journal in which she made copious notes about his tremors, sleep patterns, sinking spells, mood swings, headaches, and coughing fits; and she daily measured his urine, prepared him special meals, woke up with him in the middle of the night. "His wife is resplendent and has been a revelation to me," wrote one of O'Neill's physicians. "A beautiful girl with a brain."[309]

"There is nothing to do for Parkinson's," the despondent Monterey wrote Theresa Helburn, "it just gets worse and worse. And now that I have fallen apart I am not so brave in facing it! There are days when my heart aches so I can hardly face him—which, of course, is the worst possible thing for him. But on the whole I manage to keep on and try to make things as pleasant as possible. With war, and all it does and will mean, I am really stuck, for the first time in my life, as to what is the best thing to do regarding a future home for Gene. He should have warmth, ocean and sand (!), doctors and good nourishment."[310]

O'Neill had also become convinced that he was careening headlong toward a nervous breakdown. Often by midafternoon, he'd "crack-up—tremor ghastly—weeping." His formerly sensuous visage had solidified into what doctors treating Parkinson's refer to as the "mask." And by August 1943, Monterey noted mournfully that her husband's black Irish eyes had lost their "shine."[311]

Danville's lack of household support during World War II compelled O'Neill and Monterey to sell Tao House in February 1944. They next moved into the Huntington Hotel on San Francisco's fashionable

Nob Hill, where Monterey daily attended Mass at Grace Cathedral across the square. O'Neill refused to join her, of course. "Great and simple truth has been perverted into worldly power by organized institutions," he said. "The church is a fraud." At the same time, he had a recurring nightmare that he was drifting on an undulating sea; in each dream the seventh wave, always the seventh, towered high up above him, then curled and transformed into a huge cathedral that crashed down on his head.[312] (The number seven in the numerological world, which O'Neill had dabbled in over the years, significantly represents the artistic truth-seeker.) That summer, while they were on a drive over the Golden Gate Bridge, O'Neill said, terrifying Monterey, "God, I wish I could drink a bottle of 'Old Taylor.' "[313]

After more than a year cooped up at the Huntington, O'Neill longed for a change of scenery; anywhere, it seemed, would be better. "I'm so sick of this apartment I wish they'd give me a short stretch at Alcatraz just to enjoy the sea breezes, a change of view, and the interesting company," he complained to George Jean Nathan.[314] By then his neurological illness had become close to intolerable. "The worst part," he wrote Elizabeth Sergeant, "is the fits of extreme melancholia that go with it. God knows I have had enough of Celtic Twilight in my make-up without needing more of the same. And this isn't the same. It isn't sadness. It's an exhausted horrible apathy."[315] Still, the couple languished at their Nob Hill suite in a mutual holding pattern of solitude and infirmity, well into the summer of 1945. By then, it became undeniably apparent to O'Neill, despite his worsening health, that he'd completely fallen for a young woman named Jane Caldwell.

The daughter of Myrtle Caldwell, a classmate of Monterey's from convent school and one of the O'Neills' closest friends in California, Jane Caldwell wasn't much older than his daughter, Oona. "I think she was flirting with him," Kaye Albertoni confirmed. "She was pretty, young. And, of course he liked to play the piano [Rosie]. Oh, they danced together." The nurse found it particularly objectionable when O'Neill and the starry-eyed Caldwell, swept off her feet by the attentions heaped upon her by a world-renowned, if enfeebled, playwright, would step into his office and close the door brazenly behind them.

For her birthday, O'Neill gave Caldwell a jade-handled mirror with a note: "I must warn you that this is an enchanted, haunted mirror, for whenever you gaze in it you will see in its secret depth someone staring back at you with—well, let us say, with an emotion befitting the loveliness the surface of the mirror reflects."[316]

One day, O'Neill and Caldwell took a long walk together on the beach, and O'Neill, as he had with Alice Cuthbert back in Bermuda in 1925, wrote a love poem to her about it, "To a Stolen Moment." The last two stanzas read with a beckoning, pleading simplicity:

> The magic of love was there
> For me
> And you
> Standing there.
>
> Blue coat, buttoned up to your chin,
> So beautiful there,
> With the sea and sky in your eyes,
> And the sun and wind in your hair.[317]

Beyond a few loving inscriptions to Monterey, O'Neill's ode to Caldwell was probably the last literary writing he ever composed (and it remains the latest work of O'Neill's ever published).

When Monterey found out about his feelings for young Jane Caldwell, she first threatened suicide, then murder. "Don't you ever bring her in this house again," Monterey warned Caldwell's mother.[318] Then a terrific scene erupted after she directly confronted her husband that September: pushed to the brink, O'Neill leveled a loaded handgun at her head. She grabbed a butcher knife. He dropped the gun, grabbed her neck, and closed his fingers around it while she dug her fingernails into his hands; eventually, he let go and knocked her out with a crack to the jaw.[319]

By mid-October 1945, the O'Neills, incredibly, had reached another provisional truce before heading for New York to supervise the Theatre Guild's preparations for *The Iceman Cometh*. Maybe he'd follow his bliss, too, he thought, and open a saloon with George Jean Nathan on Long Island. They'd been discussing that retirement plan for years. Nathan and H. L. Mencken would serve drinks, and O'Neill would work the register. They'd even agreed on a name: the High Dive.[320]

Silence's End

When Saxe and Dorothy Commins joined the O'Neills for dinner in their suite at Manhattan's Hotel Barclay, Commins observed his friend appearing more anxious than usual. Then O'Neill revealed that 125,000 words of manuscript material for his Cycle, including the finished script of *A Touch of the Poet*, had gone missing. He was sure it was all there in the suite when he'd left for rehearsals that morning. Monterey denied having seen it; she also claimed that she didn't remember it being packed in San Francisco and accused O'Neill of senility. Commins suggested that he and O'Neill search the entire suite, which they did, rifling through O'Neill's towering jazz record collection, book shelves, the hallway compartments, the bedrooms and bathrooms, even, after Monterey's consent, her lingerie drawer. The manuscripts were nowhere to be found. Two days later, O'Neill told Commins to forget about it. Monterey had hidden them, Commins said, to punish O'Neill for "reasons totally obscure to him."[321]

By now, with O'Neill and Monterey's marital wounds still fresh, the proprietorship of her husband's literary legacy had become Monterey's greatest obsession. On December 5, 1945, in an attempt to mollify her, O'Neill signed a will leaving all "letters, diaries, records, unfinished plays or fragments thereof, or first drafts of any such plays, together with my private papers of every description" to Monterey or, in the event that her death preceded his, Eugene Jr. Any manuscripts Monterey didn't want for herself were to be endowed to Princeton University, except one: "I further direct and order and herewith bind my Executors, Trustees, heirs and all other persons, not to produce or cause to be produced upon the stage, in motion pictures, radio, television, or in any other dramatic form, my play 'LONG DAY'S JOURNEY INTO NIGHT.' The right to publish said play as a book I have granted to RANDOM HOUSE, INC, on condition that it not be published until twenty-five (25) years after my death." Both Eugene and Shane were bequeathed some money as well. Oona, who'd married into wealth anyway, was left nothing, "since she has amply benefited from the payments made to [her] mother" from Boulton's alimony and the property in Bermuda that had remained in his name.[322]

On September 2, 1946, O'Neill convened a press conference to promote *The Iceman Cometh*, his first public appearance since 1931. It was his first new production in twelve years, and a horde of reporters and critics eagerly descended upon the Theatre Guild's headquarters at Fifty-Third Street. They assembled in Lawrence Langner's stately oak-paneled office, chatting distractedly and perusing the Guild's promotional materials while they anticipated O'Neill's pending arrival.

When the long-absent theater giant finally stepped into the room, the members of the press corps rose from their seats in hushed silence. O'Neill looked awful. His trembling hands were racked with palsy, and his gaunt, sallow face hung loosely over an emaciated, though impeccably tailored frame. He still possessed his celebrated Irish good looks but appeared closer to seventy than his actual fifty-eight years. O'Neill's speech and mannerisms struck the journalists as strangely incongruent too—part Victorian gentleman, part Bowery bum.[323]

O'Neill started off by apologizing for his tendency to mumble. "Even my own family complains about it," he said, then steeled himself for the inquisition.[324] Instead, the reporters just sat there gawking at him, too intimidated to speak. After a dozen years of absence, O'Neill appeared to the group of scribes like a specter from Charles Dickens's *A Christmas Carol*, the Ghost of Broadway Past. O'Neill then muttered how nice it was to be back in a city where theater meant something to people. There was more awkward silence. Rosamond Gilder of *Theatre Arts Monthly* spoke up and replied that it was nice to have him back. Then another reporter asked, apropos of nothing, about O'Neill's having been born in New York. "While I was away they tore down the old Cadillac Hotel where I was born," came his laconic reply. "That was a dirty trick."[325]

More fitful seat shifting and paper rustling ensued, until finally someone asked about his intentions with his planned Cycle *A
Tale of Possessors Self-Dispossessed*, not understanding that *The Iceman
Cometh* wasn't a Cycle play. O'Neill, untroubled by the mistake, suddenly became animated: in the postwar year of triumphal American
patriotism, he declared, shocking everyone present, "I'm going on the
theory that the United States, instead of being the most successful
country in the world, is the greatest failure. It's the greatest failure because it was given everything, more than any other country. Through
moving as rapidly as it has, it hasn't acquired any real roots. Its main
idea is that everlasting game of trying to possess your own soul by the
possession of something outside of it, thereby losing your own soul
and the thing outside of it, too. America is the prime example of this
because it happened so quickly and with such immense resources.
This was really said in the Bible much better. We are the greatest
example of 'For what shall it profit a man if he shall gain the whole
world, and lose his own soul?' "[326]

"I hope to resume writing as soon as I can," O'Neill continued,
"but the war has thrown me completely off base and I have to get back
to it again. I have to get back to a sense of writing being worthwhile.
In fact, I'd have to pretend." The conference lasted about ninety minutes, and when it was over one reporter confessed, "I was going to ask
some questions . . . but I was too scared."[327] The writer James Agee,
who'd also been present, mused that after attending opening night of
The Iceman Cometh, this experience of meeting the stately dramatist
in person had been "much more affecting and revealing than the play
with which he broke his long silence as an artist."[328]

That spring of 1946, after the death of the American playwright
Edward Sheldon, O'Neill and Monterey moved out of their hotel
suite into Sheldon's majestic penthouse overlooking Central Park at
35 East Eighty-Fourth Street. It was a fitting transfer of occupancy for
the six-room apartment: not only had Sheldon also suffered terribly
from a series of debilitating illnesses in his later years, but O'Neill
respected him as perhaps his most gifted American predecessor. "Your

Salvation Nell," O'Neill had written Sheldon two decades earlier about his play from 1908, "along with the works of the Irish Players on their first trip over here, was what first opened my eyes to the existence of a real theatre as opposed to the usual—and to me, then, hateful—theatre of my father, in whose atmosphere I had been brought up."[329]

O'Neill's usual ambivalence about New York had subsided, and he was delighted to reengage the cultural nerve center of America. Monterey, on the other hand, fearful of her husband's "old cronies," had been dead set against living there. (She'd opted for Sea Island, where they'd been planning to return for some time.)[330] Her husband began going out on nightly capers at the juke joints along what was known as "The Street," at Fifty-Second Street between Fifth and Sixth avenues, to take in the latest jazz—music that Monterey reviled as "savage . . . the music of Negroes."[331] At a dinner party hosted by Russel Crouse, Irving Berlin played piano until three in the morning while O'Neill happily belted out "Alexander's Ragtime Band." He even recalled old Berlin tunes that the composer himself had long forgotten; but then O'Neill would start caterwauling through an old favorite, and Berlin played along. Another night at Bennett and Phyllis Cerf's house, O'Neill sang bawdy sea chanteys while folk singer Burl Ives accompanied him on guitar. "I will not be party to these goings-on," Monterey carped. "We're going right home, Gene." "I wouldn't dream of it," he responded. "You go home without me." "When she was gone," Cerf said, "it was as though Gene had been released from prison. . . . Carlotta didn't want him to have a good time; she wanted to own him. They loved each other—but the way she had of showing him! When Gene would go into one of his Irish furies, he would hurl things at Carlotta. He once threw a wall mirror at her, and if it had hit her, it might have killed her. There were two sides to the story—there always are."[332]

O'Neill originally hoped to direct *The Iceman Cometh* himself, but he was now far too sick for that. Yet he felt his play was in good hands with the Guild's alternative, Eddie Dowling, who'd just directed and starred in Tennessee Williams's breakout play *The Glass Menagerie* in 1944 and acted in William Saroyan's 1939 Pulitzer Prize–winning barroom drama *The Time of Your Life*. Dowling regularly accompanied O'Neill to the Martin Beck Theatre, where the production was to be staged, during which the pair of lapsed Irish Catholics talked frequently about religion. When the director introduced O'Neill to the cast members, they were as shy, at first, as O'Neill. But Dowling said they "warmed up to him after the first ten minutes; they knew he belongs in the theater." In fact, the cast grew dependent on O'Neill's reassuring presence at rehearsals and missed him on the days that he didn't appear.[333]

O'Neill took a hand in nearly every aspect of the production, and one morning during auditions, an amusing, previously unreported episode took place between two legends of American theater: O'Neill was hiding behind a folding screen while Eddie Dowling and the Guild's coproducer Margaret Webster auditioned an up-and-coming young actor. They were looking for someone to play Tom Parritt, the traitor of the anarchist movement who commits suicide in the final scene.

"How do you feel about playing [Parritt]?" Dowling started.

"I dunno," the actor replied, with an affectation of indifference that needled the director. Dowling then asked him what he thought of the play. "What did *you* think of it?" came the insolent reply. "Tell me its virtues." The actor was actually bluffing. The night before he'd fallen asleep before reading the first act and had no idea what the play was about.

Dowling spoke for a while about the merits of the work but his entreaties were clearly falling on deaf ears. "This is the greatest playwright in the world," Dowling protested. "If I were an actor being auditioned for the part, I'd certainly be eager to be in it."

"Oh, yeah?" he replied with disdain. "The guy is nuts."

"Do you like the play?" Dowling asked, incredulous.

"Na-a-a-h," the actor responded, visibly bored.

"I think I'm wasting your time, and you're wasting mine," Dowling said, and dismissed the twenty-two-year-old Marlon Brando from the building.[334]

After Brando had slumped out of view, Dowling, now fully incensed, pushed aside the screen hiding O'Neill. "Eddie," O'Neill said, grinning, "he's got something."[335]

"[O'Neill] was a very beautiful man," remembered Marcella Markham, who played the prostitute Cora in *The Iceman Cometh*. "[He was] terribly handsome and very gentle. And he loved actors, just adored actors. I find that everybody makes him out these days [the 1980s] to have been a serious, ponderous man—he wasn't."[336] Ruth Gilbert, who played another prostitute, Pearl (and had been Muriel McComber in *Ah, Wilderness!*), agreed with Markham: "Sweetness— the greatest sweetness I've ever found in a human being; that's Mr. O'Neill's outstanding quality."[337]

Before Dowling was exposed to O'Neill's charming side during auditions and rehearsals, however, what struck him most about the playwright when they first met in California was his near-myopic preoccupation with the war. "Kill, kill, kill," O'Neill kept repeating. "Kill or be killed."[338] This didn't go away when he'd arrived to work on *Iceman*. From O'Neill's perspective, despair over the false promises of human history was precisely what his tragedy was about.

When asked by the *New York Times* what significance the bums at Harry Hope's saloon might have for contemporary America, O'Neill responded that *Iceman* "is a play about pipe dreams. And the philosophy is that there is always one dream left, one final dream, no matter how low you have fallen, down there at the bottom of the bottle. I know, because I saw it." "It will take man a million years to grow up and obtain a soul," he concluded; in the meantime, all we have are our pipe dreams.[339] Larry Slade, the anarchist based on Terry Carlin, intimates this in the opening scene: "To hell with the truth! As the history of the world proves, the truth has no bearing on anything. It's irrelevant and immaterial, as the lawyers say. The lie of a pipe dream is what gives life to the whole misbegotten mad lot of us, drunk or sober" (*CP3*, 569–70).

One afternoon at a rehearsal, O'Neill, perched atop a stool at the stage bar, waved over the *PM* journalist Croswell Bowen. Fondling a prop whiskey glass, the playwright began to ruminate on his disgust over the current wave of American arrogance: "Of course," he warned, "America is due for a retribution. There ought to be a page in the history books of the United States of America of all the unprovoked, criminal, unjust crimes committed and sanctioned by our government since the beginning of our history—and before that, too."

"This American Dream stuff gives me a pain," he went on, growing increasingly agitated. "Telling the world about our American Dream! I don't know what they mean. If it exists, as we tell the whole world, why don't we make it work in one small hamlet in the United States? . . . If it's the constitution that they mean, ugh, then it's a lot of words. If we taught history and told the truth, we'd teach school children that the United States has followed the same greedy rut as every other country. We would tell who's guilty. The list of the guilty ones responsible would include some of our great national heroes. Their portraits should be taken out and burned." He went on to express glowing admiration for the American Indians who defeated Custer and his battalion at the Battle of Little Big Horn, then slammed his fist down on the stage bar. "The big business leaders in this country! Why do we produce such stupendous, colossal egomaniacs? They go on doing the most monstrous things, always using the excuse that if we don't the other person will. It's impossible to satirize them, if you wanted to."[340]

Among the ranks of the "black Irishmen" in American letters— F. Scott Fitzgerald, James T. Farrell, John O'Hara—Bowen came to believe after this meeting that O'Neill was "the blackest one of all." In a follow-up interview with Captain Tom Dorsey, who'd known O'Neill in New London, Dorsey defined "black Irish" (though a slippery term at best) as "an Irishman who has lost his Faith and who spends his life searching for the meaning of life, for a philosophy in which he can believe again as fervently as he once believed in the simple answers of the Catholic Catechism. A Black Irishman is a brooding, solitary man—and often a drinking man too—with wild words on the tip of his tongue." No wonder *The Iceman Cometh* was about pipe dreams, Bowen realized before going on to write a book about O'Neill: pipe dreams were "a Black Irishman's name for Faith."[341] The two world wars had in fact nullified any lingering desire in O'Neill for an alternative faith. "*The Iceman*," he told Bowen, "is a denial of any other experience of faith in my plays. In writing it, I felt I had locked myself in with my memories."[342]

*   *   *

The Iceman Cometh's premiere at the Martin Beck Theatre took in $600,000 at the box office for tickets sold through January. It was a Broadway record. Drama critics from Australia, South Africa, Italy, Greece, England, Norway, Sweden, and Denmark all congregated in the back of the theater and stood through the over-four-hour performance. From the street it looked more like a Hollywood premiere than a Broadway opening. Every celebrity in New York was there, even baseball legend Babe Ruth. O'Neill, of course, remained at home. When asked what he'd do opening night, he responded, "If I weren't in temperance, I'd get stinko."[343]

Instead, Bobby Jones, who'd designed the barroom set, communed with him through the night, and O'Neill left strict instructions with the Guild not to pester him with reviews the next day.[344] Staying home was expected; but refusal to read the notices was unheard of since the *Fountain* debacle in 1925. And also as with *The Fountain*, O'Neill's abstention was probably a wise choice.

The Iceman Cometh was an ill-timed production, opening as it did amid the patriotic fervor that had gripped postwar America, a time when overall confidence in national institutions had soared to historic heights. The play frustrated and bored most audiences and received respectful but lackluster reviews, with a smattering of both pans and raves. " 'The Iceman Cometh,' for all its long-windedness, has power and intensity," Ward Morehouse conceded in the *New York Sun*, capturing the general response: "If not O'Neill's finest play, it is certainly one of stature and importance. The Theatre Guild has performed a public service in bringing it to the stage and in bringing him back to combat duty." It was too long, most said, but unlike young Brando, theater critics hadn't been afforded the luxury of sleeping through it. "Someone really ought to buy him a watch," griped John Mason Brown in the *Saturday Review of Literature*.[345]

O'Neill's experiment with repetition in *Iceman* was especially lost on audiences. The play's director in 1956, José Quintero, would succeed, in part, where its first production failed because of his appreciation for O'Neill's dialogic rhythm: "[The play] resembles a complex musical form," Quintero said, "with themes repeating themselves with

The Theatre Guild's 1946 premiere of *The Iceman Cometh*, during what O'Neill called the "play's climactic scene, [Hickey's] long confessional." (COURTESY OF SHEAFFER-O'NEILL COLLECTION, LINDA LEAR CENTER FOR SPECIAL COLLECTIONS AND ARCHIVES, CONNECTICUT COLLEGE, NEW LONDON)

* * *

slight variation, as melodies do in a symphony." Quintero found that directing the play had, paradoxically, taught him "the meaning of precision in drama."[346] Theodore "Hickey" Hickman's speech at the end of act 4, the longest monologue O'Neill ever wrote, was its instrumental climax. Back when the Guild was preparing *Dynamo*, O'Neill also remarked on the musical quality of the work, "Bobby Jones once said that the difference between my plays and other contemporary work was that I always wrote primarily by the ear for the ear, that most of my plays, even down to the rhythm of the dialogue, had the definite structural quality of a musical composition. This hits the nail on the head. It is not that I consciously strive after this but that, willy-nilly, my stuff takes that form."[347]

Confronted on one too many occasions after *The Iceman Cometh*'s premiere, however, O'Neill was worn thin by the unrelenting accusation of repetition and offered a more terse response: "Have you ever been stinking drunk in your life?" he demanded. The critic admitted he hadn't. "If you had been," O'Neill said, "you'd know that a drunk says the same thing over and over again."[348]

Without question the most stinging critique of *The Iceman Cometh* was an ad hominem attack by the novelist and critic Mary McCarthy. Likening the four-and-a-half-hour play to "some stern piece of hardware ... ugly, durable, mysteriously utilitarian," McCarthy considered *Iceman* proof positive that O'Neill was simply a bad writer: "The return of a playwright who—to be frank—cannot write is a solemn and sentimental occasion." She went on to compare O'Neill to other major American authors such as Dreiser, Lewis, and James T. Farrell, "whose choice of vocation was a kind of triumphant catastrophe. ... In their last acts and chapters, they arrive not at despair but at a strange, blank nihilism." This kind of nihilism, unwelcome in postwar America, as the *Nation*'s Joseph Wood Krutch indicated in his review of the play, "was more modish twenty years ago than it is today."[349]

The following year, 1947, *A Moon for the Misbegotten*, the last play O'Neill ever wrote, would also be the last new play of his produced in his lifetime. Monterey made no secret of the fact that she despised it. A four-act play about Jim O'Neill was pointless, she insisted, after *Long Day's Journey Into Night*, and the recounting of Jim's actual drunken behavior, especially on the train from California with the prostitute and his mother's coffin in the car ahead, had made her physically ill when she read it.[350] O'Neill later admitted that he "had come to loathe" it too.[351] After many entreaties, however, the Theatre Guild inveigled him to permit a trial run in the Midwest, and *A Moon for the Misbegotten* premiered in Columbus, Ohio, on February 20, 1947.

Casting an actress for the role of Josie Hogan hadn't been easy. Lawrence Langner knew that Josie's character demanded "exactly the kind of woman who, when she comes to see you and asks whether she should attempt a career in the theatre—you look embarrassed and reply, 'Well, I'm afraid you're rather a big girl—how are we to find a man tall enough to play opposite you?' "[352] When O'Neill interviewed Mary Welch, he instantly saw that she wasn't the giantess like Christine Ell that he'd envisioned, but concluded that she was sufficiently Irish (100 percent) to carry off the role. On the night of the Columbus premiere, O'Neill sent her a dozen roses with a note that read, "Again my absolute confidence, Eugene O'Neill." "I can think of nothing finer to say to an actress on opening night," Welch recalled of the gift.[353]

"Theatrically," a local Ohioan joked of opening night, "America discovered Columbus tonight."[354] "This was a big event for Columbus," the *Columbus Citizen* affirmed. "It was our first white tie, tails and tiara affair at the legitimate theater since before the war. ... Yet this was a case where a competent cast that never obviously muffed a line or missed a stage cue wasted their time and long hours of 'line memorizing' on an unimportant play written by O'Neill, who is today still considered America's greatest dramatist."[355] One critic quipped, "The play consists of four acts. That is three too many." "Let's call it 'A Moon to Be Forgotten,' " said another.[356] More than a few reviewers favorably compared the play's realism to Erskine Caldwell's *Tobacco Road* (1932); but the juxtapositions of whiskey drinking and Christian symbolism, shanty Irishness and anticapitalism, attempted rape and tainted motherhood succeeded in affronting nearly everyone. The

Columbus Register thought the play "vile, irreverent, vulgar, immoral, and profane. . . . Among things offensive in the show were the ridicule of Catholic doctrinal practices, suggestive scenes, immoral expressions, and a profuse usage of vulgarity and profanity."[357] The *Pittsburgh Press*'s drama critic remonstrated, "I was ashamed to have my mother's old ears assaulted by the profanity and vulgarity of this play."[358]

In Detroit, the production's next stop after Columbus and Cleveland, the police censor shut it down after only two nights. "Lady, I don't care what kind of prize he's won," the censor answered the Guild producer Armina Marshall's objection that O'Neill was a Nobel Prize winner, "he can't put on a dirty show in *my* town." He charged that *A Moon for the Misbegotten* used the words *prostitute* and *mother* in the same sentence.[359] It was, he said, "a slander on American motherhood."[360] (This allegation was highly ironic, given that the main character, Jim Tyrone, recoils in disgust whenever that same connection is made. One draft even has Jim thanking Josie for not using his mother's name "in the same breath with the blonde whore on the train.")[361] If the show was to go on, the censor commanded, O'Neill must edit out several sentences and any profanity—*bastard, louse, tart, tramp,* and so on. O'Neill grudgingly agreed.

Back in the "Mad Twenties," with plays like *Desire Under the Elms* and *Strange Interlude*, such scandalous material had swept throngs of carnal-minded audiences into theaters alongside O'Neill's more intellectual, modernist theatrical base, and thus ensured a hit. Not in the forties. *A Moon for the Misbegotten*, after its final stop of St. Louis, wouldn't see a revival for another decade. (It's now one of his most commonly revived plays.) For a writer at the height of his intellectual powers, who'd dedicated his art to experimenting with anticlimax and the vagaries of ironic fate, O'Neill was at last confronted with his own anticlimactic final curtain, as a playwright if not yet as a man.

"There's a Lot to Be Said for Being Dead"

An incident at O'Neill and Monterey's penthouse on the night of January 17, 1948, gave Saxe Commins yet another shocking glimpse at Monterey's deteriorating mental state. The phone rang on the evening of his visit and Monterey answered it as usual, but then her body went rigid. "It's one of your friends," she said, handing the phone to her husband. "I won't talk to her." It was his old Province-town ally Fitzie Fitzgerald asking for a loan. Ignoring Monterey's re-proachful glare, O'Neill promised Fitzgerald $100. "Count on me," he assured her, and hung up. Turning back to Monterey, whose fury had escalated, O'Neill diffidently explained that his old friend re-quired medical attention; she likely had cancer. Fitzgerald had helped him often in the past, and it was only right to return the favor. "The lady, abandoning refinement," Commins remembered, "heaped abuse upon contempt for the people Gene knew during his days of strug-gle; they were criminals, blood-suckers, thieves, bastards, scum—and bohemians." (This last was hissed with particular venom.)[362]

At that point, Commins politely removed himself from the apart-ment. The moment the elevator door closed behind him, Monterey exploded in rage. First she smashed a glass on O'Neill's dressing table; and then, reaching down into the shards, she picked up a damaged picture of him as a baby in Ella O'Neill's arms, tore it to shreds, and screamed, "Your mother was a whore!" O'Neill slapped her hard, whereupon she dissolved into hysterics, dashed into her room to pack, then stormed out of the apartment, vowing never to see him again.

O'Neill telephoned Commins the next morning and related what had happened. It was his fault, he said in genuine contrition; he should have shown more compassion and restraint.[363] In fact, O'Neill had been drinking again, at least for a couple of weeks; it began with wine at first, but Monterey—who noted in her diary on January 2 that he "seems to be in a fog—and *loathes* me!"—was worried it would "lead to serious drinking as in times past."[364]

With Monterey gone, O'Neill required a new caretaker, so he and Commins contacted Walter "Ice" Casey, O'Neill's friend from his New London days. Casey was working, like O'Neill's character Erie Smith in *Hughie*, as a desk clerk at a shabby Manhattan hotel and was more than happy to help. On Casey's second day there, he and Commins spotted a pair of private detectives standing watch on the street outside the building and incautiously signaling each other with handkerchiefs. O'Neill then hired his own detective, who soon informed him that Monterey had checked into a Midtown hotel under an alias. "For the love of God, forgive and come back," he wrote her, culling his next entreaty from Mammy Saunders's threat to her grandson in *The Dreamy Kid*: "You are all I have in life. I am sick and I will surely die without you. You do not want to murder me, I know, and a curse will be on you for your remaining days."[365]

Over a week after the disturbing incident at the O'Neills', at six a.m. on January 29, 1948, Commins received a telephone call from Casey. He and O'Neill had been drinking the night before, and O'Neill, unsteady from a combination of alcohol and bromides, slipped in the bathroom after Casey had gone to bed, tripped over a stool, and fractured his arm. Casey was passed out cold, so O'Neill banged on the bathroom floor and shouted, unsuccessfully, to rouse the downstairs neighbors. Eventually, he blacked out.[366] A few hours later, Casey regained consciousness and frantically called O'Neill's attending physician, Dr. Shirley C. Fisk. When the two arrived at Doctors Hospital, Fisk informed Casey that "alcohol, even a little, would be potent on top of the bromides and other medications" O'Neill had been consuming daily to steady his tremors.[367]

Monterey made a brief but disquieting appearance at Doctors Hospital. With the excuse of arthritis to be admitted herself, she took a room on the floor below O'Neill's and for several days, with the aid of Herbert Freeman, monitored her husband and kept close tabs on his visitations.[368] It's unclear whether they talked themselves; but soon thereafter, O'Neill made an urgent request from his hospital bed that Commins secure his manuscripts from his penthouse and lock them in the Random House safe. If Monterey's state of mind was disturbed enough to destroy the only picture he had of him as a child in his mother's arms, his two cartons of manuscripts could well meet a similar fate. Commins immediately notified Casey, who delivered the boxes to Commins's office, after which he carefully labeled their contents and stored them in the safe. Then, on February 26, Commins's telephone rang. It was Monterey: "Have you given those scripts to Dodds of Princeton or whatever his name is?"

"What scripts?"

"The ones Gene has been lying about. You know what a God-damned liar he is."

"I won't listen to that, Carlotta. Gene is not a liar; he has never lied, and you know it."

"He has always been a liar. Did you take those scripts out of the desk?"

"You can't talk that way to me. I did not take *any* scripts out of the desk."

"I've got enough on you to send you to jail after all you've said about me."

"Carlotta, I've never mentioned your name to anyone. You ought to know that. I've always treated you with respect and I deserve a little from you."

"Respect, hell. God-damn you, I'll show you. I'll have you in jail where you've belonged for years."

"There followed," Commins reported afterwards, "a cascade of curses. The veneer of the lady had been rubbed off and the mind and the language of the show girl were exposed. The tirade devolved into a dizzying volley of obscenities." Among other insulting epithets, she called him a "Jew bastard" and declared that Hitler should have killed off more of his "kind."[369] After this, she slammed down the receiver, and Commins, by then reduced to tears, grabbed a sheet of paper, transcribed their exchange word for word, and delivered the evidence to O'Neill that evening. "Try to understand," O'Neill said to him. "She's sick, terribly sick. Don't you leave me too." Commins, still shaken but pacified for the time being, promised he wouldn't.[370]

Another hard-won truce took place between O'Neill and Monterey that April, at which point they chose to leave New York and the nightmares of the previous year and retire for good somewhere near Boston along the Massachusetts coastline. As well as having access to the sea, they would also be able to avail themselves of Boston's superior medical care. From a suite at the Ritz-Carlton, they orchestrated the purchase of a seaside cottage in Marblehead, twenty miles north of Boston. The total cost, after major renovations, came to more than

$85,000, funded principally by Monterey's trust. At the tip of Marble-head Neck, the house, built in 1880, sat perched above the shoreline on Point O'Rocks Lane. Its modest gray-shingled New England frame and long sloping eaves evoked fond memories for O'Neill of the Pink House, his family's home in New London before Monte Cristo Cottage. "It's like coming home, in a way," he wrote Kenneth Macgowan once they'd settled in, "and I feel happier than in many years."[371]

The previous year, 1947, O'Neill had signed several new drafts of his will, again leaving ownership of his literary estate to Monterey or, in the event of her death, Eugene, Jr. But now half of the remainder of his estate was bequeathed to Eugene, Monterey's daughter, Cynthia Stram, and a trust to continue paying Agnes Boulton's alimony. The other half was left to Monterey. (In the case of her death, this time, the money would go to Eugene and Cynthia and endow an annual "Eugene O'Neill Prize" to be administered by Yale University's School of Drama.) Nothing was provided for Oona, or even Shane, this time, "since they have amply benefited from the payments made to their mother" from her alimony and the Spithead property. On his tombstone, he specified, was to be carved an inscription under his name: "THERE'S A LOT TO BE SAID FOR BEING DEAD."

That summer of 1947, O'Neill and Monterey had gone over the will together. She made only a few minor alterations; significantly, one directive of O'Neill's remained untouched: that *Long Day's Journey Into Night* not be produced in any format, radio, television, film, or stage, and not be published by Random House until twenty-five years after his death. But on June 28, 1948, in a new bid to regain Monterey's trust after their contretemps in New York, O'Neill once again revised his will, this time leaving a fifth of his estate to Eugene and the remainder to Monterey. He included no reference, which he had in all of his prior wills, as to the intended fate of *Long Day's Journey*.[372]

From his new office at Marblehead Neck that fall, the ailing O'Neill, though he'd publicly joined the Euthanasia Society of America that year, wrote several friends that he planned to resume writing as soon as he was able. (Those he reached out to with this new optimism, including Saxe Commins, Dudley Nichols, and Charles Kennedy, had all been summarily banned by Monterey from calling or visiting them at Marblehead Neck.) But by early 1949, he'd lost hope again and resigned himself to the fact that he would never write another play; his straw of hopeless hope had sunk into the abyss. "As for writing a new play," he admitted to George Jean Nathan, "that pipe-dream seems as remote and unattainable as memorizing the *Encyclopedia Britannica.* . . . It is not only a matter of hand, but of mind—I just feel there is nothing more I want to say."[373]

Meanwhile, with O'Neill now lacking any future source of income, his two sons appeared incapable of providing for themselves and both were asking for money. Shane O'Neill had by this time descended into chronic drug and alcohol abuse and had repeatedly attempted suicide. He'd married a woman named Catherine Givens in 1944 and a year later she gave birth to Eugene O'Neill III. The baby, O'Neill's first grandchild and namesake to both him and his oldest son, died three months later, most likely of sudden infant death syndrome. Within three years, Shane was convicted of heroin possession and received a two-year suspended sentence. Shane confessed to a friend that he'd surrendered himself to pursuing the clear-cut path heroin provided him to his grave. Until then, he said, the drug "gives you something to live for. You have a goal in life—getting the stuff and earning enough money to pay for it. I know people who make fifteen, twenty, twenty-five thousand dollars a year just so they can earn enough to keep using H."[374]

O'Neill's stalwart lawyer Harry Weinberger had died in early 1944, a devastating blow for O'Neill, and he needed to brief his new lawyer, Winfield E. Aronberg, on Shane's perpetual legal scrapes and financial difficulties: "He cannot ever expect money from me. He has his interest in Spithead and he must make all appeals to his mother. And he might try going to work for a change. Or his wife might."[375] Shane and Catherine Givens were divorced in the early 1960s, having raised four children together.[376] Despite his reputation as an uncommonly kind person, regarded by some as almost Christlike and beloved by his children, Shane was never able to shake off his bedeviling

Shane O'Neill in 1957.

✳   ✳   ✳

addictions or ancestral demons—what Eugene Jr. had called the "but"
that invariably followed compliments about his younger brother. In
1977, Shane ended his own life by jumping from the fourth-floor
window of a friend's Brooklyn apartment.

For his part, Eugene Jr. was now drinking as much as his father
ever had. He'd quit his position teaching classics at Yale University
long before, then wound his way through part-time academic jobs—
Princeton, Fairleigh Dickinson, the New School for Social Research.
He eventually found work as a literary personality on radio and television and was billed as a "classical scholar of frightening erudition
who likes virtually nothing written since the birth of Christ." But
one night Eugene was scheduled to appear on a television panel with
the famously dapper movie star Adolphe Menjou, then considered
"the best-dressed man" in America. Eugene deliberately arrived to
the studio as "the worst-dressed"; he was also visibly drunk and thus
summarily blackballed from any future television work.[377]

In the summer of 1950, Eugene needed money to renew his
mortgage on a mountaintop property he'd bought in Woodstock,

New York; but his father refused him any financial assistance. Aronberg had been told that like Shane, Eugene "must make up his mind that he will get nothing from me and that it is necessary to find some job, and remain on that job, to plan for his future." Still, O'Neill never lost faith in his firstborn, as he had in Shane; it was Eugene who'd lost faith in himself. All of Eugene's vitriol was directed, not at his father, but at Monterey. "His hatred of Carlotta was almost maniacal," Commins recalled after meeting him on September 21, 1950. "It was she, he insisted, who was the cause of his desperation." (By this time, the feeling was mutual: when Eugene left after visits to Marblehead Neck, Monterey would burn the sheets he'd slept in.)[378]

On September 25, 1950, four days after his conference with Commins, Eugene stripped naked and, in the way of the Romans, slashed his wrist and ankles and submerged himself in a warm bath so the gashes wouldn't coagulate. His body was found near the front door of his house by his closest friend Frank Meyer's wife. Police evidence disclosed the agonizing details of his final moments: blood on the telephone indicated he'd changed his mind and tried to call for help; but he hadn't paid his bills and the phone company had cut the line. In the bathroom upstairs, a suicide note was tucked beneath an empty bottle of whiskey: "Never let it be said of an O'Neill that he failed to empty the bottle. Ave atque vale [Hail and farewell]!"[379]

Winfield Aronberg was given the unenviable task of informing his client by telephone. "Hello, Carlotta," he said when she picked up. "This is Bill Aronberg. I have terrible news for you. Try to be brave and break this gently to Gene. Young Gene has just committed suicide." "How dare you invade our privacy!" she shouted, and hung up.[380] Kathleen Jenkins was the only family member at the funeral, paid for by Eugene's brothers in Yale's elite secret society, Skull and Bones. O'Neill sent a floral arrangement of white chrysanthemums that blanketed the casket; the card attached read simply, "Father."[381]

On March 4, 1951, Kathryne Albertoni, the O'Neills' nurse from California, received a frantic phone call from Boston's McLean Hospital. "Papa needs you," a breathless Monterey pleaded. "Could you

Eugene O'Neill Jr. at his father's old desk (at which O'Neill wrote *The Emperor Jones* and *The Hairy Ape*, among other works) in the summer of 1950. This is probably the last photograph taken of Eugene Jr. before his suicide.
(PHOTO BY HARRY TEICHLAUT. COURTESY OF SHEAFFER-O'NEILL COLLECTION, LINDA LEAR CENTER FOR SPECIAL COLLECTIONS AND ARCHIVES, CONNECTICUT COLLEGE, NEW LONDON)

* * *

come?"[382] Albertoni caught the next flight out. "Oh, Kaye," Monterey greeted her, "you don't know how much this means to me. The Master hates me!"[383] Monterey, it soon became clear, hadn't summoned her because "Papa" needed her. Albertoni was there to testify for or against Monterey's sanity. She'd been institutionalized in McLean Hospital's psychiatric ward with a diagnosis of "delirium from bromide." While Monterey was fighting against accusations of insanity and the horrifying likelihood that she was gaslighted by her husband, O'Neill himself had been admitted to Salem Hospital, his leg fractured above the knee.

The tempest had begun a month earlier after a heated argument at Marblehead Neck at around nine o'clock on the night of February 5. O'Neill, infuriated, had rushed out of the house into a snowstorm; but realizing he badly needed a coat, he headed back to the house. On his way, he tripped on a rock on the pathway, fell to the ground, and broke his leg. Splayed out in the snow, he cried out for help, but Monterey, who often complained of his "falling all over the place because he *won't* do as he's told," refused him aid. For over an hour, O'Neill shouted desperately to his neighbors. Without a coat and badly injured, he was certain to die of exposure. All the while Monterey taunted him from the doorway: "I hear a little man calling in the wind, I hear a little man calling in the wind, I hear a little man calling in the wind," she repeated over and over. These were the words echoing in his head as he blacked out.[384]

About an hour later, help finally arrived in the form of Dr. Frederick B. Mayo, the local physician making his evening rounds. After checking to make sure O'Neill was alive, Mayo rushed inside and called an ambulance. Monterey was in hysterics, and he tried to coax her into the ambulance too; she refused, so he accompanied O'Neill without her to nearby Salem Hospital. The following night, a local police officer named John Snow was cruising the neighborhood of Marblehead Neck and discovered Monterey wandering the wintry roads in a fur coat. When Snow asked if he might escort her back home, she responded, "I'm not going back to that house, I'm never going back there. The air is full of people." Snow called for backup and attempted to lure her into the house with soothing assurances: "The people are all gone," he said, "there aren't any more people in the air." But she still refused, at which point Snow called Dr. Mayo, and they took her to the hospital. When informed that Monterey had just been admitted, O'Neill didn't utter a word. A few weeks later, however, when he was told his wife wanted to visit him after she'd been transferred to McLean, he cried out in terror, "Oh, don't let her near me, don't let her come here!"[385]

On February 12, 1951, O'Neill directed Winfield Aronberg to modify his will once again; three days later, the attorney arrived at the hospital to draw up the new document, which O'Neill signed on March 5. He now wished to be buried in New York City. All of his literary material would go to Princeton University, aside from the unpublished *Long Day's Journey Into Night*, since "I have already granted the right to publish said play as a book to Random House, Inc." His estate was to be administered by lawyers only, and Monterey would receive $5,000 a year. Though he'd still bequeathed nothing to Shane, in this version of his will, he left Spithead, which had remained

Eugene O'Neill at Marblehead Neck, circa 1948.
(COURTESY OF THE YALE COLLECTION OF AMERICAN LITERATURE, BEINECKE RARE BOOK
AND MANUSCRIPT LIBRARY, NEW HAVEN)

* * *

in his name after all these years as a legal convenience for him and
Boulton, to Oona O'Neill Chaplin.[386] By then O'Neill had in fact
arrived at the conclusion that Oona was the only sensible one of his
offspring, since at least she'd married into wealth.[387] (The last of his
grandchildren born his lifetime, her fifth, she named Eugene.)

O'Neill then signed a legal petition to have Monterey committed,
characterizing his wife as "an insane person . . . incapable of taking
care of herself."[388] Monterey, meanwhile, accused O'Neill of torment-

ing her with verbal and physical abuse: she said he'd threatened her with a belaying pin and that he'd entered her bedroom at night holding a shillelagh over her body while she pretended to be asleep. He was growling, according to her, "I'm going to smash her skull in, and all the blood will run down her face."[389] Whether any of this happened is impossible to know, but one thing is certain: throughout all of these scenes, both O'Neill and Monterey were heavily medicated on bromides.[390] Taking bromides in large doses, as both of them did, can lead to delusions, hallucinations, and paranoia, all of which appeared to have manifested themselves over that terrible winter.

O'Neill's Massachusetts lawyer, James E. Farley, filed a petition to have Monterey institutionalized at the Salem probate court on March 28, and the hearing was scheduled for April 23. Monterey's bank account was frozen, and her daughter Cynthia Stram couldn't help her financially; nor could she see her way to make a trip east to care for a mother who had so decisively abandoned her. When Kathryne Albertoni arrived under the impression that "Papa" needed her, a neurologist at McLean, Dr. Harry Kozol, asked Albertoni point-blank if she believed Monterey to be insane. "No," the nurse responded, "she just drives herself hard." Dr. Kozol then asked, "Is she bitchy?" Albertoni repeated, "She drives hard."[391] In the meantime, Dr. Merrill Moore, a Boston psychiatrist and Monterey's ex-husband Ralph Barton's cousin, attempted to have O'Neill institutionalized as well, but O'Neill's doctors ignored his diagnosis. Moore then visited Monterey, told her that she should never see O'Neill again, twenty-three years was enough. (He also, according to Monterey, all but propositioned her in her hospital room in front of Dr. William H. Horowitz, another attending psychiatrist on staff at McLean.)[392]

That same day Monterey sent O'Neill a bouquet of roses, and he agreed to her release on March 29. When she arrived in O'Neill's hospital room, he initially acted "high strung," according to Albertoni, but Monterey dashed into his arms and wept on his shoulder. His eyes welled up too, though he was evidently relieved to have the nurse present.[393]

On April 4, Monterey wrote Kenneth Macgowan a lengthy letter updating him about her and O'Neill's situation. She informed him that she'd been given a clean bill of mental health at McLean, but that upon hearing the news, her husband, "instead of being glad seemed to be disappointed! He *wanted* me to be a mental case!" Whatever happened, she felt condemned by the diagnosis: "Even when [it's proven that] I am *not* a mental case, the shadow will hang over me! Gene swore he'd ruin me, & he has about done it. Being a good dramatist, & Irish, & confused is a bad mixture!"[394]

Saxe Commins, Bennett Cerf, Lawrence Langner, and Russel Crouse all insisted that O'Neill be removed to New York, away from Monterey—this time, they hoped, for good. He agreed to go, and they secured a temporary room for him at the Carlyle Hotel while he convalesced for a month at Doctors Hospital. Even in traction, the ailing playwright was deemed enough of a suicide risk that a nurse was ordered to lock the windows to prevent him from jumping.[395]

Several old friends visited him there, including Jimmy Light, whom O'Neill hadn't seen since France. "Give me a cigarette, will you?" O'Neill asked when he walked in. Light gave him matches as well, but O'Neill's hands were too shaky; when Light took the book of matches and tried to help him, O'Neill snatched it back again. "Thanks for nothing," he sniped, and lit the cigarette himself. "Can you top that?" Light said later. "The guts of the man! It took him a few matches, but he finally managed to light it himself."[396] Cerf arranged for a male nurse to care for O'Neill at the Carlyle, only for the nurse to arrive at Doctors Hospital to find that O'Neill had disappeared. Monterey had located him and persuaded him to return to Boston.

Cerf and Langner were furious with O'Neill for going back to Monterey, but Commins had a more sympathetic understanding of his friend's codependent marriage. "After all," he said, "Carlotta had lived with him and [his disease] for almost a quarter of a century, and when she was not in a state of acute disturbance, she could be competent and devoted and even sacrificial in her imperious and managerial way. Hers was not a radiant future, he argued to convince himself as much as me, and she'd relinquished a life of ease as a woman of conspicuous beauty in order to be at his side through all those years, for better or for worse."[397]

On May 17, 1951, O'Neill took the train back to Boston to join Monterey at her new suite at the Shelton Hotel, across from Dr. Kozol's office. He was under sedation throughout the journey and thus missed his last chance to view New London, the only place that he could truly call home. "How could you have done that to me?" Monterey demanded once he arrived in Boston. O'Neill's face momentarily darkened, then he smiled. "Well," he said, "it was a helluva fourth act."[398]

On May 23, Monterey read over the will that he'd written at Doctors Hospital, and nearly left him on the spot. "God punish liars, traitors, + crooks!" she wrote that day, "I haven't the strength to bear much more of Gene's disloyalty + dishonesty—insane or sane, he always *attacks me!?*"[399] That week O'Neill notified his legal representatives that his June 28, 1948, version was his "true will."[400]

Monterey was once again his sole heir, her condition, apparently, for taking him back. It was the only existing will that forgoes any stipulation about *Long Day's Journey Into Night*. On June 3, 1951, O'Neill painstakingly scrawled an inscription to Monterey in a copy of *A Moon for the Misbegotten:* "To Carlotta, my beloved wife, whose love I could not possibly live without, in a spirit of the humblest gratitude for her love which has forgiven my recent shameful conduct toward her."[401] But neither his reconciliation with Monterey nor the reinstituted will ever changed his desire to withhold *Long Day's Journey* from the public eye. Ten days after his make-up note to Monterey, O'Neill requested all of his manuscripts from Random House, save one: "No, I do not want 'Long Day's Journey Into Night,' " he told Bennett Cerf. "That, as you know, is to be published twenty-five years after my death—but never produced as a play."[402]

In the winter of 1952, the intolerable possibility that some intrepid director might produce what he'd finished off his Cycle after his death moved O'Neill to a desperate act: he and Monterey must destroy the manuscripts. For hours, according to Monterey, they tore the pages up into little pieces, and she flung them into a fire. "It was awful," she recalled. "It was like tearing up children." After that, he lost any will to live. "He died when he could no longer work,"

Monterey said. "He died spiritually. And it was just a matter of drag-
ging a poor, diseased body along for a few more years until it too
died."[403] All the while, O'Neill refused any comfort from the possibility of God or an afterlife. "When I'm dying," he'd insisted, "don't let a
priest or Protestant minister or Salvation Army captain near me. Let
me die in dignity. Keep it as simple and brief as possible. No fuss, no
man of God there. If there is a God, I'll see Him and we'll talk things
over."[404]

On November 27, 1953, at four thirty-seven p.m., O'Neill, at
sixty-five, died in his two-room suite at the Shelton Hotel with Monterey and Dr. Kozol at his bedside. It was a four-day bout of pneumonia that finally claimed his life, exacerbated by his as-yet undiagnosed
neurological illness. "I knew it! I knew it!" he'd cried out between
stretches of unconsciousness. "Born in a goddamn hotel room and
dying in a hotel room!" "Don't sentimentalize him," Monterey said
after he was gone. "He was not a sweet little boy searching for a mama
or a young man ever so polite. He was a black Irishman, a rough
tough black Irishman. . . . He could have that smile that made him
appear so young; other times he'd be as old as an oriental. . . . He was
a simple man. They make a lot of nonsense and mystery out of him.
He was interested only in writing his plays."[405]

Postscript
Journey Into Light

The past is the present, isn't it? It's the future, too. We all try to lie out of that but life won't let us.

—MARY TYRONE in *Long Day's Journey Into Night*

O'NEILL'S AUTOPSY was performed that next morning, November 28, 1953, at Massachusetts General Hospital. "I wanted to know," Monterey said, "what in the name of God was the matter with this man I had nursed so long."[1] Unfortunately, given the limits of medical science at the time, the findings were a disappointment. No clear indication of Parkinson's was there, though O'Neill's cause of death was listed on his death certificate as bronchopneumonia and a "Parkinsonian Disease." The procedure did reveal that O'Neill had suffered from several lung-related ailments, including emphysema from smoking and fibrous adhesions caused by his tuberculosis from 1912 to 1913.[2] Remarkably, despite his enormous alcohol intake over a twenty-five-year period, and then intermittently, his liver and heart were in normal condition for a man of sixty-five.

Nearly five decades later, at the turn of the millennium, a new autopsy was performed using microscopical slides of the playwright's preserved brain tissue. The project was spearheaded by Dr. E. P. Richardson, a neurologist present at the original autopsy, and Dr. Bruce H. Price, a young associate enthralled by O'Neill and his work. Squinting down into the multiheaded microscope, Price recalled in 2010 that observing the legendary dramatist's brain cells for the first time "was a rather surreal, reverential moment, involving that ever elusive quest to observe and capture genius by viewing brain anatomy." Richardson and Price's investigation again found no trace of Parkinson's (nor of the elusive genius, for that matter), but developments in neuroscience did enable them to accurately diagnose "what in the name of God was the matter" with Monterey's husband. The torturous "Celtic Twilight" of O'Neill's last fifteen years was caused by a rare neurodegenerative disease: late-onset spinal cerebellar atrophy. O'Neill's particular form of the disease was "idiopathic," meaning that, contrary to popular assumption, there was little to no evidence that his drinking had anything to do with it.[3]

O'Neill's remains were laid to rest at Boston's Forest Hills Cemetery on December 2, 1953, with a plot beside him reserved for Monterey. The hearse containing O'Neill's plain black coffin, draped with a white shroud, was trailed by a car carrying three mourners: Monterey, Dr. Kozol, and a nurse. Monterey had earlier seen to the replacement of "There's a Lot to Be Said for Being Dead" on the unpretentious granite tombstone with the standard "Rest in Peace." No friends, family, or press were notified of the burial. "Everything he wished for regarding his funeral and interment was carried out to the letter," Monterey told the undertaker. "And his wishes will be carried out in everything."[4] Monterey respected O'Neill's express instructions not to have a clergyman officiate. She couldn't help bowing her head, though, to murmur the Lord's Prayer.[5]

"You are the only human being I have known who never lied to me," O'Neill wrote Monterey a month before his death. "You are the only one who never gained anything from being close to me. . . . You are the only one who really loved me!"[6] A few days after he wrote these words, with her husband's demise a certainty, Monterey swore that she had "but one reason to live & that is to carry out Gene's wishes . . . the 'twenty-five year box' is the most interesting part of it—all personal except *Long Day's Journey Into Night*—& not intended to be opened until twenty-five years after Gene's death."[7] And as late as February 1954, she wrote a diary entry that clearly indicates her understanding of his posthumous wishes: "The '25 year box' cannot be opened until 1978!"[8] But several months later, a drama behind the drama had begun to unfold.

*   *   *

In June 1954, Monterey contacted Bennett Cerf at Random House and demanded that he publish *Long Day's Journey*. Cerf consulted with Saxe Commins, and together they refused to violate their pact. Commins recalled that when Cerf informed Monterey of this, "She exploded with fury and vented most of her wrath on me, accusing me of having instigated a plot against her, of having ruined all the O'Neill plays on which I had worked with him and charging me with about as many crimes as are included in the penal code."[9] They held firm, Cerf wrote, but were soon "horrified to learn that legally all the cards were in her hand; what the author wanted, and what he had asked us to do, had no validity if *she* wanted something else—which she did."[10]

After Monterey had wrenched *Long Day's Journey* from the reluctant hands of Random House, she secured its publication by Yale University Press, with the proceeds of the American and Canadian book rights to support the Eugene O'Neill Collection at Yale's Sterling Library and the School of Drama. Next, she offered Sweden's Royal Dramatic Theatre, which had produced more of O'Neill's plays than any other theater in the world, the rights to produce the autobiographical tragedy. Then, Monterey informed the press that O'Neill had made a stunning "deathbed request" that the Swedish theater should produce *Long Day's Journey* in Swedish translation.[11]

Monterey alleged that her husband's decision to withhold the script had been meant to protect his son Eugene, but that he changed his mind after his son's death. This was untrue. On August 4, 1941, O'Neill wrote in his work diary that Eugene had read the play that day while visiting him and was "greatly moved, which pleases me a lot." No mention was made of Eugene's desire for him to quash it. Furthermore, Eugene had committed suicide nearly a year *before* O'Neill wrote Cerf to remind him of their compact on June 15, 1951.[12] On March 3, 1952, a time when his neurological illness had grown so acute that their Shelton Hotel suite was more hospice than home, O'Neill had signed a trust deed transferring the rights to his plays to Monterey, though it did not list *Long Day's Journey* on its otherwise comprehensive list of scripts, presumably because of O'Neill's well-documented decree that Random House should retain the publication rights to that particular play. Nevertheless, O'Neill had signed over to Carlotta Monterey, under these uncertain terms, the "rights, title and interest in my copyrights and literary properties."[13]

Soon after the play's release in 1956, George Jean Nathan offered a partial explanation for O'Neill's mysterious decree to withhold the script: "O'Neill had confided to me, personally, that regard for his family's feelings—chiefly his brother's and mother's—had influenced him to insist upon the play's delay."[14] Saxe Commins added that O'Neill told him that the play "should be kept from the public until everyone involved, particularly members of his family, was dead or old enough not to be hurt or even disturbed by it."[15] "To the outer world we maintained an indomitably united front and lied and lied for each other," O'Neill had told Eugene about his family. "A typical pure Irish family. The same loyalty occurs, of course, in all kinds of families, but there is, I think, among Irish still close to, or born in Ireland, a strange mixture of fight and hate and forgive, a clannish pride before the world, that is particularly our own."[16] Although it's typically Irish to bury family problems, O'Neill had effectively hung his brother's legacy out to dry with *A Moon for the Misbegotten*; and since he'd shown *Long Day's Journey* to Eugene, it's highly unlikely he would have been more concerned about Oona and Shane's reactions. If anything, the play might have explained a great deal to them about their father's behavior.

More important, O'Neill had informed the press that there was a character in *Long Day's Journey* who remained among the living, and it was out of respect for that person that he withheld the play. When asked whether it was himself he meant, he said nothing, though he was, in fact, the only one still alive.[17] But he never specified whether this character, a member of his family, as Commins indicated, was onstage or off, or even directly mentioned. (There is one other onstage character in *Long Day's Journey*, the Tyrone's Irish maid Cathleen; but she can be ruled out given his specifications about being a member of the family.) One possibility is that he meant Kathleen Jenkins, for whom he had abiding loyalty and respect—she was "the woman," as he'd told Monterey, "I gave the most trouble to" but who gave him "the least."[18]

(And in fact he'd already attempted to destroy *Exorcism* in large part, apparently, to respect Jenkins's privacy.) In fact, both Agnes Boulton and Jenkins remarked how strange it was that O'Neill neglected to mention Jenkins and Eugene Jr. in *Long Day's Journey*. "It was just that Gene was *like* that," Boulton remarked. "Who, after having seen *Long Day's Journey Into Night*, would ever realize that Edmund, the younger son, had been married and divorced and was the father of a child nearly three years old on that August evening in 1912?"[19]

Indeed Boulton, who'd retained and ensured the continued existence of the surviving copy of *Exorcism*, after countless interviews with journalists and biographers and even a memoir about her early years with O'Neill (which discusses his suicide attempt but makes no mention of *Exorcism*), respected O'Neill's privacy to her death in 1968. Nowhere did she ever betray the fact that the much-coveted script still existed. Jenkins, for her part, told the *New York Post* that she was "very glad" she and her son went unmentioned. "It was so absolutely outside anything that was between us," Jenkins said. "A great deal happened to both of us since then. It seems way back in the dark ages."[20]

But when O'Neill's remark about his "family's feelings" is taken into account, a more likely possibility exists, one that might explain his refusal to share the play: his cousin Agnes Brennan, the "only relative he ever saw," Monterey said, and one of the few of his family apprised of Ella's addiction. On May 29, 1954, at the very time that Monterey had made up her mind to contact Random House about publishing the script, Brennan came to visit. "I try to explain 'Long Day's Journey Into Night' to her," Monterey's diary reads, "which leads to her telling me all about Gene's babyhood, childhood, and boyhood—Unwanted, no love or tenderness, no care, *no discipline*, no protection! . . . If I had only known this *fully*—not in bits and pieces!" The following morning, a Sunday, Brennan attended Mass, then read *Long Day's Journey:* "It upsets her no end. But, when she has settled down—she *tells* me the play is *under* statement—spends hours weeping + telling me of the O'Neill family. . . . A sad, unnecessary mess! *What a heritage!*"[21] Brennan isn't mentioned in the play, but she's implicit in Mary Tyrone's disgust with the town of New London and *all* of its inhabitants. O'Neill's earliest work notes for *Long Day's Journey* describe his mother's character, "M," thinking of the Brennans as "obstacles to her socially, [making living in New London] impossible,"[22] and in the completed version, Mary declares venomously, "I've always hated this town and everyone in it" (*CP3*, 738).

The Brennan sisters had been "infuriated" before by what they considered O'Neill's unsavory autobiographical impulse. They believed that the Irish biddy Maggie Brennan in *The Straw* was an unfair treatment of their mother, Josephine. Josephine herself had no use for O'Neill. After reading *Thirst* in 1913, she tossed it into her furnace and proclaimed, "Someone ought to tell Eugene to get out of the gutter!"[23] Agnes Brennan and her sister Lillian's barely implicit message after *The Straw* was heard loud and clear: "Go to it, but leave the family out of it." O'Neill had mixed feelings about the "lace curtain" Brennans, but he stayed in touch. Prior to his return from France in 1931, O'Neill had written Agnes Brennan to wish her mother well on her ninety-first birthday. "I always remember with deep gratitude how kind she used to be to me when I was a boy and how I used to look forward to her visits on Pequot Avenue. . . . How I wish my Mother could have lived! It has been lonely with my Father, Mother and Jamie all gone."[24] A couple of years later, at Casa Genotta, he admitted to the director Philip Moeller that his ultimately disastrous decision to end *Days Without End* with John Loving praying at the cross and embracing God's love was "undoubtedly a wish fulfillment on his part," according to Moeller, to achieve the Brennan family's Catholic-influenced "simple trusting happiness" that his marriage to Monterey hadn't fulfilled.[25] And finally, in his penultimate will, O'Neill had bequeathed money to three people besides his wife: his stepdaughter, Cynthia, his New London friend Ice Casey, and Agnes Brennan. Agnes died in 1956, the year of *Long Day's Journey*'s release, and perhaps she was mercifully spared the worldwide news of O'Neill's shocking portrayal of her family. "Such cracks," O'Neill believed of publishing hurtful information he'd written about actual people, "are remembered, passed on, and finally appear in theatrical gossip columns and someone's feelings are hurt, even though it dates back twenty years or more."[26]

But what to make of the playwright's complete embargo on productions in any medium? This too was nothing new for him. "My interest in the productions steadily decreases," O'Neill lamented after *Dynamo's* failure in 1929, "as my interest in plays as written increases. They always—with exceptions you know—fall so far below my intent that I'm a bit weary and disillusioned with scenery and actors and the whole uninspired works of the Show Shop. . . . As it is I think I will wind up writing plays to be published with 'No Productions Allowed' in red letters on the first page. . . . The ideas for the plays I am writing and going to write are too dear to me, too much travail of blood and spirit will go into their writing, for me to expose them to what I know is an unfair test. I would rather place them directly from my imagination to the imagination of the reader."[27]

Of course he would see five more productions onto the boards after writing this; but his preference for the reader over the live audience only hardened with time. Soon after the humiliating *Days Without End* fiasco, he'd reiterated the idea to the Guild's set designer Lee Simonson: "I take my theatre too personally, I guess—so personally that before long I think I shall permanently resign from all production and confine my future work to plays in books for readers only."[28] By 1940, before Monterey had even typed up a draft of *Long Day's Journey Into Night*, O'Neill had lost faith in American drama entirely: "Now I feel out of the theatre," he told Kenneth Macgowan. "I dread the idea of production because I know it will be done by people who have really only one standard left, that of Broadway success."[29] How might a director from the future, he must have wondered, desecrate his most sacred, most personal work?

The reasons behind Monterey's premature release of *Long Day's Journey* have since remained unclear. Many believe she did it for the money. But Monterey never spent whatever profits she made on the play's international productions on a lavish lifestyle, and she'd even donated the royalties of the Swedish premiere to the Royal Dramatic Theatre's cast.[30] Others imagine she did it for attention, though she loathed (her word) publicity of any kind, and rarely agreed to be interviewed or to respond to inquiries about her husband. Perhaps she released it for O'Neill's legacy; but that was assured in any event by the play's eventual publication.

We may never know precisely why Monterey did this. But while O'Neill tormented himself over a Cycle of plays about "possessors self-dispossessed," she had dedicated her life to one purpose: the possession of her husband's legacy. "Thank God I did for him what I did do!" she concluded in her (revised for public consumption) diary of May of 1954 after making the decision to take Long Day's Journey to press; nearly a year later, while arranging the publication of the book with Yale University Press, she wrote, "No one *could* do all I've done but me—nor *would* any one but me!"³¹ O'Neill showered Monterey with loving inscriptions; but far and away his greatest gift to her was his last will and testament from 1948. Once it was probated in a Boston court less than a month after O'Neill's death, she at last possessed his legacy, with the full backing of the law. Monterey then insisted that Yale University Press include in the publication of Long Day's Journey an inscription, signed on July 22, 1941, with no further introduction:

For Carlotta, on our 12th Wedding Anniversary

Dearest: I give you the original script of this play of old sorrow, written in tears and blood. A sadly inappropriate gift, it would seem, for a day celebrating happiness. But you will understand. I mean it as a tribute to your love and tenderness which gave me the faith in love that enabled me to face my dead at last and write this play—write it with deep pity and understanding and forgiveness for *all* the four haunted Tyrones.

These twelve years, Beloved One, have been a Journey into Light—into love. You know my gratitude. And my love! (*CP3*, 714)

A previously unknown incident is also revealing for understanding her motives: O'Neill's nurse from California, Kathryne Albertoni, had come to New York with her husband, Albert, to attend a first-run performance of Long Day's Journey. (O'Neill, after all, had written much of the play while Albertoni inhabited the bedroom adjacent to his office.) Monterey gave them complimentary tickets and invited them to dine at her suite in the Carlton House on Madison Avenue. Albertoni's husband, a friend of O'Neill's back in Danville who looked and sounded like Humphrey Bogart, demanded to know why Monterey had released the play early. "Why did you do that, what you did?" he growled angrily across the dinner table. "That was not Mr. O'Neill's will." Monterey replied bluntly: because "every whore would claim she slept with him while he was writing [it]." The Albertonis took this literally, assuming she meant that some prostitutes O'Neill had caroused with as a young man might still be alive and come out of the woodwork to blackmail Monterey. "That's why she [re]wrote the will," Albertoni said as late as 2010, three years before her death. "She didn't like the way it was written. I don't blame her."[32]

But there's another way to read Monterey's response. She and O'Neill used the epithet *whore* with disturbing frequency, and he repeatedly applied it against her after she'd abandoned him at Marblehead Neck. (" 'Whore' has echoed about my ears continually," she protested that April.)[33] Monterey had several "whores" in mind after her husband's death, including Jane Caldwell. But the woman Monterey most frequently referred to as a whore was Agnes Boulton. "Where is her *pride, her self-respect?*" Monterey had fumed over Boulton's alimony payments. "*Whores* are paid for their bodies—*not wives!*"[34] If Boulton was preparing to make any claims on the profits of *Long Day's Journey*, Monterey would be ready. For over two decades, she'd voiced outrage over Boulton's financial lien on O'Neill. Additionally, Boulton was in fact present when he'd sketched out his preliminary treatment of *Long Day's Journey* back in the spring of 1927—and Boulton had that manuscript, found among her belongings after her death, to prove it if necessary. By releasing the play early, Monterey was undoubtedly forestalling Boulton's potential claims to biographers, the press, and the courts—for monetary reasons in part, perhaps, but more important to Monterey, for custodianship of the work. The glory of serving as midwife for O'Neill's most cherished child would be, and has been, hers alone.

O'Neill and Monterey's friend Carl Van Vechten responded with grave doubts to his publisher Alfred A. Knopf's query about the prospect of an O'Neill biography after *Long Day's Journey* had drummed up interest: "I think it would be impossible for any one, save in some secret way, to set down his share of the story, to write a frank O'Neill story. Undoubtedly Carlotta will have her version prepared and she has already rewritten her diary. . . . Moreover, I think she will be able to protect his reputation even after she is dead, for a generation or two." (In fact, Monterey had diligently transcribed most of her diaries before she presumably destroyed the originals, then submitted the revised transcriptions in volume form to Yale's Beinecke Library.) Van Vechten suggested collecting affidavits from those who knew O'Neill personally, with the idea being to "organize and publish these in some far distant future, without risk of getting sued."[35]

Two years later, 1958, Boulton did publish a "frank O'Neill story," a memoir about her early years with him, *Part of a Long Story: Eugene O'Neill as a Young Man in Love*. She'd planned to write two sequels before she passed away on November 25, 1968 (having signed into the hospital, in spite of her remarriage, as "Mrs. Eugene O'Neill"); but her severe alcoholism prevented their completion.[36] Over the following decade, her daughter, Oona, also began drinking heavily while nursing Chaplin until his death in 1977; later she surrendered to alcoholism and died of pancreatic cancer in 1991 at age sixty-six. Carlotta Monterey suffered a complete nervous breakdown the same month that Boulton died and was subsequently institutionalized at St. Luke's Hospital in Manhattan. She never fully recovered. Monterey had thought it likely she'd be dead herself twenty-five years after her husband's death, and she was right. She died on November 18, 1970, eight years before O'Neill's intended release date for *Long Day's Journey*.

On February 10, 1956, Stockholm's Royal Dramatic Theatre welcomed King Gustaf Adolf VI and his wife, Queen Louisa, along with a lavish, formally attired procession of Sweden's aristocrats, socialites, artists, and diplomats, to view the world premiere of *Long Day's Journey Into Night*. When the final curtain fell, the audience rose to its feet and roared applause for up to half an hour, and the cast was beckoned back for more than a dozen curtain calls.[37] The Swedish critics deemed O'Neill "the world's last dramatist of the stature of Aeschylus and Shakespeare," and the performance was hailed as the greatest theatrical event of the twentieth century.[38] Monterey, who didn't attend, next summoned José Quintero, who had directed the Greenwich Village revival of *The Iceman Cometh* at the Circle in the Square—a production that ran for 565 performances, a record for O'Neill, and prompted critics to rank *Iceman* as a masterwork. She offered Quintero and his team, including Leigh Connell and Theodore Mann, the rights to produce *Long Day's Journey* on Broadway. The *Iceman* production had starred Jason Robards Jr., whose performance as Hickey Hickman, then as Jamie Tyrone in *Long Day's Journey*, "Erie" Smith in *Hughie* in 1964, and Jim Tyrone in the legendary production of *A Moon for the Misbegotten* with Colleen Dewhurst as Josie Hogan, indelibly marked his position as O'Neill's master interpreter for the stage.

Once the final curtain had dropped on November 7, 1956, at New York's Helen Hayes Theatre, after well-received tryouts in Boston and New Haven, there was a hush of astonishment that lasted more than a minute. Then the audience rose to its feet, and the trickle of isolated clapping surged into a wave of deafening, rapturous applause; after innumerable curtain calls, a mass of theatergoers pushed forward to praise the exhausted actors onstage. Those in the audience were awed by the play's craftsmanship but also shocked by the autobiographical revelations it contained. Who could have known that the mother of America's only Nobel Prize–winning playwright had been a morphine addict for over twenty years? That O'Neill's older brother had exerted such a Mephistophelian influence on him? That his celebrated father had lived in such a painful state of regret and Irish-born terror of poverty that only alcohol and a manic acquisition of real estate could ease his suffering? Certainly no one who didn't know O'Neill intimately, and even many who did. The ghost of the playwright was a tangible presence behind the proscenium arch that night. In this drama, the dead playwright *was* the protagonist.

From left at back, Bradford Dillman as Edmund Tyrone, Jason Robards Jr. as Jamie Tyrone, Frederic March as James Tyrone, and at front, Florence Eldridge as Mary Tyrone in José Quintero's production of *Long Day's Journey Into Night* at the Helen Hayes Theatre, 1956.

✳   ✳   ✳

Long Day's Journey Into Night was hailed as O'Neill's magnum opus and Quintero's production brilliant. The *Daily News* raved that the play "exploded like a dazzling sky-rocket over the humdrum of Broadway theatricals." Brooks Atkinson wrote in the *New York Times*, "With the production of 'Long Day's Journey Into Night,' the American theatre acquires size and stature." Atkinson clarified that by "size" he didn't mean the length of the play (over three hours) but rather O'Neill's "conception of theatre as a form of epic literature."[39] The Broadway production alone ran for sixty-five weeks for a total of 390 performances and posthumously won O'Neill a Drama Critics Circle Award, an Outer Circle Award, a Tony Award, and his fourth Pulitzer Prize. Few artists, no matter their stature, had achieved this level of acclaim with a single work. O'Neill did so, implausibly, *after* having already won the Nobel Prize in Literature.

" 'Long Day's Journey' is not a play," wrote Walter Kerr in the *New York Herald Tribune*,

> It is a lacerating round-robin of recrimination, self-dramatization, lies that deceive no one, confessions that never expiate the crime. Around the whiskey bottles and the tattered leather chairs and the dangling light-cords that infest the decaying summer home of the Tyrones (read O'Neills), a family of ghosts sit in a perpetual game of four-handed solitaire, stir to their feet in a danse macabre that outlines the geography of Hell, place themselves finally on an operating table that allows for no anesthetic. When the light fails, they are still—but not saved. . . . How has O'Neill kept self-pity and vulgarity and cheap bravado out of this prolonged, unasked-for, improbable inferno? Partly by the grim determination that made him a major dramatist: the insistence that the roaring fire he could build by grinding his own two hands together was the fire of truth. You can disbelieve, but you cannot deny him his heat, his absolute passion.[40]

Carlotta Monterey's detractors, like her defenders, have been legion; but whatever her motives, the release of *Long Day's Journey* proved to be exactly the right thing to do. O'Neill's theatrical descendent Tony Kushner reminds us that Monterey's "betrayal of his wishes must be seen by us as an act of beneficence. ... He fell silent, isolated himself, withered and died. And rose again, almost immediately!"[41] Indeed, with the Broadway premieres of *A Moon for the Misbegotten* in 1957, *A Touch of the Poet* in 1958, *Hughie* in 1964, and *More Stately Mansions* in 1967, a full-scale Eugene O'Neill renaissance flourished for well over a decade. "The tallest skyscraper in New York," hailed the *Sunday Times* of London in 1958, "is the reputation of Eugene O'Neill."[42]

Just as he'd suspected all along: for all his hard work, misadventures, and suffering, there was a great deal to be said for being dead. O'Neill's posthumous resurgence in the 1950s, 1960s, and 1970s set the stage for the theatrical innovations of new generations of American dramatists—Lorraine Hansberry, Edward Albee, Neil Simon, August Wilson, William Inge, Sam Shepard, Wendy Wasserstein, David Mamet, Paula Vogel, John Patrick Shanley, Tony Kushner, David Henry Hwang, and so it goes. As time passes, O'Neill remains there among them, a ghost at the stage door.

Appendix
Selected Chronology of Works
(Date Completed)

═══

1913
A Wife for a Life
The Web
Thirst
Recklessness
Warnings

1914
Bread and Butter
Servitude
Fog
Bound East for Cardiff
Abortion
The Movie Man

1915
The Sniper
The Personal Equation

1916
Before Breakfast
Now I Ask You
"Tomorrow"
"The Screenews of War"

1917
Ile
The Long Voyage Home

The Moon of the Caribbees
In the Zone
S.O.S.

1918

Shell Shock
The Rope
Beyond the Horizon
The Dreamy Kid
Where the Cross Is Made

1919

Chris Christophersen
The Straw
Exorcism

1920

Gold
"Anna Christie"
The Emperor Jones
Diff'rent

1921

The First Man
The Hairy Ape

1922

The Fountain

1923

Welded
All God's Chillun Got Wings

1924

Desire Under the Elms

1925

Marco Millions
The Great God Brown

1926

Lazarus Laughed

1927
Strange Interlude

1928
Dynamo

1931
Mourning Becomes Electra

1932
Ah, Wilderness!

1933
Days Without End

1939
More Stately Mansions
The Iceman Cometh

1941
Long Day's Journey Into Night
Hughie

1942
A Touch of the Poet

1943
A Moon for the Misbegotten

Notes

Prologue

1. Dorothy Day, "Told in Context," ca. 1958, Dorothy Day Papers, series D-3, box 7, file 2, Special Collections and University Archives, Raynor Memorial Libraries, Marquette University, Milwaukee, Wis.

2. James Light, interview by Louis Sheaffer, August 14, 1962, Sheaffer-O'Neill Collection, Linda Lear Center for Special Collections and Archives, Connecticut College, New London.

3. Anna Alice Chapin, *Greenwich Village* (New York: Dodd, Mead, 1920), 237.

4. Croswell Bowen, "The Black Irishman" (1946), in *O'Neill and His Plays: Four Decades of Criticism*, ed. Oscar Cargill, N. Bryllion Fagin, and William J. Fisher (New York: New York University Press, 1961), 82.

5. Susan Glaspell, undated entry in notebook dated October 16, 1915, p. 20, Susan Glaspell Collection, Clifton Waller Barrett Library of American Literature, Albert and Shirley Small Special Collections Library, University of Virginia, Charlottesville.

6. A. J. Philpot, "Biggest Art Colony in the World at Provincetown," *Boston Globe*, August 27, 1916, SM9.

7. Quoted in Pierre Loving, "Eugene O'Neill," *Bookman*, August 1921, 516.

8. Hutchins Hapgood, *A Victorian in the Modern World* (New York: Harcourt, Brace, 1939), 396.

9. Harry Kemp, "O'Neill of Provincetown," *Brentano's Book Chat*, May–June 1929, 45–47.

10. Mary Heaton Vorse, *Time and the Town: A Provincetown Chronicle* (1942), ed. Adele Heller (New Brunswick, N.J.: Rutgers University Press, 1991), 120–21; Hutchins Hapgood to Mabel Dodge, July 1, 1916, Hapgood Family Papers, Beinecke Library, Yale University, New Haven.

11. Harry Kemp, "Out of Provincetown: A Memoir of Eugene O'Neill" (1930), in *Conversations with Eugene O'Neill*, ed. Mark W. Estrin (Jackson: University Press of Mississippi, 1990), 96.

12. Along with his caricatural portrayal of Mexicans in *The Movie Man*, O'Neill also employed "sight dialect," for instance, foreign-looking spellings that match proper pronunciation: "happee" for "happy," "crazee" for "crazy," "angree" for "angry," etc.

13. Frederick P. Latimer, "Eugene Is beyond Us," (New London) *Day*, February 15, 1928, 6.

14. Kemp, "Out of Provincetown," 96.

15. Vorse, *Time and the Town*, 121.

16. Kemp, "Out of Provincetown," 96.

Introduction

1. Thomas Flanagan, "Master of the Misbegotten," in *There You Are: Writings on Irish and American Literature and History*, ed. Christopher Cahill (New York: New York Review of Books, 2004), 41–61; Rohan Preston, "The Dean of Dysfunction," *Minneapolis Star Tribune*, January 18, 2013, http://www.startribune.com/entertainment/stageand-arts/187324901.html; Alan Dale, "O'Neill Play of Nine Acts and Six Hours Reviewed by Dale," *New York American*, January 31, 1928, 9.

2. Eugene O'Neill to Mary Clark, August 5, 1923, Sheaffer-O'Neill Collection, in *The Straw* file, Linda Lear Center for Special Collections and Archives, Connecticut College, New London.

3. Eugene O'Neill to Mrs. Hills, March 21, 1925, Sheaffer-O'Neill Collection, in *Desire Under the Elms* file; Alta May Coleman, "Personality Portraits No. 3: Eugene O'Neill," *Theatre Magazine*, April 1920, 264, 302. O'Neill used this exclamatory remark as an ironic mantra with which to get through difficult times.

4. Quoted in Croswell Bowen, *The Curse of the Misbegotten: A Tale of the House of O'Neill* (New York: McGraw-Hill, 1959), 310–11.

5. Quoted in Louis Sheaffer, *Son and Playwright* (Boston: Little, Brown, 1968), 419; Eugene O'Neill, *Complete Plays, 1913–1920*, ed. Travis Bogard (New York: Library of America, 1988), 1:647. Hereafter, unless otherwise indicated, all references to O'Neill's plays will be to this three-volume edition (the second and third volumes are *Complete Plays, 1920–1931*, and *Complete Plays, 1932–1943*) and will be provided in text with volume and page number: for example, *CP*1, 647. The year that each play was completed will not be identified in parentheses as they are listed in the appendix.

6. Eugene O'Neill Theater Festival, October 17, 2009, Eugene O'Neill Theater Center, Waterford, Conn.

7. Laurie Metcalf and Nathan Lane, "Two Journeys into O'Neill, via E-Mail," *New York Times*, June 14, 2012, AR7.

8. Helen Mirren, interview by Liane Hansen, "Helen Mirren, Acting Out as Tolstoy's Wild Sofya," *Weekend Edition Sunday*, January 17, 2010, NPR, http://www.npr.org/templates/story/story.php?storyId=122613323.

9. "Cornel West Commentary: The Plays of Eugene O'Neill," *The Tavis Smiley Show*, November 26, 2003, NPR, http://www.npr.org/templates/story/story .php?storyId=1522880; T. C. Boyle, "Celtic Twilight: 21st-Century Irish Americans on Eugene O'Neill," *Drunken Boat #12*, http://www.drunkenboat.com/db12/04one/boyle/ index.php.

10. Sinclair Lewis, "Nobel Prize Lecture: The American Fear of Literature," December 12, 1930, *Nobelprize.org*, http://www.nobelprize.org/nobel_prizes/literature/ laureates/1930/lewis-lecture.html.

11. "Eugene O'Neill Talks of His Own and the Plays of Others," *New York Herald Tribune*, November 16, 1924, sec. 7–8, 14; FBI memorandum, April 22, 1924 (obtained by the author through the Freedom of Information Act). The Bureau also identified him as a possible contributing editor in 1919 at poet Hart Crane's magazine the *Pagan*, which advanced individual happiness as a societal good. (That the pursuit of happiness was considered a radical philosophy is a sign of his times if there ever was one.) There is an "E. O'Neil" listed as an associate editor in the journal; ironically, the only item attributable to O'Neill (titled "Post-Lude" and appearing in volume 4, issue 1) is a few lines signed "A. Pagan Knight," in which he accuses a New York playhouse of peddling "propaganda."

12. FBI memorandum, April 22, 1924. This wasn't the last time O'Neill's name passed across a federal agent's desk. The New London *Day* reported as late as 1996 that the domestic eco-terrorist Theodore "Ted" Kaczynski, a.k.a. "the Unabomber," had applied $1 O'Neill commemorative stamps to package bombs designed to kill the addressee. After this breakthrough in the high-profile case, the FBI opened a file titled "Eugene O'Neill" and another on the Eugene O'Neill Society, which contained directories of its members from 1979 to 1992. Remnants of O'Neill stamps were found at five crime scenes associated with Kaczynski's years-long rampage, including his first attack, at Northwestern University in 1978. The FBI was tracking a bogus scent, however: in Kaczynski's handwritten response (May 20, 2013) to my letter of inquiry, he called the FBI connection "bull manure." "I've never had the faintest interest in Eugene O'Neill and I've never read anything by him, unless perhaps I was required to read something of his in a high-school English course, in which case I promptly forgot it."

13. Arthur Miller, *Timebends* (New York: Grove, 1987), 228, 229.

14. Carol Bird, "Eugene O'Neill—The Inner Man" (1924), in *Conversations with Eugene O'Neill*, ed. Mark W. Estrin (Jackson: University Press of Mississippi, 1990), 52. Bird implies in her piece that the quotations are paraphrases, given O'Neill's laconic responses to her questions.

15. Eugene O'Neill, *Selected Letters of Eugene O'Neill*, ed. Travis Bogard and Jackson R. Bryer (New Haven: Yale University Press, 1988), 206.

16. Committee for Racial Democracy in the Nation's Capital, "Eugene O'Neill Pledges No More of His Plays at National Theater unless Color Bar Is Dropped," March 24, 1947, Rev. Wilfred Parsons, SJ, Papers, box 8, file 9, Georgetown University Library, Washington, D.C.

17. O'Neill, *Selected Letters*, 515.

18. Quoted in Croswell Bowen, *The Curse of the Misbegotten: A Tale of the House of O'Neill* (New York: McGraw-Hill, 1959), 313.

19. William Faulkner, "American Drama: Eugene O'Neill," in *William Faulkner: Early Prose and Poetry* (New York: Little, Brown, 1962), 87.

20. Stella Adler, *On America's Master Playwrights* (New York: Knopf, 2012), 8.

21. James Light, "The Parade of Masks," undated, T-Mss 2001–050, Billy Rose Theatre Division, New York Public Library.

22. Tony Kushner, "The Genius of O'Neill," *Eugene O'Neill Review* 26 (2004): 248.

23. O'Neill, *Selected Letters*, 26.

24. Ibid., 545.

25. Ibid., 203.

ACT I: The Ghosts at the Stage Door

Notes to pp. 25–26: "that you write for the stupid" (Brenda Murphy, *American Realism and American Drama, 1880–1940* [New York: Cambridge University Press, 1987], 58); "What the American public always wants" (quoted in R. W. B. Lewis, *Edith Wharton: A Biography* [New York: Harper and Row, 1975], 172); "This highest of distinctions" (Eugene O'Neill, "The Nobel Prize Acceptance Letter," in *The Unknown O'Neill: Unpublished and Unfamiliar Writings of Eugene O'Neill*, ed. Travis Bogard [New Haven: Yale University Press, 1988], 427).

1. Arthur Gelb and Barbara Gelb, *O'Neill: Life with Monte Cristo* (New York: Applause, 2000), 42.

2. "Talks with Actors: James O'Neill Relates Something of His Career—An Ambition to Get into the Legitimate: A Buffalo Boy Who Has Risen," *Buffalo Express*, September 28, 1885, 5. This anecdote was circulated widely and can be found in numerous sources. James O'Neill himself quotes Neilson as saying this, referring to her as the "queen of the actresses," in "James O'Neill," *Famous Actors of the Day in America* (Boston: L. C. Page, 1899), 144. The full quotation reads: "Of all of the Romeos I have ever played with, a little Irishman named O'Neill, leading man in Chicago, was the best."

3. Quoted in Hamilton Basso, "The Tragic Sense—I," *New Yorker*, February 28, 1948, 34.

4. J. B. Russak, introduction to *"Monte Cristo" by Charles Fechter and Other Plays*, ed. J. B. Russak (Princeton, N.J.: Princeton University Press, 1941), 4.

5. Charles Webster, interview by Louis Sheaffer, October 28, 1960, Sheaffer-O'Neill Collection, Linda Lear Center for Special Collections and Archives, Connecticut College, New London.

6. James O'Neill believed he performed *Monte Cristo* six thousand times; though Louis Sheaffer argues in *O'Neill: Son and Playwright* (Boston: Little, Brown, 1968, 42) that it was probably closer to four thousand total, James told a reporter that by 1901 he'd already performed it four thousand times (Frederic Edward McKay, "O'Neill as Monte Cristo to the Bitter End," *New York Morning Telegraph*, April 1901, 2).

7. Charles Fechter, *Monte Cristo* (1870), in *"Monte Cristo" by Charles Fechter and Other Plays*, 38.

8. "Talks with Actors: James O'Neill."

9. Fechter, *Monte Cristo*, 42.

10. Quoted in Basso, "Tragic Sense—I," 34–35.

11. Sheaffer, *Son and Playwright*, 44; McKay, "O'Neill as Monte Cristo to the Bitter End," 2.

12. [No first name] Cheney, "Footlight Favorites ... The Early Promise of James O'Neill, of 'Monte Cristo' Fame—a Promise Not Entirely Fulfilled," *St. Paul Sunday Globe*, March 22, 1885, 9. The reporter also insinuates that James confessed a tragic end to his torrid affair with actress Louise Hawthorne in 1876 had exacted a heavy psychological toll, which might explain his self-removal from greatness. Hawthorne, who was married at the time, had followed James to Chicago and was staying at the Tremont Hotel. After his performance in the French melodrama *The Two Orphans*, which she attended, he apparently visited her room and broke off their relationship. "That interview must have been a stormy, crushing, heart-breaking affair," the gossip mongering went on. "Five minutes after O'Neill bade Miss Hawthorne adieu, she sprang from the fifth story window and fell to her death on the pavement below." "There are some events that murder a man's ambition," the reporter concluded, "and that terrible tragedy may have altered the whole course of O'Neill's life. He alone can tell."

13. Quoted in Basso, "Tragic Sense—I," 34–35.

14. Edmund was of course named for the Irish statesman Edmund Burke (the child's middle name was Burke), but the fact remains: given that Edmund was referred to as Edmund, James O'Neill made the connection to his stage character singularly clear. He also made it a habit to name his properties in New London after his character, such as Monte Cristo Cottage on Pequot Avenue and Monte Cristo Garage at the top of Union Street, where the words "Monte Cristo" are still inlaid above the garage doors in red brick.

15. Gelb and Gelb, *O'Neill*, 100.

16. Quoted in *Sedalia Weekly Bazoo*, March 31, 1885, 8.

17. "Autograph Manuscript, 1 page," Hammerman Collection, www.eoneill.com/manuscripts/27200.htm.

18. Sheaffer, *Son and Playwright*, 24.

19. George C. Tyler, *Whatever Goes Up: The Hazardous Fortunes of a Natural Born Gambler* (Brooklyn: Braunworth, 1934), 92–93.

20. Gelb and Gelb, *Life with Monte Cristo*, 671, note "Of the Indian"; Elizabeth Shepley Sergeant, "Casual Notes on O'Neill, the Writer," TS with handwritten corrections and notes, 1946, p. 2, Elizabeth Shepley Sergeant Papers, Beinecke Library, Yale University, New Haven.

21. "Buffalo Bill's Wild West Routes," February 2013, a list compiled at the Buffalo Bill Center of the West, Cody, Wyo. My thanks to Linda S. Clark, assistant managing editor of the Papers of William F. Cody, whose e-mail (July 8, 2013) responded to my request to verify James O'Neill and William F. Cody's crossing of paths in Chicago.

22. "In Many Theatres," *New York Dramatic Mirror*, March 13, 1893, 9; "Side-Tracked," *New York Dramatic Mirror*, April 1, 1893, 9.

23. "Well Rid of a Nuisance: Buffalo Bill Soon to Sail to Europe with the Hostile Ghost Dancers," *Pittsburgh Dispatch*, March 14, 1891, 1.

24. Bowen, "Black Irishman," 84.

25. Sergeant, "Casual Notes on O'Neill," 1.

26. Basso, "Tragic Sense—I," 34.

27. Ann-Louise S. Silver, "American Psychoanalysts Who Influenced Eugene O'Neill's *Long Day's Journey Into Night*," *Journal of the American Academy of Psychoanalysis* 29, no. 2 (2001): 315.

28. David Karsner, "Eugene O'Neill at Close Range in Maine," *New York Herald Tribune*, August 8, 1926, sec. 8, 5.

29. The complete diagram can be found in Sheaffer, *Son and Playwright*, 506.

30. Gelb and Gelb, *Life with Monte Cristo*, 164–65. This episode was conveyed to the Gelbs in an interview with Carlotta Monterey. See 675, note "Nearly fifteen."

31. Eugene O'Neill, *Selected Letters of Eugene O'Neill*, ed. Travis Bogard and Jackson R. Bryer (New Haven: Yale University Press, 1988), 210.

32. Croswell Bowen, "The Black Irishman" (1946), in *O'Neill and His Plays: Four Decades of Criticism*, ed. Oscar Cargill, N. Bryllion Fagin, and William J. Fisher (New York: New York University Press, 1961), 67.

33. Sheaffer, *Son and Playwright*, 101.

34. Carlotta Monterey, interview by Louis Sheaffer, July 29, 1962, Sheaffer-O'Neill Collection; Dorothy Day, "Told in Context," ca. 1958, Dorothy Day Papers, series D-3, box 7, file 2, Special Collections and University Archives, Raynor Memorial Libraries, Marquette University, Milwaukee, Wis. This reminiscence was written after Dorothy Day had published her autobiography *The Long Loneliness* (1952). It was apparently written as an addendum to Agnes Boulton's memoir, *Part of a Long Story*, which offers intimate details about Day's relationship with O'Neill ("Told in Context").

35. O'Neill, *Selected Letters*, 11, 14.

36. Ibid., 14, 17.

37. Eugene O'Neill, *"As Ever, Gene": The Letters of Eugene O'Neill to George Jean Nathan*, ed. Nancy L. Roberts and Arthur W. Roberts (Rutherford, N.J.: Farleigh Dickinson University Press, 1987), 116; Warren H. Hastings and Richard F. Weeks, "Episodes of Eugene O'Neill's Undergraduate Days at Princeton," *Princeton University Library Chronicle* 29, no. 3 (1968): 208–15.

38. Sheaffer, *Son and Playwright*, 116; Hastings and Weeks, "Episodes"; Croswell Bowen, *The Curse of the Misbegotten: A Tale of the House of O'Neill* (New York: McGraw-Hill, 1959), 21; doggerel quoted in Hastings and Weeks, "Episodes."

39. Hastings and Weeks, "Episodes"; Jordan Y. Miller and Winifred Frazer, *American Drama between the Wars: A Critical History* (Boston: Twayne, 1991), 32; James T. Farrell, "Some Observations on Naturalism, So-called, in Fiction" (1950), in *Documents of American Realism and Naturalism*, ed. Donald Pizer (Carbondale: Southern Illinois University Press, 1998), 253.

40. See my essay "Sad Endings and Negative Heroes: The Naturalist Tradition in American Drama," in *The Oxford Handbook to American Literary Naturalism*, ed. Keith Newlin (New York: Oxford University Press, 2011), 427–44.

41. O'Neill, *Selected Letters*, 477.

42. Hastings and Weeks, "Episodes."

43. Ibid.; George Jean Nathan, "The Bright Face of Tragedy," *Cosmopolitan*, August 1957, 66–69; Hastings and Weeks, "Episodes."

44. Bowen, *Curse of the Misbegotten*, 67.

45. Sheaffer, *Son and Playwright*, 114; Karsner, "Eugene O'Neill at Close Range in Maine."

46. O'Neill, *Selected Letters*, 170.

47. Quoted in Basso, "Tragic Sense—I," 35. The convention at the time was to spell "MacDougal Street" with a lowercase "d," and I respect that spelling here.

48. Quoted in Sheaffer, *Son and Playwright*, 104.

49. See my essay "On Eugene O'Neill's 'Philosophical Anarchism,' " *Eugene O'Neill Review* 29 (Spring 2007): 50–72.

50. Charles A. Madison, *Critics and Crusaders* (New York: Holt, 1947–48), 200; Sheaffer, *Son and Playwright*, 102, 103.

51. Quoted in Dorothy Commins, ed., *"Love and Admiration and Respect": The O'Neill-Commins Correspondence* (Durham, N.C.: Duke University Press, 1986), 1, 13.

52. Gelb and Gelb, *Life with Monte Cristo*, 243.

53. O'Neill, *Selected Letters*, 499.

54. Drew Eisenhauer, " 'A Lot of Crazy Socialists and Anarchists': O'Neill and the Artist Social Problem Play," in *Eugene O'Neill and His Early Contemporaries: Bohemians, Radicals, Progressives, and the Avant Garde*, ed. Eileen Herrmann and Robert M. Dowling (Jefferson, N.C.: McFarland, 2011), 130, 113.

55. Manuel Komroff, "Manuel Komroff," in *Anarchist Voices: An Oral History of Anarchism in America*, ed. Paul Avrich (Oakland, Calif.: AK, 2005), 203; Peter Schjeldahl, "Young and Gifted," *New Yorker*, June 25, 2012, 78–79.

56. Quoted in Sheaffer, *Son and Playwright*, 144.

57. The Division and Vital Statistics Administration of the New Jersey Department of Health lists it as October 2 (see Gelb and Gelb, *Life with Monte Cristo*, 255, 683, note "Gilpin officiated"), yet the divorce case, *Kathleen O'Neill v. Eugene G. O'Neill*, gives the date as July 26. The October date is accurate; Kathleen probably claimed the July 26 date to place Eugene Jr.'s conception within the bonds of marriage.

58. Agnes Boulton, *Part of a Long Story: "Eugene O'Neill as a Young Man in Love,"* ed. William Davies King (Jefferson, N.C.: McFarland, 2011), 166; Sheaffer, *Son and Playwright*, 149.

59. O'Neill, *Selected Letters*, 18.

60. Ibid., 18–19, 173.

61. Ibid., 19–20. O'Neill also referred to it as "the Siberia of the tropics" to his second wife, Agnes Boulton, in the summer of 1918 (see Boulton, *Part of a Long Story*, 163).

62. O'Neill, *Selected Letters*, 20, 170.

63. Gelb and Gelb, *Life with Monte Cristo*, 337; Sheaffer, *Son and Playwright*, 158, 159.

64. Sheaffer, *Son and Playwright*, 161.

65. O'Neill, *Selected Letters*, 170.

66. Quoted in Sheaffer, *Son and Playwright*, 164.

67. Eugene O'Neill, "Free" (1912), in *Poems, 1912–1944*, ed. Donald Gallup (New Haven, Conn.: Ticknor and Fields, 1980), 1.

68. See Robert A. Richter, *Eugene O'Neill and Dat Ole Davil Sea: Maritime Influences in the Life and Works of Eugene O'Neill* (Mystic, Conn.: Mystic Seaport, 2004).

69. Quoted in Joel Pfister, *Staging Depth: Eugene O'Neill and the Politics of Psychological Discourse* (Chapel Hill: University of North Carolina Press, 1995), 110.

70. Quoted in Sheaffer, *Son and Playwright*, 169; quoted in Louis Sheaffer, *O'Neill: Son and Artist* (Boston: Little, Brown, 1973), 553.

71. Richter, *Eugene O'Neill and Dat Ole Davil Sea*, 48, 50; O'Neill, *Selected Letters*, 503.

72. Richter, *O'Neill and Dat Ole Davil Sea* 52; Jason Wilson, *Buenos Aires: A Cultural and Literary History*, Cities of the Imagination Series (Oxford: Signal, 2000), 157.

73. C. J. Ballantine, "Smitty—of S. S. *Glencairn*," *New York World*, January 6, 1929; Sheaffer, *Son and Playwright*, 175; Karsner, "Eugene O'Neill at Close Range in Maine."

74. Sheaffer, *Son and Playwright*, 177; Barrett H. Clark, *Eugene O'Neill: The Man and His Plays*, rev. ed. (New York: Dover, 1947), 10; Sheaffer, *Son and Playwright*, 184.

75. Basso, "Tragic Sense—I," 36; Olin Downes, "Playwright Finds His Inspiration on Lonely Sand Dunes by the Sea" (1920), in *Conversations with Eugene O'Neill*, ed. Mark W. Estrin (Jackson: University Press of Mississippi, 1990), 9. O'Neill later claimed on several occasions that he signed onto a steamer shipping mules to Durban, South Africa. He related that he wasn't allowed to disembark in Africa because he didn't have the entry fee of £100. No record of this voyage exists, and when he signed onto the ship that would take him back to the United States, the S.S. *Ikala*, he called it his "first" ship—that is, his first berth as a working seaman (Sheaffer, *Son and Playwright*, 184).

76. Quoted in Sheaffer, *Son and Playwright*, 182–83.

77. Gelb and Gelb, *Life with Monte Cristo*, 526.

78. "The Bridegroom Weeps!" holograph poem signed "E. G. O'Neill," n.d., Henry W. and Albert A. Berg Collection of English and American Literature, New York Public Library, New York. The title is underlined by O'Neill. The manuscript was deposited at the Berg on March 27, 1974, and authenticated by his Provincetown companion Elaine Freeman, an artist who evidently spent a great deal of time with him in the summer of 1917. Freeman also gave the Berg, among other items, a letter O'Neill wrote to her from Provincetown on September 19, 1917. O'Neill's handwriting, which changed over the years, matches both, and they were both written in pencil. In 2011, a later version of this poem emerged, published on eoneill.com, in the handwriting of O'Neill's second wife, Agnes Boulton. A note at the bottom of the manuscript indicates that Agnes committed it to paper in Mt. Point Pleasant, New Jersey, in the winter of 1918–19.

79. " 'Smitty the Duke' Was a Real Man O'Neill Met," *New York Herald*, November 16, 1924.

80. Ballantine, "Smitty—of S. S. *Glencairn*."

81. Ibid.

82. Quoted in Sheaffer, *Son and Playwright*, 445.

83. Eugene O'Neill, "Inscrutable Forces," a letter to Barrett Clark (1919), in Cargill, Fagin, and Fisher, *O'Neill and His Plays*, 99.

84. Quoted in Pfister, *Staging Depth*, 109.

85. Quoted in Hamilton Basso, "The Tragic Sense—III," *New Yorker*, March 13, 1948, 38.

86. Sheaffer, *Son and Playwright*, 145, 188.

87. " 'Whisky' Kills Twelve More Men in East," *New York Tribune*, December 31, 1919, 7; "Two Men Dead, Two Ill from Bad Booze," *Brooklyn Standard Union*, December 28, 1919, 4.

88. John H. Raleigh, introduction to *Twentieth Century Interpretations of "The Iceman Cometh": A Collection of Critical Essays* (Englewood Cliffs, N.J.: Prentice-Hall, 1968), 4–5.

89. Quoted in Sheaffer, *Son and Playwright*, 190; Eugene O'Neill, *Exorcism: A Play in One Act* (1919) (New Haven: Yale University Press, 2012), 1; Herbert Corey, "Manhattan Days and Nights," *Binghamton Press and Leader*, November 14, 1924.

90. Harry Hope's bar, the setting of *The Iceman Cometh*, is based on three of O'Neill's favorite Manhattan watering holes: Jimmy the Priest's; the Garden Hotel on the northeast corner of Madison and Twenty-seventh Street across from the old Madison Square Garden; and the Hell Hole, or the Golden Swan Cafe, at Fourth Street and Sixth Avenue. But O'Neill had Jimmy's bar at the forefront of his mind when writing *Iceman*—in it, the bartender Rocky twice mentions "the Market people across the street and the waterfront workers" who come in at lunchtime, referring to people working around Washington Market, located across from Jimmy's (*CP3*, 584, 652). He also specifies that the location is a Raines-Law hotel on "the downtown West Side of New York" (*CP3*, 563). O'Neill, *Poems*, 37.

91. Gelb and Gelb, *Life with Monte Cristo*, 311; George Jean Nathan, "The Bright Face of Tragedy," *Cosmopolitan*, August 1957, 66–69; Sheaffer, *Son and Playwright*, 192; Agnes Boulton, interview by Louis Sheaffer, October 1962, Sheaffer-O'Neill Collection.

92. Steffens is quoted in Winifred Frazer's article "A Lost Poem by Eugene O'Neill," *Eugene O'Neill Newsletter* 3, no. 1 (1979). In the late 1970s, Frazer first identified "American Sovereign" as the first O'Neill poem ever published.

93. Quoted in Sheaffer, *Son and Playwright*, 194.

94. Quoted in Doris Alexander, "Eugene O'Neill as Social Critic," in Cargill, Fagin, and Fisher, *O'Neill and His Plays*, 393.

95. O'Neill's time working as a seaman comes from Louis Sheaffer's estimation (William Davies King, *Another Part of a Long Story: Literary Traces of Eugene O'Neill and Agnes Boulton* [Ann Arbor: University of Michigan Press, 2010], 254n5); Leonard Lyons, "Lyons Den," *New York Post*, November 13, 1936, Doris Alexander Papers, Linda Lear Center for Special Collections and Archives. This certificate now hangs on the wall of his study at Tao House in Danville, California. For a more complete understanding of O'Neill's maritime world, in addition to Richter, *O'Neill and Dat Ole Davil Sea*, see Patrick Chura, " 'Vital Contact': Eugene O'Neill and the Working Class" (2003), in Herrmann and Dowling, *Eugene O'Neill and His Early Contemporaries*, 9–30.

96. Mary B. Mullett, "The Extraordinary Story of Eugene O'Neill" (1922), in Estrin, *Conversations with Eugene O'Neill*, 31.

97. Louis Kalonyme [Louis Kantor], "O'Neill Lifts Curtain on His Early Days" (1924), in Estrin, *Conversations with Eugene O'Neill*, 67.

98. General Register and Record Office of Shipping and Seamen, Cardiff, to Louis Sheaffer, March 1965 (no day given), Sheaffer-O'Neill Collection.

99. http://www.ellisisland.org and http://freepages.genealogy.rootsweb.ancestry.com/
~colin/DriscollOfCork/Emigration/EllisByResidence.htm.

100. Clark, *Eugene O'Neill*, 85.

101. *Chicago Eagle*, July 16, 1904, 2; [James F. Byth], "Boer War Spectacle—Coney Island's Newest Show," *New York Times*, May 21, 1905. Given that Byth was A. W. Lewis's
press agent, I can attribute to him a press release on the Boer Spectacle and its participants that appeared above his friend James O'Neill's interview, "Mistakes of Shakespeare,"
Elmira (N.Y.) Summary, May 27, 1905, 2; O'Neill, *Selected Letters*, 306.

102. William Johnston, "To-Day's the Time," *Pleiades Club Year Book* (New York: Pleiades Club, 1912), 58.

103. Madison Cawein, "Beside the Road," *Pleiades Club Year Book*, 129.

104. See Robert M. Dowling, "Jimmy Tomorrow Revisited: New Sources for *The Iceman Cometh*," *Eugene O'Neill Review* 34, no. 3 (2013): 94–106.

105. O'Neill, *Exorcism*, 2.

106. Gelb and Gelb, *Life with Monte Cristo*, 295.

107. *Kathleen O'Neill v. Eugene G. O'Neill*, County Clerk's Index #1673, Supreme Court,
Westchester County, Westchester County Clerk's Office, White Plains, N.Y., 1912.

108. *Washington Times*, April 11, 1912, 11; *Variety*, n.d., 1913, 10.

109. O'Neill, *Selected Letters*, 128n2; Nelson O'Ceallaigh Ritschel, "J. M. Synge and the
Abbey Theatre's Leftist Influence on O'Neill," in Herrmann and Dowling, *Eugene O'Neill
and His Early Contemporaries*, 79.

110. "Staid Columbia University Shelters Radicals," *New York Times*, January 15, 1911.

111. "Sees Artist's Hope in Anarchic Ideas," *New York Times*, March 18, 1912, 8.

112. Interview with Moritz Jagendorf, February 23, 1978, in Avrich, *Anarchist Voices*,
221, 220; Komroff, "Manuel Komroff," 202; Christine Stansell, *American Moderns: Bohemian New York and the Creation of a New Century* (New York: Metropolitan, 2000), 133.

113. Robert M. Dowling, ed. "*Kathleen O'Neill v. Eugene O'Neill*: Proceedings of the
New York Supreme Court at White Plains, June 10, 1912," *Eugene O'Neill Review* 34,
no. 1 (2013): 24. O'Neill's second wife, Agnes Boulton, implies in her memoir that he
did not have sex with the prostitute, that they only talked and chain-smoked, and that
eventually he felt "as sorry for her as for himself" (*Part of a Long Story*, 168). But we should
remember that he was describing this event to his new wife.

114. See Robert M. Dowling, "Eugene O'Neill's *Exorcism*: The Lost Prequel to *Long
Day's Journey Into Night*," *Eugene O'Neill Review* 34, no. 1 (2013): 1–12.

115. O'Neill, *Exorcism*, 3, 29.

116. Ibid., 31–32.

117. Ibid., 32, 34, 55. Bearing in mind O'Neill's lifelong compulsion to project onto the
stage emotions impossible for him to express otherwise, I agree with Louis Sheaffer that
the script of *Exorcism* must be considered "the most reliable index of Eugene's frame of
mind after his suicide attempt" (Sheaffer, *Son and Playwright*, 214).

118. O'Neill, *Exorcism*, 32.

119. My characterization here refers to when O'Neill describes Stephen Murray, his
autobiographical protagonist in *The Straw*, as someone who "gives off the impression of

being somehow dissatisfied with himself but not yet embittered enough by it to take it out on others" (*CP*1, 732).

120. Gelb and Gelb, *Life with Monte Cristo*, 330; Boulton, *Part of a Long Story*, 168.

121. Boulton, *Part of a Long Story*, 169.

122. Ibid.

123. Quoted in Gelb and Gelb, *Life with Monte Cristo*, 337.

124. O'Neill, *Exorcism*, 26–29, 47.

125. See Dowling, "*Exorcism:* The Lost Prequel."

126. O'Neill, *Selected Letters*, 378.

127. Quoted in Sheaffer, *Son and Playwright*, 215. In the 1920s, O'Neill denied that he wrote the telegram, but then said it was printable because it was such a good yarn (Charles Webster, interview by Louis Sheaffer, December 18, 1962, Sheaffer-O'Neill Collection).

128. O'Neill, *Selected Letters*, 378.

129. "The New Bills," *Goodwin's Weekly* [Salt Lake City, Utah], February 3, 1912, 13; "Plays and Players at Salt Lake Theaters," *Salt Lake Tribune*, February 2 and 4, 1912, magazine section, 6; Karsner, "Eugene O'Neill at Close Range in Maine."

130. Sheaffer, *Son and Playwright*, 215; Webster, interview by Sheaffer, December 18, 1962; O'Neill, *Selected Letters*, 378; Basso, "Tragic Sense—I," 37; Sheaffer, *Son and Playwright*, 216.

131. "Orpheum," *Goodwin's Weekly*, February 10, 1912, 12; William Davies King, ed., *"A Wind Is Rising": The Correspondence of Agnes Boulton and Eugene O'Neill* (Madison, N.J.: Fairleigh Dickinson University Press, 2000), 159.

132. "Mr. James O'Neill Reaches This City After a Long Trip from New Orleans," *Ogden (Utah) Evening Standard*, February 2, 1912, 5.

133. Webster, interviews by Sheaffer, May 8, 1962, and December 18, 1962.

134. "Plays and Players at Salt Lake Theaters," 6. To view this photograph, see the Library of Congress's Web site Chronicling America (http://chroniclingamerica.loc.gov/lccn/sn83045396/1912–02–04/ed-1/seq-38/). The O'Neills also played matinee and evening performances the following Saturday, February 3, but that would not have given the *Salt Lake Tribune* enough time to publish the photograph for the Sunday paper ("No Vaudeville Thursday Night," *Ogden (Utah) Evening Standard*, January 31, 1912, 5; see also "News, Notes and Queries," *Eugene O'Neill Newsletter* 8, no. 2 [Summer–Fall, 1984], http://www.eoneill.com/library/newsletter/viii_2/viii-2n.htm).

135. Webster, interview by Sheaffer, October 28, 1960.

136. Fechter, *Monte Cristo*, 68; Webster, interviews by Sheaffer, May 8, 1962, and December 18, 1962.

137. Webster, interview by Sheaffer, December 18, 1962; Gelb and Gelb, *Life with Monte Cristo*, 322. This is an anecdote O'Neill himself liked to tell often.

138. "O'Neill Failed His Dad," *New York World*, October 19, 1929, 14 (reprinted from *St. Louis Dispatch*, 1929).

139. Ibid.

140. Fechter, *Monte Cristo*, 39.

141. Webster, interview by Sheaffer, May 8, 1962. In the interview, Webster says O'Neill uttered the line "Is he …?" which doesn't appear in the full script. It is possible they shortened the line for the vaudeville version.

142. James Light, interview by Louis Sheaffer, November 5, 1961, Sheaffer-O'Neill Collection.

143. O'Neill, *Selected Letters*, 498; quoted in Sheaffer, *Son and Playwright*, 215. The Gelbs and Sheaffer disagree about O'Neill's level of drunkenness, the former believing O'Neill that, as he said, he never drew "a sober breath," and the latter believing Webster that he didn't drink more than a few drinks a day. I agree with the Gelbs. O'Neill could hide his drunkenness well, and I don't believe that he would wish to embarrass his parents or that Webster would be privy to the insular O'Neills' actual drinking habits.

144. O'Neill, *Selected Letters*, 498.

145. "People of the Stage," *Cincinnati Commercial Tribune*, March 8, 1908, Sheaffer-O'Neill Collection; Sheaffer, *Son and Playwright*, 216. One of these was the Henry L. Brittain Company, where Eugene had once been employed.

146. Webster, interviews by Sheaffer, May 8, 1962, and December 18, 1962; Fechter, *Monte Cristo*, 65; Sheaffer, *Son and Playwright*, 220.

147. Dowling, "*Kathleen O'Neill v. Eugene O'Neill*," 16.

148. *Kathleen O'Neill v. Eugene G. O'Neill*, Westchester County Clerk's Office.

149. Sheaffer, *Son and Playwright*, 224; Gelb and Gelb, *Life with Monte Cristo*, 349; Morgan McGinley, "An Actor's Visit Stirs Memories of O'Neill's Day," (New London) *Day*, March 1, 1998, D1.

150. Basso, "Tragic Sense—I," 37; McGinley, "An Actor's Visit," D1; Sheaffer, *Son and Playwright*, 227.

151. Quoted in Clark, *Eugene O'Neill*, 19; James Light, "The Parade of Masks," T-Mss 2001-050, Billy Rose Theatre Division, New York Public Library, New York.

152. O'Neill, [untitled poem] (1912), in *Poems*, 9.

153. Frederick P. Latimer, "Eugene Is beyond Us," *New London Evening Day*, February 15, 1928, 6; J. F. O'Neill, "What a Sanatorium Did for Eugene O'Neill," *Journal of the Outdoor Life* 20, no. 6 (1923): 192; Donald Gallup, introduction to O'Neill, *Poems*, vi; Sheaffer, *Son and Playwright*, 225.

154. Sheaffer, *Son and Playwright*, 233.

155. Ibid., 289. Maibelle Scott's grandfather, Captain T. A. Scott, would also appear as Captain Dick Scott in *Beyond the Horizon*.

156. Ibid., 233, 234.

157. Ibid., 235.

158. Bowen, "Black Irishman," 65.

159. This line was written into Maibelle's friend Mildred Culver's autograph book. Quoted in Gelb and Gelb, *Life with Monte Cristo*, 434.

160. See Madeline C. Smith, "Harkness, Edward Stephen, and Hammond, Edward Crowninshield," in Dowling, *Critical Companion to Eugene O'Neill*, 2:616–17.

161. See Richard Eaton, "Dolan, John 'Dirty,' " in Dowling, *Critical Companion to Eugene O'Neill*, 2:573–75. The ice pond was actually located on Hammond's land, though O'Neill unfairly conflates him with Harkness with the Standard Oil reference.

162. Dr. Heyer appears as Dr. Hardy in *Long Day's Journey*, though Heyer was not the quack O'Neill made him out to be (Sheaffer, *Son and Playwright*, 242).

163. Ibid., 236–37.

164. Ibid, 237.

165. Ibid., 238, 240, 241.

166. Ibid., 240.

167. Ibid., 224.

168. J. F. O'Neill, "What a Sanatorium Did for Eugene O'Neill," 192.

169. O'Neill, *Selected Letters*, 25.

170. J. F. O'Neill, "What a Sanatorium Did for Eugene O'Neill," 192.

171. Gelb and Gelb, *Life with Monte Cristo*, 387; for a complete breakdown of O'Neill's reading at Gaylord, see Jean Chothia, *Forging a Language: A Study of the Plays of Eugene O'Neill* (New York: Cambridge University Press, 1979), 199.

172. Sheaffer, *Son and Playwright*, 257.

173. O'Neill, "Ye Disconsolate Poet to His 'Kitten' Anent Ye Better Farm Where Love Reigneth: Ballade" (1914), in *Poems*, 42.

174. J. F. O'Neill, "What a Sanatorium Did for Eugene O'Neill," 192.

175. O'Neill, *Selected Letters*, 533.

176. William Saroyan, *The Time of Your Life* (1939) (London: Methuen Drama, 2008), 43.

177. "Human Defects," *Lockport (N.Y.) Union-Sun and Journal*, March 18, 1940, 6.

178. Quoted in Sheaffer, *Son and Playwright*, 155.

179. Notes on James F. Byth, "The Search for Jimmy Tomorrow," Sheaffer-O'Neill Collection. Sheaffer reports that the New York Health Department Bureau of Records listed Byth's death as a suicide.

180. Quoted in Charles F. Sweeney, "Back to the Source of Plays Written by Eugene O'Neill," *New York World*, November 9, 1924, cited in Doris Alexander, *Eugene O'Neill's Last Plays: Separating Art from Autobiography* (Athens: University of Georgia Press, 2005), 23.

181. Clayton Meeker Hamilton, *Seen on the Stage* (New York: Holt, 1920), 187; Clayton [Meeker] Hamilton, "Eugene G. O'Neill," Ninth Lecture at Columbia University, April 7, 1924, in *Conversations on Contemporary Drama* (New York: Macmillan, 1925), 203, Hamilton, *Seen*, 187.

182. Boulton, *Part of a Long Story*, 222.

183. Hamilton, *Seen*, 187–88.

184. Richter, *O'Neill and Dat Ole Davil Sea*, 138, 142.

185. O'Neill, *Selected Letters*, 22.

186. Bowen, *Curse of the Misbegotten*, 114.

187. O'Neill, "Speaking, to the Shade of Dante, of Beatrices" (1915), in *Poems*, 65.

188. Beatrice Ashe, interview by Louis Sheaffer, September 1962, Sheaffer-O'Neill Collection; O'Neill, *Selected Letters*, 30.

189. Ashe, interview by Sheaffer, September 1962. (Ashe's letters from O'Neill are housed at the Berg Collection of the New York Public Library.)

190. Clayton [Meeker] Hamilton, "O'Neill's First Book: A Review of *'Thirst,'* *and Other One-Act Plays*" (1915), in Cargill, Fagin, and Fisher, *O'Neill and His Plays*, 229; Sheaffer, *Son and Playwright*, 291.

191. O'Neill, *Selected Letters*, 125.

192. Ibid.

193. Gladys Hamilton, "Untold Tales of Eugene O'Neill," *Theatre Arts* 40, no. 8 (1956): 88.

194. O'Neill, *Selected Letters*, 125.

195. Tyler, *Whatever Goes Up*, 91.

196. Gladys Hamilton, "Untold Tales," 88. *Bread and Butter* wouldn't see a performance until 1998. O'Neill claimed later that he destroyed *Servitude*, but since he copyrighted it at the Library of Congress, it was produced in 1960 at New York International Airport (now JFK). (Given *Servitude's* wooden dialogue and sexist views on love and marriage, some might feel it would have been better left to rot in Tyler's filing cabinet.)

197. O'Neill, *Selected Letters*, 125; Gladys Hamilton, "Untold Tales," 88.

198. Hamilton, *Seen*, 188; Hamilton, "Eugene G. O'Neill." As well as O'Neill, the graduates of George Pierce Baker's legendary seminar included playwrights Philip Barry, Sidney Howard, and Edward Sheldon; novelists John Dos Passos and Thomas Wolfe; renowned journalists and critics Robert Benchley, Heywood Broun, and Van Wyck Brooks; O'Neill's future producers Theresa Helburn and Kenneth Macgowan; and set designers Robert Edmond Jones and Lee Simonson, among many other literary lights (Madeline Smith, "George Pierce Baker," in Dowling, *Critical Companion to Eugene O'Neill*, 2:529).

199. O'Neill, *Selected Letters*, 26.

200. Ibid.

201. The Ebel family's house was located at 1105 Massachusetts Avenue.

202. O'Neill, *Selected Letters*, 28, 33.

203. Ibid., 52.

204. Paul D. Voelker, "Eugene O'Neill and George Pierce Baker: A Reconsideration," *American Literature* 49, no. 2 (1977): 214; O'Neill, *Selected Letters*, 36; Pfister, *Staging Depth*, 107.

205. O'Neill, *Selected Letters*, 60–61.

206. Ibid., 60.

207. Ibid., 68, 402.

208. John V. A. Weaver, "I Knew Him When—," *New York Sunday World*, February 26, 1926.

209. O'Neill, *Selected Letters*, 28, 54, 47.

210. Ibid., 42; Weaver, "I Knew Him When—."

211. Sheaffer, *Son and Playwright*, 297.

212. O'Neill, *Selected Letters*, 51.

213. Gelb and Gelb, *Life with Monte Cristo*, 482; O'Neill, *Selected Letters*, 51; Voelker, "Eugene O'Neill and George Pierce Baker," 218.

214. Webster, interview by Sheaffer, May 8, 1962; Sheaffer, *Son and Playwright*, 309–10.

215. Clark, *Eugene O'Neill*, 28; Sheaffer, *Son and Playwright*, 317.

216. This address has never been reported, but when the Canton Silk Mill took on the lease of the building in December 1919, the *New York Herald* reported, "M. & L. Hess and Holten & Leverich have sold the lease on the Garden Hotel, at 63 Madison Avenue, at the northeast corner of Twenty-seventh Street, for Welibrock & Thomforde to the Canton Silk Mill" (December 17, 1919, 23).

217. Boulton, *Part of a Long Story*, 109.

218. "A Eugene O'Neill Miscellany," *New York Sun*, January 12, 1928, 31.

219. " 'Sixty' Is Dead; Long Live Polly's! Greenwich Villagers Preparing to Give New Year Hot Welcome Dance," *New York Tribune*, December 30, 1915, 3.

220. Djuna Barnes, "The Days of Jig Cook: Recollections of Ancient Theatre History But Ten Years Old," *Theatre Guild Magazine*, January 1929, 32.

221. O'Neill, *Selected Letters*, 59, 65.

222. Mary Heaton Vorse, "Eugene O'Neill's Pet Saloon Is Gone," *New York World*, May 4, 1930, M7; Luther S. Harris, *Around Washington Square: An Illustrated History of Greenwich Village* (Baltimore: Johns Hopkins University Press, 2003), 194.

223. Vorse, "Eugene O'Neill's Pet Saloon," M7.

224. Mary Heaton Vorse, *Time and the Town: A Provincetown Chronicle* (1942), ed. Adele Heller (New Brunswick, N.J.: Rutgers University Press, 1991), 122; verse, "Eugene O'Neill's Pet Saloon," M7; Boulton, *Part of a Long Story*, 115; "Solemn Sightseers Stroll in Waldorf," *New York Times*, March 30, 1929.

225. "Sight of Revolver, Held by Policeman, Halts Gang Killing," *New York Evening World*, June 15, 1915, 5; "Gangster Outwitted by Two Detectives," *New York Evening World*, January 15, 1915, 4; Boulton, *Part of a Long Story*, 217.

226. Harry Golden, "Only in America," *Amsterdam Recorder*, June 13, 1969, 4; Vorse, "Eugene O'Neill's Pet Saloon."

227. Gelb and Gelb, *Life with Monte Cristo*, 523–24; O'Neill, *Selected Letters*, 547.

228. Quoted in Sheaffer, *Son and Playwright*, 214; Hutchins Hapgood, "Memories of a Determined Drinker; or, Forty Years of Drink" (1932), MS, Hapgood Family Papers, Beinecke Library; Boulton, *Part of a Long Story*, 254.

229. O'Neill, *Selected Letters*, 73.

230. Hutchins Hapgood, "The Case of Terry," *Revolt*, February 19, 1916, 6.

231. O'Neill, *Selected Letters*, 100.

232. Hapgood, "The Case of Terry," 6.

233. Oliver M. Sayler, "From Play at Provincetown to Work in New York and All for Native Drama Past, Present, and Future of a Brave and Fruitful Adventure" (1921), in Edna Kenton, *The Provincetown Players and the Playwrights' Theatre, 1915–1922*, ed. Travis Bogard and Jackson R. Bryer (Jefferson, N.C.: McFarland, 2004), 192.

ACT II: "To Be an Artist or Nothing"

Notes to pp. 123–24: "Now that I look back" (Louis Sheaffer, *Son and Playwright* [Boston: Little, Brown, 1968], 204); "the closed-shop, star-system, amusement racket" (Eugene O'Neill, "An Open Letter on the Death of George Pierce Baker" (January 7, 1935), in

The Unknown O'Neill: Unpublished and Unfamiliar Writings of Eugene O'Neill, ed. Travis Bogard [New Haven: Yale University Press, 1988], 420); "aimed at and almost succeeded . . . their henchmen" (quoted in Candace Barrington, *American Chaucers* [New York: Palgrave Macmillan, 2007], 47); "to establish a stage where" (Edna Kenton, *The Provincetown Players and the Playwrights' Theatre, 1915–1922*, ed. Travis Bogard and Jackson R. Bryer [Jefferson, N.C.: McFarland, 2004], 72).

1. Leona Rust Egan, *Provincetown as a Stage* (Orleans, Mass.: Parnassus, 1994), 151.

2. Wainwright J. Wainwright, *Provincetown in Picture and Story* (Cotiut, Mass.: Picture Book, 1953), 4; Mary Heaton Vorse, *Time and the Town: A Provincetown Chronicle* (1942), ed. Adele Heller (New Brunswick, N.J.: Rutgers University Press, 1991), 147, opp. p. 126.

3. The fact that O'Neill and Carlin occupied a sailmaker's loft next to Francis's Flats is mentioned with confidence in a letter from actress Kyra Markham to Louis Sheaffer, September 6, 1962 (photocopy), private collection of Jackson R. Bryer. The link between O'Neill and Boyesen with Provincetown has been given no attention to date, possibly because he was a political figure rather than a theatrical or literary one.

4. Quoted in George Monteiro, "John Francis, Go-between for Provincetown and the Players," *Laconics* 1 (2006), http://www.eoneill.com/library/laconics/1/1f.htm.

5. Ernest L. Meyer, "The First Patron of Eugene O'Neill," *Column Review* 5, no. 2 (1937): 2.

6. Ibid., 2–3.

7. Quoted in Monteiro, "John Francis."

8. Quoted in ibid.

9. On the importance of Neith Boyce's role in founding the Players, see Jeff Kennedy, "Probing Legends in Bohemia: The Symbiotic Dance between O'Neill and the Provincetown Players," in *Eugene O'Neill and His Early Contemporaries: Bohemians, Radicals, Progressives, and the Avant Garde*, ed. Eileen Herrmann and Robert M. Dowling (Jefferson, N.C.: McFarland, 2011), 163–64, as well as *The Modern World of Neith Boyce: Autobiography and Diaries*, ed. Carol DeBoer-Langworthy (Albuquerque: University of New Mexico Press, 2003).

10. Egan, *Provincetown as a Stage*, 14; Linda Ben-Zvi, *Susan Glaspell: Her Life and Times* (New York: Oxford University Press, 2005), 162; Mary Heaton Vorse vastly overstated the dimensions of the fish house in her chronicle of the Players. The figures I use here are taken from Robert Karoly Sarlós's careful estimations in his *Jig Cook and the Provincetown Players* (Boston: University of Massachusetts Press, 1982), 201; Vorse, *Time and the Town*, 118; Sartós, *Jig Cook and the Provincetown Players*, 67.

11. Susan Glaspell, *The Road to the Temple* (New York: Frederick A. Stokes, 1927), 253. In her record of this encounter, Glaspell goes on to say that she invited O'Neill and Carlin to their house that night, where the actor Frederick Burt read them *Bound East for Cardiff*. This is an inaccurate chronology of events, as it was *The Movie Man* O'Neill first read to the Players, and it was at Reed and Bryant's house, not Glaspell and Cook's. Deliberately or not, this inaccurate tale places Glaspell and Cook even more centrally in the legend of O'Neill's discovery. When Glaspell's book came out in 1927, O'Neill must have been delighted that his first disastrous night with the Players was, if only temporarily, struck from the historical record.

12. George Frame Brown, interview by Louis Sheaffer, undated, Sheaffer-O'Neill Collection, Linda Lear Center for Special Collections and Archives, Connecticut College, New London. The fact that O'Neill brought a copy of *Thirst* is recorded in Harry Kemp, "George Cram Cook and the Provincetown Players," *Lorelei* 1 (August 1924): 29–30.

13. Hutchins Hapgood to Mabel Dodge, July 1, 1916, Yale Collection of American Literature, Beinecke Library, Yale University, New Haven.

14. Bernard Holm[illegible], "Irish Players Rebel and May Quit Abbey," *New York Review*, July 1, 1916, 1. They did not, in the end, "collapse" once Ervine resigned. There's a Yeats letter pertaining to Ervine's resignation in the Henry W. and Albert A. Berg Collection of English and American Literature, New York Public Library. The dispute revolved around a leading lady named Marie O'Neill who felt she needed more time for rehearsals. Ervine demanded they rehearse twice a day. The Abbey Players were in no mood to oblige and walked out on him.

15. Egan, *Provincetown as a Stage*, xi. See Linda Ben-Zvi, "The Provincetown Players: The Success That Failed," *Eugene O'Neill Review* 27 (2005): 15; Cheryl Black, "Pioneering Theatre Managers: Edna Kenton and Eleanor Fitzgerald of the Provincetown Players," *Journal of American Drama and Theatre* 9 (Fall 1997): 58; George Cram Cook, "The Way of the Group," *Little Theatre Review*, November 18, 1920. See also George Cram Cook, [*The Emperor Jones*, by Eugene O'Neill], [1920], p. 3, unsigned MS, Henry W. and Albert A. Berg Collection of English and American Literature, New York Public Library, New York; Doris Alexander, *Eugene O'Neill's Last Plays: Separating Art from Autobiography* (Athens: University of Georgia Press, 2005), 119.

16. Vorse, *Time and the Town*, 122; Max Eastman, *Enjoyment of Living* (New York: Harper, 1948), 564–65.

17. Marsden Hartley, "The Great Provincetown Summer," MS, Yale Collection of American Literature.

18. Eastman, *Enjoyment of Living*, 565; Louise Bryant, "Christmas in Petrograd 1917," corrected TS, n.d., p. 7, Granville Hicks Papers, Special Collections Research Center, Syracuse University Libraries, Syracuse, N.Y.

19. Bryant, "Christmas in Petrograd 1917."

20. This is according to Susan Glaspell, Mary Heaton Vorse, Harry Kemp, Marsden Hartley, and other Provincetown Players in their reminiscences.

21. Egan, *Provincetown as a Stage*, 203; Marsden Hartley, "Farewell, Charles," in *The New Caravan*, ed. Alfred Kreymborg, Lewis Mumford, and Paul Rosenfeld (New York: Norton, 1936), 556; Mary V. Dearborn, *Queen of Bohemia: The Life of Louise Bryant* (Boston: Houghton Mifflin, 1996), 53.

22. Agnes Boulton, *Part of a Long Story: "Eugene O'Neill as a Young Man in Love,"* ed. William Davies King (Jefferson, N.C.: McFarland, 2011), 162; Louis Sheaffer, *Son and Playwright* (Boston: Little, Brown, 1968), 338; Susan Glaspell, undated entry in notebook dated October 16, 1915, p. 20, Susan Glaspell Collection, Clifton Waller Barrett Library of American Literature, Albert and Shirley Small Special Collections Library, University of Virginia, Charlottesville.

23. See Robert M. Dowling, " 'The Screenews of War': A Previously Unpublished Short Story by Eugene O'Neill," *Resources for American Literary Study* 31 (Fall 2007): 174.

24. This bizarre incident has been dramatized as *And Starring Pancho Villa as Himself* (2003), with Antonio Banderas as Pancho Villa and Matt Day as John Reed.

25. Quoted in Friedrich Katz, *The Life and Times of Pancho Villa* (Stanford, Calif.: Stanford University Press, 1998), 324.

26. Gary Jay Williams identifies the date as most likely July 17 (Gary Jay Williams, "Turned Down in Provincetown: O'Neill's Debut Re-Examined," *Theatre Journal* 37, no. 2 [1985]: 158).

27. Brenda Murphy, *The Provincetown Players and the Culture of Modernity* (Cambridge: Cambridge University Press, 2005), 95; Glaspell, *Road to the Temple*, 254.

28. Adele Nathan, " 'Eugene G. O'Neill': 1916," *New York Times*, October 6, 1946, SM18; Williams, "Turned Down in Provincetown," 161.

29. Vorse, *Time and the Town*, 116–17.

30. Eastman, *Enjoyment of Living*, 566.

31. Ibid.

32. Harry Kemp, "O'Neill of Provincetown," *Brentano's Book Chat*, May–June 1929, 45–47.

33. Harry Kemp, "Out of Provincetown: A Memoir of Eugene O'Neill" (1930), in *Conversations with Eugene O'Neill*, ed. Mark W. Estrin (Jackson: University Press of Mississippi, 1990), 97.

34. Edmund Wilson, *The Twenties: From Notebooks and Diaries of the Period*, ed. Leon Edel (New York: Farrar, Straus and Giroux, 1975), 110–12, 400.

35. Hutchins Hapgood, "Memories of a Determined Drinker; or, Forty Years of Drink" (1932), MS, Hapgood Family Papers, Beinecke Library.

36. Quoted in Barrett H. Clark, *Eugene O'Neill: The Man and His Plays*, rev. ed. (New York: Dover, 1947), 31.

37. Hutchins Hapgood, *A Victorian in the Modern World* (New York: Harcourt, Brace, 1939), 397.

38. Ben-Zvi, *Susan Glaspell*, 169.

39. Boulton, *Part of a Long Story*, 133; Kemp, "Out of Provincetown," 96–97.

40. Mabel Dodge Luhan, *Intimate Memories: Movers and Shakers* (New York: Harcourt, Brace and Company, 1936), 484.

41. Hapgood, "Memories."

42. Ibid., 69.

43. Vorse, *Time and the Town*, 122.

44. Quoted in Sheaffer, *Son and Playwright*, 388.

45. Quoted in "The Provincetown Players: A Theatrical Workshop for Acting Playwrights and Play-Writing Actors," *Current Opinion* 61 (July–December 1916): 323.

46. Paul Roazen, "O'Neill and Louise Bryant: New Documents," *Eugene O'Neill Review* 27 (2005): 39n1; and Stephen A. Black, *Eugene O'Neill: Beyond Mourning and Tragedy* (New Haven: Yale University Press, 1999), 202–3.

47. Brenda Murphy argues that rather than O'Neill and Bryant's affair, *The Eternal Quadrangle* more directly corresponds to Reed's passionate affair with Mabel Dodge, apparently conducted with the blessing of her wealthy husband, Edwin Dodge. See Murphy, *Provincetown Players*, 61–64.

48. O'Neill is wearing the same sweater, the same wisp of hair over his forehead. His knees are in the same position.

49. I would like to thank Professors Jackson R. Bryer and Patrick Chura for their input on the photograph. Thanks also to the artist Michael J. Peery for acting as a proxy for facial recognition software in the first stages of authentication. I realized that this photograph, which was wrongly identified at the Berg as being O'Neill and Elaine Freeman, was O'Neill and Bryant on January 18, 2013.

50. Dearborn, *Queen of Bohemia*, 53.

51. The complete poem can be found in Roazen, "O'Neill and Louise Bryant," 31.

52. Quoted in Murphy, *Provincetown Players*, 95.

53. Quoted in Dearborn, *Queen of Bohemia*, 53.

54. Quoted in Murphy, *Provincetown Players*, 95.

55. Quoted in Dearborn, *Queen of Bohemia*, 53.

56. Quoted ibid., 54.

57. Arthur Gelb and Barbara Gelb, *O'Neill: Life with Monte Cristo* (New York: Applause, 2000), 573.

58. Quoted in ibid., 562.

59. Quoted in "Provincetown Players," 323.

60. Quoted in Kenton, *Provincetown Players*, 25.

61. O'Neill destroyed the revised version of *The Movie Man*, but I found the surviving copy of the short story and published it in 2007. See Dowling, " 'The Screenews of War.' "

62. Louis Sheaffer specifies that the visit lasted only "a few days" (*Son and Playwright*, 360). Whether that count is accurate is unclear; regardless, it was a long enough stay for Jessica Rippin to recall his and Bryant's visit and for him to have written a story for which the plot had already been outlined in dramatic form; Dearborn, *Queen of Bohemia*, 65.

63. Sheaffer, *Son and Playwright*, 360.

64. Kenton, *Provincetown Players*, 59.

65. Barney Gallant to Louis Sheaffer, November 13, 1957 (photocopy), private collection of Jackson R. Bryer.

66. Quoted in Sheaffer, *Son and Playwright*, 371.

67. Clayton [Meeker] Hamilton, "Eugene G. O'Neill," Ninth Lecture at Columbia University, April 7, 1924, in *Conversations on Contemporary Drama* (New York: Macmillan, 1925), 206.

68. James Light, interview by Louis Sheaffer, October 17, 1960, Sheaffer-O'Neill Collection.

69. Kenton, *Provincetown Players*, 41; Anna Alice Chapin, *Greenwich Village* (New York: Dodd, Mead, 1920), 226. The Samovar closed when Nani Bailey signed on as a nurse and went overseas during World War I; she died in France (Kenton, *Provincetown Players*, 42).

70. Mary Heaton Vorse, "Eugene O'Neill's Pet Saloon Is Gone," *New York World*, May 4, 1930, M7.

71. Sarlós, *Jig Cook and the Provincetown Players*, 80; George Cram Cook to Susan Glaspell, December 23, 1916, copy, Sheaffer-O'Neill Collection.

72. Quoted in Sheaffer, *Son and Playwright*, 240.

73. Travis Bogard, *Contour in Time: The Plays of Eugene O'Neill*, rev. ed. (New York: Oxford University Press, 1988), 79; Gelb and Gelb, *Life with Monte Cristo*, 589; "O'Neill as an Actor is Recalled by One Who Saw Him in '17," *New York Herald Tribune*, March 17, 1929, sec. 7, 5.

74. Quoted in Gelb and Gelb, *Life with Monte Cristo*, 588.

75. William Carlos Williams to Louis Sheaffer, n.d., Sheaffer-O'Neill Collection.

76. Hapgood, *Victorian*, 399.

77. Dearborn, *Queen of Bohemia*, 65; see Alexander, *Eugene O'Neill's Last Plays*, 122, 127. For the correct date of Ella's mastectomy, see Sheaffer, *Son and Playwright*, 502n.

78. Patrick Chura, "Bryant, Louise," in *Critical Companion to Eugene O'Neill: A Literary Reference to His Life and Work*, ed. Robert M. Dowling (New York: Facts on File, 2009), 2:540; Dearborn, *Queen of Bohemia*, 60–61.

79. Gelb and Gelb, *Life with Monte Cristo*, 598–99; Kenton, *Provincetown Players*, 51. The other two plays on the "war bill" were *Ivan's Homecoming* by Irwin Granich (Mike Gold) and *Barbarisms* by Rita Wellman.

80. Nina Moise, "A Note to Edna Kenton about the Provincetown Players," in Kenton, *Provincetown Players*, 181.

81. William Davies King, *Another Part of a Long Story: Literary Traces of Eugene O'Neill and Agnes Boulton* (Ann Arbor: University of Michigan Press, 2010), 120. (Harold de Polo signed his name with two words and a lowercase "d," though he is mostly referred to in previous scholarship with the spelling "DePolo.")

82. Sheaffer, *Son and Playwright*, 380; Charles A. Merrill, "Eugene O'Neill, World-Famous Dramatist, and Family Live in Abandoned Coast Guard Station on Cape Cod" (1923), in Estrin, *Conversations with Eugene O'Neill*, 43; [untitled], *Provincetown Advocate*, March 28, 1917; Boulton, *Part of a Long Story*, 154.

83. Vorse, *Time and the Town*, 131.

84. Sheaffer, *Son and Playwright*, 381.

85. Virginia Floyd, ed., *Eugene O'Neill at Work: Newly Released Ideas for His Plays* (New York: Frederick Ungar, 1981), 305.

86. Robert A. Richter, *Eugene O'Neill and Dat Ole Davil Sea: Maritime Influences in the Life and Works of Eugene O'Neill* (Mystic, Conn.: Mystic Seaport, 2004). Quoted in Sheaffer, *Son and Playwright*, 395.

87. Bryant, "Christmas in Petrograd 1917"; Dearborn, *Queen of Bohemia*, 65, 67.

88. Eugene O'Neill, *Selected Letters of Eugene O'Neill*, ed. Travis Bogard and Jackson R. Bryer (New Haven: Yale University Press, 1988), 80.

89. Sheaffer, *Son and Playwright*, 392; O'Neill, *Selected Letters*, 79; Bryant, "Christmas in Petrograd 1917"; O'Neill, *Selected Letters*, 78.

90. Eugene O'Neill to Elaine Freeman, September 1917, Henry W. and Albert A. Berg Collection of English and American Literature; Boulton, *Part of a Long Story*, 128.

91. Mabel Collins, *Light on the Path* (1885) (Pasadena, Calif.: Theosophical University Press Online, n.d.), http://www.theosociety.org/pasadena/lightpat/lightpat.htm. See also J. Shantz, "Carlin, Terry," in Dowling, *Critical Companion to Eugene O'Neill*, 2:543–44. O'Neill frequently misspelled "it's" for "its," which leads me to believe after seeing a photograph of the rafters that he was the one who painted these words.

92. Eugene O'Neill to Elaine Freeman, September 19, 1917, and September [no day], 1917, Henry W. and Albert A. Berg Collection of English and American Literature.

93. Charles Demuth, *Letters of Charles Demuth, American Artist, 1883–1935*, ed. Bruce Kellner (Philadelphia: Temple University Press, 2000), 26; Eugene O'Neill to Elaine Freeman, September [no day], 1917; Sheaffer, *Son and Playwright*, 410; Roazen, "O'Neill and Louise Bryant," 34.

94. Dearborn, *Queen of Bohemia*, 74; Roazen, "O'Neill and Louise Bryant," 38.

95. The depth of her relationship with O'Neill remains a mystery, though a Catholic friend of hers late in life, the novelist Joseph Dever, reported, significantly while they were still in communication, "It is fairly well known that, as a budding young dramatist, Gene O'Neill was the lover of the then Bohemian, but now austere and saintly Dorothy Day" (Joseph Dever, *Cushing of Boston: A Candid Portrait* [Boston: Bruce Humphries, 1965], 282).

96. Dorothy Day, "Told in Context," ca. 1958, Dorothy Day Papers, series D-3, box 7, file 2, Special Collections and University Archives, Raynor Memorial Libraries, Marquette University, Milwaukee, Wis.; Dorothy Day, interview by Louis Sheaffer, n.d., Sheaffer-O'Neill Collection.

97. Dorothy Day, *The Long Loneliness: The Autobiography of Dorothy Day* (New York: Harper, 1952), 84. See also Eileen J. Herrmann, "Saints and Hounds: Modernism's Pursuit of Dorothy Day and O'Neill," in Herrmann and Dowling, *Eugene O'Neill and His Early Contemporaries*, 210–33.

98. Dorothy Day, interview by Sheaffer.

99. Day, *Long Loneliness*, 84.

100. Ibid., 84; Day, "Told in Context."

101. Day, "Told in Context"; Dorothy Day, interview by Sheaffer.

102. Dorothy Day, interview by Sheaffer.

103. Day, "Told in Context"; Maxwell Bodenheim, "Eugene O'Neill: Portrayed in Bold Relief," *Lorelei* 1 (August 1924): 14.

104. Kenton, *Provincetown Players*, 73.

105. "Who Is Eugene O'Neill?" *New York Times*, November 4, 1917, 7; Lewis Sherwin, "The Theatre: The Washington Square Players at the Comedy," *New York Globe and Commercial Advertiser*, November 1, 1917, 14.

106. O'Neill, *Selected Letters*, 89.

107. Black, *Eugene O'Neill*, 201.

108. "James Light Dies; O'Neill Associate," *New York Times*, February 12, 1964; "Who's Who," *New York Times*, February 8, 1925, sec. X, 2.

109. Ralph Block, "The Provincetown Players Reopen in Macdougal Street," *New York Tribune*, November 3, 1917, 13; "New Plays in New York: Eugene O'Neill, Notable Young Playwright," *Boston Evening Transcript*, November 8, 1917, 16; Kenton, *Provincetown Players*, 63; Hamilton, "Eugene G. O'Neill," 211–12; "Village Players Present Best Bill," *Journal of Commerce and Commercial Bulletin*, April 22, 1918, 9.

110. Eugene O'Neill to Maxwell Bodenheim, July 5, 1923, Sheaffer-O'Neill Collection.

111. Roazen, "O'Neill and Louise Bryant," 35, 37, 38. The word "romance" is likely but questioned by Roazen in brackets (35).

112. King, *Another Part of a Long Story*, 6.

113. Ibid., 67; Boulton, *Part of a Long Story*, 16.

114. Boulton, *Part of a Long Story*, 19; King, *Another Part of a Long Story*, 67.

115. Boulton, *Part of a Long Story*, 29, 21.

116. Ibid., 27, 31, 67.

117. Ibid., 76. The italics are Boulton's.

118. Virginia Gardner, *"Friend and Lover": The Life of Louise Bryant* (New York: Horizon, 1982), 129.

119. Roazen, "O'Neill and Louise Bryant," 36.

120. Boulton, *Part of a Long Story*, 60, 61, 57.

121. Sheaffer, *Son and Playwright*, 408.

122. Boulton, *Part of a Long Story*, 76.

123. Ibid., 77.

124. Ibid., 78, 38.

125. For a list of differing accounts, see Sheaffer, *Son and Playwright*, 410. Dorothy Day said it was the waiter, and I believe her account is the most credible.

126. Boulton, *Part of a Long Story*, 79.

127. Carlotta Monterey Diary, September 24, 1944, O'Neill Papers, Beinecke Library, Yale University, New Haven.

128. Ibid., 80.

129. Ibid., 81.

130. Roazen, "O'Neill and Louise Bryant," 38, 37. O'Neill wrote Bryant a series of final letters that her second husband, William C. Bullitt, later claimed Bryant had burned. Scholar Paul Roazen brought them to light in 2004, however, after Bullitt's papers were gifted to Yale University by Bryant and Bullitt's daughter Anne (30).

131. Quoted in Patrick Chura, "O'Neill's *Strange Interlude* and the 'Strange Marriage' of Louise Bryant," *Eugene O'Neill Review* 30 (2008): 8–9.

132. Roazen, "O'Neill and Louise Bryant," 38.

133. Boulton, *Part of a Long Story*, 85.

134. Sheaffer, *Son and Playwright*, 375.

135. Ibid. O'Neill took *The Rope* from a scenario entitled "The Reckoning." In 1924, Boulton and O'Neill later expanded this idea together into a four-act play, "The Guilty One," which was never published or produced.

136. O'Neill, *Selected Letters*, 81.

137. Ibid., 82.

138. Boulton, *Part of a Long Story*, 91, 96n12.

139. *Kathleen O'Neill v. Eugene G. O'Neill*, County Clerk's Index #1673, Supreme Court, Westchester County, Westchester County Clerk's Office, White Plains, N.Y., 1912. The earlier "Interlocutory Judgment" of July 5, signed by Judge Joseph Morschauser, stipulated that O'Neill *could* remarry but only "by express permission of this court."

140. An incomplete file, which includes the judge's order, is in O'Neill's papers at the Beinecke Library.

141. Boulton, *Part of a Long Story*, 167; Sheaffer, *Son and Playwright*, 145; Louis Sheaffer, *O'Neill: Son and Artist* (Boston: Little, Brown, 1973), 66; Sheaffer, *Son and Playwright*, 145.

142. It's likely that O'Neill received another inspiration from the boy: the name of his character Larry Slade in *The Iceman Cometh*.

143. Croswell Bowen, "The Black Irishman" (1946), in *O'Neill and His Plays: Four Decades of Criticism*, ed. Oscar Cargill, N. Bryllion Fagin, and William J. Fisher (New York: New York University Press, 1961), 74.

144. Quoted in Clark, *Eugene O'Neill*, 66.

145. Quoted in "A Letter from O'Neill," *New York Times*, April 11, 1920.

146. Quoted in Sheaffer, *Son and Playwright*, 422.

147. Boulton, *Part of a Long Story*, 111, 96.

148. Ibid., 113.

149. Ibid., 116.

150. Agnes Boulton misquotes the lines from *Light on the Path* on p. 118 of her memoir, *Part of a Long Story*, and she could not remember the source.

151. Ibid., 149.

152. Quoted in Ben-Zvi, *Susan Glaspell*, 205.

153. Quoted in Virginia Floyd, *The Plays of Eugene O'Neill: A New Assessment* (New York: Frederick Ungar, 1985), 154.

154. Roazen, "O'Neill and Louise Bryant," 36.

155. King, *Another Part of a Long Story*, 252n24.

156. Harold de Polo to Henry W. Wenning, February 2, 1960, p. 1, Clifton Waller Barrett Library of American Literature.

157. Ibid.

158. Eugene O'Neill to Sidney Howard, September 27, 1936, and November 26, 1936, Sidney Coe Howard Papers, Bancroft Library, University of California, Berkeley.

159. Harold de Polo, MS, "The Screenews of War," January 30, 1960, Clifton Waller Barrett Library of American Literature.

160. Boulton, *Part of a Long Story*, 163, 191, 161n.

161. Ibid., 153.

162. *A Theatre for America: Concerning the Provincetown Playhouse, That Famous Little Theatre, Which Has Given Americans the Best of American Drama and Many Noted Stage Personalities* (New York: Provincetown Playhouse Guild Association, ca. 1934), 1 (ten-page pamphlet at the Clifton Waller Barrett Library of American Literature); Eleanor M. Fitzgerald, "Valedictory of an Art Theatre," *New York Times*, December 22, 1929, in Kenton, *Provincetown Players*, 198; Jeff Kennedy, "Provincetown Playhouse, The (Playwrights' Theatre)," in Dowling, *Critical Companion to Eugene O'Neill*, 2:715.

163. Quoted by Gilbert Seldes, "Radio and Television in the Courtroom," September 7, 1954, *The Lively Arts*, WNYC, WNYC archives id.: 71485, New York City Municipal archives id.: LT3109, http://www.wnyc.org/shows/lively-arts-the/1954/sep/.

164. Kenton, *Provincetown Players*, 81.

165. W. Livingston Larned, "Below Washington Square," *New York Review*, November 25, 1916, 4. In this article, one of Larned's associates in the Village is a young man who "paints backgrounds in figure compositions for a large publishing house"; this is most

likely Donald Corley, the Provincetown Player who painted "Here Pegasus Was Hitched" and worked, among other jobs, as a pattern maker. Corley later designed camouflage for soldiers' uniforms during World War I; Larned became a minor celebrity for his short piece of parenting advice, "Father Forgets," which was widely circulated, translated into many languages, and eventually reprinted in Dale Carnegie's 1936 best seller *How to Win Friends and Influence People.*

166. Boulton, *Part of a Long Story*, 198; Kennedy, "Provincetown Playhouse," 2: 715. Helen Deutsch and Stella Hanau, *The Provincetown: A Story of the Theatre* (New York: Farrar and Rinehart, 1931), 43.

167. See note 78, above. Boulton, *Part of a Long Story*, 186–88.

168. Kenton, *Provincetown Players*, 82.

169. Ibid., 83, 82.

170. Quoted in Bogard, *Contour in Time*, 103.

171. Heywood Broun, "Drama," *New York Tribune*, November 25, 1918, 9.

172. Quoted in Clark, *Eugene O'Neill*, 63.

173. The following spring, 1919, the play appeared in O'Neill's second book, *"The Moon of the Caribbees" and Six Other Plays of the Sea.*

174. Quoted in Nancy Milford, *Savage Beauty: The Life of Edna St. Vincent Millay* (New York: Random House, 2002), 176. This is also mentioned in a letter from Kyra Markham to Louis Sheaffer, September 6, 1962 (photocopy), private collection of Jackson R. Bryer.

175. Sheaffer, *Son and Playwright*, 395; "Greenwich Village Sees New Dramas a la Provincetown," *New York Herald*, December 21, 1918, 8; David Karsner, "Eugene O'Neill at Close Range in Maine," *New York Herald Tribune*, August 8, 1926, sec. 8, 6.

176. Boulton, *Part of a Long Story*, 237n31, 229.

177. Ibid., 232.

178. Ibid., 224.

179. Stark Young, interview by Louis Sheaffer, n.d., Sheaffer-O'Neill Collection.

180. Quoted in King, *Another Part of a Long Story*, 102.

181. O'Neill, *Selected Letters*, 90, 137.

182. Pierre Loving, "Eugene O'Neill," *Bookman*, August 1921, 511.

183. Initially, O'Neill spelled his name Christophersen with an "e," indicating Danish rather than Swedish heritage, but later corrected the mistake.

184. Quoted in Hamilton Basso, "The Tragic Sense—II," *New Yorker*, March 6, 1948, 38.

185. Alexander, *Eugene O'Neill's Last Plays*, 21.

186. Boulton, *Part of a Long Story*, 254–57.

187. O'Neill's work diaries indicate that he wrote this play at the end of 1919 in a "Rented House, Provincetown" (Floyd, *Eugene O'Neill at Work*, 390).

188. Eugene O'Neill, *Exorcism: A Play in One Act* (1919) (New Haven: Yale University Press, 2012), 55.

189. Quoted in Sheaffer, *Son and Playwright*, 4.

190. Kenneth Macgowan, "The New Plays: The Provincetown Players, Reopening, Present One Real Oddity in Their New Bill," *New York Globe and Commercial Advertiser*, November 3, 1919, 12.

191. O'Neill, *Selected Letters*, 97.

192. William Davies King, ed., *"A Wind Is Rising": The Correspondence of Agnes Boulton and Eugene O'Neill* (Madison, N.J.: Fairleigh Dickinson University Press, 2000), 115; O'Neill, *Selected Letters*, 151.

193. O'Neill, *Selected Letters*, 103.

194. Ibid., 98, 205.

195. Ibid., 99, 98.

196. "Three Are Held in the Fake Rum Sale," *New York Sun*, December 29, 1919, 4; "61 Are Dead from Poison Whiskey Made in New York," *Brooklyn Daily Eagle*, December 28, 1919, 1.

197. O'Neill, *Selected Letters*, 105; King, *"A Wind Is Rising,"* 78; O'Neill, *Selected Letters*, 106.

198. O'Neill, *Selected Letters*, 99, 100.

199. Ibid., 105.

200. Eugene O'Neill, [untitled poem] (1919), in *Poems, 1912–1944*, ed. Donald Gallup (New Haven: Ticknor and Fields, 1980), 92. In their note on this poem in O'Neill, *Selected Letters*, Bogard and Bryer identify it as written on the morning of January 17, 1920. The date in Gallup reads "September 1919," but it was added in pencil "in an unidentified hand." In fact, Agnes Boulton quotes the poem in her memoir (*Part of a Long Story*, 260–61) and says O'Neill sent it to her in September while she was pregnant with Shane at Happy Home. I believe Bogard and Bryer are correct and that Agnes or someone else added the date to match her memoir, possibly to protect him from the above story or from *Exorcism*, the likely gift to her that goes unmentioned in her memoirs.

201. O'Neill, *Selected Letters*, 109, 108.

202. King, *"A Wind Is Rising,"* 91.

203. O'Neill, *Selected Letters*, 111.

204. *Yonkers Statesman*, January 27, 1920, 3; *"Beyond the Horizon," Yonkers Statesman*, February 3, 1920, 5.

205. O'Neill, *Selected Letters*, 112; Sheaffer, *Son and Artist*, 477.

206. King, *"A Wind Is Rising,"* 96 (of course, this wire was all in capital letters and used no italics or punctuation), 95, 96, 128.

207. O'Neill, *Selected Letters*, 112; Alexander Woollcott, "The Play: Eugene O'Neill's Tragedy," *New York Times*, February 4, 1920, 12; O'Neill, *Selected Letters*, 119.

208. Philip Mindil, "Behind the Scenes" (1920), in Estrin, *Conversations with Eugene O'Neill*, 5; O'Neill, *Selected Letters*, 129n1, 130.

209. King, *"A Wind Is Rising,"* 95, 90n2; O'Neill, *Selected Letters*, 108.

210. King, *"A Wind Is Rising,"* 120; Basso, "The Tragic Sense—II," 35; O'Neill, *Selected Letters*, 137.

211. St. John Ervine to Eugene O'Neill, February 18, 1920, Eugene O'Neill Papers, Beinecke Library. O'Neill misquotes Ervine in a letter to Boulton; see King, *"A Wind Is Rising,"* 123. Much later, in 1948, St. John Ervine wrote an eviscerating anonymous review in England of *The Iceman Cometh* titled "Counsels of Despair," in which he declaimed that "all of [O'Neill's] plays are contemptuous of people and denunciatory of human existence." [St. John Ervine] (1948), in Cargill, Fagin, and Fisher, *O'Neill and His Plays*, 369.

212. King, "*A Wind Is Rising*," 123.

213. Alta May Coleman, "Personality Portraits: No. 3, Eugene O'Neill," *Theatre Magazine*, April 1920, 264, 302.

214. King, "*A Wind Is Rising*," 116, 118; O'Neill, *Selected Letters*, 118.

215. O'Neill, *Selected Letters*, 143.

216. Ibid., 128, 120, 121.

217. Ibid., 103. O'Neill wrote Boulton in early December that he was going down to Macdougal Street "to submit my play." The unnamed play in question is *Exorcism*.

218. Kenton, *Provincetown Players*, 117. This subtitle does not appear on the surviving manuscript.

219. Jeff Kennedy, "*Exorcism:* The Context, the Critics, the Creation, and Rediscovery," *Eugene O'Neill Review* 34, no. 1 (2013): 28–38.

220. Jasper Deeter, interview by Louis Sheaffer, November 10, 1962, Sheaffer-O'Neill Collection. See also Robert M. Dowling, "Eugene O'Neill's *Exorcism:* The Lost Prequel to *Long Day's Journey Into Night*," *Eugene O'Neill Review* 34, no. 1 (2013): 1–12.

221. In the process of collecting all extant contemporary reviews for our volume *Eugene O'Neill: The Contemporary Reviews* (New York: Cambridge University Press, 2014), my coeditor Jackson R. Bryer and I found a total of five for *Exorcism*, the *New York Clipper*, the *Quill*, the *New York Tribune*, *Variety*, and the *New York Times*.

222. Quoted in Sheaffer, *Son and Artist*, 12.

223. King, "*A Wind Is Rising*," 118, 103, 113.

224. O'Neill, *Selected Letters*, 555.

225. Hamlin Garland, *Selected Letters of Hamlin Garland*, ed. Keith Newlin and Joseph B. McCullough (Lincoln: University of Nebraska Press, 1998), 349, 277, 278.

226. Light, interview by Sheaffer, March 26, 1959.

227. Hamilton, "Eugene G. O'Neill," 209, 205.

228. O'Neill, *Selected Letters*, 131, 132, 143.

229. Sheaffer, *Son and Artist*, 23–24.

230. King, "*A Wind Is Rising*," 117.

231. Boulton, *Part of a Long Story*, 132, 131.

232. Hazel Hawthorne Werner, "Recollections," n.d., TS, Sheaffer-O'Neill Collection.

233. Clark, *Eugene O'Neill*, 72; Gelb and Gelb, *Life with Monte Cristo*, 532.

234. Cornel West refers to this as an "unmasking of civilization. "Cornel West Commentary: The Plays of Eugene O'Neill," *The Tavis Smiley Show*, November 26, 2003, NPR, http://www.npr.org/templates/story/story.php?storyId=1522880.

235. *The Emperor Jones* was the first successful example of American expressionism. Scholar Keith Newlin credits Dreiser's *Laughing Gas* as the first expressionistic play ever produced in the United States. See Keith Newlin, "Expressionism Takes the Stage: Dreiser's 'Laughing Gas,' " *Journal of American Drama* 4 (Winter 1992): 5–22.

236. James Light, "The Parade of Masks," undated, T-Mss 2001-050, Billy Rose Theatre Division, New York Public Library, New York.

237. See Robert M. Dowling, "On Eugene O'Neill's 'Philosophical Anarchism,' " *Eugene O'Neill Review* 29 (Spring 2007): 50–72.

238. Max Stirner, *The Ego and His Own: The Case of the Individual Against Authority* (1844), trans. Steven T. Byington (New York: Benjamin R. Tucker, 1907), 65, 153; emphasis added.

239. Eugene O'Neill, "The Silver Bullet," MS, Eugene O'Neill Collection, Manuscripts Division, Department of Rare Books and Special Collection, Princeton University Library, Princeton, N.J.

240. King, *"A Wind Is Rising,"* 73, 117, 124, 127.

241. O'Neill, *Selected Letters*, 206; "Eugene O'Neill Talks of His Own and the Plays of Others," *New York Herald Tribune*, November 16, 1924, sec. 7–8, 14.

242. Dudley Murphy, who wrote the film script, specifies that it takes place "on the island of Haiti" (*"The Emperor Jones"* by Eugene O'Neill, Film Treatment, by Dudley Murphy, ca. 1929, p. 4, Clifton Waller Barrett Library of American Literature). Furthermore, to identify the island as Haiti in that political climate would have been damaging to his career, perhaps even dangerous. "We played Christophe," DuBose Heyward told O'Neill, after writing the 1933 film script, "as close as we dared" (DuBose Heyward to Eugene O'Neill, July 29, 1933 [photocopy], private collection of Jackson R. Bryer). The actor James Earl Jones, who decades later, in 1964, played Brutus Jones, points out that it might have been safer for O'Neill to attack capitalism over imperialism, even at the height of the Red Scare in 1920: "If O'Neill set out to write a straight play about a deposed dictator from a Caribbean island, like Haiti, it might never have been produced. . . . Brutus Jones was the ultimate capitalist, the ultimate exploiter." "And that's not black," the actor remarked, "that's American" (quoted in Donald P. Gagnon, " 'You Needn't Be Scared of Me!' Joe Mott and the Politics of Isolation and Interdependence in *The Iceman Cometh*," in Herrmann and Dowling, *Eugene O'Neill and His Early Contemporaries*, 156).

243. Kenton, *Provincetown Players*, 124–25.

244. Kennedy, "Provincetown Playhouse," 715.

245. Tragically, the legendary dome didn't survive New York University's recent renovations at the Macdougal Street address. Presumably Cook's dome is decomposing in a Staten Island or New Jersey landfill. My thanks to Jeff Kennedy for mentioning to me this all-too-true image of the dome's fate. Jimmy Light published an article at the time of the production that remains the most vivid existing description of its design, construction, and ultimate purpose.

246. Light, "Parade of Masks," 3.

247. James Light, "Lighting Effects: Secured by Use of 'Dome' Explained by James Light," *Billboard*, December 4, 1920, 20. A portion of James Light's description is misquoted in Deutsch and Hanau, *The Provincetown*, 61–62.

248. Quoted in Clark, *Eugene O'Neill*, 72. This drum technique was not unique, however. The American dramatist Austin Strong used virtually the same idea in his 1915 melodrama, *The Drums of Oude* (ibid.).

249. Kyra Markham to Louis Sheaffer, September 6, 1962 (photocopy), private collection of Jackson R. Bryer.

250. Quoted in Michael A. Morrison, "Emperors Before Gilpin: Opal Cooper and Paul Robeson," *Eugene O'Neill Review* 33, no. 2 (2012): 171n7. Morrison's account of casting the role of Brutus Jones is the most up-to-date and comprehensive.

251. "Paul Robeson," *New York Amsterdam News*, January 8, 1930, 9.

252. Morrison, "Emperors Before Gilpin," 165, 166.

253. James Light, interview by Louis Sheaffer, May 21, 1960, Sheaffer-O'Neill Collection.

254. Light, interview by Sheaffer, October 17, 1960.

255. "Paul Robeson," 9; "How Negro Actor Got His Chance in *Emperor Jones*," *New York Tribune*, November 28, 1920, 2.

256. O'Neill, *Selected Letters*, 144; Kenton, *Provincetown Players*, 126; Light, interview by Sheaffer, October 17, 1960.

257. Teddy Ballantine, interview by Louis Sheaffer, n.d., Sheaffer-O'Neill Collection; O'Neill, *Selected Letters*, 170; S. J. Woolf, "Eugene O'Neill Returns After Twelve Years" (1946), in Estrin, *Conversations with Eugene O'Neill*, 172.

258. George Cram Cook, [*The Emperor Jones*, by Eugene O'Neill], 1, 2; O'Neill, *Selected Letters*, 142.

259. Quoted in Basso, "The Tragic Sense—II," 37; Cook, "The Way of the Group." See also Cook, [*The Emperor Jones*, by Eugene O'Neill], p. 4; Kenneth Macgowan, "Curtain Calls," *New York Globe and Commercial Advertiser*, March 16, 1922; "To Close the Sunday Theatre: Directors of the Provincetown Players Charged with Violating the Law," *New York Times*, December 10, 1920.

260. James Weldon Johnson, *Black Manhattan* (1930) (New York: Da Capo, 1991), 183–85.

261. Mary Welch, "Softer Tones for Mr. O'Neill's Portrait," *Theatre Arts* 41, no. 5 (1957): 67–68.

262. Number of performances in Basso, "The Tragic Sense—II," 37. List of New York theaters in "Charles Gilpin in the Bronx," *New York Amsterdam News*, October 27, 1926, 10; also see O'Neill, *Selected Letters*, 170.

263. Hermione Lee, *Edith Wharton* (New York: Knopf, 2007), 640; R. W. B. Lewis, *Edith Wharton: A Biography* (New York: Harper and Row, 1975), 487.

264. "Charles Gilpin in the Bronx," 10; "Ku Klux Bars Charles Gilpin from the South," *Chicago Broad Ax*, January 28, 1922, 2.

265. Quoted in Hubert H. Harrison, "With the Contributing Editor: *The Emperor Jones*," *Negro World*, June 4, 1921, 6.

266. "Provincetown Players Stage Remarkable Play," *Brooklyn Daily Eagle*, November 9, 1920, sec. 2, 5.

267. Quoted in Boulton, *Part of a Long Story*, 151. William Davies King, editor of the latest edition of Boulton's memoir, notes that this section had been removed by the publishers. In his new edition, he restores the text, in brackets, for the first time (150–51).

268. Eugene O'Neill, [untitled poem], in *Poems, 1912–1944*, 77. Harlem Renaissance poet Langston Hughes, at only eighteen years old, published "The Negro Speaks of Rivers," one of his most celebrated poems, the year after *The Emperor Jones* appeared. The poem echoes O'Neill's atavistic meaning as well as referencing the riverbank—the Congo—upon which Brutus Jones is metaphorically slain. The Provincetown Players acknowledged the connection by reprinting Hughes's poem in their program for the 1924 revival of *The Emperor Jones* with Paul Robeson.

269. Harrison, "With the Contributing Editor."

270. Note on the text by Jeffrey B. Perry in Hubert Harrison, *A Hubert Harrison Reader*, ed. Jeffrey B. Perry (Watertown, Conn.: Wesleyan University Press, 2001), 194.

271. Hubert H. Harrison, "Marcus Garvey at the Bar of United States Justice" (1923), in Perry, *A Hubert Harrison Reader*, 199.

272. Eugene O'Neill to Hubert H. Harrison, June 9, 1921, p. 1, Hubert H. Harrison Papers, 1893–1927, Rare Book and Manuscript Library, Columbia University, New York.

273. Ibid., 2. It's notable that O'Neill would use this line of dialogue, "Where do I go from here?" at the point of crisis in his next expressionistic play, *The Hairy Ape*, though he probably had already used it in the lost short story of that title.

274. Ibid., 1; Floyd, *Eugene O'Neill at Work*, 38.

275. Eugene O'Neill to Hubert H. Harrison, June 9, 1921, 1; quoted in Joel Pfister, *Staging Depth: Eugene O'Neill and the Politics of Psychological Discourse* (Chapel Hill: University of North Carolina Press, 1995), 121.

276. Johnson, *Black Manhattan*, 184.

277. Quoted in Sheaffer, *Son and Artist*, 36.

278. Johnson, *Black Manhattan*, 185n1; O'Neill, *Selected Letters*, 165; Paul Robeson, "Reflections on O'Neill's Plays," in *The "Opportunity" Reader: Stories, Poems, and Essays from the Urban League's "Opportunity" Magazine*, ed. Sondra Kathryn Wilson (New York: Modern Library, 1999), 352; James Light, interview by Louis Sheaffer, June 26, 1960, Sheaffer-O'Neill Collection; O'Neill, *Selected Letters*, 177.

279. "Three Deaths," *New York Amsterdam News*, May 14, 1930, 20.

280. Murphy, *Provincetown Players*, 178; Kenton, *Provincetown Players*, 155. Bryant would die at age forty-one alone in Paris. After her failed marriage to William C. Bullitt, she surrendered herself to alcohol and drugs while suffering from the body-deforming and agonizingly painful Dercum's disease.

281. Djuna Barnes, "The Days of Jig Cook: Recollections of Ancient Theatre History But Ten Years Old," *Theatre Guild Magazine* 6 (January 1929): 32.

282. Kenneth Macgowan, review of *Diff'rent*, in Cargill, Fagin, and Fisher, *O'Neill and His Plays*, 148; Clark, *Eugene O'Neill*, 79.

283. Heywood Broun, "Grey Gods and Green Goddesses," *Vanity Fair*, April 1921, 98.

284. O'Neill, *Selected Letters*, 146.

285. Eugene O'Neill, "Damn the Optimists!" in Cargill, Fagin, and Fisher, *O'Neill and His Plays*, 104–6. This telling early statement by O'Neill was published in the *New York Tribune*, February 13, 1921, under the title "Eugene O'Neill's Credo and His Reasons for His Faith."

286. Stephen Rathbun, "O'Neill's Latest Play Presented by the Provincetown Players," *New York Sun*, December 31, 1920, 5.

287. O'Neill, *Selected Letters*, 146.

288. Heywood Broun, "*Diff'rent* Comes to Broadway at the Selwyn," *New York Tribune*, February 1, 1921, 6.

289. Quoted in Egil Törnqvist, "Philosophical and Literary Paragons," in *The Cambridge Companion to Eugene O'Neill*, ed. Michael Manheim (New York: Cambridge University Press, 1998), 22.

290. Quoted in Sheaffer, *Son and Artist*, 245.

291. Doris Alexander, *Eugene O'Neill's Creative Struggle: The Decisive Decade, 1924–1933* (University Park: Pennsylvania State University Press, 1992), 225, notes for p. 38.

292. O'Neill, "Scribbling Diary," January 20, 1925, Eugene O'Neill Papers.

293. Quoted in Törnqvist, "Philosophical and Literary Paragons," 22.

294. Quoted in Alexander, *Eugene O'Neill's Creative Struggle*, 38. O'Neill is responding to critics here about his later play *Desire Under the Elms*.

295. O'Neill, "Damn the Optimists!"

296. Dorothy Commins, ed., *"Love and Admiration and Respect": The O'Neill-Commins Correspondence* (Durham, N.C.: Duke University Press, 1986), 15; O'Neill, *Selected Letters*, 151.

297. George Jean Nathan, "The Bright Face of Tragedy," *Cosmopolitan*, August 1957, 66.

298. King, *"A Wind Is Rising,"* 171.

299. Ibid., 199.

300. Commins, *"Love and Admiration and Respect,"* 17; O'Neill, *Selected Letters*, 156.

301. Quoted in Ronald H. Wainscott, *Staging O'Neill: The Experimental Years, 1920–1934* (New Haven: Yale University Press, 1988), 67.

302. Ibid., 69.

303. Ludwig Lewisohn, *"Gold"* (1921), in *The Critical Response to Eugene O'Neill*, ed. John H. Houchin, Critical Responses in Arts and Letters, no. 5 (Westport, Conn.: Greenwood, 1993), 26.

304. Quoted in George Jean Nathan, "Eugene O'Neill After Twelve Years" (1946), in Estrin, *Conversations with Eugene O'Neill*, 177.

305. [Heywood Broun], "Animadversion on the Great-Great-Grandchildren of Ophelia—Also Shaw's Summary on Theater," *New York Tribune*, June 5, 1921, part 3, 1; Heywood Broun, *"Gold* at Frazee Shows O'Neill Below His Best," *New York Tribune*, June 2, 1921, 6.

306. Eugene O'Neill to Robert Sisk, March 11, 1929, Sheaffer-O'Neill Collection.

307. Light, "Parade of Masks."

308. Susan Glaspell, *The Verge* (1921), in *Plays by Susan Glaspell*, ed. C. W. E. Bigsby (New York: Cambridge University Press, 1987), 65, 78, 82.

309. Quoted in King, *Another Part of a Long Story*, 252n17.

310. Quoted in Sheaffer, *Son and Artist*, 48.

311. Quoted in Boulton, *Part of a Long Story*, 61.

312. Quoted in Sheaffer, *Son and Artist*, 48.

313. King, *"A Wind Is Rising,"* 195–96.

314. Heywood Broun, "It Seems to Me," *New York World*, November 11, 1921, 15.

315. James Whittaker, "O'Neill Has First Concrete Heroine," *New York Sunday News*, November 13, 1921, 21.

316. Eugene G. O'Neill, "The Mail Bag," *New York Times*, December 18, 1921, sec. Music-Drama, 72.

317. O'Neill, *Selected Letters*, 148.

318. Burns Mantle, "The New Plays: '*Anna Christie*' Vivid Drama," *New York Evening Mail*, November 3, 1921, 13; George Jean Nathan, "The Press and the Drama," *Smart Set* 67 (January 1922): 132; Alexander Woollcott, "Second Thoughts on First Nights" (1921), in Houchin, *The Critical Response to Eugene O'Neill*, 30.

319. See Katie N. Johnson, *Sisters in Sin: Brothel Drama in America, 1900–1920*, Cambridge Studies in American Theatre and Drama (New York: Cambridge University Press, 2006).

320. Kenneth Macgowan, "The New Play: Eugene O'Neill's '*Anna Christie*' a Notable Drama Notably Acted at the Vanderbilt Theatre," *New York Globe and Commercial Advertiser*, November 3, 1921, 16.

321. For a more comprehensive understanding of naturalism in drama, see my essay "Sad Endings and Negative Heroes: The Naturalist Tradition in American Drama" in *The Oxford Handbook to American Literary Naturalism*, ed. Keith Newlin (New York: Oxford University Press, 2011), 427–44.

322. Quoted in Louis Kantor, "O'Neill Defends His Play of the Negro" (1924), in Estrin, *Conversations with Eugene O'Neill*, 48.

323. O'Neill, *Selected Letters*, 121; Wainscott, *Staging O'Neill*, 92; Playgoer, "Eugene O'Neill's *The Straw* Is Gruesome Clinical Tale" (1921), in Houchin, *The Critical Response to Eugene O'Neill*, 38; Alan Dale, "Tuberculosis Dramatized in the Latest Play by Eugene O'Neill," *New York American*, November 11, 1921; Light, interview by Sheaffer, May 21, 1960.

324. Clark, *Eugene O'Neill*, 102.

325. O'Neill, *Selected Letters*, 156.

326. Memorandum of Agreement on Eugene O'Neill, Jr., between Eugene O'Neill and Kathleen Jenkins, August 15, 1921, Eugene O'Neill Papers; Sheaffer, *Son and Artist*, 65–67.

327. Charles Kennedy, "Several Sides of Mr. O'Neill," *Call Board* (Official Organ of the Catholic Actors' Guild of America), June 1948, 7.

328. Sotheby Parke-Bernet, catalogue of sales, January 26, 1977 (the eight-page, handwritten, signed letter sold on January 26, 1977). A copy of the page from this catalogue is in the private collection of Jackson R. Bryer. This would be one of the longest letters, perhaps the longest, that O'Neill ever wrote. One can only hope it resurfaces.

329. O'Neill, *Selected Letters*, 157; Commins, *"Love and Admiration and Respect,"* 20.

330. Quoted in Sheaffer, *Son and Playwright*, 383.

331. Quoted in Malcolm Mollan, "Making Plays with a Tragic End: An Intimate Interview with Eugene O'Neill, Who Tells Why He Does It" (1922), in Estrin, *Conversations with Eugene O'Neill*, 15.

332. O'Neill, *Selected Letters*, 157, and quoted in Mollan, "Making Plays with a Tragic End," 17.

333. Stirner, *The Ego and His Own*, 30; August Strindberg, "On Modern Drama and Modern Theatre" (1889), in *August Strindberg: Selected Essays*, ed. Michael Robinson (Cambridge: Cambridge University Press, 1996) 57, 59.

334. Quoted in Sheaffer, *Son and Playwright*, 239.

335. Sophus Keith Winther, *Eugene O'Neill: A Critical Study* (New York: Random House, 1934), 123.

336. Tennessee Williams, "The World I Live In" (1957), in *A Streetcar Named Desire* (New York: New Directions, 1947), 184; quoted in Sheaffer, *Son and Artist*, 44.

337. Commins, *"Love and Admiration and Respect,"* 20.

338. Oliver M. Sayler, *"The Hairy Ape* a Study in the Evolution of a Play: How O'Neill's First Expressionistic Drama Took Form from the Experiment of *The Emperor Jones," New York Globe*, May 6, 1922, 9.

339. O'Neill, *Selected Letters*, 161; Clark, *Eugene O'Neill*, 128; O'Neill, *Selected Letters*, 161.

340. George Jean Nathan. "Eugene O'Neill Is at Worst in His New Play, *First Man," Spokane Spokesman-Review*, March 26, 1922, part 5, 2.

341. Quoted in Nathan, "Eugene O'Neill After Twelve Years," 177.

342. Peter Egri, " 'Belonging' Lost: Alienation and Dramatic Form in Eugene O'Neill's *The Hairy Ape,"* in *Critical Essays on Eugene O'Neill*, ed. James J. Martine (Boston: G. K. Hall, 1984), 77; Kenneth Macgowan, "The New Play: Eugene O'Neill Sets a New Mark in *The Hairy Ape," New York Globe and Commercial Advertiser*, March 10, 1922, 12.

ACT III: "The Broadway Show Shop"

Notes to pp. 239–30: "The greatest day of the Provincetown Players" (Mary Heaton Vorse, *Time and the Town: A Provincetown Chronicle* [1942], ed. Adele Heller [New Brunswick, N.J.: Rutgers University Press, 1991], 125; "the throb of the drum" (John Dos Passos, "Is the 'Realistic' Theatre Obsolete? Many Theatrical Conventions Have Been Shattered by Lawson's 'Processional' " [1925], in *Travel Books and Other Writings, 1916–1941*, ed. Townsend Ludington [New York: Library of America, 2003], 593).

1. James Light, interview by Louis Sheaffer, October 17, 1960, Sheaffer-O'Neill Collection, Linda Lear Center for Special Collections and Archives, Connecticut College, New London; Oliver M. Sayler, *"The Hairy Ape* a Study in the Evolution of a Play: How O'Neill's First Expressionistic Drama Took Form from the Experiment of *The Emperor Jones," New York Globe*, May 6, 1922, 9; Eugene O'Neill, *Selected Letters of Eugene O'Neill*, ed. Travis Bogard and Jackson R. Bryer (New Haven: Yale University Press, 1988), 167.

2. William Davies King, ed., *"A Wind Is Rising": The Correspondence of Agnes Boulton and Eugene O'Neill* (Madison, N.J.: Fairleigh Dickinson University Press, 2000), 182.

3. Cheryl Black, "Pioneering Theatre Managers: Edna Kenton and Eleanor Fitzgerald of the Provincetown Players," *Journal of American Drama and Theatre* 9, no. 3 (1997): 46–47; Edna Kenton, *The Provincetown Players and the Playwrights' Theatre, 1915–1922*, ed. Travis Bogard and Jackson R. Bryer (Jefferson, N.C.: McFarland, 2004), 156.

4. Arthur Pollock, "About the Theater," *Brooklyn Daily Eagle*, March 12, 1922, C7.

5. Eugene O'Neill to Robert Fisk, March 15, 1935, Sheaffer-O'Neill Collection; Keith Newlin and Frederic E. Rusch, introduction to *The Collected Plays of Theodore Dreiser*, ed. Newlin and Rusch (Albany, N.Y.: Whitston, 2000), xxvi. Dreiser's full-length play *The Hand of the Potter*, a sympathetic treatment of a murderous child molester named Isadore Berchansky, based on the actual pedophilic murderer Nathan Swartz, had opened at the Provincetown Playhouse the previous December. Dreiser's plotline horrified audiences. H. L. Mencken, best known for his defense of artistic freedom, scolded his friend Dreiser for "shocking the numskulls for the mere sake of shocking them" (xxvii).

6. O'Neill, *Selected Letters*, 87.

7. Ibid., 161; Alexander Woollcott, "The Play: Eugene O'Neill at Full Tilt," *New York Times*, March 10, 1922, 18. The Wooster Group's production of the early 1990s highlighted the industrial nightmare O'Neill conceived by constructing massive, cagelike scaffolding that allowed Yank, played with ferocious intensity by Willem Dafoe, to climb about with his coal-blackened face precisely resembling the primal ancestor O'Neill envisioned; Robert C. Benchley, "Drama," *Life*, March 30, 1922, 18.

8. Yvonne Shaffer, *Performing O'Neill: Conversations with Actors and Directors* (New York: Palgrave Macmillan, 2000), 25.

9. James Light, interview by Louis Sheaffer, May 21, 1960, Sheaffer-O'Neill Collection.

10. Oliver M. Sayler, "The Yarn-Spinning Provincetown," ca. 1929, TS, Provincetown Players' Scrapbook, 1923–1929, Billy Rose Theatre Division, New York Public Library.

11. Louis Wolheim, "A Prometheus of Modern Drama," *Cincinnati Commercial Tribune*, September 24, 1922.

12. Ibid.

13. Quoted in Egil Törnqvist, *A Drama of Souls: Studies in O'Neill's Super-Naturalistic Technique* (New Haven: Yale University Press, 1969), 14. Benjamin De Casseres refers to the vultures of O'Neill's conscience and imagination in his parody "Denial without End" (*Eugene O'Neill Review* 30 [2008]: 150–55).

14. O'Neill, *Selected Letters*, 161.

15. Ibid., 165.

16. Weather described in Alexander Woollcott, "The Play: The New O'Neill Play," *New York Times*, March 6, 1922, 9; "ten bottles" from Louis Sheaffer, *O'Neill: Son and Artist* (Boston: Little, Brown, 1973), 85.

17. Sheaffer, *Son and Artist*, 86; Dorothy Commins, ed., *"Love and Admiration and Respect": The O'Neill-Commins Correspondence* (Durham, N.C.: Duke University Press, 1986), 22n29.

18. Commins, *"Love and Admiration and Respect,"* 22.

19. Ibid., 23.

20. Ibid.

21. Ibid., 24, 25.

22. Ibid., 25.

23. Sheaffer, *Son and Artist*, 87.

24. David Karsner, "Here and There and Everywhere," *New York Call*, May 20, 1922, 10.

25. James Light, interview by Louis Sheaffer, November 5, 1961, Sheaffer-O'Neill Collection.

26. Carl Hovey to Eugene O'Neill, August 13, 1918, Sheaffer-O'Neill Collection.

27. Heywood Broun, "It Seems to Me," *New York World*, April 25, 1922. Gold is quoted in this column.

28. L. E. Levick, "*The Hairy Ape* and the I.W.W.—Marine Transport Workers Turn Dramatic Critics and Praise O'Neill," *Freeman*, May 1922.

29. "O'Neill, Hopkins and *Hairy Ape* Demand Amnesty," *New York Call*, July 1, 1922, 1, 5.

30. Kenneth Macgowan, "Curtain Calls," *New York Globe and Commercial Advertiser*, March 16, 1922.

31. "Court Has Case of Provincetown Players Dropped," March 1922, Clippings Scrapbook, Eugene O'Neill Papers, Beinecke Library, Yale University, New Haven.

32. "Censorship at Its Worst," *Brooklyn Daily Eagle*, May 19, 1922; "Censors to Take Up *Hairy Ape*," *New York Call*, May 20, 1922, 1; Lawrence Reamer, "Mr. O'Neill at Home," *New York Herald*, June 4, 1922; "Calls *Hairy Ape*'s Foes 'Poor Dolts,' " *New York World*, [May] 1922.

33. Reamer, "Mr. O'Neill at Home"; Karsner, "Here and There and Everywhere," May 20, 1922, 10.

34. FBI memorandum, April 22, 1924; David Karsner, "Here and There and Everywhere," *New York Call*, June 2, 1922.

35. Patterson James, "Off the Record," *Billboard*, June 10, 1922, 18.

36. O'Neill, *Selected Letters*, 167.

37. Eleanor M. Fitzgerald, "Valedictory of an Art Theatre," *New York Times*, December 22, 1929, in Kenton, *Provincetown Players*, 199.

38. Commins, *"Love and Admiration and Respect,"* 21; Kenneth Macgowan, "Seen on the Stage," *Vogue*, May 1, 1922, 108. For Hopkins's role, see Woollcott, "The Play: Eugene O'Neill at Full Tilt," 18; "The Highbrow: At the Play; *The Hairy Ape*, at the Provincetown Playhouse," *Town Topics*, March 16, 1922, 13.

39. Kenton, *Provincetown Players*, 156; O'Neill, *Selected Letters*, 168.

40. George Cram Cook to Edna Kenton, July 8, 1922, Clifton Waller Barrett Library of American Literature, Albert and Shirley Small Special Collections Library, University of Virginia, Charlottesville.

41. Quoted in Kenton, *Provincetown Players*, 156.

42. O'Neill, *Selected Letters*, 172; Commins, *"Love and Admiration and Respect,"* 26; Sheaffer, *Son and Artist*, 66–67.

43. Quoted in Sheaffer, *Son and Artist*, 97.

44. Kyra Markham to Louis Sheaffer, September 6, 1962 (photocopy), private collection of Jackson R. Bryer.

45. See Brian Rogers, "Brook Farm," in *Critical Companion to Eugene O'Neill: A Literary Reference to His Life and Work*, ed. Robert M. Dowling (New York: Facts on File, 2009), 2:538.

46. Hamilton Basso, "The Tragic Sense—II," *New Yorker*, March 6, 1948, 38; quoted in Sheaffer, *Son and Artist*, 282.

47. Quoted in William Davies King, *Another Part of a Long Story: Literary Traces of Eugene O'Neill and Agnes Boulton* (Ann Arbor: University of Michigan Press, 2010), 145, 126. Only two charred fragments and a transcribed page of the novel, which, like *Welded*, was a fictional but deeply personal account of their marriage, has survived.

48. Teddy Ballantine's undated interview with Sheaffer indicates that this took place at Brook Farm, though he presumed it was a portrait of Agnes instead of her father. Boulton told Sheaffer it happened at Brook Farm as well (*Son and Artist*, 107).

49. Quoted in King, *Another Part of a Long Story*, 110–11.

50. See ibid., 125, 259n54.

51. Sheaffer, *Son and Artist*, 107.

52. Lloyd Goodrich, notes supplied to the author by Kathleen A. Foster, the Robert L. McNeil, Jr., Senior Curator and Director of American Art, Center for American Art, Philadelphia Museum of Fine Art.

53. Quoted in King, *Another Part of a Long Story*, 259n54.

54. Eakins biographer Gordon Hendricks saw another sketch of Teddy Boulton, but that is also lost (Kathleen A. Foster, *Thomas Eakins Rediscovered: Charles Bregler's Thomas Eakins Collection at the Pennsylvania Academy of Fine Arts* [New Haven: Yale University Press, 1997], 278n18). The physical work of the portrait published here was sold first to the Hirschl and Adler Galleries in 1987, then again to a private buyer by Sotheby's in 1997. My thanks to Hirschl and Adler's Genevieve Hulley, assistant to the senior vice president of American Paintings and Sculpture, and Kathleen A. Foster.

55. Geoff Thompson rightly shifts the psychological import for O'Neill from O'Neill's writing to his drinking in his clinical psychology master's thesis at Trinity Western University, "A Touch of the Poet: A Psychobiography of Eugene O'Neill's Recovery from Alcoholism" (2004).

56. Sheaffer, *Son and Artist*, 107; Barrett H. Clark, *Eugene O'Neill: The Man and His Plays*, rev. ed. (New York: Dover, 1947), 42; Croswell Bowen, "The Black Irishman," (1946), in *O'Neill and His Plays: Four Decades of Criticism*, ed. Oscar Cargill, N. Bryllion Fagin, and William J. Fisher (New York: New York University Press, 1961), 73; Sheaffer, *Son and Artist*, 102.

57. Louis Kantor, "O'Neill Defends His Play of the Negro" (1924), in *Conversations with Eugene O'Neill*, ed. Mark W. Estrin (Jackson: University Press of Mississippi, 1990), 49.

58. The following year, Boulton would even use the name "Elinor" as her pseudonym when she copyrighted her own marriage play, *The Guilty One*, based on a 1917 scenario of O'Neill's *The Reckoning*.

59. Agnes Boulton, *Part of a Long Story: "Eugene O'Neill as a Young Man in Love,"* ed. William Davies King (Jefferson, N.C.: McFarland, 2011), 56.

60. Friedrich Wilhelm Nietzsche, *Thus Spake Zarathustra* (1883–85), trans. Thomas Common, Project Gutenberg, Release #1988, http://onlinebooks.library.upenn.edu/webbin/gutbook/lookup?num=1998.

61. Ibid.

62. O'Neill, *Selected Letters*, 271; Virginia Floyd, *The Plays of Eugene O'Neill: A New Assessment* (New York: Frederick Ungar, 1985), 133.

63. Sheaffer, *Son and Artist*, 106, 107.

64. Ibid., 107.

65. Ibid., 116; Commins, *"Love and Admiration and Respect,"* 27.

66. Quoted in Sheaffer, *Son and Artist*, 105.

67. Ibid., 117.

68. Malcolm Cowley, "A Weekend with Eugene O'Neill," in Cargill, Fagin, and Fisher, *O'Neill and His Plays*, 41.

69. Hart Crane, *The Letters of Hart Crane, 1916–1932*, ed. Brom Weber (Berkeley: University of California Press, 1965).

70. Cowley, "A Weekend with Eugene O'Neill," 45.

71. Ibid., 47, 49.

72. O'Neill, *Selected Letters*, 378; Sheaffer, *Son and Artist*, 117.

73. During her tenure as the Players' official secretary-treasurer, Fitzgerald probably raised more money to keep Macdougal Street operational than the rest of the Players combined. "No one to whom she appealed could doubt her good sense or her competence," wrote E. E. Cummings, whose play *him* Fitzgerald would help usher onto the Macdougal Street stage in 1928 (quoted in Black, "Pioneering Theatre Managers," 52–53).

74. Helen Deutsch and Stella Hanau, *The Provincetown: A Story of the Theatre* (New York: Farrar and Rinehart, 1931), 97.

75. O'Neill, *Selected Letters*, 182.

76. George Cram Cook to Edna Kenton, July 10–23, 1922, Clifton Waller Barrett Library of American Literature.

77. Quoted in Paul Roazen, "O'Neill and Louise Bryant: New Documents," *Eugene O'Neill Review* 27 (2005): 35.

78. O'Neill, *Selected Letters*, 186; Eugene O'Neill to Susan Glaspell, June 3, 1924, Susan Glaspell Collection, Clifton Waller Barrett Library of American Literature.

79. Quoted in Black, "Pioneering Theatre Managers," 49.

80. Quoted in Clark, *Eugene O'Neill*, 31.

81. Deutsch and Hanau, *The Provincetown*, 101; Eugene O'Neill, "Strindberg and Our Theatre" (1924), in Cargill, Fagin, and Fisher, *O'Neill and His Plays*, 109; Deutsch and Hanau, *The Provincetown*, 102.

82. Agnes Boulton, "An Experimental Theatre: The Provincetown Playhouse," *Theatre Arts* 8 (March 1924): 188; Alexander Woollcott, "The Stage: The New O'Neill Work," *New York World*, December 11, 1925, 15.

83. O'Neill, "Strindberg and Our Theatre," 108; Ronald H. Wainscott, *Staging O'Neill: The Experimental Years, 1920–1934* (New Haven: Yale University Press, 1988), 117; James Light, "The Parade of Masks," undated, T-Mss 2001–050, Billy Rose Theatre Division, New York Public Library.

84. Light, "Parade of Masks."

85. Ibid.

86. Eugene O'Neill, "Memoranda on Masks," in *The Unknown O'Neill: Unpublished and Unfamiliar Writings of Eugene O'Neill*, ed. Travis Bogard (New Haven: Yale University Press, 1988), 407, 410.

87. Heywood Broun, "The New Play: At the Provincetown Playhouse," *New York World*, April 7, 1924, 9; Robert Gilbert Welsh, "Classics and Provincetown," *New York Telegram and Evening Mail*, April 7, 1924, 13.

88. E. W. Osborn, "The New Plays: *Welded*," *New York Evening World*, March 18, 1924, 10; Arthur Pollock, "The New Plays: *Welded*," *Brooklyn Daily Eagle*, March 18, 1924, 9.

89. Sheaffer, *Son and Artist*, 132; Gordon Whyte, "The New Plays on Broadway," *Billboard*, March 29, 1924, 34; Edna Kenton to Carl Van Vechten, April 4, 1924 (incomplete TS), Sheaffer-O'Neill Collection.

90. Stark Young, "Eugene O'Neill: Notes from a Critic's Diary," *Harper's Magazine*, June 1957, 66–71, 74; Macgowan, "Seen on the Stage," 92; Kantor, "O'Neill Defends," 49.

91. Deutsch and Hanau, *The Provincetown*, 108; Kenneth Macgowan, "O'Neill's Play Again," *New York Times*, August 31, 1924, X2.

92. Publicity Committee, "The Fifteen Year Record of the Class of 1910 of Princeton University," 1925, TS, Sheaffer-O'Neill Collection.

93. Kevin J. Mumford, *Interzones: Black/White Sex Districts in Chicago and New York in the Early Twentieth Century* (New York: Columbia University Press, 1997), 126–27.

94. "James Light Dies; O'Neill Associate," *New York Times*, February 12, 1964; Edmund Wilson, *The Twenties: From Notebooks and Diaries of the Period*, ed. Leon Edel (New York: Farrar, Straus and Giroux, 1975), 112; Karl Decker, "*Chillun* Roasted by 100,000 Women," *New York Morning Telegraph*, March 20, 1924.

95. Virginia Floyd, ed., *Eugene O'Neill at Work: Newly Released Ideas for His Plays* (New York: Frederick Ungar, 1981), 53 (emphasis added); "Village Man Who Helped Famous Playwright Dies," *New York Amsterdam News*, November 27, 1929, 3.

96. Floyd, *Eugene O'Neill at Work*, 176.

97. Sheaffer-O'Neill Collection.

98. Gene Fowler, "*God's Chillun* Is Staged at Provincetown," *New York American*, May 16, 1924, 10.

99. Macgowan, "O'Neill's Play Again."

100. For the date of completion, see Agnes Boulton to Harold de Polo, October 20, 1923, Clifton Waller Barrett Library of American Literature.

101. Quoted in Sheaffer, *Son and Artist*, 135.

102. Kantor, "O'Neill Defends," 46; Carol Bird, "Eugene O'Neill—The Inner Man" (1924), in Estrin, *Conversations with Eugene O'Neill*, 54.

103. TS of O'Neill's statement, March 19, 1924, is in Sheaffer-O'Neill Collection.

104. Quoted in Deutsch and Hanau, *The Provincetown*, 109.

105. Ibid., 111.

106. Sheaffer notes on *All God's Chillun*: refers to an unnamed article in the *New York American*. Sheaffer-O'Neill Collection.

107. Quoted in Sheaffer, *Son and Artist*, 140.

108. Light, interview by Sheaffer, November 5, 1961.

109. George Jean Nathan, "The Theatre," *American Mercury*, May 1924, 113; "Shieks [*sic*], Art and Uplift," *Fiery Cross*, February 29, 1924, 4.

110. Glenda Frank, "Tempest in Black and White: The 1924 Premiere of Eugene O'Neill's *All God's Chillun Got Wings*," *Resources for American Literary Study* 26, no. 1 (2000): 79.

111. T. S. Eliot, "*All God's Chillun Got Wings*," in Cargill, Fagin, and Fisher, *O'Neill and His Plays*, 169; Edmund Wilson, "*All God's Chillun* and Others," *New Republic*, May 28, 1924, 22.

112. Alain Locke, "The Negro and the American Stage," in *The Works of Alain Locke*, ed. Charles Molesworth (New York: Oxford University Press, 2012), 118; Sheaffer, *Son and Artist*, 138.

113. Quoted in Jordan Y. Miller, *Playwright's Progress: O'Neill and the Critics* (Chicago: Scott, Foresman, 1965), 39.

114. "Negroes Protest New O'Neill Play: Boston Will Ban *All God's Chillun Got Wings* as Insulting Colored Race," *Morning Telegraph*, February 24, 1924; Macgowan, "O'Neill's Play Again"; "Negro Clergy Bitter at Play," *New York American*, March 15, 1924, 24.

115. Paul Robeson, "Reflections on O'Neill's Plays," in *The "Opportunity" Reader: Stories, Poems, and Essays from the Urban League's "Opportunity" Magazine*, ed. Sondra Kathryn Wilson (New York: Modern Library, 1999), 353, 352.

116. The African American actor John Douglas Thompson, who played Jones in the Irish Repertory Theatre's production in the 2009–10 season, remarked that the only way he could justify accepting the role for himself was to fully "oppress" the white character Smithers ("O'Neill in Bohemia," Eugene O'Neill International Conference, New York City, June 22–26, 2011). A 1992 postmodern revival by the Wooster Group boldly, and highly successfully, cast Kate Valk, a white woman in blackface, as Brutus Jones.

117. T. B. Poston, "Harlem Dislikes 'Nigger' in *Emperor Jones* but Flocks to See Picture at Uptown House," *New York Amsterdam News*, September 27, 1933, 9.

118. Macgowan, "O'Neill's Play Again."

119. Sheaffer, *Son and Artist*, 140.

120. Quoted in Michael A. Morrison, "Emperors Before Gilpin: Opal Cooper and Paul Robeson," *Eugene O'Neill Review* 33, no. 2 (2012): 167.

121. Light, interview by Sheaffer, November 5, 1961; for the location of Barney Gallant's speakeasies, see Emily Kies Folpe, *It Happened on Washington Square* (Baltimore: Johns Hopkins University Press, 2002), 220, 271.

122. Heywood Broun, "Seeing Things at Night," *New York World*, June 22, 1924; Crane, *Letters*.

123. Sheaffer, *Son and Artist*, 143; Sheila Evans, "Paul Robeson, the Actor," performed by Sheila Evans and Paul Robeson Jr., Mustard Seed, 2003, CD; "*Chillun* Barred as Too Youthful, Mayor Explains," *New York Evening World*, May 16, 1924, 9.

124. Deutsch and Hanau, *The Provincetown*, 111; Percy Hammond, "The Theaters," *New York Herald Tribune*, May 16, 1924, 10; Macgowan, "O'Neill's Play Again."

125. "Hylan Stands Pat against *Chillun:* Provincetown Attorney's Plea for Reconsideration of Action Barring Children Fails," *New York Morning Telegraph*, May 17, 1924, 1; "Wings Are Folded by *God's Chillun*," *New York Morning Telegraph*, May 19, 1924, 1.

126. Publicity Committee, "The Fifteen Year Record of the Class of 1910"; Burns Mantle, "*All God's Chillun* with One Scene Cut," *New York Daily News*, May 16, 1924, 24.

127. Kelcey Allen, "*All God's Chillun Got Wings* Proves a Poignant Drama," *Women's Wear Daily*, May 16, 1924, 30. In contrast, the current drama critic for the *New Yorker*, Hilton Als, who is African American, considers *All God's Chillun Got Wings* and *Thirst* "just plain wrong but historically fascinating" plays in which O'Neill "had tackled—and made a hash of—race" (Hilton Als, "The Theatre: The Red and the Black," *New Yorker*, June 24, 2013, 82). It's interesting to note that Als did not cite *The Dreamy Kid* or *The Emperor Jones*. Langston Hughes, whose poem "The Negro Speaks of Rivers" was printed in the program for *The Emperor Jones* revival then playing on alternate nights, could not have been the poet Kelcey Allen refers to, since he was in Paris at the time of the production.

128. Karl Decker, "*All God's Chillun* Crippled at the Birth," *New York Morning Telegraph*, May 17, 1922, 2. The lady critic may well have been Ann Bridgers of Raleigh, North Carolina's *News and Observer*, who considered the play a work of "flabby sentimentalism" that succeeded only in painting "black blacker" (Ann Bridgers, "Impressions along Broadway," *Raleigh News and Observer*, July 6, 1924, sec. 10, 8).

129. Macgowan, "O'Neill's Play Again"; "*Chillun* Barred as Too Youthful, Mayor Explains," 9; Macgowan, "O'Neill's Play Again."

130. Arthur Pollock, "The New Plays: *All God's Chillun*," *Brooklyn Daily Eagle*, May 16, 1924, 5; "Prologue of *All God's Chillun* Is Read, as Child Actors Are Barred," *New York World*, May 16, 1924, 13; Robert C. Benchley, "Drama," *Life*, June 5, 1924, 22.

131. Robeson would also play Yank in a 1931 London revival of *The Hairy Ape*.

132. Robeson, "Reflections on O'Neill's Plays," 353.

133. Quoted in Deutsch and Hanau, *The Provincetown*, 110.

134. O'Neill, *Selected Letters*, 190, 189.

135. Ibid., 189, 190.

136. Ibid, 191, 188.

137. From the reviews we can glean in what order the plays were produced, a common point of confusion: *The Moon of the Caribbees, The Long Voyage Home, In the Zone*, and *Bound East for Cardiff.* On December 16, the *Glencairn* production moved uptown to the Punch and Judy Theatre and then, on January 12, to the Princess Theatre. In 1940, John Ford directed a film of the series titled *The Long Voyage Home*, with a screenplay by O'Neill's friend Dudley Nichols and with John Wayne playing the Swedish sailor Olson. It was O'Neill's favorite of the numerous film versions of his plays made while he was still alive.

138. George Jean Nathan, "The Kahn-Game," *Judge*, December 6, 1924, 17.

139. O'Neill, *Selected Letters*, 188.

140. After its run, O'Neill still accused Jones, for all his pioneering methods, of failing to produce the play "as I wrote it" (ibid., 213).

141. Quoted in Eugene O'Neill, *"The Theatre We Worked For": The Letters of Eugene O'Neill to Kenneth Macgowan*, ed. Travis Bogard and Jackson R. Bryer (New Haven: Yale University Press, 1982), 70.

142. Euphemia Van Rensselaer Wyatt, "The Drama: Eugene O'Neill on Plymouth Rock," *Catholic World*, January 1925, 520.

143. Doris Alexander, *Eugene O'Neill's Creative Struggle: The Decisive Decade, 1924–1933* (University Park: Pennsylvania State University Press, 1992), 36; Arthur Gelb, "Film Version of Play Recalls Complexity of Its Origins," *New York Times*, March 2, 1958; Eugene O'Neill, *"As Ever, Gene": The Letters of Eugene O'Neill to George Jean Nathan*, ed. Nancy L. Roberts and Arthur W. Roberts (Rutherford, N.J.: Fairleigh Dickinson University Press, 1987), 54.

144. Malcolm Mollan, "Making Plays with a Tragic End: An Intimate Interview with Eugene O'Neill, Who Tells Why He Does It" (1922), in Estrin, *Conversations with Eugene O'Neill*, 15; Alexander, *Eugene O'Neill's Creative Struggle*, 34.

145. Gilbert W. Gabriel, *"Desire Under the Elms:* Eugene O'Neill's New Tragedy of an Old Soil Staged at the Greenwich Village," *New York Telegram and Evening Mail*, November 12, 1924, 26; Alexander, *Eugene O'Neill's Creative Struggle*, 38.

146. Agnes Boulton to Harold de Polo, October 6, 1924, Clifton Waller Barrett Library of American Literature; Agnes Boulton, "Eugene's Drinking," n.d., TS (carbon copy), Beinecke Library. "Eugene's Drinking" is written in pencil on the stationary of Dr. Gilbert Van Tassel Hamilton's Bureau of Social Hygiene and Division of Psychological Research. This would date it January 1926.

147. Boulton, "Eugene's Drinking."

148. Quoted in Alexander, *Eugene O'Neill's Creative Struggle*, 33.

149. King, *"A Wind Is Rising,"* 136.

150. Juliet Throckmorton, "As I Remember Eugene O'Neill," *Yankee Magazine*, August 1968, 85, 93–95.

151. Eugene O'Neill to Harold de Polo, February 6, [probably 1925], Clifton Waller Barrett Library of American Literature.

152. For a more complete picture of the O'Neills' life in Bermuda, see Joy Bluck Waters, *Eugene O'Neill and Family: The Bermuda Interlude* (Warwick, Bermuda: Granaway), 1992.

153. O'Neill, "Scribbling Diary," January 1 and 4, 1925, Eugene O'Neill Papers.

154. Eugene O'Neill, *Eugene O'Neill Work Diary, 1924–1943* (preliminary edition), vol. 1, transcribed by Donald Gallup (New Haven: Yale University Library, 1981), January 5, 1925.

155. Boulton indicates in "Eugene's Drinking" that he stopped on January 6, but his work diary clearly shows that he'd only begun "tapering off." O'Neill maintained what he called "scribbling diaries" starting in 1924. In 1931, his third wife, Carlotta Monterey, gave him a five-year diary, which he used to transfer work-related information from the original diaries. He then destroyed the original, more personal volumes. Agnes Boulton saved one of them, for the year 1925, which enraged O'Neill, but it offers treasured biographical information about the playwright's life during this period, especially his battle with alcoholism.

156. O'Neill, "Scribbling Diary," January 27, 22, and 31, 1925.

157. Sheaffer, *Son and Artist*, 163.

158. O'Neill, "Scribbling Diary," January 9, 1925.

159. King, *Another Part of a Long Story*, 137.

160. O'Neill, "Scribbling Diary," February 8, 1925; Eugene O'Neill, "To Alice," in *Poems, 1912–1944*, ed. Donald Gallup (New Haven, Conn.: Ticknor and Fields, 1980), 95; Sheaffer, *Son and Artist*, 164.

161. O'Neill, "Scribbling Diary," February 21, 24, 25, and 27, 1925.

162. Percy Hammond, "The Theaters: Mr. O'Neill's *Desire Under the Elms* Is the Best of His Pleasing Tortures," *New York Herald Tribune*, November 12, 1924, 14; Basso, "Tragic Sense—II," 43; Louis Sheaffer, TS, n.d., in *Desire Under the Elms* folder, Sheaffer-O'Neill Collection.

163. O'Neill, "Scribbling Diary," February 10 and 16 and March 9, 1925.

164. O'Neill, *"As Ever, Gene,"* 54; Eugene O'Neill to J. O. Lief, March 28, 1925, Sheaffer-O'Neill Collection.

165. Quoted in Alexander, *Eugene O'Neill's Creative Struggle*, 38.

166. "Laughs Mark Trial of O'Neill Actors," *New York Times*, April 13, 1926.

167. Ibid.

168. Louis Sheaffer, TS, n.d., in *Desire Under the Elms* folder, Sheaffer-O'Neill Collection.

169. Sheaffer, *Son and Artist*, 315.

170. O'Neill, *Selected Letters*, 187; Travis Bogard, *Contour in Time: The Plays of Eugene O'Neill*, rev. ed. (New York: Oxford University Press, 1988), 202; Cowley, "A Weekend with Eugene O'Neill," 46; Sheaffer, *Son and Artist*, 126.

171. O'Neill, *"As Ever, Gene,"* 54; O'Neill, "Scribbling Diary," March 22 and 25, 1925.

172. Quoted in Waters, *Eugene O'Neill and Family*, 27.

173. James Light, interview by Louis Sheaffer, August 14, 1962, Sheaffer-O'Neill Collection, Linda Lear Center for Special Collections and Archives, Connecticut College, New London. Light, "Parade of Masks." Kenneth Macgowan also provides a reflection on O'Neill's use of masks in the playbill for *The Great God Brown*. Kenneth Macgowan, "The Mask in Drama," *Greenwich Playbill*, season 1925–26, no. 4: 1, 6, Albert and Shirley Small Special Collections Library.

174. Quoted in Clark, *Eugene O'Neill*, 104.

175. Sergeant, Elizabeth Shepley, "O'Neill: The Man with a Mask," *New Republic*, March 16, 1927, 94.

176. Quoted in Clark, *Eugene O'Neill*, 160.

177. Quoted in Waters, *Eugene O'Neill and Family*, 28. Oona was born the week the megastar and (thirty-six-year-old) future husband Charlie Chaplin was wrapping up the final scene of his smash hit *The Gold Rush* (1925).

178. O'Neill, "Scribbling Diary," June 6, 1925. (Note at bottom reads: "Should be Thursday," which would make it June 4.)

179. Ibid., June 15, 1925. O'Neill considered titling *Strange Interlude* "The Haunted"; *The Haunted* became the title of the third play in his 1931 trilogy *Mourning Becomes Electra* (O'Neill, *"As Ever, Gene,"* 58).

180. Agnes Boulton to Harold de Polo, June 18, 1925, Clifton Waller Barrett Library of American Literature.

181. O'Neill, "Scribbling Diary," July 17 and 18, 1925.

182. Ibid., September 11, 1925. *The Long Voyage Home* and *The Emperor Jones* opened on September 10, 1925, at the Ambassadors Theatre in London.

183. Boulton, "Eugene's Drinking"; O'Neill, "Scribbling Diary," August 2 and 6, 1925.

184. Sheaffer, *Son and Artist*, 183.

185. O'Neill, "Scribbling Diary," October 5, 1925.

186. O'Neill to Art McGinley, April 9, 1927, 1 [page 2 missing], Clifton Waller Barrett Library of American Literature. In this letter, O'Neill says this is the last time he drank, but in fact, as is clear from his "Scribbling Diary" of 1925, he continued drinking throughout that fall.

187. Quoted in Arthur Gelb and Barbara Gelb, *O'Neill: Life with Monte Cristo* (New York: Applause, 2000), 209.

188. Quoted in Lewis M. Dabney, *Edmund Wilson: A Life in Letters* (New York: Macmillan, 2005), 99.

189. O'Neill, "Scribbling Diary," November 23, 1925. O'Neill writes, "On bust with Bunnie ... stayed up all night with Bunnie and Mary." Dabney, *Edmund Wilson*, 99; Wilson, *The Twenties*, 110–12, 400; Sheaffer, *Son and Artist*, 267.

190. O'Neill, "Scribbling Diary," November 24, 1925.

191. Light, "Parade of Masks."

192. Ibid.

193. James Light, interview by Sheaffer, May 21, 1960.

194. Mary McCarthy, "Eugene O'Neill—Dry Ice" (1959), in *Twentieth Century Interpretations of "The Iceman Cometh": A Collection of Critical Essays*, ed. John H. Raleigh (Englewood Cliffs, N.J.: Prentice-Hall, 1968), 50. This essay is an expansion of her original review of *Iceman* for *Partisan Review*, November–December 1946, 577–79. The earlier version does not include the elephant metaphor.

195. O'Neill, *Selected Letters*, 122; "A Letter from O'Neill," *New York Times*, April 11, 1920; O'Neill, *Selected Letters*, 122. In his 1933 play *Days Without End* O'Neill would make his long-held frustration, one that went back at least as far as *Diff'rent*, even more transparent by titling his acts "Plot for a Novel" and "Plot for a Novel Continued."

196. James Light's reminiscence doesn't specify a date, but he makes it clear the meeting took place between O'Neill's *The Great God Brown* and *Strange Interlude*, the latter of which Light knew O'Neill had begun that spring 1925, but for which he hadn't yet begun writing the dialogue. In O'Neill's "Scribbling Diary," he remarks on November 24 that he was "disgusted" with *The Fountain*, and then went to Jimmy Light's that evening.

197. O'Neill was borrowing his analogy from Percy Bysshe Shelley's essay "A Defense of Poetry" (1821): "The greatest poet even cannot say it; for the mind in creation is as a fading coal, which some invisible influence, like an inconstant wind, awakens to transitory brightness; this power arises from within, like the color of a flower which fades and changes as it is developed, and the conscious portions of our natures are unprophetic either of its approach or its departure. Could this influence be durable in its original purity and force, it is impossible to predict the greatness of the results; but when composition

begins, inspiration is already on the decline, and the most glorious poetry that has ever been communicated to the world is probably a feeble shadow of the original conceptions of the poet."

198. Light, "Parade of Masks."

199. Ibid.

200. Eugene O'Neill to Alexander King, January 29, 1932, in the author's possession.

201. Aside from two days reviewing the proofs for the book version of *The Great God Brown*, there are no creative work days listed in his work diary from November 12, 1925, when he finished act 3, scene 1 of *Lazarus Laughed*, to March 6, 1926, when his entry reads, "Started actual work on *Lazarus Laughed*—don't like as is" (O'Neill, *Work Diary*, 23).

202. O'Neill, "Scribbling Diary," December 9, 10, and 11, 1925.

203. Gilbert W. Gabriel, "De Leon O'Neill in Search of His Spring," *New York Sun*, December 11, 1925, 34; Bogard, *Contour in Time*, 238.

204. O'Neill, "Scribbling Diary," December 27 and 31, 1925, and January 1, 1926.

205. King, *Another Part of a Long Story*, 143; Dr. G. V. Hamilton, *A Research in Marriage* (New York: Lear, 1929), 240.

206. Quoted in King, *Another Part of a Long Story*, 142–43. See also James Light, interview by Louis Sheaffer, March 26, 1959, Sheaffer-O'Neill Collection.

207. O'Neill, "Scribbling Diary," October 16, 1925.

208. Quoted in King, *Another Part of a Long Story*, 140.

209. Quoted in Edward L. Shaughnessy, *Eugene O'Neill in Ireland: The Critical Reception* (Westport, Conn.: Greenwood, 1988), 13.

210. Quoted in King, *Another Part of a Long Story*, 144.

211. Harry Kemp, "Out of Provincetown: A Memoir of Eugene O'Neill" (1930), in Estrin, *Conversations with Eugene O'Neill*, 102.

212. Quoted in Sheaffer, *Son and Artist*, 192.

213. Eugene O'Neill, "Eugene O'Neill Writes about His Latest Play, *The Great God Brown*," *New York Evening Post*, February 13, 1926.

214. Ibid.; John Anderson, "The Play: O'Neill's Newest Play Opens at the Greenwich Village," *New York Evening Post*, January 25, 1926, 6; J. Brooks Atkinson, "The Play: Symbolism in an O'Neill Tragedy," *New York Times*, January 25, 1926, 26.

215. William Harrigan [actor who played William Brown], interview by Louis Sheaffer, December 13, 1960, Sheaffer-O'Neill Collection; O'Neill, *Selected Letters*, 549.

216. Clark, *Eugene O'Neill*, 106.

217. Sheaffer, *Son and Artist*, 211.

218. Waters, *Eugene O'Neill and Family*, 49, 59.

219. O'Neill, *Selected Letters*, 204.

220. Ibid., 203.

221. Ibid., 205, 213.

222. Commins, *"Love and Admiration and Respect,"* 29.

223. For a theoretical analysis of novelistic attributes of O'Neill's plays, see Kurt Eisen, *The Inner Strength of Opposites: O'Neill's Novelistic Drama and the Melodramatic Imagination* (Athens: University of Georgia Press, 1994).

224. For more on the role of alcohol in O'Neill's late plays, see Stephen F. Bloom, "The Role of Drinking and Alcoholism in O'Neill's Late Plays," *Eugene O'Neill Newsletter* 8, no. 1 (1984), http://eoneill.com/library/newsletter/viii_1/viii-1e.htm.

225. Quoted in Sheaffer, *Son and Artist*, 205.

226. Ibid., 232; George Jean Nathan, "The Cosmopolite of the Month," *Cosmopolitan*, February 1937, 8, 11.

227. Quoted in David Karsner, "Eugene O'Neill at Close Range in Maine," *New York Herald Tribune*, August 8, 1926, sec. 8, 4.

228. Quoted in Madeline Smith, "George Pierce Baker," in Dowling, *Critical Companion to Eugene O'Neill*, 2:530.

229. Karsner, "Eugene O'Neill at Close Range in Maine," 6.

230. Quoted in Sheaffer, *Son and Artist*, 208.

231. Quoted in ibid., 209.

232. Quoted in ibid., 211. O'Neill, if not the people of New London, might have taken some consolation in the fact that the beach's Coney Island–style boardwalk and touristy shops would be washed out to sea by the hurricane of 1939.

233. David E. Philips, "Eugene O'Neill's Fateful Maine Interlude," *Down East* 28, no. 1 (1981): 106, 87.

234. O'Neill, *Selected Letters*, 206; quoted in Sheaffer, *Son and Artist*, 211.

235. O'Neill, *Selected Letters*, 210.

236. Karsner, "Eugene O'Neill at Close Range in Maine," 5.

237. Sergeant, "O'Neill," 96, 91.

238. Quoted in Sheaffer, *Son and Artist*, 213.

239. Ibid., 216; King, *Another Part of a Long Story*, 149.

240. Sheaffer, *Son and Artist*, 230; King, *Another Part of a Long Story*, 149.

241. Sheaffer, *Son and Artist*, 221–22, 223.

242. Quoted in King, *Another Part of a Long Story*, 150.

243. Philips, "Eugene O'Neill's Fateful Maine Interlude," 104; Sheaffer, *Son and Artist*, 217; O'Neill, *Work Diary*, 29.

244. Quoted in Sheaffer, *Son and Artist*, 229.

245. Quoted in Philips, "Eugene O'Neill's Fateful Maine Interlude," 106.

246. Quoted in Sheaffer, *Son and Artist*, 217.

247. O'Neill, *Selected Letters*, 207; Sheaffer, *Son and Artist*, 211.

248. Quoted in Sheaffer, *Son and Artist*, 211, 212.

249. O'Neill, *Selected Letters*, 210.

250. Philips, "Eugene O'Neill's Fateful Maine Interlude," 99.

251. Harold De Polo, "Meet Eugene O'Neill—Fisherman," *Outdoor America*, May 1928, 5–8.

252. Harold de Polo, TS, explanation for inscribed copy of *The Great God Brown*, January 16, 1960, Clifton Waller Barrett Library of American Literature.

253. Signed copy of *The Great God Brown*, from the five-volume set *"The Great God Brown," "The Fountain," "The Moon of the Caribbees" and Other Plays* (New York: Boni and Liveright, 1926), inscribed to Harold de Polo, Clifton Waller Barrett Library of American Literature.

254. O'Neill, *"As Ever, Gene,"* 72.

255. O'Neill, *Selected Letters*, 210, 201, 209; O'Neill, *"As Ever, Gene,"* 73. After their breakup in 1926, the Experimental Theatre, Inc., would carry on without O'Neill but under Macgowan and Jones's leadership for another three and a half seasons.

256. King, *"A Wind Is Rising,"* 215, 253, 269.

257. Quoted in Sheaffer, *Son and Artist*, 233.

258. O'Neill, *Work Diary*, July through September, 1926.

259. Ibid., October through November, 1926.

260. King, *"A Wind Is Rising,"* 238.

261. Waters, *Eugene O'Neill and Family*, 53–54, 59, 60; King, *"A Wind Is Rising,"* 217.

262. O'Neill, *Selected Letters*, 226, 231.

263. Ibid., 229.

264. O'Neill, *"The Theatre We Worked For,"* 128.

265. O'Neill, *Selected Letters*, 238.

266. Richard Watts Jr., "Realism Doomed, O'Neill Believes," *New York Herald Tribune*, February 5, 1928, sec. 7, 2; O'Neill, *"As Ever, Gene,"* 75; Light, "Parade of Masks."

267. See Floyd, *Eugene O'Neill at Work*, 181; and Harley Hammerman, introductory note to "Autograph Manuscript, 1 page," Hammerman Collection, http://eoneill.com/manuscripts/27200.htm.

268. Eugene O'Neill to Kenneth Macgowan, April 27, 1928 (incomplete), Sheaffer-O'Neill Collection.

269. O'Neill, *Selected Letters*, 312.

270. Eugene O'Neill, "Autograph Manuscript, 1 page," Hammerman Collection, http://eoneill.com/manuscripts/27200.htm.

271. Quoted in Floyd, *Eugene O'Neill at Work*, 181.

272. O'Neill, *Selected Letters*, 239, 240.

273. Ibid., 164.

274. Ibid., 150n2.

275. Ibid., 244.

276. Lawrence Langner, *The Magic Curtain: The Story of a Life in Two Fields, Theatre and Invention, by the Founder of the Theatre Guild* (New York: E. P. Dutton, 1951), 232.

277. Ibid. This Cine-Kodak film is located at Yale's Beinecke Library, Eugene O'Neill Collection.

278. Quoted in Sheaffer, *Son and Artist*, 253.

279. Quoted in King, *Another Part of a Long Story*, 155.

280. O'Neill, *Selected Letters*, 249, 251–52.

281. King, *"A Wind Is Rising,"* 244.

282. Ibid., 255, 261, 259.

283. O'Neill, *Selected Letters*, 229. This is O'Neill's paraphrase of her letter to him.

284. King, *"A Wind Is Rising,"* 294.

285. During her absence that December and January, Finn Mac Cool was shot and killed by a neighbor for invading his chicken coop once too often. The dog was "Shane's best friend," Shane's daughter Sheila wrote in 2008. "Seven-year-old Shane was all alone to deal with the death of his dog. I now know why Shane was so depressed all the time"

(Sheila O'Neill, afterword to *More of a Long Story*, http://www.eoneill.com/library/more/afterword.htm).

286. Quoted in King, *Another Part of a Long Story*, 266n4.

287. Quoted in Sheaffer, *Son and Artist*, 280.

288. O'Neill, *"The Theatre We Worked For,"* 34, 51; Alexander, *Eugene O'Neill's Creative Struggle*, 42.

289. Kelcey Allen, "*Marco Millions* Is Poignant O'Neill Satire," *Women's Wear Daily*, January 10, 1928, sec. 1, 4, quoted in Clark, *Eugene O'Neill*, 109; Floyd, *Plays of Eugene O'Neill*, 167; Bruce Gould, "At the Playhouses: O'Neill Takes a Crack at Babbitt," *Wall Street News*, January 12, 1928, 4.

290. Quoted in Bennett Cerf, *At Random: The Reminiscences of Bennett Cerf* (New York: Random House, 1977), 83.

291. J. Brooks Atkinson, "*Strange Interlude* Plays Five Hours," *New York Times*, January 31, 1928, 28.

292. Quoted in Sheaffer, *Son and Artist*, 287.

293. In his 1925 work diary, O'Neill unambiguously wrote, "He is bisexual" (quoted in Floyd, *Eugene O'Neill at Work*, 71). Ned Darrell describes him as "one of those poor devils who spend their lives trying not to discover which sex to belong to!" (*CP2*, 662). His name is an amalgam of two friends, the artists Charles Demuth and Marsden Hartley.

294. This argument has been convincingly argued in Brenda Murphy, "O'Neill's America: The Strange Interlude between the Wars," in *The Cambridge Companion to Eugene O'Neill*, ed. Michael Manheim (New York: Cambridge University Press, 1998), 135–47. The term "schoolboy ideals" is Murphy's.

295. Eugene O'Neill, "Memoranda on Masks," in *The Unknown O'Neill*, 426.

296. George Jean Nathan, "Eugene O'Neill as a Character in Fiction" (1929), in *The Magic Mirror: Selected Writings on the Theatre by George Jean Nathan*, ed. Thomas Quinn Curtiss (New York: Knopf, 1960), 107.

297. Wainscott, *Staging O'Neill*, 234.

298. O'Neill, *Selected Letters*, 247.

299. Quoted in Bogard, *Contour in Time*, 307n. (This Bogard *Contour* reference alone is to the 1972 edition; all other references are to the 1988 revised edition.)

300. Wainscott, *Staging O'Neill*, 235.

301. Sheaffer, *Son and Artist*, 287, 288; Thomas Van Dycke, "9-Act O'Neill Drama Opens," *New York Morning Telegraph*, January 31, 1928, 5; Dudley Nichols, "The New Play," *New York World*, January 31, 1928, 11.

302. George Jean Nathan, "Ervine Encore," *American Mercury*, February 1929, 246; Arthur H. Nethercot, "The Psychoanalyzing of Eugene O'Neill," *Modern Drama* 1, no. 3 (1960): 244; Alan Dale, "O'Neill Play of Nine Acts and Six Hours Reviewed by Dale," *New York American*, January 31, 1928, 9; Heywood Broun, "It Seems to Me," *New York World*, March 4, 1928; O'Neill, *Selected Letters*, 189.

303. These scrapbooks are at the Beinecke Library.

304. Richard Watts Jr., "Realism Doomed, O'Neill Believes," *New York Herald Tribune*, February 5, 1928, sec. 7, 2.

305. George Jean Nathan, "Eugene O'Neill" (1932), in Estrin, *Conversations with Eugene O'Neill*, 132.

306. R. A. Parker, "An American Dramatist Developing" (1921), in J. Y. Miller, ed., *Playwright's Progress: O'Neill and the Critics* (Chicago: Scott, Foresman, 1965), 28–29.

307. Joseph Wood Krutch, "Drama: *Strange Interlude*," *Nation*, February 15, 1928, 192.

308. Quoted in Arthur Gelb, "Onstage He Played the Novelist," *New York Times*, August 30, 1964, book review sec. 1.

309. O'Neill, *Selected Letters*, 247.

310. Claudia Wilsch Case, "What They Really Saw: Using Archives to Reconstruct the Censored Performance of Eugene O'Neill's *Strange Interlude*," *Laconics* 5 (2010), http://www.eoneill.com/library/laconics/5/5c.htm.

311. Alexander, *Eugene O'Neill's Creative Struggle*, 126; Case, "What They Really Saw"; "Rejects Revision of O'Neill Play: Boston Mayor Says *Strange Interlude* 'Glorifies an Abject Code of Morals,' " *New York Times*, September 24, 1929; Case, "What They Really Saw."

312. Quoted in John H. Houchin, *Censorship of the American Theatre in the Twentieth Century* (Cambridge: Cambridge University Press, 1997), 115.

313. Quoted in Edward Doherty, "Boston Bans *Strange Interlude*: A Look at a Problem of Puritanism," *Liberty*, November 16, 1929.

314. Case, "What They Really Saw." Regardless of a widespread distaste for Boston's censorship policies, they would remain in force as late as 1970. Also see Houchin, *Censorship*, 115.

315. "Providence Bans O'Neill Play," *New York Herald Tribune*, April 20, 1930.

316. Quoted in Alexander, *Eugene O'Neill's Creative Struggle*, 125.

317. Basso, "Tragic Sense—II," 44; O'Neill, *Selected Letters*, 297.

318. King, *"A Wind Is Rising,"* 304.

319. Ibid., 305.

ACT IV. Full Fathom Five

Notes to pp. 349–50: retreat from reality (Eleanor Flexner, *American Playwrights, 1918–1938: The Theatre Retreats from Reality* [New York: Simon and Schuster, 1938]); "blind alleys" (Eugene O'Neill, *Selected Letters of Eugene O'Neill*, ed. Travis Bogard and Jackson R. Bryer [New Haven: Yale University Press, 1988], 559); "There is something to be said for the Mad Twenties" (O'Neill, *Selected Letters*, 524); "O'Neill gave birth to American theatre" (Gore Vidal, "Tennessee Williams: Someone to Laugh at the Squares With," in *United States: Essays, 1952–1992* [New York: Random House, 1993], 449).

1. Quoted in Louis Sheaffer, *O'Neill: Son and Artist* (Boston: Little, Brown, 1973), 292.

2. O'Neill, *Selected Letters*, 278, 277.

3. Quoted in William Davies King, *Another Part of a Long Story: Literary Traces of Eugene O'Neill and Agnes Boulton* (Ann Arbor: University of Michigan Press, 2010), 263n21.

4. *"The Theatre We Worked For"*: *The Letters of Eugene O'Neill to Kenneth Macgowan*, ed. Travis Bogard and Jackson R. Bryer (New Haven: Yale University Press, 1982), 174; O'Neill, *Selected Letters*, 305.

5. William Davies King, ed., *"A Wind Is Rising"*: *The Correspondence of Agnes Boulton and Eugene O'Neill* (Madison, N.J.: Fairleigh Dickinson University Press, 2000), 307; O'Neill, *Selected Letters*, 278.

6. Barrett H. Clark, *Eugene O'Neill: The Man and His Plays*, rev. ed. (New York: Dover, 1947), 117.

7. "The Art of Making Masks Revealed," *Pasadena Evening Post*, May 10, 1928, 2.

8. Kenneth Macgowan, "New Line for O'Neill in *Lazarus Laughed*," *New York Telegram*, January 14, 1927.

9. O'Neill, *Selected Letters*, 257, 365.

10. George C. Warren, "*Lazarus Laughed* Produced on Coast," *New York Times*, April 10, 1928, 33; Katherine T. Von Blon, "*Lazarus* Written Not from Imagination, but from Life," *Los Angeles Times*, April 29, 1928, C17.

11. O'Neill, *Selected Letters*, 365; "Premiere of *Lazarus Laughed* This Evening to Mark Climax of Preparation at Playhouse," *Pasadena Star-News*, April 9, 1928, 9; George C. Warren, "Play at Pasadena Received with Rousing Acclaim," *San Francisco Chronicle*, April 15, 1928, 1D.

12. King, *Another Part of a Long Story*, 313; King, *"A Wind Is Rising,"* 313.

13. King, *"A Wind Is Rising,"* 170; King, *Another Part of a Long Story*, 170.

14. Quoted in Sally Cline, *Zelda Fitzgerald: Her Voice in Paradise* (New York: Arcade, 2004), 125.

15. King, *Another Part of a Long Story*, 169; King, *"A Wind Is Rising,"* 310, 312.

16. King, *"A Wind Is Rising,"* 314; O'Neill, *Selected Letters*, 298, 319.

17. Dorothy Commins, ed., *"Love and Admiration and Respect"*: *The O'Neill-Commins Correspondence* (Durham, N.C.: Duke University Press, 1986), 32, 34; O'Neill, *"The Theatre We Worked For,"* 182.

18. O'Neill, *Selected Letters*, 296.

19. Ibid., 295.

20. See ibid., 302, 315. William Davies King argues that the father was likely Boulton's *Breezy Stories* editor Courtland Young (*Another Part of a Long Story*, 189), and this has since been substantiated by Boulton's niece Dallas Cline in her recent memoir *A Formidable Shadow: The O'Neill Connection* (eoneill.com, 2014).

21. Quoted in "Eugene O'Neill's Wife Sues for Divorce in Reno," *New York Herald Tribune*, July 2, 1929.

22. *Kathleen O'Neill v. Eugene G. O'Neill*, County Clerk's Index #1673, Supreme Court, Westchester County, Westchester County Clerk's Office, White Plains, N.Y., 1912.

23. O'Neill, *Selected Letters*, 299.

24. Sheaffer, *Son and Artist*, 301.

25. Quoted in William Davies King, ed., "The Port Saïd Incident: O'Neill and Carlotta Monterey at Sea," *Eugene O'Neill Review* 33, no. 2 (2012): 235.

26. O'Neill, *Selected Letters*, 307–8.

27. Quoted in King, *"A Wind Is Rising,"* 282.

28. Daniel Aaron, *Writers on the Left: Episodes in American Literary Communism* (New York: Harcourt, Brace and World, 1961), 99–102. "I believe *The New Masses* will bear the same relationship to the commercial press as the experimental theatre does to Broadway," O'Neill wrote on behalf of the venture. "My blessing and lustiest cheers!" (Quoted in ibid., 410).

29. Quoted in Virginia Floyd, ed., *Eugene O'Neill at Work: Newly Released Ideas for His Plays* (New York: Frederick Ungar, 1981), 125. Critics also recognized the thematic and titular parallels between *Dynamo* and Henry Adams's chapter in *The Education of Henry Adams*, "The Dynamo and the Virgin"; see Joseph Wood Krutch, "The Virgin and the Dynamo," *Nation*, February 27, 1929, 264, 266; and see Euphemia Van Rennselaer Wyatt, "Plays of Some Importance," *Catholic World*, April 1929, 80–82. O'Neill hadn't read Adams in years, and it clearly wasn't in the forefront of his mind at the time of composition (see O'Neill, *Selected Letters*, 332).

30. Quoted in Floyd, *Eugene O'Neill at Work*, 126.

31. O'Neill, *Selected Letters*, 308. In this same letter, O'Neill suggests that Gold forget about writing short stories and write "a wonderful thing on East Side life . . . as much or as little disguised as you wished." Gold followed his advice and immediately began work on his groundbreaking roman à clef about Jewish life on the Lower East Side of Manhattan, *Jews without Money* (1930).

32. Eugene O'Neill, "Suggestions, Instructions, Advice, along with Sundry Snooty Remarks and Animadversions as to the Modern Theatre," September 10, 1928, Sheaffer-O'Neill Collection, Linda Lear Center for Special Collections and Archives, Connecticut College, New London.

33. O'Neill, *Selected Letters*, 301.

34. Ibid., 311.

35. Quoted in Sheaffer, *Son and Artist*, 217.

36. Quoted in Commins, *"Love and Admiration and Respect,"* 40.

37. Ibid., 33.

38. Quoted in King, *"A Wind Is Rising,"* 320.

39. Commins, *"Love and Admiration and Respect,"* 41.

40. Quoted in Floyd, *Eugene O'Neill at Work*, 170.

41. King, "Port Saïd Incident," 242; O'Neill, *Selected Letters*, 336; King, "Port Saïd Incident," 242.

42. Although the newspapers identified Renner as Austrian, both Monterey and O'Neill referred to the Renners as Hungarian (King, "Port Saïd Incident," 244; O'Neill, *Selected Letters*, 405).

43. William Weer, "Eugene O'Neill, Fleeing Prying Public Eye, Appears to Be Reverting to Old Days When He Trod the Roads of the World to Romance," *Brooklyn Daily Eagle*, December 23, 1928, A7.

44. Quoted in Sheaffer, *Son and Artist*, 314.

45. O'Neill, *Selected Letters*, 337.

46. King, "Port Saïd Incident," 247, 242. Carlotta Monterey's diaries are not entirely reliable. Monterey had a tendency to revise the past in her own and sometimes O'Neill's

favor; therefore, as a source these diaries require either corroboration or a higher than usual standard of credibility.

47. Quoted in Sheaffer, *Son and Artist*, 314.

48. Ibid., 315–16.

49. King, "Port Saïd Incident," 247; Sheaffer, *Son and Artist*, 316–17; King, "Port Saïd Incident," 247, 248.

50. "O'Neill Still in Shanghai, 'Disappearance Act' Hoax," *New York Evening Post*, December 18, 1928, 8; "Eugene O'Neill Admits Identity: Shows Passport at Manila Before Sailing," *New York Sun*, December 19, 1928, 41; "O'Neill in Manila, Fails to Find Rest," *New York Evening Post*, December 19, 1928, 2.

51. Quoted in Sheaffer, *Son and Artist*, 316–18. See also "O'Neill Still in Shanghai."

52. O'Neill, *Selected Letters*, 324; "O'Neill in Manila"; "Eugene O'Neill Admits Identity."

53. Quoted in Sheaffer, *Son and Artist*, 319.

54. King, "Port Saïd Incident," 252–53.

55. Quoted in Sheaffer, *Son and Artist*, 322.

56. O'Neill, *Selected Letters*, 323–24.

57. Ibid., 323.

58. Quoted in Floyd, *Eugene O'Neill at Work*, 210.

59. King, "Port Saïd Incident," 249.

60. Sheaffer, *Son and Artist*, 317, 319–21, 326.

61. Ibid., 278.

62. King, "Port Saïd Incident," 257, 258.

63. Quoted in Sheaffer, *Son and Artist*, 322.

64. Edna Kenton to Carl Van Vechten, n.d., Sheaffer-O'Neill Collection.

65. Eugene O'Neill, *"As Ever, Gene": The Letters of Eugene O'Neill to George Jean Nathan*, ed. Nancy L. Roberts and Arthur W. Roberts (Rutherford, N.J.: Fairleigh Dickinson University Press, 1987), 90.

66. Quoted in Doris Alexander, *Eugene O'Neill's Creative Struggle: The Decisive Decade, 1924–1933* (University Park: Pennsylvania State University Press, 1992), 147.

67. O'Neill, *Selected Letters*, 325; George Jean Nathan, "Judging the Shows," *Judge*, March 9, 1929, 18.

68. Heywood Broun, "It Seems to Me," *New York Telegram*, February 14, 1929, 2nd ed., 13.

69. Nathan, "Judging the Shows," 18.

70. O'Neill, *Selected Letters*, 330.

71. Ibid., 350.

72. Ibid., 323.

73. O'Neill, *"As Ever, Gene,"* 88; King, *"A Wind Is Rising,"* 227–28.

74. Agnes Boulton to Harold de Polo, May 31, 1929, Clifton Waller Barrett Library of American Literature, Albert and Shirley Small Special Collections Library, University of Virginia, Charlottesville.

75. O'Neill, *Selected Letters*, 336, 338, 333.

76. Sheaffer, *Son and Artist*, 330; O'Neill, *"The Theatre We Worked For,"* 188.

77. O'Neill, *"The Theatre We Worked For,"* 165; George Jean Nathan, "The Bright Face of Tragedy," *Cosmopolitan*, August 1957, 66–69; "O'Neill Gets Chateau for 13 Years for Bride," *New York Times*, July 28, 1929.

78. This title for the property has caused confusion and misidentification of the château's actual name among scholars; but along with what I suggest in my treatment of the name in this chapter, Carlotta Monterey's 1955 diary contains a card from the period in which the home is referred to as "du Plessis."

79. Commins, *"Love and Admiration and Respect,"* 55.

80. Quoted in King, *Another Part of a Long Story*, 113.

81. Commins, *"Love and Admiration and Respect,"* 61.

82. Kenneth Macgowan, "Talk of the Town: About O'Neill," *New Yorker*, September 28, 1929, 21.

83. Commins, *"Love and Admiration and Respect,"* 73.

84. O'Neill, *"The Theatre We Worked For,"* 195–97. Monterey had written Macgowan a similar note directly after the *New Yorker* article appeared, but that is currently lost.

85. Ibid., 196, 210.

86. "Eugene O'Neill's Wife Sues for Divorce in Reno"; "Eugene O'Neill Wed to Miss Monterey," *New York Times*, July 24, 1929.

87. Commins, *"Love and Admiration and Respect,"* 69.

88. Ibid., 66, 82.

89. James and Patricia Light, interview by Louis Sheaffer, November 16, 1960, Sheaffer-O'Neill Collection.

90. O'Neill, *"The Theatre We Worked For,"* 196–97.

91. James Light, interview by Louis Sheaffer, November 16, 1960, Sheaffer-O'Neill Collection.

92. O'Neill, *"The Theatre We Worked For,"* 192. Gladys Lewis would lose the suit after it went to trial on March 13, 1931. O'Neill still had to pay thousands in legal fees, and the timing of the trial doomed an offer from MGM Studios to produce *Strange Interlude* as Lillian Gish's first sound film.

93. *Lewys v. O'Neill*, District Court, Southern District of New York, #49 F.2d 603, 1931.

94. O'Neill, *Selected Letters*, 341.

95. Commins, *"Love and Admiration and Respect,"* 130.

96. O'Neill, *Selected Letters*, 395.

97. Ibid., 401.

98. Commins, *"Love and Admiration and Respect,"* 77.

99. O'Neill, *"As Ever, Gene,"* 102.

100. "Eugene O'Neill, A Playwright Not without Honor," *New York Evening Post*, January 7, 1928, 8.

101. Shivaun O'Casey, "Sean and O'Neill," in "Celtic Twilight: 21st-Century Irish-Americans on Eugene O'Neill," *Drunken Boat #12*, http://www.drunkenboat.com/db12/04one/ocasey/ocasey2.php.

102. Quoted in "Shaw Says He's out of Date; Pokes Fun at U.S. Authors," *New York Evening Post*, September 27, 1924, 6.

103. Quoted in Louis Sheaffer, *Son and Playwright* (Boston: Little, Brown, 1968), 434.

104. *Selected Letters*, 407.

105. "O'Neill, A Playwright Not without Honor."

106. O'Neill, *"As Ever, Gene,"* 102.

107. O'Neill, *Selected Letters*, 335, 339.

108. Floyd, *Eugene O'Neill at Work*, 185–86; O'Neill, *"The Theatre We Worked For,"* 168.

109. O'Neill, *"As Ever, Gene,"* 118; "O'Neill Back in France: American Worked on Next Play during Sojourn in the Canaries," *New York Times*, April 15, 1931.

110. Sheaffer, *Son and Artist*, 357; O'Neill, *Selected Letters*, 351.

111. O'Neill, *"As Ever, Gene,"* 102; Sheaffer, *Son and Artist*, 523; *"As Ever, Gene,"* 102.

112. Quoted in Tom Cerasulo, "Film Adaptations," in *Critical Companion to Eugene O'Neill: A Literary Reference to His Life and Work*, ed. Robert M. Dowling (New York: Facts on File, 2009), 2:592.

113. O'Neill, *"The Theatre We Worked For,"* 191; Sheaffer, *Son and Artist*, 363.

114. In the past, O'Neill scholars, including myself, have thought the homes along Whale Oil Row were the architectural models for the Mannon house, since it was meant to have been built in 1830. The Shaw Mansion was built in the mid-1750s, as opposed to the 1830s and 1840s, like the houses on Whale Oil Row, but the house has a stone front with white columns and more closely matches O'Neill's sketch for the set design.

115. O'Neill, *Selected Letters*, 386.

116. O'Neill, *"As Ever, Gene,"* 120.

117. O'Neill, *Selected Letters*, 390.

118. O'Neill, *"As Ever, Gene,"* 118.

119. Quoted in O'Neill, *"The Theatre We Worked For,"* 166–67.

120. "Ralph Barton Ends His Life with Pistol: Artist in Note Mourns Loss of Third Wife, Carlotta Monterey, Now Wed to Eugene O'Neill," *New York Times*, May 21, 1931.

121. Ibid.

122. Bennett Cerf, *At Random: The Reminiscences of Bennett Cerf* (New York: Random House, 1977), 83.

123. Quoted in Sheaffer, *Son and Artist*, 374, 375.

124. Ibid., 375.

125. Quoted in Ernest K. Lindley, "Exile Made Him Appreciate U.S., O'Neill Admits" (1931), in *Conversations with Eugene O'Neill*, ed. Mark W. Estrin (Jackson: University Press of Mississippi, 1990), 109.

126. Ibid., 111.

127. Quoted in Sheaffer, *Son and Artist*, 376.

128. *Mourning Becomes Electra* was published as a book on November 2, 1931.

129. O'Neill, *Selected Letters*, 363.

130. Thomas Chalmers (who played Adam Brant in *Mourning Becomes Electra*), interview by Louis Sheaffer, n.d., Sheaffer-O'Neill Collection.

131. Quoted in Paul Sifton, "A Whale of a Play," *McCall's*, May 1932, 116.

132. Sheaffer, *Son and Artist*, 384; Hamilton Basso, "The Tragic Sense—III," *New Yorker*, March 13, 1948, 44.

133. John Anderson, "O'Neill's Trilogy: Playwright's Latest Work Acclaimed as His 'Masterpiece,' " *New York Evening Journal*, October 27, 1931, 26.

134. Ibid.

135. John Mason Brown. "The Play: *Mourning Becomes Electra*, Eugene O'Neill's Exciting Trilogy, Is Given an Excellent Production at the Guild," *New York Evening Post*, October 27, 1931, 12; George Jean Nathan, "The Theatre of George Jean Nathan," *Judge*, November 21, 1931, 16.

136. Elizabeth Jordan, "Dramatics: Mr. O'Neill and Others," *America*, November 28, 1931, 187; Theresa Helburn, *A Wayward Quest: The Autobiography of Theresa Helburn* (Boston: Little, Brown, 1960), 263; Brooks Atkinson, "Tragedy Becomes Electra," *New York Times*, November 1, 1931, in *The Critical Response to Eugene O'Neill*, ed. John H. Houchin, Critical Responses in Arts and Letters, no. 5 (Westport, Conn.: Greenwood, 1993), 126.

137. Quoted in Sheaffer, *Son and Artist*, 391.

138. O'Neill, *Selected Letters*, 403–4.

139. Quoted in George Jean Nathan, "Eugene O'Neill" (1932), in Estrin, *Conversations with Eugene O'Neill*, 127–28.

140. "O'Neill Goes Mildly Pirate," *House & Garden*, January 1934, 19–21; Helburn, *Wayward Quest*, 264.

141. Quoted in Sheaffer, *Son and Artist*, 377.

142. Quoted in Alexander, *Eugene O'Neill's Creative Struggle*, 172.

143. Quoted in Hamilton Basso, "The Tragic Sense—II," *New Yorker*, March 6, 1948, 46.

144. Commins, *"Love and Admiration and Respect,"* 139.

145. O'Neill, *Selected Letters*, 408.

146. Quoted in Alexander, *Eugene O'Neill's Creative Struggle*, 181.

147. Commins, *"Love and Admiration and Respect,"* 136.

148. O'Neill, *Selected Letters*, 404.

149. Commins, *"Love and Admiration and Respect,"* 75.

150. Carlotta Monterey Diary, December 27, 1933, O'Neill Papers, Beinecke Library, Yale University, New Haven.

151. Eugene O'Neill to Robert Sisk, December 27, 1932, Clifton Waller Barrett Library of American Literature.

152. Commins, *"Love and Admiration and Respect,"* 104, 149.

153. Cerf, *At Random*, 81.

154. Quoted in Sheaffer, *Son and Artist*, 303, 417; see Dorothy Commins, *What Is an Editor: Saxe Commins at Work* (Chicago: University of Chicago Press, 1978).

155. O'Neill, *Selected Letters*, 410, 506.

156. Commins, *"Love and Admiration and Respect,"* 164.

157. O'Neill addresses his letters "Faust, New York," but that's the name of a smaller post office within the town of Tupper Lake, not a town itself. The post office was named Faust to distinguish it from the main Tupper Lake post office. The owner of Big Wolf Camp was F. L. Wurzburg, *House & Garden*'s business manager.

158. Whitney Bolton, "George M. Cohan is THE THING in O'Neill's *Ah, Wilderness!*" *New York Morning Telegraph*, October 4, 1933, 3; Elizabeth Jordan, "Mr. O'Neill Soft-Pedaled," *America*, October 28, 1933, 90.

159. O'Neill, "*As Ever, Gene*," 153; Richard Watts Jr., "O'Neill Is Eager to See Cohan in *Ah, Wilderness!*" (1933), in Estrin, *Conversations with Eugene O'Neill*, 134; Sheaffer, *Son and Artist*, 422.

160. John Mason Brown, "The Play: Mr. Cohan Gives a Magnificent Performance in Mr. O'Neill's Mellow Comedy, *Ah, Wilderness!* at the Guild," *New York Evening Post*, October 3, 1933, 26.

161. Since its 1933 premiere, *Ah, Wilderness!* has seen two film adaptations, one a musical entitled *Summer Holiday* (1948), and was later adapted into a Broadway musical, *Take Me Along* (1959), and a television miniseries.

162. Quoted in *The Unknown O'Neill: Unpublished and Unfamiliar Writings of Eugene O'Neill*, ed. Travis Bogard (New Haven: Yale University Press, 1988), 381.

163. Quoted in Sheaffer, *Son and Artist*, 256.

164. O'Neill, "*As Ever, Gene*," 133.

165. Ibid.

166. "Memoranda on Masks" (November 1932), "Second Thoughts" (December 1932), and "A Dramatist's Notebook" (January 1933).

167. Eugene O'Neill, "Memoranda on Masks," in Bogard, *Unknown O'Neill*, 407.

168. Ibid., 408. O'Neill confirms this in a letter to George Jean Nathan (O'Neill, "*As Ever, Gene*," 148).

169. O'Neill, *Selected Letters*, 403.

170. Quoted in Alexander, *Eugene O'Neill's Creative Struggle*, 202.

171. Travis Bogard contends that "the real drama was O'Neill's attempt to write the play" (*Contour in Time: The Plays of Eugene O'Neill*, rev. ed. [New York: Oxford University Press, 1988], 328), a drama Stephen A. Black thoroughly sets down in his psychoanalytic biography (*Eugene O'Neill: Beyond Mourning and Tragedy* [New Haven: Yale University Press, 1999], 377–87).

172. Quoted in John Mason Brown, "Two on the Aisle: Mr. O'Neill and His Champions—*Days Without End* Finds Some Tolerant but Sturdy Defenders," *New York Evening Post*, January 22, 1934.

173. John Mason Brown, "The Play: The Theatre Guild Presents Earle Larimore and Stanley Ridges in Mr. O'Neill's *Days Without End*," *New York Evening Post*, January 9, 1934, 17; Alexander, *Eugene O'Neill's Creative Struggle*, 207; Brooks Atkinson, "The Play: *Days Without End*," *New York Times*, January 9, 1934, 19; Bernard Sobel, "Eugene O'Neill's New Play Opens at Henry Miller," *New York Daily Mirror*, January 10, 1934, 24.

174. Monterey Diary, September 18, 1933.

175. Oscar Cargill, introduction to *O'Neill and His Plays: Four Decades of Criticism*, ed. Oscar Cargill, N. Bryllion Fagin, and William J. Fisher (New York: New York University Press, 1961), 10.

176. "O'Neill Produces the Great Catholic Play of the Age," *Queen's Work*, January 1934; Brown, "Two on the Aisle: Mr. O'Neill and His Champions"; Gerard B. Donnelly, "O'Neill's New Catholic Play," *America*, January 13, 1934, 346–47.

177. Quoted in Edward L. Shaughnessy, *Down the Nights and Down the Days: Eugene O'Neill's Catholic Sensibility* (Notre Dame: University of Notre Dame Press, 2000), 133.

178. Monterey Diary, April 30, 1933, June 28, 1933.

179. Benjamin De Casseres, " 'Denial Without End': Benjamin De Casseres's Parody of Eugene O'Neill's 'God Play' *Days Without End*," ed. Robert M. Dowling, *Eugene O'Neill Review* 30 (2008): 145–59.

180. Croswell Bowen, "The Black Irishman" (1946), in Cargill, Fagin, and Fisher, *O'Neill and His Plays*, 80.

181. O'Neill, *Selected Letters*, 425, 426.

182. Ibid., 433.

183. Brooks Atkinson, "On *Days Without End*," *New York Times*. January 14, 1934; Dorothy Day, "Told in Context," ca. 1958, Dorothy Day Papers, series D-3, box 7, file 2, Special Collections and University Archives, Raynor Memorial Libraries, Marquette University, Milwaukee, Wis.

184. O'Neill, *Selected Letters*, 424.

185. Quoted in Floyd, *Eugene O'Neill at Work*, 162–63. This letter is edited with brackets to show cross-outs by O'Neill, courtesy of Virginia Floyd, but I have deleted some confusing formatting here.

186. Quoted in Cargill, introduction to *O'Neill and His Plays*, 10. See Shaughnessy, *Down the Nights and Down the Days: Eugene O'Neill's Catholic Sensibility* (Notre Dame, Ind.: University of Notre Dame Press, 1996), for a probing and comprehensive analysis, including a complete chapter on *Days Without End*, of O'Neill's relationship to Catholicism.

187. O'Neill, *"The Theatre We Worked For,"* 208; Floyd, *Eugene O'Neill at Work*, 393.

188. "Eugene O'Neill Ill, Unable to Testify," *New York Times*, April 13, 1934; "O'Neill Loses Auto Suit," *New York Times*, April 17, 1934.

189. Eugene O'Neill to Sherwood Anderson, April 23, 1934, Contempo Records, 1930–1934, University of North Carolina Library, Chapel Hill.

190. O'Neill, *"The Theatre We Worked For,"* 209, 211.

191. O'Neill, *Selected Letters*, 435–37.

192. Arthur Gelb and Barbara Gelb, *O'Neill* (1962; rev. ed., New York: Harper and Row, 1973), 439–40.

193. This Marx Brothers line is a double allusion; the "thought aside" method is O'Neill's from *Strange Interlude*, but the line itself is a play on John Gay's 1728 *The Beggar's Opera:* "How happy could I be with either, Were t' other dear charmer away!"

194. O'Neill, *Selected Letters*, 443. Jack Benny's program was broadcast in May 1937.

195. Ibid., 431.

196. Ibid., 446.

197. *"Anna Christie,"* videocassette, produced and directed by Clarence Brown (coproduced by Paul Bern and Irving Thalberg) (MGM, 1930). *"Anna Christie"* was eventually made into the Broadway musical *New Girl in Town* in 1957.

198. Virginia Floyd, *The Plays of Eugene O'Neill: A New Assessment* (New York: Frederick Ungar, 1985), 201n; O'Neill, *Selected Letters*, 364; Alexander, *Eugene O'Neill's Creative Struggle*, 127; O'Neill, *"The Theatre We Worked For,"* 207.

199. Zoe Jones, M.D. (current owner of Casa Genotta), interview by the author, May 24, 2013. See also Nathan, "The Bright Face of Tragedy," 66–69.

200. Basso, "The Tragic Sense—III," 42.

201. Commins, *"Love and Admiration and Respect,"* 144; O'Neill, *"As Ever, Gene,"* 127; Sheaffer, *Son and Artist*, 400.

202. Monterey Diary, December 24, 1935.

203. Quoted in Sheaffer, *Son and Artist*, 448. Sheaffer does not refer to O'Neill's lapse.

204. Monterey Diary, February 21 and 22, 1936.

205. Albert Rothenberg, M.D., "Correspondence," *New England School of Medicine* 343, no. 10 (2000): 741.

206. Commins, *"Love and Admiration and Respect,"* 218.

207. P. K. Brask, *"A Tale of Possessors Self-Dispossessed,"* in Dowling, *Critical Companion to Eugene O'Neill*, 2:748. For the definitive explication of the Cycle, see Donald C. Gallup, *Eugene O'Neill and His Eleven-Play Cycle, "A Tale of Possessors Self-Dispossessed"* (New Haven: Yale University Press, 1998).

208. Quoted in Floyd, *The Plays of Eugene O'Neill*, 537.

209. Quoted in Joel Pfister, *Staging Depth: Eugene O'Neill and the Politics of Psychological Discourse* (Chapel Hill: University of North Carolina Press, 1995), 182.

210. O'Neill, *Selected Letters*, 452.

211. Ibid., 451.

212. Ibid., 452.

213. Ibid., 416.

214. Monterey Diary, August 26 and 27, 1936.

215. Ibid., November 12, 1936.

216. O'Neill, *Selected Letters*, 439; O'Neill, *"As Ever, Gene,"* 179, 180.

217. "Eugene O'Neill Receives Nobel Prize for Literature," *New York Evening Post*, November 12, 1936, 1; O'Neill, *Selected Letters*, 454; "Nobel Prize Awarded to O'Neill," *New York Times*, November 13, 1936.

218. O'Neill, *Selected Letters*, 458.

219. Ibid., 455.

220. Eugene O'Neill, "The Nobel Prize Acceptance Letter," in Bogard, *Unknown O'Neill*, 427–28.

221. O'Neill, *Selected Letters*, 456.

222. O'Neill, *"As Ever, Gene,"* 164.

223. Brenda Murphy, "Nobel Prize in Literature," in Dowling, *Critical Companion to Eugene O'Neill*, 2:680.

224. "Nobel Prize Awarded to O'Neill." O'Neill disputed that he received twice what other laureates had because of the doubling of prizes (O'Neill, *Selected Letters*, 554).

225. Per Hallström, "Award Ceremony Speech," December 10, 1936, Nobel Prize Award Ceremony, *Nobel Prizes and Laureates*, http://www.nobelprize.org/nobel_prizes/literature/laureates/1936/press.html; Helburn, *Wayward Quest*, 279.

226. O'Neill, *"As Ever, Gene,"* 164.

227. O'Neill, *"The Theatre We Worked For,"* 228; Helburn, *Wayward Quest*, 268; O'Neill, *Selected Letters*, 465.

228. Kathryne Albertoni, interview by the author, October 6, 2010.

229. Kathryne Albertoni, *Remembering Eugene O'Neill: A Memoir by Kathryne Albertoni, RN* (privately printed, 2006), 6, in the author's possession. Heinold's First and Last Chance Saloon inspired scenes and characters in several of Jack London's works, including *The Sea Wolf, The Call of the Wild* and, most evidently, his memoir of the drinking life, *John Barleycorn.*

230. O'Neill, *"The Theatre We Worked For,"* 234.

231. O'Neill, *"As Ever, Gene,"* 187.

232. O'Neill, *Selected Letters,* 467.

233. Commins, *"Love and Admiration and Respect,"* 181.

234. Sheaffer, *Son and Artist,* 471, 472.

235. Helburn, *Wayward Quest,* 277.

236. O'Neill, *Selected Letters,* 469.

237. Jane Scovell, *Oona: Living in the Shadows* (New York: Warner, 1998), 77.

238. O'Neill, *Selected Letters,* 465.

239. O'Neill, *"As Ever, Gene,"* 190.

240. O'Neill expanded the Cycle backward and forward in time, eventually arriving at eleven planned plays that could be played in repertory and separately (after their initial runs). Their final titles, which he'd shuffled around over time, in order are: *Give Me Liberty and—, The Rebellion of the Humble, Greed of the Meek, And Give Me Death, A Touch of the Poet, More Stately Mansions, The Calms of Capricorn, The Earth Is the Limit, Nothing Is Lost but Honor, The Man on Iron Horseback,* and *The Hair of the Dog.*

241. O'Neill, *Selected Letters,* 483.

242. Albertoni, interview.

243. O'Neill, *Selected Letters,* 493.

244. Albertoni, interview.

245. Albertoni, *Remembering Eugene O'Neill,* 11.

246. Scovell, *Oona,* 79.

247. Ibid.

248. Quoted in Croswell Bowen, *The Curse of the Misbegotten: A Tale of the House of O'Neill* (New York: McGraw-Hill, 1959), 267.

249. Cerf, *At Random,* 86; James Light, interview by Louis Sheaffer, ca. 1959, Sheaffer-O'Neill Collection; Sheaffer, *Son and Artist,* 419–20; Cerf, *At Random,* 87; O'Neill, *"The Theatre We Worked For,"* 250.

250. Quoted in Sheaffer, *Son and Artist,* 480.

251. O'Neill, *Selected Letters,* 486. He was commenting on Sean O'Casey's antifascist play *The Star Turns Red* (1940).

252. Ibid., 507, 486.

253. Ibid., 534.

254. Quoted in Floyd, *Eugene O'Neill at Work,* xix–xx.

255. O'Neill, *Selected Letters,* 509, 515.

256. Ibid., 508, 510.

257. Quoted in Helburn, *Wayward Quest,* 275.

258. O'Neill, *"The Theatre We Worked For,"* 256, 257.

259. My thanks to poet (and friend) Dan Donaghy, whose reading at the Harriet Beecher Stowe Center in Hartford, Connecticut, on June 27, 2010, inspired this connection of *The Iceman Cometh*, and O'Neill's state of mind while writing it, to the ancient myth of Pandora's box.

260. O'Neill, *Selected Letters*, 501.

261. Normand Berlin, "Endings," in *Modern Critical Interpretations: Eugene O'Neill's "The Iceman Cometh*," ed. Harold Bloom (New York: Chelsea House, 1987), 99.

262. O'Neill, *Selected Letters*, 502.

263. Quoted in John H. Raleigh, introduction to *Twentieth Century Interpretations of "The Iceman Cometh": A Collection of Critical Essays*, ed. John H. Raleigh (Englewood Cliffs, N.J.: Prentice-Hall, 1968), 11.

264. O'Neill, *Selected Letters*, 501, 511.

265. Ibid., 537.

266. Ibid., 508–10.

267. Quoted in Floyd, *Eugene O'Neill at Work*, 260.

268. O'Neill, *Selected Letters*, 475, 476.

269. Commins, *"Love and Admiration and Respect*," 150, 189.

270. Travis Bogard, foreword to "The Last Will and Testament of Silverdene Emblem O'Neill," by Eugene O'Neill (1940), in Bogard, *Unknown O'Neill*, 432.

271. O'Neill, "The Last Will and Testament of Silverdene," 433.

272. Bogard, foreword to "The Last Will and Testament of Silverdene."

273. Commins, *"Love and Admiration and Respect*," 192.

274. O'Neill, *Selected Letters*, 507, 519.

275. Quoted in Normand Berlin, *Eugene O'Neill* (New York: Grove, 1982), 88.

276. Quoted in Floyd, *Plays of Eugene O'Neill*, 549n.

277. O'Neill, *Selected Letters*, 506–7.

278. Quoted in Sheaffer, *Son and Artist*, 517.

279. Quoted in Virginia Floyd, ed., *Eugene O'Neill: A World View* (New York: Fredrick Ungar, 1979), 296.

280. Ingrid Bergman, "A Meeting with Eugene O'Neill," in Floyd, *Eugene O'Neill: A World View*, 294.

281. Ibid., 295.

282. Clive Barnes, "Theater: O'Neill's *More Stately Mansions* Opens," *New York Times*, November 1, 1967, 40.

283. Bergman, "A Meeting with Eugene O'Neill," 295. Yale University Press published Gierow's shortened version of the play in English in 1964. Oxford University Press published the first complete unexpurgated edition in September 1988, edited and with an introduction by Martha Gilman Bower.

284. O'Neill, *Selected Letters*, 528–29.

285. "The Visit of Malatesta" and "The Last Conquest."

286. Commins, *"Love and Admiration and Respect*," 204; O'Neill, *Selected Letters*, 538, 531.

287. O'Neill, *Selected Letters*, 531–32.

288. Ibid., 531.

289. Quoted in Judith Barlow, *Final Acts: The Creation of Three Late O'Neill Plays* (Athens: University of Georgia Press, 1985), 114.

290. O'Neill, *Selected Letters*, 532.

291. Quoted in Barlow, *Final Acts*, 116.

292. O'Neill, *"As Ever, Gene,"* 220.

293. Melville Bernstein to Louis Sheaffer, January 7, 1982, in Dallas Cline (a.k.a. D. C. Thomas), *Formidable Shadow*. Quoted in Sheaffer, *Son and Artist*, 538.

294. Eugene O'Neill Jr., "The Last Name Is Not Junior," TS carbon, corrected, 1948, pp. 2, 7, Eugene O'Neill, Jr. Collection, Beinecke Library.

295. Quoted in Scovell, *Oona*, 87; David Shields and Shane Salerno, eds. *Salinger* (New York: Simon and Schuster, 2013), 74; quoted in Scovell, *Oona*, 87.

296. Earl Wilson, "Gene O'Neill Should See Daughter Now," *New York Post*, April 13, 1942.

297. Eugene O'Neill to Oona O'Neill, November 19, 1942, Sheaffer-O'Neill Collection.

298. O'Neill, *Selected Letters*, 529.

299. Scovell, *Oona*, 100.

300. Eugene O'Neill to Oona O'Neill, November 19, 1942.

301. Ibid.

302. Scovell, *Oona*, 102.

303. Quoted in ibid., 105, 106.

304. Oona's children with Chaplin were named Geraldine, Michael, Josephine, Victoria, Eugene, Jane, Annette, and Christopher.

305. Albertoni, interview; Commins, *"Love and Admiration and Respect,"* 212.

306. Basso, "Tragic Sense—III," 42.

307. O'Neill, *"The Theatre We Worked For,"* 264.

308. O'Neill, *Selected Letters*, 566.

309. Quoted in O'Neill, *"The Theatre We Worked For,"* 219.

310. Quoted in Helburn, *Wayward Quest*, 276.

311. O'Neill, *"The Theatre We Worked For,"* 217.

312. Sheaffer, *Son and Artist*, 552, 550.

313. Monterey Diary, August 6, 1944.

314. O'Neill, *"As Ever, Gene,"* 230.

315. O'Neill, *Selected Letters*, 566.

316. Quoted in Sheaffer, *Son and Artist*, 555.

317. Eugene O'Neill, "To a Stolen Moment" (June 29, 1945), in Bogard, *Unknown O'Neill*, 376–77.

318. Albertoni, interview.

319. Sheaffer, *Son and Artist*, 558.

320. Herbert J. Stoeckel, "Memories of Eugene O'Neill," *Hartford Courant*, December 6, 1953, 3, 16.

321. Commins, *"Love and Admiration and Respect,"* 219.

322. Eugene O'Neill, "Last Will and Testament of Eugene O'Neill," December 5, 1945, Eugene O'Neill Papers, Beinecke Library.

323. James Agee, "The Ordeal of Eugene O'Neill" (1946), in Estrin, *Conversations with Eugene O'Neill*, 186; Bowen, "Black Irishman," 82.

324. John S. Wilson, "O'Neill on the World and *The Iceman*" (1946), in Estrin, *Conversations with Eugene O'Neill*, 164.

325. Ibid.

326. Ibid., 164–65.

327. Ibid., 166.

328. Agee, "The Ordeal of Eugene O'Neill," 185.

329. O'Neill, *Selected Letters*, 199.

330. Albertoni, *Remembering Eugene O'Neill*, 12.

331. Sheaffer, *Son and Artist*, 565.

332. Cerf, *At Random*, 87–88.

333. Quoted in Agee, "The Ordeal of Eugene O'Neill," 185.

334. Eddie Dowling, interview by Sheaffer.

335. Ibid.; Quoted in Marlon Brando, *Brando: Songs My Mother Taught Me* (New York: Random House, 1994), 105–6.

336. Quoted in Paul Ryan, "Eugene O'Neill: A Hundred Years On," *Drama: The Quarterly Theatre Review* 4 (1988), 27.

337. Quoted in Mary Braggiotti, "Little Girl with a Big Ideal," *New York Post*, December 20, 1946, daily magazine and comic section, 1.

338. Eddie Dowling, interview by Sheaffer.

339. Karl Schriftgiesser, "*The Iceman Cometh*," *New York Times*, October 6, 1946, 3.

340. Bowen, " Black Irishman," 83–84.

341. Ibid., 65.

342. Ibid., 84.

343. Ibid., 82.

344. Robert Sylvester, "O'Neill Won't Attend Debut," *New York Daily News*, October 10, 1946, 58.

345. Ward Morehouse, "The New Play: *The Iceman Cometh* Is Powerful Theater, Superbly Played at the Martin Beck," *New York Sun*, October 10, 1946, 18; John Mason Brown, "Seeing Things: All O'Neilling," *Saturday Review of Literature*, October 19, 1946, 26.

346. Quoted in Berlin, "Endings," 103.

347. O'Neill, "Suggestions, Instructions, Advice."

348. Robert Sylvester, "O'Neill Has a New Best Seller as Well as Another Hit Play," *New York Sunday News*, October [day unknown] 1946.

349. Mary McCarthy, "Eugene O'Neill: Dry Ice," *Partisan Review*, November–December 1946, 577; Joseph Wood Krutch, "Drama," *Nation*, October 26, 1946, 481.

350. Carlotta Monterey, interview by Louis Sheaffer, July 29, 1962, Sheaffer-O'Neill Collection.

351. O'Neill, *Selected Letters*, 589.

352. Quoted in Bogard, *Contour in Time*, 446.

353. Mary Welch, "Softer Tones for Mr. O'Neill's Portrait," *Theatre Arts*, May 1957, 67–68.

354. Elliot Norton, "O'Neill's New Drama," *Boston Post*, February 21, 1947, 3.

355. Bud Kissel, "Show Shop: Too Much Conversation in *A Moon for the Misbegotten*," *Columbus Citizen*, February 21, 1947, 5.

356. Quoted in ibid.

357. "O'Neill Drama Is Vile Sample of Playwriting," *Columbus Register*, February 28, 1947, 2.

358. Quoted in Barlow, *Final Acts*, 119.

359. Quoted in Bogard, *Contour in Time*, 452, 452n.

360. Welch, "Softer Tones for Mr. O'Neill's Portrait," 67–68.

361. Quoted in Barlow, *Final Acts*, 119.

362. Commins, *"Love and Admiration and Respect,"* 222.

363. Ibid.

364. Monterey Diary, January 2, 1948.

365. O'Neill, *Selected Letters*, 579.

366. Sheaffer, *Son and Artist*, 606. See also Russel Crouse, "Extracts from the Diaries of Russel Crouse: Eugene O'Neill," TS, Eugene O'Neill Collection, Beinecke Library. Sheaffer says he fractured his shoulder, though Crouse, Monterey, and other sources always referred to his arm.

367. Quoted in Sheaffer, *Son and Artist*, 606.

368. Ibid., 608.

369. Ibid., 609. Commins evidently censored this for his memoir.

370. Commins, *"Love and Admiration and Respect,"* 225–26.

371. O'Neill, *"The Theatre We Worked For,"* 265; Commins, *"Love and Admiration and Respect,"* 227, 228.

372. O'Neill, "Last Will and Testament of Eugene O'Neill," October 31, 1947, and June 28, 1948, Eugene O'Neill Papers, Beinecke Library. The gravestone inscription was also included in drafts of his will from February 26, 1947, and July 28, 1947. O'Neill found inspiration for it in Edward Clerihew Bentley, ed., *Biography for Beginners* (London: T. Werner Laurie, 1905), 15. The full quotation reads, "What I like about Clive / Is that he is no longer alive. / There is a great deal to be said / For being dead."

373. O'Neill, *"As Ever, Gene"*, 234, 236.

374. Quoted in Bowen, *Curse of the Misbegotten*, 335.

375. O'Neill, *Selected Letters*, 581.

376. Shane's children with Givens are named Kathleen, Maura, Theodore, and Sheila.

377. Sheaffer, *Son and Artist*, 627.

378. O'Neill, *Selected Letters*, 585; Commins, *"Love and Admiration and Respect,"* 230; Michael Burlingame, "O'Neill Recalled Warmly," (New London) *Day*, July 21, 1988, E1.

379. Commins, *"Love and Admiration and Respect,"* 231.

380. Ibid.

381. Bowen, *Curse of the Misbegotten*, 349. Kathleen Jenkins, interview by Louis Sheaffer, November 30, [no year but in the 1950 file], Sheaffer-O'Neill Collection.

382. Albertoni, *Remembering Eugene O'Neill*, 13.

383. Sheaffer, *Son and Artist*, 643.

384. Quoted in Albertoni, *Remembering Eugene O'Neill*, 13; O'Neill recounted Monterey's cry of "I hear a little man calling in the wind" to his nurse Sally Coughlin after he was later admitted to Doctors Hospital in New York (Coughlin, interview by Louis Sheaffer, n.d., Sheaffer-O'Neill Collection).

385. Quoted in Sheaffer, *Son and Artist*, 639, 642.

386. Eugene O'Neill, "Last Will and Testament of Eugene O'Neill," March 5, 1951, O'Neill Papers, Beinecke Library. O'Neill later claimed to have had "hardly any memory of signing it" (Eugene O'Neill to Albert B. Carey, June [?] 1951 [photocopy], private collection of Jackson R. Bryer).

387. Burlingame, "O'Neill Recalled Warmly," E3.

388. Quoted in Sheaffer, *Son and Artist*, 644.

389. Ibid., 646.

390. Thalia Brewer (historian, Eugene O'Neill Foundation, Tao House), notes from interview by Maxine Edie Benedict, October 18, 1977, Sheaffer-O'Neill Collection.

391. Sheaffer, *Son and Artist*, 644, 646.

392. Ibid., 643, 644.

393. Albertoni, *Remembering Eugene O'Neill*, 14.

394. Carlotta Monterey O'Neill to Kenneth Macgowan, April 4, 1951, Sheaffer-O'Neill Collection.

395. Sally Coughlin, interview by Louis Sheaffer, n.d., Sheaffer-O'Neill Collection.

396. Quoted in Sheaffer, *Son and Artist*, 654.

397. Commins, *"Love and Admiration and Respect,"* 235.

398. Quoted in Sheaffer, *Son and Artist*, 659.

399. Monterey Diary, May 23, 1951.

400. Eugene O'Neill, "Last Will and Testament of Eugene O'Neill," June 28, 1948, O'Neill Papers, Beinecke Library; Eugene O'Neill to Albert B. Carey, May 1951 [photocopy], private collection of Jackson R. Bryer. There is a note added at the bottom from Monterey: "This written (dictated) by Gene after his return to Boston and me in *May* 1951."

401. Book of inscriptions by Eugene O'Neill to Carlotta Monterey O'Neill (in Carlotta's handwriting), Billy Rose Theatre Division, New York Public Library.

402. Eugene O'Neill to Bennett Cerf, June 13, 1951, Sheaffer-O'Neill Collection.

403. Seymour Peck, "Talk with Mrs. O'Neill: Playwright's Widow Traces Long Path *Journey* Travelled to the Stage," November 4, 1956, *New York Times*, 3, 1.

404. Quoted in Sheaffer, *Son and Artist*, 668.

405. Ibid., 670; quoted in ibid., 78.

Postscript

1. Quoted in Bruce H. Price and E. P. Richardson, "The Neurologic Illness of Eugene O'Neill: A Clinicopathologic Report," *New England Journal of Medicine* 342, no. 15 (2000): 1126.

2. "Transcribed Massachusetts Death Record," Eugene O'Neill, Mass Document Retrieval, 2013; Price and Richardson, "The Neurologic Illness," 1129.

3. Bruce H. Price, "The Eugene O'Neill Autopsy Project," in "Celtic Twilight: 21st-Century Irish-Americans on Eugene O'Neill," *Drunken Boat #12*, http://www.drunken-boat.com/db12/04one/price/price.php. Price and Richardson describe it as "cerebellar cortical atrophy" ("The Neurologic Illness".)

4. Book of inscriptions by Eugene O'Neill to Carlotta Monterey O'Neill (in Carlotta's handwriting), April 11, 1954, Billy Rose Theatre Division, New York Public Library. (Monterey recorded these details regarding the burial.)

5. That she bowed her head, see Louis Sheaffer, *O'Neill: Son and Artist* (Boston: Little, Brown, 1973), 67; that she said the Lord's Prayer, see Michael Burlingame, "O'Neill Recalled Warmly," (New London) *Day*, July 21, 1988, E3. This last reported that she dropped to her knees, but Sheaffer's is an eyewitness account.

6. Book of inscriptions, October 20, 1953.

7. Quoted in Brenda Murphy, *O'Neill: Long Day's Journey Into Night* (New York: Cambridge University Press, 2001), 4.

8. Carlotta Monterey Diary, February 25, 1954, O'Neill Papers, Beinecke Library, Yale University, New Haven. My thanks to William Davies King for calling my attention to this entry.

9. Dorothy Commins, ed., *"Love and Admiration and Respect": The O'Neill-Commins Correspondence* (Durham, N.C.: Duke University Press, 1986), 239.

10. Bennett Cerf, *At Random: The Reminiscences of Bennett Cerf* (New York: Random House, 1977), 89.

11. "The Theatre: O'Neill's Last Play," *Time*, February 20, 1956, 89.

12. Eugene O'Neill, "Agreement: Carlotta Monterey O'Neill and Yale University, *Long day's Journey Into Night*," May 27, 1955, Eugene O'Neill Papers, Beinecke Library.

13. Eugene O'Neill to Carlotta Monterey O'Neill, trust agreement, March 3, 1952, Eugene O'Neill Papers, Beinecke Library. (I wrote the Suffolk County Probate Court to request the final version of O'Neill's will, and it responded, "Unfortunately, and perhaps due to his VIP status at the time of his death, his probate file at Suffolk County Probate Court is impounded and is not open to the public" [e-mail to the author, October 10, 2013].)

14. Quoted in Doris Alexander, *Eugene O'Neill's Last Plays: Separating Art from Autobiography* (Athens: University of Georgia Press, 2005), 152.

15. Commins, *"Love and Admiration and Respect,"* 199.

16. Eugene O'Neill, *Selected Letters of Eugene O'Neill*, ed. Travis Bogard and Jackson R. Bryer (New Haven: Yale University Press, 1988), 569.

17. "O'Neill's 'Self-Portrait' Play Hailed at Swedish Premiere," *Boston Daily Globe*, February 11, 1956. He also told this to Croswell Bowen (Croswell Bowen, "The Black Irishman" [1946], in *O'Neill and His Plays: Four Decades of Criticism*, ed. Oscar Cargill, N. Bryllion Fagin, and William J. Fisher [New York: New York University Press, 1961], 70).

18. Quoted in Arthur Gelb and Barbara Gelb, *O'Neill: Life with Monte Cristo* (New York: Applause, 2000), 337.

19. Agnes Boulton, *Part of a Long Story: "Eugene O'Neill as a Young Man in Love,"* ed. William Davies King (Jefferson, N.C.: McFarland, 2011), 172.

20. Jim Cook, "A Long Tragic Journey," *New York Post*, December 2, 1956.

21. Monterey Diary, May 29, 30, 1954; Brenda Murphy, "What New London Said about the O'Neills," Ninth International Conference on Eugene O'Neill, June 21, 2014, New London, Conn.; Monterey Diary, May 29, 30, 1954.

22. Eugene O'Neill, "Autograph Manuscript, 1 page," Hammerman Collection, http://eoneill.com/manuscripts/27200.htm.

23. Louis Sheaffer, *Son and Playwright* (Boston: Little, Brown, 1968), 142.

24. O'Neill, *Selected Letters*, 381.

25. Quoted in Sheaffer, *Son and Artist*, 429.

26. Ibid., 540. For more on the family's reaction to the play, see Doris Alexander, *Eugene O'Neill's Last Plays*, 122.

27. O'Neill, *Selected Letters*, 338.

28. Ibid., 435.

29. Eugene O'Neill, *"The Theatre We Worked For": The Letters of Eugene O'Neill to Kenneth Macgowan*, ed. Travis Bogard and Jackson R. Bryer (New Haven: Yale University Press, 1982), 253.

30. "The Theater: O'Neill's Last Play."

31. Monterey Diary, May 29, 30, April 21, 1954.

32. Kathryne Albertoni, *Remembering Eugene O'Neill: A Memoir by Kathryne Albertoni, RN* (privately printed, 2006), 14, in the author's possession; Kathryne Albertoni, interview by the author, October 6, 2010.

33. Quoted in Sheaffer, *Son and Artist*, 644.

34. Quoted in William Davies King, *Another Part of a Long Story: Literary Traces of Eugene O'Neill and Agnes Boulton* (Ann Arbor: University of Michigan Press, 2010), 179.

35. Carl Van Vechten to Alfred A. Knopf, October 30, 1956, in *Letters of Carl Van Vechten*, ed. Bruce Kellner (New Haven: Yale University Press, 1987), 264.

36. King, *Another Part of a Long Story*, 231. Boulton's second volume was to deal with the three-year period when O'Neill's parents and brother died, the third, with the working title "Full Fathom Five," about the couple's later years to the ruin of their marriage in 1928.

37. "The Theater: O'Neill's Last Play."

38. George Williamson, "Plaudits for O'Neill: Swedish Press Hails *Long Day's Journey Into Night*," *New York Times*, February 15, 1956.

39. John Chapman, *"Long Day's Journey Into Night* a Drama of Sheer Magnificence," *New York Daily News*, November 8, 1956, 86; Brooks Atkinson, "Theatre: Tragic Journey," *New York Times*, November 8, 1956, 47.

40. Walter Kerr, "Theater: *Long Day's Journey Into Night*," *New York Herald Tribune*, November 8, 1956, sec. 1, 20.

41. Tony Kushner, "The Genius of O'Neill," *Eugene O'Neill Review* 26 (2004): 249, 253.

42. Kenneth Pearson, "Plays and Players: The Last Touch of O'Neill," *Sunday Times* (London), October 12, 1958, 21.

Index